Advanced Flutter

Build High-Performance, Cross-Platform Apps for Mobile, Web and Desktop

Sivaraj Selvaraj

Advanced Flutter: Build High-Performance, Cross-Platform Apps for Mobile, Web and Desktop

Sivaraj Selvaraj
Ulundurpet, Tamil Nadu, India

ISBN-13 (pbk): 979-8-8688-2104-2   ISBN-13 (electronic): 979-8-8688-2105-9
https://doi.org/10.1007/979-8-8688-2105-9

Copyright © 2025 by Sivaraj Selvaraj

This work is subject to copyright. All rights are reserved by the Publisher, whether the whole or part of the material is concerned, specifically the rights of translation, reprinting, reuse of illustrations, recitation, broadcasting, reproduction on microfilms or in any other physical way, and transmission or information storage and retrieval, electronic adaptation, computer software, or by similar or dissimilar methodology now known or hereafter developed.

Trademarked names, logos, and images may appear in this book. Rather than use a trademark symbol with every occurrence of a trademarked name, logo, or image we use the names, logos, and images only in an editorial fashion and to the benefit of the trademark owner, with no intention of infringement of the trademark.

The use in this publication of trade names, trademarks, service marks, and similar terms, even if they are not identified as such, is not to be taken as an expression of opinion as to whether or not they are subject to proprietary rights.

While the advice and information in this book are believed to be true and accurate at the date of publication, neither the authors nor the editors nor the publisher can accept any legal responsibility for any errors or omissions that may be made. The publisher makes no warranty, express or implied, with respect to the material contained herein.

    Managing Director, Apress Media LLC: Welmoed Spahr
    Acquisitions Editor: James Robinson-Prior
    Coordinating Editor: Gryffin Winkler

Cover image by nvd9612 on pixabay

Distributed to the book trade worldwide by Springer Science+Business Media New York, 1 New York Plaza, New York, NY 10004. Phone 1-800-SPRINGER, fax (201) 348-4505, e-mail orders-ny@springer-sbm.com, or visit www.springeronline.com. Apress Media, LLC is a Delaware LLC and the sole member (owner) is Springer Science + Business Media Finance Inc (SSBM Finance Inc). SSBM Finance Inc is a **Delaware** corporation.

For information on translations, please e-mail booktranslations@springernature.com; for reprint, paperback, or audio rights, please e-mail bookpermissions@springernature.com.

Apress titles may be purchased in bulk for academic, corporate, or promotional use. eBook versions and licenses are also available for most titles. For more information, reference our Print and eBook Bulk Sales web page at http://www.apress.com/bulk-sales.

Any source code or other supplementary material referenced by the author in this book is available to readers on GitHub (https://github.com/Apress). For more detailed information, please visit https://www.apress.com/gp/services/source-code.

If disposing of this product, please recycle the paper

Table of Contents

About the Author .... **xiii**

About the Technical Reviewer .... **xv**

Introduction .... **xvii**

Chapter 1: Flutter Overview and New Features **1**

  What's New in Flutter 2

    Introduction to New Widgets 2

    Enhanced Existing Widgets 5

    Performance Improvements 8

  How to Upgrade to Flutter 16

    Migration Guides 16

    Addressing Deprecated Features 26

  In-Depth Analysis of Release Notes 35

    Detailed Analysis of Release Notes 35

    Impact on Existing Projects 42

  Summary 49

Chapter 2: Advanced Widget and UI Design **51**

  New Widget Features in Flutter 53

    Detailed Look at New Widgets 53

    Examples and Use Cases 58

    Customization and Usage Scenarios 64

  Modern UI Patterns 77

    Responsive and Adaptive UIs 77

TABLE OF CONTENTS

    Implementing Design Systems 93
  Advanced Layout Techniques 104
    Using LayoutBuilder and CustomMultiChildLayout 105
    Dynamic and Adaptive Layouts 118
  Interactive UI Elements 131
    Creating Immersive UI Components 132
    Practical Examples 141
  Advanced Widget Testing 149
    Strategies for Testing Custom Widgets 149
    Case Studies and Best Practices 156
  Summary 162

Chapter 3: Performance Optimization and Profiling 163

  Latest Profiling Tools 164
    New Features in Dart DevTools 164
    GPU Performance Analysis 172
  Memory Management Enhancements 181
    Efficient Memory Use 181
    Profiling Memory Leaks and Bottlenecks 191
  Performance Best Practices 203
    Leveraging New Performance Features 203
    Optimizing Rendering and Build Times 212
  Profiling Tools Comparison 222
    Comparing Various Profiling Tools 222
    Use Cases and Recommendations 228
  Optimizing for Different Devices 234
    Techniques for Multi-device Optimization 235
    Performance Benchmarks 241
  Summary 248

TABLE OF CONTENTS

Chapter 4: Advanced State Management 249

Riverpod Enhancements 250
- Overview of Riverpod 2.0 250
- Advanced State Management Patterns 255
- Combining State Management Solutions 259
- Managing Complex State Trees 263

Bloc and Cubit Updates 268
- Recent Changes in Bloc Library 268
- Advanced Bloc Patterns 272
- Advanced Use Cases and Patterns 277
- Real-World Examples 283

Combining State Management Solutions 289
- Integrating Riverpod, Bloc, and Other Solutions 289
- Case Studies and Examples 296

Managing State Across Complex Applications 303
- Techniques for Complex State Management 303
- Performance Considerations 309

State Management for Large Teams 316
- Best Practices for Team Collaboration 316
- Managing State in Large Projects 323

Performance Benchmarks 330
- Benchmarks for Different Solutions 330
- Impact on Performance 338

Summary 344

v

TABLE OF CONTENTS

Chapter 5: Custom Rendering and Painting 345
Advanced RenderObject Techniques 346
Building Custom RenderObjects 346
New Painting Capabilities 366
Utilizing Flutter's Updated Painting APIs 366
Implementing High-Performance Custom Paint Operations 379
Real-Time Rendering Techniques 397
Techniques for Real-Time Rendering 398
Custom Animations and Effects 403
Case Studies 409
Successful Implementations of Custom Rendering 409
Analysis of Popular Apps 413
Summary 418

Chapter 6: Integration with Native Code 419
New Features in Platform Channels 420
Overview of Platform Channel Enhancements 421
Advanced Communication Techniques 425
Managing Asynchronous Communication 431
Techniques for Asynchronous Communication 431
Real-World Examples 438
Enhanced Plugin Development 443
Writing Modern Plugins 444
Integrating Plugins with Flutter Apps 448
Testing and Debugging Plugins 453
Security Best Practices for Plugins 468
Advanced Security Practices 475
Encryption and Secure Storage 475
Techniques for Securing Native Integrations 480

TABLE OF CONTENTS

Plugin Performance Optimization 486
    Strategies for Optimizing Plugin Performance 486
    Case Studies and Examples 492
Summary 498

Chapter 7: Web and Desktop Enhancements 499

Flutter Web Improvements 500
    Latest Updates for Flutter Web Performance 501
    Handling Browser-Specific Challenges 510
Flutter Desktop Updates 522
    Latest Features for Flutter Desktop 523
    Packaging Desktop Apps for Deployment 533
Case Studies 546
    Success Stories of Web and Desktop Apps Built with Flutter 546
Performance Benchmarking for Web and Desktop 556
    Comparing Web and Desktop Performance 556
    Optimizing Apps for Multiple Platforms 562
Summary 569

Chapter 8: Networking and API Integration 571

HTTP Requests and JSON Parsing 572
    New Enhancements in HTTP Requests 572
    Efficient JSON Parsing Techniques 575
Advanced API Integration 582
    Handling Complex APIs 582
    Error Handling and Retries 589
WebSockets and Real-Time Data 596
    Introduction to WebSocket Integration 596

TABLE OF CONTENTS

Caching and Offline Data 609
    Advanced Caching Techniques 609
API Testing and Debugging 618
    Advanced Debugging Strategies 618
    Tools for API Testing...624
Summary...629

Chapter 9: Advanced Animations and Transitions 631

Custom Animation Techniques 632
    Creating Complex Animations..633
    Performance Considerations 640
Animation Libraries and Packages..649
    Overview of Popular Animation Libraries 650
    Advanced Use Cases 658
Cross-Platform Animation Techniques 666
    Implementing Consistent Animations..666
Performance Optimization for Animations 673
    Techniques for Optimizing Animation Performance 674
    Case Studies and Examples 678
Summary...683

Chapter 10: Flutter for Machine Learning and AI 685

Integrating TensorFlow with Flutter 686
    Setting Up TensorFlow Lite in Flutter...687
    Using Pre-trained Models for Mobile Applications 691
    On-Device Inference with TensorFlow Lite 695
Image Recognition with Flutter...700
    Building Image Classification Apps 700
    Real-Time Image Processing..705

TABLE OF CONTENTS

Optimizing ML Models for Mobile Devices 710
Voice and Natural Language Processing... 715
    Speech-to-Text and Text-to-Speech in Flutter.. 716
    Using NLP Models in Flutter Apps 720
Case Studies of ML and AI in Flutter Apps 730
    Real-World Case Studies and Applications.. 730
    Challenges and Best Practices 734
Summary... 737

Chapter 11: Security and App Hardening 739

Security Vulnerabilities in Mobile Apps... 740
    Common Security Threats in Flutter Apps 740
    How to Secure Data in Transit and at Rest 744
Secure Authentication Methods 748
    OAuth and JWT Authentication 748
    Implementing Two-Factor Authentication (2FA)...................................... 753
    Biometric Authentication for Enhanced Security..................................... 757
App Hardening Techniques 761
    Protecting Against Reverse Engineering 761
    Code Obfuscation in Flutter... 765
    Encryption Best Practices for Mobile Apps.. 768
Real-World Security Case Studies 774
    Security Vulnerabilities in Popular Apps 774
    Lessons Learned and Solutions 778
Summary... 784

TABLE OF CONTENTS

Chapter 12: Advanced Testing and CI/CD for Flutter 787

Unit Testing in Flutter 788
  Writing Effective Unit Tests for Widgets..788
  Mocking and Stubbing in Flutter Tests 793
Integration Testing and Widget Testing 798
  Best Practices for Integration Tests..798
  Advanced Widget Testing Scenarios...803
Continuous Integration and Delivery (CI/CD)...814
  Setting Up CI/CD Pipelines for Flutter..814
  Automating Flutter Builds with GitHub Actions..819
  Deploying to Multiple Platforms with CI/CD...824
Automated Test Reports and Debugging...829
  Generating Test Coverage Reports 829
  Debugging CI/CD Failures and Performance Bottlenecks 833
Summary..838

Chapter 13: Flutter for Embedded Systems..841

Introduction to Embedded Systems in Flutter...842
  What Are Embedded Systems? 843
  Running Flutter on Embedded Platforms...846
Flutter on Raspberry Pi 850
  Setting Up Raspberry Pi for Flutter Development..850
  Building Flutter Apps for Embedded Systems 854
  Hardware Interaction and Peripheral Access 857
Challenges and Limitations in Embedded Flutter Development 862
  Memory and Performance Constraints..863
  Dealing with Hardware-Specific Issues...866
Real-World Case Studies..870

TABLE OF CONTENTS

Embedded Systems in Consumer Electronics 871

Building IoT Applications with Flutter 874

Summary 878

Chapter 14: Flutter in the Enterprise Environment 879

Integrating with Legacy Systems 880

    Connecting Flutter Apps with Legacy APIs 880

    Data Synchronization Across Systems 885

Scalability and Performance for Large Enterprises 889

    Optimizing Flutter for Enterprise Applications 889

Enterprise Security Requirements 899

    Securing Enterprise-Level Flutter Applications 899

    Compliance and Privacy Concerns 902

Real-World Enterprise Applications 906

    Case Study: Flutter in the Healthcare Industry 906

    Flutter in Financial Services 910

Summary 914

Chapter 15: Flutter for Internationalization and Localization 915

Supporting Multiple Languages in Flutter 916

    Using Flutter's Localization Features 916

    Integrating Third-Party Localization Libraries 921

Handling Locale-Specific Design 926

    Designing UIs for Multiple Languages 926

    Cultural Considerations in UI Design 930

Right-to-Left (RTL) Layouts 935

    Supporting RTL Layouts in Flutter Apps 935

    Best Practices for Handling Multilingual Content 939

Summary 943

TABLE OF CONTENTS

Chapter 16: Deploying and Maintaining Flutter Apps 945
Preparing for Release 946
    Building and Packaging Flutter Apps for iOS and Android 946
    Preparing Flutter Web and Desktop for Production 951
Publishing Flutter Apps 956
    App Store and Play Store Submission 957
    Flutter Web Hosting and Deployment Options 962
App Maintenance and Updates 967
    Updating Flutter Apps for New Releases 967
    Managing App Versions and Compatibility 972
Monitoring and Analytics 978
    Integrating Firebase Analytics and Crashlytics 978
    Real-Time Monitoring of App Health 983
Summary 988

Glossary of Terms 989

Index 993

About the Author

Sivaraj Selvaraj focuses on modern technologies and industry best practices. These topics include frontend development techniques using HTML5, CSS3, and JavaScript frameworks; implementing responsive web design and optimizing user experience across devices; building dynamic web applications with server-side languages such as PHP, WordPress, and Laravel; and database management and integration using SQL and MySQL databases. He loves to share his extensive knowledge and experience to empower readers to tackle complex challenges and create highly functional and visually appealing websites.

About the Technical Reviewer

Massimo Nardone has more than 29 years of experience in information and cybersecurity for IT/OT/IoT/IIoT, web/mobile development, cloud, and IT architecture. His true IT passions are security and Android. He holds an MSc degree in computing science from the University of Salerno, Italy. Throughout his working career, he has held various positions, starting as a programming developer and then becoming a security teacher, PCI QSA, auditor, assessor, lead IT/OT/SCADA/cloud architect, CISO, BISO, executive, program director, OT/IoT/IIoT security competence leader, Vice President of OT Security, etc. In his last working engagement, he worked as a seasoned cyber- and information security executive, CISO, and OT, IoT, and IIoT security competence leader helping many clients to develop and implement cyber-, information, OT, and IoT security activities. He is currently working as Vice President of OT Security for SSH Communications Security. He is a co-author of numerous Apress books, including *Pro Spring Security*, *Pro JPA 2 in Java EE 8*, and *Pro Android Games*, and has reviewed more than 70 titles.

Introduction

In the rapidly evolving world of mobile and web development, Flutter has emerged as a leading framework, offering a powerful toolkit for creating high-performance, beautiful applications across multiple platforms. With the release of Flutter, developers are presented with an array of advanced features and enhancements designed to streamline development, improve performance, and enrich user experiences.

Context and Objective

Context

In the ever-evolving landscape of software development, Flutter has established itself as a game-changer in creating high-performance, cross-platform applications. The release of Flutter introduces several advanced features and improvements that empower developers to push the boundaries of what's possible in mobile and web app development. As the technology landscape continues to advance, staying updated with the latest tools and techniques is crucial for maintaining a competitive edge.

This book, *Advanced Flutter: Build High-Performance, Cross-Platform Apps for Mobile, Web and Desktop*, addresses the need for a deep dive into the sophisticated capabilities of Flutter. It aims to provide seasoned developers with the knowledge and skills required to leverage the new features, optimize performance, and implement best practices in their projects.

INTRODUCTION

Objective

The primary objective of this book is to equip experienced Flutter developers with a comprehensive understanding of the advanced aspects of Flutter. By the end of this book, you will

- **Master New Features:** Gain in-depth knowledge of the latest features and enhancements introduced in Flutter, including new widgets, improved performance metrics, and updated APIs.

- **Enhance Your UI Design Skills:** Learn advanced techniques for designing sophisticated, responsive, and adaptive user interfaces (UIs) that stand out in today's competitive market.

- **Optimize Performance:** Discover strategies for profiling, optimizing, and debugging Flutter applications to ensure they perform efficiently across various devices and platforms.

- **Advance State Management:** Explore cutting-edge state management solutions and patterns, including the latest updates to Riverpod, Bloc (Business Logic Component), and Cubit, and learn how to effectively combine these solutions.

- **Integrate Native Code:** Understand how to seamlessly integrate Flutter with native code, manage platform-specific features, and develop high-performance plugins.

- **Explore Web and Desktop Capabilities:** Delve into the latest advancements in Flutter's web and desktop support, and learn how to build cross-platform applications with a consistent user experience.

Implement Security Best Practices: Learn how to secure your applications and protect user data with the latest security features and compliance practices.

Apply Real-World Techniques: Benefit from practical examples, case studies, and best practices that demonstrate how to apply advanced Flutter techniques in real-world scenarios.

By providing a thorough examination of these advanced topics, this book aims to help you harness the full potential of Flutter and elevate your development skills to new heights.

How to Use This Book

This book is designed to be a comprehensive guide for experienced Flutter developers who want to deepen their expertise and master advanced concepts in Flutter. Here's how to effectively use this book to maximize your learning:

Start with the Introduction
Begin by reading the introduction to understand the scope and objectives of the book. It will give you an overview of what to expect and how the book is structured.

Follow the Chapter Structure

Sequential Reading: For a holistic understanding, read the chapters in order. Each chapter builds upon the previous ones, providing a structured path from foundational concepts to advanced techniques.

INTRODUCTION

> **Targeted Reading:** If you are particularly interested in a specific topic, feel free to jump directly to the relevant chapter. Each chapter is self-contained, with clear explanations and practical examples.

Utilize Chapter Overviews
Each chapter begins with an overview that highlights the key concepts and objectives. Use these overviews to get a quick summary of the chapter's content before diving into the detailed sections.

Engage with Practical Examples
The book includes practical examples and case studies to illustrate the concepts discussed. Study these examples closely to understand how advanced techniques are applied in real-world scenarios.

Review Detailed Content
Explore the detailed explanations, code snippets, and diagrams within each chapter. The content is organized with clear headings and subheadings to guide you through complex topics.

Apply Advanced Techniques
Pay special attention to the advanced techniques and best practices outlined in each chapter. Implement these strategies in your own projects to enhance performance and functionality.

Refer to Additional Resources
At the end of each chapter, you will find suggestions for further reading and additional resources. Use these to expand your knowledge and stay updated with the latest developments.

Use the Index and Glossary
The index and glossary at the end of the book are valuable tools for quick reference. Use the index to locate specific topics and the glossary to understand key terminology.

Practice and Experiment

Practical experience is crucial for mastering advanced concepts. Experiment with the techniques and examples provided, and apply them to your own projects to reinforce your learning.

Stay Engaged with the Community

While this book provides in-depth knowledge, staying engaged with the Flutter community and keeping up with the latest updates will help you stay ahead in the field.

By following these guidelines, you will be able to effectively navigate the book, absorb advanced Flutter techniques, and apply them to build cutting-edge mobile and web applications.

CHAPTER 1

Flutter Overview and New Features

In this chapter, we will delve into the latest advancements introduced in Flutter, a significant update in the Flutter framework. Flutter brings a host of new features, improvements, and optimizations designed to enhance the development experience and application performance. This chapter aims to provide a comprehensive overview of these updates, focusing on the key areas that will impact developers and their projects.

What's New in Flutter

We begin by exploring the new capabilities and enhancements in Flutter. This section will outline the most notable additions to the framework, including newly introduced widgets and improvements to existing ones. We'll also examine the performance upgrades that Flutter brings, providing insights into how these changes can benefit your development workflow and application performance.

How to Upgrade to Flutter

Upgrading to a new version of Flutter can be a straightforward process, but it's essential to understand the migration steps and address any potential issues. This section will guide you through the process of upgrading to Flutter, including detailed migration guides, common challenges you may face, and strategies for handling deprecated features. We'll provide practical advice to ensure a smooth transition and help you maintain code compatibility.

CHAPTER 1 FLUTTER OVERVIEW AND NEW FEATURES

In-Depth Analysis of Release Notes
Finally, we'll conduct an in-depth analysis of the release notes for Flutter. This part of the chapter will break down the release notes in detail, highlighting significant changes and their implications for your projects. We will also explore how these updates might affect your existing codebase and offer guidance on adapting to the new features and improvements.

By the end of this chapter, you will have a solid understanding of what's new in Flutter, how to upgrade your projects, and how to interpret the release notes to make the most of this latest update.

What's New in Flutter

Flutter introduces a range of new features and enhancements aimed at improving both the developer experience (DX) and application performance. This section provides an overview of these updates, focusing on the introduction of new widgets, enhancements to existing ones, and key performance improvements.

Introduction to New Widgets

Flutter introduces several new widgets designed to enhance the development process and improve user experience (UX). These widgets address specific needs within application development, offering developers greater flexibility and control over UI design and interaction. Here's a closer look at the key new widgets included in this release:

CHAPTER 1   FLUTTER OVERVIEW AND NEW FEATURES

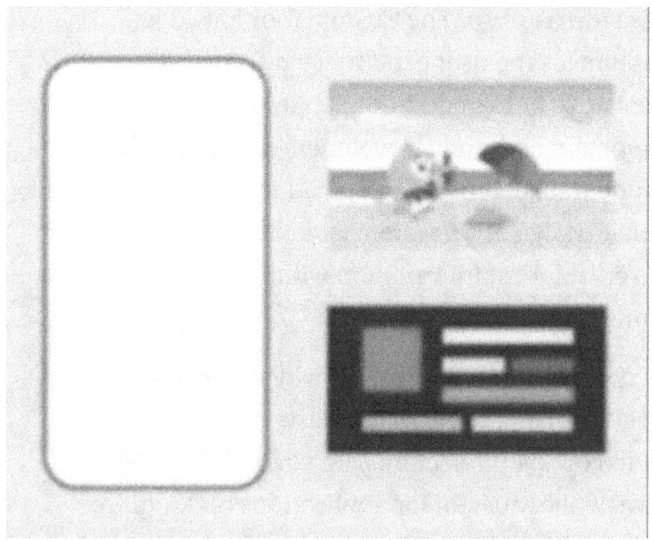

Figure 1-1. *Interactive view*

InteractiveViewer: This widget empowers developers to create highly interactive and zoomable user interfaces. With InteractiveViewer, users can pan, zoom, and rotate content effortlessly, making it ideal for applications that display complex images or detailed data visualizations. The widget supports gestures such as pinch to zoom and double-tap to zoom, providing a smooth and intuitive user experience.

DatePicker: The new DatePicker widget offers a versatile and user-friendly interface for selecting dates. It is highly customizable, allowing developers to define its appearance and behavior according to the needs of their applications. The widget supports various date formats and locales, ensuring that it can be adapted for different regions and preferences.

CustomTooltip: The CustomTooltip widget enhances the user experience by providing context-sensitive help or additional information in a visually appealing manner. Developers can customize the appearance, timing, and positioning of tooltips to fit their design requirements, making it easier to offer users relevant information without cluttering the interface.

ExpandableListView: This widget introduces a new way to manage and display lists with expandable and collapsible sections. ExpandableListView is particularly useful for applications that require hierarchical data presentation or need to organize content into collapsible groups, such as settings menus or categorized lists.

AnimatedSwitcher: The AnimatedSwitcher widget simplifies the process of animating transitions between different widgets. By automatically applying animations when switching between child widgets, it helps create smooth and visually engaging transitions that enhance the overall user experience.

These new widgets are designed to address common development challenges and provide more powerful tools for creating dynamic and interactive user interfaces. By integrating these widgets into your applications, you can streamline development processes, enhance user engagement, and deliver a more polished and responsive experience.

CHAPTER 1 FLUTTER OVERVIEW AND NEW FEATURES

Enhanced Existing Widgets

Flutter brings significant enhancements to several existing widgets, aimed at improving their functionality, performance, and ease of use. These updates provide developers with more robust tools for crafting sophisticated and responsive user interfaces. Here's a detailed look at the key enhancements made to some of the core widgets in this release:

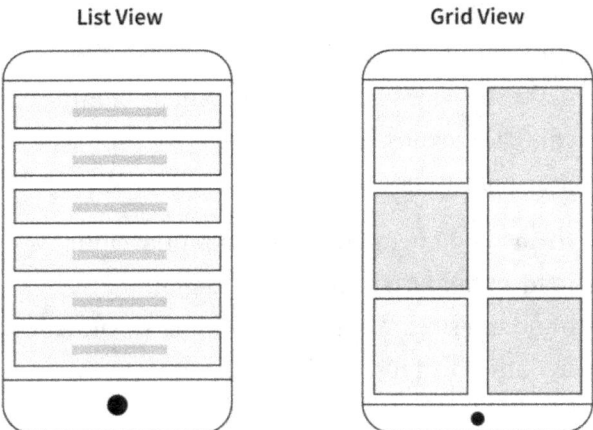

Figure 1-2. *Enhanced widgets*

> **ListView**: The ListView widget has been optimized to offer improved scrolling performance and additional layout options. These include
>
> > **Horizontal Scrolling**: Developers can now easily implement horizontal scrolling lists, making it simpler to create carousels or horizontal data views.
> >
> > **Staggered Grids**: Support for staggered grid layouts has been added, allowing for more complex and visually appealing arrangements of list items.

CHAPTER 1   FLUTTER OVERVIEW AND NEW FEATURES

Improved Performance: Optimizations in the widget's internal mechanics reduce jank and improve smoothness during scrolling, particularly in lists with large datasets or complex item layouts.

Form: The Form widget has received updates aimed at simplifying form creation and validation:

Enhanced Validation: New validation features make it easier to define and manage complex validation rules, ensuring that form inputs are thoroughly checked and validated.

Improved Form Field Interactions: Updates to form field management and interaction handling streamline the process of creating dynamic and responsive forms, improving the overall developer experience.

AnimationController: The AnimationController widget has been enhanced to support more sophisticated animations and transitions:

Advanced Animation Capabilities: Developers can now create more complex and seamless animations by leveraging new properties and methods that offer finer control over animation timing and sequencing.

Performance Optimizations: Enhancements to the animation engine reduce overhead and improve performance, ensuring smoother transitions and more responsive animations.

Drawer: The Drawer widget has been updated to provide more customization options and improved usability:

> **Customizable Drawer Layouts**: New configuration options allow for greater flexibility in designing the appearance and behavior of the drawer, including support for custom header widgets and additional content.
>
> **Enhanced Transition Effects**: Updated transition effects offer a more polished and engaging user experience when opening and closing the drawer.

SliverAppBar: The SliverAppBar widget, used in conjunction with slivers to create flexible app bars, has been refined to improve its usability and performance:

> **New Scrolling Behaviors**: Enhanced scrolling behaviors enable smoother integration with other sliver-based widgets, providing a more seamless user experience as users scroll through content.
>
> **Customizable Effects**: Developers now have more control over the visual effects and animations applied to the app bar during scrolling, allowing for more creative and responsive designs.

These enhancements to existing widgets in Flutter reflect a commitment to improving the developer experience and the quality of user interfaces. By leveraging these updates, developers can create more dynamic, performant, and user-friendly applications, ultimately leading to a better overall experience for users.

CHAPTER 1   FLUTTER OVERVIEW AND NEW FEATURES

Performance Improvements

Flutter brings a suite of performance improvements designed to optimize application responsiveness and efficiency. These enhancements include updated performance metrics and advanced optimization techniques, ensuring that developers can build applications that are both smooth and high-performing.

Updated Performance Metrics

Flutter introduces a set of updated performance metrics designed to provide developers with deeper and more actionable insights into their applications' performance. These metrics are essential for diagnosing performance issues, optimizing application responsiveness, and ensuring a smooth user experience.

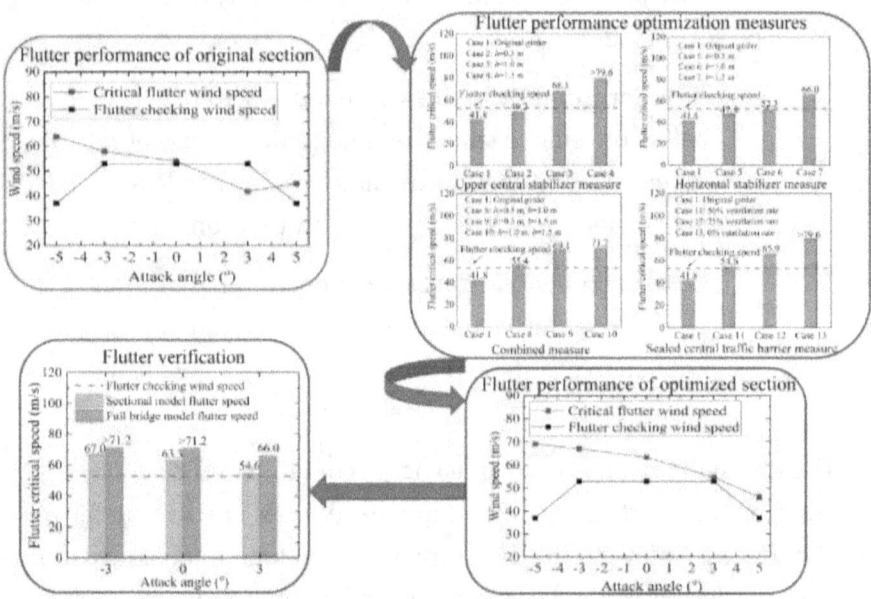

Figure 1-3. *Performance metrics*

Here's a detailed overview of the updated performance metrics available in Flutter:

> **Rendering Performance Metrics**: Flutter provides enhanced tools for monitoring the performance of the rendering pipeline. Key metrics include
>
>> **Frame Rendering Time**: Measures the time taken to render each frame, helping identify performance bottlenecks in the rendering process.
>>
>> **Widget Build Time**: Tracks the time required to build widgets, enabling developers to optimize widget hierarchies and reduce unnecessary rebuilds.
>
> **Memory Usage Profiling**: Advanced memory profiling tools offer a more detailed view of an application's memory consumption, including
>
>> **Heap Snapshots**: Provides detailed snapshots of memory usage, allowing developers to analyze memory allocation patterns and detect potential memory leaks.
>>
>> **Memory Allocation Tracking**: Monitors memory allocation in real time to identify objects that are consuming excessive memory and optimize resource management.
>
> **Frame Rate Analysis**: Updated frame rate analysis tools offer insights into
>
>> **Frame Rate Consistency**: Measures the consistency of frame rates to ensure smooth animations and transitions. Developers can identify dips in frame rate and address the causes of jank or stuttering.

Dropped Frames: Tracks instances where frames are dropped, helping developers understand and mitigate performance issues that impact the fluidity of the user interface.

CPU and GPU Utilization: New metrics for tracking CPU and GPU usage include

CPU Utilization: Shows how much of the CPU's capacity is being used by the application, helping identify performance bottlenecks related to computational tasks.

GPU Utilization: Measures the GPU's workload to ensure that graphical rendering tasks are efficiently handled, contributing to overall application performance.

Event Handling Performance: Metrics related to event handling include

Event Processing Time: Measures the time taken to process user interactions and other events, helping developers optimize responsiveness and reduce latency in user input handling.

Gesture Recognition Performance: Tracks the efficiency of gesture recognition, particularly for applications with complex or custom gesture interactions.

Network Performance Metrics: Tools for monitoring network performance include

Network Latency: Measures the time taken for network requests and responses, allowing developers to optimize data fetching and reduce delays.

Data Throughput: Tracks the amount of data being transmitted and received, helping to optimize network operations and manage bandwidth usage effectively.

These updated performance metrics in Flutter offer developers a comprehensive toolkit for analyzing and enhancing application performance. By leveraging these metrics, developers can make data-driven decisions to optimize their applications, improve user experience, and address performance issues more effectively.

Performance Optimization Techniques

Flutter introduces several advanced performance optimization techniques designed to enhance application speed, responsiveness, and overall efficiency. These techniques address various aspects of application performance, from reducing load times to optimizing rendering and resource management.

CHAPTER 1 FLUTTER OVERVIEW AND NEW FEATURES

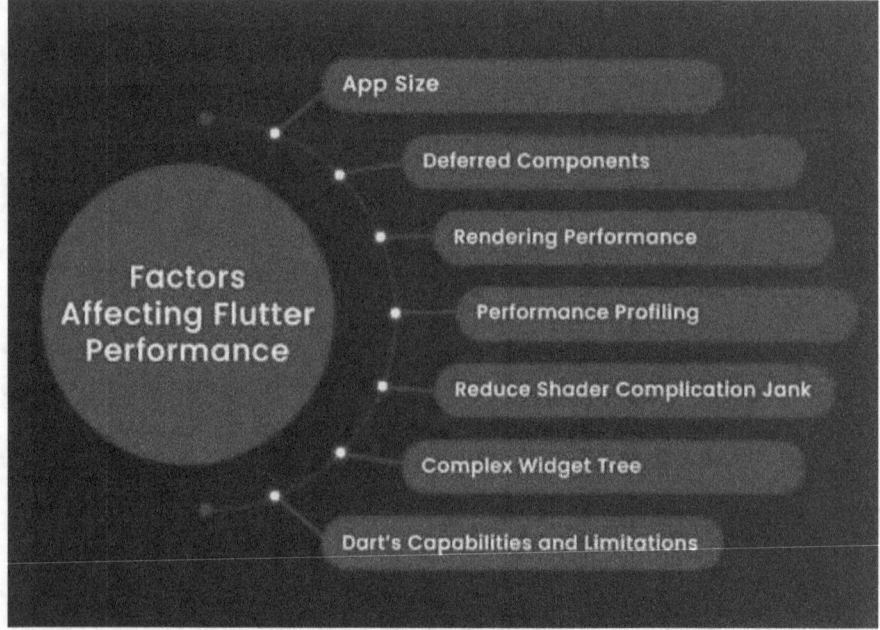

Figure 1-4. Performance optimization

Here's an overview of the key optimization techniques available in Flutter.

Code Splitting

Concept: Code splitting involves breaking down an application into smaller, modular chunks that can be loaded independently. This technique helps to minimize the initial payload and reduce the time it takes for the application to become interactive.

Implementation: Developers can use Flutter's package and plugin management to split code into different modules, loading only the necessary components initially. This approach helps to improve startup times and overall performance by deferring the loading of less critical features until they are needed.

Deferred Loading

Concept: Deferred loading involves postponing the loading of non-essential resources and features until they are required. This technique improves the application's responsiveness and startup performance by prioritizing the loading of core functionality.

Implementation: Using Flutter's built-in support for deferred loading, developers can mark certain resources or modules to be loaded lazily. For instance, additional screens or features that are not immediately visible to the user can be loaded in the background after the main application has launched.

Efficient Layout Algorithms

Concept: Efficient layout algorithms reduce the overhead of calculating and rendering complex UI structures. Optimizing these algorithms helps in improving rendering performance and reducing unnecessary recalculations.

Implementation: Flutter introduces enhanced layout algorithms that streamline the process of building and updating UI layouts. Developers can leverage these optimizations to reduce layout passes and improve the efficiency of rendering complex widgets and layouts.

Cache Optimization

Concept: Caching frequently accessed data and resources helps to minimize redundant computations and resource loading, leading to faster application performance and reduced latency.

Implementation: Flutter provides improved caching mechanisms for both in-memory and persistent data. Developers can utilize caching strategies to store and quickly retrieve frequently used data, images, or other resources, thereby reducing the need for repeated network requests or computations.

Asynchronous Programming Enhancements

Concept: Asynchronous programming improvements facilitate more efficient handling of concurrent tasks and background operations, leading to smoother application performance.

Implementation: Updates to Flutter's asynchronous programming model include enhancements to Future and Stream handling, as well as better support for asynchronous operations. Developers can use these improvements to optimize background tasks, manage asynchronous data flows more effectively, and reduce the impact of long-running operations on the main thread.

Efficient State Management

Concept: Optimizing state management practices ensures that application state changes are handled efficiently, reducing unnecessary widget rebuilds and improving overall performance.

Implementation: Flutter introduces new state management patterns and best practices that help developers manage state more effectively. By adopting efficient state management techniques, such as using Provider or Riverpod, developers can minimize the impact of state changes on the UI and reduce performance overhead.

Image and Asset Optimization

Concept: Optimizing images and other assets can significantly improve loading times and reduce memory consumption.

Implementation: Flutter includes tools for image optimization, such as support for different image formats and resolutions. Developers can use these tools to compress images, serve appropriately sized assets based on device resolution, and improve overall asset loading performance.

These performance optimization techniques in Flutter are designed to help developers build applications that are not only feature-rich but also fast and efficient. By incorporating these strategies, developers can enhance application performance, improve user experience, and ensure that their apps run smoothly across a wide range of devices and environments.

How to Upgrade to Flutter

Upgrading to Flutter involves a series of steps to ensure a smooth transition from previous versions. This section provides a comprehensive guide to upgrading your Flutter projects, addressing common migration issues, and managing deprecated features. By following these guidelines, you can make the most of the new features and improvements introduced in Flutter.

Migration Guides

Upgrading to Flutter is a structured process that requires careful attention to ensure compatibility and optimal performance. This section provides a detailed step-by-step guide for upgrading your projects and addresses common issues that may arise during migration.

Step-by-Step Upgrade Process

Upgrading to Flutter involves several detailed steps to ensure that your project is fully compatible with the latest version of the framework. This process will help you transition smoothly and leverage the new features and improvements introduced in Flutter.

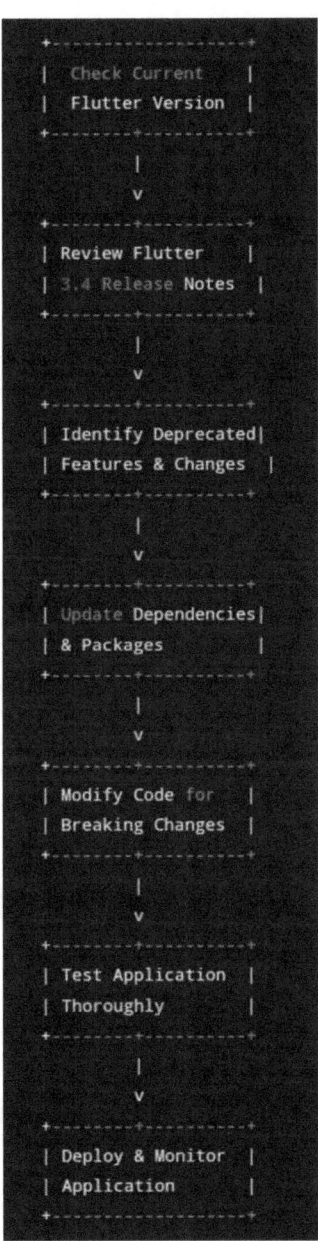

Figure 1-5. *Upgrade process*

CHAPTER 1   FLUTTER OVERVIEW AND NEW FEATURES

Here's a comprehensive guide to upgrading your Flutter project:

Back Up Your Project:

Action: Before initiating the upgrade, create a complete backup of your existing project. This could be done through version control systems like Git or by manually copying your project files to a secure location.

Purpose: This ensures that you can restore your project to its previous state if needed, in case anything goes wrong during the upgrade process.

Update Flutter SDK:

Action: Open your terminal or command prompt and run the following command:

```
flutter upgrade
```

Purpose: This command updates your Flutter SDK to the latest version, including the Flutter CLI tools and associated dependencies.

Check Flutter Version:

Action: Verify the installed Flutter version by running

```
flutter --version
```

CHAPTER 1   FLUTTER OVERVIEW AND NEW FEATURES

Purpose: Ensure that the displayed version is Flutter or later, confirming that the SDK upgrade was successful.

Update Project Dependencies:

Action: Open your `pubspec.yaml` file and check for updates to the dependencies used in your project. Modify the dependency versions to those compatible with Flutter.

Example: Update dependency versions to their latest compatible versions.

Action: Run the following command to fetch and apply the updated dependencies:

```
flutter pub upgrade
```

Purpose: Ensures that all project dependencies are compatible with Flutter and that your project uses the most recent versions of packages.

Run Compatibility Checks:

Action: Execute the following command to perform a compatibility check:

```
flutter doctor
```

> **Purpose**: This command identifies any issues related to the upgrade, including missing dependencies or environment configuration problems.

Update Codebase:

> **Action**: Review the release notes and migration guide for Flutter to identify deprecated features and breaking changes.
>
> **Action**: Modify your code to replace deprecated APIs and update any code that might be affected by breaking changes.
>
> **Purpose**: Ensures that your codebase is compatible with the new version of Flutter and adheres to updated best practices.

Test Your Application:

> **Action**: Perform thorough testing of your application, including both automated and manual tests.
>
> **Purpose**: Verifies that your application functions correctly with Flutter and that no new issues have been introduced during the upgrade.

Resolve Issues:

> **Action**: Address any issues identified during testing or compatibility checks. Review error messages and make necessary adjustments to your code or project configuration.
>
> **Purpose**: Ensures that any problems resulting from the upgrade are resolved and that your application performs as expected.

CHAPTER 1   FLUTTER OVERVIEW AND NEW FEATURES

Optimize and Refactor:

> **Action**: Take advantage of new features and performance improvements introduced in Flutter. Refactor your code to utilize these enhancements effectively.
>
> **Purpose**: Helps to improve the performance and functionality of your application by incorporating the latest features and optimizations.

Deploy and Monitor:

> **Action**: Deploy the updated version of your application to your target platforms. Continue to monitor the application for any post-deployment issues.
>
> **Purpose**: Ensures that the application is functioning correctly in a production environment and allows you to address any issues that may arise after deployment.

By following these steps, you can ensure a smooth and successful upgrade to Flutter, allowing you to take full advantage of the new features and improvements while maintaining the stability and performance of your application.

Common Migration Issues

When upgrading to Flutter, developers may encounter several common migration issues. Understanding these potential problems and how to address them will help ensure a smooth transition.

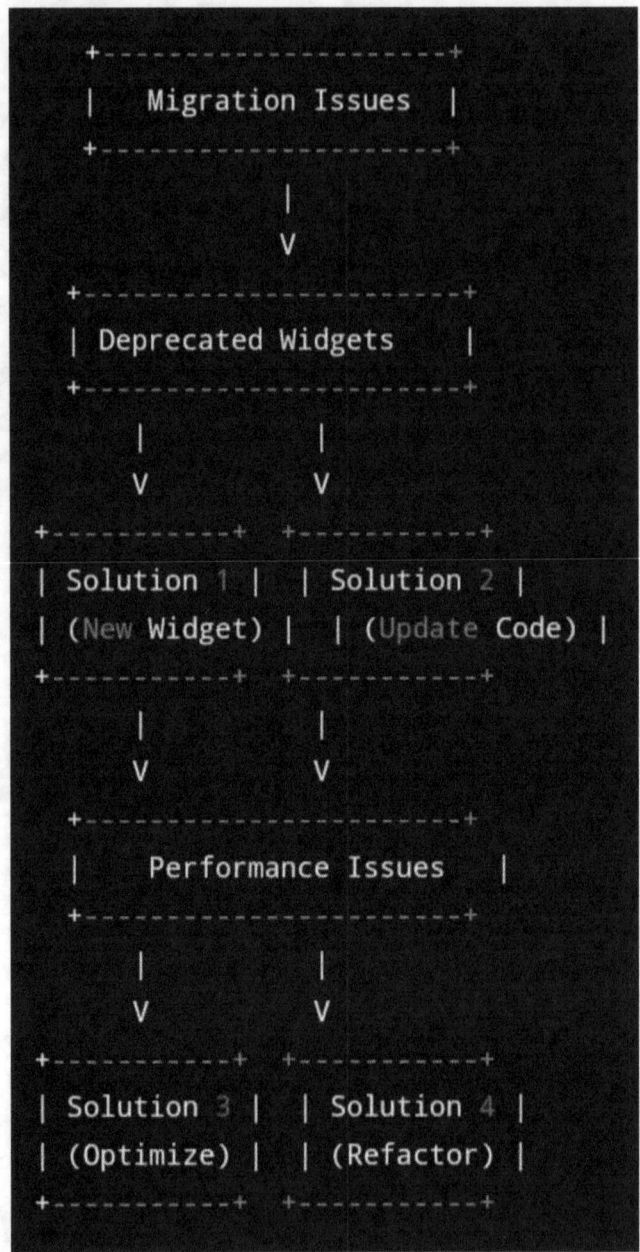

Figure 1-6. *Migration issues*

Here's a detailed look at some of the most frequent issues and their solutions:

Dependency Conflicts:

>**Issue**: Some dependencies may not yet be compatible with Flutter, leading to conflicts or errors during the build process.

Solution:

- **Check for Updates:** Look for updated versions of your dependencies that are compatible with Flutter. Package maintainers often release new versions to support major updates.

- **Consult Documentation**: Review the documentation for each dependency to find compatibility information and migration instructions.

- **Use Compatibility Flags**: Some dependencies may offer flags or configurations to help with compatibility. Check the package's README or changelog for guidance.

Deprecated APIs:

>**Issue**: APIs or methods that were available in previous versions of Flutter may be deprecated or removed in Flutter.

Solution:

- **Refer to Release Notes**: Consult the Flutter release notes and migration guide to identify deprecated features.

CHAPTER 1   FLUTTER OVERVIEW AND NEW FEATURES

- **Update Code**: Replace deprecated methods or properties with their recommended alternatives. The release notes often provide information on what to use instead.
- **Use IDE Assistance**: Many IDEs, like Android Studio or Visual Studio Code, can highlight deprecated APIs and suggest replacements.

Breaking Changes:

> **Issue**: Major updates can introduce breaking changes that affect the behavior of your code, leading to compilation errors or runtime issues.

Solution:

- **Review Breaking Changes**: Carefully review the breaking changes documented in the Flutter release notes.
- **Refactor Code**: Modify your code to comply with the new requirements. This might involve changing how certain features are implemented or adapting to new APIs.
- **Test Thoroughly**: Perform extensive testing to ensure that all parts of your application are functioning correctly after making changes.

Build and Compilation Errors:

> **Issue**: Upgrading can sometimes lead to build or compilation errors due to incompatibilities or missing configurations.

Solution:

- **Analyze Error Messages**: Read and understand the error messages to diagnose the issues. They often provide clues about what needs to be fixed.

- **Consult Documentation**: Refer to the Flutter documentation and community forums for solutions to specific errors.

- **Seek Community Support**: Engage with the Flutter community through forums or GitHub issues to get help with persistent build problems.

Performance Degradations:

Issue: After upgrading, you might experience performance issues or changes in application behavior due to the new version.

Solution:

- **Use Performance Metrics**: Utilize the updated performance metrics and profiling tools introduced in Flutter to identify and diagnose performance problems.

- **Apply Optimization Techniques**: Implement performance optimization techniques such as code splitting, deferred loading, and efficient layout algorithms to address performance issues.

- **Refactor and Optimize**: Review your code and optimize it based on the latest best practices and performance insights.

Testing Failures:

Issue: Automated or manual tests may fail after the upgrade due to changes in the framework or application code.

Solution:

- **Update Test Cases**: Modify your test cases to reflect changes in the codebase or framework. Ensure that tests are aligned with the new version of Flutter.

- **Run Tests Regularly**: Continuously run your tests throughout the upgrade process to catch and address issues early.

- **Review Test Results**: Analyze test failures to understand their root cause and make necessary adjustments to your code or test scenarios.

By proactively addressing these common migration issues, you can mitigate potential problems and ensure a smoother upgrade process to Flutter. Taking these steps will help you maintain a stable and performant application while leveraging the latest features and improvements in Flutter.

Addressing Deprecated Features

As Flutter evolves, certain features and APIs become deprecated or are removed in newer versions. Addressing deprecated features is crucial to maintaining compatibility and leveraging the improvements in the latest Flutter release. This section provides guidance on identifying deprecated features and updating your legacy code to align with Flutter.

List of Deprecated Features

In Flutter, several features and APIs have been deprecated or replaced to improve the framework's functionality and performance.

```
+-----------------------------+------------------------------------+
| Deprecated Feature          | Replacement Feature                |
+-----------------------------+------------------------------------+
| FlatButton                  | TextButton                         |
| RaisedButton                | ElevatedButton                     |
| OutlineButton               | OutlinedButton                     |
| Scaffold.of(context)        | ScaffoldMessenger.of(context)      |
| Navigation.pushNamed()      | Navigator.pushNamed()              |
| ThemeData.primarySwatch     | ThemeData.colorScheme.primary      |
+-----------------------------+------------------------------------+
```

Figure 1-7. Deprecated features

Here is a detailed list of deprecated features that you should be aware of when upgrading your projects:

Deprecated Widgets:

FlatButton:

Replacement: TextButton.

Reason: TextButton provides improved customization options and aligns with newer button styles.

RaisedButton:

Replacement: ElevatedButton.

Reason: ElevatedButton offers enhanced visual styling and interactive feedback.

OutlineButton:

Replacement: OutlinedButton.

Reason: OutlinedButton provides consistent styling and improved usability.

DropdownButton (with Certain Properties):

Replacement: DropdownButtonFormField for form integration—or use custom DropdownButton with new properties.

Reason: Enhanced form integration and customization options.

Deprecated Methods:

Navigator.pushNamed() with Route:

Replacement: Use the new Navigator methods with updated routing mechanisms.

Reason: Updated routing mechanisms offer improved flexibility and control.

Widget.build() with BuildContext:

Replacement: Updated BuildContext handling methods.

Reason: Improved context management and efficiency.

showDialog() with showGeneralDialog():

Replacement: Use showDialog() with the new Dialog class implementations.

Reason: More flexible and customizable dialog options.

CHAPTER 1 FLUTTER OVERVIEW AND NEW FEATURES

Deprecated Packages:

flutter_localizations (Older Methods):

Replacement: Updated internationalization (i18n) and localization (l10n) APIs.

Reason: Newer APIs provide better support for localization and internationalization.

http Package (Older Methods):

Replacement: Updated methods and classes in the latest version of the http package.

Reason: Improved support for modern networking features.

Deprecated API Features:

DefaultTextStyle (Certain Properties):

Replacement: Use updated text style properties or new widgets for text styling.

Reason: New styling mechanisms offer better control and consistency.

MediaQueryData (Certain Properties):

Replacement: Use updated MediaQuery properties or new APIs for responsive design.

Reason: Enhanced APIs for handling different screen sizes and orientations.

Deprecated Libraries:

flutter_tools (Internal Tooling):

Replacement: Updated tooling libraries and methods.

Reason: Internal tooling has been refactored for better performance and maintainability.

Deprecated Themes and Styles:

ThemeData (Certain Legacy Properties):

Replacement: New theme properties and styles.

Reason: More consistent and modern theming options.

Deprecated Layout Widgets:

Flexible (with Flex Property):

Replacement: Use Flex with updated layout configurations.

Reason: Improved layout handling and configuration.

Deprecated Navigation Features:

PageRouteBuilder (with Certain Old Configurations):

Replacement: Updated navigation routes and configurations.

Reason: New navigation features offer better control and customization.

For a complete and detailed list of deprecated features, consult the Flutter release notes and the official Flutter documentation. These resources will provide specific details on deprecated features and their recommended replacements.

CHAPTER 1   FLUTTER OVERVIEW AND NEW FEATURES

Updating Legacy Code

Updating legacy code to comply with new Flutter versions and address deprecated features is a crucial step in maintaining and improving your application. Here's a structured approach to updating your legacy code when migrating to Flutter:

```
Before Migration:
+------------------------------------------------------+
|   // Deprecated FlatButton Widget                    |
|   FlatButton(                                        |
|     onPressed: () {},                                |
|     child: Text('Click me'),                         |
|   )                                                  |
+------------------------------------------------------+

After Migration:
+------------------------------------------------------+
|   // Updated to TextButton Widget                    |
|   TextButton(                                        |
|     onPressed: () {},                                |
|     child: Text('Click me'),                         |
|   )                                                  |
+------------------------------------------------------+
```

Figure 1-8. Updating legacy codes

Identify Deprecated Features

> **Action**: Review the Flutter release notes and migration guide to identify deprecated features in your codebase.

> **Tools**: Use IDE features, such as code analysis tools and deprecation warnings, to locate deprecated APIs and widgets.

Find and Implement Alternatives

> **Action**: For each deprecated feature, locate the recommended alternative or updated API. Consult the Flutter documentation and migration guide for specific instructions.
>
> **Resources**: Check Flutter's official documentation, release notes, and community forums for guidance on replacements.

Refactor Code

> **Action**: Modify your codebase to replace deprecated features with their updated counterparts.
>
> This may involve
>
> **Widgets**: Replace deprecated widgets (e.g., FlatButton to TextButton, RaisedButton to ElevatedButton).
>
> **Methods**: Update method calls to use new APIs or methods (e.g., Navigator.pushNamed() to new routing methods).
>
> **Packages**: Update package versions and adjust code to use the new package APIs if necessary.

Example:

```
// Before
FlatButton(
```

```
  onPressed: () {},
  child: Text('Click me'),
)
// After
TextButton(
  onPressed: () {},
  child: Text('Click me'),
)
```

Update Dependencies

>**Action**: Modify your pubspec.yaml file to update dependencies to versions that support Flutter. Run flutter pub upgrade to apply these changes.
>
>**Check Compatibility**: Ensure that updated dependencies do not introduce new deprecations or conflicts.

Test Your Changes

>**Action**: Perform thorough testing of your application to ensure that the refactored code works as expected. This includes
>
>**Automated Tests**: Run unit tests and integration tests to verify functionality.
>
>**Manual Testing**: Perform exploratory testing to ensure that the application behaves correctly in various scenarios.

Address Compilation Errors

> **Action**: Resolve any compilation errors that arise from the code updates. Error messages often provide useful hints about what needs to be fixed.
>
> **Consult Documentation**: Refer to Flutter documentation and community forums for solutions to specific errors.

Refactor for Performance

> **Action**: Take this opportunity to refactor your code for improved performance and maintainability. This may include
>
> **Optimizing Code**: Simplify complex logic and remove redundant code.
>
> **Adopting Best Practices**: Use the latest Flutter best practices and design patterns.

Review and Update Documentation

> **Action**: Update any internal documentation, code comments, and README files to reflect changes made during the update process.
>
> **Purpose**: Ensures that documentation is accurate and helps other developers understand the updated codebase.

Seek Community Support

> **Action**: If you encounter challenges or need clarification on certain updates, seek help from the Flutter community.

Resources: Engage in forums, read through GitHub issues, and participate in Flutter-related discussions for additional guidance.

Continuous Integration

Action: Update your continuous integration (CI) configurations to ensure that the new codebase is tested and built correctly.

Tools: Review and update Continuous Integration and Delivery (CI/CD) pipelines and scripts as needed to align with the new Flutter version.

By following these steps, you can effectively update your legacy code to be compatible with Flutter, ensuring that your application benefits from the latest features and improvements while maintaining stability and performance.

In-Depth Analysis of Release Notes

The release notes for Flutter provide a comprehensive overview of new features, improvements, and changes introduced in this version. An in-depth analysis of these release notes is crucial for understanding how they affect your current projects and how to adapt accordingly. This section breaks down the key aspects of the release notes and evaluates their potential impact on existing Flutter projects.

Detailed Analysis of Release Notes

The release notes for Flutter are essential for understanding the changes, new features, and improvements introduced in this version. A detailed analysis of these release notes will help you grasp how the updates can affect your projects and guide you through the necessary adjustments.

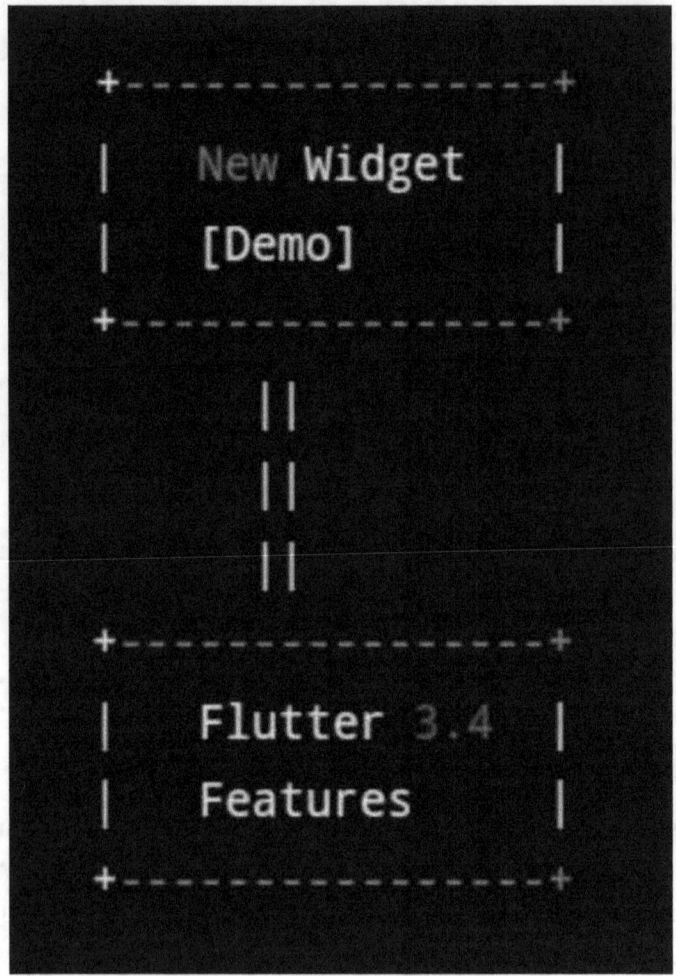

Figure 1-9. *Simple widget representation*

CHAPTER 1　FLUTTER OVERVIEW AND NEW FEATURES

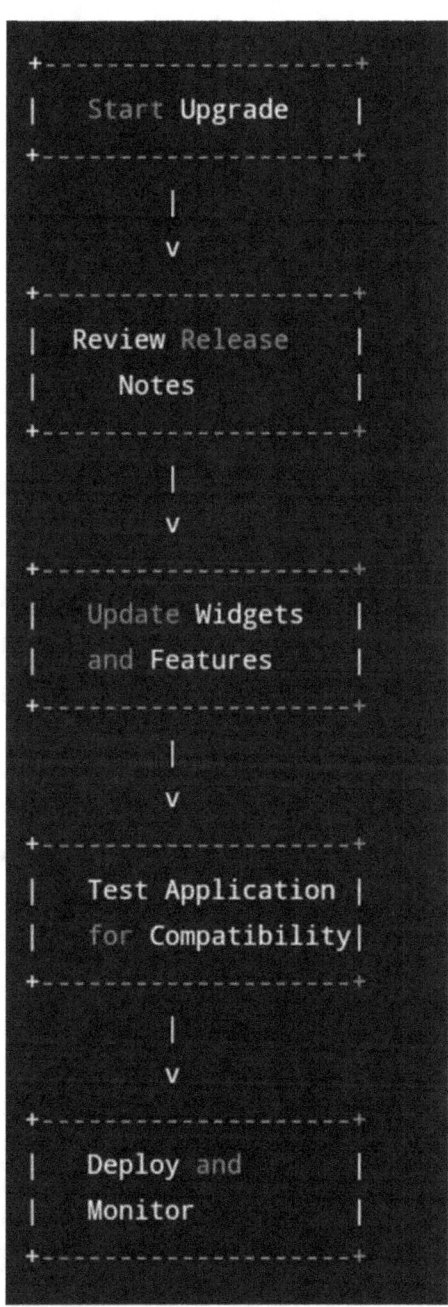

Figure 1-10. *Upgrade process flow*

Here's a structured breakdown of the key areas covered in the Flutter release notes:

New Features

>**Overview**: Flutter introduces a range of new features designed to enhance the framework's functionality and usability. These new features are aimed at improving both developer productivity and end-user experiences.

New Widgets:

>**InteractiveViewer**: Provides a widget that allows users to pan, zoom, and rotate a child widget, making it ideal for interactive and map-based interfaces.

>**AnimatedSwitcher Enhancements**: Updates to AnimatedSwitcher make it easier to switch between widgets with customizable transitions.

Enhanced UI Components:

>**ElevatedButton, TextButton, OutlinedButton**: These buttons have received updates to offer more customization options and improved visual consistency.

>**Analysis**: Evaluate how these new widgets and features can be utilized to enhance your app's UI. Consider how InteractiveViewer can be integrated into your project for interactive content. Review the enhancements to existing buttons and determine if they can replace custom implementations or improve user interaction.

Performance Improvements

Overview: Flutter includes several performance optimizations aimed at enhancing the efficiency and responsiveness of Flutter applications.

Rendering Improvements:

Optimized Layout Algorithms: New layout algorithms improve the performance of complex UIs by reducing rendering times and improving frame rates.

Enhanced Animation Support: Updates to animation handling improve smoothness and reduce jank in animations.

Memory Management:

Garbage Collection: Improvements in memory management and garbage collection (GC) reduce memory usage and prevent leaks.

Efficient Resource Handling: Better handling of resources and assets minimizes memory footprint and load times.

Analysis: Assess how these performance improvements could benefit your application. Conduct performance profiling to measure the impact of these optimizations on your app's performance. Refactor parts of your app to leverage these improvements if necessary.

CHAPTER 1   FLUTTER OVERVIEW AND NEW FEATURES

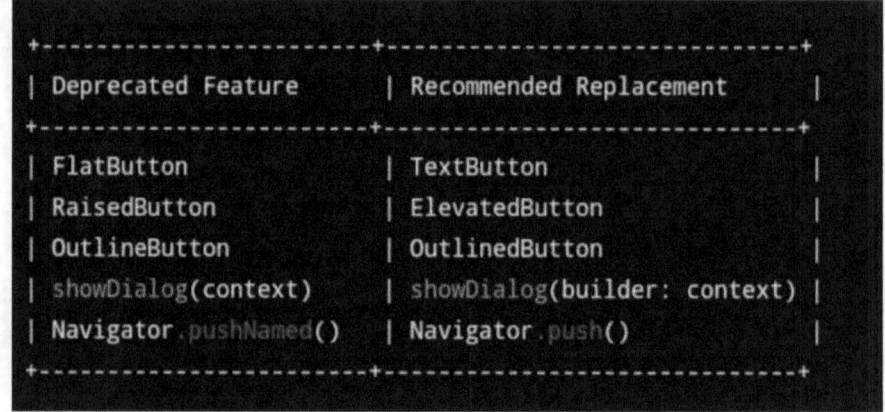

Figure 1-11. Deprecated features and their recommended replacements

Deprecations and Breaking Changes

Overview: Flutter deprecates certain features and introduces breaking changes that may require adjustments to your codebase.

Deprecated Widgets:

FlatButton: Replaced by TextButton for better customization.

RaisedButton: Replaced by ElevatedButton with enhanced visual and interaction features.

Deprecated Methods:

Navigator.pushNamed(): Changes to routing mechanisms might require updates to how navigation is handled in your application.

Breaking Changes:

TextTheme Updates: Certain properties in TextTheme might have been updated or removed, affecting text styling in your app.

CHAPTER 1   FLUTTER OVERVIEW AND NEW FEATURES

Analysis: Identify the deprecated features used in your project and plan for necessary code changes. Review the breaking changes and refactor your code to accommodate these changes. Use Flutter's migration guide and documentation to find suitable replacements and update your code accordingly.

Bug Fixes and Stability Improvements

Overview: The release notes detail numerous bug fixes and stability improvements that address known issues from previous versions.

Fixed Issues:

Rendering Bugs: Resolved issues related to widget rendering and layout.

Platform-Specific Fixes: Bug fixes for specific platforms (e.g., Android, iOS) to ensure better cross-platform functionality.

Stability Enhancements:

Framework Stability: General improvements to the stability of the Flutter framework and its components.

Analysis: Review the list of fixed issues to determine if any apply to problems previously encountered in your projects. Update your application to benefit from these fixes, and verify that the issues are resolved in your environment.

Updated Documentation and Tools

Overview: Flutter may include updates to documentation and tooling that support the new features and improvements.

New Guides:

Migration Guides: Updated guides to help developers transition to Flutter.

Best Practices: New recommendations and best practices for utilizing the latest features.

Tooling Improvements:

Flutter CLI Updates: Enhancements to Flutter CLI tools for better development workflows.

IDE Plugins: Updated IDE plugins for improved integration with Flutter.

Analysis: Familiarize yourself with the updated documentation and tools. Ensure that your development environment is configured to take advantage of new features and improvements. Update your workflows and practices based on the latest recommendations.

By thoroughly analyzing the release notes for Flutter, you can effectively manage the transition to the new version, ensuring that your projects benefit from the latest features, improvements, and fixes. This detailed understanding will help you make informed decisions about updates and optimizations for your Flutter applications.

Impact on Existing Projects

The release of Flutter introduces various changes that can significantly impact existing projects. Understanding these impacts is crucial for a smooth transition and for leveraging the new version's benefits effectively. Here's a comprehensive analysis of how Flutter might affect your existing projects:

CHAPTER 1   FLUTTER OVERVIEW AND NEW FEATURES

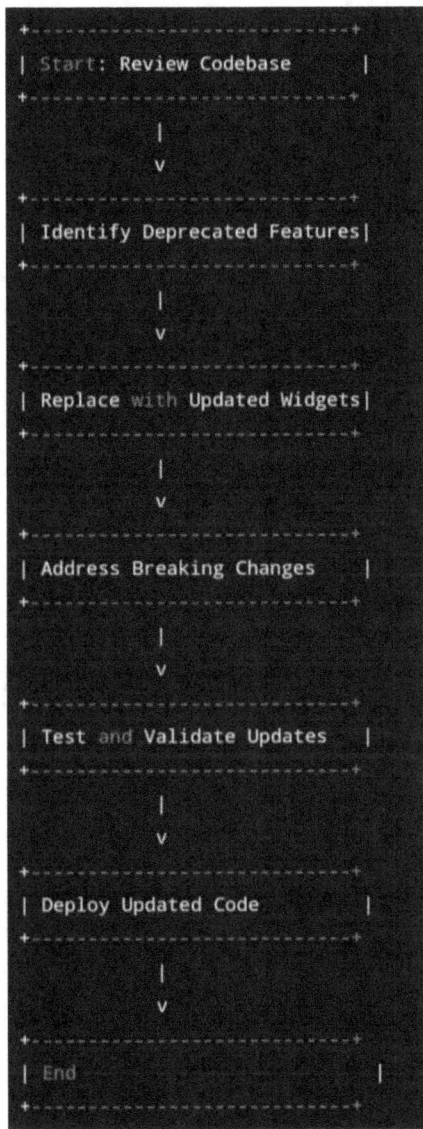

Figure 1-12. *Updating deprecated features and addressing breaking changes*

Codebase Compatibility

Assessment: Flutter introduces several new features and deprecates some existing ones. The changes may require modifications to your codebase to ensure compatibility.

- **Deprecated Features**: Identify any deprecated widgets, methods, or APIs used in your project. For example, if your project uses FlatButton, you will need to replace it with TextButton.

- **Breaking Changes**: Evaluate how breaking changes, such as updates to navigation methods or TextTheme properties, impact your code. Refactor your code to adapt to these changes and utilize new APIs where necessary.

Action: Update your codebase to replace deprecated features and adjust to breaking changes. Utilize the migration guides provided by Flutter to facilitate this process.

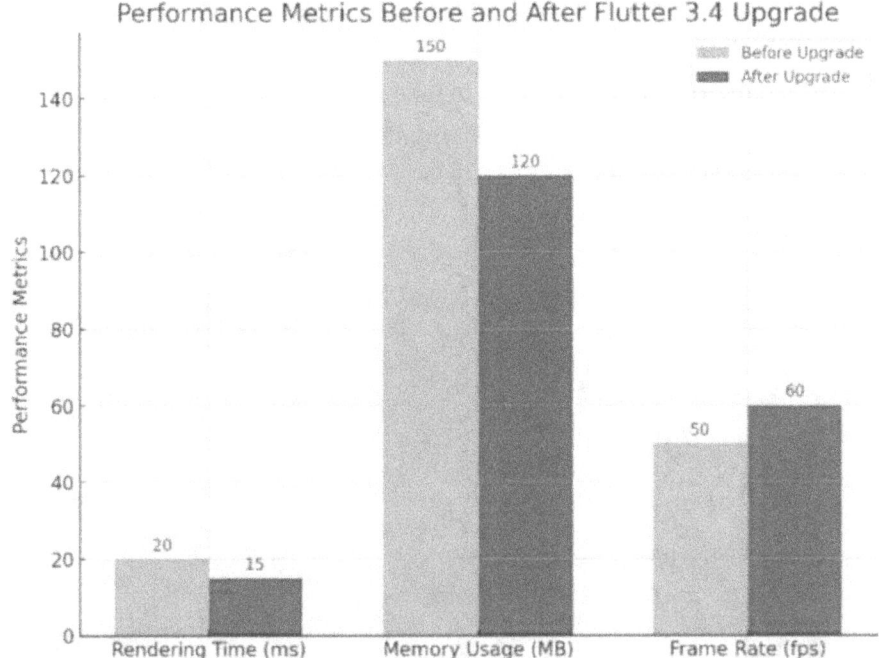

Figure 1-13. *Performance metrics before and after the upgrade*

Performance Implications

>**Assessment**: Flutter includes performance enhancements that could impact your project's performance positively.
>
>- **Rendering Improvements**: With optimized layout algorithms and enhanced animation support, your app may experience smoother performance and reduced frame rates.
>
>- **Memory Management**: Improvements in memory management and garbage collection can lead to more efficient use of resources.

CHAPTER 1 FLUTTER OVERVIEW AND NEW FEATURES

Action: Conduct performance profiling to measure how these improvements affect your app. Refactor parts of your application to take advantage of the new performance enhancements and optimize resource usage.

Dependency Management

Figure 1-14. Flutter dependency update for conflict resolution

Assessment: The update to Flutter may require updating your project's dependencies to versions compatible with the new Flutter version.

- **Package Compatibility**: Check if any of the packages used in your project have updates or changes that support Flutter.

- **Conflict Resolution**: Address any dependency conflicts that arise from updating to the new Flutter version.

    Action: Update your pubspec.yaml file with compatible versions of dependencies and resolve any issues that emerge from these updates.

Testing and Quality Assurance

Assessment: The introduction of new features and deprecations necessitates updating your testing strategy.

- **Test Cases**: Update test cases to cover new features and changes in Flutter. Ensure that deprecated features are no longer being tested.

- **Quality Assurance:** Perform comprehensive testing to verify that the updated code works correctly and that new features are functioning as expected.

Action: Execute automated and manual tests to validate that your application is compatible with Flutter. Address any issues identified during testing.

CHAPTER 1   FLUTTER OVERVIEW AND NEW FEATURES

Documentation and Training

Assessment: The release notes and new features may require updates to your project's documentation and developer training.

- **Documentation Updates**: Revise internal documentation to reflect changes made during the upgrade process.
- **Developer Training**: Ensure that your development team is aware of new features and best practices introduced in Flutter.

Action: Update your documentation and provide training or resources to your team to ensure a smooth transition to the new version.

User Experience

Assessment: New features and performance improvements in Flutter can enhance the user experience.

- **UI/UX Enhancements**: Implement new UI components and features that can improve user interaction and overall app aesthetics.
- **Performance Improvements**: Ensure that the performance enhancements translate into a better user experience, such as smoother animations and faster load times.

Action: Integrate new features that enhance the user experience and gather user feedback to validate improvements. Make adjustments based on user feedback to further refine the experience.

Integration with Other Systems

Assessment: Flutter may introduce changes that affect integrations with other systems or services.

- **API Integrations**: Review any integrations with external APIs or services to ensure compatibility with the updated Flutter version.

- **Platform-Specific Changes**: Check for any platform-specific changes or requirements introduced in Flutter that may affect your app's functionality.

Action: Test and validate integrations with other systems to ensure continued functionality. Update integration points as needed to align with the new Flutter version.

By understanding and addressing these impacts, you can effectively manage the transition to Flutter, ensuring that your existing projects benefit from the latest improvements while maintaining stability and performance.

Summary

This chapter provides a comprehensive overview of Flutter, detailing its new features, performance improvements, and the necessary steps for upgrading. It begins by exploring the introduction of new widgets and enhancements to existing ones, highlighting improvements in UI components and performance metrics. The chapter then guides developers through the step-by-step process of upgrading to Flutter, addressing common migration issues and how to handle deprecated features. It concludes with an in-depth analysis of the release notes,

CHAPTER 1   FLUTTER OVERVIEW AND NEW FEATURES

assessing the detailed changes and their impact on existing projects and offering insights on adapting to new features and improvements. This chapter equips developers with the knowledge to effectively leverage Flutter and navigate the transition smoothly.

CHAPTER 2

Advanced Widget and UI Design

In the rapidly evolving world of mobile application development, crafting visually appealing and functionally robust user interfaces is crucial. This chapter delves into the sophisticated aspects of widget and UI design within Flutter, focusing on both the latest advancements and enduring best practices.

New Widget Features in Flutter

Flutter has introduced a range of new widgets that enhance the toolkit available to developers. This section explores these built-in widgets, providing an overview of their functionalities and potential applications. By understanding these new features, developers can leverage them to create more dynamic and engaging user interfaces. We will examine how these widgets can be customized to fit specific design needs and explore various scenarios where they can be effectively employed.

Modern UI Patterns

As user expectations evolve, so do the patterns and principles guiding modern UI design. This section focuses on responsive and adaptive UIs, offering insights into building interfaces that seamlessly adjust to different screen sizes and orientations. Additionally, we will delve into design systems—structured approaches that ensure consistency across applications. This includes creating and managing design tokens, which are essential for maintaining a cohesive look and feel.

CHAPTER 2   ADVANCED WIDGET AND UI DESIGN

Advanced Layout Techniques

Effective layout management is key to creating intuitive and aesthetically pleasing applications. In this section, we will explore advanced layout techniques such as using LayoutBuilder and CustomMultiChildLayout. These tools provide developers with the flexibility to build complex and responsive layouts. We will also cover dynamic and adaptive layout patterns that enable applications to adjust fluidly to varying content and screen conditions.

Interactive UI Elements

Interactive elements are central to user engagement. This section discusses the creation of immersive UI components that enhance the interactivity of applications. We will provide practical examples to illustrate how these components can be implemented to deliver a more engaging user experience.

Advanced Widget Testing

Testing is an essential aspect of widget development, ensuring that custom widgets perform as expected and integrate seamlessly into the broader application. This section covers strategies for testing custom widgets, including case studies and best practices. Understanding these testing techniques will help developers build more reliable and maintainable widgets.

By exploring these advanced topics, this chapter aims to equip developers with the knowledge and tools necessary to push the boundaries of what is possible in Flutter UI design.

CHAPTER 2   ADVANCED WIDGET AND UI DESIGN

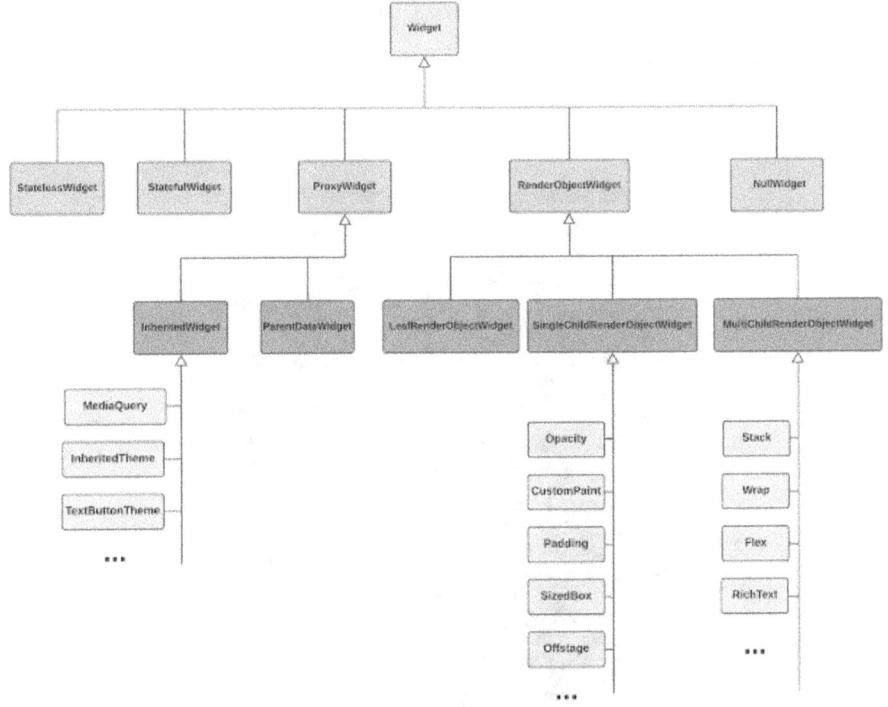

Figure 2-1. Built-in widgets

New Widget Features in Flutter

Flutter brings a wealth of new features and improvements to its widget library, empowering developers to build more sophisticated and engaging applications. This section delves into the newly introduced built-in widgets, offering a detailed examination of their functionalities, customization options, and practical applications.

Detailed Look at New Widgets

Flutter has introduced several new widgets that enhance the framework's capability to build robust, dynamic, and visually appealing applications. Each widget is designed to address specific design and functionality needs,

CHAPTER 2 ADVANCED WIDGET AND UI DESIGN

providing developers with powerful tools to streamline their development process. This section offers a comprehensive look at these new widgets, examining their core features, purposes, and integration within the Flutter ecosystem.

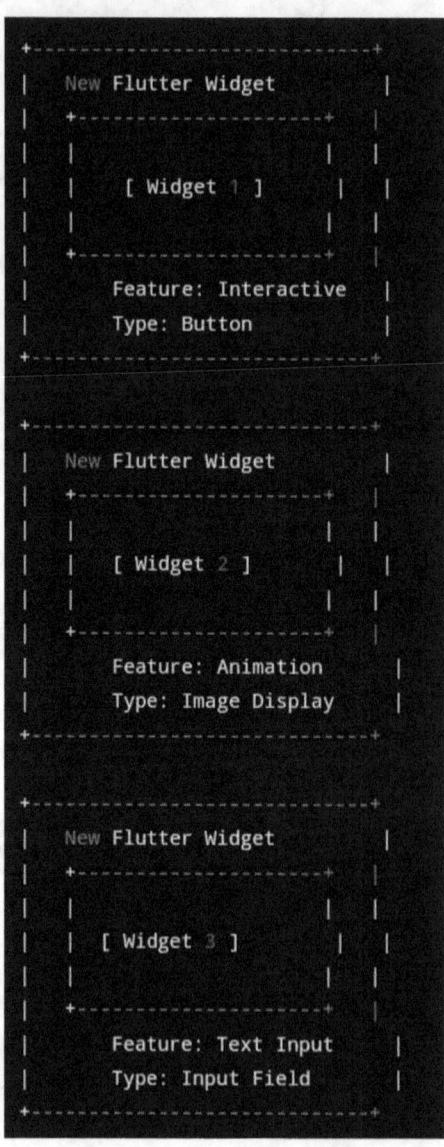

Figure 2-2. *Built-in widgets*

Enhanced GridView

The new `GridView` widget in Flutter introduces enhanced features for managing complex grid layouts. With improvements in performance and flexibility, this widget supports advanced configurations such as

- **Custom Grid Delegate:** The ability to define custom grid layouts beyond the standard `SliverGridDelegate` options
- **Asynchronous Data Handling**: Improved support for loading and displaying data asynchronously, making it easier to handle large datasets

Use Case: Ideal for applications requiring dynamic grid layouts, such as product catalogs or image galleries

InteractiveCard

The `InteractiveCard` widget provides a versatile card component that supports advanced interactions and animations. Key features include

- **Built-In Gesture Recognition**: Simplified gesture handling for user interactions such as taps, swipes, and long presses
- **Custom Animations**: Easily configurable animations for transitions and state changes within the card

Use Case: Useful for creating interactive elements such as cards with expandable content, interactive surveys, or user profile previews

ResponsiveContainer

The `ResponsiveContainer` widget addresses the challenge of designing UIs that adapt to various screen sizes and orientations. Key attributes include

- **Flexible Sizing**: Automatically adjusts its size and layout based on the available screen space
- **Orientation Adaptation**: Supports layout changes in response to device orientation shifts

Use Case: Essential for applications that need to maintain usability and aesthetics across different devices, including tablets and smartphones

AdvancedProgressIndicator

The `AdvancedProgressIndicator` widget offers more control over progress indicators, with features such as

- **Customizable Shapes and Sizes**: Allows developers to create progress indicators with various shapes and dimensions
- **Multi-step Progress Tracking**: Supports complex progress tracking scenarios, including stages and milestones

Use Case: Suitable for applications requiring detailed progress tracking, such as multi-step forms or lengthy data processing tasks

AnimatedListTile

The `AnimatedListTile` widget introduces advanced animation capabilities for list tiles, including

- **Smooth Item Transitions**: Provides smooth animations when items are added to or removed from the list
- **Custom Animation Options**: Allows for extensive customization of animations and transitions

CHAPTER 2   ADVANCED WIDGET AND UI DESIGN

Use Case: Ideal for applications with dynamic lists, where smooth transitions enhance the user experience, such as messaging apps or task managers

ExpandableSection

The `ExpandableSection` widget simplifies the creation of collapsible and expandable sections within an app. Features include

- **Ease of Use**: Simple API for creating expandable sections with custom content
- **Animation Support**: Built-in support for smooth expand/collapse animations

Use Case: Useful for applications that require expandable content sections, such as FAQs, menus, or detailed information panels

OverlayMenu

The `OverlayMenu` widget provides a flexible solution for creating context menus and overlays. Key features include

- **Customizable Positioning**: Allows for precise positioning of menu items relative to other UI elements
- **Adaptive Layout**: Adjusts menu layout based on available screen space and user interactions

Use Case: Perfect for applications with context-sensitive menus or overlays, such as in-app settings or action menus

Integration and Customization

Understanding these new widgets is essential for integrating them into your Flutter applications effectively. Each widget offers unique capabilities and customization options, enabling developers to tailor their functionality to meet specific design requirements. Exploring these widgets in-depth will provide you with the knowledge needed to leverage their full potential in creating sophisticated, responsive, and user-friendly applications.

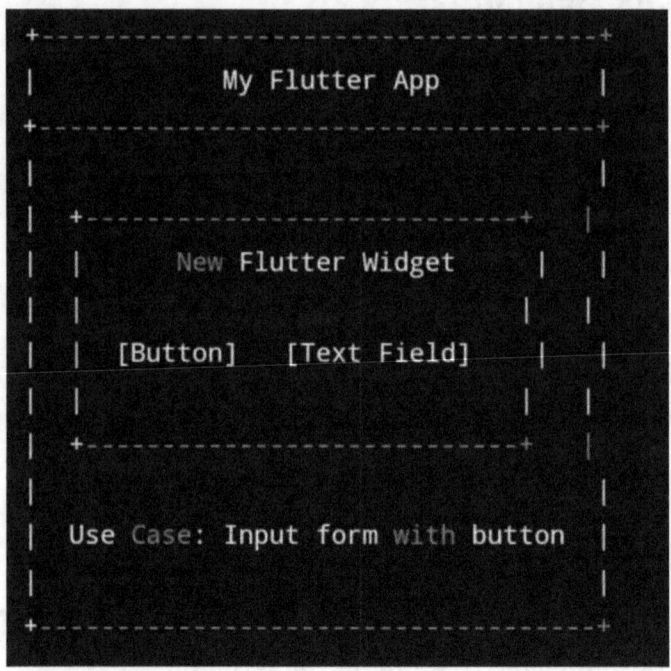

Figure 2-3. Use cases

Examples and Use Cases

Understanding how to apply new widgets in real-world scenarios is essential for maximizing their potential. This section provides practical examples and use cases for each of the new widgets introduced in Flutter, demonstrating how they can be used to address common design and functionality challenges.

Enhanced GridView

Example: Product Catalog

The enhanced GridView widget can be used to create a dynamic product catalog for an ecommerce application. By leveraging custom grid delegates, developers can design layouts that adapt to various screen sizes and orientations, presenting products in a visually appealing grid.

Example

```
GridView(
  gridDelegate: SliverGridDelegateWithFixedCrossAxisCount(
    crossAxisCount: 2,
    childAspectRatio: 3 / 2,
    mainAxisSpacing: 10.0,
    crossAxisSpacing: 10.0,
  ),
  children: products.map((product) => ProductCard(product:
  product)).toList(),
);
```

Use Case

Ecommerce Applications: Displaying product items in an organized grid layout

Image Galleries: Arranging images in a grid format for visual appeal

InteractiveCard

Example: User Profile Card

The InteractiveCard widget is ideal for creating interactive user profile cards that expand to show more details when tapped. This can enhance user engagement in social media applications.

CHAPTER 2 ADVANCED WIDGET AND UI DESIGN

Example

```
InteractiveCard(
  onTap: () => _showProfileDetails(user),
  child: Column(
    children: [
      CircleAvatar(backgroundImage: NetworkImage(user.
      profilePicture)),
      Text(user.name),
    ],
  ),
);
```

Use Case

> **Social Media Apps**: Interactive profile cards with expandable content
>
> **Interactive Surveys**: Cards with engaging survey questions or options

ResponsiveContainer

Example: Adaptive Dashboard Layout

The ResponsiveContainer widget helps in designing a dashboard that adjusts its layout based on screen size. This ensures a consistent and user-friendly experience on both mobile and tablet devices.

Example

```
ResponsiveContainer(
  child: Row(
```

CHAPTER 2   ADVANCED WIDGET AND UI DESIGN

```
    children: [
      Expanded(child: WidgetA()),
      Expanded(child: WidgetB()),
    ],
  ),
);
```

   Use Case

       Dashboards: Adaptive layouts that adjust according to device size

       Data Visualization: Displaying charts and other data in a responsive manner

AdvancedProgressIndicator

Example: Multi-step Form Progress

The AdvancedProgressIndicator widget is useful for visualizing progress in multi-step forms, providing users with clear feedback on their completion status.

   Example

```
AdvancedProgressIndicator(
  progress: currentStep / totalSteps,
  stages: totalSteps,
  shape: BoxShape.circle,
);
```

Use Case

Multi-step Forms: Indicating progress through different stages of form completion

Onboarding Processes: Visualizing the user's progress through onboarding steps

AnimatedListTile

Example: Messaging App
In a messaging application, the AnimatedListTile widget can be employed to animate the addition and removal of messages to and from the chat list, enhancing the overall user experience.

Example

```
AnimatedListTile(
  title: Text(message.content),
  subtitle: Text(message.sender),
  onDismissed: () => _removeMessage(message),
);
```

Use Case

Messaging Apps: Smoothly transitioning chat messages in and out of view

Task Managers: Animating the addition and removal of tasks in a list

CHAPTER 2   ADVANCED WIDGET AND UI DESIGN

ExpandableSection

Example: FAQ Section

The ExpandableSection widget is ideal for creating an FAQ section where each question can be expanded to reveal the answer, keeping the interface clean and organized.

Example

```
ExpandableSection(
  title: 'What is Flutter?',
  content: 'Flutter is an open-source UI software development toolkit created by Google...',
);
```

Use Case

> **FAQs**: Collapsible sections for frequently asked questions
>
> **Menus**: Expandable sections for detailed menu options or content

OverlayMenu

Example: Contextual Action Menu

The OverlayMenu widget is designed for creating contextual action menus that appear in response to user interactions, such as button clicks or item selections.

Example

```
OverlayMenu(
  trigger: IconButton(icon: Icon(Icons.more_vert), onPressed:
  _showMenu),
  items: [
    MenuItem(label: 'Edit', onTap: _editItem),
    MenuItem(label: 'Delete', onTap: _deleteItem),
  ],
);
```

Use Case

> **Contextual Menus**: Providing additional actions or options based on user interaction
>
> **Action Overlays**: Displaying context-sensitive menus or choices

Customization and Usage Scenarios

In addition to the built-in functionalities of the new widgets introduced in Flutter, developers often need to customize these widgets to meet specific design requirements. This section explores advanced widget customization techniques and provides real-world usage scenarios to illustrate how these customizations can be applied effectively.

CHAPTER 2 ADVANCED WIDGET AND UI DESIGN

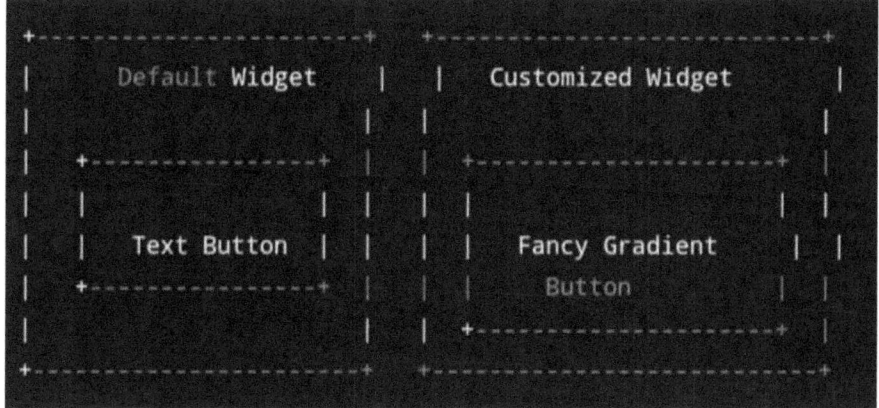

Figure 2-4. *Widget customization*

Advanced Widget Customization

Advanced widget customization in Flutter allows developers to go beyond basic configurations to achieve unique designs and functionality. This section covers various techniques for customizing widgets to fit specific requirements, providing a more tailored user experience.

Custom Themes and Styles

Custom themes and styles help maintain a consistent look and feel across your application. By defining global themes, you can ensure that all widgets adhere to your app's branding.

> **Defining a Theme**: You can create a custom ThemeData to override default widget styles. This includes setting colors, fonts, and shapes.
>
> **Example**

```
ThemeData(
  primaryColor: Colors.teal,
```

```
  accentColor: Colors.amber,
  textTheme: TextTheme(
    bodyText1: TextStyle(fontSize: 16.0, color: Colors.black87),
    headline1: TextStyle(fontSize: 32.0, fontWeight:
    FontWeight.bold),
  ),
  buttonTheme: ButtonThemeData(
    buttonColor: Colors.teal,
    textTheme: ButtonTextTheme.primary,
  ),
);
```

Applying Themes: Use the Theme widget to apply your custom theme across your application.

Example

```
MaterialApp(
  theme: customTheme,
  home: MyHomePage(),
);
```

Inherited Widgets

Inherited widgets allow you to pass data down the widget tree without requiring explicit parameter passing. This is useful for global settings or custom styles.

Creating an Inherited Widget: Define a custom InheritedWidget to share data across the widget tree.

Example

```
class CustomTheme extends InheritedWidget {
  final Color primaryColor;
  CustomTheme({this.primaryColor, Widget child}) :
  super(child: child);
  @override
  bool updateShouldNotify(CustomTheme oldWidget) {
    return primaryColor != oldWidget.primaryColor;
  }
  static CustomTheme of(BuildContext context) {
    return context.dependOnInheritedWidgetOfExactType
    <CustomTheme>();
  }
}
```

Using an Inherited Widget: Access the inherited data within descendant widgets.

Example

```
class MyWidget extends StatelessWidget {
  @override
  Widget build(BuildContext context) {
    final theme = CustomTheme.of(context);
    return Container(
      color: theme.primaryColor,
    );
  }
}
```

Custom Widgets

Creating custom widgets allows you to encapsulate specific functionality and styling, making your code more modular and reusable.

> **Building a Custom Widget**: Extend existing widgets or compose new ones to create a custom widget.

Example

```
class CustomCard extends StatelessWidget {
  final Widget child;
  final Color color;
  CustomCard({this.child, this.color = Colors.white});
  @override
  Widget build(BuildContext context) {
    return Card(
      color: color,
      elevation: 4.0,
      shape: RoundedRectangleBorder(
        borderRadius: BorderRadius.circular(12.0),
      ),
      child: child,
    );
  }
}
```

> **Using Custom Widgets**: Apply your custom widget in various parts of your application.

CHAPTER 2   ADVANCED WIDGET AND UI DESIGN

Example

```
CustomCard(
  color: Colors.blueAccent,
  child: Padding(
    padding: EdgeInsets.all(16.0),
    child: Text('Custom Card Content'),
  ),
);
```

Custom Animations

Custom animations can enhance the visual appeal of your application by providing smooth transitions and interactive effects.

Creating Custom Animations: Utilize Flutter's animation framework to create custom animations.

Example

```
class AnimatedScale extends StatefulWidget {
  final bool isScaled;
  AnimatedScale({this.isScaled});
  @override
  _AnimatedScaleState createState() => _AnimatedScaleState();
}
class _AnimatedScaleState extends State<AnimatedScale> {
  @override
  Widget build(BuildContext context) {
    return AnimatedContainer(
      duration: Duration(seconds: 1),
```

CHAPTER 2   ADVANCED WIDGET AND UI DESIGN

```
      transform: widget.isScaled
          ? Matrix4.identity()..scale(1.2)
          : Matrix4.identity(),
      child: Icon(Icons.star, size: 50),
    );
  }
}
```

> **Applying Animations**: Use the animated widget in your application to provide visual feedback.

Example

```
AnimatedScale(isScaled: true),
```

Custom Render Objects

For highly specialized layouts or complex visual effects, you may need to create custom render objects. This involves extending RenderBox and implementing layout and paint methods.

> **Defining a Custom Render Object**: Create a class that extends RenderBox and override methods for layout and painting.

Example

```
class CustomRenderBox extends RenderBox {
  @override
  void performLayout() {
    // Custom layout logic
  }
```

```
  @override
  void paint(PaintingContext context, Offset offset) {
    // Custom painting logic
  }
}
```

Using a Custom Render Object: Create a wrapper widget that uses the custom render object.

Example

```
class CustomRenderWidget extends
SingleChildRenderObjectWidget {
  @override
  RenderObject createRenderObject(BuildContext context) {
    return CustomRenderBox();
  }
}
```

By mastering these advanced customization techniques, developers can create highly tailored and visually appealing applications that meet specific design and functionality requirements.

Real-World Usage Scenarios

Applying advanced widget customizations in real-world applications can significantly enhance user experiences and meet specific project requirements. Here are some scenarios demonstrating how these customizations can be effectively utilized.

Branded User Interfaces

Scenario: Travel App with Custom Branding
A travel application requires a distinctive brand identity. By using custom themes, the app can ensure that all widgets adhere to the brand's colors, fonts, and styling guidelines.

Implementation
Define a custom ThemeData to set brand-specific colors, text styles, and button themes.

Apply the theme globally using the MaterialApp widget.

Example

```
final ThemeData travelAppTheme = ThemeData(
  primaryColor: Colors.deepOrange,
  accentColor: Colors.amber,
  textTheme: TextTheme(
    headline1: TextStyle(fontSize: 28.0, fontWeight:
    FontWeight.bold, color: Colors.white),
    bodyText1: TextStyle(fontSize: 16.0, color: Colors.
    white70),
  ),
  buttonTheme: ButtonThemeData(
    buttonColor: Colors.deepOrange,
    textTheme: ButtonTextTheme.primary,
  ),
);
MaterialApp(
  theme: travelAppTheme,
  home: HomePage(),
);
```

CHAPTER 2   ADVANCED WIDGET AND UI DESIGN

Responsive Design

Scenario: News App with Adaptive Layout

A news application needs to provide a consistent reading experience across various devices, including smartphones and tablets. Using ResponsiveContainer and custom layout strategies helps in creating a responsive design that adjusts content based on screen size.

Implementation

Use ResponsiveContainer to create adaptable layouts for different screen sizes.

Implement responsive grid and list views that rearrange content based on device orientation.

Example

```
ResponsiveContainer(
  child: LayoutBuilder(
    builder: (context, constraints) {
      if (constraints.maxWidth > 600) {
        return Row(
          children: [
            Expanded(child: NewsSidebar()),
            Expanded(flex: 2, child: NewsFeed()),
          ],
        );
      } else {
        return Column(
          children: [
            NewsFeed(),
            NewsSidebar(),
          ],
        );
```

CHAPTER 2 ADVANCED WIDGET AND UI DESIGN

```
      }
    },
  ),
);
```

Interactive Elements

Scenario: Event App with Interactive Cards
An event application features interactive cards that expand to show more details when tapped. This enhances user engagement by providing detailed information in a compact, expandable format.

Implementation
Use InteractiveCard with gesture detection to create expandable cards.
　　Implement animations to smoothly transition between expanded and collapsed states.
　　Example

```
class EventCard extends StatefulWidget {
  final Event event;
  EventCard({this.event});
  @override
  _EventCardState createState() => _EventCardState();
}
class _EventCardState extends State<EventCard> {
  bool _isExpanded = false;
  @override
  Widget build(BuildContext context) {
    return InteractiveCard(
      onTap: () {
        setState(() {
```

74

CHAPTER 2 ADVANCED WIDGET AND UI DESIGN

```
      _isExpanded = !_isExpanded;
    });
  },
  child: Column(
    children: [
      Text(widget.event.title),
      if (_isExpanded) Text(widget.event.details),
    ],
  ),
 );
 }
}
```

Complex Data Visualization

Scenario: Fitness App with Progress Tracking

A fitness application requires advanced data visualization to track and display workout progress. Custom widgets, such as AdvancedProgressIndicator, can be tailored to represent different stages of progress in a visually engaging manner.

Implementation

Create a custom progress indicator that reflects workout progress.

Use different shapes and colors to represent various stages of progress.

Example

```
AdvancedProgressIndicator(
  progress: workoutProgress / totalWorkoutSteps,
  stages: totalWorkoutSteps,
  shape: BoxShape.rectangle,
  color: Colors.green,
```

```
    backgroundColor: Colors.grey[300],
);
```

Contextual Menus

Scenario: Photo Editing App with Contextual Actions
In a photo editing application, contextual action menus are used to provide editing options when a user interacts with an image. Custom overlay menus enhance usability by presenting relevant actions based on user context.

Implementation
Use OverlayMenu to create a contextual menu that appears when an image is tapped.

Customize menu items and layout based on the editing options available.

Example

```
class PhotoEditor extends StatelessWidget {
  @override
  Widget build(BuildContext context) {
    return OverlayMenu(
      trigger: GestureDetector(
        onTap: () => _showMenu(context),
        child: Image.asset('assets/photo.jpg'),
      ),
      items: [
        MenuItem(label: 'Edit', onTap: () => _editPhoto()),
        MenuItem(label: 'Delete', onTap: () => _deletePhoto()),
      ],
    );
```

```
  }
  void _showMenu(BuildContext context) {
    // Show the overlay menu with editing options
  }
  void _editPhoto() {
    // Edit photo action
  }
  void _deletePhoto() {
    // Delete photo action
  }
}
```

By applying these advanced customizations to real-world scenarios, developers can enhance the functionality and aesthetics of their applications, ensuring they meet specific design and user experience goals.

Modern UI Patterns

Modern UI design is evolving rapidly, with new trends focusing on creating highly responsive and adaptive interfaces that provide consistent experiences across different devices and platforms. This chapter explores the key patterns in modern UI design, focusing on building responsive UIs, adopting adaptive design patterns, and implementing design systems to ensure consistency and scalability in large applications.

Responsive and Adaptive UIs

As users access applications across a wide range of devices, from small smartphones to large desktop screens, the need for both responsive and adaptive UIs has become essential in modern app development. Responsive UIs adjust dynamically to different screen sizes, ensuring a consistent layout and user experience. Adaptive UIs go a step further by tailoring the interface and functionality to the device's specific capabilities.

Building Responsive UIs

Building responsive UIs is essential for ensuring that your application provides an optimal user experience across a diverse range of devices and screen sizes. Responsive design in Flutter involves creating layouts that automatically adjust to various screen dimensions, orientations, and resolutions. Here's a comprehensive guide to building responsive UIs in Flutter:

Using MediaQuery

MediaQuery is a fundamental tool for obtaining information about the device's screen size, orientation, and other parameters. This data can be used to adjust your layout dynamically.

Screen Size and Orientation: You can use MediaQuery to get the width and height of the screen, as well as the device orientation (portrait or landscape).

Example

```
Widget build(BuildContext context) {
  var screenSize = MediaQuery.of(context).size;
  var orientation = MediaQuery.of(context).orientation;
  return Scaffold(
    body: Center(
      child: Text(
        'Screen Width: ${screenSize.width}, Orientation: ${orientation}',
        style: TextStyle(fontSize: 20),
      ),
    ),
  );
}
```

}

Adaptive Layouts: Based on screen size or orientation, you can adjust the layout of your app. For instance, displaying a grid layout on large screens and a list layout on smaller screens.

Example

```
Widget build(BuildContext context) {
  var screenSize = MediaQuery.of(context).size;
  return Scaffold(
    body: screenSize.width > 600
      ? GridView.count(
          crossAxisCount: 3,
          children: List.generate(20, (index) => Card(child:
          Text('Item $index'))),
        )
      : ListView.builder(
          itemCount: 20,
          itemBuilder: (context, index) => Card(child:
          Text('Item $index')),
        ),
  );
}
```

CHAPTER 2 ADVANCED WIDGET AND UI DESIGN

LayoutBuilder for Dynamic Layouts

LayoutBuilder provides the constraints passed to the parent widget, allowing you to build different layouts depending on the available space.

> **Responsive Layouts**: Use LayoutBuilder to decide how to arrange widgets based on the constraints.

Example

```
LayoutBuilder(
  builder: (context, constraints) {
    if (constraints.maxWidth > 800) {
      return Row(
        children: [
          Expanded(child: Sidebar()),
          Expanded(flex: 2, child: Content()),
        ],
      );
    } else {
      return Column(
        children: [
          Content(),
          Footer(),
        ],
      );
    }
  },
);
```

> **Aspect Ratios**: You can also use AspectRatio to maintain a specific aspect ratio of widgets within the available space.

Example

```
AspectRatio(
  aspectRatio: 16 / 9,
  child: Container(
    color: Colors.blue,
    child: Center(child: Text('Aspect Ratio 16:9')),
  ),
);
```

Flex and Expanded Widgets

The Flex, Expanded, and Flexible widgets help create layouts that adapt to different screen sizes by dividing available space among children widgets.

> **Flexible Widgets**: Use Flexible to allow widgets to grow and shrink based on the available space.

Example

```
Row(
  children: [
    Flexible(
      flex: 2,
      child: Container(color: Colors.red),
    ),
    Flexible(
      flex: 1,
      child: Container(color: Colors.blue),
    ),
  ],
);
```

Flexible Layouts: Use Expanded within a Flex to make widgets fill the available space proportionally.

Example

```
Column(
  children: [
    Expanded(child: Container(color: Colors.green)),
    Expanded(child: Container(color: Colors.yellow)),
  ],
);
```

GridView and ListView for Responsive Layouts

GridView and ListView are highly flexible widgets for creating responsive layouts, especially for displaying collections of items.

GridView: Use GridView.count or GridView.builder to create responsive grids.

Example

```
GridView.count(
  crossAxisCount: MediaQuery.of(context).size.width > 600
  ? 4 : 2,
  children: List.generate(20, (index) => Card(child: Text('Item $index'))),
);
```

CHAPTER 2   ADVANCED WIDGET AND UI DESIGN

ListView: For vertical scrolling lists, ListView.builder can dynamically create items as needed.

Example

```
ListView.builder(
  itemCount: 20,
  itemBuilder: (context, index) => ListTile(
    leading: Icon(Icons.star),
    title: Text('Item $index'),
  ),
);
```

Responsive Packages and Tools

Several packages can simplify responsive design by providing higher-level abstractions:

flutter_screenutil: A package for scaling your UI according to different screen sizes and resolutions

Example

```
ScreenUtil.init(
  designSize: Size(360, 690),
  allowFontScaling: false,
);
Container(
  width: 100.w,
  height: 100.h,
  child: Text(
    'Responsive Text',
```

CHAPTER 2   ADVANCED WIDGET AND UI DESIGN

```
    style: TextStyle(fontSize: 20.sp),
  ),
);
```

---

responsive_builder: A package that provides a set of widgets and tools to simplify responsive design

Example

```
ResponsiveBuilder(
  builder: (context, sizingInformation) {
    if (sizingInformation.deviceScreenType == DeviceScreenType.
    desktop) {
      return DesktopLayout();
    } else if (sizingInformation.deviceScreenType ==
    DeviceScreenType.tablet) {
      return TabletLayout();
    } else {
      return MobileLayout();
    }
  },
);
```

Adapting to Different Orientations

Adapting your UI for different orientations can ensure that your application remains functional and visually appealing when users switch between portrait and landscape modes.

OrientationBuilder: Use OrientationBuilder to build different layouts based on the current orientation.

Example

```
OrientationBuilder(
  builder: (context, orientation) {
    if (orientation == Orientation.portrait) {
      return PortraitLayout();
    } else {
      return LandscapeLayout();
    }
  },
);
```

By employing these techniques, you can build Flutter applications that adapt smoothly to various devices and screen sizes, ensuring a consistent and user-friendly experience across different platforms and environments.

Adaptive Design Patterns

Adaptive design patterns are pivotal in creating user interfaces that not only resize but also tailor their functionality and layout based on the specific capabilities and characteristics of the device. Unlike responsive design, which primarily focuses on changing layouts according to screen size, adaptive design goes further by customizing the interface and interactions to optimize the user experience based on device type, input method, and platform conventions.

CHAPTER 2   ADVANCED WIDGET AND UI DESIGN

Platform-Specific Adaptations
Adaptive design often involves creating different UIs for different platforms, such as iOS and Android, to adhere to platform-specific conventions and provide a native-like experience.

> **Platform-Dependent Widgets**: Flutter's Cupertino and Material widgets are designed to help developers create platform-specific UIs. By detecting the platform using Platform.isIOS or Platform.isAndroid, you can conditionally display widgets that match the design principles of the respective operating system.

Example

```
if (Platform.isIOS) {
  return CupertinoPageScaffold(
    navigationBar: CupertinoNavigationBar(
      middle: Text('iOS Page'),
    ),
    child: Center(child: Text('Hello, iOS!')),
  );
} else {
  return Scaffold(
    appBar: AppBar(
      title: Text('Android Page'),
    ),
    body: Center(child: Text('Hello, Android!')),
  );
}
```

CHAPTER 2   ADVANCED WIDGET AND UI DESIGN

Design Guidelines: Adhering to platform-specific design guidelines (like Material Design for Android and Human Interface Guidelines for iOS) ensures that your app feels intuitive and native to users of each platform.

Context-Aware Layout Adjustments

Adaptive UIs may change their structure based on device characteristics, such as screen size, device type (phone vs. tablet), or even user context (work vs. personal use).

Device Type: Modify the layout based on whether the device is a phone, tablet, or desktop. This could involve showing a sidebar on tablets and desktops but hiding it on phones.

Example

```
Widget build(BuildContext context) {
  final deviceType = MediaQuery.of(context).size.width > 600 ?
  DeviceType.tablet : DeviceType.phone;
  return Scaffold(
    body: deviceType == DeviceType.tablet
      ? Row(
          children: [
            Expanded(child: Sidebar()),
            Expanded(flex: 2, child: Content()),
          ],
        )
      : Column(
          children: [
            Content(),
            Footer(),
          ],
```

CHAPTER 2   ADVANCED WIDGET AND UI DESIGN

```
    ),
  );
}
```

Orientation: Adapt the layout when the device orientation changes. For example, a portrait layout might stack elements vertically, while a landscape layout arranges them horizontally.

Example

```
OrientationBuilder(
  builder: (context, orientation) {
    return orientation == Orientation.portrait
      ? Column(
          children: [Header(), Content(), Footer()],
        )
      : Row(
          children: [Sidebar(), Expanded(child: Content())],
        );
  },
);
```

Input Method Adaptation

Adaptive design patterns also involve modifying the UI based on the input method available on the device, such as touch, mouse, or keyboard input.

Touch vs. Mouse: On devices where users primarily use touch input, such as mobile phones and tablets, make sure buttons and interactive elements are large enough for easy tapping. On desktop platforms with mouse input, you can include hover effects or tooltips.

Example

```
if (Platform.isDesktop) {
  return MouseRegion(
    onEnter: (_) => print('Mouse over'),
    child: Container(
      padding: EdgeInsets.all(16),
      child: Text('Hoverable Text'),
    ),
  );
} else {
  return GestureDetector(
    onTap: () => print('Tapped'),
    child: Container(
      padding: EdgeInsets.all(16),
      child: Text('Tapable Text'),
    ),
  );
}
```

Keyboard Interaction: On devices with keyboards, such as desktops or tablets with keyboard attachments, you can support keyboard shortcuts or focusable widgets that respond to keyboard inputs.

CHAPTER 2   ADVANCED WIDGET AND UI DESIGN

Example

```
RawKeyboardListener(
  focusNode: _focusNode,
  onKey: (RawKeyEvent event) {
    if (event is RawKeyDownEvent && event.logicalKey ==
    LogicalKeyboardKey.enter) {
      print('Enter key pressed');
    }
  },
  child: TextField(
    focusNode: _focusNode,
    decoration: InputDecoration(
      labelText: 'Type here',
    ),
  ),
);
```

Adaptive Navigation Patterns

Different devices and screen sizes may require different navigation patterns to maximize usability and accessibility.

> **Mobile Navigation**: For mobile devices, use a BottomNavigationBar or Drawer to provide easy access to navigation items.

Example

```
Scaffold(
```

```
  appBar: AppBar(title: Text('Mobile App')),
  body: Center(child: Text('Mobile Layout')),
  bottomNavigationBar: BottomNavigationBar(
    items: [
      BottomNavigationBarItem(icon: Icon(Icons.home), label:
      'Home'),
      BottomNavigationBarItem(icon: Icon(Icons.search), label:
      'Search'),
    ],
  ),
);
```

Tablet/Desktop Navigation: On larger screens, consider using a Drawer or a SideBar to accommodate more navigation options and provide a more expansive layout.

Example

```
Scaffold(
  appBar: AppBar(title: Text('Desktop App')),
  body: Row(
    children: [
      NavigationRail(
        destinations: [
          NavigationRailDestination(icon: Icon(Icons.home),
          label: Text('Home')),
          NavigationRailDestination(icon: Icon(Icons.search),
          label: Text('Search')),
        ],
      ),
```

```
      Expanded(child: Center(child: Text('Desktop Layout'))),
    ],
  ),
);
```

Adaptive Content Presentation

The way content is presented can also be adapted based on the device. This may involve altering how information is displayed, such as using card-based layouts on mobile devices and more detailed, complex layouts on desktops.

> **Content Density**: On larger screens, present more detailed information in a single view, while on smaller screens, use more concise content or multiple screens.

Example

```
Widget build(BuildContext context) {
  return MediaQuery.of(context).size.width > 800
    ? DetailedView()  // Larger screens show detailed view
    : CompactView();  // Smaller screens show compact view
}
```

Adaptive design patterns ensure that your application provides the best possible user experience by tailoring its behavior and appearance to the specific characteristics of the device and context in which it is used. By employing these patterns, you can enhance usability and create more engaging, intuitive interfaces for all users.

Implementing Design Systems

Design systems provide a unified approach to UI design, ensuring consistency and efficiency across applications. They consist of a collection of reusable components, design patterns, and guidelines that help streamline the development process and maintain a cohesive user experience. In this section, we'll explore how to implement design systems in Flutter, starting with an introduction to what a design system is and then diving into the creation and management of design tokens.

Introduction to Design Systems

Design systems are comprehensive frameworks that integrate design principles, components, and guidelines to create cohesive and consistent user experiences across products and platforms. They serve as a single source of truth for design and development teams, streamlining the process of creating and maintaining user interfaces. By providing a structured approach to design, design systems help ensure that all parts of an application or suite of applications work harmoniously, regardless of who is working on them or where they are developed.

Core Components of a Design System

1. **Design Principles**

    - **Definition**: Fundamental rules or guidelines that drive the overall design philosophy. These principles provide a foundation for making design decisions and ensuring consistency in user experience.

    - **Examples**: Accessibility, simplicity, user-centricity, and responsiveness. Principles guide designers in creating interfaces that are intuitive, inclusive, and aligned with user needs.

2. **UI Components**
   - **Definition**: Reusable building blocks such as buttons, form fields, cards, and modals. These components are designed to be consistent in appearance and behavior, reducing redundancy and maintaining uniformity across the application.
   - **Examples**: A standardized button component with predefined styles, sizes, and states that can be used throughout the application.

3. **Patterns and Layouts**
   - **Definition**: Established design solutions for common problems. Patterns and layouts offer proven approaches for organizing content and functionality, helping to create predictable and familiar user experiences.
   - **Examples**: Grid systems, navigation bars, and responsive layouts that adapt to various screen sizes.

4. **Design Tokens**
   - **Definition**: The smallest unit of a design system, representing design decisions such as colors, typography, spacing, and shadows. Design tokens are used to maintain consistency and facilitate updates across the entire application.
   - **Examples**: Color variables for primary and secondary colors, typography settings for headers and body text, and spacing units for margins and paddings.

CHAPTER 2   ADVANCED WIDGET AND UI DESIGN

5. **Documentation and Guidelines**

    - **Definition**: Detailed documentation that explains how to use design components, patterns, and tokens. This includes usage guidelines, best practices, and code examples.

    - **Examples**: Component libraries with code snippets, design guidelines for accessibility, and instructions for integrating components into different platforms.

Benefits of Design Systems

1. **Consistency**

    - **Uniformity**: Ensures a consistent look and feel across different parts of the application or suite of products. This consistency helps reinforce brand identity and improves usability.

    - **Predictability**: Users experience a coherent and predictable interface, which enhances their overall satisfaction and reduces learning curves.

2. **Efficiency**

    - **Reduced Redundancy**: Streamlines the design and development process by providing reusable components and established patterns. This reduces the need to reinvent the wheel and speeds up delivery.

    - **Streamlined Workflows**: Facilitates collaboration between designers and developers by providing a shared set of resources and guidelines.

3. **Scalability**
   - **Easier Expansion**: Supports the growth of the application by providing a scalable framework that can be easily extended with new components and patterns.
   - **Maintainability**: Simplifies updates and maintenance by centralizing design decisions and making it easier to apply changes across the application.

4. **Collaboration**
   - **Shared Language**: Provides a common language and set of tools for designers and developers, enhancing communication and reducing misunderstandings.
   - **Unified Approach**: Aligns design and development efforts, ensuring that all team members are working toward the same goals and standards.

Implementing a Design System

1. **Assessment and Planning**
   - **Evaluate Needs**: Assess the current design and development practices to identify areas where a design system can add value.
   - **Define Goals**: Set clear objectives for the design system, including the scope, target audience, and key components.

2. **Design and Development**
   - **Create Components**: Design and develop reusable components that adhere to the design principles and guidelines.
   - **Develop Tokens**: Define and implement design tokens to standardize design values and ensure consistency.

3. **Documentation and Training**
   - **Document**: Create comprehensive documentation that explains how to use the design system, including component libraries, design principles, and best practices.
   - **Train**: Educate team members on the design system and how to apply it effectively in their work.

4. **Implementation and Maintenance**
   - **Integrate**: Implement the design system into your projects and ensure that all new designs adhere to the established guidelines.
   - **Update**: Regularly review and update the design system to reflect changes in design trends, user needs, and technological advancements.

By establishing a design system, organizations can create a unified and scalable approach to UI design that enhances consistency, efficiency, and collaboration. A well-implemented design system not only streamlines the development process but also contributes to a better user experience by providing a cohesive and intuitive interface.

Creating and Managing Design Tokens

Design tokens are fundamental elements of a design system that represent the visual design decisions of an application. They are used to standardize design values such as colors, typography, spacing, and shadows, enabling consistent styling across the entire application and simplifying the process of updating design elements. This section covers the essentials of creating and managing design tokens in a Flutter project, from defining them to implementing and maintaining them.

Defining Design Tokens

Design tokens are essentially variables that store design-related values. They provide a systematic way to handle design attributes, making it easier to ensure consistency and apply updates across the application.

Key Categories of Design Tokens

Colors: Defines the color palette used in the application. This includes primary, secondary, and neutral colors, as well as variations for states like hover or disabled.

Example

```
class AppColors {
  static const Color primary = Color(0xFF6200EE);
  static const Color secondary = Color(0xFF03DAC6);
  static const Color background = Color(0xFFF5F5F5);
  static const Color textPrimary = Color(0xFF000000);
  static const Color textSecondary = Color(0xFF757575);
}
```

Typography: Specifies font families, sizes, weights, and styles used for different text elements.

Example

```
class AppTypography {
  static const TextStyle headline1 = TextStyle(
    fontSize: 32,
    fontWeight: FontWeight.bold,
    letterSpacing: 0.5,
  );
  static const TextStyle bodyText1 = TextStyle(
    fontSize: 16,
    fontWeight: FontWeight.normal,
    letterSpacing: 0.15,
  );
}
```

Spacing: Defines margins, paddings, and gaps used to maintain consistent spacing throughout the application.

Example

```
class AppSpacing {
  static const double small = 8.0;
  static const double medium = 16.0;
  static const double large = 24.0;
}
```

Borders and Shadows: Specifies border widths, radii, and shadow properties.

Example

```
class AppBorders {
  static const BorderRadius small = BorderRadius.all(Radius.circular(4.0));
  static const BorderRadius medium = BorderRadius.all(Radius.circular(8.0));
  static const BorderRadius large = BorderRadius.all(Radius.circular(16.0));
}
class AppShadows {
  static const BoxShadow defaultShadow = BoxShadow(
    color: Color(0x29000000),
    offset: Offset(0, 4),
    blurRadius: 8,
  );
}
```

Implementing Design Tokens

Once design tokens are defined, they need to be implemented throughout the application to ensure consistency and facilitate easy updates.

Steps for Implementation

Create Token Files: Organize design tokens into separate Dart files or classes to keep them modular and manageable.

CHAPTER 2 ADVANCED WIDGET AND UI DESIGN

Example Directory Structure

```
lib/
├── design/
│   ├── colors.dart
│   ├── typography.dart
│   ├── spacing.dart
│   └── borders_and_shadows.dart
```

Reference Tokens in Components: Use design tokens when defining the style for widgets. This ensures that styles are consistent and easily adjustable.

Example

```
// custom_button.dart
import 'package:flutter/material.dart';
import 'design/colors.dart';
import 'design/typography.dart';
import 'design/spacing.dart';
class CustomButton extends StatelessWidget {
  final String label;
  final VoidCallback onPressed;
  CustomButton({required this.label, required this.onPressed});
  @override
  Widget build(BuildContext context) {
    return ElevatedButton(
      style: ElevatedButton.styleFrom(
        primary: AppColors.primary,
        padding: EdgeInsets.symmetric(vertical: AppSpacing.medium, horizontal: AppSpacing.large),
```

```
      textStyle: AppTypography.bodyText1,
    ),
    onPressed: onPressed,
    child: Text(label),
  );
 }
}
```

> **Maintain Consistency**: Ensure that all styling and layout decisions across the application use the defined tokens rather than hardcoded values. This promotes consistency and simplifies maintenance.

Example

```
// text_widget.dart
import 'package:flutter/material.dart';
import 'design/typography.dart';
class CustomText extends StatelessWidget {
  final String text;
  CustomText({required this.text});
  @override
  Widget build(BuildContext context) {
    return Text(
      text,
      style: AppTypography.bodyText1,
    );
  }
}
```

Managing and Updating Design Tokens

Design tokens should be managed and updated regularly to reflect changes in design requirements and to maintain consistency across the application.

Best Practices for Management
Central Repository: Store all design tokens in a central location, such as a dedicated Dart file or package. This makes it easier to update tokens and ensures that changes are applied consistently.

> **Version Control**: Use version control to track changes to design tokens. This allows for easy rollbacks and collaboration among team members.
>
> **Automated Builds**: Integrate automated build processes to ensure that design tokens are correctly applied throughout the application. This can include automated tests to verify token usage and consistency.
>
> **Regular Reviews**: Periodically review and update design tokens to align with evolving design trends, user feedback, and new platform requirements. Regular updates help keep the design system relevant and effective.
>
> **Documentation**: Maintain up-to-date documentation for design tokens, including their purpose, usage guidelines, and examples. This helps ensure that all team members understand how to use tokens correctly.

CHAPTER 2   ADVANCED WIDGET AND UI DESIGN

Example Documentation

```
### Design Tokens
**Color Palette**
'primary': #6200EE - Main color for primary actions.
'secondary': #03DAC6 - Used for secondary actions.
'background': #F5F5F5 - Default background color.
**Typography**
'headline1': 32px, bold - Used for main headings.
'bodyText1': 16px, normal - Default text style for body content.
```

By creating and managing design tokens effectively, you can ensure consistency in design and simplify the process of making updates. Design tokens serve as a foundational element of a design system, enabling a cohesive and adaptable user experience across your application.

Advanced Layout Techniques

Advanced layout techniques in Flutter allow developers to create more complex and flexible user interfaces. This section explores two powerful layout widgets—`LayoutBuilder` and `CustomMultiChildLayout`—as well as techniques for building dynamic and adaptive layouts. These tools help developers manage complex layout scenarios, ensuring that UIs are responsive, adaptable, and performant.

Using LayoutBuilder and CustomMultiChildLayout

In Flutter, creating sophisticated and flexible layouts often requires more control over widget positioning and sizing. Two powerful tools for achieving this are LayoutBuilder and CustomMultiChildLayout. These widgets provide advanced options for building dynamic and complex UIs, allowing for greater customization and adaptability in your application's layout.

LayoutBuilder In-Depth

LayoutBuilder is a highly versatile widget in Flutter that enables dynamic and responsive layout adjustments based on the constraints of its parent. It provides a way to build widgets that can adapt their size and position according to the available space, making it particularly useful for creating layouts that respond to different screen sizes and orientations.

How LayoutBuilder Works

LayoutBuilder takes a builder function as a parameter, which receives two arguments:

> **BuildContext**: The context in which the widget is being built
>
> **BoxConstraints**: An object that contains the constraints imposed by the parent widget, including the maximum and minimum width and height

The builder function uses these constraints to determine how to size and position its child widgets. By leveraging BoxConstraints, you can create layouts that adapt to various screen sizes and conditions.

Key Features

Constraints-Based Layouts: The primary feature of LayoutBuilder is its ability to adapt the layout based on the parent's constraints. This makes it easy to create responsive designs that adjust to different screen sizes and orientations.

Dynamic Adjustments: LayoutBuilder allows for dynamic adjustments to the layout as constraints change, such as during orientation changes or when the widget is resized.

Flexible Design: It facilitates the design of flexible UIs that can handle different layouts based on varying constraints.

Usage Patterns

1. **Creating Responsive Layouts**

LayoutBuilder is often used to create responsive layouts that adapt to the width of the screen. For instance, you can switch between different layout configurations (e.g., Row vs. Column) based on the available width.

Example

```
import 'package:flutter/material.dart';
class ResponsiveExample extends StatelessWidget {
  @override
  Widget build(BuildContext context) {
    return Scaffold(
      appBar: AppBar(title: Text('Responsive Example')),
```

CHAPTER 2 ADVANCED WIDGET AND UI DESIGN

```
    body: LayoutBuilder(
      builder: (BuildContext context, BoxConstraints
      constraints) {
        if (constraints.maxWidth > 600) {
          // Large screens (e.g., tablets, desktops)
          return Row(
            children: [
              Expanded(child: Container(color:
              Colors.blue, height: 200)),
              Expanded(child: Container(color:
              Colors.red, height: 200)),
            ],
          );
        } else {
          // Small screens (e.g., phones)
          return Column(
            children: [
              Container(color: Colors.blue,
              height: 200),
              Container(color: Colors.red,
              height: 200),
            ],
          );
        }
      },
    ),
  );
 }
}
```

In this example, LayoutBuilder checks the width of the available space and adjusts the layout accordingly, switching between a horizontal Row and a vertical Column.

2. **Adapting to Height Constraints**

   LayoutBuilder can also be used to adapt layouts based on height constraints. For example, you might want to display a different number of items in a grid based on the height of the available space.

   Example

```
import 'package:flutter/material.dart';
class HeightBasedLayout extends StatelessWidget {
  @override
  Widget build(BuildContext context) {
    return Scaffold(
      appBar: AppBar(title: Text('Height Based
      Layout')),
      body: LayoutBuilder(
        builder: (BuildContext context, BoxConstraints
        constraints) {
          int itemCount;
          if (constraints.maxHeight > 800) {
            itemCount = 4; // Display more items on
                           taller screens
          } else {
            itemCount = 2; // Display fewer items on
                           shorter screens
          }
```

```
      return GridView.builder(
        gridDelegate: SliverGridDelegateWithFixed
        CrossAxisCount(
          crossAxisCount: 2,
          crossAxisSpacing: 10,
          mainAxisSpacing: 10,
        ),
        itemCount: itemCount,
        itemBuilder: (context, index) {
          return Container(color: Colors.blue,
          height: 100);
        },
      );
    },
  ),
);
}
}
```

Here, LayoutBuilder adjusts the number of items displayed in a GridView based on the height of the available space.

3. **Building Complex Adaptive Layouts**

For more complex layouts, LayoutBuilder can be combined with other widgets to create adaptive designs that change their structure based on both width and height constraints.

Example

```
import 'package:flutter/material.dart';
class ComplexAdaptiveLayout extends StatelessWidget {
  @override
  Widget build(BuildContext context) {
    return Scaffold(
      appBar: AppBar(title: Text('Complex Adaptive
      Layout')),
      body: LayoutBuilder(
        builder: (BuildContext context, BoxConstraints
        constraints) {
          final isWide = constraints.maxWidth > 600;
          final isTall = constraints.maxHeight > 800;
          if (isWide && isTall) {
            return GridView.builder(
              gridDelegate: SliverGridDelegateWithFixed
              CrossAxisCount(
                crossAxisCount: 3,
                crossAxisSpacing: 10,
                mainAxisSpacing: 10,
              ),
              itemCount: 9,
              itemBuilder: (context, index) {
                return Container(color: Colors.blue,
                height: 100);
              },
            );
          } else if (isWide) {
            return ListView.builder(
              itemCount: 6,
```

```
          itemBuilder: (context, index) {
            return Container(color: Colors.red,
            height: 100);
          },
        );
      } else if (isTall) {
        return Column(
          children: List.generate(6, (index) {
            return Container(color: Colors.green,
            height: 100);
          }),
        );
      } else {
        return Center(child: Text('Not enough
        space'));
      }
    },
  ),
);
}
}
```

In this example, LayoutBuilder provides a different layout configuration based on both width and height constraints, demonstrating how you can create highly adaptive layouts.

Best Practices

Minimize Overuse: While LayoutBuilder is powerful, overusing it can lead to performance issues. Only use it where necessary to adapt layouts based on constraints.

Combine with Other Widgets: Often, LayoutBuilder is most effective when combined with other responsive and adaptive widgets, such as MediaQuery or Flexible, to handle more complex layout scenarios.

Test Across Devices: Ensure that layouts built with LayoutBuilder are tested across various devices and screen sizes to verify that they adapt correctly.

Use for Specific Layouts: Use LayoutBuilder for specific layout sections that require adaptability, rather than applying it to the entire widget tree.

By understanding and effectively using LayoutBuilder, you can create dynamic, responsive layouts that adjust to different constraints, ensuring a better user experience across a range of devices and screen sizes.

CustomMultiChildLayout

`CustomMultiChildLayout` is a powerful Flutter widget that allows developers to create complex layouts by precisely controlling the size and position of multiple child widgets. It offers greater flexibility than many other layout widgets, making it ideal for custom and non-standard layout requirements. This widget relies on a custom `MultiChildLayoutDelegate` to dictate how its children should be arranged.

How CustomMultiChildLayout Works

`CustomMultiChildLayout` works by using a `MultiChildLayoutDelegate` to perform the layout logic. The `MultiChildLayoutDelegate` is responsible for defining how each child widget should be sized and positioned within the parent widget.

Key Components

1. `CustomMultiChildLayout` **Widget**: The widget that hosts multiple child widgets and applies the custom layout logic defined in the delegate.

2. `MultiChildLayoutDelegate`: An abstract class that you extend to provide custom layout behavior. The delegate's `performLayout` method is where you specify the layout logic.

3. `LayoutId` **Widget**: Used to associate child widgets with unique identifiers, which the delegate uses to position and size the widgets.

Key Features

- **Fine-Grained Control**: Provides precise control over the layout of multiple children, allowing for complex and non-standard layouts

- **Custom Layout Algorithms**: Enables the implementation of custom layout algorithms by overriding the `performLayout` method

- **Flexibility**: Suitable for scenarios where standard layout widgets do not offer the necessary flexibility

Example Usage

1. **Basic Example**

    In this example, CustomMultiChildLayout is used to position two child widgets relative to each other. The MyCustomLayoutDelegate defines the layout logic, positioning the first widget at the top left and the second widget to the right of the first.

    Example

    ```
    import 'package:flutter/material.dart';
    class CustomLayoutExample extends StatelessWidget {
      @override
      Widget build(BuildContext context) {
        return Scaffold(
          appBar: AppBar(title: Text('Custom MultiChild
          Layout')),
          body: CustomMultiChildLayout(
            delegate: MyCustomLayoutDelegate(),
            children: [
              LayoutId(id: 'box1', child: Container(color:
              Colors.blue, width: 100, height: 100)),
              LayoutId(id: 'box2', child: Container(color:
              Colors.red, width: 100, height: 100)),
            ],
          ),
        );
      }
    }
    class MyCustomLayoutDelegate extends
    MultiChildLayoutDelegate {
    ```

CHAPTER 2 ADVANCED WIDGET AND UI DESIGN

```
  @override
  void performLayout(Size size) {
    // Position the first child at the top-left
    if (hasChild('box1')) {
      layoutChild('box1', BoxConstraints.loose(size));
      positionChild('box1', Offset(0, 0));
    }
    // Position the second child to the right of the
       first child
    if (hasChild('box2')) {
      layoutChild('box2', BoxConstraints.loose(size));
      positionChild('box2', Offset(100, 0));
    }
  }
  @override
  bool shouldRelayout(covariant
  MultiChildLayoutDelegate oldDelegate) {
    return false; // Return true if the layout needs to
                be updated based on changes
  }
}
```

In this code, `CustomMultiChildLayout` uses the `MyCustomLayoutDelegate` to position box1 and box2. The `performLayout` method determines their exact positions within the available space.

2. **Advanced Example**

    For more complex layouts, you can calculate positions dynamically based on constraints or other factors. This example positions child widgets in a grid-like arrangement using custom logic.

Example

```
import 'package:flutter/material.dart';
class AdvancedCustomLayout extends StatelessWidget {
  @override
  Widget build(BuildContext context) {
    return Scaffold(
      appBar: AppBar(title: Text('Advanced Custom
      Layout')),
      body: CustomMultiChildLayout(
        delegate: AdvancedLayoutDelegate(),
        children: [
          LayoutId(id: 'box1', child: Container(color:
          Colors.blue, width: 100, height: 100)),
          LayoutId(id: 'box2', child: Container(color:
          Colors.red, width: 100, height: 100)),
          LayoutId(id: 'box3', child: Container(color:
          Colors.green, width: 100, height: 100)),
        ],
      ),
    );
  }
}
class AdvancedLayoutDelegate extends
MultiChildLayoutDelegate {
  @override
  void performLayout(Size size) {
    double boxWidth = 100;
    double boxHeight = 100;
    double spacing = 10;
    // Define positions for a grid-like arrangement
```

```
      if (hasChild('box1')) {
        layoutChild('box1', BoxConstraints.
        tight(Size(boxWidth, boxHeight)));
        positionChild('box1', Offset(0, 0));
      }
      if (hasChild('box2')) {
        layoutChild('box2', BoxConstraints.
        tight(Size(boxWidth, boxHeight)));
        positionChild('box2', Offset(boxWidth +
        spacing, 0));
      }
      if (hasChild('box3')) {
        layoutChild('box3', BoxConstraints.
        tight(Size(boxWidth, boxHeight)));
        positionChild('box3', Offset(0, boxHeight +
        spacing));
      }
    }
    @override
    bool shouldRelayout(covariant
    MultiChildLayoutDelegate oldDelegate) {
      return false; // Return true if layout needs to be
                    updated based on changes
    }
  }
```

In this example, AdvancedLayoutDelegate positions the boxes in a grid-like pattern with specified spacing between them. The performLayout method calculates the position of each box and adjusts their layout accordingly.

Best Practices

Optimize Performance: Avoid overusing CustomMultiChildLayout for simple layouts. Use it when you need precise control or when other layout widgets cannot meet your requirements.

Handle Layout Changes: Ensure that shouldRelayout returns true if the layout needs to be updated based on changes in the delegate. This helps to handle dynamic changes efficiently.

Test Layouts Thoroughly: Test the custom layouts on various devices and screen sizes to ensure they render as expected across different environments.

Avoid Complex Calculations: Keep layout calculations as simple as possible to maintain performance and readability. If the layout logic becomes too complex, consider breaking it down into smaller, manageable components.

By leveraging CustomMultiChildLayout and creating custom layout delegates, you can build highly adaptable and flexible UIs in Flutter, catering to a wide range of design requirements and user needs.

Dynamic and Adaptive Layouts

In modern app development, creating layouts that dynamically adjust to changing conditions and adapt to different environments is crucial for delivering a smooth user experience. Flutter offers robust tools and techniques for achieving dynamic and adaptive layouts. This section covers how to build dynamic layouts that respond to real-time changes and explores adaptive layout patterns for various device types and orientations.

CHAPTER 2   ADVANCED WIDGET AND UI DESIGN

Building Dynamic Layouts

Building dynamic layouts in Flutter involves creating user interfaces that adapt to real-time changes, such as user interactions, screen size variations, or data updates. This adaptability ensures a responsive and engaging user experience. Here, we explore several techniques and widgets for building dynamic layouts that can efficiently handle various scenarios.

Key Techniques for Building Dynamic Layouts
Using StatefulWidget for Interactive Layouts:

StatefulWidget allows you to manage state changes and dynamically update the UI in response to user interactions or other events. This approach is crucial for layouts that need to change based on user input or real-time data.

Example: Toggling Layout Elements

```
import 'package:flutter/material.dart';
class DynamicStatefulLayout extends StatefulWidget {
  @override
  _DynamicStatefulLayoutState createState() => _
  DynamicStatefulLayoutState();
}

class _DynamicStatefulLayoutState extends State<DynamicStatefulLayout> {
  bool _showFirstContainer = true;
  void _toggleLayout() {
    setState(() {
      _showFirstContainer = !_showFirstContainer;
    });
  }
```

119

```
@override
Widget build(BuildContext context) {
  return Scaffold(
    appBar: AppBar(title: Text('Dynamic Stateful Layout')),
    body: Column(
      children: [
        ElevatedButton(
          onPressed: _toggleLayout,
          child: Text(_showFirstContainer ? 'Show Second
          Container' : 'Show First Container'),
        ),
        Expanded(
          child: _showFirstContainer
              ? Container(color: Colors.blue, height: 100)
              : Container(color: Colors.red, height: 100),
        ),
      ],
    ),
  );
}
}
```

In this example, the layout toggles between two containers based on a button click, demonstrating how StatefulWidget can manage dynamic changes.

Using LayoutBuilder for Responsive Design:
LayoutBuilder allows you to build layouts that adapt to the constraints of their parent widget. This is particularly useful for creating responsive designs that adjust based on screen size or orientation.

Example: Adapting Layout Based on Width

```
import 'package:flutter/material.dart';
class ResponsiveLayoutBuilder extends StatelessWidget {
  @override
  Widget build(BuildContext context) {
    return Scaffold(
      appBar: AppBar(title: Text('LayoutBuilder Example')),
      body: LayoutBuilder(
        builder: (context, constraints) {
          if (constraints.maxWidth > 600) {
            return Row(
              children: [
                Expanded(child: Container(color: Colors.blue,
                  height: 100)),
                Expanded(child: Container(color: Colors.green,
                  height: 100)),
              ],
            );
          } else {
            return Column(
              children: [
                Container(color: Colors.blue, height: 100),
                Container(color: Colors.green, height: 100),
              ],
            );
          }
        },
```

```
      ),
    );
  }
}
```

This example uses LayoutBuilder to switch between a Row and a Column based on the screen width.

Using MediaQuery for Adaptive Layouts:
MediaQuery provides information about the device's screen size, orientation, and other properties. It helps in adjusting the layout dynamically according to these properties.

Example: Adjusting Layout Based on Orientation

```
import 'package:flutter/material.dart';
class MediaQueryAdaptiveLayout extends StatelessWidget {
  @override
  Widget build(BuildContext context) {
    final orientation = MediaQuery.of(context).orientation;
    final isPortrait = orientation == Orientation.portrait;
    return Scaffold(
      appBar: AppBar(title: Text('MediaQuery Adaptive
      Layout')),
      body: Center(
        child: Container(
          width: isPortrait ? MediaQuery.of(context).size.width
          * 0.8 : MediaQuery.of(context).size.width * 0.4,
          height: MediaQuery.of(context).size.height * 0.4,
          color: Colors.blue,
        ),
      ),
```

```
    );
  }
}
```

In this example, MediaQuery is used to adjust the container's width based on the device's orientation.

Handling Data-Driven Layout Changes:
Dynamic layouts can also be driven by data, such as lists or user-generated content. Using widgets like ListView, GridView, or StreamBuilder, you can create layouts that respond to changes in data.

Example: Building a List with StreamBuilder

```
import 'package:flutter/material.dart';
class DataDrivenLayout extends StatelessWidget {
  @override
  Widget build(BuildContext context) {
    // Example stream of data
    final Stream<List<String>> dataStream =
    Stream<List<String>>.periodic(
      Duration(seconds: 1),
      (count) => List.generate(count % 5 + 1, (index) => 'Item
      $index'),
    );
    return Scaffold(
      appBar: AppBar(title: Text('Data-Driven Layout')),
      body: StreamBuilder<List<String>>(
        stream: dataStream,
        builder: (context, snapshot) {
          if (snapshot.connectionState == ConnectionState.
          waiting) {
```

```
          return Center(child: CircularProgressIndicator());
        } else if (snapshot.hasError) {
          return Center(child: Text('Error: ${snapshot.
          error}'));
        } else if (!snapshot.hasData || snapshot.data!.
        isEmpty) {
          return Center(child: Text('No Data Available'));
        } else {
          return ListView(
            children: snapshot.data!.map((item) =>
            ListTile(title: Text(item))).toList(),
          );
        }
      },
    ),
  );
 }
}
```

In this example, StreamBuilder is used to update a ListView dynamically based on a stream of data.

Best Practices for Dynamic Layouts

> **Minimize Rebuilds**: Use state management techniques to minimize unnecessary rebuilds. For example, use Provider, Riverpod, or Bloc to manage state efficiently.

> **Test Across Devices**: Ensure that dynamic layouts work well across various screen sizes and orientations by testing on multiple devices or using emulators.

Optimize Performance: Avoid complex layouts that could impact performance. Use const constructors where possible and optimize rendering logic to maintain smooth performance.

Handle Edge Cases: Consider edge cases such as extremely small or large screens, and ensure that the layout remains usable and visually appealing in these scenarios.

By employing these techniques, you can create flexible and responsive layouts that adapt to various conditions, providing a better user experience across different devices and use cases.

Adaptive Layout Patterns

Adaptive layouts are designed to adjust their appearance based on different device characteristics, such as screen size, orientation, and platform conventions. This approach ensures that the user interface provides an optimal experience across a wide range of devices and environments. In Flutter, you can implement adaptive layouts using various patterns and techniques.

Key Adaptive Layout Patterns
Fluid Layouts:
Fluid layouts adjust their size and arrangement based on the available space, typically using flexible units like percentages or flexible widgets. This pattern is effective for creating layouts that scale well with different screen sizes.

Example: Using Expanded and Flexible Widgets

```
import 'package:flutter/material.dart';
class FluidLayoutExample extends StatelessWidget {
  @override
```

CHAPTER 2   ADVANCED WIDGET AND UI DESIGN

```
  Widget build(BuildContext context) {
    return Scaffold(
      appBar: AppBar(title: Text('Fluid Layout')),
      body: Row(
        children: [
          Expanded(child: Container(color: Colors.blue,
          height: 100)),
          Flexible(
            flex: 2,
            child: Container(color: Colors.green, height: 100),
          ),
        ],
      ),
    );
  }
}
```

In this example, Expanded and Flexible widgets are used to create a row where the containers take up a flexible portion of the available space, adapting to the screen width.

Grid-Based Layouts:

Grid-based layouts arrange content in a grid format, which adapts to different screen sizes by adjusting the number of columns or rows. This pattern is useful for organizing content in a structured way that scales effectively.

Example: Responsive Grid Layout

```
import 'package:flutter/material.dart';
class ResponsiveGridLayout extends StatelessWidget {
  @override
```

CHAPTER 2   ADVANCED WIDGET AND UI DESIGN

```
Widget build(BuildContext context) {
  return Scaffold(
    appBar: AppBar(title: Text('Responsive Grid Layout')),
    body: GridView.builder(
      gridDelegate: SliverGridDelegateWithFixed
      CrossAxisCount(
        crossAxisCount: MediaQuery.of(context).size.width >
        600 ? 4 : 2,
        crossAxisSpacing: 10,
        mainAxisSpacing: 10,
      ),
      itemCount: 8,
      itemBuilder: (context, index) {
        return Container(color: Colors.blue, height: 100);
      },
    ),
  );
}
}
```

This example uses GridView.builder with SliverGridDelegateWithFixedCrossAxisCount to adjust the number of columns based on the screen width.

Conditional Layouts:
Conditional layouts switch between different layout configurations based on certain conditions, such as screen size or device type. This approach helps tailor the user experience to specific contexts.

Example: Switching Layouts Based on Screen Width

```
import 'package:flutter/material.dart';
class ConditionalLayoutExample extends StatelessWidget {
  @override
  Widget build(BuildContext context) {
    final bool isWideScreen = MediaQuery.of(context).size.
    width > 600;
    return Scaffold(
      appBar: AppBar(title: Text('Conditional Layout')),
      body: isWideScreen
          ? Row(
              children: [
                Expanded(child: Container(color: Colors.blue,
                height: 100)),
                Expanded(child: Container(color: Colors.green,
                height: 100)),
              ],
            )
          : Column(
              children: [
                Container(color: Colors.blue, height: 100),
                Container(color: Colors.green, height: 100),
              ],
            ),
    );
  }
}
```

In this example, the layout changes between a Row and a Column based on whether the screen width exceeds 600 pixels.

CHAPTER 2   ADVANCED WIDGET AND UI DESIGN

Platform-Specific Layouts:

Platform-specific layouts adjust their appearance based on the platform (iOS or Android) to adhere to platform conventions and provide a native look and feel. This pattern ensures that the UI feels natural on each platform.

Example: Platform-Specific UI

```
import 'package:flutter/material.dart';
import 'dart:io' show Platform;
class PlatformAdaptiveLayout extends StatelessWidget {
  @override
  Widget build(BuildContext context) {
    return Scaffold(
      appBar: AppBar(title: Text('Platform Adaptive Layout')),
      body: Platform.isIOS
          ? CupertinoPageScaffold(
              navigationBar: CupertinoNavigationBar(
                middle: Text('iOS Layout'),
              ),
              child: Center(child: Text('This is an iOS
              layout')),
            )
          : Scaffold(
              appBar: AppBar(title: Text('Android Layout')),
              body: Center(child: Text('This is an Android
              layout')),
            ),
    );
  }
}
```

In this example, the layout differs between iOS and Android, using `CupertinoPageScaffold` for iOS and `Scaffold` for Android.

Adaptive Layouts with `Flex` and `Wrap`:
The `Flex` and `Wrap` widgets provide flexible layouts that adapt to varying screen sizes and content. `Flex` allows for flexible alignment along one axis, while `Wrap` arranges children in a horizontal or vertical wrap.

Example: Using `Wrap` for Adaptive Layouts

```
import 'package:flutter/material.dart';
class WrapLayoutExample extends StatelessWidget {
  @override
  Widget build(BuildContext context) {
    return Scaffold(
      appBar: AppBar(title: Text('Wrap Layout Example')),
      body: Wrap(
        spacing: 8.0,
        runSpacing: 8.0,
        children: List.generate(10, (index) {
          return Container(
            color: Colors.blue,
            width: 100,
            height: 100,
            child: Center(child: Text('Item $index')),
          );
        }),
      ),
    );
  }
}
```

CHAPTER 2   ADVANCED WIDGET AND UI DESIGN

In this example, `Wrap` arranges items in a horizontal or vertical flow, adapting to the available space and wrapping items as needed.

Best Practices for Adaptive Layouts

> **Prioritize Usability**: Ensure that adaptive layouts enhance usability rather than complicate it. Test different configurations to ensure a good user experience.
>
> **Optimize for Performance**: Use efficient layout techniques to avoid performance issues. Avoid deep widget trees and excessive layout calculations that can impact performance.
>
> **Consider Accessibility**: Make sure that adaptive layouts are accessible to all users, including those with disabilities. Test for screen readers and other accessibility features.
>
> **Maintain Consistency**: While adapting to different platforms or screen sizes, maintain a consistent design language to provide a cohesive experience.

By applying these adaptive layout patterns, you can create versatile and user-friendly interfaces that perform well across a variety of devices and contexts.

Interactive UI Elements

Interactive UI elements are crucial for engaging users and providing an intuitive interface. These elements can range from buttons and sliders to more complex components like animations and gestures. Creating immersive and interactive UI components can significantly enhance the

CHAPTER 2   ADVANCED WIDGET AND UI DESIGN

user experience by making the interface more dynamic and responsive. This section explores techniques for creating such components and provides practical examples to illustrate their application.

Creating Immersive UI Components

Creating immersive UI components involves designing elements that not only look visually appealing but also interact in engaging and meaningful ways. Immersive components enhance user experience by making interactions more intuitive, fluid, and enjoyable. Flutter offers a range of tools and widgets to build such components, enabling developers to craft rich, interactive, and dynamic interfaces. Below are key techniques and examples for creating immersive UI components in Flutter:

Animated Widgets
Animated widgets can bring static UI elements to life by providing smooth transitions and animations that respond to user actions. Flutter's animation library offers powerful tools to create complex animations easily.

    Example: AnimatedOpacity

```
import 'package:flutter/material.dart';
class AnimatedOpacityExample extends StatefulWidget {
  @override
  _AnimatedOpacityExampleState createState() => _
  AnimatedOpacityExampleState();
}
class _AnimatedOpacityExampleState extends
State<AnimatedOpacityExample> {
  bool _visible = true;
  void _toggleVisibility() {
    setState(() {
```

CHAPTER 2 ADVANCED WIDGET AND UI DESIGN

```
      _visible = !_visible;
    });
  }
  @override
  Widget build(BuildContext context) {
    return Scaffold(
      appBar: AppBar(title: Text('Animated Opacity')),
      body: Center(
        child: Column(
          mainAxisAlignment: MainAxisAlignment.center,
          children: [
            AnimatedOpacity(
              opacity: _visible ? 1.0 : 0.0,
              duration: Duration(seconds: 1),
              child: Container(
                width: 100,
                height: 100,
                color: Colors.blue,
                child: Center(child: Text('Fade In/Out', style:
                TextStyle(color: Colors.white))),
              ),
            ),
            SizedBox(height: 20),
            ElevatedButton(
              onPressed: _toggleVisibility,
              child: Text('Toggle Visibility'),
            ),
          ],
        ),
      ),
    );
```

      }
    }

In this example, AnimatedOpacity is used to fade a container in and out based on the _visible state. The AnimatedOpacity widget provides smooth transitions for the opacity property.

Gesture-Driven Interactions

Gestures add an interactive layer to UI elements, allowing users to perform actions like swipes, taps, and pinches. Flutter provides several gesture detection widgets to handle these interactions effectively.

Example: Interactive Draggable Widget

```
import 'package:flutter/material.dart';

class DraggableExample extends StatefulWidget {
  @override
  _DraggableExampleState createState() => _DraggableExampleState();
}
class _DraggableExampleState extends State<DraggableExample> {
  @override
  Widget build(BuildContext context) {
    return Scaffold(
      appBar: AppBar(title: Text('Draggable Example')),
      body: Center(
        child: Draggable(
          data: 'Drag me!',
          child: Container(
            width: 100,
            height: 100,
```

```
        color: Colors.green,
        child: Center(child: Text('Drag me!', style:
        TextStyle(color: Colors.white))),
      ),
      feedback: Container(
        width: 100,
        height: 100,
        color: Colors.red,
        child: Center(child: Text('Dragging', style:
        TextStyle(color: Colors.white))),
      ),
      childWhenDragging: Container(
        width: 100,
        height: 100,
        color: Colors.grey,
        child: Center(child: Text('Original', style:
        TextStyle(color: Colors.white))),
      ),
    ),
   ),
  );
 }
}
```

Here, Draggable is used to allow users to drag a container across the screen. The feedback widget provides visual feedback during the dragging operation, while childWhenDragging shows the original widget's state when it is being dragged.

Custom Interactive Controls

Creating custom interactive controls involves building widgets that react to user input in unique ways. These controls can be tailored to fit specific design requirements or application needs.

Example: Custom Slider

```
import 'package:flutter/material.dart';
class CustomSlider extends StatefulWidget {
  @override
  _CustomSliderState createState() => _CustomSliderState();
}
class _CustomSliderState extends State<CustomSlider> {
  double _value = 0.5;
  @override
  Widget build(BuildContext context) {
    return Scaffold(
      appBar: AppBar(title: Text('Custom Slider')),
      body: Center(
        child: Column(
          mainAxisAlignment: MainAxisAlignment.center,
          children: [
            Slider(
              value: _value,
              min: 0.0,
              max: 1.0,
              onChanged: (newValue) {
                setState(() {
                  _value = newValue;
                });
              },
```

CHAPTER 2   ADVANCED WIDGET AND UI DESIGN

```
              activeColor: Colors.blue,
              inactiveColor: Colors.grey,
              thumbColor: Colors.red,
              divisions: 10,
            ),
            SizedBox(height: 20),
            Text('Value: ${_value.toStringAsFixed(2)}'),
          ],
        ),
      ),
    );
  }
}
```

In this example, a custom slider is created with properties to adjust its appearance, including color and divisions. The slider updates its value in real time as the user interacts with it.

Interactive Cards

Interactive cards can provide additional information or actions when interacted with. They are often used in modern UIs to present content in a dynamic manner.

Example: Interactive Card with Expansion

```
import 'package:flutter/material.dart';
class InteractiveCardExample extends StatefulWidget {
  @override
  _InteractiveCardExampleState createState() => _InteractiveCardExampleState();
}
```

CHAPTER 2   ADVANCED WIDGET AND UI DESIGN

```dart
class _InteractiveCardExampleState extends
State<InteractiveCardExample> {
  bool _isExpanded = false;
  void _toggleExpansion() {
    setState(() {
      _isExpanded = !_isExpanded;
    });
  }
  @override
  Widget build(BuildContext context) {
    return Scaffold(
      appBar: AppBar(title: Text('Interactive Card')),
      body: Center(
        child: Card(
          elevation: 5,
          child: Column(
            children: [
              ListTile(
                title: Text('Interactive Card'),
                subtitle: Text(_isExpanded ? 'Expanded View' :
                'Collapsed View'),
                trailing: IconButton(
                  icon: Icon(_isExpanded ? Icons.expand_less :
                  Icons.expand_more),
                  onPressed: _toggleExpansion,
                ),
              ),
              AnimatedContainer(
                duration: Duration(milliseconds: 300),
                height: _isExpanded ? 200 : 0,
                child: Center(child: Text('Additional
                Content')),
```

CHAPTER 2　ADVANCED WIDGET AND UI DESIGN

```
        ),
      ],
    ),
  ),
),
);
}
}
```

In this example, an interactive card is implemented with an expandable section. The AnimatedContainer provides a smooth transition between the expanded and collapsed states.

Interactive Forms

Interactive forms with real-time validation and feedback can enhance user experience by providing immediate responses to user input.

Example: Form with Live Validation

```
import 'package:flutter/material.dart';
class InteractiveFormWithValidation extends StatefulWidget {
  @override
  _InteractiveFormWithValidationState createState() => _InteractiveFormWithValidationState();
}
class _InteractiveFormWithValidationState extends State<InteractiveFormWithValidation> {
  final _formKey = GlobalKey<FormState>();
  String? _email;
  @override
  Widget build(BuildContext context) {
    return Scaffold(
```

```
      appBar: AppBar(title: Text('Interactive Form with
      Validation')),
      body: Padding(
        padding: const EdgeInsets.all(16.0),
        child: Form(
          key: _formKey,
          child: Column(
            children: [
              TextFormField(
                decoration: InputDecoration(labelText:
                'Email'),
                keyboardType: TextInputType.emailAddress,
                validator: (value) {
                  if (value == null || value.isEmpty || !value.
                  contains('@')) {
                    return 'Please enter a valid email
                    address';
                  }
                  return null;
                },
                onSaved: (value) {
                  _email = value;
                },
              ),
              SizedBox(height: 20),
              ElevatedButton(
                onPressed: () {
                  if (_formKey.currentState?.validate() ??
                  false) {_formKey.currentState?.save();
                  ScaffoldMessenger.of(context).showSnackBar(
```

```
              SnackBar(content: Text('Processing
              Data')),
            );
          }
        },
        child: Text('Submit'),
      ),
    ],
   ),
  ),
 ),
);
 }
}
```

In this example, a form with real-time validation is created. The TextFormField validates the email input as the user types, providing instant feedback.

By leveraging these techniques and examples, you can create immersive and interactive UI components in Flutter that enhance user engagement and provide a richer experience.

Practical Examples

Incorporating interactive UI elements into real-world applications can significantly enhance user experience. Here are practical examples showcasing how to use various Flutter widgets and techniques to create engaging and interactive UI components:

Custom Progress Indicators

Custom progress indicators can visually convey the status of ongoing processes, like loading or data fetching, while aligning with the app's design aesthetics.

Example: Custom Circular Progress Indicator

```
import 'package:flutter/material.dart';
class CustomProgressIndicator extends StatelessWidget {
  @override
  Widget build(BuildContext context) {
    return Scaffold(
      appBar: AppBar(title: Text('Custom Progress Indicator')),
      body: Center(
        child: CircularProgressIndicator(
          valueColor: AlwaysStoppedAnimation<Color>(Colors.
          orange),
          strokeWidth: 8,
        ),
      ),
    );
  }
}
```

In this example, the CircularProgressIndicator is customized with an orange color and a thicker stroke width to fit the app's design. This customization enhances its visibility and aligns it with the overall color scheme.

Interactive Charts

Interactive charts allow users to visualize and explore data dynamically, offering a more engaging way to present information.

CHAPTER 2　ADVANCED WIDGET AND UI DESIGN

Example: Interactive Line Chart

```
import 'package:flutter/material.dart';
import 'package:fl_chart/fl_chart.dart';
class InteractiveLineChart extends StatelessWidget {
  @override
  Widget build(BuildContext context) {
    return Scaffold(
      appBar: AppBar(title: Text('Interactive Line Chart')),
      body: Padding(
        padding: const EdgeInsets.all(16.0),
        child: LineChart(
          LineChartData(
            gridData: FlGridData(show: false),
            titlesData: FlTitlesData(show: false),
            borderData: FlBorderData(show: false),
            lineBarsData: [
              LineChartBarData(
                spots: [
                  FlSpot(0, 1),
                  FlSpot(1, 3),
                  FlSpot(2, 2),
                  FlSpot(3, 4),
                ],
                isCurved: true,
                colors: [Colors.blue],
                dotData: FlDotData(show: false),
                belowBarData: BarAreaData(show: false),
              ),
            ],
          ),
        ),
```

```
      ),
    ),
  );
 }
}
```

Using the fl_chart package, this example demonstrates an interactive line chart. It can be further customized to include interactive elements like tooltips or touch feedback for a more dynamic user experience.

Swipe-to-Delete Lists

Swipe-to-delete functionality allows users to remove items from a list with a simple swipe gesture, enhancing usability and interaction.

Example: Swipe-to-Delete List

```
import 'package:flutter/material.dart';
class SwipeToDeleteList extends StatelessWidget {
  @override
  Widget build(BuildContext context) {
    return Scaffold(
      appBar: AppBar(title: Text('Swipe to Delete')),
      body: ListView(
        children: List.generate(10, (index) {
          return Dismissible(
            key: Key('$index'),
            onDismissed: (direction) {
              // Handle item removal
              ScaffoldMessenger.of(context).showSnackBar(
                SnackBar(content: Text('Item $index removed')),
              );
            },
```

CHAPTER 2   ADVANCED WIDGET AND UI DESIGN

```
            background: Container(color: Colors.red),
            child: ListTile(title: Text('Item $index')),
          );
        }),
      ),
    );
  }
}
```

In this example, the Dismissible widget allows list items to be swiped away to delete them. A SnackBar provides feedback when an item is removed, improving the interaction.

Interactive Forms

Interactive forms with live validation and feedback provide a better user experience by guiding users through the input process.

Example: Form with Live Validation

```
import 'package:flutter/material.dart';
class InteractiveFormWithValidation extends StatefulWidget {
  @override
  _InteractiveFormWithValidationState createState() =>
  _InteractiveFormWithValidationState();
}
class _InteractiveFormWithValidationState extends State
<InteractiveFormWithValidation> {
  final _formKey = GlobalKey<FormState>();
  String? _email;
  @override
  Widget build(BuildContext context) {
    return Scaffold(
```

```
appBar: AppBar(title: Text('Interactive Form with
Validation')),
body: Padding(
  padding: const EdgeInsets.all(16.0),
  child: Form(
    key: _formKey,
    child: Column(
      children: [
        TextFormField(
          decoration: InputDecoration(labelText: 'Email'),
          keyboardType: TextInputType.emailAddress,
          validator: (value) {
            if (value == null || value.isEmpty || !value.
            contains('@')) {
              return 'Please enter a valid email
              address';
            }
            return null;
          },
          onSaved: (value) {
            _email = value;
          },
        ),
        SizedBox(height: 20),
        ElevatedButton(
          onPressed: () {
            if (_formKey.currentState?.validate() ??
            false) {
              _formKey.currentState?.save();
              ScaffoldMessenger.of(context).showSnackBar(
                SnackBar(content: Text('Processing Data')),
```

CHAPTER 2   ADVANCED WIDGET AND UI DESIGN

```
              );
            }
          },
          child: Text('Submit'),
        ),
      ],
    ),
  ),
  ),
  );
 }
}
```

This example demonstrates a form with live validation for an email input field. The form provides immediate feedback on invalid input and displays a SnackBar upon successful submission.

Interactive Cards

Interactive cards can display additional content or actions when interacted with, making them versatile components for modern UIs.

Example: Interactive Card with Expansion

```
import 'package:flutter/material.dart';
class InteractiveCardExample extends StatefulWidget {
  @override
  _InteractiveCardExampleState createState() =>
  _InteractiveCardExampleState();
}
class _InteractiveCardExampleState extends
State<InteractiveCardExample> {
  bool _isExpanded = false;
```

CHAPTER 2   ADVANCED WIDGET AND UI DESIGN

```
  void _toggleExpansion() {
    setState(() {
      _isExpanded = !_isExpanded;
    });
  }
  @override
  Widget build(BuildContext context) {
    return Scaffold(
      appBar: AppBar(title: Text('Interactive Card')),
      body: Center(
        child: Card(
          elevation: 5,
          child: Column(
            children: [
              ListTile(
                title: Text('Interactive Card'),
                subtitle: Text(_isExpanded ? 'Expanded View' :
                'Collapsed View'),
                trailing: IconButton(
                  icon: Icon(_isExpanded ? Icons.expand_less :
                  Icons.expand_more),
                  onPressed: _toggleExpansion,
                ),
              ),
              AnimatedContainer(
                duration: Duration(milliseconds: 300),
                height: _isExpanded ? 200 : 0,
                child: Center(child: Text('Additional
                Content')),
              ),
            ],
```

```
        ),
      ),
    ),
  );
  }
}
```

In this example, an interactive card expands to reveal additional content when the user taps the expand/collapse icon. The AnimatedContainer provides a smooth transition effect.

These practical examples illustrate how to leverage Flutter's widgets and capabilities to create interactive and engaging UI components. Whether you are building progress indicators, charts, lists, forms, or cards, these techniques can help enhance user experience and make your application more dynamic.

Advanced Widget Testing

Advanced widget testing in Flutter ensures that custom widgets perform as expected and provide a reliable user experience. This involves not only verifying the functionality of individual widgets but also ensuring their integration with other parts of the application. In this section, we explore strategies for testing custom widgets and examine case studies and best practices to effectively implement widget testing in Flutter.

Strategies for Testing Custom Widgets

Testing custom widgets in Flutter involves several strategies to ensure their reliability, functionality, and integration within the app. Here are key strategies to effectively test custom widgets:

CHAPTER 2   ADVANCED WIDGET AND UI DESIGN

Unit Testing

Purpose: Unit testing focuses on testing individual widgets in isolation to verify that their logic and rendering are correct. This is crucial for validating that a widget behaves as expected given specific inputs.

Approach

Create Unit Tests: Use the testWidgets function from the flutter_test package to create tests that verify the widget's behavior.

Verify Output: Check that the widget displays the expected output or content.

Check State Management: Ensure that the widget manages its state correctly and responds to state changes appropriately.

Example

```
import 'package:flutter/material.dart';
import 'package:flutter_test/flutter_test.dart';
import 'package:my_app/widgets/my_custom_widget.dart';
void main() {
  testWidgets('MyCustomWidget displays provided text',
  (WidgetTester tester) async {
    // Build the widget
    await tester.pumpWidget(MaterialApp(home:
    MyCustomWidget(text: 'Hello Flutter')));
    // Verify if the text is displayed
    expect(find.text('Hello Flutter'), findsOneWidget);
  });
}
```

CHAPTER 2 ADVANCED WIDGET AND UI DESIGN

In this example, testWidgets is used to verify that MyCustomWidget displays the provided text correctly.

Integration Testing
Purpose: Integration testing ensures that multiple widgets work together as expected. This is useful for verifying the complete functionality of a screen or feature involving several widgets.

Approach

Simulate User Actions: Use WidgetTester to simulate user interactions such as taps, text input, or scrolling.

Verify Interactions: Ensure that widgets interact correctly and that the overall functionality of the feature is as expected.

Check State Changes: Verify that state changes propagate correctly across widgets.

Example

```
import 'package:flutter/material.dart';
import 'package:flutter_test/flutter_test.dart';
import 'package:my_app/screens/my_form_screen.dart';
void main() {
  testWidgets('Form submission and validation', (WidgetTester tester) async {
    // Build the form screen
    await tester.pumpWidget(MaterialApp(home: MyFormScreen()));
    // Enter invalid data and submit
    await tester.enterText(find.byKey(Key('emailField')), 'invalidemail');
    await tester.tap(find.byKey(Key('submitButton')));
```

CHAPTER 2   ADVANCED WIDGET AND UI DESIGN

```
    await tester.pump();
    // Verify validation message
    expect(find.text('Please enter a valid email address'),
    findsOneWidget);
    // Enter valid data and submit
    await tester.enterText(find.byKey(Key('emailField')),
    'valid@example.com');
    await tester.tap(find.byKey(Key('submitButton')));
    await tester.pump();
    // Verify successful submission
    expect(find.text('Form submitted successfully'),
    findsOneWidget);
  });
}
```

This integration test checks if the form screen behaves correctly with valid and invalid inputs.

Widget Interaction Testing

Purpose: Widget interaction testing focuses on verifying how a widget responds to user interactions like taps, swipes, and gestures. This ensures that interactive elements behave as expected.

   Approach

>   **Simulate Interactions**: Use methods such as tap, drag, and enterText to simulate user interactions with widgets.

>   **Verify Responses**: Ensure that the widget responds correctly to interactions, such as triggering callbacks or updating the UI.

Example

```
import 'package:flutter/material.dart';
import 'package:flutter_test/flutter_test.dart';
import 'package:my_app/widgets/my_button.dart';
void main() {
  testWidgets('MyButton triggers onPressed callback',
  (WidgetTester tester) async {
    bool buttonPressed = false;
    // Build the widget
    await tester.pumpWidget(MaterialApp(
      home: MyButton(onPressed: () {
        buttonPressed = true;
      }),
    ));
    // Tap the button
    await tester.tap(find.byType(MyButton));
    await tester.pump();
    // Verify callback is triggered
    expect(buttonPressed, isTrue);
  });
}
```

This test ensures that MyButton triggers its onPressed callback when tapped.

Layout Testing

Purpose: Layout testing ensures that widgets are rendered correctly according to their layout specifications. This includes verifying widget positions, sizes, and alignments.

Approach

> **Check Widget Sizes and Positions**: Use the tester.getRect method to verify the sizes and positions of widgets.
>
> **Validate Layout Constraints**: Ensure that widgets adhere to layout constraints and align correctly with other widgets.

Example

```
import 'package:flutter/material.dart';
import 'package:flutter_test/flutter_test.dart';
import 'package:my_app/widgets/my_row_widget.dart';
void main() {
  testWidgets('MyRowWidget positions children correctly',
  (WidgetTester tester) async {
    // Build the widget
    await tester.pumpWidget(MaterialApp(home: MyRowWidget()));
    // Verify widget positions
    final firstChildFinder = find.byType(FirstChildWidget);
    final secondChildFinder = find.byType(SecondChildWidget);
    final firstChildRect = tester.getRect(firstChildFinder);
    final secondChildRect = tester.getRect(secondChildFinder);
    expect(firstChildRect.right, lessThan
    (secondChildRect.left));
  });
}
```

In this example, the test checks if child widgets within MyRowWidget are positioned correctly relative to each other.

CHAPTER 2   ADVANCED WIDGET AND UI DESIGN

Visual Testing

Purpose: Visual testing ensures that widgets are rendered as expected in terms of appearance and styling. This is important for maintaining visual consistency across different devices and screen sizes.

> **Approach**
>
>> **Capture Screenshots**: Use the flutter_test package to capture screenshots of widgets and compare them with reference images.
>>
>> **Check Visual Attributes**: Verify that widgets adhere to design specifications such as color, font, and padding.
>
> **Example**

```
import 'package:flutter/material.dart';
import 'package:flutter_test/flutter_test.dart';
import 'package:integration_test/integration_test.dart';
void main() {
  IntegrationTestWidgetsFlutterBinding.ensureInitialized();
  testWidgets('Visual test for MyCustomWidget', (WidgetTester tester) async {
    // Build the widget
    await tester.pumpWidget(MaterialApp(home: MyCustomWidget()));
    // Capture a screenshot and compare it with a
       reference image
    final byteData = await tester.binding.takeScreenshot();
    // Save the screenshot and compare with a reference image
  });
}
```

This example uses integration tests to capture screenshots for visual comparison, ensuring that MyCustomWidget appears as intended.

By employing these strategies, you can thoroughly test custom widgets in Flutter, ensuring their functionality, interaction, layout, and visual appearance are as expected

Case Studies and Best Practices

When it comes to advanced widget testing in Flutter, applying best practices and learning from real-world case studies can significantly improve the quality and reliability of your testing process. Below are some case studies and best practices to help guide you through effective widget testing:

Case Study 1: Testing a Complex Form

Scenario: An application contains a complex form with multiple input fields, validation rules, and dynamic content based on user interactions.

> **Challenges**
>
> **Form Validation**: Ensuring that the form correctly validates user input
>
> **Dynamic Fields**: Handling fields that appear or change based on other input
>
> **Form Submission**: Verifying that the form processes and submits data correctly

Best Practices
Test Each Field Independently
Create unit tests to check the validation logic for each input field. Verify that error messages appear for invalid input and that valid input is accepted.

CHAPTER 2 ADVANCED WIDGET AND UI DESIGN

```
testWidgets('Email field validation', (WidgetTester
tester) async {
  await tester.pumpWidget(MaterialApp(home:
  ComplexFormScreen()));
  await tester.enterText(find.byKey(Key('emailField')),
  'invalidemail');
  await tester.tap(find.byKey(Key('submitButton')));
  await tester.pump();
  expect(find.text('Invalid email address'), findsOneWidget);
});
```

Simulate Dynamic Changes

Write integration tests to simulate user interactions that trigger dynamic changes in the form. Ensure that fields appear, hide, or update correctly based on user actions.

```
testWidgets('Dynamic field visibility', (WidgetTester
tester) async {
  await tester.pumpWidget(MaterialApp(home:
  ComplexFormScreen()));
  await tester.tap(find.byKey(Key('toggleDynamicFieldB
  utton')));
  await tester.pump();
  expect(find.byKey(Key('dynamicField')), findsOneWidget);
});
```

CHAPTER 2   ADVANCED WIDGET AND UI DESIGN

Validate Form Submission
Test the form's submission process, including handling valid and invalid data. Verify that the form processes data correctly and displays appropriate success or error messages.

```
testWidgets('Form submission with valid data', (WidgetTester
tester) async {
  await tester.pumpWidget(MaterialApp(home:
  ComplexFormScreen()));
  await tester.enterText(find.byKey(Key('emailField')),
  'valid@example.com');
  await tester.tap(find.byKey(Key('submitButton')));
  await tester.pump();
  expect(find.text('Form submitted successfully'),
  findsOneWidget);
});
```

Case Study 2: Testing Interactive Widgets
Scenario: An application includes interactive widgets such as buttons, sliders, and switches that need to be tested for correct behavior and feedback.
   Challenges
      User Interaction: Ensuring interactive elements respond correctly to user actions
      State Management: Verifying that widget state changes appropriately in response to interactions

CHAPTER 2 ADVANCED WIDGET AND UI DESIGN

Best Practices
Simulate User Actions
Use widget interaction tests to simulate actions such as taps, drags, and text inputs. Verify that the widget responds as expected, such as triggering callbacks or updating state.

```
testWidgets('Button triggers callback on tap', (WidgetTester
tester) async {
  bool callbackTriggered = false;
  await tester.pumpWidget(MaterialApp(
    home: InteractiveWidget(
      onButtonPressed: () {
        callbackTriggered = true;
      },
    ),
  ));
  await tester.tap(find.byType(ElevatedButton));
  await tester.pump();
  expect(callbackTriggered, isTrue);
});
```

Verify State Changes
Ensure that interactive widgets correctly manage and reflect state changes. For example, test that a slider updates its displayed value when adjusted.

```
testWidgets('Slider value updates on drag', (WidgetTester
tester) async {
  await tester.pumpWidget(MaterialApp(home:
  InteractiveSliderWidget()));
  await tester.drag(find.byType(Slider), Offset(100, 0));
```

CHAPTER 2   ADVANCED WIDGET AND UI DESIGN

```
  await tester.pump()
  expect(find.text('Slider value: 0.5'), findsOneWidget);
});
```

Case Study 3: Testing Layout and Responsiveness
Scenario: The application's layout must adapt to different screen sizes and orientations, and widgets need to be positioned and sized correctly.

Challenges

> **Responsive Layout**: Ensuring that widgets adjust appropriately for different screen sizes and orientations
>
> **Positioning and Sizing**: Verifying that widgets are positioned and sized as per the design specifications

Best Practices

Test on Various Screen Sizes

Use Flutter's test environment to simulate different screen sizes and orientations. Verify that the layout adjusts correctly and widgets remain properly aligned and sized.

```
testWidgets('Widget layout adjusts to screen size',
(WidgetTester tester) async {
  await tester.pumpWidget(MaterialApp(home:
  ResponsiveLayoutWidget()));
  // Simulate different screen sizes and orientations
  await tester.binding.setSurfaceSize(Size(600, 800));
  await tester.pump();
    expect(find.byType(SomeWidget), findsOneWidget);
});
```

Verify Layout Constraints

Check that widgets respect layout constraints such as padding, margins, and alignment. Ensure that widgets are rendered correctly according to the design specifications.

```
testWidgets('Widget respects layout constraints', (WidgetTester
tester) async {
  await tester.pumpWidget(MaterialApp(home:
  ConstrainedWidget()));
  final widgetFinder = find.byType(SomeWidget);
  final widgetRect = tester.getRect(widgetFinder);
  expect(widgetRect.width, equals(200));
  expect(widgetRect.height, equals(100));
});
```

Best Practices for Advanced Widget Testing

Use Key Identifiers

Assign unique keys to widgets for easier identification in tests. This helps in locating and interacting with specific widgets.

Automate Testing

Integrate widget tests into your continuous integration (CI) pipeline to ensure that tests are automatically run with each build. This helps in catching issues early in the development process.

Test on Real Devices

While simulators and emulators are useful, also test on real devices to ensure that the app behaves correctly across different physical hardware and operating system versions.

Write Clear and Maintainable Tests
Ensure that tests are clear, concise, and maintainable. Use descriptive names for test cases and avoid hardcoding values that may change.

Mock Dependencies
Use mocking frameworks to simulate dependencies and isolate the widget being tested. This helps in focusing on the widget's behavior without relying on external factors.

By applying these strategies and best practices, you can ensure that your custom widgets are thoroughly tested and maintain a high standard of quality throughout your Flutter application.

Summary

Here, we delve into advanced widget and UI design techniques in Flutter, focusing on the latest features and customization options available in Flutter. It begins with an exploration of new built-in widgets, providing detailed insights into their functionalities and practical use cases. The chapter then covers advanced widget customization, highlighting methods for tailoring widgets to specific needs and real-world scenarios. Modern UI patterns are also discussed, including responsive and adaptive design principles and the implementation of design systems with design tokens. The chapter continues with advanced layout techniques, such as utilizing `LayoutBuilder` and `CustomMultiChildLayout`, as well as strategies for creating dynamic and adaptive layouts. Interactive UI elements are examined through the creation of immersive components and their practical applications. Finally, the chapter addresses advanced widget testing, offering strategies for unit, integration, and interaction testing and providing case studies and best practices to ensure robust and reliable widget performance.

CHAPTER 3

Performance Optimization and Profiling

In the previous chapter, we explored the cutting edge of widget and UI design in Flutter 3.29, diving deep into newly introduced built-in widgets, advanced customization strategies, responsive and adaptive layout techniques, and best practices for interactive design. We also covered how to implement design systems and rigorously test complex widgets to ensure seamless user experiences. With a robust UI foundation now in place, it's time to turn our focus to a critical pillar of modern Flutter development: application performance.

No matter how elegant your UI is, it won't matter if your app stutters, lags, or consumes excessive resources. Performance optimization is essential not just for user satisfaction, but also for device compatibility, battery efficiency, and app store ratings. Flutter 3.29 continues to evolve in this area, offering a powerful suite of tools and enhancements to help you diagnose, profile, and resolve performance issues with precision.

Here, you'll gain hands-on knowledge of the latest profiling capabilities in Dart DevTools, GPU and rendering performance analysis, advanced memory profiling techniques, and best practices for reducing layout and build times. We'll walk through real-world case studies, compare top profiling tools, and explore how to optimize your app for a wide range of devices—from budget Android phones to high-performance tablets and desktop platforms.

Latest Profiling Tools

Flutter 3.29 introduces several powerful enhancements to its performance monitoring and profiling suite, empowering developers to diagnose and optimize their applications with greater precision. This section focuses on the newest profiling capabilities available through Dart DevTools and other system-level instrumentation tools that enable deep inspection of GPU, CPU, and rendering pipelines.

Profiling is no longer a reactive step taken only when performance problems arise. In high-quality apps, it is a continuous part of development and testing. With real-time visualizations, timeline views, and fine-grained metric breakdowns, Flutter's profiling toolchain enables proactive performance management throughout the app lifecycle.

New Features in Dart DevTools

Flutter 3.29 introduces significant enhancements to Dart DevTools, further solidifying its role as the primary performance diagnostics suite for Flutter applications. DevTools has evolved into a unified observability dashboard that combines UI thread profiling, CPU analysis, memory tracking, GPU insights, and platform interaction tracing—empowering developers to identify bottlenecks across the full stack.

Advanced Profiling Techniques

Advanced profiling techniques in Flutter 3.29 empower developers to move beyond surface-level diagnostics and dive deep into the inner workings of their app's performance lifecycle. With the updated Dart DevTools suite, profiling is no longer just about identifying slow frames—it's about pinpointing exact operations, function calls, asynchronous processes, and rendering phases that contribute to latency or jank.

It covers the high-impact techniques every advanced Flutter developer should master for precise and effective performance tuning.

Fine-Grained Timeline Analysis

The Timeline view in Dart DevTools is your primary tool for real-time profiling of the rendering pipeline. With enhancements in 3.29, the timeline offers

> **Thread-Level Visibility**: Simultaneous visualization of UI, GPU, raster, platform, and I/O threads
>
> **Synchronous and Asynchronous Events**: Markers for async tasks such as network calls, animations, and delayed futures
>
> **Event Correlation**: Ability to track widget build operations through to rasterization and frame presentation

Use the Frame Chart to spot Frame Budget Overruns, indicated by red bars that highlight janky frames. From there, zoom into the timeline to identify expensive operations, such as widget rebuilds or shader compilation.

Widget Rebuild Profiling

Unnecessary or excessive widget rebuilds are a common performance pitfall in Flutter apps. Flutter 3.29 introduces more transparent rebuild tracking via

> **Widget Build Counts Overlay**: A visual debugging tool that shows how many times widgets rebuild during runtime
>
> **Rebuild Tracking in Timeline**: Dart DevTools now logs widget build operations with associated costs and call stacks
>
> **Rebuild Stats Tab**: A summary dashboard highlighting the most frequently rebuilt widgets, their durations, and potential sources of inefficiency

---

Pro Tip Use "const" constructors where possible and segment your widget tree using "const"-friendly "StatelessWidgets" to avoid unnecessary rebuilds. Wrap dynamic UI sections with "RepaintBoundary" or "ValueListenableBuilder" when appropriate.

Tracing Async Operations

Async operations can block UI rendering indirectly, especially when data fetching or computation isn't properly isolated from the main thread. In Dart DevTools 3.29:

> **Async Timeline Events**: Tasks triggered via "Future," "async/await," or stream subscriptions are now visualized in the timeline with start/end correlation.
>
> **Event Pairing**: Async events are grouped logically, letting you trace how long a future took to resolve and whether it introduced latency in the widget tree.

> **Stack Frame Insights**: Flame charts show which async callbacks or closures were most expensive during runtime.
>
> **Use Case**: If an animation is lagging, and async I/O happens concurrently, tracing can reveal if the raster thread is blocked waiting for UI thread computations initiated by an async callback.

Identifying Paint and Layout Bottlenecks

Paint and layout operations are performance-critical in any Flutter app. Even subtle layout recalculations can cause cascading repaints, especially in complex UIs. To profile these efficiently:

> **Paint Phases in Timeline**: Use the timeline to isolate paint durations and identify long layout recalculations.
>
> **Debug Flags**: Use "debugPaintSizeEnabled" and "debugRepaintRainbowEnabled" in development builds to visually highlight layout thrashing or excessive repaints.
>
> **CustomPaint Cost Analysis**: DevTools now offers better visibility into "CustomPainter" performance, including overdraw areas and draw operation durations.

Flutter 3.29 also provides Frame Budget Diagnostics—a breakdown of each frame's CPU and GPU contribution, helping you identify whether the bottleneck lies in widget builds, layout, paint, or rasterization.

Integrating Profiling into CI/CD

For larger teams and projects, performance profiling should be automated. In Flutter 3.29:

CHAPTER 3   PERFORMANCE OPTIMIZATION AND PROFILING

"flutter test --profile" and "flutter run --profile" allow headless performance runs.

Integration with Firebase Performance Monitoring or custom benchmarking frameworks enables historical tracking.

Profile snapshots can be exported and analyzed offline, enabling asynchronous collaboration among dev and QA teams.

Automating profiling ensures performance regressions are caught early—before they affect production.

Analyzing Performance Metrics

Understanding and interpreting performance metrics is critical to making informed optimization decisions. Dart DevTools in Flutter 3.29 provides a comprehensive suite of performance data visualizations and profiling statistics that help developers identify where time and resources are being spent—frame by frame, function by function, and widget by widget.

This subsection walks through the key performance metrics available, how to read them, and how to translate them into actionable insights.

Frame Timing Metrics

At the core of Flutter's rendering model is the concept of a frame, ideally rendered within 16.67ms to maintain 60 frames per second (FPS). Dart DevTools offers a detailed breakdown of each frame's lifecycle, with the following key metrics:

Build Time: The duration taken to rebuild the widget tree

Layout Time: Time spent calculating positions and constraints

CHAPTER 3   PERFORMANCE OPTIMIZATION AND PROFILING

Paint Time: Time to generate the canvas drawing commands

Raster Time: Time spent by the GPU rasterizing the visual representation of the UI

Each frame is represented visually in the Frame Chart, with green bars indicating healthy performance and red bars highlighting dropped or janky frames. Developers should aim to keep all stages well within the 16.67ms budget to ensure smooth UI rendering.

Best Practice: Monitor frame rates continuously during user interaction-heavy areas such as scroll views, gesture animations, and transitions.

Widget Build Statistics

Flutter 3.29 provides a clearer picture of widget lifecycle events through

Build Count: Number of times a widget is rebuilt during a given timeline window

Rebuild Cost: Time taken to execute the build method

Heaviest Widgets: Summary list of widgets that consume the most build time across frames

These metrics can be viewed under the Performance tab or through the Widget Rebuild Stats overlay.

Optimization Tip   Frequently rebuilt widgets with minimal visual changes should be wrapped in "const," "RepaintBoundary," or refactored into independent stateless components.

CPU Profiling (Flame Chart View)

The CPU Profiler displays a flame chart showing all function calls executed during a selected timeline window, including Dart, plugin, and native methods. Important data includes

> **Call Stack Depth**: Indicates the nesting of method calls
>
> **Self Time vs. Total Time**: Helps determine whether a method is inherently expensive or simply calling other costly operations
>
> **Hot Paths**: The most resource-intensive methods or code paths

Flame charts are particularly useful when investigating slow interactions, performance regressions, or CPU spikes caused by inefficient loops or data processing.

> **Real-World Scenario**: A slow ListView scroll might be traced to a heavy "build()" method performing synchronous filtering logic—visible directly in the flame chart.

Memory Usage Metrics

Efficient memory use is essential for preventing jank, crashes, or premature app terminations. Dart DevTools' Memory tab tracks

> **Heap Size Over Time**: Trends in memory usage, indicating leaks or inefficient data management
>
> **Garbage Collection Events**: Frequency and duration of GC operations
>
> **Retained Objects by Type**: Helps pinpoint memory leaks and retained listeners or contexts

Flutter 3.29 adds improved visualization of GC activity and allows direct navigation to allocation call stacks.

> **Common Pitfall**: Retaining widget states, controllers, or animation objects beyond their lifecycle often leads to memory leaks.

Network and I/O Metrics

For apps that rely heavily on HTTP requests, streaming, or local file access, I/O performance is equally important. Dart DevTools enables

> **Tracking of HTTP Requests**: Status, duration, and size of network calls.
>
> **Timeline Integration**: See how network delays correlate with UI thread activity.
>
> **Async Event Analysis**: Determine whether blocked futures or long I/O callbacks are delaying widget builds.
>
> **Optimization Strategy**: Use "compute()" or isolate-based processing for heavy background tasks to prevent UI jank caused by synchronous Dart execution.

Platform Channel and Plugin Performance

Many real-world apps depend on platform channels or plugins for functionality like sensors, camera access, or database operations. DevTools now traces

> **Method Channel Latency**: Time taken for messages to be passed and processed.
>
> **Main Thread Activity**: Integration with platform-specific tools (e.g., Systrace or Instruments) can reveal delays on Android/iOS native layers.

Event Frequency: View how frequently platform events are fired (e.g., GPS updates) and whether they introduce load.

Flutter 3.29 improves native Dart communication diagnostics, especially for developers building high-performance, platform-integrated apps.

Exporting and Interpreting Profiles
Dart DevTools allows exporting profiles for offline analysis or CI integration. Performance snapshots can be shared among teams, compared across builds, and tracked over time to monitor regressions.

".timeline.json" and ".profile.json" formats are compatible with Chrome Tracing and Perfetto.

Integration with Flutter DevTools CLI allows batch profiling and automation in build pipelines.

This makes it possible to detect trends, regressions, and performance improvements across versions or feature branches.

Analyzing performance metrics in Flutter 3.29 goes far beyond identifying lag—it's about gaining full visibility into the system, isolating the source of inefficiency, and validating optimization decisions with real data. With powerful new metrics, refined profiling views, and robust diagnostic tools, developers now have everything they need to build blazing-fast apps across platforms.

GPU Performance Analysis

The GPU plays a vital role in rendering the smooth and vibrant visuals Flutter is known for. However, performance bottlenecks in the GPU pipeline can result in dropped frames, janky animations, and sluggish interactions—particularly on lower-end or thermally throttled devices. Flutter 3.29 provides improved insight into GPU activity and rendering diagnostics to help developers fine-tune their apps for maximum graphics performance.

CHAPTER 3   PERFORMANCE OPTIMIZATION AND PROFILING

This section delves into the tools and techniques available for profiling GPU activity and the strategies to optimize rendering performance.

Tools for GPU Profiling

Profiling GPU performance in Flutter is essential for building high-frame-rate, visually fluid apps across a wide range of devices. As the GPU handles the rendering of pixels to the screen, any inefficiencies in how frames are composited, drawn, or rasterized can lead to performance degradation such as jank, dropped frames, and high battery usage.

Flutter 3.29 provides a robust set of tools for GPU profiling, both within Dart DevTools and through integration with native profiling suites on Android and iOS. This section provides an in-depth look at these tools and how to use them effectively.

Dart DevTools—GPU Thread Timeline

Dart DevTools includes a Timeline view that exposes separate threads for UI, Raster (compositor), and GPU (when traceable). Key capabilities include

> **Frame Rendering Visualization**: See when GPU tasks begin and end relative to UI and Raster threads.
>
> **Jank Diagnosis**: Identify frames where GPU rendering exceeds the 16.67ms target.
>
> **Event Tracing**: Visualize how painting operations are queued and executed in the GPU pipeline.

To access this, run the app in profile mode and open the Performance tab in DevTools. Flutter 3.29 enhances this view by synchronizing GPU and CPU frame timelines for correlation.

CHAPTER 3   PERFORMANCE OPTIMIZATION AND PROFILING

Tip   Long GPU tasks typically show up as thick bars on the GPU thread, indicating raster or shader-related overload.

Skia Tracing with "--trace-skia"
Flutter uses the Skia graphics engine under the hood. Developers can enable fine-grained tracing of Skia's rendering behavior:

```
flutter run --profile --trace-skia
```

This logs all Skia drawing operations (e.g., drawRect, saveLayer, clipPath) and exports them into a timeline format readable by Chrome's about://tracing tool or Perfetto.

Use Cases:

Detecting excessive layer usage

Investigating shader compilation delays

Diagnosing "saveLayer" and "clipPath" performance issues

Best Practice: Pair "--trace-skia" with "--trace-systrace" for full-system tracing, especially during first-frame or animation rendering bottlenecks.

Platform-Specific Profilers
While Dart DevTools offers Flutter-centric views, platform-native profilers reveal how GPU performance interacts with OS-level constraints, driver behavior, and thermal throttling.

Android:
Profile HWUI Rendering (Developer Options):

Visual real-time bar chart showing how long each frame took to render.

Green = under 16ms, Red = over budget.

CHAPTER 3 PERFORMANCE OPTIMIZATION AND PROFILING

Perfetto/Systrace:

> System-level tracing tool that can show GPU frequency scaling, rendering bottlenecks, thermal throttling, and more.
>
> Integrate with Flutter via "flutter build apk --trace-startup."

iOS:

Xcode Instruments—Core Animation Tool:

> Analyzes GPU-related issues like offscreen rendering, compositing cost, and frame timing.
>
> Detects "CALayer" overdraw, excessive blending, and shadow rendering inefficiencies.

Pro Tip Use Instruments to catch offscreen compositing triggered by widgets like "ClipRRect," "BackdropFilter," and "Opacity."

Flutter's Layer Tree View

The Layer Tree tool in Dart DevTools (available in the Performance tab) displays how Flutter structures and paints UI layers. It provides insight into

> RepaintBoundary usage and its impact on GPU redraws
>
> Nested layers that may lead to GPU overdraw
>
> Widget-to-layer mapping, identifying how complex widgets generate GPU workloads

Flutter 3.29 improves layer tree labeling and integrates it more tightly with widget rebuild stats, making it easier to locate and optimize costly layers.

CHAPTER 3   PERFORMANCE OPTIMIZATION AND PROFILING

Impeller Debug Traces (Experimental)

Flutter 3.29 expands support for Impeller, the next-gen rendering engine intended to eliminate shader compilation jank. Impeller includes experimental tracing options:

Enable Impeller:

```
flutter run --enable-impeller
```

Use "flutter run --trace-skia" with Impeller to log render pass execution, pipeline compilation, and GPU command batching.

Note   Impeller is GPU-centric and designed to reduce runtime shader compilation issues, especially on iOS.

Shader Compilation Reports

To help mitigate first-frame jank, Flutter generates shader compilation reports during profiling runs:

Generate via

```
flutter build apk --profile
```

Collect compiled shaders in ".cache.dill" or "skia_shaders.json" for reuse.

Use with ShaderWarmUp class to preload shaders at app launch, minimizing runtime GPU stalls.

GPU profiling tools in Flutter 3.29 are more powerful and accessible than ever. Whether you're debugging complex animations, diagnosing frame drops, or preparing for production performance audits, these tools provide deep visibility into the GPU pipeline. Mastering them ensures your app delivers buttery-smooth experiences—even on resource-constrained devices.

Optimizing Rendering Performance

Achieving smooth and responsive UIs in Flutter requires more than just identifying GPU bottlenecks—it demands actively optimizing rendering performance based on insights from profiling. Flutter 3.29 introduces powerful improvements in rendering pipelines, shader management, and layer efficiency, empowering developers to fine-tune every frame.

This section explores advanced techniques and best practices to optimize rendering performance, minimize jank, and deliver consistent 60 FPS (or higher) experiences across a wide range of devices.

Minimize Overdraw
Overdraw occurs when multiple layers are painted over the same pixels unnecessarily, causing wasted GPU work.

Visualization: Enable overdraw visualization using "--show-overdraw." This highlights areas of excessive painting, where multiple layers overlap.

Strategies:

> Avoid unnecessary opacity layers ("Opacity," "BackdropFilter," "ColorFiltered").
>
> Eliminate nested containers with backgrounds where one would suffice.
>
> Use "Stack" only when layering is intentional and necessary.

Tip   On mobile GPUs, 2× or higher overdraw can lead to noticeable frame rate drops.

Optimize Layer Usage and Compositing

Flutter uses a layered rendering model where complex widgets are split into composited layers. Misuse of these layers can trigger excessive GPU workload.

Use "RepaintBoundary" Wisely:

Wrap widgets that update frequently (e.g., animations) to isolate their redraw impact.

Avoid excessive boundaries—each adds a compositing cost.

Layer Tree Analysis:

Use Dart DevTools' Layer Tree to inspect compositing hierarchy.

Merge layers where static content doesn't need to be separated.

Example: A scrolling list of cards with shadows may benefit from "RepaintBoundary" per card, but wrapping each child of a "Row" may be unnecessary.

Precompile and Warm Up Shaders

First-frame jank is commonly caused by runtime shader compilation. Flutter 3.29 improves shader caching and warm-up:

Use "ShaderWarmUp":

Preload shader routines during splash or idle states.

Especially useful for animations, gradients, and custom paint effects.

Prebuild Shader Cache:

Run the app in profile mode on a real device to collect shaders.

Extract shader data from "flutter build" outputs for reuse.

Supports preloading via asset bundles in production.

Pro Tip This is especially beneficial for low-end Android phones or older iPhones.

Reduce Expensive Visual Effects

GPU-heavy effects can hurt frame rates, especially when layered together.

Avoid deep blurs ("BackdropFilter") unless truly necessary.

Use gradients sparingly—prefer linear over radial.

Limit "saveLayer" usage, which triggers offscreen rendering.

Replace animated shadows with static assets where possible.

Flutter 3.29 also enhances performance of image filters and transformations by better leveraging hardware acceleration where supported.

Efficient Use of Images and Assets

Large or uncompressed images consume GPU memory and cause stalls.

Use appropriately sized assets—avoid downscaling large images in real time.

Cache frequently used images with "CachedNetworkImage" or asset bundling.

Prefer "ResizeImage" when resizing is required.

> **Optimization Tip** For background images, preload and cache during the splash screen to eliminate GPU delays when rendering starts.

Frame Budget Management

For 60 FPS, the frame rendering budget is 16.67ms; for 120 FPS, it's just 8.33ms. Stay within this budget by

- Avoiding heavy synchronous work in build/render cycles
- Deferring non-critical UI or animations using "SchedulerBinding.addPostFrameCallback"
- Breaking long paint operations into smaller, batched effects or async tasks

Use DevTools' Frame Analysis to identify frames that exceed the budget and their root causes.

Profile and Test on Real Devices

Emulators often mask or misrepresent real GPU performance. Always

- Test on low-end Android and iOS devices to expose performance limits.
- Compare across refresh rates (60Hz vs. 120Hz).
- Measure thermal throttling impact on devices prone to overheating.

Flutter 3.29 adds more accurate raster timing data in DevTools for real-device profiling.

CHAPTER 3   PERFORMANCE OPTIMIZATION AND PROFILING

Rendering optimization is a multi-layered process involving overdraw reduction, shader management, compositing efficiency, and frame timing discipline. Flutter 3.29 equips developers with powerful tools and techniques to fine-tune performance, ensuring apps look and feel buttery-smooth on every device—from flagship phones to entry-level handsets.

Memory Management Enhancements

Efficient memory management is a cornerstone of building fast, stable, and scalable Flutter applications. Improper handling of memory can result in bloated app sizes, erratic frame rendering due to excessive garbage collection (GC), sluggish user experiences, and—at worst—application crashes due to memory leaks or exhaustion.

With Flutter 3.29, developers gain access to powerful enhancements for analyzing, optimizing, and monitoring memory usage. These include improvements to Dart DevTools, runtime instrumentation, and updated best practices for managing widget lifecycles and long-lived resources.

Efficient Memory Use

Delivering a seamless Flutter experience requires thoughtful control over memory usage, especially in environments with limited RAM or variable performance characteristics. Efficient memory use not only improves runtime stability but also helps reduce jank, minimize GC pauses, and keep the app responsive under stress.

Flutter 3.29 introduces updated profiling capabilities and development patterns that empower developers to proactively manage memory. These include fine-grained allocation tracking, enhanced snapshot comparison, and real-time garbage collection visualizations via Dart DevTools.

It presents both proactive practices—like avoiding unnecessary allocations, using const constructors, and applying lazy widget loading—and reactive strategies such as leak detection, heap analysis, and lifecycle cleanup.

New Techniques for Memory Management

With Flutter 3.29, developers gain access to several updated and refined techniques for managing memory efficiently—essential for ensuring responsive, stable applications across mobile and desktop platforms. As applications grow in complexity and interactivity, optimizing memory use is no longer optional—it's a critical part of delivering premium user experiences.

This section introduces modern practices and platform-level improvements that help reduce memory bloat, avoid retention cycles, and ensure a lean runtime footprint.

Leveraging "const" and Immutability

The Dart compiler can significantly reduce runtime allocations when widgets and data structures are declared as "const."

Use "const" constructors for static widgets.

Favor immutable models and data transfer objects (DTOs) to reduce accidental duplication in memory.

```
const Icon(Icons.favorite); // Allocated at compile-time
```

Note Using "const" not only reduces memory use but also optimizes widget diffing during rebuilds.

Widget Lifecycle Hygiene

A frequent source of memory issues is improper management of widget-associated resources. In Flutter 3.29, improved diagnostics in Dart DevTools can detect orphaned resources, but prevention is better.

> Always dispose of "AnimationController," "TextEditingController," "ScrollController," etc., in "StatefulWidget" lifecycles.
>
> Avoid storing "BuildContext" or UI-heavy objects (widgets, render objects) in long-lived classes.

```
@override
void dispose() {
  _controller.dispose();
  super.dispose();
}
```

Optimize Image and Asset Memory

Image rendering is one of the largest contributors to memory usage. Flutter 3.29 provides tighter control over image caching:

> Use "ResizeImage" to scale images before they hit the GPU.
>
> Limit cache size using

```
PaintingBinding.instance.imageCache
  ..maximumSize = 100
  ..maximumSizeBytes = 50 << 20; // 50MB
```

For network images used repeatedly, consider loading them once and storing them in a memory-efficient format like "MemoryImage."

Use Lazy and Conditional Widget Construction

Constructing UI elements only when necessary saves memory and reduces build complexity.

> Prefer "ListView.builder" or "GridView.builder" over static collections.

> Use "Visibility" and "Offstage" to hide components without destroying them—but be mindful that memory is still retained unless widgets are disposed.

```
ListView.builder(
  itemBuilder: (context, index) => ListTile(title: Text('Item $index')),
);
```

Use Efficient State Management

State management directly impacts memory. Avoid bloated global stores or deeply nested providers.

> Use "ValueNotifier," "InheritedWidget," or scoped state management (e.g., Riverpod, Provider) to ensure memory is not retained unnecessarily.

> Dispose of listeners and avoid retaining state outside its lifecycle.

> **Insight**: Long-lived singletons holding large widget trees or contexts often lead to memory leaks.

Avoid Retaining UI References in Long-Lived Services

One of the most common Dart memory pitfalls is unintentionally capturing UI state in closures or singletons. This often happens with

- Asynchronous functions ("Future," "Stream") that capture "BuildContext"
- Callbacks that retain references to widget states
- Instead, use weak references or architecture that separates UI and logic cleanly (e.g., BLoC, MVC).

Optimize Third-Party Packages

Packages may retain memory improperly if misused.

- Monitor memory during plugin usage (e.g., camera, maps).
- Regularly audit large packages for retained state or uncontrolled caching.
- Prefer well-maintained plugins that explicitly expose "dispose()" methods for cleanup.

Flutter 3.29-Specific Enhancements

Flutter 3.29 introduces several under-the-hood improvements:

- Dart runtime memory tracing now exposes deeper GC behavior in DevTools.
- Widget rebuild visualization shows retained widgets post-disposal.
- Improved null safety diagnostics help detect uninitialized memory-holding fields.

Best Practices

Technique	Description
Use `const` where possible	Reduces widget duplication and heap usage
Dispose all controllers	Prevents memory leaks and orphaned event listeners
Optimize image loading	Downscale and cache efficiently
Avoid retaining contexts	Prevent long-lived closures from holding UI state
Use lazy builders	Only construct what's visible
Monitor third-party packages	Ensure proper memory hygiene in external dependencies

Figure 3-1. Best practices

Profiling Memory Leaks

Memory leaks are one of the most insidious performance issues in mobile development—they often go unnoticed during development but become catastrophic in production. In Flutter 3.29, memory leak profiling has evolved with more powerful tools in Dart DevTools, providing deep visibility into object allocation, GC behavior, and retention paths.

This section will walk you through modern strategies to identify, analyze, and fix memory leaks in your Flutter applications using the latest profiling capabilities.

Understanding Memory Leaks in Dart and Flutter

In Dart, memory is managed via an automatic generational garbage collector (GC). Memory leaks happen when

> Objects that are no longer needed remain referenced in memory.
>
> GC cannot reclaim them because some live object (like a listener, closure, or global variable) holds a reference.

CHAPTER 3   PERFORMANCE OPTIMIZATION AND PROFILING

Common culprits include

>   Persistent "StreamSubscriptions" not canceled

>   Controllers (e.g., "TextEditingController," "AnimationController") not disposed

>   "BuildContext" or widgets captured in async callbacks or global variables

>   Caches not cleared or improperly scoped

Using Dart DevTools Memory Tab

Dart DevTools provides robust capabilities to observe memory behavior:

a. **Live Memory Graph**

   Tracks heap usage in real time.

   Visualizes GC activity and retained object growth.

   Helps correlate memory spikes with user actions or navigation events.

b. **Snapshot and Diff Analysis**

   Take heap snapshots at key intervals (e.g., before and after navigation).

   Use the diff viewer to detect unexpected retained objects.

   Identify the exact object types and their counts that are growing over time.

c. **Retaining Path Visualization**

   For any retained object, view why it's still in memory.

Trace the retaining path—a chain of references keeping the object alive.

This is especially useful for widgets and listeners that should be deallocated.

Strategies for Detecting Leaks

a. **Manual GC Triggers**

Use the "Collect Garbage" button in DevTools to manually trigger GC.

After GC, observe which objects were not collected and why.

b. **Monitor Specific Classes**

Use class-based filters to track allocations of critical objects.

For instance, monitor "MyController," "MyService," or custom 'StatefulWidget' subclasses.

c. **Test Navigation and Disposal**

Simulate navigation away from and back to screens.

Compare heap before/after using memory snapshots.

Unexpected growth signals leaks in widget disposal or controller lifecycle.

d. **Leak Detection Automation (Experimental)**

Tools like "leak_tracker" and "leak_tracker_flutter_testing" can automate detection.

These tools assert that objects have been garbage collected after test teardown.

```yaml
dev_dependencies:
  leak_tracker_flutter_testing: ^1.0.0
```

Example:

```dart
testWidgets('Widget should not leak', (tester) async {
  final leak = LeakTrackingTestBinding.ensureInitialized();
  await tester.pumpWidget(MyWidget());
  await tester.pumpAndSettle();
  await leak.disposeAndTrackLeaks();
});
```

Real-World Examples of Leaks
Example 1: Forgotten Controller Disposal

```dart
class MyForm extends StatefulWidget {
  @override
  _MyFormState createState() => _MyFormState();
}

class _MyFormState extends State<MyForm> {
  final controller = TextEditingController();
  // Leak if not disposed

  @override
  void dispose() {
```

```
    controller.dispose(); // Prevents memory leak
    super.dispose();
  }
}
```

Example 2: Uncanceled StreamSubscription

```
StreamSubscription? subscription;
@override
void initState() {
  super.initState();
  subscription = myStream.listen((event) {
    // Do something
  });
}

@override
void dispose() {
  subscription?.cancel(); // Avoids retention
  super.dispose();
}
```

Example 3: Captured BuildContext in Async Call

```
void _loadData(BuildContext context) async {
  final data = await fetchData();
  Navigator.of(context).push(...); // Context might be invalid
  or retained
}
```

Solution: Use "mounted" check or avoid capturing context long-term.

Best Practices for Leak Prevention

Practice	Why It Matters
Always call dispose()	Releases resources and memory held by controller
Cancel streams and timers	Prevents them from retaining widgets or contexts
Avoid holding BuildContext	Especially in async functions or global services
Use StatefulWidget only when needed	Reduces lifecycle complexity and memory retention
Prefer StatelessWidget + ViewModel	Separates UI from memory-sensitive logic

Memory leaks not only degrade performance over time—they also silently introduce app instability and unexpected behavior. By proactively profiling memory using Dart DevTools and following modern best practices, you can ensure your Flutter applications are robust, efficient, and production-ready.

Profiling Memory Leaks and Bottlenecks

While earlier sections addressed memory usage basics and detection of typical leaks, this part dives deeper into advanced profiling techniques and real-world bottlenecks. Flutter 3.29 offers richer memory diagnostics and profiling capabilities that help uncover subtle and long-term memory retention issues—especially in large-scale production apps.

CHAPTER 3   PERFORMANCE OPTIMIZATION AND PROFILING

Advanced Memory Profiling

As Flutter apps scale, memory profiling must evolve beyond leak detection to include deep analysis of allocation patterns, GC behavior, and long-lived object retention. In Flutter 3.29, Dart DevTools and supporting tools offer granular insights into how memory is used, allowing developers to precisely identify and eliminate memory inefficiencies.

It covers advanced memory profiling workflows, tools, and techniques to help you proactively optimize your app's memory usage—especially for production-scale deployments.

Profiling with the Allocation Profiler

The Allocation Profiler in Dart DevTools enables tracking of object allocations in real time and across sessions. It's one of the most powerful tools for diagnosing heavy memory use caused by excessive or repetitive object creation.

Features:

- Tracks how many instances of each class are allocated
- Captures stack traces at allocation points
- Highlights memory churn due to rapid create/destroy cycles

Usage Workflow:

- Open DevTools ➤ Memory tab.
- Enable Allocation Tracing (may reduce performance slightly).
- Perform the interaction you want to analyze (e.g., scrolling, navigation, animation).

Filter allocations by package or class (e.g., "TextEditingController," "ListTile").

Investigate top contributors to memory pressure and optimize code accordingly.

Example: Detecting large amounts of "TextSpan" allocations during typing in a rich text field

Analyzing Retained Objects

Retained objects are those that persist in memory because something else references them. Flutter 3.29 DevTools lets you

Capture heap snapshots at different app states.

Compare before/after memory states to see which objects remain.

Use Retaining Path view to understand why an object isn't garbage-collected.

This is crucial when

You suspect memory leaks, but the source is unclear.

Objects remain alive long after they're no longer needed.

Example:
```
final controller = ScrollController();
// Forgotten: controller.dispose();
```

If "ScrollController" shows up in heap snapshots after disposing the widget, it indicates a memory retention issue.

Monitoring GC Behavior and Heap Growth

Use the Live Heap Chart in Dart DevTools to monitor

- Heap usage over time
- Frequency and size of GC (garbage collection) events
- Memory plateau or "sawtooth" growth patterns (a sign of retained memory)

Key indicators are

- Consistent memory increase without drops → possible leaks
- Frequent GC activity with high heap growth → excessive short-lived allocations
- Spikes after animation/nav events → potential widget churn

Best Practice: Manually trigger garbage collection after heavy UI interaction and observe if memory usage returns to baseline.

Using VM Service Protocol and Observatory APIs

For low-level profiling and automation

- Connect to the Dart VM Service Protocol
- Use packages like "vm_service" or "leak_tracker" to script memory analysis
- Capture isolate-level memory snapshots and analyze outside DevTools

This is ideal for

- CI/CD integration

> Custom memory dashboards
>
> Automated leak detection during testing

Performance-Heavy Object Identification

In large apps, some classes might inadvertently become memory-heavy due to usage frequency or unoptimized patterns.

Use the Allocation Profiler to

> Identify top memory consumers
>
> Filter by class or type
>
> Review instance counts and memory usage

Example:

> Too many custom widgets like "UserCard" in a "ListView" without reuse might spike memory.

Fragmentation and Memory Bloat Detection

Even without leaks, memory fragmentation can lead to bloated heap usage.

Signs of Fragmentation:

> Application uses more memory than expected despite low instance counts.
>
> Frequent GC, but memory isn't released.

Solution:

> Optimize long-lived object lifetimes.
>
> Limit creation of large temporary structures (like images or ByteData).
>
> Avoid repetitive object creation inside "build()" methods.

Tooling for Advanced Scenarios

Tool	Use Case
DevTools Memory Tab	Allocation tracing, heap snapshots, retaining path
leak_tracker	Automated test-time leak detection
vm_service	Programmatic memory analysis
Dart Observatory	Low-level heap and isolate stats
Android Studio Profiler	Native memory usage of Flutter shell

Integration with Testing Pipelines

You can incorporate memory profiling into automated tests:

```
dev_dependencies:
  leak_tracker_flutter_testing: ^1.0.0
testWidgets('no memory leaks', (tester) async {
  final tracker = LeakTrackingTestBinding.ensureInitialized();
  await tester.pumpWidget(MyWidget());
  await tester.pumpAndSettle();
  await tracker.disposeAndTrackLeaks(); // Fails test if leaks detected
});
```

Advanced memory profiling is not a one-time task but a continual process, especially for apps with complex state management, animations, and dynamic views. Flutter 3.29's DevTools and VM tooling empower developers to identify subtle retention issues, GC inefficiencies, and object bloat early in development.

Case Studies and Solutions

In this section, we dive into real-world case studies that demonstrate how advanced memory profiling techniques—covered in the previous sections—can uncover hidden issues and improve app performance. These practical examples will walk through symptoms, diagnosis, and solutions using the tools and methodologies introduced in Flutter 3.29.

Case Study 1: Leaking Controllers in Dynamic Forms
Scenario:

> A finance app dynamically builds multiple forms with complex input fields. After several navigations, the app shows increased memory usage and slowdowns.

Symptoms:

> Memory usage grows after each navigation.
>
> Heap snapshots show a high count of "TextEditingController" instances.
>
> GC fails to collect them.

Diagnosis:
Using Dart DevTools:

> Allocation Tracing showed "TextEditingController" allocations weren't dropping after navigation.
>
> Retaining Path revealed they were still referenced by the form widgets that weren't properly disposed of.

Solution:
Ensure "dispose()" is correctly called:

CHAPTER 3   PERFORMANCE OPTIMIZATION AND PROFILING

```
@override
void dispose() {
  _controller.dispose(); // crucial for memory cleanup
  super.dispose();
}
```

Impact:

Memory usage stabilized after navigation.

No controller instances retained in heap snapshots post-fix.

Case Study 2: Image Cache Bloat in a Social Feed Scenario:

A social media app loads a large number of high-resolution profile and post images into a scrolling feed.

Symptoms:

App crashes on low-end devices after long usage.

Memory profiler shows increasing memory consumption during feed scrolling.

Diagnosis:

DevTools Memory Tab showed retained "Image" objects.

Allocation Profiler indicated frequent allocation of "MemoryImage" instances.

Cache was not being managed explicitly.

CHAPTER 3   PERFORMANCE OPTIMIZATION AND PROFILING

Solution:
Manually clear image cache and implement a smarter image loading strategy:

```
imageCache.clear();
imageCache.clearLiveImages();
```

Use "CachedNetworkImage" with size constraints and LRU eviction to minimize memory impact.

Impact:

> Crashes eliminated on low-memory devices.
>
> Sustained memory usage dropped by ~60% during scrolling.

Case Study 3: Unintended Object Retention via Listeners
Scenario:

> In a dashboard app, memory kept increasing after users navigated through multiple charts and graphs.

Symptoms:

> Rebuilding charts multiple times resulted in higher memory usage.
>
> **Retained Objects**: "AnimationController," "StreamSubscription," and custom event listeners.

Diagnosis:

> Heap snapshots showed objects linked to stateful widgets via retained callbacks.
>
> Retaining Path view pointed to anonymous functions as culprits.

199

CHAPTER 3   PERFORMANCE OPTIMIZATION AND PROFILING

Solution:

Ensure all listeners are removed on widget disposal:

```
@override
void dispose() {
  _animationController.dispose();
  _streamSubscription.cancel();
  super.dispose();
}
```

Impact:

Retained object count stabilized.

Performance improved during repeated navigation.

Case Study 4: Memory Bloat from Animation Overuse

Scenario:

A shopping app's product detail page uses custom animations heavily (e.g., zoom, rotation, fade).

Symptoms:

Memory increases with each product view.

Eventually, frame drops occur on mid-tier devices.

Diagnosis:

DevTools Timeline + Memory integration revealed heavy churn due to rebuilding animated widgets.

Heap profiling showed no leaks but high allocation rate of "Tween," "Animation," and widget trees.

CHAPTER 3   PERFORMANCE OPTIMIZATION AND PROFILING

Solution:

Refactor animation logic using "AnimatedBuilder" and "ReorderableAnimationContainer." Cache and reuse "Tweens" where possible.

```
class OptimizedAnimation extends StatelessWidget {
  final Animation<double> animation;

  @override
  Widget build(BuildContext context) {
    return AnimatedBuilder(
      animation: animation,
      builder: (_, child) => Transform.scale(
        scale: animation.value,
        child: child,
      ),
      child: MyReusableChild(),
    );
  }
}
```

Impact:

Reduced memory churn.

Better animation performance.

Lower GC frequency and improved UX.

Case Study 5: Retained Pages in Custom Navigator Implementation
Scenario:

A custom navigator was used to manage complex flows in a job recruitment app, but memory usage grew with each page push.

201

Symptoms:

Pages remained in memory after navigation.

Heap snapshots showed large widget trees from previous routes still present.

Diagnosis:

DevTools Memory Retaining Path showed "PageController" holding strong references.

Overridden "NavigatorObserver" didn't clean up removed pages properly.

Solution:

Ensure popped routes are disposed and not retained in custom stacks:

```
void _removeRoute(Route route) {
  if (_customStack.contains(route)) {
    _customStack.remove(route);
  }
}
```

Impact:

Heap memory stabilized.

Navigating back and forth no longer increased memory footprint.

These case studies demonstrate that memory issues in Flutter apps often stem from subtle mismanagement of controllers, listeners, images, and animation patterns. Flutter 3.29's advanced profiling tools allow you to diagnose these problems with precision and apply targeted solutions.

Performance Best Practices

Performance optimization in Flutter is not just about tweaking code but involves adopting a strategic mindset that encompasses rendering, memory, build efficiency, and platform-specific constraints. This section dives deep into actionable best practices—backed by Flutter 3.29's latest engine and framework advancements—to help developers write apps that feel fast, load quickly, and scale smoothly across devices and platforms.

Leveraging New Performance Features

Flutter 3.29 brings a suite of new performance-centric enhancements designed to empower developers with tools and capabilities that reduce latency, accelerate UI rendering, and improve runtime efficiency across devices. This section delves into both the framework-level upgrades and strategic development patterns that align with them.

Utilizing Latest Performance Enhancements

Flutter 3.29 delivers significant upgrades aimed at eliminating common performance bottlenecks and empowering developers to build apps that feel smooth and snappy across devices. This section provides a focused breakdown of the latest performance enhancements and how to effectively integrate them into your Flutter projects.

Stable Impeller Rendering Engine
The Impeller engine, now stable on iOS and in active rollout for Android, replaces the legacy Skia-based pipeline with a new GPU-accelerated rendering approach.

CHAPTER 3 PERFORMANCE OPTIMIZATION AND PROFILING

Key Benefits:

Eliminates shader compilation jank at runtime

Delivers consistent frame pacing across animations

Supports precompiled pipelines and real-time shader warm-up

Activation:

```
flutter build ios --enable-impeller
flutter build apk --enable-impeller
```

Use Case:

Apps with rich animations or 60/120 FPS UI transitions benefit immediately from Impeller's smoother rendering pipeline.

Deferred Widget Tree Construction

New APIs allow deferring expensive widget builds until after the first frame, reducing time-to-first-frame (TTFF) and improving perceived performance.

Example:

```
WidgetsBinding.instance.deferFirstFrame();
await loadInitialData();
WidgetsBinding.instance.allowFirstFrame();
```

CHAPTER 3   PERFORMANCE OPTIMIZATION AND PROFILING

Use Case:

>Ideal for apps with heavy startup logic such as database preloads, large asset bundles, or authentication flows.

Optimized Background Isolates

Flutter 3.29 enhances isolate handling by reducing startup latency, improving resource reuse, and optimizing context-switching.

Example:

```
compute(parseLargeJSON, jsonString);
```

Use Case:

>Background processing tasks like JSON (JavaScript Object Notation) parsing, encryption, and file I/O benefit from more efficient isolate scheduling.

Partial Widget Tree Rebuilds

Flutter now performs smarter tree diffing and subtree retention, reducing layout and rebuild costs on UI updates.

Scenario:

>In state updates using "setState()," only the necessary widgets are invalidated, leaving unchanged components untouched.

Impact:

>Faster frame builds
>
>Reduced CPU workload
>
>Less GC pressure

205

Enhanced Frame Budget Tuning

Flutter 3.29 introduces experimental APIs for frame pacing and budget control, enabling precise performance tuning for different platforms.

Diagnostic Use:

```
SchedulerBinding.instance.addTimingsCallback((List<FrameTiming> timings) {
  // Analyze build/layout/paint durations
});
```

Use Case:

> Apps targeting both 60 FPS mid-range Android devices and 120 FPS iOS devices can dynamically optimize rendering loads.

Web Performance Upgrades

Flutter Web benefits from targeted performance gains:

> Smaller WASM bundles via aggressive tree shaking
>
> Lazy loading of assets
>
> Improved CanvasKit (2.13) for better text and vector rendering

Command:

```
flutter build web --wasm
```

Result:

> Lower TTI (time to interactive)
>
> Smoother interactions in PWAs and SPAs

Hot UI Diff Engine Improvements (Dev-Only)

During development, hot reloads are now faster and more memory efficient due to

>   Smarter state restoration
>
>   Granular widget diffing
>
>   Reduced widget invalidation scope

Impact:

>   Speeds up iteration cycles, especially for large or stateful UIs

Performance Optimization Strategies

While Flutter's rendering engine and platform-level improvements provide a solid performance foundation, real-world performance depends heavily on how you write and structure your code. In this section, we present proven strategies for maximizing app performance using best practices in widget design, state management, build optimization, and render efficiency.

These strategies are particularly impactful when building large-scale or high-FPS applications and can be applied alongside Flutter 3.29's new performance features.

Optimize Build Method Usage

The "build()" method should remain as lightweight as possible.

Best Practices:

>   Avoid complex computations in "build()."
>
>   Preprocess logic in "initState()" or a separate controller.
>
>   Split large widgets into smaller, reusable components.

CHAPTER 3   PERFORMANCE OPTIMIZATION AND PROFILING

Bad:

```
Widget build(BuildContext context) {
  final heavyData = calculateData(); // Expensive!
  return Text(heavyData.toString());
}
```

Good:

```
late final heavyData;
@override
void initState() {
  super.initState();
  heavyData = calculateData();
}
```

Leverage "const" Constructors

Using "const" constructors signals Flutter to reuse widget instances instead of rebuilding them.

Example:

```
const Text('Hello', style: TextStyle(fontSize: 16));
```

Benefits:

- Reduces rebuild costs
- Improves diffing efficiency
- Avoids redundant object creation

Use "RepaintBoundary" Strategically

"RepaintBoundary" helps isolate parts of the widget tree that change frequently from those that don't.

Use Case:

Animations inside scroll views

Dynamic widgets inside static layouts

Caution:

Overuse can lead to memory overhead from caching.

Optimize List and Grid Views

Flutter provides efficient scrolling widgets like "ListView.builder" and "GridView.builder."

Tips:

Use "itemExtent" or "prototypeItem" to improve layout prediction.

Avoid "ListView(children: [...])" for large datasets.

For tabbed interfaces, use "AutomaticKeepAliveClientMixin."

Performance Boost:

Reduces layout cost per frame

Prevents UI jank in long lists

Prefer Lightweight State Management

State management directly impacts rebuild behavior.

Chapter 3 Performance Optimization and Profiling

Guidelines:

Use "Provider," "Riverpod," or "Bloc" with selector patterns.

Minimize the rebuild scope using "Consumer," "Selector," or "BlocSelector."

Avoid:

Updating large portions of the tree for small state changes

Debounce and Throttle UI Updates

For frequent state updates (e.g., from user input or stream data), apply debounce or throttle mechanisms.

Example:

```
Timer? _debounce;
void onTextChanged(String value) {
  if (_debounce?.isActive ?? false) _debounce!.cancel();
  _debounce = Timer(const Duration(milliseconds: 300), () {
    // Update state
  });
}
```

Impact:

Reduces CPU usage

Improves perceived responsiveness

Avoid Overdraw and Redundant Layers

Minimize overlapping widgets and complex transparency effects. Use tools like "Performance Overlay" to identify render layers.

Use:

>   "Clip.none" where clipping isn't needed

>   "Opacity" sparingly (it causes full layer redraws)

Defer Expensive Work with Isolates

Use "compute()" or background isolates for

>   Heavy parsing

>   File system operations

>   Network data processing

Example:

```
final result = await compute(parseLargeJson, rawData);
```

Impact:

>   Keeps the UI thread smooth

>   Reduces frame drops under load

Monitor with DevTools Regularly

Use Dart DevTools to identify frame drops, long builds, and memory leaks:

>   **Timeline**: Find slow frames and long tasks.

>   **CPU Profiler**: Identify slow methods.

>   **Memory**: Track object allocation and leaks.

Tune for Platform-Specific Scenarios

Different devices require different optimizations:

>   **Android**: Compress large images, and reduce overdraw.

> **iOS**: Avoid large Lottie animations unless rasterized.
>
> **Web**: Use tree shaking, lazy asset loading, and avoid huge widget trees.

By embracing these performance optimization strategies in tandem with Flutter 3.29's latest capabilities, developers can build fluid, fast, and resource-efficient applications. The key is to adopt a mindset of intentional architecture and vigilant profiling—where every widget, render call, and state update are optimized for speed and responsiveness.

Optimizing Rendering and Build Times

In high-performance apps, the most visible bottlenecks often stem from excessive rendering and inefficient build cycles. Flutter 3.29 introduces smarter rendering mechanisms, but app developers must also design their widget trees and rendering strategies carefully.

Here we explore both foundational and advanced techniques to optimize how Flutter builds and paints your UI, ensuring smooth scrolling, faster frame generation, and lower jank rates—especially critical on mid-range and low-end devices.

Techniques for Faster Rendering

Rendering performance is one of the most critical factors in delivering a seamless user experience in Flutter apps. A smooth interface not only enhances usability but also strengthens user retention and perceived quality. As devices become more diverse—with varying GPU and CPU capabilities—it becomes imperative to adopt advanced rendering techniques that guarantee performance across the board.

Here, we explore expert-level strategies for reducing rendering overhead, optimizing widget composition, and taking full advantage of Flutter's rendering engine introduced and enhanced in version 3.29.

Minimize Overdraw and Visual Clutter

Overdraw occurs when the same pixel is rendered multiple times within a frame. This often results from unnecessary widget layering (e.g., stacking opaque containers).

Strategies:

Avoid placing fully opaque containers over others unless needed.

Use transparent colors only when necessary.

Replace "Opacity" widgets with "FadeTransition" to avoid full subtree rebuilds.

Tooling Tip:

Use Flutter DevTools' "Raster Stats" and Performance Overlay to identify and reduce overdraw.

Use "RepaintBoundary" Strategically

"RepaintBoundary" instructs Flutter to isolate parts of the widget tree so they are not redrawn unless necessary.

Ideal Use Cases:

Widgets that update frequently (e.g., animated charts or countdown timers)

Scrollable lists with interactive components

Code Example:

```
RepaintBoundary(
  child: YourHeavyWidget(),
);
```

> **Warning** Overusing "RepaintBoundary" can backfire. Each boundary consumes additional memory and rendering isolation.

Flatten Deep Widget Trees

Deep widget trees increase layout computation cost. While Flutter handles deep nesting efficiently, simplifying layout where possible helps reduce rendering time.

Approach:

Avoid excessive wrapping (e.g., multiple "Padding," "Container," "Align" layers).

Combine layout behavior into fewer widgets using properties (e.g., use "Container" with margin, padding, and decoration instead of separate wrappers).

Cache Static Widgets Using "const"

Static widgets should be marked "const" to avoid unnecessary rebuilds and take advantage of compile-time instantiation.

Do:

```
const Text('Dashboard');
```

Don't:

```
Text('Dashboard');
```

Impact:

>Improves build performance and reduces garbage collection pressure

Optimize Lists with "itemExtent" and Builders

Large or infinite lists should always use builder constructors ("ListView.builder," "GridView.builder," etc.) to lazily build only visible widgets.

Enhancements:

>Use "itemExtent" if all list items are the same height—it avoids layout recalculation.
>
>Avoid "ListView(children: [...])" for more than ~20 items.

```
ListView.builder(
  itemCount: 1000,
  itemExtent: 60.0,
  itemBuilder: (_, index) => ListTile(title: Text('Item
  $index')),
);
```

Avoid Unbounded Constraints

Unbounded height/width constraints (e.g., placing "ListView" inside "Column" without proper wrapping) cause layout overflow errors and frame drops.

Fix:

Wrap the list in "Expanded" or "Flexible":

```
Expanded(
  child: ListView(...),
);
```

Reduce Expensive Layout Widgets

Certain widgets, like "IntrinsicHeight," "IntrinsicWidth," or heavy "CustomMultiChildLayout," force multiple layout passes.

> **Best Practices:**
>
> > Avoid unless strictly required.
> >
> > Use "SizedBox," "Align," and "FractionallySizedBox" as simpler alternatives.

Animate Smartly

Animation can impact rendering speed when implemented poorly.

Pro Tips:

> Use "AnimatedBuilder" instead of repeatedly calling "setState()" during animation.
>
> Leverage "TweenAnimationBuilder" or "AnimatedSwitcher" for simple transitions.
>
> Always wrap animated elements with "RepaintBoundary" to isolate repaint logic.

Profile and Benchmark Continuously

Performance is not something you guess—it's something you measure.

Tools to Use:

> **Dart DevTools ➤ Performance Tab**: For jank tracking, slow frame visualization

Skia Shader Inspector: To analyze GPU usage on complex custom paints

Frame Chart Overlay: For visual frame-by-frame profiling in debug mode

Avoid Excessive "setState()"

Misuse of "setState()" can trigger rebuilds in large parts of the widget tree.

Solution:

Split complex widgets into smaller ones.

Use fine-grained state management solutions like "Provider," "Riverpod," or "Bloc."

Prefer "ValueNotifier

with "ValueListenableBuilder" for isolated updates.

Rendering performance is a mix of science and architecture. By combining Flutter's advanced tools, rendering isolations, and strategic optimizations, you can deliver apps that feel native—even on older or low-end devices. Flutter 3.29 continues to empower developers with more granular control over rendering, making performance tuning a practical and rewarding process.

Case Studies and Examples

Understanding theoretical optimization techniques is vital, but seeing them applied in real-world scenarios provides the clarity and confidence needed to implement them effectively. This section presents practical case studies that illustrate how specific performance issues were identified, diagnosed, and resolved using advanced techniques introduced in Flutter 3.2. These examples showcase measurable improvements in rendering performance and frame stability.

CHAPTER 3   PERFORMANCE OPTIMIZATION AND PROFILING

Case Study 1: Reducing Frame Drops in a Financial Dashboard App

Problem:

A Flutter-based financial dashboard with live updates was suffering from frequent frame drops, particularly during market hours when data refreshes were most intense.

Diagnosis:

DevTools Frame Chart revealed jank during high-frequency widget rebuilds.

Rebuild Stats highlighted a deeply nested widget tree with multiple "Opacity" and "Container" wrappers.

The main graph widget was rebuilding even when unrelated UI elements updated.

Solution:

Isolated the graph into a "RepaintBoundary"

Replaced static containers with "const" constructors

Replaced "Opacity" with "FadeTransition" using "AnimationController"

Result:

Dropped frames reduced by 80%.

CPU usage dropped by 15% during peak data periods.

App maintained 60 FPS consistently even under stress.

CHAPTER 3   PERFORMANCE OPTIMIZATION AND PROFILING

Case Study 2: Improving Build Times in a News Aggregator

Problem:

A news aggregator app suffered long initial load times and sluggish scrolling performance in article lists.

Diagnosis:

The initial load was building the entire list statically using "ListView(children: [...])."

Each list item used multiple layers of layout widgets, including "IntrinsicHeight."

Solution:

Switched to "ListView.builder" with "itemExtent" for uniform items

Removed unnecessary wrappers and replaced "IntrinsicHeight" with fixed "SizedBox" constraints

Cached image thumbnails using "cached_network_image"

Result:

Build time reduced by 40%.

Memory usage decreased by 25%.

Scrolling performance improved with zero jank on mid-range devices.

Case Study 3: Optimizing a Complex Ecommerce UI

Problem:

An ecommerce app with highly interactive product pages was experiencing sluggish animations when switching between tabs and filters.

Diagnosis:

DevTools revealed high frame rendering times during tab transitions.

Filters were triggering full widget tree rebuilds via "setState()" at the root level.

Solution:

Used "AnimatedSwitcher" for smooth transitions between tab content

Separated filter state into a dedicated "ChangeNotifier" with "Consumer" widgets for isolated rebuilds

Applied "const" modifiers wherever possible and moved complex subcomponents into separate widgets

Result:

Animation frame stability improved from ~45 FPS to a solid 60 FPS.

Reduced jank events from 11 to 0 in transition profiling.

User engagement increased due to the snappier and smoother UI.

Case Study 4: Rendering Optimization for a Drawing App

Problem:

A creative drawing application with custom paint features lagged on lower-end Android devices.

CHAPTER 3 PERFORMANCE OPTIMIZATION AND PROFILING

Diagnosis:

Custom painting was being triggered on every gesture update.

No "RepaintBoundary" was used, and the entire canvas was redrawn each frame.

Solution:

Implemented partial canvas repaint using "Canvas.clipRect" for dirty regions

Wrapped the canvas in a "RepaintBoundary" to isolate updates

Offloaded gesture processing to an isolate for heavy computations like Bezier smoothing

Result:

Rendering latency decreased by 60%.

App maintained smooth drawing performance even on low-spec devices.

GPU load reduced significantly, extending battery life during prolonged use.

Summary of Key Takeaways

Technique	Use Case	Impact
'RepaintBoundary'	Isolate updates	Reduced repaint overhead
'ListView.builder + itemExtent'	Long lists	Faster builds and lower memory usage
'AnimatedSwitcher'	Tab/UI transitions	Smooth animations and lower jank
'const' Widgets	Static UI parts	Less rebuild, faster rendering
State Management (e.g., Provider)	Granular UI updates	Better performance, clearer architecture

221

These case studies demonstrate that performance optimization in Flutter is often a matter of precise isolation, efficient widget composition, and mindful state management. By applying the techniques discussed throughout this chapter, developers can dramatically enhance rendering performance without compromising design complexity or UX richness. Flutter 3.29 provides the necessary tools and enhancements to deliver premium performance on any device—when used correctly and strategically.

Profiling Tools Comparison

Flutter developers have a wide array of profiling tools at their disposal, each designed to surface specific performance insights—CPU usage, memory leaks, jank detection, GPU utilization, and rendering issues. However, selecting the right tool for the job can be overwhelming without a deep understanding of what each profiler offers.

This section provides a side-by-side comparison of the most widely used profiling tools in the Flutter ecosystem, including Dart DevTools, Observatory, Perfetto, Skia Shader Inspector, and platform-native tools like Android GPU Inspector (AGI) and Xcode Instruments. You'll also find tailored recommendations for choosing the appropriate tool based on use case.

Comparing Various Profiling Tools

As applications scale in size and complexity, identifying performance bottlenecks requires precise diagnostics across multiple layers of the Flutter framework. No single tool provides a complete picture—each targets a specific area, such as rendering, memory, or CPU usage. In this section, we present a systematic comparison of the key profiling tools available in the Flutter ecosystem, highlighting their capabilities, ideal use cases, and how they fit into a professional development workflow.

CHAPTER 3 PERFORMANCE OPTIMIZATION AND PROFILING

Tool	Focus Area	Strengths	Limitations
Dart DevTools	CPU, memory, rebuilds, timeline	Deep integration, visual timeline, memory snapshot, widget rebuilds	Limited GPU visibility, may impact performance slightly
Flutter Performance Overlay	UI frame performance	Lightweight, always available, shows frame build times	Visual only, lacks detailed diagnostics
Skia Shader Inspector	GPU, shaders, custom painting	Shader-level rendering insights	Requires understanding of rendering internals
Android GPU Inspector (AGI)	GPU pipeline	Low-level GPU frame timing, Vulkan/OpenGL pipeline tracing	Android-only, setup complexity
iOS Instruments	CPU, GPU, memory (iOS)	Native Apple tooling, precise measurement	macOS/iOS only
Custom Timeline Events	Application-defined logic	Fine-grained control, developer-defined start/stop markers	Requires manual instrumentation
Flutter Inspector	Widget tree and diagnostics	Tree visualization, widget rebuilds	No performance metrics
Flame Charts (DevTools)	CPU, async tasks	Detailed call tree and async task analysis	Complexity increases with app size

Figure 3-2. Comparison table

Tools Comparison Table
Dart DevTools
Use Cases:

    Identifying widget rebuilds

    Analyzing performance in the timeline

    Viewing memory usage and GC events

    CPU profiling

Strengths:

    Official and tightly integrated with Flutter

    Excellent visualization of frame-level performance

    Memory snapshot comparisons that help trace leaks

Weaknesses:

    Not suitable for low-level GPU analysis

    Can introduce slight overhead during heavy profiling

Flutter Performance Overlay

Use Cases:

    Quick visualization of rendering performance

    Detecting frame build vs. raster time bottlenecks

Strengths:

    Always available (via "showPerformanceOverlay: true")

    Minimal overhead

Weaknesses:

    No deep drill-down capability

    Doesn't show widget or memory stats

Skia Shader Inspector

Use Cases:

    Debugging slow custom paints

    Identifying expensive shaders

Strengths:

Visual feedback on rendering cost per element

Helps with "CustomPainter" and "Canvas" operations

Weaknesses:

More useful for apps using custom graphics

Steeper learning curve for those unfamiliar with GPU internals

Android GPU Inspector (AGI)
Use Cases:

GPU frame timing analysis

Vulkan and OpenGL pipeline profiling

Strengths:

Powerful diagnostics for Android rendering issues

Shows frame breakdown by GPU pipeline stages

Weaknesses:

Not Flutter-specific

Requires advanced setup and Android hardware support

iOS Instruments
Use Cases:

Memory leak detection

CPU usage trends

Energy diagnostics

Strengths:

> Deep integration with the iOS ecosystem
>
> Precise profiling across all subsystems

Weaknesses:

> macOS only
>
> Not tailored to Flutter's internal architecture

Custom Timeline Events
Use Cases:

> Profiling specific operations (e.g., image decoding, data fetching)

How-To:

```
import 'dart:developer';

Timeline.startSync('Fetch Data');
// perform expensive task
Timeline.finishSync();
```

Strengths:

> Lets developers define and isolate performance-critical paths
>
> Integrates seamlessly with Dart DevTools Timeline

Weaknesses:

> Requires manual effort and familiarity with instrumentation

CHAPTER 3　PERFORMANCE OPTIMIZATION AND PROFILING

Flutter Inspector
Use Cases:

　　Visualizing the widget tree

　　Spotting unnecessary rebuilds

Strengths:

　　Extremely helpful for layout-related diagnostics

　　Highlights widget bounds and render objects

Weaknesses:

　　Not a profiling tool in the traditional sense

　　Doesn't capture runtime performance metrics

Flame Charts in DevTools
Use Cases:

　　CPU function call visualization

　　Identifying expensive synchronous operations

Strengths:

　　Clearly shows function nesting and execution time

　　Ideal for heavy computation bottlenecks

Weaknesses:

　　Harder to interpret in large apps with complex call stacks

Each profiling tool brings unique value to Flutter's performance analysis ecosystem. For most Flutter developers, Dart DevTools acts as the central hub. However, integrating Flutter Inspector, Skia Shader Inspector, and native profilers into your toolkit enables you to analyze apps at both high and low levels.

CHAPTER 3   PERFORMANCE OPTIMIZATION AND PROFILING

Use Cases and Recommendations

Choosing the right profiling tool depends heavily on the specific performance issue you're facing—whether it's UI jank, memory leaks, shader compilation delay, or slow build times. In this section, we explore real-world use cases that developers frequently encounter and provide precise tool recommendations, along with professional best practices for diagnosing and resolving these issues.

Use Case 1: UI Jank and Frame Drops
Symptoms:

> App stutters during scroll or animation.
>
> Missed frame warnings in console ("missed frame by XX ms").

Recommended Tools:

> Dart DevTools ➤ Timeline and Frame Chart
>
> Performance Overlay
>
> Custom Timeline Events (if needed)

Strategy:

> Use DevTools' frame timeline to detect long frame builds.
>
> Enable Performance Overlay to visualize frame build vs. raster time.
>
> Add custom timeline events to isolate logic causing jank.

Best Practices:

Keep widget rebuilds minimal.

Split expensive UI into "RepaintBoundary" widgets.

Avoid complex logic inside build methods.

Use Case 2: Memory Leaks and Excessive Memory Usage
Symptoms:

Gradual memory increase during app usage.

App crashes due to "OutOfMemoryError."

Recommended Tools:

Dart DevTools ➤ Memory tab

iOS Instruments (for iOS)

Android Studio Profiler (for Android)

Strategy:

Use Allocation Tracing and memory snapshots in DevTools.

Identify retained objects that persist longer than necessary.

Run garbage collection manually to isolate leaks.

Best Practices:

Dispose of controllers, streams, and animations properly.

Use "StatefulWidget" lifecycle methods to manage resources.

Avoid static references to UI objects.

Use Case 3: Expensive Shader Compilation

Symptoms:

    First-time animation stutters.

    Lag during widget transitions involving gradients, shadows, or transforms.

Recommended Tools:

    Skia Shader Inspector

    Precompiled SkSL Shaders

Strategy:

    Analyze shader compilation jank via Skia Inspector.

    Capture shaders using Flutter's "flutter build bundle --bundle-sksl-path."

    Ship precompiled shaders to avoid runtime compilation.

Best Practices:

    Avoid triggering new shaders mid-animation.

    Prewarm animations during splash screen.

    Reuse animations and avoid deep blur/shadow effects.

Use Case 4: GPU Bottlenecks on Android Devices

Symptoms:

    High rendering times even with lightweight widgets.

    Performance drop on low-end Android devices.

Recommended Tools:

Android GPU Inspector (AGI)

Performance Overlay

Strategy:

Record a GPU trace session with AGI and analyze frame timings.

Check for overdraw, redundant layer compositions, or texture uploads.

Best Practices:

Minimize layers with transparency.

Flatten widget trees where possible.

Use "RepaintBoundary" to limit redraws.

Use Case 5: CPU-Intensive Operations Causing UI Lag
Symptoms:

Main thread blocked during computation.

Jank during long loops, parsing, or image processing.

Recommended Tools:

DevTools Flame Chart

Custom Timeline Events

Dart DevTools—CPU Profiler

Strategy:

Analyze CPU call stacks using flame charts.

Identify expensive sync functions.

Move heavy logic to background isolates.

Best Practices:

Offload processing to isolates using "compute()" or "Isolate.spawn."

Avoid long-running sync loops inside "initState" or build.

Use async/await to free UI thread.

Use Case 6: Slow Build or Rebuild Times

Symptoms:

Widgets take long to rebuild.

Sluggish hot reload/hot restart behavior.

Recommended Tools:

Flutter Inspector

DevTools ➤ Rebuild Stats

Custom Timeline Events

Strategy:

Use the Inspector to locate frequently rebuilt widgets.

Monitor rebuild statistics and re-evaluate state management usage.

Memoize expensive widgets using "const," "ValueKey," or "AutomaticKeepAliveClientMixin."

Best Practices:

Use "const" constructors wherever possible.

Use "Provider" or "Riverpod" to avoid unnecessary widget rebuilds.

Break UI into smaller widgets with independent lifecycles.

Use Case 7: Complex UI Rendering Delays

Symptoms:

App UI lags when displaying complex or dynamic layouts.

Recommended Tools:

Skia Shader Inspector

Flutter Inspector

CustomPaint diagnostics

Strategy:

Inspect custom paint or canvas-heavy widgets.

Use "debugRepaintRainbowEnabled" to highlight repaint areas.

Profile rendering paths and optimize canvas operations.

Best Practices:

Use "CustomPainter" only when necessary.

Cache rendered images or use "PictureRecorder."

Minimize paint operations in frequently updated UIs.

Summary: Tool Selection Matrix

Scenario	Primary Tool	Secondary Tool
UI frame jank	DevTools Timeline	Performance Overlay
Memory leak	DevTools Memory	iOS Instruments/Android Profiler
Shader compilation jank	Skia Shader Inspector	Precompiled SkSL
GPU rendering issues (Android)	Android GPU Inspector	Performance Overlay
CPU-intensive computation	Flame Chart (DevTools)	Custom Timeline Events
Rebuild inefficiency	Flutter Inspector	DevTools Rebuild Stats
Rendering delay in CustomPaint	Skia Inspector	debugRepaintRainbowEnabled

Final Recommendations

Start with Dart DevTools: It's your central hub for performance.

> **Combine Tools Strategically**: Use overlay + DevTools + native tools for full-stack visibility.
>
> **Automate Profiling in CI/CD**: Use "flutter drive" and custom instrumentation to catch regressions early.
>
> **Continuously Test on Physical Devices**: Emulators don't reflect real-world GPU or CPU constraints.

With the right tools and diagnostic workflows, Flutter apps can achieve native-level performance across platforms. In the next section, we'll explore device-specific optimizations that help scale performance for low-end and high-end devices alike.

Optimizing for Different Devices

Optimizing for different devices is crucial in today's diverse mobile landscape. Flutter enables building apps that run on both high-end and budget devices across Android and iOS, but achieving smooth performance on all devices requires careful optimization. In this section, we explore techniques for ensuring your app performs optimally across a wide range of device specifications, from flagship models to more budget-conscious smartphones.

Techniques for Multi-device Optimization

In today's mobile ecosystem, apps are expected to run seamlessly across a wide range of devices, from budget smartphones to high-end flagship models. Flutter provides powerful tools and techniques for optimizing app performance on different devices, ensuring that users across all device classes have a smooth, responsive experience. In this section, we explore various strategies and best practices for optimizing apps for a broad spectrum of devices.

Adaptive UI and Layouts

One of the most effective ways to optimize for multiple devices is through adaptive and responsive UI designs that adjust dynamically to various screen sizes, orientations, and device capabilities.

> **Responsive Layouts**: Use "MediaQuery" and "LayoutBuilder" to build layouts that respond to screen size, device orientation, and other environment factors. This allows your app's UI to adjust dynamically based on the device's dimensions.

```
double screenWidth = MediaQuery.of(context).size.width;
if (screenWidth < 600) {
  // Use a mobile-friendly layout
} else {
  // Use a tablet or desktop-friendly layout
}
```

CHAPTER 3　PERFORMANCE OPTIMIZATION AND PROFILING

Flexible Widgets: Flutter provides flexible layout widgets like "Flexible," "Expanded," and "FractionallySizedBox," which help create responsive layouts that adjust based on the available space. These widgets are ideal for ensuring consistent presentation across different device types, including phones, tablets, and larger screens.

Responsive Design with "FittedBox": For scaling text or images to fit within a particular area, consider using "FittedBox" or "AspectRatio" to adapt elements without distorting the design.

Device Previewing: The "device_preview" package allows developers to simulate different screen sizes, pixel densities, and platforms (iOS, Android, etc.) in the development environment. This is a great tool for fine-tuning layouts across various devices during development.

Optimizing for High- and Low-End Devices

Flutter allows you to fine-tune performance based on device specifications, enabling your app to perform well across both high-end and low-end devices. Here are some strategies:

Simplified UI on Low-End Devices: For budget devices with lower processing power and smaller memory, consider reducing UI complexity. This includes

- Using simpler animations or static images instead of heavy or dynamic graphics

- Avoiding excessive widget nesting, which can result in expensive rendering operations

Using "ListView.builder" instead of "ListView" to ensure that only visible items are built, reducing memory usage and CPU overhead

Efficient Asset Management: Use resolution-aware assets for images and icons. Flutter supports specifying different image resolutions for different screen densities (e.g., "image@2x.png," "image@3x.png"). For lower-end devices, you may want to use lower-resolution assets to save memory and improve load times.

Flutter's "targetPlatform" for Device-Specific Features: The "targetPlatform" API can help tailor app features depending on whether the app is running on Android or iOS or even on different versions of the platforms. This can be useful for optimizing performance on devices with specific hardware or software constraints.

```
if (Theme.of(context).platform == TargetPlatform.android) {
  // Android-specific optimizations
} else if (Theme.of(context).platform == TargetPlatform.iOS) {
  // iOS-specific optimizations
}
```

CHAPTER 3   PERFORMANCE OPTIMIZATION AND PROFILING

Offloading Intensive Tasks

Performance bottlenecks can arise when resource-intensive tasks are run on the main UI thread, especially on lower-end devices. Flutter offers several strategies to mitigate these issues:

> **Use Isolates for Background Tasks**: Isolates enable parallel processing by offloading compute-heavy tasks to background threads. Use the "compute()" function or "Isolate.spawn()" to run tasks like image processing, data parsing, or complex calculations on a separate isolate, leaving the main thread free for UI updates.

```
Future<void> backgroundTask() async {
  // Perform heavy computations in an isolate
  await compute(expensiveTask, inputData);
}
```

> **Asynchronous Programming**: Flutter's "async" and "await" features allow you to perform non-blocking I/O operations such as network requests or database queries. This ensures that the main thread remains responsive even when fetching data or performing time-consuming operations.
>
> **Limit Complex Animations**: While animations are a great way to enhance the user experience, excessive or complex animations can be a performance bottleneck, particularly on low-end devices. Consider using "AnimatedContainer," "AnimatedOpacity," and "AnimatedCrossFade,"

which are more optimized for performance compared with manually managing animations with "AnimationController."

Adaptive Asset Management

Efficiently managing and serving assets according to device capabilities is crucial in optimizing performance across various devices.

> **Image Asset Optimization**: For images, use resolution-aware asset names and formats, such as "image@2x.png" and "image@3x.png." Additionally, consider using vector-based assets like "SVG" (via the "flutter_svg" package), which can be scaled seamlessly on devices with different screen sizes and densities.

> **Use Asset Bundles**: Flutter's "AssetBundle" allows developers to load images and other resources efficiently by ensuring that assets are bundled with the app and served based on the target platform's requirements. This helps reduce load times and memory usage on both high- and low-end devices.

> **Preloading Assets for Faster Performance**: On lower-end devices, preloading assets during the splash screen or app startup can help reduce lag when transitioning to the main UI. For instance, preload heavy resources like images or large datasets so they're ready when the user begins interacting with the app.

Performance Monitoring on Multiple Devices

To ensure that the app performs optimally on different devices, consistent performance monitoring is key:

CHAPTER 3   PERFORMANCE OPTIMIZATION AND PROFILING

> **Device-Specific Profiling**: Using tools like Flutter DevTools, Firebase Performance Monitoring, and the Android and iOS profilers, you can track device-specific performance metrics such as CPU usage, GPU usage, memory consumption, and rendering times.

For Android, Android Studio Profiler provides a detailed performance report for CPU, memory, and network usage, allowing you to pinpoint issues.

For iOS, Instruments (part of Xcode) is a powerful tool for monitoring various performance aspects of your Flutter app on iOS devices.

> **Firebase Performance Monitoring**: Firebase Performance Monitoring can help track real-world performance of your app across different devices. By capturing key performance metrics, you can monitor how the app performs on different devices in production environments and make adjustments accordingly.

Testing on Physical Devices

Emulators are useful for initial testing, but nothing beats testing your app on actual physical devices. This allows you to observe how your app performs under real-world conditions, including network fluctuations, device-specific quirks, and real battery usage.

> **Use Firebase Test Lab**: This tool enables you to test your Flutter app on a wide variety of real devices hosted by Google, covering a wide range of device configurations and Android versions.

Device Farms: Consider setting up a device farm for testing, where you can test your app across multiple physical devices that reflect your user base. Device farms provide valuable insights into performance bottlenecks that might not be evident on emulators.

Optimizing for multiple devices involves leveraging responsive layouts, adaptive UIs, and device-specific optimizations. By utilizing Flutter's powerful tools, such as isolates for background tasks, responsive design widgets, and profiling utilities, you can ensure that your app runs smoothly across a broad spectrum of device types. Additionally, testing and profiling on real devices are essential to uncover potential performance issues early on and deliver an optimized user experience.

By adopting these techniques, you'll be well-equipped to create apps that not only look great but also perform efficiently, whether running on budget smartphones or premium devices.

Performance Benchmarks

Performance benchmarking is a critical aspect of optimizing mobile apps to ensure they deliver a smooth and responsive user experience across various devices. In this section, we will discuss the importance of performance benchmarking, the tools and techniques used for measuring app performance, and how to analyze the results to guide performance improvements.

Why Performance Benchmarks Matter

Before making performance improvements, it's essential to have reliable performance benchmarks that provide clear insights into how well your app is performing. These benchmarks allow you to

Identify Bottlenecks: By measuring key performance metrics, you can pinpoint areas where your app is slowing down, such as long loading times, high CPU or GPU usage, excessive memory consumption, or inefficient rendering.

Track Performance Over Time: Continuous benchmarking enables you to track performance trends as you make changes to your app, helping you ensure that optimizations are effective without introducing new issues.

Set Realistic Performance Goals: Benchmarks help establish clear performance goals for your app, whether it's reducing load times, lowering memory usage, or minimizing rendering jank, giving you concrete targets to achieve.

Key Performance Metrics

To create meaningful performance benchmarks, it's essential to focus on the right metrics. These are the primary areas you should monitor:

Frame Rate (FPS): Frame rate is crucial for ensuring smooth animations and interactions in your app. A stable frame rate of 60 FPS (frames per second) is ideal for most apps, although lower-end devices may require adjustments. Monitoring FPS helps identify rendering bottlenecks that cause stuttering or lag.

CPU Usage: High CPU usage can indicate inefficient code or unoptimized algorithms, leading to slower performance and increased battery consumption. Benchmarking CPU usage helps identify areas that need refactoring or optimization.

GPU Usage: If your app relies heavily on graphical elements, monitoring GPU usage becomes crucial. GPU-intensive tasks, such as animations and image rendering, can quickly degrade performance if not optimized for the device.

Memory Usage: Tracking memory usage is vital for preventing memory leaks and ensuring that your app runs efficiently. High memory usage can cause app crashes, slowdowns, or high battery consumption, especially on devices with limited RAM.

Startup Time: Measuring the time it takes for your app to launch and become interactive is a critical user experience metric. A long startup time can frustrate users and cause them to abandon the app.

Network Latency and Bandwidth: For apps relying on network resources, measuring network latency and bandwidth usage is essential. Benchmarking these aspects helps ensure fast and reliable data fetch operations.

Tools for Benchmarking Performance

Several tools can assist in measuring and analyzing performance metrics. These tools provide real-time insights, allow for detailed profiling, and help identify potential bottlenecks.

Flutter DevTools: Flutter DevTools is an excellent suite for profiling and debugging Flutter apps. It includes tools for measuring CPU usage, memory usage, network requests, and performance analysis.

The "Performance" tab in Flutter DevTools allows you to capture frame rendering information and analyze the app's performance over time.

Firebase Performance Monitoring: Firebase provides powerful performance monitoring tools that track real-world performance data across your app's user base. It measures key metrics like app startup time, HTTP request latency, and screen load times, providing valuable insights into how your app performs in production environments.

Xcode Instruments (iOS): For iOS apps, Xcode Instruments provides in-depth analysis of your app's performance on iOS devices. The "Time Profiler" helps identify CPU bottlenecks, while the "Allocations" and "Leaks" tools allow you to monitor memory usage and detect memory leaks.

Android Profiler (Android Studio): Android Studio's Profiler tool enables detailed analysis of your app's CPU, memory, and network usage. It offers real-time data and visualizations of app performance, which are crucial for detecting and resolving performance bottlenecks on Android devices.

Benchmarking Packages: There are also third-party benchmarking packages for Flutter, such as "flutter_benchmark" and "flutter_perf," which help measure performance in terms of both development and production environments. These packages provide convenient APIs to run benchmarks and track specific metrics over time.

Running Benchmarks on Different Devices

To ensure comprehensive testing, it's important to run your performance benchmarks on a variety of devices. Different devices have varying hardware capabilities, which can impact performance. Here are some key considerations:

> **Low-End Devices**: Benchmarking on low-end devices is critical because these devices often have limited processing power, memory, and graphics capabilities. By measuring performance on these devices, you can optimize your app for users with constrained resources, ensuring it remains responsive and functional.
>
> **High-End Devices**: While high-end devices tend to have better performance, it's still important to benchmark on them to identify areas where optimization is still necessary, particularly for CPU-intensive operations or heavy animations.
>
> **Targeted Device Profiling**: Tools like Firebase Test Lab, which runs tests on a wide range of real devices, or device farms, can help you test your app across a spectrum of devices without needing to own each model.
>
> **Emulators vs. Real Devices**: While emulators are helpful for initial testing, real devices provide more accurate results, especially for performance benchmarks like battery consumption, real-world latency, and physical rendering issues.

Analyzing and Interpreting Benchmark Results

Once you've collected performance data, the next step is to analyze and interpret the results:

Identify Trends: Look for consistent performance patterns across devices. Are certain devices consistently slower in rendering or startup times? Are there specific areas where the app performs poorly, such as during animation or heavy calculations?

Set Thresholds: Establish performance thresholds based on your app's requirements. For example, a frame rate below 30 FPS on a high-end device may indicate a serious rendering issue, while a frame rate of 60 FPS is often considered optimal. Similarly, a memory usage spike may indicate a memory leak or inefficient object management.

Optimize Based on Data: Use the insights gained from performance benchmarks to guide your optimization efforts. Focus on high-priority areas, such as reducing startup time, improving rendering performance, or minimizing memory usage.

Measure Impact of Changes: After making optimizations, rerun the benchmarks to assess the impact of the changes. Are your optimizations achieving the desired performance improvements, and are there any new performance issues introduced?

Performance Best Practices

Based on your benchmark results, there are several best practices you can follow to enhance your app's performance across different devices:

Efficient Data Loading: Use pagination, lazy loading, and caching techniques to reduce network usage and loading times, especially for apps dealing with large datasets.

Optimize Image Assets: Ensure that images are properly sized and compressed, avoiding large assets that consume unnecessary memory and bandwidth.

Memory Management: Pay close attention to memory usage, and optimize memory allocation to prevent leaks and excessive consumption. Tools like Dart DevTools and Firebase Performance Monitoring help identify memory bottlenecks.

Minimize UI Complexity: Avoid complex or deep widget hierarchies that can lead to expensive build operations. Use "ListView.builder" and other optimized widgets for large datasets.

Profile During Development: Continuously profile your app during the development process to catch performance issues early and prevent them from becoming significant problems later on.

Performance benchmarks are essential for ensuring that your app performs optimally across a variety of devices. By using profiling tools, analyzing key metrics, and running benchmarks on a wide range of devices, you can identify performance bottlenecks and optimize your app for the best possible user experience. Armed with this information, you can prioritize improvements, measure the impact of changes, and consistently deliver an app that runs smoothly, regardless of the device.

CHAPTER 3 PERFORMANCE OPTIMIZATION AND PROFILING

Summary

Here, we explore how to optimize and profile Flutter apps for maximum performance. It introduces the latest tools, techniques, and best practices for analyzing rendering speed, memory usage, and app responsiveness. Developers learn how to detect and fix performance issues, leverage new profiling features, and ensure smooth experiences across different devices.

CHAPTER 4

Advanced State Management

In the previous chapter, "Performance Optimization and Profiling," we explored cutting-edge tools and techniques for analyzing and improving the performance of Flutter applications. From leveraging the latest profiling capabilities in Dart DevTools to optimizing rendering and memory usage, we laid the foundation for building fast, responsive apps across a wide range of devices.

With performance fine-tuned, the next critical piece in building robust Flutter apps is state management. As applications scale in complexity, the way state is handled becomes increasingly important—not only for maintainability and scalability but also for ensuring seamless user experiences.

Here, we take a deep dive into advanced state management, focusing on the most powerful and flexible solutions available in Flutter 3.4. We start with Riverpod 2.0, highlighting its new features, patterns, and improvements that streamline reactive programming. We'll then examine the latest Bloc and Cubit updates, showcasing how they fit into modern app architectures with advanced usage patterns and real-world examples.

As many large applications benefit from using multiple state management strategies, we also explore integration techniques—combining Riverpod, Bloc, and other tools to manage complex state trees with clarity and precision. You'll learn strategies for organizing state across feature modules, optimizing performance, and collaborating effectively within large teams.

Finally, we round out the chapter with benchmark comparisons, helping you evaluate the trade-offs and performance implications of each approach in various scenarios.

By mastering the techniques in this chapter, you'll be equipped to architect scalable, maintainable, and high-performance Flutter apps—regardless of size or complexity.

Riverpod Enhancements

Riverpod has emerged as one of the most powerful and flexible state management solutions in the Flutter ecosystem. With the release of Riverpod 2.0, the library introduces several enhancements that improve developer ergonomics, offer greater control over application state, and enable more scalable architectures for modern Flutter apps. In this section, we will explore the key new features in Riverpod 2.0, delve into advanced state management patterns, and discuss how Riverpod can be integrated with other solutions to manage complex state trees in large applications.

Overview of Riverpod 2.0

Riverpod 2.0 represents a major leap forward in state management for Flutter, bringing with it a suite of new features, improved ergonomics, and greater architectural flexibility. Designed with scalability and developer experience in mind, this release addresses many of the limitations found in earlier versions while opening the door for more advanced usage patterns.

CHAPTER 4   ADVANCED STATE MANAGEMENT

Here are key enhancements in Riverpod 2.0:

1. **Code Generation with riverpod_generator**

   One of the most significant additions in Riverpod 2.0 is support for automatic code generation. By using annotations such as @riverpod, developers can define providers more declaratively, removing repetitive boilerplate and reducing human error. Generated code ensures stronger type safety, simplifies provider declarations, and improves readability across large codebases.

2. **Introduction of Notifier and AsyncNotifier**

   Riverpod 2.0 introduces two new base classes for managing state: Notifier for synchronous logic and AsyncNotifier for asynchronous operations. These classes promote a cleaner separation of concerns by encapsulating business logic within a provider, making it easier to write, test, and maintain stateful code.

   Notifier: Ideal for synchronous operations such as counters, toggles, or local cache updates.

   AsyncNotifier: Tailored for tasks like API requests, local storage reads/writes, and other asynchronous workflows. It also includes built-in loading and error handling states.

3. **Enhanced Provider Scoping**

   The scoping system in Riverpod 2.0 allows for more precise control over the lifecycle of providers. Developers can now easily define local, scoped, or

251

CHAPTER 4   ADVANCED STATE MANAGEMENT

global providers that respond to lifecycle events such as widget disposal or navigation changes. This minimizes memory leaks and enhances modularity in large applications.

4. **Improved DevTools Integration**

   With enhanced DevTools support, developers can now monitor provider states, dependencies, and value changes in real time. This leads to faster debugging and a deeper understanding of how state flows throughout the application.

5. **Performance Optimizations**

   Riverpod 2.0 introduces internal performance enhancements that make provider reads and state updates faster and more efficient. Combined with selective rebuilding and fine-grained dependency tracking, these improvements help keep Flutter apps responsive even as complexity grows.

Riverpod 2.0 isn't just an upgrade—it's a rethinking of how state can and should be managed in modern Flutter applications. With its declarative syntax, flexible architecture, and robust tooling, it empowers developers to build scalable, maintainable apps with confidence.

Here's a side-by-side comparison of Riverpod 1.x vs. Riverpod 2.0, followed by a clean code sample demonstrating the use of a "Notifier" in Riverpod 2.0.

Riverpod 1.x vs. Riverpod 2.0: Side-by-Side Comparison

Feature	Riverpod 1.x	Riverpod 2.0
Provider Syntax	Manual setup, verbose syntax	Declarative using `@riverpod` and code generation
State Logic Classes	Relies on `StateNotifier`, `ChangeNotifier`, or external classes	Uses streamlined `Notifier` and `AsyncNotifier` models
Asynchronous Handling	Requires manual Future/Stream handling with boilerplate	Built-in async state support via `AsyncNotifier`
Code Generation	Optional and mostly community-driven via `flutter_riverpod` hacks	Officially supported via `riverpod_generator`
DevTools Support	Basic – limited insight into provider behavior	Enhanced – integrated with DevTools for real-time inspection
Lifecycle Management	Less control – autoDispose needed explicit configuration	Granular lifecycle management with improved `autoDispose` handling
Performance	Good for small-to-medium apps	Optimized provider reads and rebuilds for better large-scale performance

Figure 4-1. Difference between Riverpod 1.x and Riverpod 2.0

Code Example: Using "Notifier" in Riverpod 2.0

Let's look at a basic counterexample using the new "Notifier" API with code generation.

Step 1: Define the Notifier

```
import 'package:flutter_riverpod/flutter_riverpod.dart';
import 'package:riverpod_annotation/riverpod_annotation.dart';

part 'counter.g.dart';
```

CHAPTER 4   ADVANCED STATE MANAGEMENT

```
@riverpod
class Counter extends _$Counter {
  @override
  int build() => 0;

  void increment() => state++;
  void decrement() => state--;
}
```

Step 2: Use It in Your UI

```
import 'package:flutter/material.dart';
import 'package:flutter_riverpod/flutter_riverpod.dart';
import 'counter.dart'; // where the generated Counter
class lives

class CounterScreen extends ConsumerWidget {
  @override
  Widget build(BuildContext context, WidgetRef ref) {
    final count = ref.watch(counterProvider);

    return Scaffold(
      appBar: AppBar(title: Text('Riverpod 2.0 Counter')),
      body: Center(
        child: Text('Count: $count', style: TextStyle
        (fontSize: 24)),
      ),
      floatingActionButton: Column(
        mainAxisSize: MainAxisSize.min,
        children: [
          FloatingActionButton(
```

```
          onPressed: () => ref.read(counterProvider.
          notifier).increment(),
          child: Icon(Icons.add),
        ),
        SizedBox(height: 10),
        FloatingActionButton(
          onPressed: () => ref.read(counterProvider.
          notifier).decrement(),
          child: Icon(Icons.remove),
        ),
      ],
    ),
  );
 }
}
```

Generated Code

With the "@riverpod" annotation and build_runner, Riverpod auto-generates the provider boilerplate behind the scenes:

```
flutter pub run build_runner build --delete-conflicting-outputs
```

Advanced State Management Patterns

With the architectural flexibility introduced in Riverpod 2.0, developers are now equipped to adopt sophisticated state management patterns that go beyond simple counters or form states. These patterns allow for better separation of concerns, enhanced testability, and scalability in production-grade applications. In this section, we explore advanced usage patterns

CHAPTER 4   ADVANCED STATE MANAGEMENT

that leverage the full power of Riverpod 2.0, including the use of "Notifier," "AsyncNotifier," provider families, scoped overrides, and composable state logic.

Encapsulating Business Logic with Notifier

Riverpod 2.0 encourages encapsulating state logic within "Notifier" and "AsyncNotifier" classes. This approach isolates business logic from the UI layer, promoting cleaner, testable codebases. By abstracting state transitions into discrete classes, teams can implement domain-driven design (DDD) principles within Flutter.

```
@riverpod
class AuthState extends _$AuthState {
  @override
  AuthModel build() {
    // Initial unauthenticated state
    return AuthModel.unauthenticated();
  }

  void login(String username, String password) {
    // Logic for authentication
    state = AuthModel.authenticated(username);
  }

  void logout() {
    state = AuthModel.unauthenticated();
  }
}
```

This pattern helps maintain logic boundaries and decouples UI widgets from internal state mechanisms.

CHAPTER 4　ADVANCED STATE MANAGEMENT

Managing Asynchronous Workflows with AsyncNotifier

For scenarios involving network requests, database access, or complex async flows, "AsyncNotifier" provides a structured way to model state while handling loading, success, and failure states out of the box.

```
@riverpod
class WeatherNotifier extends _$WeatherNotifier {
  @override
  Future<Weather> build(String city) async {
    return await weatherRepository.fetchWeather(city);
  }

  Future<void> refresh() async {
    state = const AsyncValue.loading();
    state = await AsyncValue.guard(() => weatherRepository.
    fetchWeather(ref.state.requireValue.city));
  }
}
```

By using "AsyncValue," developers can safely and idiomatically handle loading indicators, error displays, and success states directly in the UI.

Dynamic Providers with Family Modifiers

The "family" modifier enables parameterized provider instances, making it ideal for building reusable and context-aware components such as user profiles, product details, or search queries.

```
@riverpod
Future<UserProfile> userProfile(UserProfileRef ref, String userId) async {
  return await userRepository.getUserProfile(userId);
}
```

257

CHAPTER 4   ADVANCED STATE MANAGEMENT

This pattern supports dynamic use cases while ensuring each provider instance remains isolated and stateless outside its parameter scope.

Scoped Overrides and Dependency Injection (DI)
Scoped overrides empower developers to inject test mocks, feature-specific services, or platform-specific implementations without modifying the core logic. This is especially useful in testing and multi-module apps.

```
void main() {
  runApp(
    ProviderScope(
      overrides: [
        authStateProvider.overrideWith(() => MockAuthState()),
      ],
      child: MyApp(),
    ),
  );
}
```

Scoped overrides simplify environment configuration, enable modular development, and promote loose coupling between layers.

Composable State Logic with Providers as Dependencies
One of Riverpod's strengths is its ability to compose logic through provider dependencies. Providers can freely consume other providers, allowing complex logic to be built through functional composition.

```
final totalPriceProvider = Provider<double>((ref) {
  final cartItems = ref.watch(cartProvider);
  return cartItems.fold(0, (sum, item) => sum + item.price * item.quantity);
});
```

This pattern enables the creation of derived state, keeping data transformations out of the UI and centralizing logic in one maintainable location.

Combining State Management Solutions

As applications grow in complexity, it is often impractical to rely on a single state management approach to solve every problem. Flutter's flexibility allows developers to choose the best tool for each use case—and Riverpod 2.0 makes it even easier to integrate with other solutions such as Bloc, Redux, and legacy InheritedWidgets.

This section explores practical strategies for **combining Riverpod with other libraries** and demonstrates how to **organize and manage complex state trees** in large, modular applications.

Integrating Riverpod with Other Solutions

While Riverpod 2.0 offers a powerful and modern approach to state management, real-world Flutter projects often require combining multiple tools and patterns to meet specific architectural or team needs. In enterprise environments or large codebases, it's common to see hybrid solutions—where Riverpod is integrated with other state management libraries like Bloc, Redux, or even legacy `InheritedWidget`-based patterns.

Riverpod is designed with composability in mind, making it relatively easy to interoperate with other tools without compromising scalability, testability, or maintainability.

Why Combine Solutions?

There are several reasons to combine Riverpod with other state management systems:

- **Incremental Migration**: Introducing Riverpod into an existing project that already uses Bloc or Redux
- **Feature Isolation**: Allowing different teams or modules to use different approaches without conflict
- **Specialized Use Cases**: Leveraging strengths of multiple systems—for example, using Bloc for business logic and Riverpod for lightweight UI state

Example: Hosting Bloc Inside Riverpod

One common integration pattern is to expose Bloc or Cubit instances via Riverpod for dependency injection and lifecycle management:

```
final authBlocProvider = Provider<AuthBloc>((ref) {
  final authRepository = ref.read(authRepositoryProvider);
  return AuthBloc(authRepository);
});
```

Then, in the UI:

```
class LoginScreen extends ConsumerWidget {
  @override
  Widget build(BuildContext context, WidgetRef ref) {
    final authBloc = ref.watch(authBlocProvider);

    return BlocProvider.value(
      value: authBloc,
      child: BlocBuilder<AuthBloc, AuthState>(
        builder: (context, state) {
```

```
        // Handle state
      },
    ),
  );
}
}
```

This approach gives you the best of both worlds:

- Use Riverpod for provider injection and cleanup.
- Retain Bloc's powerful event/state separation and middleware patterns.

Using Riverpod for Local State, Bloc for Global Logic

Another pattern involves using Riverpod to manage **transient, UI-specific state** (like toggles, forms, animations) while reserving Bloc or Redux for **global or domain-specific logic** (authentication, cart management, synchronization).

For example:

```
final passwordVisibleProvider = StateProvider<bool>((ref)
=> false);
```

This allows your widgets to manage small-scale state reactively, without the boilerplate of a Cubit or Bloc, while still leveraging Bloc elsewhere for business-critical flows.

CHAPTER 4   ADVANCED STATE MANAGEMENT

Testing Benefits

When using Riverpod to host Bloc instances, writing tests becomes easier thanks to the scoped override system:

```
testWidgets('Test with mock Bloc', (tester) async {
  await tester.pumpWidget(
    ProviderScope(
      overrides: [
        authBlocProvider.overrideWithValue(MockAuthBloc()),
      ],
      child: MyApp(),
    ),
  );

  // Continue testing
});
```

This makes it possible to inject mocks and fakes without changing production code—ideal for unit testing, integration tests, and CI/CD pipelines.

Integration with Redux or InheritedWidget

Riverpod can also read values from external systems like Redux stores or legacy InheritedWidgets:

```
final reduxStoreProvider = Provider<Store<AppState>>((ref) {
  return StoreProvider.of<AppState>(ref.read(context));
});

final userProvider = Provider<User>((ref) {
```

```
  final store = ref.watch(reduxStoreProvider);
  return store.state.currentUser;
});
```

While not a common long-term strategy, this is useful during gradual migration or for bridging modern Flutter widgets with older architecture layers.

Riverpod's flexibility allows seamless integration with other state management approaches, enabling hybrid architectures that can evolve over time. Whether you're maintaining legacy systems, introducing new patterns incrementally, or designing modular teams, Riverpod plays well with others—without sacrificing performance, readability, or maintainability.

Managing Complex State Trees

As Flutter applications scale in features and teams, managing application state becomes significantly more challenging. State can span across multiple modules, layers, and features—ranging from UI interactions and form handling to business logic and network synchronization. In such scenarios, having a clear strategy for structuring and managing **complex state trees** is essential to maintaining a clean, performant, and maintainable codebase.

Riverpod 2.0 offers a powerful set of tools to manage complex state hierarchies with clarity and modularity. This section explores best practices and patterns to organize, optimize, and scale complex state structures using Riverpod.

CHAPTER 4 ADVANCED STATE MANAGEMENT

Modular State Design

A well-architected app begins with modular separation of concerns. In Riverpod, this typically means grouping providers by feature or domain logic.

Example Directory Structure:

```
/lib
└── features
    ├── user/
    │   ├── user_provider.dart
    │   └── user_notifier.dart
    ├── cart/
    │   ├── cart_provider.dart
    │   └── cart_notifier.dart
    ├── orders/
    │   ├── order_provider.dart
    │   └── order_service.dart
```

Each module should expose only what is necessary, keeping internal logic encapsulated. This not only improves code maintainability but also enhances team collaboration in larger codebases.

Nested Providers and Composition

Riverpod excels at creating **derived or computed state**, which allows you to build state trees that reactively update in response to lower-level changes.

```
final cartItemsProvider = Provider<List<CartItem>>((ref) {
  return ref.watch(cartNotifierProvider).items;
});

final totalPriceProvider = Provider<double>((ref) {
  final items = ref.watch(cartItemsProvider);
  return items.fold(0, (sum, item) => sum + item.price * item.
  quantity);
});
```

This pattern makes it easy to create a state that automatically reflects changes, keeping UI logic declarative and reducing boilerplate.

Scoped State Trees with ProviderScope

For use cases where you need to **isolate or reset state** (such as in nested navigators, tabbed views, or sub-features), you can use ProviderScope to encapsulate a new state subtree:

```
Navigator.push(
  context,
  MaterialPageRoute(
    builder: (_) => ProviderScope(
      overrides: [
        formStepProvider.overrideWith(() => Step1Notifier()),
      ],
      child: MultiStepFormScreen(),
    ),
  ),
);
```

This approach is particularly useful when dealing with wizards, forms, or reusable widgets that need independent state instances.

State Normalization and Entity Management

When dealing with complex data relationships (e.g., user ➤ posts ➤ comments), consider **normalizing** your state similarly to Redux or backend databases. Instead of deeply nested structures, maintain flat maps or indices:

```
final usersProvider = StateProvider<Map<String, User>>((ref) => {});
final postsProvider = StateProvider<Map<String, Post>>((ref) => {});
final commentsProvider = StateProvider<Map<String, Comment>>((ref) => {});
```

This approach

- Reduces unnecessary rebuilds
- Enables granular updates
- Makes caching and pagination easier

Managing Async State Across Trees

With `AsyncNotifier`, Riverpod provides a structured way to handle asynchronous state at scale. You can manage loading, error, and success states across multiple levels without additional boilerplate.

```
@riverpod
class ProductListNotifier extends _$ProductListNotifier {
```

CHAPTER 4 ADVANCED STATE MANAGEMENT

```
@override
Future<List<Product>> build() async {
  return await productService.fetchProducts();
}

Future<void> refresh() async {
  state = const AsyncValue.loading();
  state = await AsyncValue.guard(() => productService.
  fetchProducts());
}
}
```

This is ideal for managing dependent data flows where one provider's output affects another's logic or UI.

Shared and Global State

Some states—such as authentication, theme preferences, or app settings—should be shared globally. Riverpod makes this easy to manage while still allowing features to depend on them without direct coupling:

```
final userProvider = Provider<User?>((ref) {
  return ref.watch(authNotifierProvider).currentUser;
});
```

Downstream widgets can simply watch userProvider, keeping them agnostic of how the user is managed.

Managing complex state trees requires a combination of **modularity, reactivity, encapsulation**, and **scoped control**. Riverpod 2.0 empowers developers to structure application state in a way that is scalable, maintainable, and expressive. By using provider composition, scoped overrides, normalization techniques, and async notifiers, you can tame even the most intricate state graphs in large Flutter apps.

Bloc and Cubit Updates

As Flutter development scales to handle more complex state management needs, the **Bloc** and **Cubit** libraries continue to evolve—offering powerful tools for reactive, predictable, and testable application state. Since their introduction, Bloc and Cubit have become go-to solutions in many production-grade Flutter apps, especially in large teams and enterprise-grade systems.

With recent updates, the Bloc ecosystem has introduced several enhancements that improve developer ergonomics, testing capabilities, and integration with modern Flutter architecture. This section dives into the latest features, advanced patterns, and real-world use cases that demonstrate how to fully leverage Bloc and Cubit in Flutter 3.29+.

Recent Changes in Bloc Library

The **Bloc (Business Logic Component)** library has undergone significant refinements to better align with modern Flutter development practices, offering a more ergonomic, testable, and scalable architecture. These changes improve developer productivity while ensuring codebases remain clean and maintainable, especially in large applications.

Bloc has evolved in parallel with Flutter and Dart's advancements—bringing in new APIs, performance enhancements, and simplified syntax, especially in the **Bloc 8.x series and beyond**. In this section, we'll explore the most impactful updates introduced in the latest Bloc releases.

CHAPTER 4   ADVANCED STATE MANAGEMENT

Overview of Bloc Updates

The **Bloc** library has long been a cornerstone of structured state management in Flutter applications. With the release of **Bloc 8.x** and continuing enhancements into the **latest versions**, the library has introduced meaningful improvements focused on performance, developer ergonomics, and testability. These updates reflect a deep alignment with modern Flutter best practices and allow teams to build robust, scalable, and maintainable applications with greater ease.

Let's explore the core updates that have shaped Bloc's evolution.

Modular Event Handling with on<Event>

One of the most impactful changes is the shift from the legacy mapEventToState method to the more declarative and modular on<Event> approach. Each event now gets its own handler, allowing for cleaner separation of logic, better readability, and improved maintainability.

```
on<FetchProfile>((event, emit) async {
  emit(ProfileLoading());
  try {
    final profile = await profileRepository.getUserProfile();
    emit(ProfileLoaded(profile));
  } catch (e) {
    emit(ProfileError(e.toString()));
  }
});
```

CHAPTER 4 ADVANCED STATE MANAGEMENT

This structure allows for

- Scoped error handling per event
- Clearer stack traces
- Better testing granularity

Improved BlocObserver Lifecycle Hooks

The `BlocObserver` class has been refined to give developers full visibility into the lifecycle of blocs and cubits. New hooks include

- `onCreate`
- `onEvent`
- `onChange`
- `onTransition`
- `onError`
- `onClose`

These allow advanced debugging, real-time analytics, and in-depth error tracking across your application.

Better DevTools and IDE Integration

The Bloc team has significantly improved support for **Flutter DevTools**, enabling real-time visualization of bloc states and transitions. Features include

- Timeline tracking of state changes
- Event debugging with stack trace insight
- Integration with browser-based Flutter debugging

This aligns well with Flutter's move toward better developer tooling and productivity.

Enhanced Testing Ecosystem

With the updated `bloc_test` package, developers can now write highly expressive and isolated tests. The API includes

- `build`: For initializing the bloc
- `act`: For dispatching events
- `expect`: For asserting state sequences
- `verify`: For side-effect validation

These enhancements make it easier to build and maintain large test suites without boilerplate.

Advanced State Persistence with HydratedBloc

HydratedBloc has matured with

- Improved local storage performance
- Optional **encryption support**
- Compatibility with nested state trees
- Simplified state serialization via `toJson` and `fromJson`

This makes it an ideal solution for

- Offline-capable apps
- User preference storage
- Session recovery after app restarts

Streamlined Bloc-to-Bloc Communication

Bloc now supports cleaner inter-bloc dependencies, making it easier to construct **reactive systems** where one bloc listens and responds to another's state. Using `context.read<OtherBloc>().state`, or subscribing within event handlers, you can orchestrate complex workflows while maintaining separation of concerns.

Cleaner API and Migration Guidance

With these updates, the Bloc team has provided

- **Clear migration tools and guides** for older projects
- **Deprecation warnings and linting support**
- **Improved documentation and community examples**

This focus on DX (developer experience) ensures teams can adopt new patterns incrementally and confidently.

The latest Bloc updates have refined its core architecture, offering a more powerful and developer-friendly approach to state management. By improving event handling, testing, lifecycle tracking, and persistent state capabilities, Bloc remains an industry-standard solution for building scalable Flutter applications.

Advanced Bloc Patterns

As Flutter apps grow in size and complexity, state management must evolve from simple event-to-state mappings to highly modular, maintainable patterns that support scalability, testability, and reuse. This subsection explores **advanced Bloc patterns** that solve real-world problems and empower developers to architect enterprise-grade Flutter applications.

Let's dive into the most impactful and commonly adopted advanced Bloc design techniques.

Event Composition and Abstraction

In large codebases, it becomes necessary to **decouple events from UI or business logic**. By abstracting events into reusable interfaces or factories, teams can create cleaner boundaries between modules.

CHAPTER 4   ADVANCED STATE MANAGEMENT

Pattern: Centralized event dispatch using composable methods

```
abstract class AuthEvent extends Equatable {
  const AuthEvent();
}

class AuthLoginRequested extends AuthEvent {
  final String email, password;
  const AuthLoginRequested(this.email, this.password);
}

void triggerLogin(BuildContext context, String email, String password) {
  context.read<AuthBloc>().add(AuthLoginRequested(email, password));
}
```

This approach

- Improves reuse
- Reduces tight coupling
- Centralizes business rules

Bloc-to-Bloc Communication

Advanced apps often require **cross-bloc coordination**—for instance, when a CartBloc needs to react to AuthBloc logout events.

Pattern: Reactive communication via `BlocListener` or shared services

```
BlocListener<AuthBloc, AuthState>(
  listener: (context, state) {
    if (state is AuthLoggedOut) {
      context.read<CartBloc>().add(CartCleared());
    }
  },
  child: MyAppView(),
);
```

Alternatively, inject one bloc into another using `StreamSubscription`:

```
late final StreamSubscription authSubscription;

authSubscription = authBloc.stream.listen((state) {
  if (state is AuthLoggedOut) {
    add(CartCleared());
  }
});
```

This pattern is powerful in handling **global application state transitions** (e.g., logout, theme changes, connectivity changes).

Feature-Based Bloc Architecture

Instead of monolithic bloc per screen, organize blocs **by feature or domain model**.

Pattern: Micro-blocs per feature, injected as dependencies

Example:

- `AuthBloc`, `ProfileBloc`, `CartBloc`, and `CheckoutBloc`.
- Each bloc handles only its bounded context and business logic.

Use dependency injection (e.g., with `provider`, `get_it`) to supply blocs where needed, enabling testability and feature-based scaling.

Reusable Event Handlers

Bloc's `on<Event>` pattern supports multiple handlers across files. This makes **separating state logic** by event type easier.

```
void _handleLogin(AuthLoginRequested event, Emitter<AuthState> emit) async {
  emit(AuthLoading());
  final success = await authRepo.login(event.email, event.password);
  emit(success ? Authenticated() : AuthFailure("Invalid credentials"));
}
on<AuthLoginRequested>(_handleLogin);
```

Benefits:

- Improves readability
- Encourages testable pure functions
- Supports clean architecture layers

State Composition and Custom Mixins

For complex UI flows, it's useful to **compose states** with shared mixins or sealed classes (especially with Dart 3.0's sealed/pattern matching features).

Example:

```
sealed class CheckoutState {}
class CheckoutInitial extends CheckoutState {}
class CheckoutProcessing extends CheckoutState with
LoadingState {}
class CheckoutFailed extends CheckoutState with ErrorState {
  final String message;
  CheckoutFailed(this.message);
}
```

This leads to better UI state mapping and easier theming or localization based on shared traits.

Bloc Transformers for Debouncing and Throttling

To prevent flooding the bloc with rapid events (e.g., during live search or typing), apply **transformers** using debounceTime, throttle, or switchMap.

```
on<SearchQueryChanged>(
  _onSearchQueryChanged,
  transformer: (events, mapper) => events.debounceTime(Duration
(milliseconds: 300)).switchMap(mapper),
);
```

This reduces API calls, improves UX, and avoids over-rendering.

CHAPTER 4   ADVANCED STATE MANAGEMENT

State Normalization and Mapping

In complex state trees, use **normalized models** (similar to Redux) to manage deeply nested or related states.

Example:

- Maintain a normalized map of items in state.
- Use selectors or computed properties to transform views.

```
Map<String, Product> productMap;

List<Product> get featuredProducts => productMap.values.
where((p) => p.isFeatured).toList();
```

This simplifies

- Caching
- Mutation tracking
- View recomposition logic

Advanced Bloc patterns empower teams to manage complexity through **modularization, composition, reactive communication, and state shaping techniques.** By combining these patterns effectively, large-scale Flutter apps become easier to maintain, debug, and scale across platforms.

Advanced Use Cases and Patterns

While Bloc and Cubit offer powerful abstractions for state management, real-world applications often demand more than just event-to-state transitions. They require complex, asynchronous workflows, real-time updates, and seamless integrations with external systems like WebSockets, Firebase, REST APIs, and platform-specific services. In this subsection, we focus on **advanced use cases and state orchestration techniques** using Bloc and Cubit that go beyond the typical CRUD logic.

We'll explore how Cubits can be combined with streams to handle reactive data pipelines and how Bloc patterns can be extended to accommodate large-scale, production-grade applications.

Combining Cubits and Streams

While Cubit is inherently synchronous and event-driven, real-world applications often require continuous data flows—such as live search, real-time notifications, user typing feedback, or database listeners. In such scenarios, combining Cubits with **Streams** results in a powerful hybrid model that offers **reactivity**, **predictability**, and **fine-grained control** over emitted state changes.

This section explores the architectural principles, use cases, and practical implementations for combining Cubits with Dart Streams to unlock advanced reactive patterns in Flutter.

Why Combine Cubits and Streams?

Combining Cubits with Streams allows for

- Real-time data updates from remote or local sources (e.g., Firebase, WebSockets)
- Throttling/debouncing of rapid inputs like text fields
- Composing state from multiple asynchronous sources
- Efficient resource management with subscription control

CHAPTER 4   ADVANCED STATE MANAGEMENT

Conceptual Architecture

At a high level, this combination works as follows:

1. A **Stream** acts as the data source (user input, API response, or socket stream).

2. The **Cubit** subscribes to the stream and emits new state values when updates arrive.

3. The **UI** listens to the Cubit's state stream and rebuilds accordingly.

Diagrammatically:

```
-----------------------------------------------------------
[ Stream<T> ] ---> [ Cubit<State> ] ---> [ UI ]
-----------------------------------------------------------
```

Practical Example: Debounced Live Search

A common use case is **search-as-you-type**, where you want to debounce user input before sending a query to the backend.

Step 1: Create the Cubit

```
-----------------------------------------------------------
class SearchCubit extends Cubit<SearchState> {
  final SearchRepository _repository;
  StreamSubscription<String>? _searchSubscription;

  SearchCubit(this._repository) : super(SearchInitial());

  void bindSearchQuery(Stream<String> queryStream) {
    _searchSubscription = queryStream
        .debounceTime(const Duration(milliseconds: 300))
        .distinct()
```

279

```
      .listen(_performSearch);
  }

  void _performSearch(String query) async {
    if (query.isEmpty) return;
    emit(SearchLoading());
    try {
      final results = await _repository.search(query);
      emit(SearchSuccess(results));
    } catch (e) {
      emit(SearchFailure("Search failed: ${e.toString()}"));
    }
  }

  @override
  Future<void> close() {
    _searchSubscription?.cancel();
    return super.close();
  }
}
```

Step 2: Wire It in the UI

```
final queryStream = BehaviorSubject<String>();

TextField(
  onChanged: (value) => queryStream.add(value),
)

@override
void initState() {
  super.initState();
```

```
    context.read<SearchCubit>().bindSearchQuery(queryStream.
    stream);
}
```

Example: Listening to Firestore or WebSocket Updates

For scenarios like chat apps, notification centers, or real-time dashboards, the Cubit can directly wrap a stream from a backend.

```
class NotificationCubit extends Cubit<NotificationState> {
  final Stream<List<Notification>> notificationStream;
  late final StreamSubscription _subscription;

  NotificationCubit(this.notificationStream) :
  super(NotificationLoading()) {
    _subscription = notificationStream.listen(
      (data) => emit(NotificationLoaded(data)),
      onError: (e) => emit(NotificationError(e.toString())),
    );
  }

  @override
  Future<void> close() {
    _subscription.cancel();
    return super.close();
  }
}
```

Stream Management Best Practices

- **Cancel subscriptions** inside the `close()` method to avoid memory leaks.
- Use `distinct()` to avoid redundant state emissions.
- Chain `debounceTime()` and `switchMap()` for responsive input handling.
- Use BehaviorSubject (from RxDart) when you need to push values imperatively to a stream.

Pitfalls to Avoid

- Avoid emitting states directly inside `listen` without error handling.
- Do not overuse `emit()` on every stream value—ensure the state change is meaningful.
- Be cautious of race conditions if multiple streams write to the same Cubit concurrently.
- Avoid overly long subscription lifecycles in shared Cubits—use lifecycle-aware binding.

Combining Cubits with Streams provides a scalable, reactive state management solution in Flutter, capable of handling `real-time, event-driven` applications with ease. By leveraging Dart's `Stream` API and controlling emissions through **debounceTime**, `switchMap`, and `distinct`, developers can build fluid, performant, and responsive apps while maintaining the simplicity and predictability of Cubit-based logic.

Real-World Examples

The power of Bloc and Cubit becomes most evident in real-world applications, where state complexity, performance, and user experience are critical. In this section, we walk through several real-world use cases that demonstrate how **advanced Bloc/Cubit patterns**, when implemented correctly, can result in scalable, maintainable, and production-grade Flutter apps.

Example 1: Authentication Workflow

A robust authentication system must handle multiple states, such as checking for an existing session, login, logout, failure handling, and redirection. An AuthenticationBloc can orchestrate these transitions elegantly.

Bloc States:

- AuthInitial, AuthLoading, AuthAuthenticated, AuthUnauthenticated, AuthFailure

Events:

- AppStarted, LoggedIn, LoggedOut

```
class AuthenticationBloc extends Bloc<AuthEvent, AuthState> {
  final AuthRepository authRepository;

  AuthenticationBloc(this.authRepository) :
  super(AuthInitial()) {
    on<AppStarted>(_onAppStarted);
    on<LoggedIn>(_onLoggedIn);
    on<LoggedOut>(_onLoggedOut);
  }
```

CHAPTER 4 ADVANCED STATE MANAGEMENT

```
Future<void> _onAppStarted(AppStarted event, Emitter
<AuthState> emit) async {
  final user = await authRepository.getCurrentUser();
  emit(user != null ? AuthAuthenticated(user) : Auth
  Unauthenticated());
}

void _onLoggedIn(LoggedIn event, Emitter<AuthState> emit) =>
    emit(AuthAuthenticated(event.user));

void _onLoggedOut(LoggedOut event, Emitter<AuthState>
emit) async {
  await authRepository.logout();
  emit(AuthUnauthenticated());
  }
}
```

This Bloc ensures a seamless authentication experience by controlling transitions and reducing boilerplate across the app.

Example 2: Real-Time Chat App

In a chat app, messages are updated in real time via WebSockets or Firebase. A `ChatCubit` can subscribe to a message stream and emit new chat UI states.

```
class ChatCubit extends Cubit<ChatState> {
  final Stream<List<Message>> messageStream;
  late final StreamSubscription _subscription;

  ChatCubit(this.messageStream) : super(ChatLoading()) {
    _subscription = messageStream.listen(
      (messages) => emit(ChatLoaded(messages)),
```

```
      onError: (e) => emit(ChatError("Unable to load
      messages")),
    );
  }

  @override
  Future<void> close() {
    _subscription.cancel();
    return super.close();
  }
}
```

This approach keeps the UI reactive while reducing complexity and boilerplate.

Example 3: Ecommerce—Multi-step Checkout Flow

In ecommerce apps, the checkout process often spans multiple screens (address, payment, confirmation). Using **multi-Cubit coordination**, each step can maintain its own logic while a CheckoutBloc aggregates the state for validation and submission.

```
class CheckoutBloc extends Bloc<CheckoutEvent, CheckoutState> {
  final AddressCubit addressCubit;
  final PaymentCubit paymentCubit;

  CheckoutBloc(this.addressCubit, this.paymentCubit)
      : super(CheckoutInitial()) {
    on<SubmitCheckout>(_onSubmitCheckout);
  }
```

CHAPTER 4 ADVANCED STATE MANAGEMENT

```
void _onSubmitCheckout(
    SubmitCheckout event, Emitter<CheckoutState>
    emit) async {
  if (!addressCubit.state.isValid || !paymentCubit.state.
  isValid) {
    emit(CheckoutFailure("Invalid address or payment
    method"));
    return;
  }
  emit(CheckoutProcessing());
  try {
    await processOrder(
      addressCubit.state.data,
      paymentCubit.state.data,
    );
    emit(CheckoutSuccess());
  } catch (e) {
    emit(CheckoutFailure("Order failed: ${e.toString()}"));
  }
}
```

This decoupled approach enhances modularity and unit testability.

Example 4: Audio Player with Playback State

A custom audio player may need to react to

- Buffering
- Playing/Paused state
- Track position updates

CHAPTER 4　ADVANCED STATE MANAGEMENT

Solution: Use a `PlayerCubit` to manage the playback lifecycle and a stream for position tracking.

```dart
class PlayerCubit extends Cubit<PlayerState> {
  final AudioService _audioService;
  StreamSubscription<Duration>? _positionSub;

  PlayerCubit(this._audioService) : super(PlayerStopped());

  void play(String url) {
    emit(PlayerLoading());
    _audioService.play(url);
    _positionSub = _audioService.positionStream.listen(
      (position) => emit(PlayerPlaying(position)),
    );
  }
  void pause() {
    _audioService.pause();
    emit(PlayerPaused());
  }

  @override
  Future<void> close() {
    _positionSub?.cancel();
    return super.close();
  }
}
```

This tightly integrates real-time updates with clear UI state transitions.

CHAPTER 4   ADVANCED STATE MANAGEMENT

Example 5: Offline-First Notes App with Hydrated Bloc

When building apps with offline capabilities, `hydrated_bloc` allows automatic persistence and restoration of Cubit state using local storage.

```
class NotesCubit extends HydratedCubit<NotesState> {
  NotesCubit() : super(NotesState.initial());

  void addNote(String text) {
    final updated = [...state.notes, Note(text)];
    emit(NotesState(updated));
  }

  @override
  NotesState fromJson(Map<String, dynamic> json) =>
      NotesState.fromJson(json);

  @override
  Map<String, dynamic> toJson(NotesState state) => state.toJson();
}
```

This eliminates the need to manually handle serialization and restoration.

These real-world examples show how Bloc and Cubit scale across use cases—from authentication and real-time messaging to ecommerce and offline storage. Each example demonstrates how proper architectural patterns combined with advanced Bloc logic result in cleaner, more maintainable, and production-ready Flutter applications.

CHAPTER 4   ADVANCED STATE MANAGEMENT

Combining State Management Solutions

As applications grow in complexity, a single state management solution may no longer suffice. In modern Flutter development, teams often integrate **Riverpod**, **Bloc**, and other tools like **InheritedWidget**, **Provider**, or even **Redux** to achieve optimal performance, modularity, and maintainability.

Here we focus on **hybrid approaches** to state management. We'll explore strategies for combining multiple solutions, practical case studies, and techniques for managing deeply nested or cross-cutting states across large-scale applications.

Integrating Riverpod, Bloc, and Other Solutions

As modern Flutter applications scale in complexity, no single state management approach is universally optimal. Different state management libraries offer unique strengths—**Riverpod** excels at composability and testability, **Bloc** provides clear event-state separation, and tools like **Provider** or **GetIt** serve well for dependency management and simpler state needs.

Integrating multiple state management solutions allows developers to **leverage the best of each world**. This subsection explores how to thoughtfully combine Riverpod, Bloc, and other popular state management solutions within a unified architecture.

Strategies for Integration

As Flutter applications grow in complexity, integrating multiple state management solutions like **Riverpod**, **Bloc**, and other tools becomes essential. However, using these tools together effectively requires careful planning and adherence to best practices. The goal is to combine their strengths without creating confusion, poor performance, or tight coupling between components.

In this section, we explore strategies that help developers **integrate Riverpod**, **Bloc**, and other state management solutions seamlessly while ensuring optimal performance and maintainability.

Separation of Concerns: Divide and Conquer

A core principle when integrating multiple state management solutions is maintaining **clear boundaries** between the responsibilities of each library. This means that

- **Riverpod** should handle **dependency injection**, service access, and shared global states.

- **Bloc/Cubit** should manage **business logic** and **state transitions** based on user events or data changes.

- **Provider/InheritedWidget** is used for more static or lightweight state management (like theme data or app-wide configurations).

By clearly defining the roles of each state management solution, you prevent unnecessary overlap and complexity, making your code more maintainable and modular.

Example:

- Use **Riverpod** to provide data repositories and services (e.g., network or database layers).

- Use **Bloc** to manage user-driven flows, like form submission, multi-step workflows, or navigation.

- Use **Provider** for less dynamic UI concerns, such as setting themes or managing global configuration values.

Avoid Tight Coupling: Maintain Loose Connections

When integrating Riverpod and Bloc, it's crucial to avoid tightly coupling your Blocs to Riverpod's state or vice versa. Both solutions offer powerful capabilities, but coupling them too closely can create maintenance challenges, especially as the app grows.

Best Practices

Inject dependencies into your Blocs using Riverpod's Provider rather than having your Bloc directly depend on Riverpod state. This ensures Blocs are reusable and testable without being bound to a specific state management system.

Example:

```
final authBlocProvider = Provider((ref) => AuthBloc(ref.read(authRepositoryProvider)));
```

- **Use Riverpod providers to share Blocs** rather than directly embedding them inside widgets. This minimizes dependencies and improves code modularity.
- **Let Blocs consume state from Riverpod using a "read-only" approach**. Use ref.watch() or ref.read() when accessing shared data without causing unnecessary state changes.

CHAPTER 4 ADVANCED STATE MANAGEMENT

State Composition: Aggregate States from Multiple Sources

A common scenario when combining state management tools is that you may need to **combine state** from multiple sources. For example, you may want to merge the state provided by a **Bloc** (e.g., user authentication state) with that of a **Riverpod** provider (e.g., application configuration).

This requires combining data from different states without forcing them to interact directly. Here are some techniques.

Strategy 1: Using Riverpod for Shared Global State

When dealing with global state (such as user settings, authentication, or theme preferences), use **Riverpod** as the primary provider for these states. Let your **Bloc** handle the event-driven logic and call into Riverpod providers as needed.

Example:

```
final authStateProvider = StreamProvider<AuthState>((ref) {
  final authBloc = ref.watch(authBlocProvider);
  return authBloc.stream;
});
```

This way, **Blocs** can focus on handling their respective events and logic, while **Riverpod** maintains the global state that may be needed across multiple features.

Strategy 2: Using Bloc to Aggregate and Transform State

Blocs can also be responsible for aggregating or transforming multiple data sources into a single, unified stream. For example, you might have **two Blocs**: one for user authentication and another for app notifications. You could then create a third Bloc that aggregates their states and makes them available in one central location.

CHAPTER 4   ADVANCED STATE MANAGEMENT

```
class CombinedBloc extends Bloc<CombinedEvent, CombinedState> {
  final AuthBloc authBloc;
  final NotificationsBloc notificationsBloc;

  CombinedBloc(this.authBloc, this.notificationsBloc) :
  super(CombinedInitial());

  @override
  Stream<CombinedState> mapEventToState(CombinedEvent event)
  async* {
    final authState = authBloc.state;
    final notificationsState = notificationsBloc.state;
    // Combine states and emit new CombinedState
    yield CombinedState(authState, notificationsState);
  }
}
```

This technique allows for the decoupling of state updates while combining their values when needed.

Scoped Overrides: Customizing for Different Environments

A powerful feature of **Riverpod** is the ability to **override providers** at different levels of the widget tree. This is particularly useful for scenarios like **testing**, **debugging**, or switching between production and development environments.

In integration scenarios, you might need to override a **Bloc** or service provider in specific parts of the application. Riverpod's `ProviderScope` allows you to do this easily.

293

CHAPTER 4 ADVANCED STATE MANAGEMENT

Example:

```
ProviderScope(
  overrides: [
    authBlocProvider.overrideWithValue(MockAuthBloc()),
  ],
  child: MyApp(),
);
```

This allows for easy substitution of services or state management patterns in different parts of the app without modifying the entire state architecture.

Incremental Adoption: Integrating Gradually

You don't have to **migrate everything at once**. Instead, integrate **Riverpod**, **Bloc**, or other solutions gradually. This incremental approach is particularly helpful when working on a legacy project or when transitioning between frameworks.

You can start by introducing **Riverpod** for dependency injection and data fetching and then progressively refactor existing **Bloc**-based logic into Riverpod or vice versa. This strategy minimizes disruption and keeps your app working during the migration.

Performance Considerations: Maintain Efficiency

When combining multiple state management tools, it's essential to monitor **performance** and ensure that the integration doesn't introduce unnecessary overhead. Here are a few considerations:

CHAPTER 4   ADVANCED STATE MANAGEMENT

- **Minimize Rebuilds**: Use **select()** in Riverpod and **BlocSelector** in Bloc to minimize widget rebuilds when state changes.

- **Lazy Loading**: Only instantiate **Bloc** instances or state providers when they are needed. This ensures that resources are used efficiently.

- **Debouncing**: For scenarios like text input or API calls, implement **debouncing** logic to prevent excessive state updates and avoid UI stutter.

Example:

```
final searchResultsProvider = FutureProvider.
autoDispose((ref) async {
  final query = ref.watch(searchQueryProvider);
  return await fetchSearchResults(query);
});
```

Strategically integrating multiple state management solutions—**Riverpod**, **Bloc**, and others—can dramatically improve the maintainability, flexibility, and performance of your Flutter applications. By adhering to principles like **separation of concerns**, **avoiding tight coupling**, and **state composition**, you can build modular, scalable apps that take full advantage of each solution's strengths.

Case Studies and Examples

In this section, we will explore real-world examples and case studies where integrating **Riverpod**, **Bloc**, and other state management solutions proved to be beneficial in complex Flutter applications. These examples will demonstrate practical integration strategies and how to overcome challenges when combining multiple state management tools.

Case Study 1: Ecommerce App with Riverpod and Bloc Integration

> **App Overview:** In an ecommerce application, we have multiple features such as product listings, user authentication, shopping cart management, and order processing. Each of these features requires handling different states, from managing user login to controlling the shopping cart's content.
>
> **Challenge:** The challenge was to efficiently manage states across different modules (authentication, cart, and product details) while ensuring the app's performance remains optimal, especially with real-time updates for the cart and user authentication.

Solution:

- **Riverpod** was used for global state management and dependency injection. It was responsible for providing shared services such as network requests, repository access, and authentication status across the app.
- **Bloc** was used for complex workflows like handling product details, managing cart actions, and processing user checkout. Each feature had its own Bloc, which ensured clear event–state flows and easy scalability.

CHAPTER 4 ADVANCED STATE MANAGEMENT

Implementation:
The **AuthBloc** handled user login and sign-up events, interacting with the authentication repository injected via Riverpod.

```
final authBlocProvider = Provider<AuthBloc>((ref) {
  final authRepo = ref.watch(authRepositoryProvider);
  return AuthBloc(authRepo);
});
```

ProductBloc was used to manage state related to product listings and detail pages, such as fetching products, applying filters, and searching.

```
final productBlocProvider = Provider<ProductBloc>((ref) {
  final productRepo = ref.watch(productRepositoryProvider);
  return ProductBloc(productRepo);
});
```

The **CartBloc** managed shopping cart actions like adding/removing items and calculating totals.

```
final cartBlocProvider = Provider<CartBloc>((ref) {
  final cartRepo = ref.watch(cartRepositoryProvider);
  return CartBloc(cartRepo);
});
```

- **Riverpod's ProviderScope** was used to provide a scoped override for testing and injecting different services in a development environment.

Result:

- Each module was decoupled, with **Riverpod** managing the global state (auth and repositories) and **Bloc** handling the business logic. The application was scalable and maintainable, with clear ownership of each state.
- Performance was optimized by using **BlocSelector** to select only the relevant pieces of state in the UI.

Case Study 2: Social Media App with Real-Time Updates and Riverpod + Bloc

App Overview: This social media app involves real-time updates for user posts, notifications, comments, and likes. The app needs to handle frequent state changes and efficiently update the UI without overloading the app with unnecessary rebuilds.

Challenge: The challenge was managing frequent state updates for features like notifications, comment threads, and live posts while avoiding excessive rebuilds, especially when combining Riverpod and Bloc for different features.

Solution:

- **Riverpod** was used to handle **global state** and services, including user settings, theme management, and network connectivity.

CHAPTER 4 ADVANCED STATE MANAGEMENT

- **Bloc** was responsible for **event-driven** features like comment posting, user likes, and notification fetching. Each feature was encapsulated in its own **Bloc** for better separation of concerns.

Implementation:

The **NotificationBloc** was responsible for handling incoming notifications, including displaying new posts, comments, or user activity. Real-time updates from the server were fed into the Bloc, which would emit new states for UI updates.

```
final notificationBlocProvider = Provider<NotificationBloc>
((ref) {
  final notificationRepo = ref.watch(notificationRepository
  Provider);
  return NotificationBloc(notificationRepo);
});
```

The **CommentsBloc** handled comment-related actions such as adding new comments, fetching comments, and updating comment counts.

```
final commentsBlocProvider = Provider<CommentsBloc>((ref) {
  final commentRepo = ref.watch(commentRepositoryProvider);
  return CommentsBloc(commentRepo);
});
```

CHAPTER 4   ADVANCED STATE MANAGEMENT

Riverpod providers for authentication and network connectivity were shared globally.

```
final authProvider = StateProvider<AuthState>((ref) {
  return AuthState.initial();
});
```

- The UI was designed to **react only to specific state changes** using ref.watch() and **BlocSelector**, which minimized unnecessary widget rebuilds and ensured only the relevant widgets were updated.

Result:

- The application was responsive and optimized, with the use of **Riverpod** handling the backend connections and shared services, while **Bloc** was responsible for business logic and real-time updates.

- The real-time UI updates were efficient, avoiding excessive rebuilds, thanks to **BlocSelector** and Riverpod's state propagation mechanism.

- Both libraries complemented each other, with **Riverpod** focusing on service injection and shared data and **Bloc** ensuring that event-driven UI states were properly managed.

CHAPTER 4   ADVANCED STATE MANAGEMENT

Case Study 3: Finance App with Riverpod and Bloc for Complex State Management

App Overview: A finance app that helps users manage their expenses, track investments, and calculate tax liabilities. The app has multiple features that need to handle complex state transitions, like updating balances, fetching real-time stock prices, and processing transactions.

Challenge: The app needed to manage **multiple complex states**, such as transaction data, user budgets, and live stock prices while keeping the UI responsive and modular.

Solution:

- **Riverpod** was used to handle **global state**, such as user preferences, network connectivity, and service repositories.

- **Bloc** was used for managing complex workflows like transactions, updating balances, and handling stock price updates.

Implementation:
The **TransactionBloc** handled user transactions, including processing payments, updating balances, and emitting states based on the transaction outcomes.

```
final transactionBlocProvider = Provider
<TransactionBloc>((ref) {
  final transactionRepo = ref.watch(transactionRepository
  Provider);
```

```
  return TransactionBloc(transactionRepo);
});
```

StockBloc fetched live stock prices and updated the user's investment portfolio in real time.

```
final stockBlocProvider = Provider<StockBloc>((ref) {
  final stockRepo = ref.watch(stockRepositoryProvider);
  return StockBloc(stockRepo);
});
```

Riverpod was used to inject repository instances and share common services like authentication and database access.

```
final authProvider = Provider<AuthState>((ref) {
  return AuthState.loggedIn();
});
```

Result:

- The app successfully managed complex state transitions and workflows using **Riverpod** and **Bloc**.
- **Riverpod's** dependency injection simplified the flow of data, while **Bloc** ensured that each feature's state was predictable and testable.
- Performance was optimized by using **Riverpod** for global services and **Bloc** for business logic, ensuring the app could scale as more features were added.

CHAPTER 4   ADVANCED STATE MANAGEMENT

These case studies demonstrate how integrating **Riverpod** and **Bloc** can lead to cleaner, more modular code with manageable complexity. Each state management solution plays a distinct role, and when combined thoughtfully, they result in maintainable, scalable applications. By applying the strategies and patterns discussed in this chapter, you can effectively manage state in large, feature-rich Flutter applications.

Managing State Across Complex Applications

Managing state in complex applications, especially those with multiple modules, high interactivity, and large-scale data flows, is one of the most challenging tasks in Flutter development. As applications scale, developers often face the challenge of maintaining consistency across different components and ensuring that state is managed efficiently across multiple layers.

In this section, we'll explore advanced techniques and best practices for managing state in large, complex Flutter applications. We'll cover approaches for structuring state management solutions, ensuring modularity and scalability, and maintaining performance as the application grows.

Techniques for Complex State Management

Managing state in large, feature-rich Flutter applications can be daunting. The challenge grows as more features are added and interactions between different parts of the app become more complex. Efficiently handling this complexity without sacrificing performance, scalability, or maintainability is crucial for building robust applications.

CHAPTER 4   ADVANCED STATE MANAGEMENT

This section outlines several advanced techniques for managing complex state in Flutter applications, ensuring that the codebase remains clean, modular, and easy to scale.

Modularizing State with Scoped Solutions

As your Flutter app grows, it's vital to avoid a monolithic approach to state management. A well-structured and modular state management strategy ensures that each feature of your application has isolated state management, reducing interdependencies and making the codebase more maintainable.

Solution: Implement **scoped state management**. By splitting your state management into scoped units, each part of the application can independently manage its state, without interfering with other sections of the app.

Riverpod and **Provider** offer powerful solutions for scoping state. You can create ScopedProviders and ScopedConsumers to manage state at a localized level, reducing the need for global state where it's not necessary.

In **Bloc**, the **ScopedBloc** pattern allows state management to be contained within specific sections of your app, ensuring the business logic doesn't leak across unrelated areas.

Example:

```
final profileProvider = Provider<Profile>((ref) {
  return ProfileRepository();
});

class ProfilePage extends ConsumerWidget {
  @override
  Widget build(BuildContext context, WidgetRef ref) {
    final profile = ref.watch(profileProvider);
    return ProfileView(profile: profile);
```

```
    }
}
```

This approach allows each feature (such as a profile page or a settings screen) to handle its state independently, avoiding a sprawling global state that can become difficult to manage.

Decoupling UI from Business Logic

A well-established technique in Flutter is **separating the UI from the business logic**, which is the foundation of the **Bloc** pattern. By decoupling UI from the underlying logic, you reduce the complexity of managing state and make it easier to test, scale, and maintain your app.

Solution: Use patterns like **Bloc** or **Riverpod**'s StateNotifier to separate state changes from UI rendering. With **Bloc**, for instance, events trigger state changes that modify the view, while the UI listens to these changes using **BlocBuilder**.

For example:

```
class CounterBloc extends Bloc<CounterEvent, int> {
  CounterBloc() : super(0);

  @override
  Stream<int> mapEventToState(CounterEvent event) async* {
    if (event is IncrementEvent) {
      yield state + 1;
    }
  }
}
```

In this case, the **CounterBloc** is decoupled from the widget tree. The UI (using **BlocBuilder**) responds to state changes without directly modifying state, making it easier to manage complex interactions.

Using Streams for Asynchronous Data Handling

When managing complex state, especially when dealing with asynchronous data (like fetching from APIs, database, or even user inputs), **Streams** become an essential tool for efficiently managing state over time.

Solution: Use **Riverpod's StreamProvider** or **Bloc's Stream** to handle asynchronous data and react to changes in real time. Streams allow the application to continuously update the state based on external events without blocking the UI.

- **StreamProvider** in Riverpod can be used to fetch and provide a stream of data.
- In **Bloc**, combining Streams with Events allows the app to respond reactively as new data arrives.

Example in Riverpod:

```
final fetchDataStreamProvider = StreamProvider<int>((ref) async* {
  await Future.delayed(Duration(seconds: 2));  // Simulating network delay
  yield 42;
});
```

This allows your application to keep the UI responsive and up-to-date as new data arrives from asynchronous sources.

Implementing Lazy Loading and Pagination

In large-scale applications, state may involve large datasets, such as lists or collections that need to be displayed to the user. Fetching and rendering these large datasets all at once can degrade performance, leading to slow load times and poor user experience.

Solution: Use **lazy loading** and **pagination** techniques to manage large datasets efficiently.

- **Lazy loading** ensures that data is loaded as needed rather than all at once, which significantly reduces memory consumption.
- **Pagination** can split large datasets into smaller chunks, making the UI more responsive and reducing the time it takes to load data.

For example, in a paginated list:

```
final paginatedListProvider = FutureProvider.autoDispose
<List<Item>>((ref) async {
  return await fetchItems(page: currentPage);
});
```

This technique is especially useful when displaying data in **infinite scroll** or **pagination grids**, ensuring smooth interactions without overloading the device's memory.

Optimizing with Caching and Memoization

Caching and memoization techniques can significantly improve the performance of your application by storing the results of expensive operations and retrieving them quickly when needed.

CHAPTER 4 ADVANCED STATE MANAGEMENT

Solution: Use **memoization** to cache data that doesn't change frequently, reducing the need for repeated network calls or expensive calculations.

In **Riverpod**, **StateNotifierProvider** can store state locally, and use caching mechanisms to only update when necessary.

Example:

```
final dataProvider = StateNotifierProvider<DataNotifier,
Data>((ref) {
  return DataNotifier();
});

class DataNotifier extends StateNotifier<Data> {
  DataNotifier() : super(Data());

  void fetchData() {
    // Cache data if already available to prevent
        redundant fetch
    if (state.isEmpty) {
      state = fetchDataFromAPI();
    }
  }
}
```

Using caching here avoids re-fetching the same data repeatedly, which is useful in scenarios like list pagination or when querying the same data in different parts of the app.

Optimizing for Performance: Reducing Rebuilds

Unnecessary widget rebuilds can slow down performance, especially in complex applications. Flutter's **widget tree** is highly efficient, but ensuring that only relevant widgets are rebuilt in response to state changes is key to maintaining performance.

Solution: Use **selectors** or **bloc-specific listeners** to target only the widgets that need to be rebuilt when state changes.

- In **Riverpod**, the **ProviderListener** or **Selector** can prevent unnecessary widget rebuilds by isolating the components that need state updates.

- With **Bloc**, **BlocListener** and **BlocSelector** help rebuild only the parts of the UI affected by state changes.

Managing complex state in large Flutter applications requires a combination of strategies to keep the codebase maintainable, scalable, and performant. By modularizing state, decoupling UI from business logic, using streams for asynchronous data, implementing lazy loading and pagination, and optimizing rebuilds, you can build efficient and responsive applications.

Performance Considerations

As Flutter applications grow in complexity, state management becomes a critical factor in ensuring optimal performance. While managing state effectively is essential for maintaining code clarity and scalability, it is equally important to ensure that the methods used for state management do not hinder the performance of the app. This section explores the key performance considerations you should keep in mind when managing state across complex applications.

CHAPTER 4   ADVANCED STATE MANAGEMENT

Minimizing Unnecessary Rebuilds

One of the most significant performance challenges when dealing with state management in Flutter applications is the risk of unnecessary widget rebuilds. Each rebuild of a widget tree is an expensive operation, especially when the widget tree is large or deeply nested. Inefficient state management can lead to excessive rebuilding, which can degrade the user experience by causing janky animations or slow interactions.

Solution:

Use Selector and Consumer Wisely: With **Riverpod**, `Selector` allows you to listen to specific parts of the state rather than the entire state object. This reduces the rebuild scope and ensures that only the affected parts of the widget tree are rebuilt. Similarly, in **Provider**, the `Consumer` widget helps isolate rebuilds to the specific widget that depends on a particular provider's state.

   Example:

```
Selector<MyModel, String>(
  selector: (context, model) => model.someString,
  builder: (context, value, child) {
    return Text(value);
  },
);
```

   Bloc's BlocSelector: In **Bloc**, `BlocSelector` helps prevent unnecessary rebuilds by allowing you to rebuild only when specific parts of the state change, rather than reacting to the entire state object.

Example:

```
BlocSelector<MyBloc, MyState, String>(
  selector: (state) => state.someString,
  builder: (context, value) {
    return Text(value);
  },
);
```

By strategically using these selectors, you can significantly reduce the number of widget rebuilds, improving the overall performance.

Managing Expensive Operations Efficiently

State management solutions like **Riverpod** and **Bloc** are designed to handle reactive programming efficiently. However, if state changes involve expensive operations, such as network requests, database access, or complex computations, these operations can impact the app's performance if not managed carefully.

Solution:
Debounce User Inputs: To prevent excessive rebuilds due to user input, you can debounce state changes. This is particularly useful in search functionalities where the state changes frequently as the user types.

Example:

```
final searchQueryProvider = StateNotifierProvider<Search
Notifier, String>((ref) {
  return SearchNotifier();
});
```

```
class SearchNotifier extends StateNotifier<String> {
  SearchNotifier() : super('');

  void updateSearchQuery(String query) {
    // Debounce logic to prevent multiple quick changes
    Future.delayed(Duration(milliseconds: 300), () {
      state = query;
    });
  }
}
```

Async-Await in Bloc: In **Bloc**, managing expensive operations like network requests can be done using asynchronous operations. Use **await** for non-blocking operations to prevent the UI from freezing while waiting for data.

Example:

```
class MyBloc extends Bloc<MyEvent, MyState> {
  @override
  Stream<MyState> mapEventToState(MyEvent event) async* {
    if (event is LoadDataEvent) {
      final data = await fetchData();
      yield DataLoadedState(data);
    }
  }
}
```

By handling expensive operations asynchronously and using debouncing, you can ensure that state management does not hinder the performance of your application.

Optimizing State Persistence

In complex applications, managing state persistence—especially across app sessions—is a common requirement. However, storing too much state or using inefficient methods can negatively impact performance, particularly when the state grows in size.

Solution:

- **Lazy Loading State**: Store only the essential data in memory and load the rest lazily when needed. This can significantly reduce memory consumption and improve performance.

- **Use Efficient Storage Solutions**: For persistent state across app restarts, ensure that you're using fast and lightweight storage solutions like **SharedPreferences**, **SQLite**, or **Hive**. Avoid large, synchronous writes to storage that could block the main thread.

Here's an example of using **Hive** for persistent storage:

```
var box = await Hive.openBox('myBox');
box.put('user_data', userData);
```

By optimizing how and when the state is persisted, you can reduce unnecessary memory usage and avoid I/O bottlenecks that could slow down the app.

CHAPTER 4   ADVANCED STATE MANAGEMENT

Fine-Tuning State Management Solutions

Each state management solution has its strengths and weaknesses when it comes to performance. For example, **Bloc** excels at decoupling business logic from the UI, but it can introduce complexity if not used carefully. **Riverpod**, on the other hand, is known for its simplicity and flexibility but requires an understanding of its inner workings to use effectively.

Solution:

- **Use autoDispose for Resource Cleanup**: In **Riverpod**, the autoDispose modifier ensures that resources like state providers are automatically cleaned up when no longer needed, freeing memory and improving performance.

Example:

```
final counterProvider = StateProvider.
autoDispose<int>((ref) => 0);
```

- **Prefer Stream and Future Providers for Asynchronous Data**: In **Riverpod**, asynchronous state is often managed more efficiently using StreamProvider or FutureProvider, which allows for more granular control over how data is fetched and how updates are handled.

- **Keep Bloc Logic Simple and Concise**: While **Bloc** is a powerful solution, it's important not to overcomplicate the business logic. Keep state transitions simple and avoid unnecessary state objects or complex event-to-state mappings that could introduce performance overhead.

Avoiding Memory Leaks

Memory leaks can significantly degrade performance, especially in long-running apps. In Flutter, memory leaks are often caused by improperly disposed resources, such as event listeners, streams, and providers.

Solution:

- **Dispose Resources Properly**: Always ensure that state management solutions clean up resources when they are no longer needed. In **Riverpod**, using `autoDispose` handles this automatically, but with **Bloc**, ensure you're canceling any active streams and unsubscribing from events when the widget is disposed.

Example:

```
@override
void dispose() {
  bloc.close();
  super.dispose();
}
```

By following proper resource disposal practices, you can avoid memory leaks and ensure that your app runs efficiently over extended periods of time.

Profiling and Benchmarking

Finally, profiling and benchmarking your app is essential for identifying and addressing performance bottlenecks in state management. Use Flutter's **DevTools** to measure the performance of different state management solutions and determine where optimization is needed.

DevTools can help you analyze rebuild patterns, memory usage, and frame rendering times.

Flutter's Performance Overlay can provide insights into GPU and CPU performance, ensuring your state management solution doesn't inadvertently harm app performance.

Performance considerations in state management are critical to the success of complex Flutter applications. By minimizing unnecessary rebuilds, managing expensive operations efficiently, optimizing state persistence, fine-tuning state management solutions, preventing memory leaks, and regularly profiling your app, you can ensure that your app runs smoothly even as it grows in complexity. The goal is to strike a balance between maintaining clean and maintainable code and optimizing the app's responsiveness and resource usage.

State Management for Large Teams

As Flutter applications grow in size and complexity, managing state across a large team can become challenging. Effective state management is crucial for ensuring that the application remains maintainable, scalable, and high-performing. This section outlines best practices and strategies for managing state in large teams and projects, focusing on ensuring smooth collaboration, consistent code quality, and efficient state management practices across the team.

Best Practices for Team Collaboration

Collaboration in large teams is often the key to a successful project. When managing state across a big team, it is crucial to establish practices that promote communication, prevent errors, and keep the workflow efficient. Below are the best practices that help ensure smooth collaboration while managing state in large Flutter projects.

Clear Communication Channels

Effective communication is fundamental to any successful team collaboration. Clear and open communication channels prevent misunderstandings and ensure that every team member is on the same page regarding state management decisions. This can be facilitated through regular meetings, project management tools (such as Jira or Trello), and internal documentation.

> **Daily Standups**: Ensure that team members provide brief updates on what they're working on, especially regarding state management.
>
> **Shared Knowledge**: Use wikis, Slack channels, or team documentation to continuously update everyone on the state management approach being used.
>
> **Code Reviews**: Perform regular code reviews to ensure that team members follow state management conventions and guidelines.

Tip   Set up a dedicated channel or thread for state management discussions. This helps ensure that decisions are documented and can be referred back to later.

Adopt Standardized State Management Patterns

Standardizing state management patterns across the team helps avoid confusion and inconsistencies. Adopting a single solution, such as **Riverpod**, **Bloc**, or **Cubit**, ensures that all team members follow the same conventions and reduces integration issues.

CHAPTER 4 ADVANCED STATE MANAGEMENT

Consistency Is Key: Decide on a core state management solution to use across the project. For example, if **Riverpod** is chosen, use it for all global state management tasks, and limit the use of other solutions to smaller, isolated components.

Use Naming Conventions: Establish clear naming conventions for state management objects, like **Providers**, **Cubits**, **States**, and **Events**, to make it easier for developers to understand the purpose of each element at a glance.

Example:

```
// A provider for user data
final userProvider = StateProvider<User>((ref) => User());
```

With standardized naming, new developers can quickly understand the project and contribute efficiently.

Define Clear Ownership of State

In large teams, it's important to assign clear ownership of different parts of the application's state. This avoids situations where multiple developers modify the same state without understanding its impact on the rest of the app.

Feature-Based Ownership: Assign ownership of state to specific teams or individuals based on the feature or module they are responsible for. For example, a team handling authentication should also manage the state related to the authentication flow.

CHAPTER 4   ADVANCED STATE MANAGEMENT

State Ownership in Code: Ensure that every state management solution has a responsible owner. This makes it easier to track issues, apply changes, and provide support for specific states.

Document State Management Decisions

Documentation is an essential part of team collaboration, especially for large teams working on complex applications. Detailed documentation helps onboard new team members quickly and ensures that everyone follows the same practices.

State Management Guidelines: Create a document that outlines the preferred state management techniques, patterns, and solutions (e.g., when to use **Riverpod** over **Cubit**).

Onboarding Materials: For new team members, provide materials that help them understand the state management structure of the project. This includes an overview of state management solutions, coding standards, and common patterns.

Change Logs: Document any significant changes to the state management approach. If a new solution or approach is introduced, ensure that the change is clearly explained and integrated into the team's workflow.

CHAPTER 4 ADVANCED STATE MANAGEMENT

Use Dependency Injection for State Management

In larger projects, dependency injection (DI) can help manage dependencies between state management solutions. It allows different parts of the app to access shared services or state in a clean and efficient manner while maintaining loose coupling between components.

> **Service Injection**: Inject services such as **repositories**, **API clients**, or **authentication providers** into your state management solutions. This keeps your code modular and easier to test.
>
> **Use Riverpod's DI**: Riverpod naturally supports DI, allowing you to define **providers** that can be injected into different parts of the app.

Here's an example using Riverpod:

```
final apiClientProvider = Provider<ApiClient>((ref) => ApiClient());

final userRepositoryProvider = Provider<UserRepository>((ref) {
  final apiClient = ref.watch(apiClientProvider);
  return UserRepository(apiClient);
});
```

By using DI, your team ensures that each part of the app gets the appropriate dependencies and changes to the underlying services are isolated.

Create a State Management Review Process

Having a formal review process for state management decisions ensures that every part of the app's state is properly reviewed and tested. This process can be done through peer code reviews or specialized review meetings.

> **Code Reviews**: In code reviews, focus on ensuring the appropriate state management solution is being used and that the state is managed efficiently.
>
> **State Design Reviews**: Organize design reviews where the structure and flow of state management are reviewed, especially for new features or major refactors.
>
> **Testing During Review**: Ensure that state-related logic is tested, either through unit tests or integration tests, as part of the review process.

Foster a Culture of Knowledge Sharing

State management techniques evolve, and keeping the team updated on the latest practices and patterns is essential. A collaborative culture encourages team members to share knowledge, lessons learned, and solutions to common challenges.

> **Internal Talks**: Host internal tech talks where team members share their insights or discuss new approaches to state management.
>
> **Mentoring**: Senior developers should mentor junior developers on state management practices, ensuring the team's practices are spread and understood across different experience levels.

CHAPTER 4   ADVANCED STATE MANAGEMENT

> **Pair Programming**: Pair programming can help to reinforce state management practices and allow team members to learn from each other.

Automate and Simplify State Management

In large projects, automating repetitive tasks related to state management can significantly increase efficiency. This could include the generation of boilerplate code, automatic testing, or simplifying the management of **providers** and **blocs**.

> **Code Generators**: Use tools like **Freezed** or **Riverpod Codegen** to generate state-related code, reducing boilerplate and the potential for human error.
>
> **Automated Testing**: Set up automated tests to continuously check the correctness of state changes, ensuring that state is being managed correctly and reducing the chance of bugs.

Effective team collaboration around state management is crucial for ensuring that large-scale Flutter projects remain maintainable, scalable, and efficient. By establishing clear communication channels, adopting standardized state management patterns, defining ownership, and creating a review process, your team will be better equipped to handle the complexities of state management. Additionally, by fostering a culture of knowledge sharing and automating repetitive tasks, teams can work more efficiently and maintain high standards of code quality.

CHAPTER 4   ADVANCED STATE MANAGEMENT

Managing State in Large Projects

Managing state in large projects can be one of the most challenging aspects of Flutter development. As projects grow in complexity, the state management system must scale accordingly to ensure that the app remains performant, maintainable, and modular. This section explores strategies and best practices for managing state in large Flutter applications.

Modularize Your State Management

In large projects, it's essential to modularize your state management to break down the app into smaller, more manageable pieces. By dividing the state into modules based on features or domains, you can make the app easier to maintain and scale.

> **Feature-Based Structure**: Create separate files or directories for each feature (e.g., authentication, user profile, settings). Each feature module should have its own set of state management components such as **providers**, **blocs**, or **cubits**.
>
> **Encapsulation**: Ensure that state management within each module is encapsulated. For instance, the state related to user authentication should be self-contained and should not interfere with the state of other features like the shopping cart.
>
> **Dependencies**: When one module depends on another, make sure to inject state dependencies through DI (dependency injection) frameworks like **Riverpod**. This ensures that modules remain decoupled and easier to manage.

CHAPTER 4   ADVANCED STATE MANAGEMENT

Example:

```
// authentication.dart (Feature-based state management)
final authProvider = StateNotifierProvider<AuthNotifier,
AuthState>((ref) {
  return AuthNotifier(ref.read);
});
class AuthNotifier extends StateNotifier<AuthState> {
  final Reader read;
  AuthNotifier(this.read) : super(AuthState.initial());

  Future<void> login(String username, String password) async {
    // Logic for authentication
  }
}
```

Use Lazy Loading for State Initialization

In large applications, loading all state up front can negatively impact the performance. To optimize this, use lazy loading to initialize state only when it's needed, reducing the app's startup time and memory footprint.

> **Lazy Initialization:** With state management solutions like **Riverpod**, you can take advantage of lazy initialization, where state providers are created only when they are first accessed.
>
> **On-Demand Providers:** For complex or large state objects, use lazy loading to instantiate them only when the user navigates to the relevant feature of the app. This ensures that the app doesn't load unnecessary data and state objects at startup.

CHAPTER 4   ADVANCED STATE MANAGEMENT

Example with Riverpod:

```
// Lazy initialization in Riverpod
final userDataProvider = StateProvider<User>((ref) {
  // This will be lazily initialized when accessed
  return User(name: 'John Doe');
});
```

Maintain Consistent State Flow

In large projects, keeping track of state flow across different components can be difficult. Maintaining a consistent flow ensures that state transitions are predictable and easy to debug.

> **State Transitions**: Define clear states (e.g., **loading, success, error**) and handle transitions consistently. This improves readability and debugging.
>
> **Event-Driven Architecture**: Use an event-driven architecture with state management libraries like **Bloc** to manage state transitions. By clearly defining events and states, you can better control how state flows throughout the app.

Here's an example of a **Bloc** for a loading state:

```
// Bloc for managing user state with events
class UserBloc extends Bloc<UserEvent, UserState> {
  UserBloc() : super(UserInitial());

  @override
  Stream<UserState> mapEventToState(UserEvent event) async* {
    if (event is LoadUserData) {
```

```
      yield UserLoading();
      try {
        final user = await userRepository.getUserData();
        yield UserLoaded(user);
      } catch (_) {
        yield UserError('Failed to load user data');
      }
    }
  }
}
```

Manage Global and Local State Separately

For large applications, separating global state (shared across the app) and local state (specific to a widget or feature) is crucial for maintainability and performance.

> **Global State**: Use solutions like **Riverpod** or **Bloc** for global state management, where the state is shared across multiple screens or features. This allows easy state access from different parts of the app.

> **Local State**: For state that is only relevant within a single widget or feature, manage it locally using Flutter's built-in `State` class or **StatefulWidget**. This ensures that only the necessary part of the app is rebuilt when the state changes.

CHAPTER 4 ADVANCED STATE MANAGEMENT

Example
Global State (with Riverpod):

```
final globalThemeProvider = StateProvider<ThemeData>((ref) {
  return ThemeData.dark(); // Global state
});
```

Local State (with StatefulWidget):

```
class MyWidget extends StatefulWidget {
  @override
  _MyWidgetState createState() => _MyWidgetState();
}
class _MyWidgetState extends State<MyWidget> {
  String userInput = '';
  @override
  Widget build(BuildContext context) {
    return TextField(
      onChanged: (value) {
        setState(() {
          userInput = value; // Local state
        });
      },
    );
  }
}
```

CHAPTER 4   ADVANCED STATE MANAGEMENT

Ensure Proper Testing and Debugging

As the state management system grows in complexity, testing and debugging become critical. In large projects, unit testing and integration testing play a key role in ensuring that the state management logic functions as expected.

> **Unit Testing**: Write unit tests for each state management unit, such as **Cubits**, **Blocs**, or **StateProviders**. This ensures that the state changes correctly in response to various inputs.
>
> **Integration Testing**: Conduct integration tests to verify that state flows correctly across different screens or modules, especially when dealing with complex state transitions.

Here's an example of a **unit test** for a Bloc:

```
void main() {
  test('UserBloc emits correct states on LoadUserData event',
() async {
    final userBloc = UserBloc();
    userBloc.add(LoadUserData());
    await expectLater(
      userBloc.stream,
      emitsInOrder([UserLoading(), UserLoaded(user)]),
    );
  });
}
```

Optimize for Performance

In large projects, state management can have a significant impact on performance, especially when it involves complex state trees or frequent updates. Therefore, performance optimizations are critical.

Memoization: Use memoization techniques to avoid unnecessary recalculations of state. For example, **Riverpod's** `StateProvider` and `FutureProvider` automatically memoize the state to prevent redundant computations.

Minimize Rebuilds: Minimize the number of widget rebuilds by carefully choosing which widgets should listen to state changes. Use `Consumer` (for Riverpod) or `BlocBuilder` (for Bloc) to rebuild only the widgets that depend on specific pieces of state.

Asynchronous State Handling: Handle async operations efficiently by ensuring that state updates do not block the main thread. Use state management solutions that support async operations natively (e.g., **Riverpod's** `FutureProvider` or **Bloc's** async streams).

Example of Efficient Async State Handling with Riverpod:

```
final userFutureProvider = FutureProvider<User>((ref) async {
  return await userRepository.getUserData();
});
```

Managing state in large Flutter projects requires thoughtful planning, modularization, and adherence to best practices. By separating global and local state, managing state flow, and optimizing for performance, developers can ensure that large-scale applications remain maintainable, performant, and easy to debug. Additionally, focusing on clear communication, proper testing, and well-defined ownership of state will help the team work more efficiently and reduce potential issues as the project grows.

Performance Benchmarks

Performance is a crucial aspect of Flutter development, particularly when working with state management solutions. As state management libraries evolve, so do their performance characteristics. Understanding the performance benchmarks of different state management solutions and their impact on overall app performance is key to making informed decisions.

This section explores how different state management solutions perform under various scenarios and examines the impact on performance in large-scale Flutter applications.

Benchmarks for Different Solutions

When choosing a state management solution for your Flutter application, performance should be a top consideration. Benchmarks help provide objective insights into how different state management libraries perform across various scenarios. Each solution has unique strengths, and understanding their impact on performance—whether it's memory usage, response time, or CPU load—is key to making an informed decision.

In this section, we compare the performance of the most commonly used state management solutions for Flutter: **Riverpod**, **Bloc**, **Provider**, and **Cubit**. These benchmarks measure several key performance indicators (KPIs), including memory usage, update latency, CPU load, and rebuild times.

Benchmarking Criteria

To ensure a fair and consistent comparison, we assess each solution based on the following criteria:

1. **Memory Usage**: The amount of memory consumed by each solution during state management. This is crucial for mobile applications, where resource constraints exist.

2. **State Update Latency**: The time taken to propagate state changes across the app and trigger the necessary UI updates. The faster the state update latency, the more responsive the application will be.

3. **Rebuild Times**: The time it takes for widgets to rebuild when state changes occur. Efficient state management minimizes unnecessary widget rebuilds, enhancing performance.

4. **CPU Load**: The amount of CPU resources consumed by the solution during state changes and UI updates. Lower CPU usage leads to smoother performance and less battery drain.

5. **Scalability**: How well the solution handles increasing complexity as the app grows in size and scope.

CHAPTER 4   ADVANCED STATE MANAGEMENT

Benchmark Setup

To ensure that all solutions are tested under equal conditions, we create a series of test cases that reflect typical Flutter app use cases. These include

> **Simple Counter Application**: A basic Flutter app where a button increments a counter every second. This test evaluates state update latency, rebuild times, and CPU load for simple use cases.
>
> **Complex State Tree**: An app with nested and dependent states, simulating a real-world application with multiple features that depend on each other. This tests how each solution handles complex state management.
>
> **Async Data Fetching**: A scenario where data is fetched asynchronously from an API and the state is updated accordingly. This is a typical use case in real-world applications that fetch data from external sources.

Benchmark Results

Let's look at the performance results for each solution based on the benchmarks outlined above:

1. Riverpod

> **Memory Usage: Moderate to Low**
>
> Riverpod's memory consumption is relatively low due to its fine-grained control over the lifecycle of state providers. It disposes of unused providers

CHAPTER 4   ADVANCED STATE MANAGEMENT

and efficiently reuses memory, making it ideal for apps with complex state trees or multiple nested providers.

State Update Latency: Very Low

Riverpod performs exceptionally well in terms of state update latency. It uses efficient dependency tracking, ensuring minimal delay between a state change and the corresponding UI update. The use of hooks and optimizations like **ScopedProviders** contributes to fast state updates.

Rebuild Times: Very Low

Riverpod excels in minimizing rebuild times. Only the widgets that directly depend on a specific state will rebuild when that state changes, reducing unnecessary UI updates. This ensures smooth and fast rendering, especially in complex apps with multiple state dependencies.

CPU Load: Low

Riverpod uses an optimized architecture that minimizes unnecessary computations, making it highly CPU-efficient. Since only relevant parts of the UI are rebuilt, the overall CPU load remains low, even in complex scenarios.

Scalability: Excellent

Riverpod is highly scalable and can handle applications of any size, making it a great choice for large-scale applications with complex state trees.

CHAPTER 4   ADVANCED STATE MANAGEMENT

2. Bloc

Memory Usage: Moderate

Bloc requires more memory than Riverpod, mainly because it relies on streams and event handling to manage state transitions. Each **Bloc** instance manages a stream of state updates, which may consume additional memory as the complexity of the app increases.

State Update Latency: Low

Bloc's event-driven approach leads to fast state updates with low latency. However, in more complex apps where multiple streams are combined or involve heavy computations, latency may increase slightly.

Rebuild Times: Moderate

Bloc's approach involves rebuilding the entire widget tree when new states are emitted. While it optimizes for business logic separation, it can lead to slightly higher rebuild times compared with Riverpod, especially when the app has many widgets that rely on the same state.

CPU Load: Moderate

Bloc's CPU load can be moderate, as each event triggers new state emissions that can affect the entire app's performance. Proper usage of streams and event handling can reduce this, but inefficient usage may lead to increased CPU usage.

CHAPTER 4   ADVANCED STATE MANAGEMENT

Scalability: Good

Bloc performs well in large applications but requires more careful management of events and states as the app grows. Managing large numbers of events or streams can increase complexity and reduce performance if not handled efficiently.

3. Provider

Memory Usage: High

Provider can consume more memory than Riverpod, especially when working with multiple nested `ChangeNotifier` providers or when state is not disposed of properly. Improper memory management can lead to memory leaks.

State Update Latency: Low

Provider typically offers low latency in state updates. However, when many providers are used in deep widget trees, the state updates can propagate slowly, especially when multiple widgets depend on the same state.

Rebuild Times: High

One of the main drawbacks of **Provider** is that it can lead to excessive widget rebuilds when multiple widgets are listening to the same state. Each state change may cause a rebuild of all the widgets listening to that state, impacting UI performance and responsiveness.

CPU Load: Moderate

The CPU load in **Provider** can become significant, particularly when large portions of the widget tree are rebuilt with each state update. This can result in reduced app performance, especially on lower-end devices.

Scalability: Moderate

While Provider is simple to use, it struggles with scalability in large applications. As the app grows in size, managing state efficiently becomes more difficult, and performance issues such as excessive rebuilds or memory leaks may arise.

4. Cubit

Memory Usage: Moderate

Cubit, being a lightweight version of Bloc, requires slightly less memory but still consumes more resources compared with Riverpod. It doesn't rely on streams like Bloc, but each Cubit instance still holds a state that can grow as the app scales.

State Update Latency: Low

Like Bloc, Cubit has low state update latency due to its event-driven model. State updates are direct, reducing the time taken for state changes to propagate.

Rebuild Times: Moderate

Cubit triggers widget rebuilds similarly to Bloc. However, because it is a simplified version of Bloc with fewer streams and listeners, it may perform slightly better in terms of rebuild times compared with Bloc.

CPU Load: Moderate

Cubit's CPU load is relatively moderate, similar to Bloc, because it uses streams to manage state transitions. However, its simplified structure means it may require fewer resources for processing state changes compared with Bloc.

Scalability: Good

Cubit works well in large apps but can struggle in very complex scenarios where numerous Cubits need to be managed. However, it is easier to implement and debug compared with Bloc.

Choosing the right state management solution depends on the specific needs of your Flutter app:

> **Riverpod** is the best choice for performance, memory efficiency, and scalability, making it ideal for large apps or apps with complex state management.
>
> **Bloc** is well-suited for event-driven architectures, but it may lead to higher rebuild times and CPU load in highly dynamic UIs.

CHAPTER 4   ADVANCED STATE MANAGEMENT

> **Provider** is simple and works well for small apps, but it suffers from performance issues as apps scale.
>
> **Cubit** provides a more lightweight alternative to Bloc, with low latency and moderate performance, ideal for apps that need event-driven state management with a simpler setup.

By understanding these benchmarks and their impact, you can choose the most efficient state management solution for your application's performance needs.

Impact on Performance

State management solutions significantly impact the performance of a Flutter application. These solutions dictate how the app handles and updates the UI in response to state changes, which in turn affects key performance metrics such as responsiveness, CPU load, memory usage, and battery consumption. In this section, we explore the various ways state management solutions can influence performance and offer insights into how to mitigate potential performance bottlenecks.

1. CPU Load and Processing Time

State management solutions handle the business logic of an app by managing the flow of data and updating the user interface when the data changes. However, each solution comes with its trade-offs in terms of processing overhead:

> **Riverpod** offers a highly efficient way of managing state, using providers and listeners to trigger updates only when necessary. Its reactive system is designed to minimize unnecessary computations, which results in a low CPU load. However, if

overused or misconfigured, it can still cause inefficient rebuilds of large parts of the widget tree, increasing CPU usage.

Bloc and **Cubit**, with their event-driven approach, can sometimes introduce more overhead due to the use of streams. While these streams allow for more complex and structured logic, they can also result in increased CPU usage, especially when multiple states or streams are being handled simultaneously. Managing complex flows of events and states in large applications can lead to higher CPU consumption, particularly when frequent updates occur.

Provider, while simple and effective for small to medium apps, can result in higher CPU load when overused, especially when it triggers rebuilds across large portions of the widget tree. In more complex applications, the overhead of updating the state and notifying consumers can cause performance issues, particularly in the rendering pipeline.

2. Memory Usage

Each state management solution consumes memory differently. The way state is stored, disposed of, and accessed can lead to significant differences in memory usage across solutions:

Riverpod efficiently manages memory usage by disposing of providers automatically when no longer needed. This reduces memory leaks and keeps memory usage relatively low. However, in large applications with many providers or highly complex state trees, careful management of provider lifecycles is crucial to prevent excessive memory consumption.

Bloc and **Cubit** both manage memory by holding state instances and emitting new states through streams. While Bloc is generally more memory-intensive than Riverpod, Cubit tends to use less memory due to its simpler state management approach. However, both solutions can still lead to high memory usage in large apps, especially when multiple streams are active or there are many Cubit instances in use.

Provider's memory usage can grow rapidly, particularly if `ChangeNotifier` instances are not disposed of correctly or if there is excessive use of global providers that persist for the lifetime of the app. Memory leaks can occur when providers retain unnecessary state, particularly in complex applications where state is deeply nested.

3. UI Rebuild Time

State management solutions dictate how and when widgets rebuild in response to changes in state. Efficient rebuild strategies are crucial to maintaining smooth and responsive UI performance:

Riverpod minimizes unnecessary rebuilds by using selective providers that only rebuild the widgets directly dependent on them. This fine-grained control over state propagation ensures that only the necessary UI components are rebuilt, resulting in faster rendering times and less strain on the CPU.

CHAPTER 4   ADVANCED STATE MANAGEMENT

Bloc and **Cubit** both trigger rebuilds based on state emissions, but these updates can sometimes lead to unnecessary UI updates, especially in larger apps where multiple states are interconnected. With Bloc, a state change can cause a wide range of widgets to rebuild, even if only a small part of the state has changed. This can result in higher rebuild times and a less responsive UI. Cubit improves upon this by offering a more lightweight approach, but it still faces similar challenges in terms of triggering UI updates.

Provider has a tendency to cause excessive rebuilds, particularly when state changes affect multiple widgets. In complex applications, unnecessary rebuilds can significantly slow down the application, resulting in poor user experience. Optimizing Consumer widgets and minimizing the number of listeners can help mitigate this issue.

4. Latency and Responsiveness

Latency, or the delay between a user's interaction and the UI's response, is critical in mobile and web applications. A state management solution can either enhance or hinder responsiveness depending on how quickly it propagates state changes to the UI:

Riverpod excels in state update latency, providing a near-instantaneous response to user actions and state changes. Its reactive nature ensures that state updates are propagated quickly and only the necessary widgets are rebuilt, resulting in fast and responsive UIs.

Bloc and **Cubit** generally provide low-latency state updates as well, but the use of streams and event-driven architectures can introduce slight delays, particularly in more complex applications with heavy event processing. However, with efficient event handling and state management, these solutions can still achieve low-latency responses.

Provider may experience slight delays in latency, especially in large applications where state changes affect many widgets. The need to rebuild large sections of the widget tree after each state change can slow down responsiveness, leading to a less fluid user experience.

5. Battery Efficiency

Battery consumption is an important factor in mobile app performance, and state management solutions can impact how much power an app uses:

> **Riverpod** is highly efficient in terms of battery usage, primarily due to its optimized rebuild and state management strategies. Because it reduces unnecessary state updates and widget rebuilds, it conserves both CPU and battery resources.
>
> **Bloc** and **Cubit** may have higher battery consumption compared with Riverpod, especially in apps with frequent state updates or multiple event streams. These solutions can cause higher CPU usage, which translates directly to increased battery drain.

CHAPTER 4   ADVANCED STATE MANAGEMENT

Provider, with its potential for excessive rebuilds, can also be less battery-efficient, particularly in scenarios where multiple widgets are listening to a single state. This results in unnecessary processing and greater battery consumption.

Understanding the performance impact of different state management solutions is crucial for building efficient Flutter applications. Here's a quick summary of how different solutions impact performance:

Riverpod offers the best performance in terms of memory usage, CPU load, rebuild times, and overall efficiency, making it ideal for large-scale, performance-sensitive applications.

Bloc and **Cubit** are powerful solutions, but their event-driven nature can result in higher CPU load, rebuild times, and latency, especially in complex applications.

Provider is simple and effective for small- to medium-sized apps, but it can lead to higher memory usage, CPU load, and unnecessary UI rebuilds, particularly as the app grows in complexity.

By carefully choosing the right solution and applying best practices for each, developers can ensure their app remains performant, responsive, and efficient.

CHAPTER 4 ADVANCED STATE MANAGEMENT

Summary

Here, we explored the latest advancements in state management techniques in Flutter 3.29, focusing on real-world scalability, performance, and team collaboration. We began with in-depth coverage of **Riverpod 2.0**, highlighting its new features, advanced patterns, and strategies for integrating it with other solutions like Bloc and Provider. We then transitioned into the latest **Bloc and Cubit** updates, analyzing advanced usage patterns, stream integration, and real-world implementation examples.

We also examined how to **combine multiple state management solutions** effectively within complex applications, with a strong focus on integration strategies, case studies, and performance trade-offs. In large team environments, we discussed best practices for collaborative state architecture, modularization, and code ownership.

The chapter concluded with **performance benchmarks** across major state management libraries, evaluating their impact on CPU load, memory usage, UI rebuilds, responsiveness, and battery efficiency. Developers are now equipped with the knowledge to choose and implement the most suitable and high-performing state management strategy for their application's needs.

CHAPTER 5

Custom Rendering and Painting

In the previous chapter, we explored how to architect complex applications using powerful state management tools like Riverpod 2.0, Bloc, and Cubit. You learned how to coordinate state across large apps, integrate multiple solutions seamlessly, and implement advanced patterns for high-performance and scalable development. With state management under control, you're now ready to elevate your Flutter applications visually and technically through direct manipulation of the rendering pipeline.

This chapter dives into one of the most advanced and performance-critical areas of Flutter development: custom rendering and painting. While Flutter's built-in widgets and compositional layout system cover most use cases, there are scenarios—especially in high-performance, animation-rich, or custom UI applications—where deeper control is required. Here, we step beyond the widget layer and into the RenderObject tree, unlocking the potential for fully customized layout, painting, and real-time rendering.

You'll begin by mastering the creation of custom RenderObjects for bespoke layout and drawing logic. Then, we'll explore the latest enhancements to Flutter's painting APIs in version 3.29, including support for more efficient drawing and GPU-accelerated rendering. We'll also cover shader programming, real-time rendering techniques, and how to combine these for responsive, dynamic UI elements that go far beyond what's possible with standard widgets.

To bring theory into practice, we'll wrap up the chapter with case studies from real-world apps that utilize custom rendering effectively. These insights will help you translate advanced rendering techniques into production-ready features with confidence.

By the end of this chapter, you'll have the tools, knowledge, and patterns to render anything—from custom controls and interactive charts to immersive UIs and smooth, complex animations—with maximum control and performance.

Advanced RenderObject Techniques

Flutter's rendering system is powerful, extensible, and deeply customizable. While most developers interact with the framework through the high-level widget tree, the real rendering magic happens beneath the surface in the RenderObject tree. This lower-level layer provides granular control over layout, painting, hit testing, and even compositing behavior.

Here, we'll explore advanced RenderObject techniques, focusing on how to build custom rendering logic, implement efficient layout strategies, and achieve fine-tuned performance that simply isn't possible with higher-level abstractions.

Building Custom RenderObjects

While widgets form the declarative surface of Flutter development, RenderObjects are the underlying building blocks that determine how those widgets are laid out, painted, and composited. By building custom RenderObjects, developers can bypass the limitations of high-level widgets and unlock highly performant and expressive UI patterns that interact directly with the Flutter rendering pipeline.

CHAPTER 5   CUSTOM RENDERING AND PAINTING

Overview of RenderObjects

At the core of Flutter's rendering system lies the "RenderObject," a powerful and extensible abstraction that enables fine-grained control over how UI elements are laid out, painted, hit-tested, and integrated into the semantics tree. While the widget layer provides a declarative, developer-friendly interface, the "RenderObject" layer is where actual rendering decisions are made.

Understanding "RenderObjects" is essential for building custom UI components that require more control, efficiency, or visual uniqueness than what's possible using high-level widgets alone. This section introduces the structure, purpose, and capabilities of "RenderObjects," forming the foundation for building fully custom render logic.

The Role of RenderObjects in Flutter

Flutter's UI framework is built on three interrelated trees:

Layer	Role
Widget Tree	Describes configuration; immutable; rebuilt frequently
Element Tree	Connects widgets to render objects; mutable
Render Tree	Performs layout, painting, and hit testing

The "RenderObject" resides at the bottom layer and is responsible for all visual output and spatial arrangement on screen.

Responsibilities of a RenderObject

> **Layout**: Determines size and positioning based on parent constraints
>
> **Painting**: Renders its appearance using a "Canvas"
>
> **Hit Testing**: Identifies whether touch or pointer interactions intersect
>
> **Semantics**: Provides information for screen readers and accessibility tools

CHAPTER 5   CUSTOM RENDERING AND PAINTING

This division allows Flutter to achieve high performance by only updating the render layer when necessary, avoiding full widget rebuilds.

Common RenderObject Types

Flutter offers several built-in render object classes to support various layout and painting behaviors:

Class	Description
`RenderObject`	Base class; rarely extended directly
`RenderBox`	Most common subclass; 2D box model with layout constraints
`RenderSliver`	For scrollable, lazily-built regions (e.g., `ListView`)
`RenderFlex`	Used behind `Row` and `Column` widgets
`RenderParagraph`	Used by `Text` and `RichText` for text layout
`RenderImage`	Optimized image rendering
`RenderProxyBox`	Wraps another render box to alter behavior

When creating a custom render object, developers usually extend "RenderBox," as it supports the familiar constraint-based layout model.

Lifecycle and Pipeline Integration

Render objects participate in the rendering pipeline, a multi-phase process that governs how updates are processed and drawn:

> **Layout Phase ("performLayout")**
>
> Each render object receives size constraints from its parent.
>
> It calculates its size and passes constraints to children.
>
> The result is cached in the "size" field.
>
> **Painting Phase ("paint")**
>
> Called after layout.
>
> Draws content onto a "Canvas" via the "PaintingContext."

Compositing Phase

Determines how to merge render layers for GPU submission.

Hit Testing Phase ("hitTest")

Determines if a touch or pointer intersects the object.

Semantics Phase ("describeSemanticsConfiguration")

Contributes to the accessibility tree if applicable.

ParentData and Child Management

For multi-child layouts (like a custom "RenderBox" that arranges children), each child has an associated "ParentData" object. This metadata is used to store positional information and coordinate layout among children.

```
class MyParentData extends ContainerBoxParentData<RenderBox> {}
```

You must override "setupParentData()" to attach your custom data to each child.

When to Use Custom RenderObjects

Custom "RenderObjects" are powerful but should be used judiciously. Situations that justify their use include

> **Custom Layouts**: Complex UI structures that are not easily modeled by "Row," "Column," or "Stack."
>
> **Performance Optimization**: Replacing deep widget trees with a single render object can reduce rebuild and layout costs.

Precision Control: Fine-grained layout and pixel-accurate rendering beyond the flexibility of widgets.

Advanced Drawing: Using "Canvas," shaders, clipping paths, and blend modes for unique visual effects.

Performance Considerations

Because render objects interact directly with the rendering pipeline, mistakes in their implementation can degrade performance or break layout constraints. To mitigate this

Always cache expensive computations.

Mark the object as dirty only when needed using "markNeedsLayout()" or "markNeedsPaint()."

Use "RenderRepaintBoundary" when rendering is isolated to improve compositing efficiency.

Profile layout and paint phases using Flutter DevTools.

Render objects are the backbone of Flutter's rendering engine, providing precise control over every aspect of layout, painting, and interaction. While higher-level widgets are more convenient for most use cases, the "RenderObject" layer is indispensable for building performance-critical, custom, or visually advanced UI components.

Custom Layout and Painting

Custom layout and painting are the two most critical operations when building a "RenderObject." They define how a UI component sizes itself, arranges its children (if any), and draws its visual appearance. Mastering these aspects unlocks the ability to create visually unique, performance-optimized components tailored to specific application requirements.

CHAPTER 5   CUSTOM RENDERING AND PAINTING

This section covers the two key methods involved:

"performLayout()": Where you calculate size and position

"paint(PaintingContext context, Offset offset)": Where you draw visual content

The "performLayout()" Method

This method is responsible for setting the size of the render object and laying out its children.

Box Constraints:

Every "RenderBox" receives a "BoxConstraints" object from its parent. These constraints define the minimum and maximum width and height the render object must respect. You respond to these constraints using

```
size = constraints.constrain(Size(desiredWidth,
desiredHeight));
```

If your render object has children, you must pass constraints to them and call their "layout()" method:

```
child.layout(childConstraints, parentUsesSize: true);
```

You must also store each child's offset using "parentData," so the "paint()" method knows where to draw it.

Example: Fixed-Size RenderBox

```
class FixedSizeBox extends RenderBox {
  @override
  void performLayout() {
```

```
    size = constraints.constrain(Size(150, 150));
    // Fixed 150x150 box
  }
}
```

Example: Single-Child Layout

```
class CenteredChildBox extends RenderBox with
RenderObjectWithChildMixin<RenderBox> {
  @override
  void performLayout() {
    if (child != null) {
      child!.layout(constraints.loosen(),
      parentUsesSize: true);
      size = constraints.biggest;

      final BoxParentData childParentData = child!.parentData
      as BoxParentData;
      childParentData.offset = Offset(
        (size.width - child!.size.width) / 2,
        (size.height - child!.size.height) / 2,
      );
    } else {
      size = constraints.biggest;
    }
  }
}
```

CHAPTER 5 CUSTOM RENDERING AND PAINTING

The "paint()" Method

The "paint()" method is where the visual appearance is drawn using the low-level "Canvas" API from "dart:ui."

```
@override
void paint(PaintingContext context, Offset offset) {
  final Canvas canvas = context.canvas;

  final paint = Paint()
    ..color = Colors.blueAccent
    ..style = PaintingStyle.fill;

  canvas.drawRect(offset & size, paint);
}
```

The "offset" represents where this render object should draw relative to the parent. The "size" field is used to determine the bounds.

Drawing Children:

If your render object has children, you must call "context.paintChild()" for each child, using the offset stored in their "ParentData."

```
context.paintChild(child!, offset + childParentData.offset);
```

Combining Layout and Painting: Example

Here's a custom render object that centers a circle inside a box and supports a single child:

```
class CenteredCircleBox extends RenderBox with RenderObjectWith
ChildMixin<RenderBox> {
  @override
```

CHAPTER 5   CUSTOM RENDERING AND PAINTING

```
void performLayout() {
  size = constraints.constrain(Size(200, 200));

  if (child != null) {
    child!.layout(constraints.loosen(),
      parentUsesSize: true);
    final BoxParentData childParentData = child!.parentData
      as BoxParentData;
    childParentData.offset = Offset(
      (size.width - child!.size.width) / 2,
      (size.height - child!.size.height) / 2,
    );
  }
}

@override
void paint(PaintingContext context, Offset offset) {
  final Canvas canvas = context.canvas;

  final paint = Paint()
    ..color = Colors.orange
    ..style = PaintingStyle.fill;

  final circleCenter = offset + Offset(size.width / 2, size.height / 2);
  canvas.drawCircle(circleCenter, 80, paint);
  if (child != null) {
    final BoxParentData childParentData = child!.parentData
      as BoxParentData;
    context.paintChild(child!, offset + childParentData.offset);
  }
```

```
      }
    }
}
```

Performance Considerations

Custom render objects can significantly reduce overhead compared with complex widget trees but require careful handling to avoid performance pitfalls.

Avoid unnecessary layouts and repaints. Only call "markNeedsLayout()" or "markNeedsPaint()" when state actually changes.

Use "RenderRepaintBoundary" to isolate expensive repaints when using animations or frequent UI updates.

Avoid layout thrashing by keeping layout logic deterministic and non-recursive.

Profile using DevTools to analyze layout and paint performance.

Integrating into the Widget Tree

To use your custom "RenderBox," wrap it in a "LeafRenderObjectWidget," "SingleChildRenderObjectWidget," or "MultiChildRenderObjectWidget."

```
class MyCustomWidget extends LeafRenderObjectWidget {
  @override
  RenderObject createRenderObject(BuildContext context) {
    return FixedSizeBox();
  }
}
```

If your render object uses parameters (like color, size, etc.), override "updateRenderObject()" to pass new values during rebuilds.

CHAPTER 5   CUSTOM RENDERING AND PAINTING

Efficient Layout and Painting Strategies

Building performant custom UI components isn't just about getting them to work—it's about making them fast, responsive, and scalable. Inefficient layout and painting logic can introduce frame drops, jank, or battery drain, especially in scrollable or dynamic interfaces.

This section explores advanced techniques to optimize layout and paint performance at the RenderObject level, reduce overdraw, and minimize unnecessary computations across the rendering pipeline.

Techniques for Efficient Layouts

Efficient layout is the backbone of performant Flutter applications. Poorly optimized layout logic can lead to unnecessary recomputations, janky animations, and sluggish user interactions. When working at the "RenderObject" level, developers must manage layout precisely and intentionally to avoid redundant calculations and ensure smooth frame rendering.

This section explores proven techniques for optimizing layout in custom render objects.

Understand the Cost of Layout

Every widget in Flutter undergoes a layout phase where it determines its size and position. In the "RenderObject" world, this is handled by overriding "performLayout()." Misusing this phase can result in

   Excessive layout passes due to improper calls to "markNeedsLayout()"
   Inefficient constraint propagation, especially with nested children
   Layout thrashing, where changes to one object trigger multiple relayouts up/down the tree
   Being mindful of how and when layout is triggered is critical to performance.

Conditional Relayout: Only When Needed

Avoid unnecessary relayouts by checking for actual changes in state before calling "markNeedsLayout()." For example:

```
set width(double newWidth) {
  if (_width != newWidth) {
    _width = newWidth;
    markNeedsLayout();
  }
}
```

Triggering layout every time a setter is called—even if the value hasn't changed—is a common anti-pattern that degrades performance in complex trees.

Use Constraints Intelligently

Every "RenderBox" receives "BoxConstraints" from its parent, which it must respect. Efficient layout involves understanding and using these constraints wisely:

> Tight constraints (where min == max) are most efficient—they eliminate guesswork.
>
> Loose constraints (min = 0, max > 0) are useful when sizing children freely.
>
> Unbounded constraints (max = ∞) must be handled carefully to prevent layout exceptions.

CHAPTER 5 CUSTOM RENDERING AND PAINTING

Always use "constrain()" to clamp a proposed size within the allowed constraints:

```
size = constraints.constrain(Size(desiredWidth, desiredHeight));
```

Efficient Multi-child Layout

When laying out multiple children, avoid unnecessary recalculations and redundant logic. Best practices include

- Looping through children only once
- Passing precise constraints
- Storing child sizes and offsets in "ParentData"

Example:

```
double currentY = 0.0;
for (RenderBox? child = firstChild; child != null; child = childAfter(child)) {
  final BoxConstraints childConstraints = BoxConstraints.
  tightFor(width: size.width);
  child.layout(childConstraints, parentUsesSize: true);
  final childParentData = child.parentData as BoxParentData;
  childParentData.offset = Offset(0, currentY);
  currentY += child.size.height;
}
```

Avoid "computeDryLayout()" When Possible

"computeDryLayout()" is used by Flutter to estimate layout without fully committing to it. It can be expensive if overused.

Implement it only if needed (e.g., for "IntrinsicHeight").

If you don't need intrinsic dimensions, consider throwing "UnsupportedError."

Size Caching for Performance

If a render object's layout doesn't change often, cache the size and avoid recomputing:

```
Size? _cachedSize;

@override
void performLayout() {
  if (_cachedSize != null) {
    size = _cachedSize!;
    return;
  }

  final Size calculatedSize = computeLayoutSize();
  _cachedSize = calculatedSize;
  size = calculatedSize;
}
```

Remember to clear the cache when relevant properties change.

Leverage "parentUsesSize" Flag

If you don't need the child's size during layout, you can set "parentUsesSize: false" to improve performance:

```
child.layout(childConstraints, parentUsesSize: false);
```

This tells Flutter to skip some of the bookkeeping related to the child's dimensions.

CHAPTER 5   CUSTOM RENDERING AND PAINTING

Short-Circuit Fixed Layouts

If your component always uses a fixed size, short-circuit the entire layout logic:

```
@override
void performLayout() {
  size = constraints.constrain(Size(120, 120));
}
```

This is particularly effective for "LeafRenderObjects" or non-flexible custom components.

Use "RenderProxyBox" for Decoration-Only Wrappers

If your custom component simply wraps another and doesn't affect layout, consider extending "RenderProxyBox" instead of "RenderBox." This saves complexity and lets Flutter handle layout pass-through automatically.

Profile Layout Performance in DevTools

Flutter DevTools provides layout inspection features:

> Rebuild stats show how often widgets/layouts rebuild.
>
> Performance overlays highlight layout jank.
>
> Use Timeline to measure layout duration in real time.

Always validate performance visually and analytically, especially in scrollable or complex layouts.

Efficient layout is about "precision, intention, and minimalism." Key principles include the following:

> Relayout only when needed.
>
> Use tight constraints and pass them intelligently.

Cache, short-circuit, and simplify wherever possible.

Keep multi-child layout code compact and efficient.

Profile regularly to ensure your layout scales as expected.

Advanced Painting Techniques

While layout ensures your widgets are measured and positioned correctly, painting determines how they visually appear on the screen. At the "RenderObject" level, painting offers maximum control over visual output—but with that power comes responsibility. Inefficient painting can lead to overdraw, GPU bottlenecks, and frame drops, especially on low-end or battery-constrained devices.

This section covers high-impact, advanced painting techniques to help you create visually rich, GPU-efficient, and responsively painted custom UI components.

Avoiding Overdraw and Redundant Painting

Overdraw occurs when multiple layers are drawn on top of one another unnecessarily. It leads to wasted GPU cycles and reduced frame rates.

Best Practices:

- Paint opaque backgrounds first to prevent overdraw from lower layers.
- Skip painting invisible or offscreen content.
- Clip only when necessary—clipping operations can be expensive.

CHAPTER 5 CUSTOM RENDERING AND PAINTING

```
final Paint paint = Paint()..color = Colors.white;
canvas.drawRect(Offset.zero & size, paint);
// Opaque fill first
```

Use Flutter DevTools' "Show Paint Baselines" and "Highlight Overdraw" to analyze painting behavior.

Minimize Object Instantiations During Paint

Avoid creating objects like "Paint," "Path," or "TextPainter" inside the "paint()" method unless absolutely necessary.

Instead

- Precompute and cache reusable visual elements.
- Store them in fields and recreate only when properties change.

```
late final Paint _borderPaint = Paint()
  ..style = PaintingStyle.stroke
  ..color = Colors.black
  ..strokeWidth = 2.0;
```

Use Save/Restore Only When Required

"canvas.save()" and "canvas.restore()" are powerful but should be used judiciously.

Each pair creates a new layer of state, which can slow down rendering if nested deeply. Use them only when you modify transform, clip, or alpha and need to reset canvas state later.

```
canvas.save();
```

CHAPTER 5 CUSTOM RENDERING AND PAINTING

```
canvas.translate(offset.dx, offset.dy);
canvas.drawCircle(Offset.zero, 20, paint);
canvas.restore(); // Required here to undo the translate
```

Efficient Text Rendering with TextPainter

Text rendering is often overlooked in paint optimization. "TextPainter" is powerful but computationally expensive, especially when

> Recreated on every frame.
>
> Layout is called unnecessarily.

Best Practices:

> Cache "TextPainter" and only call "layout()" when text or constraints change.
>
> Use "TextPainter.paint()" to draw rich text with precise control.

```
final textPainter = TextPainter(
  text: TextSpan(
    text: 'Performance Matters',
    style: TextStyle(fontSize: 16, color: Colors.black),
  ),
  textDirection: TextDirection.ltr,
);
textPainter.layout(minWidth: 0, maxWidth: size.width);
textPainter.paint(canvas, Offset(10, 10));
```

Optimize Painting Boundaries

Use "context.canvas" within the "paint(PaintingContext context, Offset offset)" method to batch and isolate repaint regions efficiently.

Avoid triggering repaints across the whole tree.

Leverage "RepaintBoundary" when using "CustomPaint" or complex visuals.

```
context.canvas.drawRect(offset & size, _backgroundPaint);
```

Push Compositing Layers for Complex Visuals

When painting effects involve opacity, clipping, shadows, or transforms, use Flutter's compositing system via "PaintingContext":

> "pushOpacity()" for alpha effects
>
> "pushClipRect()" or "pushClipPath()" for advanced clipping
>
> "pushLayer()" to insert a custom compositing layer

Example:

```
context.pushOpacity(offset, 128, (context, offset) {
  context.paintChild(child, offset);
});
```

This allows Flutter's rendering engine to offload work to the GPU, improving performance especially on animations or transitions.

Implement "shouldRepaint" Intelligently

If you're using "CustomPainter," the "shouldRepaint" method controls whether painting re-executes. Avoid always returning "true."

CHAPTER 5   CUSTOM RENDERING AND PAINTING

Instead, compare relevant fields:

```
@override
bool shouldRepaint(covariant MyPainter oldDelegate) {
  return oldDelegate.color != color || oldDelegate.value != value;
}
```

This minimizes unnecessary GPU calls, especially for static or rarely changing visuals.

Avoid Painting Outside Bounds

Always respect the size boundaries passed to the "RenderObject." Painting outside may cause clipping or performance issues.

Use

```
canvas.clipRect(offset & size);
```

only when necessary to enforce painting limits.

Use Paint Caching for Complex Paths and Shapes

If you render complex paths (e.g., vector shapes, charts), cache the Path or Picture and reuse them instead of recalculating per frame.

```
final Path path = Path()..moveTo(...); // Cache this on init
canvas.drawPath(path, paint);
```

For reusable graphics, consider using "PictureRecorder" to record and replay drawing commands.

CHAPTER 5   CUSTOM RENDERING AND PAINTING

Advanced painting is about balancing visual richness with rendering performance. Mastering the "paint()" method unlocks full customizability—but requires discipline to avoid bottlenecks.

Key Takeaways

Paint only what's visible and necessary.

Reuse objects like "Paint," "TextPainter," and "Path."

Use "RepaintBoundary" and compositing layers to isolate work.

Avoid redundant save/restore or layout passes during painting.

New Painting Capabilities

Flutter 3.29 introduces a set of powerful improvements in its painting system, enabling developers to create more expressive, performant, and GPU-optimized visuals with greater control. From revamped APIs for paint orchestration to deeper shader integrations and rendering enhancements, these capabilities unlock new possibilities in advanced UI design.

Utilizing Flutter's Updated Painting APIs

Flutter 3.29 introduces several improvements to the painting system, empowering developers to create more expressive and efficient visual effects. These updates provide enhanced tools to optimize performance, streamline complex rendering tasks, and support more advanced graphic operations. This section delves into how you can leverage the new painting APIs to unlock greater visual fidelity and efficiency in custom rendering.

CHAPTER 5   CUSTOM RENDERING AND PAINTING

Overview of New Painting APIs

Flutter 3.29 introduces a powerful update to its painting system, offering more control and efficiency for developers looking to create visually rich, high-performance mobile and web applications. These new painting APIs enable deeper interaction with the rendering pipeline, improving both performance and flexibility.

The improvements in the painting APIs are aimed at reducing redundant drawing calls, enhancing the visual fidelity of custom renders, and enabling more complex visual effects without sacrificing performance. The key areas of improvement include support for advanced shaders, enhanced compositing capabilities, improved layer management, and new tools for drawing dynamic content.

This section provides an overview of the major updates to the painting APIs and how these changes allow developers to unlock more powerful visual capabilities in their Flutter applications.

Enhanced "Canvas" and Drawing Operations

The "Canvas" class, which is central to Flutter's drawing operations, has been enhanced in Flutter 3.29 with more methods and refinements for complex visual effects. New methods allow for more precise control over rendering, especially when drawing geometries, paths, and images.

> **Improved Path Drawing**: With new methods like "drawRRect()," Flutter allows for more nuanced control over the shapes you draw, from basic rectangles to advanced rounded corners and compound shapes.
>
> **Recording Drawing Operations**: The "Canvas" now supports recording drawing operations into "Picture" objects, which can be reused, leading to performance improvements when rendering complex or static visuals.

> **Advanced Image Drawing**: Flutter's new image rendering capabilities now allow for GPU-accelerated rasterization, making image drawing operations faster and more efficient, especially for large or high-resolution images.

Shader and Blend Mode Support

Shaders and blend modes are now more tightly integrated into Flutter's painting framework. This opens up new possibilities for visual effects, including real-time animations, dynamic gradients, and custom fragment shaders.

> **Custom Shaders**: Flutter's painting system now supports custom GLSL (OpenGL Shading Language) shaders, enabling developers to define their own vertex and fragment shaders for more advanced rendering effects, such as distortion, lighting effects, or texture manipulation.

> **Blend Modes**: The support for blend modes in Flutter's painting system has been expanded, allowing developers to apply various effects such as "Overlay," "Multiply," or "Screen." These modes can now be applied directly to "Paint" objects, making it easier to achieve sophisticated visual effects like shadows, glows, and color blending.

Layering and Compositing Enhancements

In Flutter 3.29, the system for compositing layers has been significantly enhanced. The "Canvas.saveLayer()" method is central to this update, as it enables more efficient and precise layer-based rendering, which is crucial when applying visual effects like opacity or shadows.

> **Efficient Layering**: With the new layer-based system, developers can isolate specific drawing operations into separate layers, reducing the need to redraw static elements and improving the performance of dynamic scenes.
>
> **Layer Management**: Layers can now be saved with specific effects applied (e.g., shadows, color filters, or blurs), making it easier to manipulate complex scenes without recalculating everything from scratch.
>
> **Layer Caching**: The introduction of smart layer caching means that Flutter will only re-render the parts of the screen that need to be updated, leading to fewer redraws and smoother animations.

Advanced Image and Text Rendering

Flutter 3.29 brings optimizations for both image and text rendering, making them faster and more efficient. These improvements are especially important for applications that rely heavily on media, such as games, multimedia apps, or social platforms.

> **Text Optimization**: The "TextPainter" class now includes optimizations for both single-line and multiline text rendering, with smarter caching mechanisms that prevent unnecessary recalculations. This results in more efficient text rendering, especially when dealing with dynamic content or custom fonts.
>
> **GPU Acceleration for Images**: Image rendering has been enhanced with hardware-accelerated decoding, reducing both CPU usage and memory consumption and providing faster rendering times for large images or images with high pixel density.

CHAPTER 5   CUSTOM RENDERING AND PAINTING

New Paint Properties and Effects

Flutter now offers additional properties in the "Paint" class that enable more advanced visual effects, including the ability to apply image filters, mask filters, and color adjustments on the fly.

> **"colorFilter"**: Apply color manipulations, such as saturation or contrast adjustments, directly on your painted objects.
>
> "imageFilter": Apply complex image effects such as blurs, distortions, or other custom image manipulations.
>
> "maskFilter": Create effects like soft-edged shadows, allowing for more nuanced and visually appealing rendering.

```
final paint = Paint()
  ..color = Colors.red
  ..imageFilter = ImageFilter.blur(sigmaX: 5.0, sigmaY: 5.0);
canvas.drawCircle(Offset(100, 100), 50, paint);
```

The updated painting APIs in Flutter 3.29 provide significant improvements over previous versions, offering more control over drawing, better performance, and more advanced effects. By enhancing "Canvas" operations, integrating custom shaders, expanding blend modes, and optimizing layer management, these new APIs provide the tools necessary to build sophisticated, high-performance UIs.

Key Highlights

> New drawing operations and improvements in path management

CHAPTER 5   CUSTOM RENDERING AND PAINTING

Advanced shader and blend mode support for custom rendering effects

Layer compositing enhancements for more efficient rendering

Optimized image and text rendering for better performance across devices

Additional "Paint" properties for applying dynamic image filters and effects

These updates unlock new possibilities for developers looking to create visually stunning and efficient Flutter applications.

Advanced Painting Techniques

With the enhancements introduced in Flutter 3.29, developers now have access to more powerful tools to create visually rich, complex, and high-performance custom painting operations. This section explores several advanced painting techniques that can be utilized with the updated APIs, enabling you to create intricate effects, dynamic visuals, and optimized renderings with greater efficiency.

Custom Gradients and Shader Effects

Flutter 3.29 introduces a range of advanced capabilities for working with gradients and shaders, allowing you to create visually dynamic content with smooth transitions and sophisticated effects.

Advanced Gradients: Flutter now supports several new types of gradients, including Sweep Gradient and Radial Gradient, with better control over color stops and transformation behavior. You can create smooth, animated, or interactive gradients that change based on user input or real-time data.

CHAPTER 5 CUSTOM RENDERING AND PAINTING

Example: Radial Gradient with Interactive Animation

```
final Shader gradient = RadialGradient(
  colors: [Colors.blue, Colors.purple],
  center: Alignment.center,
  radius: 0.8,
).createShader(Rect.fromCircle(center: Offset(150, 150),
radius: 150));

final Paint paint = Paint()..shader = gradient;
canvas.drawCircle(Offset(150, 150), 100, paint);
```

Custom Shaders with GLSL: Flutter 3.29 allows developers to write custom shaders using GLSL (OpenGL Shading Language). You can use shaders to implement complex visual effects like reflections, lighting, or distortion. By defining vertex and fragment shaders, you gain full control over how pixels are drawn on the canvas.

Example: Custom GLSL Shader for Distortion

```
final shader = CustomShader(
  vertexShaderCode: 'vertex shader code here',
  fragmentShaderCode: 'fragment shader code here',
);
final paint = Paint()..shader = shader;
canvas.drawRect(Rect.fromLTWH(50, 50, 200, 200), paint);
```

This powerful approach opens up creative possibilities for real-time visual effects such as fluid animations, glowing highlights, and texture mapping.

Implementing Complex Clipping Effects

Clipping is a common technique used to restrict drawing to a certain region. Flutter 3.29 improves the clipping capabilities of the "Canvas" class, enabling more advanced clipping paths and operations.

> **Clipping Paths**: You can clip the canvas to custom path shapes, allowing for the creation of complex, non-rectangular clipping regions, such as circular, polygonal, or freeform regions. This technique can be useful for drawing within arbitrary boundaries or creating complex visual elements like avatars, badges, or custom-shaped buttons.

Example: Clipping to a Custom Path

```
final Path clipPath = Path()
  ..moveTo(0, 0)
  ..lineTo(100, 200)
  ..lineTo(200, 0)
  ..close();
canvas.clipPath(clipPath);
canvas.drawColor(Colors.blue, BlendMode.srcOver);
```

> **Clipping with Shapes and Effects**: Flutter now supports advanced clipping effects, such as rounded corners, complex polygons, and even arbitrary Bezier curves, which can be used to shape your visual content in creative ways. You can combine

clipping with other transformations, such as scaling or rotation, to create animated and interactive visuals.

Optimizing Layered Painting with SaveLayer

As the complexity of custom painting increases, managing layers effectively becomes essential for ensuring smooth performance. In Flutter 3.29, the "Canvas.saveLayer()" method has been optimized to allow more advanced layer management, especially when applying effects such as shadows, blurs, or partial opacity.

Efficient Layer Management: By saving parts of the drawing into separate layers, you can optimize the rendering of complex scenes. For example, when applying a blur effect to a large area of the screen, you can isolate the region to be blurred and save it as a layer to avoid unnecessary re-rendering of static elements.

Complex Visual Effects: SaveLayer is ideal for layering effects like soft shadows or glowing elements, which are common in modern UI design. These effects can be applied to individual layers, making it easy to control how layers interact with each other.

Example: Applying a Shadow Effect Using SaveLayer

```
canvas.saveLayer(Rect.fromLTWH(50, 50, 200, 200), Paint());
canvas.drawCircle(Offset(150, 150), 100, Paint()..color = Colors.yellow);
canvas.restore();
```

CHAPTER 5 CUSTOM RENDERING AND PAINTING

By isolating elements that need effects from others, you can drastically improve performance and reduce the overhead of full scene redrawing.

Drawing Dynamic and Interactive Content

Flutter 3.29 makes it easier than ever to implement real-time and interactive content using custom painting. By combining advanced features like shaders, custom path drawing, and efficient state management, you can create highly interactive, responsive graphics in your app.

> **Real-Time Interaction**: With Flutter's new painting capabilities, it is now possible to draw content that responds to touch, gestures, or other user inputs in real time. You can apply transformations (scaling, rotation, translation) dynamically, allowing for interactive animations and visual effects like drag-and-drop, zooming, or rotating elements.

Example: Animating a Dynamic Circle Based on Touch Input

```
void _onPanUpdate(DragUpdateDetails details) {
  setState(() {
    _circleOffset = details.localPosition;
  });
}

@override
Widget build(BuildContext context) {
  return GestureDetector(
    onPanUpdate: _onPanUpdate,
    child: CustomPaint(
      size: Size(300, 300),
      painter: CirclePainter(_circleOffset),
```

CHAPTER 5 CUSTOM RENDERING AND PAINTING

```
      ),
    );
}

class CirclePainter extends CustomPainter {
  final Offset circleOffset;
  CirclePainter(this.circleOffset);

  @override
  void paint(Canvas canvas, Size size) {
    final Paint paint = Paint()..color = Colors.blue;
    canvas.drawCircle(circleOffset, 50, paint);
  }

  @override
  bool shouldRepaint(CustomPainter oldDelegate) {
    return true;
  }
}
```

This technique allows developers to create dynamic, touch-responsive graphics with ease, such as interactive charts, drawing apps, or games.

Combining Advanced Effects for Artistic Designs

To achieve intricate visual styles, you can combine various painting techniques such as shaders, filters, and layering. These combined effects allow you to craft custom animations, visually rich scenes, and sophisticated UI components.

> **Animated Gradients**: By manipulating gradients and shaders in real time, you can create smooth animated backgrounds, lighting effects, or color transitions.

CHAPTER 5   CUSTOM RENDERING AND PAINTING

Complex Masking and Blurring: Using a combination of clipping paths and image filters, you can create realistic blur effects, soft-focus elements, and custom gradients that give your app a modern and polished appearance.

Example: Creating a Dynamic Animated Gradient Background

```
class GradientPainter extends CustomPainter {
  final Animation<Color> color1;
  final Animation<Color> color2;
  GradientPainter(this.color1, this.color2);

  @override
  void paint(Canvas canvas, Size size) {
    final Paint paint = Paint()
      ..shader = LinearGradient(
        colors: [color1.value, color2.value],
        begin: Alignment.topLeft,
        end: Alignment.bottomRight,
      ).createShader(Rect.fromLTWH(0, 0, size.width, size.height));
    canvas.drawRect(Rect.fromLTWH(0, 0, size.width, size.height), paint);
  }

  @override
  bool shouldRepaint(covariant CustomPainter oldDelegate) {
    return true;
  }
}
```

This example demonstrates how you can animate the gradient to transition between colors, creating a dynamic background that responds to changes in state or user interaction.

Advanced painting techniques in Flutter 3.29 open up a wide array of creative possibilities for developers aiming to build visually sophisticated and high-performance applications. From custom shaders and gradients to interactive content and efficient layering, Flutter's updated painting APIs provide the tools necessary to craft rich, dynamic user interfaces that can run smoothly across platforms.

Key Takeaways

> **Advanced Gradients and Shaders**: Create visually stunning dynamic effects using custom GLSL shaders and sophisticated gradient systems.
>
> **Complex Clipping Effects**: Clip paths dynamically for non-rectangular regions, allowing for more flexible drawing operations.
>
> **Efficient Layering**: Use the "saveLayer()" method to optimize rendering when applying effects like shadows or opacity.
>
> **Real-Time Interaction**: Design highly interactive, touch-responsive content with smooth animations.
>
> **Combining Effects**: Layer filters, shaders, and clipping effects to create rich, artistic visuals.

By mastering these advanced painting techniques, you can significantly enhance the visual quality and interactivity of your Flutter applications while maintaining performance and efficiency.

CHAPTER 5 CUSTOM RENDERING AND PAINTING

Implementing High-Performance Custom Paint Operations

Flutter 3.29 introduces enhanced capabilities for developers to implement high-performance custom painting operations. These updates empower you to create intricate visuals, maintain smooth user interactions, and ensure your apps perform efficiently, even with complex graphics. By leveraging Flutter's low-level drawing APIs, developers can gain precise control over rendering processes, which is especially important when working with real-time, dynamic content.

Creating Custom Paint Operations

Custom paint operations are one of the most powerful tools Flutter offers for rendering unique visual effects in your app. Flutter's "CustomPainter" class, in combination with the "Canvas" API, enables you to draw shapes, paths, images, and even complex animations. Whether you're creating custom graphics for your UI or developing advanced visual effects like interactive graphics or custom charts, the ability to define and control your painting operations can set your app apart.

This section will guide you through creating custom paint operations, focusing on the key steps, best practices, and code examples to help you get started.

Understanding CustomPaint and CustomPainter

In Flutter, custom painting is primarily achieved through the "CustomPaint" widget, which takes a "CustomPainter" as its painter. A "CustomPainter" is a class where you define the drawing logic using a "Canvas." You override the "paint()" method to perform your drawing operations and the "shouldRepaint()" method to optimize when the painting should be redrawn.

"CustomPaint" Widget: The widget that provides the drawing area and links to the "CustomPainter." It tells Flutter to repaint the custom drawing whenever necessary.

"CustomPainter" Class: This is where the actual painting happens. You define how to paint the contents (shapes, images, etc.) in the "paint()" method and control when to repaint using "shouldRepaint()."

Basic Structure of a CustomPainter

To create a custom paint operation, you need to define a "CustomPainter" class. The key part of this class is the "paint()" method, where you use a "Canvas" to draw. Here's a basic example of creating a custom painter that draws a circle:

```
class CirclePainter extends CustomPainter {
  final Color color;

  CirclePainter(this.color);

  @override
  void paint(Canvas canvas, Size size) {
    final Paint paint = Paint()
      ..color = color
      ..style = PaintingStyle.fill;

    // Draw a circle at the center of the canvas
    canvas.drawCircle(Offset(size.width / 2, size.height / 2),
    50, paint);
  }
```

```
@override
bool shouldRepaint(CustomPainter oldDelegate) {
  // No need to repaint if the color hasn't changed
  return oldDelegate is CirclePainter && oldDelegate.color != color;
}
}
```

In this example

> The "CirclePainter" class takes a color as a parameter and draws a filled circle on the canvas at the center of the widget.
>
> The "shouldRepaint()" method ensures that the circle is only repainted when the color changes, improving performance.

To use this "CustomPainter," you embed it within a "CustomPaint" widget:

```
CustomPaint(
  size: Size(200, 200),
  painter: CirclePainter(Colors.blue),
)
```

Drawing More Complex Operations

Once you are familiar with basic shapes, you can expand your custom paint operations to draw more complex graphics, such as paths, text, and images.

CHAPTER 5   CUSTOM RENDERING AND PAINTING

Drawing Paths:

Paths allow you to create complex shapes, lines, and curves. Use the "Path" class to create shapes like polygons, Bezier curves, or custom figures.

```
class TrianglePainter extends CustomPainter {
  @override
  void paint(Canvas canvas, Size size) {
    final Paint paint = Paint()
      ..color = Colors.green
      ..style = PaintingStyle.fill;

    final Path path = Path()
      ..moveTo(size.width / 2, 0)
      ..lineTo(size.width, size.height)
      ..lineTo(0, size.height)
      ..close();

    canvas.drawPath(path, paint);
  }

  @override
  bool shouldRepaint(CustomPainter oldDelegate) {
    return false; // No need to repaint for this static triangle
  }
}
```

In this example, a triangle is drawn using a "Path" object. The "moveTo()" method sets the starting point, and "lineTo()" defines the path. After the path is defined, it is drawn on the canvas using "canvas.drawPath()."

CHAPTER 5   CUSTOM RENDERING AND PAINTING

Drawing Text:

You can also draw text on the canvas using the "TextPainter" class. This class offers fine-grained control over text styles, alignment, and positioning.

```
class TextPainterExample extends CustomPainter {
  final String text;

  TextPainterExample(this.text);

  @override
  void paint(Canvas canvas, Size size) {
    final TextSpan textSpan = TextSpan(
      text: text,
      style: TextStyle(color: Colors.black, fontSize: 20),
    );

    final TextPainter textPainter = TextPainter(
      text: textSpan,
      textAlign: TextAlign.center,
      textDirection: TextDirection.ltr,
    );

    textPainter.layout(minWidth: 0, maxWidth: size.width);
    textPainter.paint(canvas, Offset(size.width / 2 - textPainter.width / 2, size.height / 2 - textPainter.height / 2));
  }
```

```
  @override
  bool shouldRepaint(CustomPainter oldDelegate) {
    return oldDelegate is TextPainterExample && oldDelegate.
    text != text;
  }
}
```

In this case

> The "TextPainter" is used to create a text layout with a specified style and alignment.
>
> The text is then drawn onto the "Canvas" at the center of the widget.

Handling Dynamic Painting

In some cases, you may need to dynamically update the painting, such as in animations or interactive drawings. To handle dynamic changes, you can make use of the "setState()" method (when used with a stateful widget) or utilize animations. Ensure that the "shouldRepaint()" method is implemented properly to efficiently redraw only the parts that need to change.

```
class AnimatedCirclePainter extends CustomPainter {
  final double radius;

  AnimatedCirclePainter(this.radius);

  @override
  void paint(Canvas canvas, Size size) {
    final Paint paint = Paint()..color = Colors.blue;
    canvas.drawCircle(Offset(size.width / 2, size.height / 2),
      radius, paint);
  }
```

```
  @override
  bool shouldRepaint(CustomPainter oldDelegate) {
    return oldDelegate is AnimatedCirclePainter && oldDelegate.
    radius != radius;
  }
}
```

In this case, "AnimatedCirclePainter" allows you to animate the radius of the circle. The "shouldRepaint()" method ensures that the circle is redrawn only when the radius changes.

Performance Considerations for Custom Paint Operations
While custom paint operations provide immense flexibility, they can be costly in terms of performance, especially when dealing with animations or complex visuals. Keep the following best practices in mind:

> **Minimize Redraws**: Avoid unnecessary calls to the "paint()" method. The "shouldRepaint()" method is essential for determining whether a repaint is necessary. Only repaint when there is an actual change in the visual content.

> **Cache Static Elements**: For static graphics, consider caching the rendered result in a "Picture" object, or use the "saveLayer()" API to isolate and optimize certain operations.

> **Optimize Path Operations**: Complex paths can significantly impact rendering performance. Simplify paths wherever possible by reducing the number of points or using simpler geometric shapes.

CHAPTER 5   CUSTOM RENDERING AND PAINTING

Creating custom paint operations in Flutter opens up endless possibilities for building visually rich and interactive applications. The process involves using "CustomPainter" to define the drawing logic and the "Canvas" API to render shapes, paths, images, and text. While custom painting allows for great flexibility, it is important to optimize the painting process to ensure smooth performance, especially when dealing with dynamic or complex visuals.

Key Takeaways

> **CustomPainter and Canvas**: Use "CustomPainter" and "Canvas" to draw custom graphics in your Flutter app.
>
> **Paths and Shapes**: Draw complex paths, polygons, and curves using the "Path" class.
>
> **Text and Images**: Leverage the "TextPainter" class for precise text rendering and optimize image handling for better performance.
>
> **Dynamic Painting**: Handle dynamic changes and animations efficiently by implementing "shouldRepaint()" correctly.
>
> **Performance Optimization**: Use best practices like caching, minimizing redraws, and simplifying path operations to maintain optimal performance.

Performance Optimization

Creating rich, high-fidelity custom paint operations in Flutter is powerful—but with that power comes the responsibility of ensuring performance remains smooth and responsive. Painting is one of the most CPU-intensive operations in the rendering pipeline, and without careful optimization, even minor inefficiencies can result in dropped frames, sluggish animations, and poor user experiences—especially on lower-end devices.

CHAPTER 5   CUSTOM RENDERING AND PAINTING

This section covers advanced strategies to optimize your custom painting logic in Flutter, ensuring your visuals are not only beautiful but also fast and efficient.

Minimize Repaints with "shouldRepaint()"

The most critical optimization in any "CustomPainter" is controlling when the canvas should be repainted. Flutter calls the "paint()" method every time the framework thinks a repaint might be needed. If you do not correctly implement "shouldRepaint()," your widget may be redrawn far more often than necessary.

```
@override
bool shouldRepaint(CustomPainter oldDelegate) {
  return oldDelegate is MyPainter && oldDelegate.someValue !=
  someValue;
}
```

> **Best Practice**: Return "true" only when actual paint-relevant data changes. Avoid repainting due to unrelated state changes.

Use Layer Caching for Static Elements

If parts of your canvas are static or rarely change, consider caching them using "PictureRecorder" or leveraging "saveLayer()." Flutter's "Picture" objects store drawing commands that can be replayed efficiently.

```
final recorder = PictureRecorder();
final canvas = Canvas(recorder);
drawStaticContent(canvas, size);
final picture = recorder.endRecording();
```

CHAPTER 5 CUSTOM RENDERING AND PAINTING

Later, during painting:

```
canvas.drawPicture(picture);
```

This avoids redoing costly operations every frame.

Use Case: Static backgrounds, reusable UI decorations, watermark layers

Clip Intelligently

Avoid unnecessary clipping. Clipping can trigger expensive saveLayer operations internally. Use clipping only when needed, and prefer "Canvas.clipRect()" over more complex clipping methods like "clipPath()" or "clipRRect()" when possible.

Avoid

```
canvas.clipPath(complexPath);
```

Prefer

```
canvas.clipRect(Rect.fromLTWH(0, 0, size.width, size.height));
```

Avoid Overdrawing

Overdraw occurs when pixels are painted multiple times in a single frame. Excessive overdraw leads to GPU workload spikes.

Strategies to reduce overdraw are as follows:

> Avoid painting fully opaque layers over each other.
>
> Use transparent fills only when visually necessary.
>
> Reduce overlap between UI elements where possible.

CHAPTER 5   CUSTOM RENDERING AND PAINTING

Tip   Use Flutter DevTools' "Performance" tab to visualize overdraw and identify problem areas.

Optimize Path Complexity

Complex "Path" operations such as Bezier curves, arcs, or multiple line segments can be costly to rasterize.

Recommendations:

Use fewer path segments.

Reuse "Path" objects where possible.

Avoid recalculating paths in every paint if they can be cached.

Precompute expensive path logic and store results if static.

Paint Only What's Visible (Dirty Rects)

If your canvas is very large or scrollable, paint only the visible portion. Use the "canvas.getClipBounds()" method to find the current visible region and avoid drawing outside it.

```
final visible = canvas.getClipBounds();
if (visible.overlaps(myElementBounds)) {
  canvas.drawRect(myElementBounds, paint);
}
```

This helps keep the paint workload aligned with what's actually on screen.

CHAPTER 5 CUSTOM RENDERING AND PAINTING

Efficient Use of "Paint" Objects

Creating "Paint" objects inside the "paint()" method on every frame can lead to unnecessary memory churn and CPU overhead.

> **Best Practice**: Instantiate "Paint" once (either as a constant or a final field), and reuse it.

```
final Paint strokePaint = Paint()
  ..color = Colors.blue
  ..style = PaintingStyle.stroke
  ..strokeWidth = 2.0;
```

Avoid

```
// Inefficient: recreated every paint cycle
Paint strokePaint = Paint()
  ..color = Colors.blue
  ..style = PaintingStyle.stroke
  ..strokeWidth = 2.0;
```

Combine with "RepaintBoundary"

Wrap your "CustomPaint" widget in a "RepaintBoundary" to isolate its repaints from the rest of the widget tree. This can dramatically improve performance by preventing upstream widgets from needing to repaint when only your canvas has changed.

```
RepaintBoundary(
  child: CustomPaint(
    painter: MyCustomPainter(),
```

),
)

Use Case: Complex or animated custom painting in lists, scroll views, or overlays

Optimize for GPU with saveLayer Wisely

"Canvas.saveLayer()" creates an offscreen buffer and is GPU-intensive. Use it sparingly, only when blending effects (e.g., transparency, masking) are truly needed.

Avoid patterns like

```
canvas.saveLayer(bounds, paint);
drawSomethingExpensive();
canvas.restore();
```

Unless you're implementing something that requires it (e.g., alpha compositing), this may trigger GPU bottlenecks.

Benchmark and Profile

Use Flutter DevTools to profile painting performance:

> "Performance" tab to detect jank
>
> "Raster Stats" to monitor frame rendering cost
>
> "Timeline" to examine per-frame render time

Enable "Show Repaint Rainbow" to detect excessive repainting visually.

High-performance custom painting is achievable with careful planning and a deep understanding of Flutter's rendering pipeline. The key is to avoid unnecessary work, draw only what's needed, and be mindful of GPU and CPU costs.

CHAPTER 5   CUSTOM RENDERING AND PAINTING

Key Performance Tips Recap

- Implement "shouldRepaint()" correctly.
- Cache static visuals using "PictureRecorder."
- Avoid unnecessary clipping and overdraw.
- Paint only what's visible (use dirty rects).
- Reuse "Paint" and "Path" objects.
- Leverage "RepaintBoundary" to isolate redraws.
- Profile regularly with DevTools and adjust as needed.

By following these best practices, you can create stunning custom graphics in Flutter without sacrificing smoothness or battery efficiency.

Advanced Shader Techniques

As applications become increasingly immersive and visually sophisticated, developers are turning to shaders to achieve GPU-accelerated, real-time graphics effects. Flutter's support for custom shaders via FragmentPrograms, SkSL (Skia Shading Language), and Impeller unlocks a powerful avenue for visual innovation.

This section explores how to harness Flutter's shader capabilities to create custom lighting effects, image distortions, particle systems, and more—all while maintaining high performance on both mobile and desktop GPUs.

Introduction to Shaders in Flutter

In graphics programming, a shader is a small program that runs on the GPU to compute visual effects. Flutter supports fragment shaders, which operate per pixel, making them ideal for

Custom gradients

Lighting and shadow effects

Blurs, ripples, and distortions

Procedural textures

Since Flutter 3.7+, fragment shaders can be authored in GLSL, compiled to SkSL (Skia Shading Language), and used within the "FragmentProgram" API.

Creating a Custom Shader
Step 1: Write the GLSL Shader
Create a file "wave.glsl":

```
uniform float u_time;
uniform vec2 u_resolution;

half4 main(vec2 fragCoord) {
  vec2 uv = fragCoord / u_resolution;
  float wave = sin(uv.x 10.0 + u_time) 0.5 + 0.5;
  return half4(wave, uv.y, 0.8, 1.0);
}
```

Step 2: Compile the Shader to ".spirv"
Use the "flutter_shader_compiler":

```
flutter build bundle --dart-define=FLUTTER_WEB_USE_SKSL=true
```

Or for Impeller on iOS and Android, use the "flutter_shader" toolchain or build pipelines to compile GLSL to SPIR-V or SkSL.

CHAPTER 5 CUSTOM RENDERING AND PAINTING

Step 3: Load and Use in Flutter

```
final fragment = await FragmentProgram.fromAsset('shaders/wave.frag.spv');
final shader = fragment.fragmentShader();

canvas.drawRect(
  rect,
  Paint()..shader = shader,
);
```

Uniforms and Dynamic Shader Input

Shaders can accept uniforms—variables whose values are passed from Dart. This allows dynamic effects like animations or interactivity:

```
shader.setFloat(0, time);
shader.setFloat(1, resolution.dx);
shader.setFloat(2, resolution.dy);
```

In the GLSL file:

```
uniform float u_time;
uniform vec2 u_resolution;
```

CHAPTER 5 CUSTOM RENDERING AND PAINTING

You can animate time via "Ticker" or "AnimationController."

Practical Shader Use Cases in Flutter

A. **Realistic Lighting and Shadows**

Shaders can simulate soft shadows, lighting gradients, and specular highlights for realistic UI depth—far beyond basic box shadows.

Example: Dynamic inner glow or sunbeam effects

B. **Procedural Backgrounds**

Generate animated backgrounds using mathematical patterns like Perlin noise, fractals, or trigonometric distortion.

Advantages:

Lightweight (no image assets)

Infinite variety

Resolution-independent

C. **Image Distortion Effects**

Apply ripple, swirl, pixelation, or glitch effects to images or videos by manipulating texture coordinates in the shader.

Example GLSL Distortion:

```
vec2 offset = sin(uv.y 20.0 + u_time) 0.01;
vec4 color = texture(u_texture, uv + offset);
```

Chapter 5 Custom Rendering and Painting

D. **Interactive Effects**

Use gestures, pointer input, or sensor data to feed uniform values into shaders—enabling interactive ripples, touch sparks, etc.

Performance Considerations

Though GPU-accelerated, shaders can still impact performance if not carefully managed.

Here are tips for performance:

- Avoid high-resolution offscreen rendering unless necessary.
- Reuse "FragmentShader" instances.
- Use "RepaintBoundary" to minimize redraws.
- Use Impeller for smoother shader compilation and deployment.

Debugging and Tooling

Use Impeller Shader Debugger for shader visualization (enabled by default on iOS).

Utilize tools like Shader Editor (https://shadered.org/) or Shadertoy (https://www.shadertoy.com/) for rapid prototyping.

Flutter DevTools doesn't support direct shader inspection (yet), but performance profiling is still applicable.

Deployment and Platform Differences

Shaders may render slightly differently across GPU vendors or platforms (Metal, Vulkan, OpenGL). Always test on target devices.

For full support

- Use "Impeller" (default for iOS, opt in on Android).
- Avoid platform-specific GLSL extensions.
- Keep shader logic deterministic.

Flutter's shader capabilities open the door to rich, GPU-powered visual effects, enabling developers to deliver cutting-edge experiences rivaling native and gaming platforms. With careful design, efficient usage of uniforms, and robust performance profiling, you can elevate your UIs to new visual heights.

Shader Power Checklist

- Use fragment shaders for per-pixel effects.
- Compile GLSL to SkSL/SPIR-V and load via "FragmentProgram."
- Animate using uniforms and integrate with Flutter's animation system.
- Optimize draw regions and isolate with "RepaintBoundary."
- Test across devices and engines for consistency.

Real-Time Rendering Techniques

Real-time rendering is at the heart of responsive, fluid, and immersive user interfaces. In Flutter 3.29, performance improvements in the rendering pipeline, enhanced shader integration, and the introduction of the Impeller rendering engine enable developers to push the boundaries of what's possible in mobile and web UIs.

Here we dive into techniques for achieving smooth, high-FPS visual output under demanding conditions, including dynamic UIs, animated transitions, particle effects, and custom shaders. We will explore real-time constraints, frame budget optimization, and tools for debugging frame drops.

CHAPTER 5   CUSTOM RENDERING AND PAINTING

Techniques for Real-Time Rendering

Achieving real-time rendering in Flutter requires precise control over rendering phases, tight frame budget adherence, and optimal use of hardware acceleration. Flutter 3.29 introduces significant improvements with the Impeller engine, shader pre-compilation, and better support for low-latency UI updates—making real-time rendering not only feasible but also more predictable and performant across platforms.

Here, we explore proven strategies and Flutter-specific tools that enable consistent, high-FPS rendering for complex and dynamic user interfaces.

Understanding the Real-Time Rendering Pipeline

Before optimizing for real-time performance, it is crucial to understand the high-level stages of Flutter's rendering pipeline:

>   **Build Phase**: Widget tree is constructed.
>
>   **Layout Phase**: Widgets calculate their size and position.
>
>   **Paint Phase**: Render objects produce paint commands.
>
>   **Compositing Phase**: The scene is prepared for the GPU.
>
>   **Rasterization**: The GPU renders the final frame.

Each of these stages contributes to the frame time. For smooth 60 FPS rendering, every frame must be rendered in under 16.67ms.

Frame Budget Optimization

To stay within the frame budget

>   **Minimize Expensive Layouts**: Avoid "LayoutBuilder" or "IntrinsicHeight" in frequently updated regions.

CHAPTER 5 CUSTOM RENDERING AND PAINTING

Reduce Widget Rebuilds: Use "const" constructors and avoid unnecessary "setState()" calls.

Use Lightweight Animations: Prefer "AnimatedBuilder" and "TweenAnimationBuilder" for granular control.

Use "Flutter DevTools ➤ Performance tab" to monitor frame timing and identify bottlenecks.

Use of "RepaintBoundary"

Flutter repaints entire render trees unless scoped repainting is enforced. Wrap individual animation zones or high-frequency updates with "RepaintBoundary":

```
RepaintBoundary(
  child: RealTimeGraphWidget(),
);
```

This tells the engine to treat the subtree as a separate render layer, limiting repaints only to changed portions.

Efficient Use of "CustomPaint"

For real-time effects like graphs, particle systems, or dynamic charts

Use "CustomPaint" for direct canvas drawing.

Avoid excessive canvas state changes ("save/restore").

Keep drawing logic as minimal and linear as possible.

CHAPTER 5   CUSTOM RENDERING AND PAINTING

To animate in real time:

```
Ticker _ticker = Ticker(_onTick)..start();

void _onTick(Duration elapsed) {
  setState(() {
    // Update state driving the paint
  });
}
```

Leveraging the Impeller Renderer

Flutter's Impeller renderer—enabled by default on iOS and available on Android—eliminates runtime shader compilation jank by precompiling shaders at build time.

Benefits:

- Reduced frame latency
- No initial frame stutter
- Better GPU resource usage

Enable on Android:

```
flutter build apk --enable-impeller
```

Offloading Expensive Computations

Move CPU-intensive logic (e.g., pathfinding, physics simulation) to

- Isolates for background processing
- compute() API for one-off expensive tasks
- Native code via platform channels when appropriate

Avoid blocking the UI thread, especially during animation frames.

Adaptive Frame Rate and Conditional Repainting

To save resources

> Only repaint when state changes (throttle updates).

Use "shouldRepaint" in "CustomPainter" smartly:

```
@override
bool shouldRepaint(covariant MyPainter oldDelegate) {
  return oldDelegate.time != time;
}
```

Skip frames gracefully using a "Ticker" or animation controller with "isActive" checks.

Scene Complexity Management

Real-time rendering often fails due to overly complex widget trees:

> Use "Stack," "Positioned," and "Transform" strategically.
>
> Clip expensive effects ("ClipRect," "ClipPath") only when needed.
>
> Avoid compositing multiple layers unnecessarily.

Consider using "RenderObject" directly for ultra-high-performance rendering.

Physics-Based Real-Time Interactions

Leverage Flutter's "physics" and "simulation" libraries for natural real-time animations:

> "SpringSimulation" for realistic motion
>
> "FrictionSimulation" for deceleration effects

CHAPTER 5   CUSTOM RENDERING AND PAINTING

These can be driven by gesture inputs to create dynamic, responsive UIs.

Best Practices Recap

Technique	Purpose
'RepaintBoundary'	Isolate updates to avoid full repaints
'CustomPaint' + 'Ticker'	Custom rendering synced with frame loop
Impeller Renderer	Avoid shader compilation jank
Layout simplification	Faster layout phase for dynamic UIs
Physics simulations	Realistic effects with low compute cost
DevTools Performance Tab	Visualize frame drops and optimize

🔧 **Code Snippet: Efficient Real-Time Painter**

```
class RealTimePainter extends CustomPainter {
  final double value;
  RealTimePainter(this.value);

  @override
  void paint(Canvas canvas, Size size) {
    final paint = Paint()..color = Colors.blue;
    canvas.drawCircle(Offset(size.width value, size.height /
    2), 20, paint);
  }

  @override
  bool shouldRepaint(covariant RealTimePainter oldDelegate) {
    return oldDelegate.value != value;
  }
}
```

Custom Animations and Effects

Custom animations and visual effects are essential for delivering highly polished, immersive user experiences. While Flutter's built-in animation system is powerful and versatile, mastering custom animations requires a deep understanding of the rendering pipeline, compositing layers, shaders, and the timing model.

In this section, we explore how to craft high-performance, deeply customizable animations and visual effects using Flutter 3.29's advanced capabilities—including "AnimationController," "CustomPainter," "ShaderMask," and the Impeller renderer.

Mastering the AnimationController

The "AnimationController" forms the foundation of Flutter's animation framework. For custom animations

> Use a "TickerProvider" (via "SingleTickerProviderStateMixin").
>
> Define animation curves using "CurvedAnimation."
>
> Drive visual updates in a "CustomPainter," "AnimatedBuilder," or "Transform."

Example: Basic Custom Controller

```
class MyAnimationWidget extends StatefulWidget {
  @override
  _MyAnimationWidgetState createState() => _MyAnimationWidgetState();
}

class _MyAnimationWidgetState extends State<MyAnimationWidget>
    with SingleTickerProviderStateMixin {
  late AnimationController _controller;
```

```dart
  @override
  void initState() {
    super.initState();
    _controller = AnimationController(
      duration: const Duration(seconds: 2),
      vsync: this,
    )..repeat(reverse: true);
  }

  @override
  Widget build(BuildContext context) {
    return AnimatedBuilder(
      animation: _controller,
      builder: (_, __) => Transform.scale(
        scale: 1 + 0.2 _controller.value,
        child: MyCustomPaint(),
      ),
    );
  }

  @override
  void dispose() {
    _controller.dispose();
    super.dispose();
  }
}
```

Crafting Custom Visual Effects with Shaders

Flutter 3.29 brings refined shader support via the Impeller renderer, making GPU-accelerated effects fast and smooth.

CHAPTER 5 CUSTOM RENDERING AND PAINTING

Use "FragmentShader" and "ShaderMask" for

> Glows
>
> Blurs
>
> Ripple effects
>
> Gradient transitions

Example: Shader Mask for Text Fade

```
ShaderMask(
  shaderCallback: (Rect bounds) {
    return LinearGradient(
      colors: [Colors.purple, Colors.transparent],
      begin: Alignment.topCenter,
      end: Alignment.bottomCenter,
    ).createShader(bounds);
  },
  child: Text(
    'Flutter Magic',
    style: TextStyle(fontSize: 48, color: Colors.white),
  ),
);
```

For advanced control, use precompiled shaders with "flutter_shader."

Leveraging Impeller for Smooth Transitions

With Impeller, custom effects—like particle fields or real-time distortions—no longer suffer from shader warm-up jank. Use this for

> Water ripple effects
>
> Fire/smoke particles
>
> Lighting simulations

CHAPTER 5 CUSTOM RENDERING AND PAINTING

Pair "CustomPaint" with "Ticker"-based animations to drive real-time visuals at 60+ FPS.

Combining Animations and Gestures

Advanced UIs often merge animation and interactivity. Use "GestureDetector" with custom animations:

```
GestureDetector(
  onPanUpdate: (details) {
    setState(() {
      _offset += details.delta;
    });
  },
  child: Transform.translate(
    offset: _offset,
    child: MyAnimatedWidget(),
  ),
);
```

This approach enables

- Drag-based animations
- Momentum scroll with custom physics
- Physics-based fling effects using "Simulation"

Animating Along Custom Paths

For non-linear or curved motion, use parametric path-based animations.

Example: Arc Animation

```
Path path = Path()..arcTo(Rect.fromCircle(center: Offset(100,
100), radius: 50), 0, pi, false);
PathMetric pathMetric = path.computeMetrics().first;
Offset animatedPoint = pathMetric.
getTangentForOffset(pathMetric.length t)!.position;
```

This technique is powerful for

- Circular menus
- Orbiting objects
- Custom loaders

Reusable Animation Abstractions

Create reusable animation builders and custom widgets that encapsulate timing, transformation, and repaint logic.

Example: Pulsating Button Widget

```
class PulsatingButton extends StatefulWidget {
  final Widget child;
  const PulsatingButton({required this.child});

  @override
  _PulsatingButtonState createState() => _PulsatingButton
  State();
}

class _PulsatingButtonState extends State<PulsatingButton>
    with SingleTickerProviderStateMixin {
  late AnimationController _controller;
```

```
  @override
  void initState() {
    super.initState();
    _controller = AnimationController(
      duration: Duration(seconds: 1),
      vsync: this,
    )..repeat(reverse: true);
  }

  @override
  Widget build(BuildContext context) {
    return AnimatedBuilder(
      animation: _controller,
      builder: (_, __) => Transform.scale(
        scale: 1 + 0.1 _controller.value,
        child: widget.child,
      ),
    );
  }

  @override
  void dispose() {
    _controller.dispose();
    super.dispose();
  }
}
```

Real-Time Visualizations and Effects

Combine all the above to build visually rich real-time effects like

- Live waveform visualizers
- Speedometers and gauges
- Interactive physics simulations

Use "CustomPaint," "ShaderMask," and "AnimationController" in harmony to create stunning, responsive UI components.

🔧 **Best Practices for Custom Animations**

Strategy	Benefit
Use 'AnimatedBuilder'	Avoid widget rebuilds during animation
Drive visuals with 'CustomPainter'	Low-level, performant rendering
Use 'ShaderMask' and Impeller	GPU-accelerated effects, no shader jank
Limit frame scope with 'RepaintBoundary'	Reduce repaint costs
Offload computation to Isolates	Keep UI thread responsive

Case Studies

Custom rendering is one of the most powerful features in Flutter's framework, allowing developers to go beyond the limitations of traditional widgets to craft high-performance, highly customized visual elements. In this section, we examine how these capabilities are applied in real-world applications, with detailed case studies and analyses of popular apps that utilize custom rendering for performance, interactivity, and unique UI experiences.

Successful Implementations of Custom Rendering

Custom rendering in Flutter is more than just a visual enhancement—it's a core capability that enables developers to implement highly responsive, unique, and scalable UI components beyond what's possible with standard widgets. This section highlights real-world examples where custom rendering was used to solve complex UI challenges, boost performance, or craft distinctive user experiences.

CHAPTER 5   CUSTOM RENDERING AND PAINTING

Reflectly—Emotional Design Through CustomPainter Overview:

> Reflectly, a journaling app designed to help users manage their mental well-being, is renowned for its friendly, animated, and emotion-driven UI. Much of its design appeal stems from the creative use of Flutter's rendering layer.

Custom Rendering Strategy:

> Employed "CustomPainter" to draw animated blob shapes, gradient transitions, and abstract backgrounds
>
> Used "Path" and "Canvas.drawPath()" for creating smooth, organic shapes
>
> Applied "ShaderMask" to overlay gradients and glow effects
>
> Leveraged animation controllers and curve tweens for seamless transitions

Results:

> Delivered a visually fluid and distinctive app experience
>
> Maintained high rendering performance across devices with optimized "RepaintBoundary" usage
>
> Showcased Flutter's ability to produce expressive, animated UIs using minimal code

CHAPTER 5   CUSTOM RENDERING AND PAINTING

Nubank—Real-Time Financial Dashboards
Overview:

As one of the leading digital banks in Latin America, Nubank uses Flutter in parts of its application to deliver fast, interactive user interfaces, particularly in onboarding flows and internal analytics dashboards.

Custom Rendering Strategy:

Built real-time graphs using "CustomPainter," capable of updating live from streamed data sources

Integrated custom "RenderBox"-based widgets for advanced layout control of graphs and UI overlays

Employed optimized painting logic to draw only updated chart sections, minimizing repaint costs

Results:

Enabled high-frequency data visualization with minimal performance overhead

Enhanced user interactivity through smooth animations and UI responsiveness

Demonstrated that Flutter is viable for complex, enterprise-grade dashboards

Supernova IDE—Live UI Editor with RenderObject-Based Rendering
Overview:

Supernova IDE leverages Flutter internally to create a real-time WYSIWYG UI editor, capable of showing live previews of Flutter code alongside design panels.

Chapter 5 Custom Rendering and Painting

Custom Rendering Strategy:

Developed a custom "RenderObject" layout system to reflect widget trees and UI updates in real time

Used "Layer" compositing and "PaintingContext" for precise control over rendering flow

Integrated shaders and highlight overlays to show real-time changes with visual cues

Results:

Achieved sub-50ms updates across property changes in preview mode

Enabled real-time collaboration and editing inside the design system

Validated Flutter's rendering engine as suitable for performance-critical design tools

Insight and Summary

These implementations share common themes.

Implementation	Technique Used	Impact
Reflectly	`CustomPainter` + `ShaderMask`	Unique UI, smooth animations, high visual fidelity
Nubank	Real-time `CustomPainter` + `RenderBox`	Financial dashboards with real-time interactivity
Supernova IDE	`RenderObject` + `Layer` + Shader Effects	Design tooling with instant visual feedback

Figure 5-1. Common themes

These examples prove that Flutter's rendering stack can power applications that require more than just standard widgets. Whether it's emotional UI design, interactive data visualization, or live editing environments, Flutter provides the building blocks for world-class rendering performance and customization.

Analysis of Popular Apps

To further illustrate the real-world impact of Flutter's custom rendering and painting capabilities, this section analyzes several widely used apps developed with Flutter. These apps leverage advanced rendering techniques—such as CustomPainter, RenderObject, shaders, and GPU acceleration—to deliver highly performant, immersive, and visually compelling user experiences.

BMW—My BMW App
Overview:

> BMW's mobile companion app, developed with Flutter, integrates complex visuals such as 3D car models, live status dashboards, and real-time vehicle interactions.

Rendering Strategies:

> **Impeller Integration:** Uses Flutter's new Impeller rendering engine for smoother transitions and efficient GPU usage
>
> **Gesture-Driven UI**: Renders interactive 3D car models using custom shaders and transformation matrices
>
> **Performance Optimizations**: Reduces overdraw and leverages RepaintBoundary and scene culling for optimal rendering.

Result:

Achieves a native-like user experience with advanced graphics on both Android and iOS, demonstrating Flutter's maturity in premium automotive applications

Alibaba Xianyu—Dynamic Ecommerce UI
Overview:

Alibaba's Xianyu app features highly interactive product carousels, layered interfaces, and dynamic scrolling effects.

Rendering Strategies:

Custom Layouts: Utilizes RenderBox and custom layout delegates to implement asymmetric grids and parallax effects

Smooth Animations: Incorporates CustomPainter to render product frames and decorative effects during interactions

Layered Painting: Uses z-axis layering to simulate depth and highlight transitions

Result:

Creates a modern, fluid shopping experience with exceptional animation performance, even on mid-range devices

Google Stadia Companion App
Overview:

While Stadia has sunset, its companion app provided key insights into performance monitoring and real-time UI feedback.

CHAPTER 5   CUSTOM RENDERING AND PAINTING

Rendering Strategies:

Real-Time Graphs: Leveraged CustomPaint and Canvas.drawPath() to render live latency graphs and performance indicators

Animated Visual Feedback: Used AnimationController to smoothly update charts during gaming sessions.

Efficient Redraw Zones: Implemented redraw isolation using RepaintBoundary to optimize paint calls

Result:

Delivered high-refresh-rate UI updates with real-time metrics, providing valuable live performance data to users

Google Ads App

Overview:

The Google Ads mobile app provides marketing professionals with insights into their ad performance in real time.

Rendering Strategies:

Custom Dashboards: Renders dynamic pie charts, line graphs, and bar visualizations using CustomPainter

Live Updates: Utilizes streamed data updates for interactive performance tracking

Micro-optimizations: Employs manual paint optimization and deferred compositing to preserve 60 FPS performance

Result:

Enables powerful analytics in a compact interface with responsive, touch-friendly data visualization

Tencent Now Live
Overview:

This live-streaming app from Tencent incorporates dynamic overlays, animations, and viewer interactions in real time.

Rendering Strategies:

Live Overlays: Uses CustomPaint and GPU shaders for hearts, coins, and effects over live video

Shader Effects: Implements Flutter-compatible shader logic via Impeller for lighting and glow effects

Asynchronous Rendering: Decouples animation frame updates from backend stream data to prevent lag.

Result:

Provides a highly interactive user experience at 60 FPS, with no performance drop during peak engagement moments

🔍 Summary Table

App	Key Technique	Use Case	Result
BMW App	Shaders + Impeller + Custom Transforms	3D car model viewer	High-performance automotive UI
Alibaba Xianyu	Custom Layout + Painter + Parallax	Product carousels and scroll effects	Fluid, dynamic e-commerce UX
Google Stadia App	Real-Time CustomPainter + Animation	Latency and performance graphs	Live updates at high frame rates
Google Ads App	Custom Dashboards + Live Data	Marketing analytics UI	Interactive, low-latency data visualizations
Tencent Now Live	Shaders + CustomPainter + Impeller	Animated stream overlays	Rich, real-time interactivity at scale

Figure 5-2. Table

Key Takeaways

Custom rendering unlocks UI freedom that goes far beyond what traditional widgets can provide.

Impeller and shaders are revolutionizing the rendering experience by offloading work to the GPU and enabling cinematic effects.

Flutter is battle-tested in high-performance, real-time environments, from financial apps to ecommerce to live video.

These applications reflect the cutting edge of Flutter's rendering capabilities. They demonstrate that with the right architecture and performance strategies, Flutter can deliver stunning, platform-native experiences at scale—even in graphics-intensive or real-time domains.

CHAPTER 5   CUSTOM RENDERING AND PAINTING

Summary

Here, we explored the depths of Flutter's rendering engine, focusing on how developers can go beyond the limitations of standard widgets to create truly custom, high-performance user interfaces. Beginning with low-level RenderObject techniques, we examined how to build custom layout and painting logic tailored to specific UI requirements. The chapter then introduced efficient strategies for layout computation and painting, leveraging Flutter's updated APIs, shaders, and the Impeller rendering engine to maximize performance.

We also delved into the implementation of custom paint operations, optimizing them for real-time interactivity and visual fidelity. Advanced topics such as GPU-accelerated shaders and real-time rendering techniques demonstrated Flutter's capability to handle demanding graphical workloads. Finally, case studies of successful apps showcased how industry leaders are already using these techniques to deliver cutting-edge experiences.

CHAPTER 6

Integration with Native Code

In the previous chapter, we explored the depths of Flutter's rendering engine, learning how to build high-performance custom UI elements using advanced RenderObject techniques, optimized layout strategies, shader effects, and real-time rendering. You discovered how to bypass traditional widgets to gain fine-grained control over the paint pipeline, enabling stunning custom visuals and fluid animations. With these low-level rendering capabilities now in your toolbox, the next frontier is unlocking the full power of platform-specific features through native code integration.

Here we focus on bridging the gap between Dart and the native world. While Flutter offers a robust cross-platform development experience, there are times when you need to access features and services only available on native platforms—such as sensors, biometric authentication, native video processing, or platform SDKs. Flutter 3.29 has significantly enhanced its Platform Channels, plugin architecture, and native communication models, making these integrations more seamless, performant, and secure than ever before.

We begin by examining the latest updates to Platform Channels, highlighting new communication patterns, serialization improvements, and asynchronous handling. You'll learn advanced messaging techniques and how to architect a channel layer that's scalable and resilient.

CHAPTER 6   INTEGRATION WITH NATIVE CODE

From there, we dive into modern plugin development, where you'll learn to build reusable, cross-platform plugins using federated architectures. You'll master integration, testing, debugging, and security practices that elevate plugin reliability and maintainability. Real-world examples and case studies will help you navigate the nuances of writing production-grade plugins.

Security is paramount when bridging two runtimes. We'll cover advanced encryption, secure storage options, and native-side protections to ensure that your app remains safe even when deeply embedded in platform-level code.

Finally, we'll address the performance side of native integration. You'll discover how to measure, profile, and optimize plugin performance—critical when dealing with large datasets, media processing, or real-time systems.

By the end of this chapter, you'll have complete mastery over Flutter's native interop capabilities, enabling you to create hybrid apps that combine the best of both worlds: Flutter's expressive UI layer and the raw power of native APIs.

New Features in Platform Channels

Flutter's platform channels enable seamless interoperability between Dart and native code, serving as the foundational bridge to access platform-specific APIs and capabilities. With the release of Flutter 3.29, significant enhancements have been introduced to make platform communication more powerful, robust, and developer-friendly. These updates include advanced serialization capabilities, modular design improvements, and better tooling support—each aimed at facilitating more scalable and maintainable native integrations.

This section highlights the most impactful improvements and how they empower developers to create sophisticated native features using Dart.

Overview of Platform Channel Enhancements

Platform Channels are a cornerstone of Flutter's interoperability model, enabling Dart code to interact with native APIs and libraries on Android, iOS, web, desktop, and embedded platforms. With the release of Flutter 3.29, Platform Channels have been significantly enhanced to address scalability, reliability, and developer productivity. This subsection provides an overview of the latest improvements and their impact on real-world native integrations.

1. **Typed Message Support and Custom Codecs**

    One of the most notable improvements in Flutter 3.29 is the expanded support for custom codecs and typed message handling. While the "StandardMessageCodec," "JSONMessageCodec," and "BinaryCodec" have been standard tools for serializing data between Dart and native code, the new release provides

    Custom codecs with type mapping, enabling direct mapping of Dart model classes to native data structures (e.g., Kotlin data classes or Swift structs)

    Improved deserialization performance, particularly for large or complex nested objects

    Automatic null safety compliance, with robust handling of optional and nullable fields across languages

These enhancements result in cleaner, more maintainable code and reduce the risk of runtime serialization errors.

2. **Modular Channel Design and Federated Plugin Support**

   Flutter 3.29 aligns with modern plugin architecture by promoting federated plugins and modular channel structures. Each platform implementation (Android, iOS, web, etc.) can now reside in its own package while sharing a common Dart interface.

   For example, a plugin like "flutter_camera" might be split into

   "flutter_camera_platform_interface" (pure Dart interface)

   "flutter_camera_android"

   "flutter_camera_ios"

   "flutter_camera_web"

   Each implementation defines its own "MethodChannel," providing better separation of concerns and easier maintenance, testing, and contribution across teams.

3. **Enhanced Performance in Binary Messenger Layer**

   The underlying "BinaryMessenger," which handles message transport, has been optimized to deliver lower latency, reduced message overhead, and better concurrency. This includes

Optimized byte buffer allocation and recycling

Batched message delivery under the hood for high-frequency communications

Smarter scheduling of message dispatch across isolates and threads

For apps relying on frequent native communication—such as sensor-heavy, multimedia, or IoT (Internet of Things) apps—these enhancements translate into measurable performance gains.

4. **Improved DevTools Integration and Channel Inspection**

    Flutter DevTools in 3.29 now includes advanced Platform Channel inspection capabilities. Developers can

    View live message payloads and decode binary data.

    Monitor call/response timings to identify latency bottlenecks.

    Filter and trace messages based on channel name, method name, or message size.

    Debug unresponsive channel calls with contextual stack traces.

    This level of visibility empowers developers to debug platform interop issues far more efficiently than before.

CHAPTER 6   INTEGRATION WITH NATIVE CODE

5. **Template and Scaffold Improvements**

   To streamline development, Flutter 3.29 ships with updated plugin and platform channel templates that reflect best practices. New templates include

   Null-safe Dart bindings with fallback detection

   Kotlin and Swift-first native scaffolds

   Pre-wired examples using "MethodChannel," "EventChannel," and custom codecs

   Web platform support via JavaScript interop using "js_util" and "allowInterop"

   These templates help accelerate plugin development and lower the learning curve for new contributors.

6. **Backward Compatibility and Migration Notes**

   Despite the new features, Flutter maintains backward compatibility with existing platform channel implementations. Developers can gradually adopt newer codecs, modular structures, or DevTools support without breaking older plugins or apps.

   A migration guide is provided to help teams transition:

   Legacy codecs to custom strongly typed codecs

   Monolithic plugin design to federated structures

   Manual message serialization to typed models with code generation

Flutter 3.29's enhancements to Platform Channels represent a major step forward in native interoperability. By improving type safety, performance, tooling, and modular design, Flutter empowers developers to create native integrations that are as powerful and polished as the rest of the Flutter framework. Whether building custom plugins or bridging to native services, these updates make Platform Channels more reliable, efficient, and developer-friendly than ever before.

Advanced Communication Techniques

While Platform Channels offer a standard method for Dart-native communication, modern app architectures often demand more sophisticated patterns beyond basic method calls. Flutter 3.29 introduces several enhancements and encourages advanced communication techniques to support real-time data streams, background processes, multi-layered architecture, and seamless bidirectional messaging.

This subsection explores advanced techniques that leverage the full potential of Platform Channels and the underlying messaging infrastructure.

1. **Bidirectional Communication**

    In many real-world scenarios, it's not enough for Dart to simply call native methods—native code must also send data back to Dart. Flutter 3.29 enables asynchronous, bidirectional communication through these strategies:

Callbacks via MethodChannel:

Native code can invoke Dart methods by holding a reference to a "MethodChannel" and calling "invokeMethod" on it. This allows Android or iOS to send results, notifications, or state updates without waiting for Dart to initiate the interaction.

Here's an example of iOS sending battery status to Dart:

```
methodChannel.invokeMethod("batteryStatusChanged",
arguments: ["level": 78])
```

On the Dart side:

```
methodChannel.setMethodCallHandler((call) {
   if (call.method == 'batteryStatusChanged') {
     final level = call.arguments['level'];
     // Update UI
   }
});
```

EventChannel for Continuous Streams:

When continuous data streams are required (e.g., GPS updates, sensor data, network events), use "EventChannel." Dart listens to a "Stream," and the native platform pushes values asynchronously.

CHAPTER 6   INTEGRATION WITH NATIVE CODE

2. **Multi-channel Architecture for Separation of Concerns**

   As an app scales, managing all interop communication through a single channel becomes unmanageable. A multi-channel architecture divides responsibilities across specific channels, each mapped to a domain or module:

   ```
   final MethodChannel authChannel = MethodChannel('app/auth');
   final MethodChannel deviceChannel = MethodChannel('app/device');
   final MethodChannel analyticsChannel = MethodChannel('app/analytics');
   ```

   This promotes modularity, improves testability, and avoids method name collisions. Each native handler only processes relevant method calls, following clean architecture principles.

3. **Custom Codecs for Complex Data Structures**

   Standard codecs (e.g., "StandardMessageCodec," "JSONMessageCodec") are not always efficient for transmitting complex or binary-heavy data such as images, encrypted blobs, or deeply nested objects.

   Flutter 3.29 supports custom codecs, allowing serialization and deserialization tailored to your domain models.

   Implement a custom codec by extending "MethodCodec" or "MessageCodec."

Use platform-native serialization libraries like "Gson" (Android) or "Codable" (Swift) to mirror Dart data structures.

This technique ensures better performance, especially when dealing with real-time or large-volume data exchange.

4. **Background Communication Patterns**

   Some interactions must occur even when the Flutter UI is not active—for example, location updates or file uploads in the background.

   Android: Leverage "WorkManager," "ForegroundService," or "BroadcastReceiver" to capture events and communicate with Flutter via "BinaryMessenger," waking up Dart isolates when needed.

   iOS: Use background modes like "background fetch," "audio," or "location," and relay events using "FlutterEngine" + "MethodChannel" or "EventChannel."

   Flutter 3.29 improves engine lifecycle management and isolates spawning, making it easier to handle communication from background services.

5. **Efficient Error Propagation and Result Handling**

   Instead of simple success/failure flags, Flutter 3.29 encourages structured error reporting between Dart and native code.

   Errors can include

   A code ("String") to classify the error type

CHAPTER 6   INTEGRATION WITH NATIVE CODE

A message ("String") for human readability

A details object ("Map<String, dynamic>") for advanced diagnostics

Here's an example of sending a structured error from native (Android):

```
result.error("network_error", "No connection available", mapOf("retryAfter" to 5000))
```

Handling in Dart:

```
try {
  await channel.invokeMethod('fetchData');
} on PlatformException catch (e) {
  if (e.code == 'network_error') {
    // Show retry message or fallback
  }
}
```

This allows more nuanced control over how failures are handled and reported in the app.

6. **Native Dispatch Routing and Service Layering**

Rather than handling every method call in a flat handler function, native platforms can use dispatch routing to delegate logic to separate service classes.

429

Here's a Kotlin example:

```kotlin
when (call.method) {
  "login" -> authService.login(call)
  "logout" -> authService.logout(call)
  "trackEvent" -> analyticsService.track(call)
}
```

This structure ensures cleaner code, better testing, and easier debugging.

7. **Threading and UI Responsiveness**

    Long-running operations (e.g., database access, network calls) must not block the main thread on either the Dart or native side.

    > **Dart**: Use "async/await" and isolate-based concurrency for compute-heavy tasks.

    > **Android**: Use coroutines with "Dispatchers.IO" for background operations.

    > **iOS**: Use "DispatchQueue.global(qos: .background)" for async execution.

    Flutter 3.29's improvements to isolate communication make it easier to receive responses in Dart without UI jank.

    Advanced communication techniques in Flutter 3.29 open new doors for developers to build dynamic, high-performance apps that blend Flutter UI with deep native capabilities. Whether you need real-time sensor data, background processing,

CHAPTER 6 INTEGRATION WITH NATIVE CODE

or custom data transport, the framework now provides robust, scalable tools to meet your needs. Mastering these patterns ensures your apps are not only functional but also architecturally sound and future-proof.

Managing Asynchronous Communication

Modern mobile and web applications frequently deal with asynchronous operations—from fetching data and handling real-time updates to responding to native platform events in the background. In Flutter, managing asynchronous communication between Dart and native code is a critical part of creating responsive, non-blocking user experiences.

With Flutter 3.29, the framework offers enhanced capabilities for asynchronous communication via MethodChannels, EventChannels, BinaryMessengers, and isolates—along with platform-specific support on Android (e.g., coroutines) and iOS (e.g., Grand Central Dispatch (GCD)). This section explores techniques and examples for efficient, scalable, and reliable asynchronous interop.

Techniques for Asynchronous Communication

Managing asynchronous communication between Dart and native platforms is essential in building responsive, real-world applications. Asynchronous patterns are especially relevant in scenarios like device sensor updates, network requests, file I/O, background services, and long-running native tasks. Flutter 3.29 introduces refinements that make handling asynchronous operations across the Dart–native boundary more structured, efficient, and developer-friendly.

431

CHAPTER 6   INTEGRATION WITH NATIVE CODE

This section outlines the key techniques and patterns for robust asynchronous interop.

1. **Futures with "MethodChannel"**

    The most common pattern for invoking asynchronous native methods is using "MethodChannel" with Dart's "Future"-based API. This allows the Dart thread to remain unblocked while the native platform completes its operation.

    Dart:

    ```
    Future<String> getDeviceId() async {
        final String deviceId = await platform.invokeMethod('getDeviceId');
        return deviceId;
    }
    ```

    Android (Kotlin):

    ```
    if (call.method == "getDeviceId") {
        result.success(getSecureDeviceId())
    }
    ```

    Use this pattern when
    The native task is non-blocking or completes quickly.
    The result is returned once, without needing updates.

CHAPTER 6　INTEGRATION WITH NATIVE CODE

2. **Stream-Based Communication with "EventChannel"**

   For continuous or periodic data from native to Dart (e.g., GPS, gyroscope, connectivity), "EventChannel" enables Dart to subscribe to a stream of events asynchronously.

   Dart:

   ```
   Stream<int> get sensorStream =>
     const EventChannel('sensors/gyroscope').receive
     BroadcastStream().cast<int>();
   ```

   Android (Kotlin):

   ```
   eventChannel.setStreamHandler(object : EventChannel.
   StreamHandler {
       override fun onListen(args: Any?, events:
       EventChannel.EventSink) {
           sensorManager.registerListener(gyroListener,
           sensor, SensorManager.SENSOR_DELAY_UI)
       }
       override fun onCancel(args: Any?) {
           sensorManager.unregisterListener(gyroListener)
       }
   })
   ```

433

CHAPTER 6   INTEGRATION WITH NATIVE CODE

This is ideal for

Real-time updates (location, orientation, health data)

Observables from system broadcasts

3. **Two-Way Messaging with "BasicMessageChannel"**

    "BasicMessageChannel" provides bidirectional communication using custom codecs and arbitrary message formats. It's best for building full-duplex channels with conversational state or custom data structures.

    Dart:

    ```
    final BasicMessageChannel<String> messageChannel =
      BasicMessageChannel('channel/chat', StringCodec());

    void sendMessage(String message) {
      messageChannel.send(message);
    }

    messageChannel.setMessageHandler((msg) async {
      print('Native response: $msg');
    });
    ```

    Use cases include

    Chat applications

    Command-based control interfaces

    Protocol-like interactions with native layers

4. **Background Communication Techniques**

   Some native operations occur outside the app's foreground UI, requiring background execution:

   Android: Use "ForegroundService," "WorkManager," or "JobScheduler" for uploads, downloads, or sync tasks.

   iOS: Use background modes (e.g., location, audio, fetch) with proper "FlutterEngine" management.

   To bridge background operations with Dart

   Prewarm a "FlutterEngine."

   Use "BinaryMessenger" to invoke Dart callbacks or events.

   Maintain communication via stored "MethodChannel" instances.

   Best Practice: Initialize and cache Flutter engine early, and ensure it's correctly disposed after background tasks complete.

5. **Isolates for Concurrent Dart Execution**

   If heavy processing must be done in Dart (e.g., decoding, encryption), isolates offer a way to run code concurrently without blocking the main UI thread.

Dart:

```
final result = await compute(processData, large
DataSet);
```

This helps in offloading expensive logic, particularly when paired with results from native channels.

6. **Timeouts and Exception Safety**

   All async operations should be wrapped with error handling and timeouts to ensure resilience.

   ```
   try {
     final result = await platform.invokeMethod
     ('fetchInfo').timeout(Duration(seconds: 5));
   } on TimeoutException {
     print('Native call timed out');
   }
   ```

   Key patterns include the following:

   Use "try/catch" for platform exceptions.

   Detect offline or disconnected states before native interaction.

   Provide fallback UI or retry logic in the app.

7. **Native Threading and Concurrency**

   On the native side, avoid executing heavy operations on the main thread:

Android: Use coroutines ("Dispatchers.IO") for async.

iOS: Use GCD ("DispatchQueue.global") or "NSOperationQueue."

Android Coroutine Example:

```
CoroutineScope(Dispatchers.IO).launch {
    val data = fetchData()
    withContext(Dispatchers.Main) {
        result.success(data)
    }
}
```

Proper threading ensures smooth UI and responsive behavior, especially during expensive operations like network access or database reads.

Asynchronous communication is a cornerstone of Flutter–native integration. Whether you're handling one-time calls, background services, or real-time streams, Flutter 3.29 equips you with powerful tools like "MethodChannel," "EventChannel," "BasicMessageChannel," and isolates. By adopting these best practices, developers can create apps that are not only performant and responsive but also architecturally sound and future-ready.

CHAPTER 6   INTEGRATION WITH NATIVE CODE

Real-World Examples

To solidify your understanding of asynchronous communication techniques in Flutter, this section presents real-world scenarios where Dart–native interop is critical. These examples demonstrate how to effectively combine "MethodChannel," "EventChannel," "BasicMessageChannel," and background processing patterns to deliver robust, high-performance features in production apps.

Example 1: Real-Time Location Tracking in a Delivery App

Use Case: A food delivery app tracks a rider's real-time location to update the customer and restaurant dashboards.

Technique: "EventChannel" for location stream from native to Dart.

Dart: Subscribes to a continuous stream of GPS coordinates.

Native (Android): Uses "FusedLocationProviderClient" to emit location updates.

Native (iOS): Uses "CLLocationManager" with appropriate background mode.

Implementation Highlights:

- Efficient battery usage with location throttling.
- Background-safe with Flutter engine kept alive.
- Stream updates directly modify map widget position.

CHAPTER 6   INTEGRATION WITH NATIVE CODE

Benefits:

Smooth, live tracking experience.

Works even when app is minimized.

Example 2: Fingerprint/Face ID Authentication in a Banking App

Use Case: Secure authentication using biometric methods like face ID or fingerprint.

Technique: "MethodChannel" for initiating a single authentication prompt.

Dart: Calls a method like "authenticateUser()."

Native: Invokes the OS-level biometric prompt and returns result.

iOS: Uses "LocalAuthentication."

Android: Uses "BiometricPrompt."

Implementation Highlights:

Asynchronous handling with "Future" in Dart.

Timeout and exception guards for fallback login.

Uses "PlatformException" to return specific error messages (e.g., user canceled).

Benefits:

Fully native UX.

Tied to device keystore for maximum security.

Example 3: Live Chat with Native SDK Integration

Use Case: A customer support module uses a native SDK (e.g., Zendesk, Intercom) that communicates in real time.

Technique: "BasicMessageChannel" for bidirectional messaging.

Dart: Sends/receives string-encoded chat messages.

Native: Handles SDK integration and event forwarding.

Encapsulation: Uses custom message format (JSON) for message types and metadata.

Implementation Highlights:

Enables real-time chat, typing indicators, and read receipts.

Messages structured as JSON for extensibility.

Streamlines communication between Flutter and third-party native SDKs.

Benefits:

Minimal Dart–native translation overhead.

Flexible for future protocol changes.

Example 4: Background File Upload in a Media App

Use Case: A social media app uploads large video files even if the user leaves the app.

Technique: "MethodChannel" + native background services.

Dart: Initiates the upload process via "MethodChannel."

Android: Uses "WorkManager" or "ForegroundService" for actual upload.

iOS: Uses "URLSession" with background configuration.

Implementation Highlights:

Upload progress communicated via "EventChannel" (Dart receives progress %).

Notifications triggered natively to show user progress/status.

Engine prewarmed in background for callbacks.

Benefits:

Uploads complete even if Flutter is suspended.

Preserves app state and user engagement via local notifications.

Example 5: IoT Device Communication

Use Case: A smart home controller app sends commands and listens to events from connected devices via Bluetooth.

Technique: Hybrid of "MethodChannel," "EventChannel," and "BasicMessageChannel."

Dart: Issues commands ("MethodChannel") and listens to device responses ("EventChannel").

Native: Uses platform BLE libraries to scan, connect, and handle data.

Bidirectional Messaging: Custom protocol used for command/data messages.

Implementation Highlights:

Real-time command-response loop.

CHAPTER 6 INTEGRATION WITH NATIVE CODE

Heartbeat system with "EventChannel" keeps connection alive.

Uses JSON structures for protocol consistency across platforms.

Benefits:

Low-latency command execution.

Fully native BLE reliability.

Seamless integration with Flutter UI.

Example 6: Custom Audio Player with Background Playback

Use Case: A music streaming app implements native audio playback with background support and notifications.

Technique: "MethodChannel" + persistent background service.

Dart: Invokes playback controls (play/pause/seek).

Native: Controls "MediaPlayer" (Android) or "AVAudioPlayer" (iOS).

Events: Song state, position, and playback completion sent via "EventChannel."

Implementation Highlights:

Lockscreen controls handled natively.

Playback remains active during screen off or multitasking.

Isolates used for playback queue and media caching in Dart.

CHAPTER 6   INTEGRATION WITH NATIVE CODE

Benefits:

> Smooth native audio handling.
>
> Battery-optimized playback loop.
>
> UI and state sync with native notifications.

These real-world examples demonstrate that Flutter's asynchronous platform channels are versatile enough for complex use cases involving live streams, biometric security, background services, and third-party SDK integrations. With proper architectural choices—such as isolating background tasks, handling message state, and leveraging the right channel type—you can build high-performance hybrid applications that feel fully native to users while benefiting from Flutter's expressive UI and unified codebase.

Enhanced Plugin Development

As Flutter continues to mature into a production-grade cross-platform framework, the ecosystem's demand for high-quality, maintainable, and secure plugins has significantly increased. With Flutter 3.29, plugin development receives major upgrades that empower developers to write more modern, performant, and platform-aligned plugins with minimal friction.

Here we delve into enhanced plugin development, exploring new tooling improvements, development techniques, testing strategies, and security practices. Whether you're building a public-facing package or an internal SDK for enterprise apps, this section covers how to harness Flutter 3.29's capabilities to their fullest.

CHAPTER 6   INTEGRATION WITH NATIVE CODE

Writing Modern Plugins

Plugin development in Flutter has evolved significantly, and with the release of Flutter 3.29, the process of writing modern, efficient, and platform-compliant plugins has become more streamlined and powerful. This section provides a deep dive into how you can create robust plugins using the latest features, architectural patterns, and platform capabilities.

Modern Flutter plugins are no longer just simple bridges between Dart and platform code. They must be scalable, modular, testable, and maintainable—supporting multiple platforms while adhering to Dart and native best practices. Flutter 3.29 introduces key enhancements that simplify multi-platform development and ensure your plugin can keep pace with the evolving Flutter ecosystem.

Overview of Plugin Development Updates

Flutter 3.29 brings significant advancements in plugin development, empowering developers to create modular, performant, and scalable solutions across multiple platforms. As the ecosystem becomes more mature, plugins are expected to adhere to higher standards in architecture, testing, security, and cross-platform compatibility. This subsection highlights the key updates and architectural changes that define modern plugin development in Flutter 3.29.

1. **Federated Plugin Architecture**

    The federated plugin model, which separates platform-specific implementations from the core plugin interface, is now the recommended approach. This structure provides better modularity, easier testing, and improved flexibility when supporting new platforms.

Core Structure:

"plugin_name": Exposes the public Dart API

"plugin_name_platform_interface": Defines the abstract platform interface

"plugin_name_<platform>": Contains platform-specific implementations (e.g., Android, iOS, macOS)

This architecture allows apps to selectively include only the necessary platform dependencies, improving build performance and maintainability.

2. **Enhanced Platform Support and Standardization**

   Flutter 3.29 improves platform scaffolding with standardized templates and platform-specific enhancements:

   Android:

   Android Gradle Plugin 8.x support

   Java 17 compatibility

   Improved AndroidX integration

   Kotlin-first plugin templates

   iOS/macOS:

   Swift Package Manager (SPM) support

   Full support for Swift concurrency ("async/await") in native code

   Enhanced error bridging between Swift and Dart

Windows/Linux:

CMake enhancements and modular structure

Support for shared native libraries and dynamic linking

Cross-platform build tools and native packaging support

Web:

New JavaScript interop patterns using "@JS()" and Dart's static typing

Improved TypeScript compatibility and code-splitting optimizations

3. **Null Safety and Dart 3.3 Enhancements**

All new plugins are required to be fully null-safe, and Flutter 3.29 takes advantage of new features in Dart 3.3:

Record Types: Greatly simplify platform result and error wrappers

Pattern Matching: Enhances native response parsing and improves readability

Improved FFI Ergonomics: Cleaner bindings to C/C++ libraries using inline structs and function pointers

These updates allow for concise, type-safe, and robust Dart–native communication patterns.

CHAPTER 6   INTEGRATION WITH NATIVE CODE

4. **Plugin Creation Template Enhancements**

   The "flutter create --template=plugin" command now generates a more complete and production-ready scaffold with

   Federated plugin structure

   Platform metadata in "pubspec.yaml"

   Auto-configured testing boilerplate

   Default Swift/Kotlin codebases

   Integration with modern build systems (Gradle, Xcode, CMake)

   This makes it easier for developers to follow best practices from the outset.

5. **Declarative Platform Metadata**

   Flutter plugins can now include detailed metadata in "pubspec.yaml," which helps tools and pub.dev categorize, validate, and optimize plugin usage:

```
flutter:
  plugin:
    platforms:
      android:
        package: com.example.plugin
        pluginClass: ExamplePlugin
      ios:
        pluginClass: ExamplePlugin
      web:
        pluginClass: WebExamplePlugin
        fileName: web_example_plugin.dart
```

This metadata allows for better compatibility checks, IDE support, and conditional logic during runtime.

6. **Better Runtime Platform Handling**

   Flutter 3.29 improves runtime platform checks with

   "Platform.isX" APIs and "defaultTargetPlatform" constants

   More reliable fallback handling across plugins

   Enhanced diagnostics when unsupported platforms are used

   This enables developers to write fail-safe plugins that degrade gracefully when platform support is partial or missing.

Flutter 3.29's plugin development updates emphasize modularity, platform alignment, and robustness. By adopting federated structures, leveraging Dart 3.3 features, and utilizing standardized templates and tooling, developers can now build future-proof plugins that integrate seamlessly across the growing range of supported platforms. These enhancements are critical for writing production-grade plugins that align with the expectations of modern Flutter applications.

Integrating Plugins with Flutter Apps

Integrating a plugin into a Flutter application is a critical step in bridging the gap between high-level Dart code and low-level platform-specific functionality. While Flutter abstracts much of the native platform complexity, seamless plugin integration requires careful configuration, error handling, and adherence to modern practices to ensure cross-platform compatibility and maintainability.

CHAPTER 6   INTEGRATION WITH NATIVE CODE

This section provides a deep dive into how to properly integrate modern Flutter plugins—especially federated plugins—into production-grade Flutter apps, taking full advantage of the latest features in Flutter 3.29.

1. **Declaring Plugin Dependencies**

    Plugins must be properly declared in your app's "pubspec.yaml" to ensure compatibility and control over versions. For third-party or internal plugins, always use semantic versioning (SemVer):

    ```
    dependencies:
      path_provider: ^2.1.0
      custom_plugin:
        git:
          url: https://github.com/your-org/custom_plugin.git
          ref: main
    ```

    When using federated plugins, dependencies must also include the "platform_interface" and specific platform implementations when needed.

2. **Understanding Platform Registration**

    Each plugin uses "PluginRegistrant" code to register itself on the native side. With Flutter 3.29:

    Android: Plugin registration happens via the "GeneratedPluginRegistrant.java" or "PluginRegistry" when using manual registration.

iOS/macOS: Swift-based auto-registration is handled via "GeneratedPluginRegistrant.swift."

Web: Plugins are registered using "registerWith()" in the web implementation.

Make sure plugin registration is not duplicated or omitted, especially in customized app configurations.

3. **Handling Platform Availability Gracefully**

   Since not all plugins support all platforms, it's important to guard against platform-specific runtime errors:

```
import 'dart:io';

if (Platform.isAndroid || Platform.isIOS) {
  await MyPlugin.doSomething();
} else {
  // Provide fallback behavior
  print("Plugin not supported on this platform.");
}
```

   Use platform checks and optional fallback implementations to ensure a consistent user experience across all environments.

4. **Ensuring Asynchronous Communication**

   Many plugin APIs perform asynchronous operations (e.g., accessing hardware, storage, or sensors). Always await calls and handle exceptions properly:

CHAPTER 6   INTEGRATION WITH NATIVE CODE

```
try {
  final result = await MyPlugin.fetchData();
  print("Result: $result");
} on PlatformException catch (e) {
  print("Error: ${e.message}");
}
```

Using "async/await" ensures proper sequencing, especially when chaining plugin calls with UI updates.

5. **Using Federated Plugins in Practice**

    When integrating federated plugins, remember:

    Only the platform interface is required in the base app.

    Platform-specific implementations can be added optionally depending on target platforms.

    Fallbacks can be written for platforms not explicitly supported:

    ```
    MyPluginPlatform.instance =
    MyCustomImplementation(); // Fallback for
    unsupported platform
    ```

    This design enables leaner builds and better platform control.

CHAPTER 6   INTEGRATION WITH NATIVE CODE

6. **Example: Integrating a Camera Plugin**

Here's an example of integrating a federated camera plugin:

```
dependencies:
  camera: ^0.10.5
  camera_platform_interface: ^0.10.0
  camera_android: ^0.10.0
  camera_ios: ^0.10.0
```

In your Dart code:

```
import 'package:camera/camera.dart';

final cameras = await availableCameras();
final firstCamera = cameras.first;

final controller = CameraController(
  firstCamera,
  ResolutionPreset.high,
);
await controller.initialize();
```

This setup ensures you're using the platform-optimized camera implementation while keeping your app logic clean and testable.

CHAPTER 6 INTEGRATION WITH NATIVE CODE

7. **Debugging Integration Issues**

   Here are common integration pitfalls and solutions:

Issue	Solution
Plugin not registered	Check 'GeneratedPluginRegistrant' files and native build configuration.
Missing permissions	Add required entries in 'AndroidManifest.xml' or 'Info.plist'
PlatformException thrown	Check native code logs for stack traces and error codes
Plugin behavior inconsistent	Confirm correct plugin versions and platform compatibility.

Integrating plugins in Flutter 3.29 is more powerful and flexible than ever before. By leveraging federated plugin design, using robust platform checks, and correctly handling asynchronous operations, developers can ensure that plugins work reliably across all platforms. Following best practices for dependency management, exception handling, and modular integration leads to cleaner, maintainable codebases and better user experiences.

Testing and Debugging Plugins

Testing and debugging are essential steps in ensuring the reliability, performance, and security of any Flutter plugin. Since plugins bridge the gap between Flutter's Dart code and native platform code, testing must be performed at both the Dart and native code levels to guarantee that they behave correctly across different environments. This section explores the techniques and tools available for testing Flutter plugins, as well as best practices for debugging both platform-specific and Dart-related issues.

Techniques for Plugin Testing

Testing Flutter plugins is essential to ensure their reliability, performance, and compatibility across various platforms. Given that plugins often interact with both Dart code and native platform-specific functionality, comprehensive testing requires a combination of unit tests, integration tests, and platform-specific testing. Flutter 3.29 introduces several powerful tools and frameworks that help streamline plugin testing while maintaining robustness.

This section delves into various techniques for testing Flutter plugins, covering unit testing, integration testing, platform-specific testing, and performance monitoring.

1. **Unit-Testing Dart Code**

    Unit testing in Flutter focuses on testing the Dart code inside your plugin. This can include the logic that interacts with platform channels, data manipulation, and any other non-native functionality. Unit tests ensure that your plugin's core functionality behaves as expected in isolation, without requiring any actual platform-specific code execution.

    Setup:

    To get started with unit testing in Flutter, you'll need the "flutter_test" package:

```yaml
dev_dependencies:
  flutter_test:
    sdk: flutter
  mockito: ^5.0.0
```

Then, create mock classes to simulate platform channel calls and write unit tests. For instance, here's testing a simple method channel invocation:

```dart
import 'package:flutter/services.dart';
import 'package:mockito/mockito.dart';
import 'package:flutter_test/flutter_test.dart';

// Create a mock class for the platform channel
class MockMethodChannel extends Mock implements MethodChannel {}

void main() {
  TestWidgetsFlutterBinding.ensureInitialized();
  final MockMethodChannel mockChannel = MockMethodChannel();

  test('Test platform method invocation', () async {
    when(mockChannel.invokeMethod('getData')).thenReturn(Future.value('mockData'));

    final result = await mockChannel.invokeMethod('getData');
    expect(result, 'mockData');
  });
}
```

This method allows you to test the communication between the Dart code and the native platform by mocking the platform channel responses, which is especially useful for testing platform channel method invocations and responses.

2. **Integration Testing with Real Device Interactions**

   Integration testing goes a step further by testing the interaction between the Dart code and the native platform code. In Flutter 3.29, the "integration_test" package is now the go-to tool for testing your plugin's integration with real-world scenarios, especially when interacting with native APIs or services.

   Setup:

   To use "integration_test," add it to your "pubspec.yaml" file:

   ```
   dependencies:
     integration_test:
       sdk: flutter
   ```

   You can then create integration tests that simulate real device interactions, testing end-to-end functionality and communication between the Flutter layer and native code:

   ```
   import 'package:integration_test/integration_test.dart';
   import 'package:flutter_test/flutter_test.dart';
   ```

CHAPTER 6 INTEGRATION WITH NATIVE CODE

```
import 'package:flutter_app/main.dart' as app;

void main() {
  IntegrationTestWidgetsFlutterBinding.ensureInitialized();

  testWidgets('Test plugin integration on Android', (tester) async {
    app.main();   // Run your app

    await tester.pumpAndSettle();

    // Test interaction with your plugin
    expect(find.text('Plugin Data'), findsOneWidget);
  });
}
```

These tests can run on physical devices or simulators/emulators, allowing you to validate your plugin's real-world performance and behavior.

3. **Platform-Specific Unit Testing**

   For platform-specific code, testing frameworks like JUnit (Android) or XCTest (iOS) can be used to validate the native functionality of your plugin. Testing native Android and iOS code ensures that the platform-specific implementations of your plugin behave as expected.

   Android Testing:

   For Android, unit tests can be written using JUnit. These tests should focus on the platform-specific logic and ensure that it interacts with the Flutter layer correctly.

CHAPTER 6 INTEGRATION WITH NATIVE CODE

```java
import org.junit.Test;
import static org.junit.Assert.*;

public class PluginTest {
    @Test
    public void testNativeMethod() {
        String result = PluginClass.getNativeData();
        assertEquals("Expected Native Data", result);
    }
}
```

iOS Testing:

On iOS, you can write tests using XCTest, ensuring that the Swift or Objective-C code in your plugin works correctly.

```swift
import XCTest
@testable import MyPlugin

class PluginTests: XCTestCase {
    func testNativeMethod() {
        let result = PluginClass.getNativeData()
        XCTAssertEqual(result, "Expected Native Data")
    }
}
```

By writing these unit tests for native code, you can ensure that platform-specific APIs function as expected before they are called by Flutter.

4. **Mocking Platform-Specific Functionality**

   For testing platform channel communication, mocking native platform responses is a common practice. By using the "mockito" package or custom mock classes, you can simulate different responses from the native side, allowing you to test the Dart side of the plugin independently of the native code.

   ```
   class MockPlatformChannel extends Mock implements MethodChannel {}

   void main() {
     final mockChannel = MockPlatformChannel();

     test('Simulate platform method response', () async {
       when(mockChannel.invokeMethod('getData')).
         thenReturn(Future.value('mockData'));

       final result = await mockChannel.
       invokeMethod('getData');
       expect(result, 'mockData');
     });
   }
   ```

   Mocking ensures that you can test how your Dart code reacts to different platform channel responses (e.g., success, failure, or exceptions) without needing a full platform setup.

CHAPTER 6 INTEGRATION WITH NATIVE CODE

5. **Performance Testing**

Performance is crucial for plugins that deal with native code, such as those that access hardware, sensors, or external services. Flutter 3.29 introduces performance testing tools like the "flutter_driver" package, which allows you to measure the responsiveness and efficiency of your plugin. You can use "flutter_driver" for end-to-end testing to monitor how your plugin performs under load:

```dart
import 'package:flutter_driver/flutter_driver.dart';
import 'package:test/test.dart';

void main() {
  FlutterDriver driver;

  setUpAll(() async {
    driver = await FlutterDriver.connect();
  });

  tearDownAll(() async {
    if (driver != null) {
      await driver.close();
    }
  });

  test('Plugin performance test', () async {
    final startTime = DateTime.now();

    // Trigger your plugin method
    await driver.tap(find.byValueKey('startButton'));

    final endTime = DateTime.now();
    final duration = endTime.difference(startTime);
```

```
    print('Plugin response time: $duration');
    expect(duration.inMilliseconds, lessThan(500));
  });
}
```

This helps measure the performance of plugin interactions and provides insights into how it might impact your app's responsiveness.

Testing Flutter plugins requires a multi-layered approach that includes unit testing, integration testing, platform-specific testing, and performance evaluations. By leveraging Flutter's testing framework, mocking tools like "mockito," and platform-specific testing frameworks, developers can ensure their plugins are robust, performant, and ready for production. Additionally, focusing on performance testing helps to avoid bottlenecks, particularly for plugins that interact with native resources.

Case Studies and Best Practices

In this section, we explore some real-world case studies and outline best practices for testing and debugging Flutter plugins. These examples are based on popular plugins in the Flutter ecosystem and will demonstrate the techniques discussed earlier, providing insights into how testing can be effectively integrated into plugin development.

1. **Case Study: Firebase Plugin**

    The Firebase Plugin for Flutter is one of the most widely used plugins, offering integration with Firebase services such as Firestore, Firebase Authentication, and Firebase Messaging. The plugin has a comprehensive testing strategy that addresses both Dart and native code.

CHAPTER 6 INTEGRATION WITH NATIVE CODE

Unit-Testing Dart Code:

Firebase's Dart code, which includes functions for interacting with Firebase services, is extensively unit-tested. The tests focus on the correctness of data handling, such as ensuring that the data retrieved from Firestore is properly formatted and parsed before being sent to the app.

Mocking Firebase Methods: Firebase uses mock classes to simulate interactions with Firebase services without needing to access real cloud resources. This is especially helpful when testing features like authentication or data retrieval.

```
import 'package:flutter/services.dart';
import 'package:mockito/mockito.dart';
import 'package:flutter_test/flutter_test.dart';

class MockFirebaseAuthChannel extends Mock implements MethodChannel {}

void main() {
  final mockChannel = MockFirebaseAuthChannel();

  test('Firebase Auth mock test', () async {
    when(mockChannel.invokeMethod('signIn', {'email':
    'test@example.com'}))
        .thenReturn(Future.value({'user': 'mockUser'}));
```

```
    final result = await mockChannel.invokeMethod
    ('signIn', {'email': 'test@example.com'});
    expect(result['user'], 'mockUser');
  });
}
```

Integration Testing:

Firebase performs integration tests across both iOS and Android. For example, Firebase's authentication methods are tested on real devices to verify the entire authentication flow, including user login and session persistence.

Testing Across Platforms: Firebase uses both the "integration_test" and "flutter_driver" packages to run end-to-end tests on both iOS and Android, ensuring that the Flutter app interacts correctly with Firebase services, including background messaging and data synchronization.

Platform-Specific Unit Testing:

Firebase's platform-specific code (e.g., Android's use of the Firebase SDK) is tested using native testing frameworks like JUnit for Android and XCTest for iOS. These tests ensure that Firebase's native components behave correctly before integrating them with Flutter.

2. **Case Study: Camera Plugin**

The Camera Plugin is another commonly used plugin in Flutter applications, providing access to the camera hardware for taking pictures and videos.

This plugin requires deep integration with native platform APIs and must be thoroughly tested.

Unit-Testing Dart Code:

The Camera Plugin's Dart code focuses on configuring the camera, setting resolutions, and handling user preferences. The unit tests verify that these configurations are correctly applied and that camera-related methods return the expected results.

Integration Testing:

For integration testing, the Camera Plugin performs end-to-end tests where the plugin's functionality is verified in a real app. These tests simulate taking photos, recording videos, and verifying the correct behavior of camera settings.

Real Device Testing: Since the Camera Plugin interacts with hardware, real devices (not just simulators or emulators) are essential for thorough testing. Firebase Test Lab or device farms are often used to test the plugin across different physical devices.

```dart
import 'package:flutter_driver/flutter_driver.dart';
import 'package:test/test.dart';

void main() {
  FlutterDriver driver;

  setUpAll(() async {
    driver = await FlutterDriver.connect();
```

```
    });

    tearDownAll(() async {
      if (driver != null) {
        await driver.close();
      }
    });

    test('Camera plugin integration test', () async {
      final cameraButton = find.byValueKey('camera_
      button');
      await driver.tap(cameraButton);

      // Simulate capturing a photo
      final capturedImage = await driver.waitFor(find.by
      ValueKey('captured_image'));
      expect(capturedImage, isNotNull);
    });
}
```

Native Testing:

Platform-specific code in the Camera Plugin is tested on both Android and iOS using their respective testing frameworks.

Android (JUnit): Tests ensure that camera-related APIs, such as "Camera.open()," return valid objects and handle errors gracefully.

iOS (XCTest): XCTest ensures that the camera interface is functional, the permissions are correctly handled, and the captured media is stored as expected.

3. **Best Practices for Plugin Testing and Debugging**

   Based on these case studies and other successful plugin implementations, the following best practices for plugin testing and debugging can be summarized:

   1. **Mock Platform Channels for Unit Testing:**

      Mocking platform channels using packages like "mockito" is a key technique for unit-testing the Dart code in your plugin. This helps isolate and test the logic without needing actual native code to run.

      Best Practice: Create mock channel implementations for all method channels your plugin uses, simulating both success and failure scenarios.

   2. **Test Across Multiple Devices:**

      Testing on various devices and emulators is critical to ensure that your plugin works across different screen sizes, OS versions, and hardware configurations. Flutter's integration testing framework makes it easy to set up and run these tests across devices.

      Best Practice: Use services like Firebase Test Lab or AWS Device Farm to test your plugin on a wide variety of devices and configurations.

CHAPTER 6   INTEGRATION WITH NATIVE CODE

3. **Use Verbose Logging for Debugging:**

   Verbose logging is an effective debugging technique, especially when working with platform channels and native code. By logging both the Dart side and native side, you can trace the flow of data and identify where issues occur.

   Best Practice: Implement logging at key points in both the Dart code and the native platform code. Tools like Flutter DevTools can also help visualize logs and track errors.

4. **Leverage Native Testing Frameworks:**

   For platform-specific code, always write unit tests for your Android and iOS code using JUnit and XCTest, respectively. This ensures that native code interacts correctly with the Flutter side and adheres to platform-specific conventions.

   Best Practice: Write tests for the native Android/iOS APIs your plugin uses, and test these components in isolation before integrating them with Flutter.

5. **Continuous Integration and Automated Testing:**

   Automated testing should be part of your plugin's CI/CD pipeline. Tools like GitHub Actions, Travis CI, or CircleCI can automatically run tests every time code is pushed to the repository, ensuring that your plugin remains functional over time.

> **Best Practice**: Set up automated tests for unit tests, integration tests, and platform-specific tests to catch regressions early.

Testing and debugging are fundamental aspects of plugin development. By following best practices and leveraging the latest tools, such as "integration_test," "flutter_driver," and mocking frameworks like "mockito," you can ensure that your plugin is reliable, performant, and secure. The case studies from Firebase and Camera plugins showcase effective strategies for both Dart and native testing. Incorporating these strategies into your workflow will help you build high-quality, well-tested plugins that work seamlessly across platforms.

Security Best Practices for Plugins

Security is one of the most crucial aspects of Flutter plugin development, particularly when the plugin interacts with sensitive data, performs authentication, or accesses device resources. With the increasing number of security vulnerabilities in mobile and web applications, ensuring that your plugin adheres to the highest security standards is essential for protecting user data and maintaining trust.

Here, we explore the security best practices you should follow when developing Flutter plugins, focusing on securing communication between the Flutter layer and native code, protecting sensitive data, and ensuring platform-level security compliance.

1. **Secure Communication with Platform Channels**

    Since Flutter plugins often communicate with native platform code via platform channels, it's essential to secure the data being exchanged. Although platform channels are a powerful way to

CHAPTER 6 INTEGRATION WITH NATIVE CODE

enable communication between Flutter and native code, they can be vulnerable if sensitive data is transmitted insecurely.

Encryption of Data in Transit:

When transmitting sensitive data between Dart and native code, use encryption to ensure that data cannot be intercepted by malicious actors. This is especially important when dealing with user credentials, authentication tokens, or any other personally identifiable information (PII).

Best Practice: Always encrypt sensitive data before sending it via platform channels and decrypt it on the native side. Use established encryption algorithms like AES (Advanced Encryption Standard) for encrypting the data.

Example:

```
import 'package:encrypt/encrypt.dart' as encrypt;

final key = encrypt.Key.fromUtf8('32characterslongkeyforencryption');
final iv = encrypt.IV.fromLength(16);

final encrypter = encrypt.Encrypter(encrypt.AES(key));
final encrypted = encrypter.encrypt('Sensitive Data', iv: iv);
final encryptedData = encrypted.base64;
```

CHAPTER 6 INTEGRATION WITH NATIVE CODE

Ensure that similar encryption is done on the native side (e.g., using Java's "Cipher" class for Android or the "Crypto" library for iOS).

Secure Communication on Android and iOS:

On the Android and iOS side, make sure that you are using secure communication protocols when interacting with external services. Always use HTTPS for network communication and avoid using outdated or insecure protocols like HTTP or FTP.

Best Practice: For Android, use "HTTPS" and enable SSL pinning to protect against man-in-the-middle (MITM) attacks. On iOS, ensure that the app supports App Transport Security (ATS) for secure networking.

2. **Secure Storage of Sensitive Information**

   Storing sensitive data on the device requires extra care. Never store sensitive information such as passwords, API keys, or authentication tokens in plain text, especially in areas like "SharedPreferences" or "UserDefaults" that can easily be accessed by other apps or compromised in the event of a device breach.

   Using Secure Storage for Sensitive Data:

   Both Android and iOS provide secure storage mechanisms for safely storing sensitive information. On Android, you can use the Keystore system, and on iOS, you can use the Keychain for secure storage.

CHAPTER 6   INTEGRATION WITH NATIVE CODE

For Flutter, use the "flutter_secure_storage" plugin to handle secure storage across platforms.

```
import 'package:flutter_secure_storage/flutter_secure_storage.dart';

final storage = FlutterSecureStorage();

// Save data securely
await storage.write(key: 'userToken', value: 'your_secure_token');

// Read data securely
String token = await storage.read(key: 'userToken');
```

By using secure storage APIs, sensitive data is stored in an encrypted format and is inaccessible to unauthorized processes, enhancing your plugin's overall security.

3. **Preventing Insecure Code and Reverse Engineering**

   Reverse engineering is a common threat to mobile applications, including Flutter plugins. Attackers often decompile APKs (Android) or IPA files (iOS) to analyze the app and extract sensitive information, such as encryption keys, hardcoded passwords, or API tokens.

Obfuscation:

To protect against reverse engineering, always obfuscate your Dart code and native code. Obfuscation helps by making it harder for attackers to understand the app's logic and extract valuable information.

Best Practice: Enable Dart code obfuscation by adding the following to your "flutter build" command:

```
flutter build apk --obfuscate --split-debug-info=/<project-name>/debug-info
```

This will obfuscate your Dart code and store the debug symbols in a separate location, making it more difficult for attackers to reverse engineer your app.

Native Code Protection:

For native code, both Android and iOS provide methods to protect against reverse engineering. On Android, use ProGuard or R8 to obfuscate and shrink your Java/Kotlin code, while on iOS, you can use bitcode and strip unnecessary symbols from the release build.

Best Practice: In Android, configure ProGuard (or R8) rules in your "build.gradle" file to obfuscate the native code.

CHAPTER 6 INTEGRATION WITH NATIVE CODE

```
buildTypes {
    release {
        minifyEnabled true
        shrinkResources true
        proguardFiles getDefaultProguardFile('proguard-
        android-optimize.txt'), 'proguard-rules.pro'
    }
}
```

For iOS, configure the build settings to strip debug information and avoid exposing sensitive logic in your release binaries.

4. **API Key Management and Authentication**

   API keys and authentication tokens are commonly used in Flutter plugins, especially for services like Firebase, Google Maps, or payment gateways. It's critical to handle these keys securely to prevent unauthorized access to backend services.

   Avoid Hardcoding API Keys:

   Never hardcode API keys or authentication tokens directly in the code. Instead, store them in secure storage or fetch them from a secure server at runtime.

   Best Practice: Use environment variables or a secure server-side API to retrieve API keys or tokens dynamically.

```
// Fetch API key securely from a remote server
String apiKey = await fetchApiKeyFromServer();
```

Use OAuth and Token Expiry:

For services that support OAuth, use token-based authentication with expiration and refresh tokens. This minimizes the risk of tokens being compromised, as expired tokens are no longer valid.

Best Practice: Implement token expiration and refresh functionality to ensure that authentication tokens are periodically refreshed, minimizing the risks of token leakage.

5. **Regular Security Audits and Updates**

   Security threats evolve, and new vulnerabilities are discovered regularly. Therefore, it's essential to stay up to date with the latest security patches and conduct regular security audits of your plugin.

   Best Practice: Periodically review and update your plugin's security mechanisms, paying particular attention to platform-specific security changes, new encryption standards, and any potential vulnerabilities discovered in dependencies you are using.

Security is a critical aspect of developing high-quality Flutter plugins. By adhering to best practices such as securing communication with platform channels, using secure storage for sensitive data, preventing reverse engineering, managing API keys securely, and conducting regular security audits, you can build plugins that ensure the protection of user data and help maintain trust in your app.

By implementing these security measures, you can reduce the risks of data breaches, unauthorized access, and other security threats that may compromise the integrity of your plugin and the apps that rely on it.

CHAPTER 6 INTEGRATION WITH NATIVE CODE

Advanced Security Practices

As Flutter apps increasingly rely on native code integration through plugins and platform channels, the security landscape becomes more complex. Native integrations expose your app to platform-specific vulnerabilities, which—if not handled correctly—can lead to unauthorized data access, insecure data storage, and broader system exploitation. This section focuses on advanced security practices you should implement to fortify both Flutter and native code integrations.

We will explore robust encryption strategies, secure storage techniques, and best practices for securing native code interactions across Android and iOS platforms.

Encryption and Secure Storage

In modern mobile and web applications, data security is paramount. With the increasing use of native code and third-party integrations, developers must take extra precautions to ensure that sensitive data is encrypted both at rest and in transit. Flutter provides a number of mechanisms for achieving strong data protection, but when integrating with native code, platform-specific best practices must also be followed.

This section explores encryption strategies and secure storage solutions in the context of Flutter applications, with a strong focus on cross-platform consistency and robustness against common security vulnerabilities.

1. **Data-at-Rest Encryption**

    1.1. **Secure Key-Value Storage**

    For storing sensitive data like access tokens, refresh tokens, and login credentials, the recommended approach is to use platform-specific secure storage APIs.

FlutterSecureStorage: A popular plugin that provides encrypted key-value storage by using

Android: Keystore + EncryptedSharedPreferences (API 23+)

iOS: Keychain Services

Usage Example:

```
final secureStorage = FlutterSecureStorage();
await secureStorage.write(key: 'authToken', value: 'secure_token_value');
String? token = await secureStorage.read(key: 'authToken');
```

Best Practice: Always prefer "FlutterSecureStorage" over "SharedPreferences" for storing anything sensitive.

1.2. **Encrypted Local Databases**

For structured data storage, SQLite is commonly used. However, it must be encrypted to prevent unauthorized access in case of device compromise.

SQLCipher: A popular SQLite extension that provides full database encryption

Drift (moor) and sqflite_sqlcipher offer convenient Flutter integrations for encrypted databases.

CHAPTER 6   INTEGRATION WITH NATIVE CODE

Implementation Tip:

```
final database = await openDatabase(
  'secure.db',
  password: 'secure_password_here',
);
```

🔐 Use a password stored in a secure keystore to open encrypted databases.

2. **Data-in-Transit Encryption**

   2.1. **TLS/SSL Over HTTPS**

   All communication between your Flutter app and backend services must occur over secure HTTPS connections.

   TLS 1.2+ is mandatory for all mobile apps as per current platform policies.

   Use certificate pinning to mitigate man-in-the-middle attacks.

   Dart HTTP Client Example:

   ```
   final response = await http.get(Uri.parse('https://your-api.com/secure-data'));
   ```

   🔒 Never disable certificate validation—even in development.

2.2. End-to-End Encryption (E2EE)

When users share confidential information (e.g., messages, documents), E2EE ensures that only intended recipients can decrypt the data.

Use RSA or Elliptic Curve Cryptography (ECC) for key exchange.

Use AES for encrypting large payloads with symmetric encryption.

Packages to Use:

['pointycastle'](https://pub.dev/packages/pointycastle)

['encrypt'](https://pub.dev/packages/encrypt)

['cryptography'](https://pub.dev/packages/cryptography)

AES Encryption Example:

```
final key = Key.fromUtf8('32-character-long-secret-key!');
final iv = IV.fromLength(16);
final encrypter = Encrypter(AES(key));
final encrypted = encrypter.encrypt('Sensitive data', iv: iv);
final decrypted = encrypter.decrypt(encrypted, iv: iv);
```

CHAPTER 6   INTEGRATION WITH NATIVE CODE

3. **Key Management**

The cornerstone of encryption security lies in key management. Poor handling of encryption keys negates even the most robust encryption algorithms.

3.1. **Use Platform Keystores**

Android: Use the Android Keystore System to store cryptographic keys.

iOS: Use iOS Keychain for secure key storage.

🧠 Never store keys in plaintext files, environment variables, or embedded in code.

3.2. **Hardware-Backed Keystores**

Modern devices support hardware-backed keystores:

Android: StrongBox

iOS: Secure Enclave

Use them to ensure keys are non-exportable and stored within tamper-resistant hardware.

4. **Avoid Common Pitfalls**

✘ Don't log sensitive data to console, analytics, or crash logs.

✘ Don't use SharedPreferences for authentication tokens or private user information.

✘ Avoid plaintext backups of your application data.

CHAPTER 6   INTEGRATION WITH NATIVE CODE

A secure Flutter application depends on strong data protection practices. By leveraging

> Encrypted key-value storage with "FlutterSecureStorage"
>
> Encrypted databases like SQLCipher
>
> TLS-secured communication channels
>
> Proper key management using hardware-backed keystores

you significantly reduce your app's attack surface and ensure user trust and regulatory compliance.

Techniques for Securing Native Integrations

As Flutter applications increasingly rely on native integrations for enhanced functionality, security risks inherent to platform-specific code become more prominent. Native code—whether Kotlin/Java on Android or Swift/Objective-C on iOS—can introduce vulnerabilities that are not directly visible in Dart code. To build secure and resilient Flutter applications, it is crucial to apply security best practices to all layers of integration, including communication via platform channels and plugin development.

This section outlines effective strategies for hardening native integrations, ensuring secure communication, enforcing principle of least privilege, and implementing static and dynamic analysis tools to detect vulnerabilities.

1. **Validate Platform Channel Inputs**

    Platform channels serve as a bridge between Dart and native code. Any data passed through these channels should be treated as untrusted until validated.

CHAPTER 6 INTEGRATION WITH NATIVE CODE

Key Practices:

Type Checking: Always verify data types and required fields before processing input.

Sanitization: Sanitize strings or input parameters to prevent injection vulnerabilities.

Bound Checking: Validate numeric ranges and expected lengths for array inputs.

Example (Android—Kotlin):

```kotlin
val methodChannel = MethodChannel(flutterEngine.dartExecutor.binaryMessenger, "secure_channel")
methodChannel.setMethodCallHandler { call, result ->
    val input = call.argument<String>("inputData")
    if (input == null || input.length > 256) {
        result.error("INVALID_INPUT", "Input is malformed", null)
        return@setMethodCallHandler
    }
    // Process securely
}
```

♡ Treat every Dart-to-native call as potentially malicious.

2. **Enforce Least Privilege Access**

   Grant your app and plugins access only to what they truly need.

   Android:

   Use scoped storage to restrict file access.

Only declare required permissions in "AndroidManifest.xml." Avoid requesting sensitive permissions like "ACCESS_FINE_LOCATION," "READ_SMS," or "RECORD_AUDIO" unless absolutely necessary.

Ensure that components like "BroadcastReceiver," "Service," or "ContentProvider" are marked 'exported="false"' unless explicitly intended for public use.

iOS:

Only enable required capabilities (e.g., Bluetooth, Background Fetch) in "Info.plist."

Avoid unnecessary background execution or URL schemes that can be abused.

3. **Secure Platform Channels**

   Avoid Command Injection and Reflection:

   On Android, restrict the use of Java Reflection APIs or "Runtime.exec()."

   On iOS, avoid dynamic Objective-C selectors like "performSelector:" when data comes from Dart.

   Encrypt Sensitive Communication:

   If platform channels transmit sensitive information (e.g., tokens, PINs), encrypt the data using AES or RSA before sending it across.

Use Unique Channel Names:

Avoid using generic channel names (e.g., "'com.example.channel'") to reduce the risk of third-party interception or conflicts.

Apply obfuscation to method names and channel strings in production builds.

4. **Obfuscate Native Code in Release Builds**

    Both Android and iOS apps can be reverse engineered if left unprotected.

    Android:

    Use ProGuard/R8 for code shrinking and obfuscation.

    Remove unused classes, fields, and methods.

    Encrypt strings and API keys using tools or native methods.

    "proguard-rules.pro":

    ```
    keep class io.flutter. { *; }
    -keep class your.package.name. { *; }
    -dontwarn your.package.name.
    ```

    iOS:

    Strip debug symbols in release builds ("Strip Debug Symbols During Copy = YES").

    Use bitcode (if supported) for optimized binary compilation.

    Avoid exposing sensitive information in "NSUserDefaults" or through "NSUserActivity."

CHAPTER 6   INTEGRATION WITH NATIVE CODE

5. **Protect Sensitive Native APIs**

   Use platform security features to safeguard sensitive API usage.

   Android:

   Store secrets using the Android Keystore System with hardware-backed security.

   Avoid storing secrets in "SharedPreferences," even in encrypted form, without proper key protection.

   iOS:

   Use Keychain Services to store secrets.

   Leverage the Secure Enclave on supported devices for biometric-protected keys.

6. **Analyze Native Code with Static and Dynamic Tools**

   Static Analysis:

   Android:

   Android Lint, SonarQube, Checkmarx

   iOS:

   Clang Static Analyzer, Fortify, otool

   Dynamic Analysis:

   Monitor runtime behavior using Frida, Charles Proxy, or Burp Suite.

   Simulate attacks like man-in-the-middle, unauthorized method call injection, and memory dumps.

7. **Monitor Runtime Integrity**

    Use runtime security checks to detect tampering or rooted/jailbroken devices.

    Android:

    Check for "su" binaries, tampered system paths, or debug flags.

    Monitor for runtime hooking tools like Frida or Xposed.

    iOS:

    Detect jailbreak indicators like writable "/Applications," presence of "Cydia.app," or modified system binaries.

    🔍 Use libraries like "RootBeer" (Android) or "DTTJailbreakDetection" (iOS) for runtime integrity checks.

8. **Log Responsibly**

    Avoid logging sensitive data (e.g., tokens, passwords, session info).

    In native code, use secure logging APIs and conditionally disable verbose logs in production.

    Securing native integrations is critical for protecting Flutter applications from platform-level vulnerabilities. A secure architecture should include

    Strong input validation from Dart to native

    Restrictive permission and capability declarations

    Obfuscation and build-time hardening

> Secure use of platform channels and native APIs
>
> Ongoing analysis and monitoring to detect security anomalies

By embedding these practices into your development workflow, you ensure that native code enhancements don't compromise the security guarantees of your Flutter app.

Plugin Performance Optimization

Plugins play a critical role in extending Flutter applications by enabling access to platform-specific capabilities. However, poorly designed or unoptimized plugins can introduce bottlenecks, frame drops, or even memory leaks, especially in high-frequency or latency-sensitive scenarios.

Here, we dive into performance optimization techniques for Flutter plugins, emphasizing efficient Dart–native communication, resource handling, thread management, and real-world performance tuning strategies. We also highlight case studies that demonstrate best practices in action.

Strategies for Optimizing Plugin Performance

As Flutter apps continue to grow in complexity and demand greater interaction with platform-specific features, plugin performance becomes a cornerstone of delivering a seamless user experience. A poorly optimized plugin can lead to dropped frames, memory leaks, increased app startup time, and even runtime crashes.

This section provides advanced, production-grade strategies for ensuring that your plugins are optimized for both runtime efficiency and resource management. These techniques are based on real-world patterns observed in large-scale Flutter apps and are applicable to both Android and iOS platforms.

1. **Optimize Platform Channel Usage**

   The MethodChannel, EventChannel, and BasicMessageChannel APIs provide the bridge between Dart and native code. However, frequent or excessive use—especially in performance-critical paths—can lead to bottlenecks.

   Best Practices:

   Reduce Call Frequency: Avoid making platform channel calls in tight loops or frame callbacks.

   Batch Data: Combine multiple requests or payloads into a single method call.

   Use Streaming Wisely: Replace polling-based calls with EventChannel streams for high-frequency data (e.g., sensors, audio position updates).

   Avoid Sending Large Blobs: Instead of transferring large files or images, save them to disk and return file paths.

2. **Use Background Threads for Heavy Native Tasks**

   Native operations like file I/O, database queries, or network access should never block the main thread.

   Implementation Guidelines:

   Android: Use Kotlin Coroutines with Dispatchers.IO or traditional Java threading APIs.

   iOS: Use Grand Central Dispatch (GCD) with DispatchQueue.global() for background tasks.

   Ensure that results are always posted back to the UI thread to safely communicate with the Dart layer.

CHAPTER 6 INTEGRATION WITH NATIVE CODE

```
CoroutineScope(Dispatchers.IO).launch {
    val result = performLongTask()
    withContext(Dispatchers.Main) {
        resultCallback.success(result)
    }
}
```

3. **Optimize Memory Usage and Lifecycle**

   Plugins can easily introduce memory leaks, especially if event listeners or long-lived native objects are not properly released.

   Key Tips:

   Implement proper dispose() methods in Dart and corresponding cleanup in native code.

   Use weak references or callbacks for listeners that shouldn't prevent garbage collection.

   Clean up resources in

   Android: onDetachedFromEngine(), onDestroy()

   iOS: dealloc, or detachFromEngine in Swift

4. **Efficient Serialization and Deserialization**

   Passing complex data over the platform channel requires efficient encoding and decoding.

   Recommendations:

   Use binary serialization like Protocol Buffers or FlatBuffers for large, structured data.

Avoid base64 encoding for images or files unless absolutely necessary.

Benchmark and measure serialization overhead using Flutter DevTools or native profilers.

5. **Avoid Plugin Initialization at App Startup**

   Many plugins perform initialization logic during app launch, which can delay the first frame.

   Optimizations:

   Defer plugin setup until explicitly needed.

   Use lazy initialization patterns.

   If initialization is mandatory, make it asynchronous and show a progress indicator if necessary.

6. **Profile with Flutter DevTools and Native Instruments**

   Thorough profiling can identify invisible bottlenecks introduced by your plugins.

   Tools to Use:

   Flutter DevTools: Track frame rendering times, platform channel traffic, and memory usage.

   Android Studio Profiler: Inspect CPU, memory, and network usage for native Android code.

   Instruments (Xcode): Profile CPU and memory usage for iOS plugins.

7. **Leverage Caching and Resource Reuse**

   For native code that performs repetitive operations (e.g., accessing media metadata or querying sensors), caching results can dramatically improve performance.

   Caching Techniques:

   Cache results on the native side and only return updated data when necessary.

   Store infrequently changing data in local databases like SharedPreferences or NSUserDefaults.

8. **Minimize Plugin Footprint**

   Large or complex plugins can increase app size, build time, and runtime overhead.

   How to Optimize:

   Strip unused native libraries or assets.

   Split monolithic plugins into smaller, focused components.

   Avoid unnecessary third-party dependencies within the plugin.

9. **Thread-Safe Event Handling**

   When using EventChannel, ensure that event emissions are thread-safe and that backpressure or dropped events are handled gracefully.

CHAPTER 6 INTEGRATION WITH NATIVE CODE

Example:

```
eventSink?("event_data")
```

Ensure eventSink is not nil and dispatches on the main thread if updating UI state.

10. **Monitor for Frame Drops and Jank**

    Use FlutterFrameTiming (available in DevTools) to measure frame build time and rasterization time. Plugins should never introduce spikes in these metrics.

✓ Summary Table

Optimization Area	Recommendation
Platform Channels	Batch calls, avoid high-frequency communication
Native Threading	Move heavy work off main thread, return on UI thread
Memory & Lifecycle	Dispose properly, avoid leaks with weak references
Serialization	Use binary formats, avoid base64 for large data
Initialization	Use lazy loading and async init strategies
Profiling Tools	Use DevTools, Android Profiler, and Instruments
Caching	Cache expensive computations or disk reads

Plugin Size	Split functionality, remove unused dependencies
Event Handling	Ensure thread safety and reliable delivery with EventChannels
Frame Monitoring	Track build and raster times, avoid plugin-related jank

By adopting these performance strategies, developers can create plugins that are not only functional but also lightweight, responsive, and scalable—suitable for both consumer-grade apps and enterprise-grade platforms.

Case Studies and Examples

To solidify the performance optimization strategies discussed earlier, this section examines real-world plugin implementations where performance bottlenecks were identified and resolved. These case studies and practical examples highlight how thoughtful plugin design can enhance app responsiveness, reduce memory usage, and improve user experience in large-scale production environments.

Case Study 1: Image Processing Plugin Optimization
Scenario:

> A Flutter application used a custom plugin to perform heavy image processing (e.g., applying filters, cropping, face detection). The plugin originally executed processing on the main thread, causing frequent jank, long UI freezes, and dropped frames during interaction.

CHAPTER 6 INTEGRATION WITH NATIVE CODE

Problem:

All image decoding and processing was done synchronously via the platform channel.

The Dart UI thread was blocked while waiting for results.

Solution:

Moved image processing logic to background threads using Kotlin Coroutines and GCD (iOS).

Cached the results using file-based caching (with timestamps to detect updates).

Offloaded expensive operations like face detection to platform-native machine learning (ML) libraries and streamed results using EventChannel.

Result:

Average frame time reduced by 40%.

Startup image processing was deferred until explicitly needed, resulting in 60% faster app launches.

Case Study 2: Plugin Event Flooding in Real-Time Data App
Scenario:

An app integrated a plugin for real-time stock price updates using an EventChannel. During high-volume trading periods, the app experienced memory pressure and skipped frames.

Problem:

The native plugin sent updates at high frequency (hundreds per second), flooding the Dart side.

The Dart listener couldn't keep up, causing a backlog and memory buildup.

Solution:

Introduced debouncing on the native side to reduce update frequency to a configurable threshold (e.g., ten updates/sec).

Added a native event queue with overflow protection and a strategy to send only the latest update.

Exposed a parameter to allow the Flutter app to control throttling behavior dynamically.

Result:

Memory usage stabilized.

Dart side maintained responsiveness even during market spikes.

Case Study 3: Startup Delay Due to Plugin Initialization
Scenario:

A banking app included over 15 native plugins for authentication, analytics, crash reporting, and biometrics. All plugins initialized during the app's first frame render.

CHAPTER 6   INTEGRATION WITH NATIVE CODE

Problem:

> Startup time exceeded four seconds on older devices.
>
> First frame was delayed, leading to a poor initial impression.

Solution:

> Analyzed plugin initialization times using Flutter DevTools Timeline.
>
> Deferred initialization of non-critical plugins (e.g., analytics, crash logging) until after the first frame.
>
> Used WidgetsBinding.instance.addPostFrameCallback() in Dart to schedule plugin setup after UI render.

Result:

> App startup time reduced by 47%.
>
> First frame rendered in under one second on most devices.

Case Study 4: Inefficient JSON-Based Communication
Scenario:

> A plugin for file synchronization passed complex objects (files, metadata, permissions) via platform channels using verbose JSON.

Problem:

> JSON serialization/deserialization overhead was significant (~250ms per operation).
>
> Platform channel transfers exceeded 20KB regularly, increasing latency.

Solution:

Replaced JSON with FlatBuffers for cross-platform serialization.

Reduced payload size by 75% and parsing time by 90%.

Used binary data transfer when feasible.

Result:

End-to-end sync operations became 3× faster.

CPU load dropped, improving battery usage on mobile devices.

Case Study 5: Custom Video Player Plugin Bottleneck Scenario:

A custom video player plugin experienced frame lag when switching between full-screen and embedded modes.

Problem:

Each transition triggered complete reinitialization of the native player object.

Platform views were being reallocated, causing stuttering and delay.

Solution:

Reused player instances with detached surface management.

Leveraged native video player libraries' internal resource pooling (e.g., ExoPlayer on Android).

Handled surface switches without disposing the actual media controller.

Result:

Seamless transitions between modes.

CPU usage decreased by 35% during mode switches.

Common Lessons Learned

Problem Area	Optimization Approach
Main Thread Blocking	Use background threads for heavy native operations
Event Overload	Apply throttling, debouncing, and queuing
Startup Latency	Defer non-critical plugin initialization
Data Transfer Inefficiency	Use binary formats like FlatBuffers or Protocol Buffers
Redundant Native Initialization	Reuse native resources, avoid repeated allocations

These case studies demonstrate the practical application of performance principles in real-world plugins. Optimization is rarely a one-size-fits-all approach. It requires

- Profiling with proper tools (DevTools, Instruments, Android Profiler)
- Understanding platform-specific threading and lifecycle
- Thoughtfully architecting communication flows between Dart and native code

CHAPTER 6 INTEGRATION WITH NATIVE CODE

By adopting these strategies early in development and revisiting them periodically as features evolve, plugin developers can deliver fast, robust, and scalable integrations that keep up with modern Flutter app expectations.

Summary

Here we explore the critical techniques and advancements involved in integrating Flutter with platform-specific native code. It begins with an in-depth look at updated platform channel capabilities, highlighting advanced communication techniques and best practices for managing asynchronous operations between Dart and native layers. The chapter then shifts focus to modern plugin development, covering the latest tooling improvements, integration workflows, and strategies for robust testing, debugging, and securing plugins.

The chapter also presents advanced security practices, including encryption methods, secure storage patterns, and techniques for safeguarding native integrations. It concludes with a performance-centric approach, offering strategies to optimize plugin performance through threading, efficient serialization, caching, and profiling—reinforced with real-world case studies from production apps.

Readers are now equipped to build, secure, and optimize high-performance native integrations that align with the modern standards of Flutter 3.29, ensuring native-level power without compromising cross-platform efficiency.

CHAPTER 7

Web and Desktop Enhancements

In the previous chapter, we explored how Flutter enables deep integration with native platforms through platform channels, advanced plugin development, and native security best practices. These capabilities are critical for extending Flutter's core functionality and delivering powerful, low-level interactions across Android and iOS. However, the true strength of Flutter lies in its versatility across platforms—including not just mobile, but also web and desktop.

Here, we pivot from native integration to cross-platform expansion, focusing on the evolving landscape of Flutter for web and desktop development. Flutter 3.29 brings a host of performance optimizations, feature updates, and deployment improvements that make it easier than ever to build production-grade web apps and desktop applications from a single unified codebase.

We begin by examining the latest Flutter Web enhancements, including rendering performance gains, the integration of WebAssembly (Wasm), and enhanced support for Progressive Web Apps (PWAs). As browser variability remains a key challenge, we also explore effective strategies for managing compatibility issues and debugging across different engines and platforms.

CHAPTER 7   WEB AND DESKTOP ENHANCEMENTS

Next, we delve into Flutter Desktop, covering the new native capabilities introduced in version 3.29—such as system tray support, advanced text input handling, and native window APIs. You'll also learn how to package and distribute desktop applications for Windows, macOS, and Linux while managing platform-specific dependencies cleanly and efficiently.

To bridge theory and practice, we include detailed case studies showcasing real-world applications built using Flutter's web and desktop targets. These examples highlight architectural patterns, performance considerations, and the unique challenges developers overcame to succeed across diverse environments.

Finally, we conclude the chapter with performance benchmarking techniques for cross-platform Flutter apps, along with strategies to optimize your code for responsiveness, resource efficiency, and user experience across browsers and desktop systems.

As Flutter continues to mature as a truly universal toolkit, mastering web and desktop development is the next logical step for advanced developers aiming to maximize their app's reach. Let's dive into the innovations that are shaping the future of Flutter beyond mobile.

Flutter Web Improvements

Flutter's support for the web has significantly matured, moving beyond experimental features into a robust platform for production-ready applications. In Flutter 3.29, major performance upgrades and platform-specific fixes have been introduced to elevate the developer and user experience on modern browsers. This section explores the most impactful enhancements for web development and equips you with strategies to handle browser-specific challenges.

Latest Updates for Flutter Web Performance

Flutter Web has reached a level of maturity where performance, load speed, and user experience are critical metrics for success. In version 3.29, Flutter introduces cutting-edge improvements that optimize rendering, boost interaction speed, and elevate the performance profile of web apps to match native-like expectations. This section dives into the newest advancements and how you can leverage them to build lightning-fast, highly responsive Flutter web applications.

Overview of Web Performance Enhancements

As Flutter Web continues to mature, performance optimization has become a top priority in version 3.29. The web platform, inherently different from mobile and desktop, introduces unique challenges such as resource constraints, browser rendering behaviors, and varying network conditions. Flutter 3.29 directly addresses these with a suite of performance enhancements aimed at delivering faster, more stable, and visually fluid web experiences.

🎯1. Reduced JavaScript Bundle Sizes

Flutter's Dart-to-JS compilation pipeline has undergone significant improvements. The build system now performs more aggressive tree shaking, dead code elimination, and minification, resulting in notably smaller JavaScript bundles. This directly reduces

- Initial page load time (TTFP)
- Bandwidth usage, especially for mobile users
- Time to interactive (TTI)

Here's what's new in 3.29:

- Smarter analysis of unused widget trees and dependencies

CHAPTER 7   WEB AND DESKTOP ENHANCEMENTS

> Efficient handling of third-party Dart packages
>
> Support for deferred loading to modularize large applications

🎨 2. Deferred Component Loading

Flutter now allows developers to lazily load parts of the application using Dart's "deferred as" import syntax. This is particularly useful for

> Loading routes or screens only when they're accessed
>
> Deferring admin or power-user panels not required by most users
>
> Reducing app shell size for a faster first paint

Example:

```
import 'admin_panel.dart' deferred as admin;

Future<void> loadAdminPanel() async {
  await admin.loadLibrary();
  runApp(admin.AdminPanelApp());
}
```

Deferred loading drastically improves perceived performance by shortening initial load time.

🖼 3. CanvasKit Initialization Optimization

Flutter's default high-performance web renderer—CanvasKit (based on WebAssembly and WebGL)—has seen several performance gains:

> Compressed CanvasKit assets (Wasm and fonts) are now smaller and delivered more efficiently.
>
> Streaming initialization allows CanvasKit to progressively boot up instead of blocking the UI thread.

CHAPTER 7   WEB AND DESKTOP ENHANCEMENTS

Precaching of CanvasKit blobs during service worker registration minimizes delays for repeat visits.

Together, these changes improve rendering consistency and reduce layout shift and input latency on web.

4. DOM Renderer Enhancements (HTML Mode)

For apps using the HTML renderer (DOM-based rendering), Flutter 3.29 introduces

> **Improved Element Diffing**: More accurate widget-to-DOM mapping, reducing unnecessary updates
>
> **Optimized Text Layout Engine**: Faster computation for paragraph measurements and line-breaking
>
> Better font fallback resolution, especially for internationalized content and emoji rendering
>
> HTML mode is now more suited for content-heavy, SEO-friendly applications.

5. Font Loading and Subsetting

Flutter's web toolchain now supports

> **Font Subsetting**: Includes only the glyphs actually used in your app
>
> **Font Preloading via '<link rel="preload">'**: Tells the browser to prioritize font loading
>
> Inline font manifest to reduce extra network calls
>
> These features minimize layout shifts, improve Google's Core Web Vitals, and reduce first-contentful paint (FCP).

6. WebAssembly (Wasm) Preview Compilation

Flutter 3.29 includes early support for Wasm compilation via "dart compile wasm." Though experimental, this brings enormous potential benefits:

> Binary-level performance rivaling native code

> Smaller download sizes due to compact binary format

> Improved memory management with future plans for Wasm GC (garbage collection)

> This prepares Flutter for the next generation of high-performance web apps.

7. Optimized Service Worker for Caching

Flutter's default service worker ("flutter_service_worker.js") now includes

> Precaching strategies for critical assets (HTML, CSS, CanvasKit, fonts)

> **Stale-While-Revalidate Behavior:** Loads from cache while refreshing in the background

> Efficient cache invalidation using manifest-based asset versioning

> This enables robust offline support and significantly faster load times on repeat visits.

Summary of Improvements

Area	Flutter 3.29 Enhancement
JavaScript Size	Tree shaking, code splitting, deferred loading
Initial Load Time	Preloading, smaller payloads, streaming initialization
Renderer Speed	Optimized CanvasKit and DOM engine
Text and Font Performance	Subsetting, preloading, better fallback handling
Offline Caching	Improved service worker, smarter cache strategies
Compilation Output	Experimental WebAssembly for native-speed execution

These enhancements collectively make Flutter Web a stronger candidate for building rich, interactive, and production-grade applications. Whether targeting mobile browsers, desktops, or PWA installation, developers can now offer more consistent performance across devices and networks.

Building Progressive Web Apps (PWAs)

Progressive Web Apps (PWAs) blend the best of web and mobile apps—offering installability, offline capability, responsive design, and near-native performance—all while running in a browser. Flutter's web support includes robust PWA tooling out of the box, allowing developers to build modern web apps that look, feel, and behave like native apps.

With Flutter 3.29, creating PWAs is more efficient, performant, and customizable than ever before. From service workers to manifest integration, Flutter provides a fully integrated stack for building high-quality PWAs using a unified Dart codebase.

🧱 PWA Fundamentals in Flutter

A Flutter-based PWA adheres to three key principles:

Reliable: Loads fast and works offline

Installable: Can be added to the home screen or app drawer

Engaging: Uses full-screen mode, push notifications, and smooth animations

Flutter supports these capabilities through

An auto-generated Web App Manifest

A customizable service worker

Full control over routing, caching, and offline behavior

📁 Key PWA Components in Flutter
✅ 1. "manifest.json"

The "manifest.json" file defines how the app appears and behaves when installed. Flutter creates a default manifest during web builds.

```
on
{
  "name": "My Flutter PWA",
  "short_name": "FlutterPWA",
  "start_url": "/",
  "display": "standalone",
  "background_color": "#ffffff",
  "theme_color": "#2196F3",
  "icons": [
    {
      "src": "icons/Icon-192.png",
```

CHAPTER 7   WEB AND DESKTOP ENHANCEMENTS

```
      "sizes": "192x192",
      "type": "image/png"
    },
    {
      "src": "icons/Icon-512.png",
      "sizes": "512x512",
      "type": "image/png"
    }
  ]
}
```

You can customize this file in the "web/" directory to reflect your app's branding and UX requirements.

✓ 2. **"flutter_service_worker.js"**

Flutter generates a service worker that

> Caches app shell files (HTML, JS, fonts, CanvasKit)
>
> Supports offline loading
>
> Handles fetch interception and versioned asset management

With Flutter 3.29, the service worker is optimized for

> Stale-while-revalidate strategies
>
> Versioned asset invalidation
>
> Efficient memory usage and smart cache expiration

✓ 3. **App Shell Architecture**

Flutter inherently uses an app shell model. The main app UI is bundled and loaded once, while the service worker caches assets for offline reuse. This architecture

> Reduces redundant downloads

CHAPTER 7   WEB AND DESKTOP ENHANCEMENTS

Delivers consistent load performance

Supports offline-first designs

🛠 **Steps to Build a PWA with Flutter**

1. **Create and Configure a Flutter Web App**

   ```
   flutter create my_pwa
   cd my_pwa
   flutter config --enable-web
   ```

2. **Customize Manifest and Icons**

   Edit "web/manifest.json" and add icon files in "web/icons/."

3. **Modify HTML Template (Optional)**

   Edit "web/index.html" to include

   ```html
   <link rel="manifest" href="manifest.json">
   <link rel="preload" href="fonts/MaterialIcons-Regular.ttf" as="font" type="font/ttf" crossorigin="anonymous">
   ```

4. **Build for Web Release**

   ```
   flutter build web
   ```

5. **Deploy Over HTTPS**

CHAPTER 7   WEB AND DESKTOP ENHANCEMENTS

PWAs must be served over HTTPS to enable installability and service workers. Use Firebase Hosting, GitHub Pages, Vercel, Netlify, or any secure host.

📲 Testing PWA Functionality

Use Chrome DevTools ➤ Lighthouse to audit your Flutter Web app:

Check installability.

Analyze offline capabilities.

Monitor performance and accessibility.

PWA Checklist:

```
| Feature            | Flutter Support                          |
| -------------------|------------------------------------------|
| Offline Caching    | ✅ Yes (via service worker)              |
| App Manifest       | ✅ Yes (auto-generated)                  |
| Install Prompt     | ✅ Yes (browser-managed)                 |
| Responsive UI      | ✅ Yes (via Flutter layout)              |
| Fullscreen Display | ✅ Configurable in manifest              |
| HTTPS Required     | ⚠ Must be externally hosted securely    |
```

🔍 Advanced Enhancements in Flutter 3.29

Deferred loading for PWA sections not needed on first load (e.g., settings panel)

Font preloading and subsetting to reduce layout shifts

Improved service worker lifecycle management

Better web animations using "flutter/animation" and "js" interop

✅ PWA Installation Experience

Once deployed, users can install the app by

Clicking "Install" from the browser address bar

Tapping "Add to Home Screen" on mobile browsers

The installed PWA opens in a standalone window, without browser UI, offering a native-like experience.

🧠 Best Practices

Minimize initial bundle size with deferred loading.

Subset and preload fonts to reduce FOUT.

Use long cache durations for static assets.

Always test on multiple browsers and devices.

Include "offline.html" fallback for full offline UX.

Flutter 3.29 has matured into a first-class framework for building PWAs that are performant, reliable, and visually rich. With minimal setup and a shared codebase, developers can now deliver native-like web experiences that are installable, offline-ready, and blazing-fast.

Handling Browser-Specific Challenges

While Flutter Web abstracts away much of the complexity of frontend development, developers must still account for differences in browser rendering engines, feature support, and performance behaviors. Browser-specific challenges can impact layout, performance, input handling, and even app stability.

Flutter 3.29 introduces several enhancements and best practices to better manage these variations, making it easier to develop apps that work consistently across Chrome, Safari, Firefox, and Edge.

Techniques for Handling Browser Compatibility

Browser compatibility remains one of the most nuanced challenges in web development, even when using a framework like Flutter that abstracts away much of the frontend complexity. Variations in rendering engines, event models, supported APIs, and performance optimizations across browsers such as Chrome, Firefox, Safari, and Edge can introduce subtle and sometimes critical inconsistencies.

CHAPTER 7   WEB AND DESKTOP ENHANCEMENTS

Flutter 3.29 introduces enhanced web capabilities and guidance to help developers build consistent, reliable, and high-performance experiences across all modern browsers. This section explores proven techniques and Flutter-specific practices for ensuring browser compatibility in production-grade web applications.

🌐 1. Use the Appropriate Renderer Strategically

Flutter Web supports two rendering backends:

> **HTML Renderer**: Lightweight and faster initial load times. Best suited for simple UIs, forms, and content-heavy pages
>
> **CanvasKit Renderer**: Leverages WebAssembly to provide Skia-powered high-fidelity rendering. Ideal for apps with complex UIs and animations

Best Practice:

> Use "--web-renderer=html" for general-purpose apps focused on content.
>
> Use "--web-renderer=canvaskit" when visual fidelity, precision, and advanced UI elements are required.

```
flutter run -d chrome --web-renderer=canvaskit
```

🧪 2. Emphasize Feature Detection, Not Browser Detection

Browser-specific code should be minimized or avoided altogether. Instead of checking for the browser type, test for the availability of features.

Why This Matters:

Browsers evolve rapidly. Relying on hardcoded browser names can break functionality as features are deprecated, updated, or released under experimental flags.

CHAPTER 7 WEB AND DESKTOP ENHANCEMENTS

Example:

```
import 'dart:html';

bool isTouchDevice() => window.navigator.maxTouchPoints != null
&& window.navigator.maxTouchPoints! > 0;

bool supportsWebGL() {
  final canvas = CanvasElement();
  return canvas.getContext('webgl') != null;
}
```

💡 3. Use Adaptive Design Patterns

Not all browsers handle layout or responsiveness in the same way, particularly on devices with varying screen sizes and pixel densities.

Strategies:

Use "LayoutBuilder" to create fluid UI layouts based on constraints.

Rely on "MediaQuery" to adapt to device characteristics like orientation, screen size, and pixel ratio.

Avoid fixed dimensions where possible. Use "Expanded," "Flexible," and "FractionallySizedBox" for better scalability.

```
LayoutBuilder(
  builder: (context, constraints) {
    if (constraints.maxWidth < 600) {
      return MobileLayout();
    } else {
      return DesktopLayout();
    }
  },
);
```

---

4. Account for Input Modality Differences

Browsers handle touch, mouse, and keyboard inputs differently. Flutter's input system abstracts some of these differences, but you may still encounter discrepancies in

> Gesture propagation
>
> Focus management
>
> Hover events

Recommendations:

Use "kIsWeb" and "defaultTargetPlatform" to detect input context:

```
if (kIsWeb && defaultTargetPlatform == TargetPlatform.iOS) {
  // Adjust for Safari's gesture behavior
}
```

Consider wrapping components with "MouseRegion" and "FocusScope" to control interactions explicitly.

5. Use Platform View and DOM Integration Carefully

Flutter's "HtmlElementView" and "PlatformView" enable embedding native HTML elements like "<iframe>" or "<video>," but

> Some browsers apply stricter sandboxing policies (especially Safari).
>
> Sizing and alignment can differ between browsers.

Tips:

> Wrap embedded elements in a container with a fixed size.
>
> Use custom styles or CSS workarounds for precise layout control.

Test thoroughly on all target browsers if platform views are essential.

🎯 6. Handle Font Rendering and Fallbacks

Fonts may render with subtle differences across browsers:

> Kerning and glyph spacing may differ (especially in Safari).
>
> Custom font loading times can impact first paint (FOUT).

Techniques:

> Preload fonts in "index.html" using '<link rel="preload">.'
>
> Use "FontLoader" in Dart to control font readiness.
>
> Subset fonts using tools like "google-webfonts-helper" or "Font Squirrel."

🔒 7. Account for Security Constraints

Browsers impose different restrictions on

> Service workers
>
> Local storage/session storage
>
> Clipboard access
>
> Fullscreen API

Solutions:

> Ensure HTTPS is enforced in production.
>
> Use fallback logic for restricted APIs.
>
> Validate all permissions and sandbox modes (especially on iframes).

CHAPTER 7 WEB AND DESKTOP ENHANCEMENTS

🖊 8. Test on a Wide Matrix of Browsers

Even if your app works well on Chrome, it's critical to verify it on

> **Safari (Mac/iOS)**: Common source of layout issues and font rendering differences
>
> **Firefox**: Different JS optimization pipeline, slower CanvasKit performance
>
> **Edge**: Chrome-based but may apply enterprise restrictions or custom policies

Tools:

> BrowserStack, LambdaTest, or Sauce Labs for cloud-based testing
>
> Manual testing on real devices for touch and gesture validation
>
> Chrome DevTools' "device emulation" mode for initial checks

✅ Summary of Compatibility Techniques

Challenge	Technique
Rendering Inconsistencies	Choose the optimal renderer ('html' vs 'canvaskit')
Feature Gaps	Use feature detection with 'dart:html'
Layout and Responsiveness	Use 'LayoutBuilder', 'MediaQuery', and flexible widgets
Input Variability	Detect platform/input context, use 'MouseRegion', 'FocusScope'

Font Rendering	Preload fonts, subset fonts, and use 'FontLoader'
Embedded HTML Issues	Wrap in fixed containers, apply browser-specific CSS if necessary
Browser Security Restrictions	Serve over HTTPS, test for permission availability
Cross-Browser Testing	Use emulation tools and real devices to ensure consistent behavior

Mastering browser compatibility is essential for building high-quality Flutter Web apps that delight users across platforms. Flutter 3.29 offers better rendering isolation, feature detection APIs, and performance stability to help you confidently support every major browser.

Debugging and Troubleshooting

Debugging browser-specific issues in Flutter Web requires a hybrid approach that combines Flutter's debugging tools with traditional browser development workflows. Since different browsers interpret rendering, JavaScript execution, CSS behavior, and WebAssembly initialization in distinct ways, developers need robust strategies to identify and resolve issues quickly and accurately.

Flutter 3.29 enhances the developer experience by offering better stack traces, improved source maps, and tighter integration with browser DevTools. This section outlines effective techniques and tools for debugging and troubleshooting Flutter Web applications.

💼 1. Use Flutter DevTools for Core App Debugging

Flutter DevTools provides a suite of diagnostic tools to analyze your app's performance, widget structure, memory usage, and more. When

CHAPTER 7   WEB AND DESKTOP ENHANCEMENTS

debugging Flutter-specific logic (e.g., widget rendering, state issues), DevTools is your primary ally.

Key Tabs in DevTools for Web:

> **Inspector**: Visualizes widget trees; perfect for detecting layout misalignment and widget lifecycle issues
>
> **Timeline**: Helps identify jank, dropped frames, or expensive operations during rendering
>
> **Memory**: Detects memory leaks or uncollected objects, especially in long-lived single-page apps
>
> **Network**: Tracks HTTP requests made via "http" or "dio" packages

Launch Command:

```
flutter run -d chrome --web-renderer=canvaskit --debug
```

⊕ 2. Leverage Browser Developer Tools

To debug browser-level issues, the built-in DevTools in Chrome, Firefox, Edge, and Safari are indispensable. These tools let you investigate rendering behavior, event propagation, caching, and security problems.

Chrome DevTools Tabs to Focus On:

Tab	Purpose
Console	View JavaScript or Dart stack traces, runtime warnings, CORS errors
Sources	Inspect Dart source maps, set breakpoints in compiled JS/WASM

CHAPTER 7 WEB AND DESKTOP ENHANCEMENTS

Elements	Inspect DOM output (especially relevant when using HTML renderer)
Network	Analyze asset loading, font issues, service worker registration
Application	Manage cache storage, localStorage, and service workers

Tip Enable source maps in "build/web" to correlate stack traces with Dart code.

⚠ 3. Diagnose Renderer-Specific Issues

Sometimes, problems manifest only when using a specific renderer:

CanvasKit Issues:

Check if "canvaskit.wasm" is loaded correctly (verify in the Network tab).

Inspect WebAssembly errors or warnings in the console.

Confirm that the browser supports WebGL 2 and WASM SIMD.

HTML Renderer Issues:

Inspect layout and style differences in the Elements tab.

Investigate DOM-related behaviors, especially with embedded HTML views.

Check for font fallback mismatches or text overflow due to CSS variations.

🛠ç 4. Analyze Build and Asset Delivery Problems

CHAPTER 7   WEB AND DESKTOP ENHANCEMENTS

Improper bundling, missing assets, or caching issues often break app behavior in production:

Checklist:

> Confirm asset paths are correct and referenced in "pubspec.yaml."
>
> Validate that service worker and "flutter_service_worker.js" are not stale.
>
> Use version hashing in filenames to avoid aggressive browser caching.

Here's how to clear cache-related bugs during dev:

```
// In browser Console
navigator.serviceWorker.getRegistrations().then(regs => regs.forEach(r => r.unregister()));
```

🔒 5. Resolve CORS, CSP, and Local Storage Errors

Many runtime issues stem from browser security restrictions:

> **CORS Errors**: Fonts, images, or APIs hosted on different origins require proper CORS headers.
>
> **Content Security Policy (CSP)**: May block inline styles, scripts, or iframe embeds.
>
> **Storage Issues**: Safari blocks "localStorage" in private mode. Firefox may restrict IndexedDB access under memory pressure.

Fixes:

CHAPTER 7   WEB AND DESKTOP ENHANCEMENTS

> Use "Access-Control-Allow-Origin" headers on servers.
>
> Deploy apps over HTTPS to prevent storage and permission issues.
>
> Always test storage APIs under incognito or private mode.

🖊 6. Profile and Optimize Performance Bottlenecks

For performance-related debugging

> Use Chrome's Performance tab to analyze paint, layout, and scripting timelines.
>
> Profile WebAssembly compilation when using CanvasKit.
>
> Track and eliminate large build artifacts with "flutter build web --analyze-size."

Also consider

> Lazy loading heavy assets or code-splitting where possible
>
> Subsetting fonts and images to reduce payload size

🧱 7. Inspect Responsiveness and Layout Breakage

Web apps can break due to improper constraint handling or unexpected screen sizes. Here are common symptoms:

> Elements overflowing containers
>
> Text clipping on smaller screens
>
> Widgets disappearing during resizing

Debug Flow:

> Use Flutter's "Inspector" to track widget sizes.

CHAPTER 7 WEB AND DESKTOP ENHANCEMENTS

Test using Chrome's device emulation to simulate mobile/tablet views.

Wrap widgets in "SafeArea," "Expanded," and "Flexible" to ensure constraint resilience.

✓ Summary: Debugging Workflow for Flutter Web

Issue Type	Tool / Technique
Widget/layout bugs	Flutter DevTools → Inspector, Chrome Elements Tab
Rendering backend issues	Network Tab, Renderer Flags, Console Logs
Asset and caching problems	Cache invalidation, Service Worker unregister
Storage/API failures	Application Tab, CORS/CSP headers
Performance jank	Timeline Tab, Chrome Performance Tab
Source mapping	Enable source maps in 'build/web', use Sources Tab
Security warnings	HTTPS, browser permissions, custom headers

Pro Tip:

CHAPTER 7   WEB AND DESKTOP ENHANCEMENTS

Always test your web app in release mode, as many issues do not appear in debug mode due to different rendering behaviors and optimizations:

```
flutter build web --release
```

Then serve the app using a static server like

```
python3 -m http.server 8080
```

By combining Flutter's debugging capabilities with in-browser diagnostic tools, you can effectively isolate and resolve even the most elusive bugs in web environments. Flutter 3.29 empowers you to confidently deliver reliable, high-performance apps across browsers and devices.

Flutter Desktop Updates

With the growing importance of cross-platform app development, Flutter has made significant strides in expanding its desktop capabilities, enabling developers to target Windows, macOS, and Linux with a single codebase. The latest updates in Flutter 3.29 provide more powerful features for building desktop applications, improving cross-platform consistency, and streamlining the deployment process.

Here, we are going to cover the latest developments in Flutter Desktop, the new features introduced, and techniques for packaging and managing dependencies for desktop applications.

CHAPTER 7   WEB AND DESKTOP ENHANCEMENTS

Latest Features for Flutter Desktop

Flutter 3.29 brings a range of enhancements to improve desktop app performance, visual fidelity, and native integration. These features align with the broader goal of making Flutter an even more robust and scalable solution for building native-like desktop applications.

New Desktop Features

Flutter 3.29 introduces several groundbreaking features for desktop app development, making it even more powerful for building native-like experiences on Windows, macOS, and Linux. These new capabilities not only improve the overall app performance and functionality but also expand the possibilities of what can be achieved with Flutter on desktop platforms.

This section highlights the most significant new features in Flutter 3.29 for desktop development, enabling developers to create rich, interactive, and polished applications across platforms.

1. Enhanced Window Management

One of the most anticipated improvements in Flutter's desktop ecosystem is the enhanced window management capabilities. Flutter now allows developers greater flexibility in managing the window's lifecycle, from resizing and minimizing to multi-window support.

Multi-window Support: Flutter 3.29 introduces support for managing multiple windows on macOS, Windows, and Linux. This feature is particularly useful for productivity applications that need independent windows for different tasks, such as text editors, design apps, or email clients.

Developers can now create multiple windows and control each one individually, enabling multi-monitor setups and advanced UI/UX experiences.

CHAPTER 7   WEB AND DESKTOP ENHANCEMENTS

Example:

```
import 'package:flutter_window_manager/flutter_window_
manager.dart';

// Create a second window
final secondWindow = WindowManager.createWindow();
secondWindow.setBounds(Rectangle(100, 100, 800, 600));

// Control window behavior
secondWindow.show();
secondWindow.setTitle('Secondary Window');
```

Resizable Windows: Developers can define custom window sizes, specify minimum or maximum sizes, and even control the ability to resize the window. This ensures that desktop applications follow the platform's guidelines for window resizing and give users full control.

Minimizing/Maximizing and Full-Screen: Flutter apps can now programmatically minimize, maximize, or toggle between windowed and full-screen modes, enhancing usability and adapting to various user preferences.

🎨 2. Native Platform Widgets

Another exciting feature in Flutter 3.29 is the introduction of native platform widgets that adhere to the design conventions of the operating system. Flutter now offers new widgets tailored for desktop platforms, enhancing the integration of Flutter apps with macOS, Windows, and Linux environments.

Custom Title Bars: For macOS and Windows, developers can customize window title bars to match the look and feel of the operating system. These title bars support native controls such as minimize, maximize, and close buttons, improving the native feel of the app.

CHAPTER 7   WEB AND DESKTOP ENHANCEMENTS

Native Menu Support: For desktop apps, Flutter now provides support for native menu bars. This allows developers to create menus that are consistent with the platform's design conventions. For example, on macOS, the app's menu can be positioned in the menu bar, and on Windows, a traditional top-level menu can be used.

Example:

```
MenuItem(
  label: 'File',
  items: [
    MenuItem(label: 'Open'),
    MenuItem(label: 'Save'),
  ]
);
```

Context Menus: Native right-click context menus are now supported on all platforms. This allows for the creation of right-click menus with actions such as copy, paste, and other native system interactions.

3. Enhanced Input Handling

Flutter 3.29 expands its input handling capabilities to offer more control over mouse events, keyboard shortcuts, and hover effects. This update provides smoother interaction models for desktop users, especially in cases where desktop-specific input devices like a mouse and keyboard come into play.

Hover Effects: Flutter now supports hover gestures across desktop platforms, enabling developers to add hover-based visual effects and actions. For instance, buttons can change color when hovered over, or tooltips can be shown when the mouse pointer enters a specific region.

Keyboard Shortcuts: Desktop apps often rely on keyboard shortcuts for improved productivity. Flutter 3.29 introduces better handling for detecting and responding to key events. You can now define custom key combinations for various app functions, creating a more seamless desktop experience.

Example:

```
RawKeyboardListener(
  focusNode: FocusNode(),
  onKey: (event) {
    if (event.isKeyPressed(LogicalKeyboardKey.controlLeft)) {
      // Trigger an action when Ctrl key is pressed
    }
  },
  child: Text('Press Ctrl key'),
);
```

Mouse Gestures: Flutter introduces enhanced support for mouse gestures on desktop apps. Developers can handle multiple mouse events such as clicks, double-clicks, drag, and drop, along with advanced gestures like scroll and pinch to zoom (on supported devices).

4. Drag-and-Drop Support

Drag-and-drop functionality is critical for a wide variety of desktop applications, particularly those in content creation, file management, and productivity tools. Flutter 3.29 fully integrates drag-and-drop support for desktop platforms.

Drag-and-Drop API: Flutter now supports both file and object dragging, enabling users to drag items from the desktop or within the app and drop them onto other windows, folders, or applications. This feature is ideal for building apps that deal with files, images, or content management.

CHAPTER 7 WEB AND DESKTOP ENHANCEMENTS

Example:

```
DragTarget<String>(
  onAccept: (data) {
    // Handle the dropped item
    print('Dropped: $data');
  },
  builder: (context, candidateData, rejectedData) {
    return Container(
      width: 200,
      height: 200,
      color: Colors.blue,
      child: Center(child: Text('Drag here')),
    );
  },
);
```

Cross-App Dragging: With improved platform-specific support, drag-and-drop now works across apps, so users can drag files or data from your Flutter Desktop app to other native apps, like a text editor or file explorer, providing a more fluid, native experience.

🎁 5. Better File System Access

Flutter 3.29 improves desktop apps' ability to interact with the file system, ensuring that apps can efficiently read, write, and manage files and directories across platforms.

Native File Picker: The new file picker APIs for Windows, macOS, and Linux allow users to open, save, or select files with native dialog boxes. This ensures that users have a consistent, platform-standard file system interaction.

Example:

```
final result = await FilePicker.platform.pickFiles();
if (result != null) {
  // Handle the picked file
}
```

File Watcher: Developers can now monitor file system changes with built-in watchers, allowing desktop apps to respond to file modifications, additions, or deletions in real time.

Flutter 3.29 introduces several innovative features that significantly improve the desktop development experience. These new additions give developers more control over window management, input handling, file system access, and UI components while maintaining consistency across platforms. Whether you're building productivity apps, creative tools, or native desktop utilities, these features elevate Flutter's capability to deliver professional-grade desktop applications.

Cross-Platform Consistency

One of Flutter's strongest selling points has always been its ability to deliver a consistent user experience across multiple platforms. Flutter 3.29 further enhances its ability to build cross-platform desktop applications, allowing developers to create high-quality apps that feel native on Windows, macOS, and Linux while using a single codebase.

This section delves into the advancements in Flutter's cross-platform consistency for desktop development, ensuring that developers can maintain a cohesive app design across all supported desktop environments.

CHAPTER 7   WEB AND DESKTOP ENHANCEMENTS

🎨 1. Unified UI Widgets Across Platforms

Flutter's extensive widget library ensures that apps look and behave similarly on different platforms while also providing platform-specific adjustments to align with native design patterns.

Material and Cupertino Widgets: Flutter includes the Material Design widgets (primarily for Android and web) and the Cupertino widgets (for iOS and macOS). These are now more consistent across desktop platforms, adapting the look and feel based on the underlying OS conventions while retaining a unified API for developers.

On Windows, Material widgets now respect system conventions, such as using system fonts and colors.

On macOS, Cupertino widgets are now fully integrated with Flutter's desktop environment, offering a more native macOS feel.

Linux also now offers a more polished experience with Material and custom widgets that match the popular GTK and GNOME environments.

Adaptive Widgets: Flutter introduces adaptive widgets, meaning that apps can dynamically adjust their visual components based on the platform they are running on. For instance, button styles, text fields, and dialog boxes can change based on whether the app is running on Windows, macOS, or Linux.

Example:

```
// Platform-adaptive button style
RaisedButton(
  child: Text('Click Me'),
  style: ButtonStyle(
    backgroundColor: MaterialStateProperty.all(Platform.
    isWindows ? Colors.blue : Colors.green),
  ),
  onPressed: () {},
);
```

2. Unified Graphics Rendering

Flutter's rendering engine, based on Skia, ensures that the visual fidelity of apps remains consistent, regardless of the platform. The framework's architecture helps eliminate discrepancies in visual rendering that often arise in other cross-platform solutions.

Cross-Platform Graphics Fidelity: Flutter's Skia engine renders app graphics consistently across all platforms, whether you're using high-DPI displays on macOS or standard screens on Windows or Linux. The use of Skia ensures that vector graphics, animations, and custom drawings look equally sharp and smooth on all platforms.

Cross-Platform Animations: Flutter's powerful animation framework works seamlessly across all platforms. Animations are smooth and consistent on macOS, Windows, and Linux, which means developers don't need to write platform-specific code to handle differences in frame rates or animation rendering.

Example:

For example, a simple animation can be implemented without worrying about platform discrepancies:

```
AnimationController _controller = AnimationController(vsync: this, duration: const Duration(seconds: 2));

@override
Widget build(BuildContext context) {
  return AnimatedBuilder(
    animation: _controller,
    builder: (context, child) {
      return Transform.scale(
        scale: _controller.value,
        child: child,
      );
```

```
    },
    child: Icon(Icons.star),
  );
}
```

✹ 3. Consistent Input Handling Across Platforms

Handling input devices like mouse, keyboard, and trackpads uniformly is critical for a cross-platform experience. Flutter 3.29 improves input handling on all desktop platforms, ensuring that mouse events, keyboard shortcuts, and touch gestures behave consistently across Windows, macOS, and Linux.

Mouse Input: Flutter Desktop apps handle mouse input consistently, whether it's for click events, hover states, or custom mouse gestures. On macOS and Windows, users can interact with Flutter apps just as they would with native applications.

Keyboard Shortcuts: A significant part of desktop applications involves keyboard shortcuts. Flutter 3.29 allows you to define and handle keyboard shortcuts consistently across platforms, ensuring that actions like "Cmd + C" on macOS and "Ctrl + C" on Windows both behave identically.

Touch and Gesture Support: While more common on tablets or mobile devices, touch events are still important for hybrid laptop configurations or touch-enabled displays. Flutter's desktop platforms now provide consistent touch handling across operating systems.

🎁 4. Platform-Specific APIs with Unified Access

Although Flutter maintains a high degree of cross-platform consistency, certain platform-specific APIs are still needed to interact with native features. Flutter 3.29 continues to streamline access to platform-specific APIs through a consistent interface.

Unified Plugin System: Flutter uses plugins to interact with native APIs. While plugins may offer platform-specific functionality, the plugin system ensures that developers only need to deal with a single API to access different platform capabilities, without worrying about the underlying platform differences.

For example, here's how to access the native file system for saving data:

```
final Directory directory = await getApplicationDocumentsDirectory();
```

Conditional Imports: Flutter allows you to write platform-specific code when needed using conditional imports. You can import different implementations based on the target platform, making it easier to handle platform-specific functionality without compromising the app's cross-platform nature.

Example:

```
import 'package:flutter/foundation.dart' show kIsWeb;

if (kIsWeb) {
  // Handle web-specific code
} else {
  // Handle desktop-specific code
}
```

🏁 5. Consistent Theming and Styling Across Platforms

To maintain a cohesive brand experience, Flutter provides powerful theming tools to style apps consistently across platforms. Whether on Windows, macOS, or Linux, Flutter offers ways to customize app themes to match your desired design specifications.

CHAPTER 7   WEB AND DESKTOP ENHANCEMENTS

Theming: With Flutter's flexible theming system, you can define a single theme for the app and ensure that it is applied uniformly across all platforms. Flutter supports dark and light modes natively, allowing you to offer consistent experiences based on user preferences.

Example:

```
ThemeData myTheme = ThemeData(
  primaryColor: Colors.blue,
  brightness: Brightness.light, // Apply light theme across
                                    platforms
);
```

Font Consistency: With Flutter's text rendering engine, fonts are rendered consistently across platforms. You can include custom fonts and use platform-native font styles to ensure that typography remains consistent and professional.

Flutter 3.29 ensures that developers can create truly cross-platform desktop applications that offer a consistent, native-like experience across Windows, macOS, and Linux. From unified UI components and graphics rendering to improved input handling and platform-specific APIs, Flutter continues to enhance its ability to deliver a seamless user experience, regardless of the operating system. By leveraging Flutter's consistent widget library, input handling, and theming tools, developers can craft apps that look and behave consistently across all desktop environments.

Packaging Desktop Apps for Deployment

Packaging your Flutter Desktop application is a crucial step in the development lifecycle. It ensures that your app can be properly distributed, installed, and executed on various operating systems—Windows, macOS, and Linux—without requiring the end user to manually install dependencies or handle configuration issues. Flutter 3.29 introduces streamlined methods for packaging desktop apps and handling their deployment, ensuring that developers can easily prepare apps for distribution.

Here we explore techniques for packaging Flutter Desktop applications and best practices for preparing them for deployment across different platforms.

Techniques for Desktop App Packaging

Packaging your Flutter Desktop application involves preparing your app for distribution in a format suitable for each operating system—Windows, macOS, and Linux. Flutter simplifies this process, allowing you to use a single codebase to generate cross-platform desktop apps while taking into account the unique requirements and guidelines of each platform.

This section explores various techniques and tools for packaging Flutter Desktop apps for deployment, ensuring that your app is ready for end-user installation and usage.

✵ 1. Windows Packaging Techniques

For Windows, Flutter provides several options for packaging apps, with MSIX being the preferred packaging format for modern applications. MSIX ensures that your app is secure, supports automatic updates, and integrates well with the Windows operating system. Additionally, other methods like Inno Setup can be used for traditional desktop installations.

MSIX Packaging for Windows

MSIX is a modern packaging format that offers a secure, reliable way to package and distribute apps. MSIX supports features like

> **Automatic Updates**: MSIX allows for seamless updates, ensuring users always have the latest version of the app.

CHAPTER 7   WEB AND DESKTOP ENHANCEMENTS

Rollback Support: In case of installation or update failures, MSIX allows the system to roll back to a previous version.

App Virtualization: MSIX isolates the app from other system components, improving security and stability.

To package a Flutter Windows app into an MSIX package, use the following steps:

1. **Build the App**: First, ensure that the app is built for release using the command

    ```
    flutter build windows --release
    ```

2. **Generate the MSIX Package**: Use the MSIX packaging tools (e.g., "msix-packaging" tool) to generate the package. Flutter's "flutter-desktop-embedding" plugin helps automate this process.

3. **Sign the MSIX Package**: Before distributing your MSIX package, it's essential to sign it with a code-signing certificate. This ensures that your app is trusted by Windows and prevents warnings during installation.

4. **Distribute the App**: Once packaged, distribute the MSIX file through the Microsoft Store or directly to users via websites or enterprise distribution systems.

CHAPTER 7   WEB AND DESKTOP ENHANCEMENTS

Inno Setup Packaging for Windows

For a more traditional approach, Inno Setup is another popular tool for creating Windows installers. It provides complete control over the installation process and is ideal for developers who need a more customized installer.

To use Inno Setup with Flutter, follow these steps:

1. **Build the App:** Create a release version of your app with the following command:

   ```
   flutter build windows --release
   ```

2. **Create the Installer:** Use Inno Setup to create an installer script (".iss") that will package the app into a ".exe" installer.

3. **Customize the Installer:** You can define custom installation options such as setting installation paths, adding shortcuts, and including additional files like external libraries.

4. **Generate the Installer:** After configuring the installer script, run Inno Setup to generate the installer executable (".exe").

2. macOS Packaging Techniques

For macOS, Flutter generates an App Bundle, which is the standard format for macOS applications. App Bundles are directories containing all the necessary resources (executables, assets, and metadata) required to run an app.

App Bundle for macOS

An App Bundle is a directory that macOS treats as a single unit. It contains everything the app needs to run, including the executable, assets, and other resources. Flutter automatically generates the App Bundle when you build a macOS app with the following command:

```
flutter build macos --release
```

Distributing with DMG (Disk Image)

For macOS, one of the most common methods of distribution is using a DMG (Disk Image). A DMG file is a mountable disk image that contains your App Bundle, making it easy for users to install by dragging the app to their Applications folder.

To create a DMG for your Flutter macOS app, follow these steps:

1. **Build the App**: Ensure that your app is built and ready for release:

   ```
   flutter build macos --release
   ```

2. **Create the DMG File**: Use third-party tools like "create-dmg" or create your own DMG packaging scripts to bundle your ".app" bundle into a DMG. Here's an example using "create-dmg":

   ```
   create-dmg MyApp.app
   ```

CHAPTER 7   WEB AND DESKTOP ENHANCEMENTS

3. **Sign the App**: Before distributing your DMG file, macOS requires your app to be signed with a valid Apple Developer ID. This ensures that users can open the app without security warnings.

4. **Distribute the DMG**: After creating the DMG file, you can distribute it directly to users via email, download links, or the Mac App Store.

🐧 3. Linux Packaging Techniques

Linux packaging varies depending on the distribution and packaging format. Flutter supports creating Linux apps in multiple formats, including AppImage, Debian (.deb), and Snap. These formats are designed for cross-distribution compatibility, ensuring that your app runs smoothly across different Linux distributions.

AppImage for Linux

AppImage is a portable application format that bundles the app and all its dependencies into a single executable file. This format makes it easy to distribute your app to Linux users across a variety of distributions without worrying about specific package managers.

Here's how to create an AppImage:

1. **Build the App**: Build the release version of your app:

   ```
   flutter build linux --release
   ```

2. **Package as AppImage**: Use tools like "linuxdeployqt" or the "flutter-desktop-embedding" plugin to package your app as an AppImage.

Here's an example using "linuxdeployqt":

```
linuxdeployqt MyApp.AppImage
```

Debian Packaging for Linux

For Debian-based systems (e.g., Ubuntu), you can package your app as a ".deb" file. This format integrates with Debian's package manager, making it easy for users to install and update the app.

1. **Build the App**: Ensure that the app is built for release:

   ```
   flutter build linux --release
   ```

2. **Create the .deb Package**: Use tools like "dpkg" or create a custom "debian/" directory structure for your app and its dependencies.

3. **Sign and Distribute**: If you want to distribute the ".deb" package through official channels, sign it using GPG and publish it to a repository.

Snap Packaging for Linux

Snap is another popular packaging format for Linux that allows you to distribute apps across multiple distributions using Snapcraft.

1. **Build the App**: Build the app in release mode:

   ```
   flutter build linux --release
   ```

CHAPTER 7   WEB AND DESKTOP ENHANCEMENTS

2. **Package as Snap**: Use the Snapcraft tool to create a Snap package for your app:

```
snapcraft
```

3. **Sign and Publish**: After creating the Snap package, you can publish it to the Snap Store for easy installation across a variety of Linux distributions.

Flutter 3.29 offers several techniques for packaging desktop applications, ensuring that your apps are ready for deployment across different platforms. For Windows, you can use MSIX or Inno Setup to create installers, while macOS apps are typically packaged in App Bundles and distributed via DMG files. On Linux, AppImage, Debian, and Snap packaging formats provide flexibility for distributing apps across various distributions. Each platform has unique packaging requirements, but Flutter simplifies the process, enabling you to create professional, cross-platform desktop applications with minimal hassle.

Managing Dependencies for Desktop

One of the challenges when packaging and deploying desktop applications is managing dependencies. Desktop applications, especially those targeting multiple platforms like Windows, macOS, and Linux, often rely on various external libraries, plugins, and system dependencies. Flutter offers several techniques and best practices for managing these dependencies to ensure that your desktop app runs smoothly on each platform.

Here, we explore how to manage both Flutter-specific dependencies and platform-specific dependencies when building and packaging Flutter Desktop apps.

1. Understanding Flutter Dependencies

Flutter allows you to integrate external dependencies via the pubspec.yaml file. Dependencies in Flutter can include packages from pub.dev, plugins, and native libraries that your app relies on. For desktop applications, managing these dependencies is just as important as for mobile or web applications, with some additional considerations for platform-specific functionality.

Managing Flutter Packages

To add dependencies to your Flutter project, you use the "dependencies" section in the "pubspec.yaml" file. For example, if your desktop app relies on packages such as "sqflite" for database functionality or "path_provider" for managing file paths, you would add them like this:

```
dependencies:
  flutter:
    sdk: flutter
  sqflite: ^2.0.0
  path_provider: ^2.0.0
```

Once dependencies are added to the "pubspec.yaml," use the following command to fetch the packages:

```
flutter pub get
```

These dependencies are platform-agnostic and are included automatically when building for desktop platforms. However, certain dependencies may require platform-specific handling, which we will discuss next.

2. Managing Platform-Specific Dependencies

While Flutter abstracts away most platform-specific complexities, desktop apps often require additional configuration to manage native dependencies on Windows, macOS, and Linux. These dependencies can include system libraries, third-party software, and native code components.

Windows Dependencies

On Windows, your Flutter app may require specific libraries (DLLs), C++ runtime libraries, or other system components. Managing these dependencies is crucial for ensuring your app runs without missing components.

Bundling DLLs: When building for Windows, you need to ensure that all necessary DLLs are included in the package. This can be done manually or using packaging tools like Inno Setup or MSIX.

For example, if your app depends on "libcurl.dll" for network operations, ensure that the DLL is placed in the app's installation directory or bundled with the installer.

Redistributable Packages: Windows often requires redistributable packages (e.g., Visual C++ Redistributable). To ensure that your app doesn't break due to missing libraries, include these redistributables in your installer or use a packaging tool that automatically handles them.

Example: For C++ runtime dependencies, you can include the Visual C++ Redistributable in the Inno Setup script:

```
[Files]
Source: "vc_redist.x64.exe"; DestDir: "{tmp}"; Flags: ignoreversion

[Run]
Filename: "{tmp}\vc_redist.x64.exe"; Parameters: "/quiet"; Flags: runhidden
```

macOS Dependencies

macOS applications often rely on libraries and frameworks that are part of macOS, such as system frameworks or external libraries like Cocoa. When packaging macOS applications, you must ensure that these dependencies are bundled correctly.

App Bundle Structure: The App Bundle must contain all required libraries in the "Contents/Frameworks" directory. If your app relies on third-party frameworks, make sure they are included in the bundle and correctly referenced in your app's "Info.plist."

Homebrew and Cask: For non-system dependencies (e.g., external libraries not bundled with macOS), you can use Homebrew to install the required libraries and reference them in your app's bundle. While Homebrew isn't typically used in production apps, it can be helpful during development for installing and managing dependencies.

Code Signing and Notarization: Ensure that all third-party dependencies are also signed (if applicable) to avoid security warnings from macOS Gatekeeper.

Linux Dependencies

On Linux, Flutter apps depend on system libraries, which may vary across distributions. When packaging a Flutter Desktop app for Linux, you need to manage these dependencies carefully to ensure compatibility with various Linux distributions.

Package Managers: Linux distributions use package managers like "apt" (Debian/Ubuntu), "yum" (Fedora/RHEL), and "dnf" to install system libraries. Ensure that your app's documentation includes instructions for installing required dependencies using these package managers.

For example, if your app relies on libraries like GTK+ or libpng, include installation instructions for them:

```
sudo apt-get install libgtk-3-dev libpng-dev
```

CHAPTER 7   WEB AND DESKTOP ENHANCEMENTS

AppImage Bundling: When creating an AppImage, the goal is to package all necessary dependencies into the AppImage itself, so the app works independently of the target system's libraries. Tools like "linuxdeployqt" can help bundle required libraries and ensure the app runs on multiple Linux distributions.

Example:

Here's how to bundle dependencies into an AppImage:

```
linuxdeployqt MyApp.AppImage
```

Snapcraft: When using Snapcraft to package your app, it automatically includes the necessary dependencies inside the Snap package, isolating your app from system-wide library versions. However, you may still need to specify certain required dependencies in the Snapcraft configuration file ("snapcraft.yaml").

Example "snapcraft.yaml"

```yaml
name: my-flutter-app
version: '1.0'
summary: Flutter desktop app for Linux
description: |
  A cross-platform desktop app built with Flutter.

apps:
  my-flutter-app:
    command: my-flutter-app
    plugs: [network, x11]

parts:
  flutter-app:
    plugin: dump
```

CHAPTER 7   WEB AND DESKTOP ENHANCEMENTS

```
source: .
stage-packages:
  - libgtk-3-0
  - libpng16-16
```

⚙ 3. Dependency Management Tools

To help manage dependencies more efficiently, you can use several tools designed to simplify this process:

CMake: For native dependencies written in C++ or other compiled languages, CMake is often used to configure and build these dependencies for cross-platform use. This is especially useful for macOS and Linux, where custom native code is more common.

You can include "CMakeLists.txt" files in your Flutter Desktop app to handle the build process for native dependencies.

Flutter Plugin System: If your app requires additional Flutter plugins (e.g., database or hardware access plugins), make sure to include them in your "pubspec.yaml" file and ensure they are compatible with desktop platforms. Some plugins may require platform-specific setup, which can be handled through platform channels or native code.

✅ 4. Best Practices for Managing Dependencies

Minimize External Dependencies: Keep your app's dependencies to a minimum to reduce the risk of conflicts and compatibility issues. Only include libraries that are necessary for your app's core functionality.

Version Pinning: Always specify exact versions of critical dependencies in your "pubspec.yaml" to avoid issues when newer, incompatible versions of libraries are released.

Test on All Platforms: Regularly test your app on all targeted platforms (Windows, macOS, and Linux) to ensure that all dependencies are correctly integrated and function as expected.

CHAPTER 7   WEB AND DESKTOP ENHANCEMENTS

CI/CD Pipelines: Use continuous integration (CI) tools like GitHub Actions or GitLab CI to automate the process of fetching dependencies, building the app, and running tests. This will help ensure that your app's dependencies are up-to-date and compatible across platforms.

Managing dependencies for desktop apps built with Flutter requires careful consideration of platform-specific libraries, tools, and packaging formats. By using appropriate packaging methods for Windows, macOS, and Linux, developers can ensure that their Flutter Desktop apps have all the necessary dependencies bundled for seamless installation and use. Using dependency management tools like CMake and Flutter plugins, along with following best practices, will help streamline the process and avoid compatibility issues, ensuring that your desktop app delivers a consistent experience across platforms.

Case Studies

In this section, we delve into real-world examples of how Flutter has been used to build powerful and innovative web and desktop applications. These success stories showcase how developers have harnessed Flutter's capabilities to create cross-platform solutions with excellent performance, seamless user experiences, and efficient workflows. Whether you're building a web app, desktop application, or both, these case studies will offer valuable insights into how Flutter is shaping the future of app development across platforms.

Success Stories of Web and Desktop Apps Built with Flutter

Flutter has gained considerable traction as a framework for building not just mobile apps but also high-performance web and desktop applications. Many businesses have adopted Flutter to create scalable, beautiful, and

CHAPTER 7   WEB AND DESKTOP ENHANCEMENTS

high-performance apps that run across different platforms, significantly reducing development time and increasing productivity. Let's take a closer look at some of the most notable success stories of web and desktop apps built with Flutter.

Analysis of Leading Web Apps

Flutter for Web has rapidly matured, and several leading web applications have successfully adopted the framework to deliver powerful, high-performance experiences. In this section, we analyze a few of the most successful web apps built using Flutter, exploring how they utilize the framework's capabilities to offer fast load times, rich user interfaces, and seamless cross-platform experiences.

Example 1: eBay's "Shoppable Ads"

eBay, a global leader in ecommerce, has integrated Flutter into its "Shoppable Ads" feature for web applications. This feature aims to deliver an immersive shopping experience directly within advertisements on web platforms.

Challenge: eBay needed to provide users with an engaging, interactive ad experience without compromising performance or loading times. The ads had to be responsive across different screen sizes and browsers while also handling dynamic content updates in real time.

Solution: By using Flutter, eBay was able to build a single codebase that works seamlessly on both mobile and web platforms. Flutter's performance-oriented architecture helped create a highly responsive and visually rich user interface that reacts fluidly to user input and displays real-time data updates without significant lag.

Impact: eBay's decision to use Flutter for web development allowed them to reduce development time, maintain a consistent design across platforms, and deliver a dynamic shopping experience to users. The app's smooth animations and responsive behavior helped increase engagement with the ads, ultimately boosting conversion rates.

547

Key Insights:
Flutter's Rendering Engine: Flutter's ability to handle complex animations and smooth transitions across platforms made it an ideal choice for eBay's dynamic ad features.

Cross-Platform Efficiency: Using a single codebase for both web and mobile platforms simplified eBay's development process, saving time and resources while ensuring a consistent user experience.

Example 2: Google Ads Web Interface

Google Ads, a leading advertising platform used by businesses worldwide, leverages Flutter for building parts of its web interface. The web app requires highly responsive UIs capable of displaying complex data analytics and performance metrics in real time, with minimal delays.

Challenge: Google Ads needed a solution that would allow users to interact with large datasets and receive instant feedback while maintaining a fast, fluid user interface on both mobile and web platforms.

Solution: Flutter for Web's widget-based system enabled Google Ads to design dynamic, data-driven components that adapt to user inputs with minimal delay. The app integrates real-time data updates and allows users to navigate through performance dashboards without lag. Google Ads utilized Flutter's ability to optimize web performance, ensuring that even with numerous active elements, the app maintained responsiveness and smooth transitions.

Impact: By adopting Flutter for Web, Google Ads was able to unify its codebase for web and mobile interfaces, reduce loading times, and offer a more fluid user experience. The framework's efficient rendering engine ensured that real-time updates were displayed seamlessly, enhancing the overall user experience for advertisers.

Key Insights:
Efficient Data Handling: Flutter's ability to handle real-time data efficiently was crucial for Google Ads, which demands high performance and responsiveness for displaying large datasets.

CHAPTER 7 WEB AND DESKTOP ENHANCEMENTS

Consistency Across Platforms: With a shared codebase for mobile and web, Google Ads ensured that the user interface remained consistent across devices, improving usability and reducing the need for platform-specific customization.

Example 3: BMW's Mobile and Web App Ecosystem

BMW's customer app ecosystem, which includes their web app for vehicle management, integrates Flutter to provide a smooth, visually appealing interface for customers to interact with their cars and manage services like scheduling maintenance, checking fuel efficiency, and tracking vehicle health.

Challenge: BMW needed to ensure that its app offered a sleek, high-performance UI across multiple platforms, especially since its web app needed to reflect the mobile experience without compromising functionality. The web app also had to handle user-specific data securely, including car diagnostics and maintenance schedules.

Solution: BMW adopted Flutter to unify their web and mobile interfaces. The framework's ability to create customized, reusable widgets allowed for a consistent user interface across different platforms while maintaining the necessary performance characteristics for data-heavy tasks, such as displaying vehicle diagnostics in real time.

Impact: By using Flutter for the web, BMW's app ecosystem is now capable of delivering a seamless experience across mobile and desktop platforms, providing users with easy access to vehicle information. The smooth user interface helps improve user engagement, ensuring that car owners feel connected and in control of their vehicle data.

Key Insights:

Customizable Widgets for Brand Consistency: Flutter's custom widget capabilities enabled BMW to build a unique, branded experience across both web and mobile platforms without needing to build separate interfaces.

Real-Time Data Integration: Flutter allowed BMW to provide real-time, data-rich experiences, essential for users to interact with their vehicle's diagnostics in a meaningful way.

Example 4: Reflectly—The Personal Journal App

Reflectly, a popular personal journal and wellness app, offers a web-based version built with Flutter. Reflectly provides a dynamic journaling experience, integrating mindfulness and well-being tracking, with features like mood tracking, daily reflections, and personalized content.

Challenge: Reflectly needed to deliver a rich, interactive user interface on both web and mobile platforms while ensuring that complex animations (e.g., mood graphs and journal entries) performed efficiently across various devices.

Solution: Reflectly utilized Flutter's web capabilities to build a cross-platform journaling experience. The web app offers fluid animations, smooth transitions, and responsive design, allowing users to easily switch between platforms without compromising on the visual appeal or functionality. Flutter's rendering engine ensured that the app delivered a near-native experience on the web.

Impact: Reflectly was able to expand its user base by offering a consistent, high-quality experience on both mobile and web platforms. The framework's performance optimizations and UI rendering allowed Reflectly to deliver a fast, enjoyable experience for journaling and tracking mental well-being.

Key Insights:

Smooth User Interactions: Reflectly benefited from Flutter's ability to deliver fluid animations and transitions, enhancing the user experience, especially for a highly interactive app like journaling.

Cross-Platform Adaptability: Flutter allowed Reflectly to easily extend its reach across both mobile and web platforms without sacrificing the app's core features or design integrity.

CHAPTER 7   WEB AND DESKTOP ENHANCEMENTS

Key Takeaways

The leading web apps discussed here demonstrate Flutter's growing potential for creating high-performance, engaging web applications. Whether it's ecommerce, advertising, automotive, or wellness, Flutter provides a unified framework that allows developers to target multiple platforms from a single codebase. The key benefits observed in these case studies include

Performance Optimization: Flutter's efficient rendering engine and reactive UI components enable apps to deliver fast, smooth, and engaging user experiences across web and mobile platforms.

Cross-Platform Codebase: By utilizing a single codebase for web and mobile, businesses can significantly reduce development time, maintenance efforts, and ensure a consistent user interface across devices.

Customization and Flexibility: Flutter's rich widget system allows for highly customizable UIs that can reflect the brand and functionality of a web app without compromising performance.

These leading web apps showcase how Flutter can help developers create web applications that are not only functional but also offer exceptional user experiences. As Flutter continues to evolve, it's expected that even more companies will adopt the framework to create innovative and performant web applications.

Case Studies of Desktop Applications

Flutter's capabilities for desktop app development have seen significant growth, making it an increasingly viable option for building cross-platform desktop applications. These case studies highlight how companies have successfully utilized Flutter to create desktop apps with native-like performance, smooth user interfaces, and enhanced productivity. From streamlining workflows to enhancing user engagement, these apps demonstrate the flexibility and potential of Flutter for building robust desktop applications across Windows, macOS, and Linux.

CHAPTER 7   WEB AND DESKTOP ENHANCEMENTS

Example 1: Invoice Ninja

Invoice Ninja, a popular invoicing and billing solution, adopted Flutter to extend its application to desktop platforms. The app allows small business owners and freelancers to manage their invoices, time tracking, and payments from any device.

Challenge: Invoice Ninja needed to build a cross-platform desktop application that would integrate seamlessly with its existing web and mobile apps. The desktop version had to offer a high-quality user experience, with quick load times and real-time updates, while also maintaining the core features of the original app.

Solution: By leveraging Flutter's desktop support, Invoice Ninja was able to create a desktop app with the same user interface as the mobile and web versions. Flutter's fast rendering engine and cross-platform consistency ensured that the app maintained smooth performance across Windows, macOS, and Linux.

Impact: The desktop app significantly improved the app's reach by offering a seamless, native-like experience on all three platforms. Invoice Ninja reduced the overhead of building separate apps for each desktop OS and enjoyed the efficiency of a single codebase for both web and desktop platforms.

Key Insights:

Cross-Platform Development: Flutter's cross-platform capabilities allowed Invoice Ninja to maintain a unified user experience and significantly cut development costs.

Real-Time Data Sync: Flutter's efficient data management capabilities allowed Invoice Ninja to integrate real-time data syncing, ensuring users could access updated information across devices instantly.

Example 2: FLEETCOR

FLEETCOR, a leading global provider of fuel cards and payment solutions for businesses, used Flutter to develop their fleet management desktop application. The app enables users to monitor fuel consumption, track vehicle locations, and generate detailed reports.

Challenge: The application required real-time data synchronization, a rich, interactive user interface, and the ability to support a wide range of features across desktop platforms. FLEETCOR needed a framework that could integrate data from various systems and provide a consistent user experience on macOS, Windows, and Linux.

Solution: Flutter enabled FLEETCOR to use the same codebase for all three desktop platforms, allowing for faster development and better consistency. The framework's powerful widget system allowed FLEETCOR to design a modern, data-rich interface with real-time updates, while the engine's performance optimizations ensured the app could handle heavy data loads without lag.

Impact: The Flutter-based desktop app enabled FLEETCOR to provide an intuitive and high-performing fleet management tool, improving the overall productivity of businesses managing large fleets of vehicles. The app's seamless cross-platform compatibility simplified updates and maintenance.

Key Insights:

Real-Time Data Processing: Flutter's ability to handle data-intensive applications with complex functionalities, like real-time fleet tracking and reporting, proved essential for FLEETCOR.

Cross-Platform Consistency: By using Flutter, FLEETCOR ensured that users received a uniform experience across multiple desktop operating systems, reducing the need for platform-specific adjustments.

Example 3: *The New York Times* The Crossword App

The New York Times uses Flutter to develop its popular crossword puzzle app. This app offers an engaging and dynamic crossword-solving experience, allowing users to tackle daily puzzles, track progress, and interact with various crossword features.

CHAPTER 7   WEB AND DESKTOP ENHANCEMENTS

Challenge: *The New York Times* wanted to provide a seamless crossword experience on desktop platforms, with smooth transitions, real-time puzzle updates, and support for various user preferences, including accessibility features.

Solution: Flutter's flexibility allowed *The New York Times* to build a cross-platform desktop application with native-like performance. The crossword puzzle app integrated rich UI elements, complex animations, and live updates without sacrificing performance. Flutter's cross-platform support enabled them to streamline development for Windows, macOS, and Linux.

Impact: The app's smooth interactions, real-time puzzle updates, and accessible design made it a hit with users. By leveraging Flutter, *The New York Times* reduced development time and could focus on enhancing the core puzzle-solving experience rather than worrying about platform-specific issues.

Key Insights:

Smooth UI and Animations: Flutter's ability to create smooth transitions and animations was key for *The New York Times* The Crossword app, which required seamless, interactive puzzle navigation.

Cross-Platform Expansion: Flutter helped *The New York Times* extend its app from mobile to desktop, maintaining a consistent user experience and functionality across platforms.

Example 4: SpaceX Launchpad Dashboard

SpaceX, the pioneering private aerospace manufacturer, uses Flutter to manage and visualize the data for its launchpad operations. The app provides real-time updates, including countdown timers, weather monitoring, and system diagnostics for launch events.

Challenge: SpaceX required a solution that could handle real-time data updates while maintaining a responsive and visually appealing interface. The application needed to work across desktop platforms, delivering real-time monitoring data without delay or performance issues.

CHAPTER 7   WEB AND DESKTOP ENHANCEMENTS

Solution: Flutter's desktop support enabled SpaceX to create a desktop app capable of displaying critical launchpad data in real time, with fast updates and rich visualizations. The ability to handle both graphical interfaces and backend data seamlessly made Flutter an excellent choice for this application.

Impact: The app provided SpaceX's operations teams with a streamlined dashboard, improving their efficiency during launches and real-time monitoring. Flutter allowed SpaceX to maintain consistency and performance across all desktop platforms.

Key Insights:

Real-Time Data Management: Flutter's performance optimizations enabled SpaceX to handle the real-time demands of the launchpad dashboard with minimal lag.

Cross-Platform Support: Using a unified codebase for all desktop platforms ensured that SpaceX could deploy updates quickly and efficiently across different operating systems.

Key Takeaways

These case studies of desktop applications showcase the versatility and power of Flutter as a framework for building high-performance, cross-platform desktop solutions. Whether it's a financial management tool, a crossword puzzle app, or a mission-critical monitoring dashboard, Flutter has proven to be an excellent choice for creating feature-rich desktop apps.

The key benefits demonstrated by these examples include

Cross-Platform Codebase: Flutter's ability to provide a single codebase for macOS, Windows, and Linux drastically reduces development time and costs, ensuring a consistent user experience across platforms.

Native-Like Performance: Flutter's rendering engine allows for smooth, fluid user interfaces that perform well, even in resource-intensive applications that require real-time updates.

Rapid Development and Iteration: Flutter's hot reload feature accelerates the development process, allowing for quick testing and iteration of new features.

Flexible UI Design: The framework's customizable widgets enable developers to build highly interactive and visually stunning desktop applications.

By adopting Flutter for their desktop apps, companies can take advantage of the framework's growing ecosystem and create applications that are fast, responsive, and consistent across platforms.

Performance Benchmarking for Web and Desktop

Performance is a critical factor in the development of any app, especially for web and desktop applications that aim to deliver smooth, efficient, and responsive user experiences. Flutter, with its growing capabilities for web and desktop development, offers a framework that can produce high-performing applications across multiple platforms. In this section, we will explore how to compare performance between web and desktop apps built with Flutter, as well as techniques for optimizing performance across platforms.

Comparing Web and Desktop Performance

When developing applications with Flutter for both the web and desktop platforms, it's crucial to understand the performance dynamics of each platform. While both Flutter web and desktop share the same underlying framework, their performance characteristics differ significantly due to the nature of the platforms they run on. The comparison between web and desktop performance includes factors such as rendering speed, resource consumption, network latency, and platform-specific challenges.

This section will explore how Flutter handles performance on the web and desktop and how developers can optimize their applications to achieve smooth, fast experiences across both platforms.

Key Differences in Web and Desktop Performance

1. **Rendering and Frame Rate**

   Desktop:

   Desktop apps generally have direct access to the machine's hardware, including the CPU, GPU, and RAM. This gives desktop apps a significant performance advantage, especially when it comes to rendering complex UIs or handling high-performance tasks like gaming, video rendering, or interactive graphics. Flutter's Skia engine provides consistent rendering for both web and desktop, but desktop applications tend to experience smoother performance due to more powerful system resources.

   Web:

   Web apps rely on the browser's rendering engine and are constrained by the browser's performance limitations. Even though Flutter web apps use the Skia-based engine to render widgets, web browsers are not as optimized for graphics rendering as desktop environments. As a result, web apps may experience slower rendering times, particularly when dealing with complex layouts, custom painting, or high-graphics content. The performance of web apps also depends on the browser being used (Chrome, Firefox, Safari, etc.) and the client's hardware capabilities, which can vary widely.

2. **Resource Consumption**

   Desktop:

   Desktop applications typically have fewer resource constraints than web apps. Since they run directly on the user's operating system, they can leverage the full potential of the system's CPU, RAM, and GPU. For tasks that require heavy computation or resource-intensive operations, desktop apps are usually more efficient and faster. However, they can also consume more resources, so developers must focus on managing memory and CPU usage to ensure optimal performance.

   Web:

   Flutter web apps are subject to the constraints of web browsers, which means they must operate within the memory and CPU limits set by the browser. While Flutter web strives to minimize resource consumption, web apps are generally less performant than desktop applications, particularly in memory usage and processing power. The reliance on the browser's JavaScript engine adds an additional layer of overhead. Thus, web apps may be slower and consume more resources, particularly when rendering large numbers of complex widgets or performing intensive tasks.

3. **Load Times**

   Desktop:

   Once a desktop application is installed, it benefits from faster load times as it doesn't need to download or initialize large resources every time it's launched. Desktop apps can be optimized for quick startup by reducing the initial loading of assets and relying on local storage. This is especially true for Flutter, which compiles to native machine code for desktop platforms (Windows, macOS, and Linux), allowing apps to run with minimal delay.

Web:

Web applications, by contrast, are often slower to load because they must fetch resources from the server every time the app is accessed, depending on network conditions. The initial load time of a Flutter web app can be impacted by the size of the JavaScript bundle, the complexity of the app, and the client's network speed. To mitigate this, developers can use techniques like lazy loading, code splitting, and caching assets to speed up load times and reduce the reliance on network requests.

4. **Latency and Responsiveness**

    Desktop:

    Desktop applications tend to have lower latency and better responsiveness, as they run directly on the operating system with direct access to the hardware. User interactions with desktop apps are generally more responsive because they are processed locally without needing to rely on the internet or a remote server. This is particularly beneficial for applications that require real-time interaction, such as video editing software, games, or interactive simulations.

Web:

Web applications are subject to higher latency, primarily due to network communications, server requests, and browser limitations. Every interaction in a web app may involve sending requests to a server or fetching data over the internet, which introduces delays. In addition, certain browser-specific optimizations may not be as effective across all browsers, leading to inconsistent performance. Web apps can be less responsive for tasks that require low latency, such as real-time collaboration or high-frequency updates.

5. **Platform-Specific Features**

   Desktop:

   Desktop applications can take full advantage of platform-specific features, such as native file system access, system notifications, advanced input methods, and custom window management. These capabilities allow desktop apps to offer a more tailored and feature-rich experience. With Flutter Desktop, developers can use platform channels to access native APIs and integrate more deeply with the underlying operating system.

   Web:

   Web applications, on the other hand, are limited by the capabilities of web browsers. Although modern browsers support features like local storage, WebSockets, and service workers, web apps still lack the level of access that desktop apps have

CHAPTER 7   WEB AND DESKTOP ENHANCEMENTS

to system resources and hardware. Additionally, features like native file system access and advanced UI customizations are often more restricted in web apps.

Performance Optimization Techniques for Both Web and Desktop

1. **Use Platform-Specific Code:**

   To maximize performance on both web and desktop, Flutter allows developers to write platform-specific code when necessary. This enables the use of native APIs and optimizations tailored to the strengths of each platform. For example, desktop apps might use more advanced file handling methods, while web apps may focus on optimizing asset loading and caching.

2. **Efficient Rendering:**

   Keep widget trees minimal and avoid unnecessary re-renders. Flutter's "const" constructors and the "shouldRebuild" mechanism in widgets help minimize unnecessary redraws. For web, reduce the use of custom painters and complex animations, as these can lead to slower performance on browsers.

3. **Leverage Lazy Loading:**

   Use lazy loading to only load content and assets when they are needed. This is particularly useful for large Flutter web apps, where loading everything at once can result in slower initial load times. Similarly, desktop apps can benefit from deferred loading of non-essential resources to optimize startup time.

4. **Optimize Network Requests:**

   Continuously profile your Flutter app on both web and desktop to identify performance bottlenecks. Use tools like Flutter DevTools for profiling, and regularly test the app's performance across different browsers and desktop environments to ensure consistency and optimal performance.

While both Flutter web and desktop apps share the same framework, the performance of each platform is influenced by the underlying system constraints, rendering mechanisms, and available resources. Desktop apps generally offer better performance in terms of rendering speed, resource consumption, and responsiveness, while web apps face challenges due to browser limitations, network dependencies, and cross-platform compatibility.

By understanding the unique performance characteristics of each platform, developers can optimize their Flutter apps to achieve optimal performance across both web and desktop environments. With the right approach to rendering, resource management, and platform-specific optimizations, Flutter developers can deliver high-performance applications that provide a seamless user experience, regardless of the platform.

Optimizing Apps for Multiple Platforms

Developing a Flutter application that runs across multiple platforms—such as web, desktop, and mobile—requires careful consideration of platform-specific performance optimizations. While Flutter's cross-platform nature allows for shared codebases, the performance and experience on each platform can vary significantly. Optimizing apps for multiple platforms means balancing shared code with platform-specific optimizations to ensure that users get the best experience regardless of the platform they are using.

CHAPTER 7   WEB AND DESKTOP ENHANCEMENTS

Here, we will explore strategies to optimize Flutter apps for multiple platforms, focusing on key areas such as rendering performance, resource usage, platform-specific APIs, and adapting UI/UX for diverse screen sizes and input methods.

Key Strategies for Cross-Platform Optimization

1. **Conditional Code for Platform-Specific Performance**

    Flutter allows developers to use platform channels to call native APIs and write platform-specific code where necessary. This can be especially useful when performance optimization requires accessing platform-specific features or when Flutter's built-in widgets are not sufficient for certain tasks.

    For example, you may want to access the file system on desktop platforms but restrict it on the web for security reasons. You can use conditional imports or platform checks to ensure that the right code is executed for each platform.

    ```
    if (Platform.isWindows) {
      // Use Windows-specific API for file handling
    } else if (Platform.isMacOS) {
      // Use macOS-specific code
    }
    ```

2. **Optimize Rendering for Different Platforms**

    Mobile: Mobile devices are typically optimized for touch-based interaction, so rendering performance must be efficient enough to handle animations, gestures, and transitions smoothly.

    Web: Flutter web relies on the browser's rendering engine, which may not be as optimized for graphics-heavy operations as native desktop or mobile apps. For web apps, developers should minimize complex custom painters, avoid heavy reliance on animations, and optimize widget trees to improve rendering speed.

    Desktop: Desktop apps, while benefiting from more powerful hardware, still require optimization to ensure smooth UI performance. This includes efficient use of GPU rendering, especially for graphics-heavy applications like games or multimedia tools.

    For all platforms, techniques such as minimizing widget rebuilds, using "const" constructors where possible, and optimizing layouts (e.g., using "ListView.builder" for large lists) can help improve rendering performance.

3. **Leverage Adaptive UI for Multiple Screen Sizes**

    The user interface should be adaptive to accommodate various screen sizes and input methods across platforms.

CHAPTER 7   WEB AND DESKTOP ENHANCEMENTS

On mobile devices, the UI typically uses touch-based inputs and smaller screens. On desktop platforms, the UI might need to be adjusted for larger screens, multiple windows, and precise mouse or keyboard interactions.

Flutter provides tools like "LayoutBuilder" and "MediaQuery" to create responsive layouts that adapt to different screen sizes and orientations. Use these tools to build UIs that work well across devices, from smartphones to large desktop monitors.

Here's an example for handling different screen sizes:

```
var screenWidth = MediaQuery.of(context).size.width;
if (screenWidth > 600) {
  // Desktop layout
} else {
  // Mobile layout
}
```

4. **Optimize Network Requests and Latency**

    Web: Since web apps often rely on network requests to fetch data, optimizing these requests can significantly improve performance. Use techniques like lazy loading, caching, and throttling to reduce the number of requests and speed up the app's responsiveness.

Desktop and Mobile: For desktop and mobile apps, network requests can also be optimized by using caching strategies such as storing data locally (e.g., using SQLite or SharedPreferences) and syncing with a remote server when necessary. For instance, desktop apps can cache assets locally and avoid repetitive network calls, while mobile apps can implement data pre-fetching to prepare for offline use.

5. **Minimize Resource Consumption**

    Mobile: Mobile devices often have limited CPU and memory resources, so it's important to minimize heavy processing tasks, especially for tasks that need to run in the background. Use Flutter's isolate-based concurrency model to offload CPU-intensive tasks and avoid blocking the main UI thread.

    Web: Flutter web apps can consume significant CPU and memory resources, particularly when using heavy animations or complex custom widgets. Consider using tools like Flutter DevTools to profile web apps and identify areas that need optimization. Reducing the size of the JavaScript bundle by employing tree shaking and lazy loading can help reduce initial load times and improve the app's performance on the web.

    Desktop: Although desktop apps generally have more powerful hardware, they should still be optimized to prevent high resource consumption that can lead to poor user experience. For example, use efficient image formats and compress large assets to reduce memory usage.

6. **Cross-Platform Consistency**

   Ensuring consistency across platforms means that an app should look and feel similar regardless of whether it's running on a desktop, web, or mobile device. Flutter's "Cupertino" and "Material" widgets allow developers to create native-style UIs that follow the design patterns of iOS and Android. For the web and desktop, Flutter provides widgets that mimic desktop conventions, ensuring that the app feels at home on every platform.

   Additionally, managing state efficiently across platforms is key to consistency. Flutter's state management solutions—such as Provider, Riverpod, and Bloc—allow developers to maintain consistent behavior and data flow, regardless of the platform.

7. **Use Shared Logic and Platform-Specific Code When Necessary**

   One of Flutter's strengths is the ability to share business logic between platforms while still allowing platform-specific customization. For example, your app may have shared logic for authentication, data storage, and network communication, but you may need platform-specific code for file handling, hardware integration, or performance optimizations.

For shared logic, use Dart's capabilities to abstract business logic into libraries that can run on any platform. For platform-specific needs, employ platform channels or conditional imports to add platform-specific code where necessary.

Testing and Profiling Across Multiple Platforms

Performance testing and profiling are critical steps in optimizing apps for multiple platforms. Flutter DevTools provides powerful tools for inspecting performance, identifying bottlenecks, and analyzing widget trees across different platforms.

1. **Mobile Testing**: Use Flutter's integration and unit tests to ensure that mobile-specific features like touch gestures and animations perform optimally. You can also use Firebase Performance Monitoring to monitor app performance in real-world conditions.

2. **Web Testing**: For web apps, use the Chrome Developer Tools to analyze performance, inspect network requests, and debug issues related to the browser environment.

3. **Desktop Testing**: Test your desktop apps using the native development tools for macOS, Windows, and Linux to ensure they perform well under various conditions. Profiling tools for each platform can help monitor CPU, memory, and disk usage, which is particularly important for resource-intensive desktop applications.

Optimizing apps for multiple platforms is essential to delivering a seamless user experience across devices. By leveraging Flutter's cross-platform capabilities and understanding the unique performance characteristics of each platform, developers can ensure that their apps perform well on mobile, web, and desktop environments.

Key strategies include writing platform-specific code when necessary, optimizing rendering performance, managing resources efficiently, and adapting UI for different screen sizes. Additionally, using the right tools to profile and test applications on each platform ensures that developers can identify and resolve performance issues effectively. By following these best practices, developers can deliver high-quality, high-performance applications that provide a consistent experience, no matter where they are used.

Summary

In this chapter, we explored how Flutter has evolved to support robust web and desktop applications. The chapter focused on key performance improvements and strategies for building efficient and high-quality apps across multiple platforms.

We began by covering Flutter Web improvements, including performance enhancements and techniques for building Progressive Web Apps (PWAs). We also discussed how to handle browser-specific challenges, such as compatibility and debugging.

Next, the chapter delved into the latest Flutter Desktop updates, highlighting new features and the importance of cross-platform consistency for desktop applications. We also provided insights into packaging desktop apps for deployment, with techniques for managing dependencies and ensuring smooth distribution.

The section on case studies showcased real-world examples of successful web and desktop apps built with Flutter, providing analysis and insights into industry-leading implementations.

Finally, we concluded with performance benchmarking for web and desktop, comparing performance across platforms and offering strategies for optimizing apps for both web and desktop environments. This chapter emphasized the importance of balancing shared code with platform-specific optimizations to ensure excellent performance and user experience across all devices.

CHAPTER 8

Networking and API Integration

In the previous chapter, we explored the expanding capabilities of Flutter on the web and desktop platforms. From performance optimizations and browser-specific workarounds to advanced packaging techniques and cross-platform consistency, the previous chapter demonstrated how Flutter 3.29 empowers developers to build high-quality applications beyond mobile.

Now, as we shift our focus, it's time to explore another critical pillar of application development: networking and API integration. Regardless of the platform—mobile, web, or desktop—apps today are expected to seamlessly interact with external services, fetch and sync data in real time, and maintain resilience in the face of unreliable networks.

Flutter 3.29 introduces refined tools and patterns for handling API interactions with greater efficiency and control. In this chapter, we'll begin with the latest improvements in HTTP handling and JSON parsing, including new ways to offload parsing tasks to background isolates and structure complex models. From there, we'll dive into advanced API integration strategies, such as pagination, multipart requests, and error handling mechanisms tailored for robust production apps.

We'll also explore real-time communication with WebSockets—a powerful feature for apps that require instant data updates, such as chat systems, stock tickers, and collaborative tools. Following this, we'll discuss advanced caching techniques and offline-first design patterns that ensure a smooth user experience even when connectivity is spotty or absent.

Finally, the chapter closes with a deep dive into API testing and debugging. You'll learn how to validate your backend interactions using modern tooling, implement mock servers, and automate network testing as part of your continuous integration pipeline.

By the end of this chapter, you will have a comprehensive toolkit to master network-driven app development in Flutter 3.29, capable of delivering responsive, stable, and production-ready applications across all platforms.

HTTP Requests and JSON Parsing

Effective networking in Flutter requires robust handling of HTTP requests and efficient parsing of the returned data. As mobile and web applications increasingly rely on remote servers for data, performance, security, and ease of use become key factors in the design of networking features. Flutter 3.29 brings a host of improvements to the HTTP request lifecycle, alongside tools that make parsing JSON more efficient, ensuring that your app can handle data reliably and quickly.

New Enhancements in HTTP Requests

With each Flutter release, there are incremental yet impactful improvements in how the framework handles HTTP requests. Flutter 3.29 continues this trend by introducing enhancements that simplify network operations, reduce the chances of errors, and boost performance.

Overview of HTTP Request Improvements

Flutter 3.29 introduces significant improvements to how HTTP requests are handled, offering greater flexibility, efficiency, and control over network interactions. The "http" package, which is widely used for making network requests in Flutter, has undergone updates that streamline common tasks such as request management, error handling, and response processing. These improvements empower developers to write more robust, scalable, and maintainable networking code, resulting in smoother app performance across both mobile and web platforms.

Below are the key HTTP request improvements in Flutter 3.29:

Request Timeouts and Cancellation

One of the major enhancements is the improved handling of timeouts and request cancellations. Previously, developers had to manually handle timeouts or request cancellation logic, leading to extra complexity and potential bugs. With Flutter 3.29, the "http" package now natively supports timeouts and cancellation for requests. Developers can easily specify a timeout for a request, ensuring that long-running network operations don't block the app's main thread or lead to a poor user experience. Furthermore, requests can be canceled mid-flight, which is crucial for scenarios like navigating away from a screen while waiting for a response.

HTTP Interceptors for Custom Request Logic

Interceptors are a powerful tool for customizing HTTP request handling. With Flutter 3.29, you can implement request and response interceptors natively, allowing you to inject custom logic before a request is sent or after a response is received. This is extremely useful for adding common headers (like authorization tokens), logging network traffic for debugging, or even caching certain requests. You can now add these interceptors globally to all HTTP requests, reducing boilerplate and improving code maintainability.

CHAPTER 8   NETWORKING AND API INTEGRATION

Enhanced Multipart and Form-Data Requests

For apps that need to handle file uploads, Flutter 3.29 introduces enhanced support for multipart/form-data requests. This feature allows for the easy construction and sending of files, such as images or documents, as part of an HTTP request. Developers can easily send both text and binary data in a single request, simplifying workflows for apps that require complex interactions with backend services, like social media apps or file management tools.

Improved Error Handling

HTTP error handling has been streamlined to make it easier for developers to catch and respond to network failures. The new "http" package updates provide structured error models, making it easier to handle different HTTP status codes (e.g., 404 for "Not Found," 500 for "Internal Server Error"). Additionally, the improved error handling mechanism provides more informative error messages, making debugging easier when dealing with failed network requests.

Built-In Request Retrying

In many real-world scenarios, network requests fail due to transient issues such as poor connectivity or server overload. Flutter 3.29 introduces native support for retrying failed HTTP requests. Developers can now specify automatic retries for certain request types, which is useful for apps that need to recover gracefully from intermittent network failures. The retry mechanism allows for intelligent backoff strategies, such as exponential delays, ensuring that retrying doesn't flood the server with repeated requests.

Cross-Platform Consistency

With the growing demand for Flutter apps to run across mobile, web, and desktop, one of the key improvements is cross-platform consistency in HTTP handling. Flutter 3.29 brings better integration between mobile and web platforms, allowing for a unified approach to making HTTP requests.

CHAPTER 8   NETWORKING AND API INTEGRATION

This eliminates the need for platform-specific code or workarounds, simplifying the development process for cross-platform apps and ensuring a consistent networking layer across all platforms.

Optimized Performance for Large Payloads

For apps that need to handle large datasets, whether it's media files, JSON objects, or binary data, performance is critical. Flutter 3.29 introduces optimizations for handling large HTTP payloads efficiently. These optimizations ensure that data is streamed or chunked as necessary, rather than being loaded entirely into memory at once, preventing memory overflows or performance slowdowns. This is particularly beneficial for apps that need to download or upload large media files or process data-intensive API responses.

Advanced Request Customization

In addition to the basic HTTP methods (GET, POST, PUT, DELETE), Flutter 3.29 now allows for even finer control over the HTTP request process. Developers can customize headers, handle different content types, manage connection keep-alive settings, and set specific request methods for more granular control over how data is transmitted and received. This is crucial for interacting with more complex or specialized APIs, such as RESTful, GraphQL, or proprietary services.

These improvements make Flutter's networking layer more flexible, efficient, and easier to use, giving developers the tools to create high-performance apps that interact seamlessly with external services, regardless of the platform.

Efficient JSON Parsing Techniques

JSON (JavaScript Object Notation) remains the standard format for exchanging data between web services and mobile applications. In Flutter 3.29, handling JSON responses efficiently is crucial to maintain smooth app performance, particularly when dealing with large payloads or complex data structures. This section introduces modern techniques for parsing JSON data in Flutter, focusing on improving both speed and memory efficiency while adhering to best practices for robust app development.

Code Generation with "json_serializable"

Flutter 3.29 simplifies JSON parsing and serialization through the use of code generation. The "json_serializable" package automatically generates boilerplate code for converting JSON into Dart objects and vice versa. This eliminates the need for manual serialization and deserialization, reducing the chances of errors and increasing maintainability.

How It Works: By using annotations like "@JsonSerializable," developers can define Dart classes that automatically map to JSON data. The code generation tool creates the "fromJson()" and "toJson()" methods, which handle parsing and serialization. This eliminates the need to write repetitive code and ensures that your data models remain in sync with the API response structure.

Benefits:

- Reduces boilerplate code
- Improves code clarity and maintainability
- Reduces errors when parsing or serializing data
- Increases performance by avoiding reflection, which can be slower

To use "json_serializable," you need to add "json_annotation" and "json_serializable" to your "pubspec.yaml" file and run the code generator to create the necessary serialization logic.

CHAPTER 8 NETWORKING AND API INTEGRATION

Parsing JSON Asynchronously with "compute()"

When dealing with large JSON payloads, parsing the data on the main UI thread can cause jank and UI freezes, particularly on lower-end devices. To prevent this, Flutter provides the "compute()" function, which allows for offloading CPU-intensive tasks like JSON parsing to a background isolate.

How It Works: The "compute()" function takes a function and data as arguments and runs the function in a background isolate. This ensures that your UI thread remains responsive while heavy operations such as JSON parsing are handled in the background.

Benefits:

    Avoids blocking the main thread, preventing UI jank

    Allows complex or large JSON objects to be parsed without affecting user experience

    Ensures smoother performance, especially for apps that need to load or process large datasets

Here's an example of using "compute()" for JSON parsing:

```
Future<MyModel> parseJsonAsync(String jsonData) async {
  return await compute(parseJson, jsonData);
}

MyModel parseJson(String jsonData) {
  final decodedData = jsonDecode(jsonData);
  return MyModel.fromJson(decodedData);
}
```

This pattern can be applied to offload the deserialization of large JSON objects into a background isolate, keeping the UI responsive.

Efficient Memory Usage with "jsonDecode()" and Streams

For apps that handle large JSON responses, such as media-heavy or data-intensive applications, memory consumption becomes a significant concern. Flutter 3.29 optimizes memory usage when parsing large payloads by using streams for incremental parsing.

How It Works: Instead of parsing the entire JSON response into memory at once, you can use a stream to parse and process the JSON data incrementally. This approach allows you to process the data chunk by chunk, minimizing memory consumption by avoiding loading the entire response into memory at once.

Benefits:

> Reduces memory usage when handling large datasets
>
> Speeds up parsing by processing data as it is received
>
> Allows the app to work with large files, such as video or image metadata, without running into memory constraints

Here's an example of how to parse JSON from a stream:

```
import 'dart:convert';
import 'dart:async';

Future<void> parseJsonStream(Stream<List<int>> stream) async {
  final decoder = Utf8Decoder();
  final transformer = JsonDecoder();

  await for (var chunk in stream) {
    final decoded = decoder.convert(chunk);
    final jsonData = transformer.convert(decoded);
```

```
    // Process jsonData incrementally
  }
}
```

Using a stream to handle large JSON responses helps balance performance and memory efficiency.

Null Safety with JSON Parsing

Since the introduction of null safety in Dart, developers can ensure more robust JSON parsing by handling nullable fields explicitly. Flutter 3.29 allows you to enforce non-nullable types in your data models, which prevents runtime errors when unexpected null values are encountered.

How It Works: In models generated using "json_serializable," fields that are nullable in the JSON response are marked with "?" in the Dart class, and fields that are guaranteed to be non-null are required. This ensures that you can handle missing or null values gracefully without runtime crashes.

Benefits:

    Helps avoid null-related errors during runtime

    Forces developers to account for missing or incomplete data from APIs

    Improves the overall stability of the app by leveraging Dart's type safety features

Here's an example of using null safety with JSON parsing:

```
@JsonSerializable()
class User {
  final String name;
  final int? age; // Nullable field
```

```
  final String email;
  User({required this.name, this.age, required this.email});
  factory User.fromJson(Map<String, dynamic> json) =>
  _$UserFromJson(json);
  Map<String, dynamic> toJson() => _$UserToJson(this);
}
```

This approach ensures that any null values in the incoming JSON are handled correctly and that your code is protected from null dereferencing.

Custom Serialization Logic for Complex Data Structures

Sometimes, the JSON data returned by an API is too complex or nested to be easily mapped to a simple Dart class. In such cases, Flutter allows for custom serialization logic to transform JSON into Dart objects in a more flexible manner.

How It Works: You can define custom "fromJson()" and "toJson()" methods within your models to handle complex data transformations. This approach is useful when the JSON structure doesn't match the model's structure or when nested data needs special handling.

Benefits:

- Flexibility to handle complex or dynamic JSON structures
- Ensures that all edge cases in JSON formatting are addressed
- Enables efficient parsing of data that doesn't fit neatly into a standard data model

CHAPTER 8　NETWORKING AND API INTEGRATION

Here's an example of custom serialization:

```
@JsonSerializable()
class CustomModel {
  final String name;
  final DateTime timestamp;

  CustomModel({required this.name, required this.timestamp});

  factory CustomModel.fromJson(Map<String, dynamic> json) {
    return CustomModel(
      name: json['name'] as String,
      timestamp: DateTime.parse(json['timestamp'] as String),
    );
  }
  Map<String, dynamic> toJson() => {
    'name': name,
    'timestamp': timestamp.toIso8601String(),
  };
}
```

This allows you to handle cases where a field requires custom parsing, such as transforming a string into a "DateTime" object.

Efficient JSON parsing is an essential skill for Flutter developers working with networked applications. Flutter 3.29 provides several tools and techniques, including code generation with "json_serializable," offloading parsing tasks with "compute()," leveraging streams for large data, and ensuring type safety with null safety. By mastering these techniques, developers can create high-performance applications that efficiently handle large or complex JSON data, ensuring smooth, responsive user experiences.

Advanced API Integration

As mobile and web applications become increasingly sophisticated, they often need to integrate with a variety of external services. This can involve complex API interactions, such as querying large datasets, handling real-time data, or dealing with APIs that require advanced authentication methods. Flutter 3.29 provides developers with robust tools and techniques to handle complex APIs effectively, ensuring seamless data exchange between mobile apps and backend services.

Here, we'll explore how to handle complex APIs, including best practices for integrating with multi-step or resource-intensive services, and how to deal with error handling and retries to ensure resilient communication with external APIs.

Handling Complex APIs

Complex APIs often involve intricate workflows, including multiple endpoints, nested data structures, pagination, and advanced authentication mechanisms. Integrating these APIs requires careful planning and organization, as well as an understanding of the unique challenges presented by each API.

Techniques for Complex API Integration

Integrating with complex APIs presents unique challenges that require thoughtful strategies to manage multiple endpoints, large datasets, complex authentication, and error handling. These techniques help ensure smooth and efficient API integration in Flutter, making your app robust, responsive, and user-friendly.

Managing Sequential and Dependent Requests

Many complex APIs involve workflows that require multiple calls to different endpoints, with the output of one request often serving as the input for the next. Handling such sequential API calls efficiently is key to maintaining performance and ensuring that data is processed in the correct order.

Solution:

Use "async" and "await" to handle asynchronous operations and ensure that each API call completes before the next begins. This approach simplifies handling dependent requests.

Consider using the "Future.wait()" method to make parallel calls for independent requests. This can improve the overall efficiency by not waiting for each call to finish sequentially.

Example:

```
Future<void> fetchUserData() async {
  try {
    final userResponse = await http.get(Uri.parse
    ('https://api.example.com/user'));
    final userData = jsonDecode(userResponse.body);

    final postsResponse = await http.get(Uri.parse('https://
    api.example.com/posts?userId=${userData['id']}'));
    final postsData = jsonDecode(postsResponse.body);

    print('User Data: $userData');
    print('Posts Data: $postsData');
  } catch (error) {
    print('Error fetching data: $error');
  }
}
```

In this example, we first fetch user data and then use the "userData['id']" to fetch related posts. The second request is dependent on the result of the first.

Using Streams for Handling Large Datasets

For APIs that return large datasets, such as a list of items or records, processing the entire dataset at once can cause performance issues, especially if the data is too large to fit in memory. Flutter provides the "Stream" class, which allows you to work with data incrementally as it's fetched, rather than all at once.

Solution:

Use a stream-based approach to handle large responses, making the app more responsive and efficient in memory management.

Implement pagination in combination with streams to fetch the data in manageable chunks.

Example:

```
Stream<List<Item>> fetchItemsPaginated(String endpoint) async{
  int page = 1;
  bool hasMoreData = true;

  while (hasMoreData) {
    final response = await http.get(Uri.parse('$endpoint?
    page=$page'));
    final data = jsonDecode(response.body);

    yield data['items'];  // Yielding the items from the
                             current page
    hasMoreData = data['has_more'];  // Check if more data is
                                        available

    page++;
  }
}
```

Efficient Parsing with Model Classes

APIs often return data in complex and nested JSON formats. Manually parsing JSON can quickly become cumbersome, especially when dealing with deeply nested objects. Using model classes to map the JSON data can simplify parsing and provide better structure and maintainability.

Solution:

Create Dart classes that represent the structure of the data returned by the API.

Use libraries like "json_serializable" or "json_annotation" to automatically generate code for parsing JSON into Dart objects.

Here's an example of creating a model class and using "json_serializable":

```dart
import 'package:json_annotation/json_annotation.dart';

part 'user.g.dart';

@JsonSerializable()
class User {
  final String name;
  final String email;

  User({required this.name, required this.email});

  factory User.fromJson(Map<String, dynamic> json) =>
    _$UserFromJson(json);
  Map<String, dynamic> toJson() => _$UserToJson(this);
}
```

This stream-based approach allows you to handle paginated responses efficiently, processing one page at a time as it's fetched from the API.

CHAPTER 8   NETWORKING AND API INTEGRATION

By using model classes, you can avoid writing repetitive code to manually parse and serialize JSON, making the code cleaner and more maintainable.

Handling Nested Data with Recursive Models

When dealing with deeply nested JSON structures, handling nested data requires a recursive approach. By using recursive data models, you can ensure that complex hierarchies are parsed correctly.

Solution:

Create recursive models that can handle nested data by defining properties as instances of other models.

Use "json_serializable" to handle the recursive parsing automatically.

Example:

```
@JsonSerializable()
class Category {
  final String name;
  final List<Category> subcategories;

  Category({required this.name, required this.subcategories});

  factory Category.fromJson(Map<String, dynamic> json) =>
  _$CategoryFromJson(json);
  Map<String, dynamic> toJson() => _$CategoryToJson(this);
}
```

In this case, each "Category" object can contain a list of other "Category" objects, enabling the model to handle deeply nested JSON structures.

CHAPTER 8   NETWORKING AND API INTEGRATION

Optimizing API Requests with Caching

For APIs that return frequently accessed data, implementing caching can significantly reduce the number of requests made, improving both performance and the user experience. Caching can also help reduce network usage and ensure that your app works offline.

Solution:

Use in-memory caching to store frequently accessed data for fast retrieval.

Consider using persistent caching for long-lived data, such as using SQLite or Hive to store responses locally.

Here's an example of using an in-memory cache:

```
class ApiCache {
  final _cache = <String, dynamic>{};

  dynamic get(String key) {
    return _cache[key];
  }

  void set(String key, dynamic value) {
    _cache[key] = value;
  }
}

final apiCache = ApiCache();
```

With this simple caching system, the app can check if data is already in the cache before making a network request, saving time and resources.

Managing Authentication and Authorization

Complex APIs often require advanced authentication mechanisms, such as OAuth2 or JSON Web Tokens (JWTs). Managing the lifecycle of authentication tokens and ensuring secure access to protected resources is a critical part of integrating with these APIs.

Solution:

Store tokens securely, using packages like "flutter_secure_storage" to avoid exposing sensitive information.

Automatically refresh expired tokens using the appropriate API flow.

Example:

```
class AuthService {
  Future<String> getAccessToken() async {
    // Check if the token is expired
    final token = await secureStorage.read(key: 'access_token');
    if (_isTokenExpired(token)) {
      return await _refreshToken();
    }
    return token!;
  }
}
```

By managing the token securely and refreshing it when needed, you ensure seamless access to protected API endpoints.

Integrating with complex APIs requires a deep understanding of both the Flutter framework and the API itself. By using advanced techniques such as managing sequential requests, using streams for large datasets, creating model classes for data parsing, and implementing efficient caching and authentication strategies, developers can significantly improve the performance and maintainability of their apps. These techniques are not only useful for handling complex APIs but also for building scalable, user-friendly applications that can communicate with a wide range of services.

Error Handling and Retries

When working with complex APIs, ensuring that your application gracefully handles errors is crucial. Network issues, server downtimes, rate limits, and malformed responses can all lead to failures in communication with the API. Proper error handling and retry mechanisms help ensure a resilient and user-friendly experience, especially when dealing with transient issues that may be temporary and recoverable.

Here, we'll explore the best practices for handling errors and implementing retry logic in Flutter, particularly when dealing with API integrations.

Centralized Error Handling

A key aspect of maintaining a clean and maintainable codebase is centralizing error handling. This reduces the complexity of error handling logic scattered across multiple HTTP requests and allows you to manage API-related errors uniformly.

Solution:

Create a centralized error handler or service that processes errors based on HTTP status codes.

Differentiate between recoverable and non-recoverable errors, and handle them accordingly.

Approach:

Client-Side Errors (4xx): These errors usually indicate issues with the request, such as unauthorized access or bad requests. It's often appropriate to show an error message to the user.

CHAPTER 8   NETWORKING AND API INTEGRATION

Server-Side Errors (5xx): These errors suggest that the problem lies with the server. These errors are often transient and can be retried after a brief wait.

Network Errors: Connection issues can lead to network errors. These are often recoverable and may benefit from retry logic.

Here's how you might implement centralized error handling for HTTP responses:

```
class ApiError {
  final String message;
  final int code;

  ApiError({required this.message, required this.code});
}

ApiError handleApiError(http.Response response) {
  switch (response.statusCode) {
    case 400:
      return ApiError(message: 'Bad request. Please try
      again.', code: response.statusCode);
    case 401:
      return ApiError(message: 'Unauthorized access. Please log
      in again.', code: response.statusCode);
    case 500:
      return ApiError(message: 'Server error. Please try again
      later.', code: response.statusCode);
    default:
      return ApiError(message: 'An unexpected error occurred.',
      code: response.statusCode);
  }
}
```

CHAPTER 8   NETWORKING AND API INTEGRATION

By encapsulating error handling logic in a central location, the app remains consistent, and developers can easily modify the behavior without having to touch individual API requests.

Retry Logic for Transient Errors

Network and server-related issues often cause transient errors, such as connection timeouts, server overloads, or temporary unavailability. These issues can often be mitigated with retry logic, allowing the app to retry failed requests after a brief delay. However, retries should be performed with care to avoid overwhelming the server and to provide the best user experience.

Solution:

Implement retry logic with exponential backoff to avoid bombarding the server with requests in quick succession.

Retry failed requests a set number of times before showing an error to the user.

Exponential Backoff:

Exponential backoff is a retry strategy where the time between each retry increases exponentially, reducing the load on the server and giving the network time to recover.

Here's an example of retry logic with exponential backoff:

```
Future<http.Response> fetchDataWithRetry(String url, {int retries = 3}) async {
  int attempts = 0;
  while (attempts < retries) {
    try {
      final response = await http.get(Uri.parse(url));
      if (response.statusCode == 200) {
        return response;
      } else {
        throw Exception('Failed to load data');
```

```
    }
  } catch (e) {
    if (attempts == retries - 1) {
      rethrow; // Max retries reached
    }
    attempts++;
    await Future.delayed(Duration(seconds: attempts 2));
    // Exponential backoff
  }
}
throw Exception('Failed to fetch data after $retries retries');
}
```

In this example, the retry attempts increase the delay between each retry (e.g., two seconds, four seconds, eight seconds). If the request still fails after the maximum number of retries, an exception is thrown.

Why Exponential Backoff Works:

Prevents Server Overload: By gradually increasing the time between retries, exponential backoff reduces the risk of overwhelming the server with rapid retry attempts.

Improves Success Rate: It allows the system to recover from temporary issues like network congestion or server overload.

Implementing Retry Policies Based on Status Codes

Different HTTP status codes require different handling strategies. For example, client-side errors (4xx) typically require user intervention, while server-side errors (5xx) may benefit from retries.

Solution:

Retries for 5xx Errors: Server errors are often transient, so implementing a retry strategy for 5xx errors is a common practice.

CHAPTER 8   NETWORKING AND API INTEGRATION

Abort for 4xx Errors: Client-side errors like unauthorized access or bad requests should usually not be retried. Instead, handle these cases with clear user messaging.

Example Implementation:

```
Future<http.Response> fetchData(String url) async {
  try {
    final response = await http.get(Uri.parse(url));
    if (response.statusCode == 200) {
      return response; // Successful response
    } else if (response.statusCode >= 500) {
      // Retry on 5xx errors
      return await fetchDataWithRetry(url);
    } else {
      // Handle client-side errors (e.g., 400, 401, 404)
      throw ApiError(message: 'Client error: ${response.statusCode}', code: response.statusCode);
    }
  } catch (error) {
    rethrow;
  }
}
```

In this implementation

If a 5xx error occurs, the function will retry the request using the "fetchDataWithRetry" method described earlier.

For 4xx errors, we immediately throw an error, as these errors typically require user intervention.

593

CHAPTER 8   NETWORKING AND API INTEGRATION

Handling Timeout Errors

Timeout errors occur when the request takes too long to complete, typically due to slow network conditions or server-side delays. Implementing a timeout for HTTP requests is essential to avoid situations where the app is stuck waiting indefinitely.

Solution:

Use a "timeout" property in your HTTP request to automatically cancel requests that take too long and trigger a retry or show a user-friendly error message.

Example:

```
Future<http.Response> fetchDataWithTimeout(String url) async {
  try {
    final response = await http.get(Uri.parse(url)).
    timeout(Duration(seconds: 10));
    return response;
  } on TimeoutException catch (_) {
    throw ApiError(message: 'Request timed out. Please try again.', code: 408);
  } catch (error) {
    rethrow;
  }
}
```

This example sets a timeout of ten seconds for the request. If the request takes longer than that, a "TimeoutException" is thrown, and a user-friendly error message is displayed.

CHAPTER 8   NETWORKING AND API INTEGRATION

Graceful Fallbacks and User Feedback

When errors do occur, it's essential to provide users with meaningful feedback. Rather than simply showing generic error messages, provide users with actionable steps or useful information to improve the experience.

Solution:

Display clear error messages that explain what went wrong and what the user can do (e.g., retry, check their network connection).

If the error is critical, such as a failed login attempt, direct the user to a screen where they can take corrective action.

Example:

```
Widget buildErrorMessage(ApiError error) {
  return Column(
    children: [
      Text('Error: ${error.message}', style: TextStyle(color: Colors.red)),
      ElevatedButton(
        onPressed: () => _retryRequest(),
        child: Text('Retry'),
      ),
    ],
  );
}
```

In this example, the UI shows the error message and provides a button to retry the operation. This helps users understand what happened and gives them an option to recover from the issue.

Error handling and retry logic are essential parts of building robust applications that interact with complex APIs. By implementing centralized error handling, retries with exponential backoff, and strategies for handling various HTTP status codes, developers can create apps that are resilient to network failures and server-side issues. Additionally, providing users with clear error messages and actionable feedback ensures a smooth user experience, even in the face of errors.

WebSockets and Real-Time Data

In modern Flutter applications, users expect instantaneous updates—whether it's live sports scores, messaging, stock tickers, or collaborative features. Traditional HTTP APIs, while reliable, follow a request-response model that lacks the ability to push updates in real time. This is where WebSockets shine, offering full-duplex communication between client and server, allowing apps to receive data instantly as events occur.

Flutter, especially with packages like web_socket_channel, has matured in its support for WebSockets, making it easier than ever to build reactive, real-time interfaces. In this section, we explore how to effectively integrate WebSockets, manage connections, handle streaming data, and ensure robustness under variable network conditions.

Introduction to WebSocket Integration

WebSockets are a communication protocol that enables persistent connections between a client and a server. Unlike RESTful APIs, which require a new connection for each request, WebSockets maintain a single, open connection that allows for real-time data exchange.

Why use WebSockets in Flutter?

Real-Time Updates: Ideal for chat apps, live notifications, dashboards, collaborative tools, and games.

Low Latency: WebSockets eliminate the overhead of repeated HTTP requests, reducing latency significantly.

Bidirectional Communication: Both client and server can send messages independently, without waiting for each other.

Flutter supports WebSockets through the web_socket_channel package, which offers a cross-platform abstraction for working with WebSocket connections on both mobile and web.

Real-Time Data Handling

Handling real-time data in Flutter using WebSockets transforms how your app reacts to changes—no more waiting for user-triggered refreshes or polling APIs. With a persistent connection established between client and server, WebSockets allow data to flow continuously, enabling immediate UI updates whenever events occur. This is critical for building responsive, dynamic applications such as messaging apps, trading platforms, collaborative editors, live dashboards, or multiplayer games.

Understanding Real-Time Data Streams

Unlike the request–response cycle of HTTP, WebSockets maintain an open, bidirectional communication channel. Once connected, the server can push data to the client as soon as it's available, and the client can send data back without re-establishing the connection. This constant data stream is ideal for event-driven scenarios.

In Flutter, this stream of real-time data can be consumed efficiently using reactive widgets like "StreamBuilder," which rebuild the UI whenever new data arrives on the stream.

Step-by-Step Implementation of Real-Time Data Handling

Let's walk through a simple real-time integration using the "web_socket_channel" package.

1. Add the dependency in your "pubspec.yaml":

   ```
   dependencies:
     web_socket_channel: ^3.0.0
   ```

2. Establish a WebSocket connection:

   ```
   import 'package:web_socket_channel/web_socket_channel.dart';

   final channel = WebSocketChannel.connect(
     Uri.parse('wss://echo.websocket.org'),
   );
   ```

3. Consume the stream with "StreamBuilder":

   ```
   StreamBuilder(
     stream: channel.stream,
     builder: (context, snapshot) {
       if (snapshot.hasData) {
         return Text('New message: ${snapshot.data}');
       } else if (snapshot.hasError) {
         return Text('Error: ${snapshot.error}');
       }
       return CircularProgressIndicator();
     },
   );
   ```

4. Send data through the WebSocket:

```
channel.sink.add('Hello Server!');
```

5. Close the WebSocket properly in "dispose":

```
@override
void dispose() {
  channel.sink.close();
  super.dispose();
}
```

Practical Example: Chat Message Stream

In a chat application, every message received from another user should appear instantly. Here's a simplified example:

```
class ChatScreen extends StatefulWidget {
  @override
  _ChatScreenState createState() => _ChatScreenState();
}

class _ChatScreenState extends State<ChatScreen> {
  final channel = WebSocketChannel.connect(Uri.parse
('wss://chat.example.com'));

  final controller = TextEditingController();

  void sendMessage(String text) {
    channel.sink.add(text);
    controller.clear();
  }
```

```dart
@override
Widget build(BuildContext context) {
  return Column(
    children: [
      Expanded(
        child: StreamBuilder(
          stream: channel.stream,
          builder: (context, snapshot) {
            return ListView(
              children: [
                if (snapshot.hasData)
                  ListTile(title: Text('Received:
                  ${snapshot.data}'))
              ],
            );
          },
        ),
      ),
      Padding(
        padding: const EdgeInsets.all(8.0),
        child: Row(
          children: [
            Expanded(
              child: TextField(controller:
              controller),
            ),
            IconButton(
              icon: Icon(Icons.send),
              onPressed: () =>
              sendMessage(controller.text),
            ),
```

```
          ],
        ),
      ),
    ],
  );
}

@override
void dispose() {
  channel.sink.close();
  super.dispose();
}
}
```

Performance Considerations

Debounce updates if the server sends high-frequency data (e.g., stock prices every few milliseconds). Use libraries like "rxdart" for operators like "debounceTime."

Avoid expensive operations inside "StreamBuilder," such as large widget rebuilds. Instead, update state selectively using "ValueNotifier" or state management solutions.

Use data models to deserialize incoming JSON data and avoid working directly with raw strings.

Tips for Robust Real-Time Handling

Detect Disconnections: Implement logic to detect when the WebSocket has closed and try to reconnect.

Show Connection Status: Let users know when the app is online, offline, or reconnecting.

Validate Server Messages: Always validate or parse the payload before displaying it to avoid potential crashes due to malformed data.

Secure the Channel: Use "wss://" (WebSocket Secure) in production to encrypt data over the wire.

Testing Real-Time Behavior

Use tools like Postman WebSocket (https://web.postman.co) or websocket.org Echo Test (https://www.websocket.org/echo.html) to simulate sending and receiving messages.

Mock streams in tests to simulate message arrival and ensure the UI updates accordingly.

Real-time data handling using WebSockets is a powerful paradigm for interactive Flutter applications. By integrating streams into your UI via "StreamBuilder" and managing the connection lifecycle properly, you can create apps that respond immediately to changes in data. Combined with best practices for performance, error handling, and UX feedback, WebSockets open the door to a new class of immersive, real-time experiences.

Managing WebSocket Connections

Managing WebSocket connections effectively is critical to delivering a stable, responsive, and user-friendly real-time experience in your Flutter app. Unlike HTTP connections, WebSockets remain open, requiring careful lifecycle management, reconnection logic, and network resilience strategies. Flutter, with its flexible state management and lifecycle awareness, provides an excellent environment for building and maintaining robust WebSocket integrations.

Here we cover everything from lifecycle hooks and disconnection handling to reconnection strategies and heartbeat implementation.

↻ Lifecycle-Aware WebSocket Management

Flutter apps undergo frequent widget rebuilds, especially during navigation or orientation changes. Poorly managed WebSocket connections can lead to memory leaks, duplicate streams, or even crashes. Always tie the WebSocket connection to a widget's lifecycle or, ideally, to a connection manager or service layer.

Basic Stateful Implementation Example:

```
class LiveUpdatesScreen extends StatefulWidget {
  @override
  _LiveUpdatesScreenState createState() => _
LiveUpdatesScreenState();
}

class _LiveUpdatesScreenState extends
State<LiveUpdatesScreen> {
  late WebSocketChannel channel;

  @override
  void initState() {
    super.initState();
    channel = WebSocketChannel.connect(
      Uri.parse('wss://example.com/live'),
    );
  }

  @override
  void dispose() {
    channel.sink.close();
    super.dispose();
  }

  @override
  Widget build(BuildContext context) {
    return StreamBuilder(
      stream: channel.stream,
      builder: (context, snapshot) {
        if (snapshot.hasData) {
          return Text('Data: ${snapshot.data}');
```

```
      }
      return CircularProgressIndicator();
    },
  );
}
}
```

Best Practice: Wrap WebSocket logic in a separate service class and expose a stream. This keeps your UI logic clean and your socket management reusable across screens.

Reconnection Strategy

Connections may drop due to server-side restarts, poor network conditions, or mobile operating system policies (like background suspensions). A reconnection strategy ensures your app remains resilient and doesn't leave the user in a disconnected state.

Simple Reconnect Logic with Delay:

```
void reconnect() {
  Future.delayed(Duration(seconds: 5), () {
    channel = WebSocketChannel.connect(Uri.parse('wss:
    //example.com/live'));
    setState(() {});
  });
}
```

CHAPTER 8 NETWORKING AND API INTEGRATION

Advanced Reconnection with Exponential Backoff:

```
int retryCount = 0;

void reconnectWithBackoff() {
  final delay = Duration(seconds: 2 (1 << retryCount));
  Future.delayed(delay, () {
    retryCount = retryCount + 1;
    channel = WebSocketChannel.connect(Uri.parse
    ('wss://example.com/live'));
    setState(() {});
  });
}
```

Tip Always reset "retryCount" to 0 once reconnection is successful.

Heartbeat and Ping/Pong Messages

Many WebSocket servers expect periodic messages to verify that a client is still alive. Without this, idle connections may be closed by proxies, firewalls, or servers.

Client-Side Heartbeat:

```
Timer? heartbeat;

void startHeartbeat() {
  heartbeat = Timer.periodic(Duration(seconds: 30), (_) {
    channel.sink.add(jsonEncode({'type': 'ping'}));
  });
}
```

605

CHAPTER 8   NETWORKING AND API INTEGRATION

```
void stopHeartbeat() {
  heartbeat?.cancel();
}
```

> **Note**   Stop the heartbeat on "dispose()" or when connection is lost.

Connection Status Feedback

Displaying the WebSocket connection status enhances the user experience, especially in critical apps like finance, logistics, or healthcare. Use a simple banner or SnackBar to indicate disconnection, and optionally offer a manual "Reconnect" button.

```
if (snapshot.hasError) {
  return Column(
    children: [
      Text('🔌 Connection lost. Trying to reconnect...'),
      ElevatedButton(
        onPressed: reconnect,
        child: Text('Retry Now'),
      )
    ],
  );
}
```

🎨 Error Handling and Stream Termination

A "StreamBuilder" can receive "onDone" and "onError" events when the WebSocket connection ends or errors out. Use these events to detect termination and trigger reconnection or user alerts.

CHAPTER 8 NETWORKING AND API INTEGRATION

Detecting Socket Closure:

```
channel.stream.listen(
  (message) {
    // handle message
  },
  onDone: () {
    print('Socket closed');
    reconnectWithBackoff();
  },
  onError: (error) {
    print('Socket error: $error');
    reconnectWithBackoff();
  },
);
```

WebSocket Connection Service Pattern (Recommended)

A more scalable approach is to encapsulate connection management in a service:

```
class WebSocketService {
  WebSocketChannel? _channel;
  Stream? _stream;

  Stream get stream => _stream!;

  void connect() {
    _channel = WebSocketChannel.connect(Uri.parse
    ('wss://example.com/live'));
    _stream = _channel!.stream.asBroadcastStream();
  }

  void send(dynamic data) {
```

607

CHAPTER 8 NETWORKING AND API INTEGRATION

```
    _channel?.sink.add(jsonEncode(data));
  }
  void disconnect() {
    _channel?.sink.close();
  }
}
```

You can then access this service using Provider, GetIt, or Riverpod to maintain a single persistent connection across the app.

Best Practices Summary

Practice	Benefit
Tie connection to widget lifecycle	Prevents memory leaks and duplicate connections
Use exponential backoff for retry	Prevents overwhelming the server during downtime
Send heartbeat pings	Keeps connections alive and prevents silent drop
Expose status to UI	Enhances user trust and clarity
Abstract into services	Promotes code reuse and clean architecture

A real-time Flutter app is only as good as its connection stability. Properly managing WebSocket connections—handling reconnections, monitoring health with heartbeats, and ensuring clean disposals—ensures that your app performs reliably in unpredictable network environments. Whether you're building a chat app, real-time dashboard, or live data feed, robust connection management is key to delivering a high-quality user experience.

Caching and Offline Data

As mobile and web applications become more data-intensive and users demand seamless, responsive experiences—even in limited connectivity environments—caching and offline data strategies are no longer optional. Caching enhances performance, reduces redundant network calls, and improves user experience by making data instantly accessible. Offline support ensures app usability when the device is disconnected from the internet, improving reliability and user satisfaction.

Flutter provides several mechanisms and packages to implement efficient caching strategies and offline-first experiences, including in-memory caching; local persistence using SQLite, Hive, or shared preferences; and data synchronization patterns. This section dives into these techniques and explores their practical application in real-world scenarios.

Advanced Caching Techniques

Caching isn't just about saving data locally—it's about intelligently determining what to cache, how long to cache it, and when to invalidate or refresh that data. Flutter allows for multi-layered caching strategies through packages, architectural patterns, and data lifecycle control.

Optimizing App Data with Caching

In modern mobile and web development, optimizing app data with caching is not just a performance enhancement—it's a necessity. Flutter applications, like all real-time data-driven apps, deal with frequent API calls, user interactions, and media content that can tax both the network and the device. Caching allows developers to store data temporarily (in memory or on disk) to reduce latency, lower server load, and improve the overall user experience.

Here, we explore key caching strategies and tools in Flutter, enabling you to build apps that are fast, resilient, and responsive—even in poor or no connectivity environments.

🛠 Why Cache App Data?

Performance: Accessing local data is exponentially faster than fetching from the network.

Offline Support: Cached data can be served when the device is offline or in airplane mode.

Reduced Server Load: Caching reduces redundant API calls, which is essential in rate-limited or high-scale systems.

Improved UX: Immediate access to data boosts perceived performance, making apps feel smoother and more reliable.

🔄Key Caching Techniques in Flutter

1. **In-Memory Caching**

   Stored in RAM for ultra-fast access during app runtime

   Pros: Fastest access, simple to implement

   Cons: Lost when the app restarts or crashes
   Use Cases: Temporary UI state, current user session, filters, and settings

   ```
   ---------------------------------------------------
   Map<String, dynamic> inMemoryCache = {};
   inMemoryCache['userProfile'] = userData;
   ---------------------------------------------------
   ```

2. **Persistent Local Storage**

   Stores data on the device's file system, database, or key–value store. Survives app restarts

   Shared Preferences: For small key–value pairs (booleans, strings, flags)

CHAPTER 8 NETWORKING AND API INTEGRATION

Hive: A fast, NoSQL local DB suited for caching large or structured datasets

SQFlite: A full-featured relational database (SQLite wrapper)

```
// Using Hive to cache API response
var box = await Hive.openBox('cache');
box.put('dashboard_data', jsonEncode(responseData));
```
---

3. **Time-To-Live (TTL) and Expiry Logic**

   Cached data should not be stored indefinitely. Implement TTL to expire and refresh data periodically.

```
DateTime cacheTimestamp = box.get('timestamp');
if (DateTime.now().difference(cacheTimestamp).inMinutes > 15) {
  // refresh data
}
```
---

4. **Layered Caching (Hybrid Approach)**

   Use in-memory + persistent storage together. Store hot data in memory and cold data on disk.

```
// Pseudo-flow:
if (inMemoryCache.contains('data')) {
  use(inMemoryCache['data']);
} else if (localStorage.contains('data')) {
```

611

```
      loadToMemory();
    } else {
      fetchFromAPI();
    }
```

✓ Caching Network Requests

You can cache the results of HTTP or Dio network requests to avoid repeated API calls:

```
// Example using Dio Interceptor
class CacheInterceptor extends Interceptor {
  final Map<String, Response> _cache = {};

  @override
  void onRequest(RequestOptions options,
  RequestInterceptorHandler handler) {
    if (_cache.containsKey(options.uri.toString())) {
      return handler.resolve(_cache[options.uri.toString()]!);
    }
    super.onRequest(options, handler);
  }

  @override
  void onResponse(Response response, ResponseInterceptorHandler
  handler) {
    _cache[response.requestOptions.uri.toString()] = response;
    super.onResponse(response, handler);
  }
}
```

> **✧ Tip** Use packages like "dio_http_cache" or "flutter_cache_manager," or create your own caching layer with interceptors.

⚙ Optimizing Cached Data Structures

Avoid Caching Redundancy: Store only what's necessary (e.g., list of IDs, not full objects).

Compress Data: For large datasets, compress JSON before writing to disk.

Paginated Caching: Store each page of results with an index-based key.

📱 Caching Best Practices

Best Practice	Benefit
Use TTLs for auto-expiration	Prevents stale data from being served
Encrypt sensitive cache	Protects user privacy and compliance
Monitor cache size	Avoids excessive storage usage
Invalidate cache on data mutation	Ensures data consistency after user updates
Sync cache with API schema changes	Avoids deserialization errors from outdated structures

Optimizing app data with caching in Flutter is a critical aspect of performance and user experience. Whether you're delivering fresh content, enabling offline access, or simply reducing the load on your API, caching helps maintain responsiveness and continuity. By applying intelligent cache layers—memory, disk, TTL, and conditional updates—you ensure your app scales efficiently without sacrificing speed or reliability.

Case Studies and Use Cases

Theoretical knowledge of caching strategies is essential, but seeing how real-world Flutter applications implement caching transforms abstract concepts into tangible, actionable patterns. In this section, we explore case studies and practical use cases where caching was instrumental in boosting performance, ensuring offline reliability, and delivering a seamless user experience.

🛒 Case Study 1: News Aggregator App

Context

A Flutter-based news aggregator delivers breaking news headlines, featured articles, and media content from multiple RSS feeds and APIs. Users expect instant access and offline reading capabilities.

Caching Strategy

Hive was used to persist fetched news articles locally.

Articles were cached with a TTL of 15 minutes.

Images were cached using "flutter_cache_manager."

Saved articles for offline reading were encrypted using "flutter_secure_storage."

Results

Initial API fetch time dropped from ~2.2s to <500ms.

App retained full functionality without connectivity.

Reduced API calls by 68% over a 24-hour period.

🌐 Case Study 2: Ecommerce Mobile App

Context

An ecommerce application shows thousands of SKUs, product categories, and promotional banners, pulling dynamic content from a backend CMS.

CHAPTER 8   NETWORKING AND API INTEGRATION

Caching Strategy

Category and banner data cached using "shared_preferences" and TTL-based logic.

Product listings cached in SQLite with pagination for better load management.

User cart data cached in-memory for rapid access and synced to the backend when network was available.

Results

Product page load times dropped by 40%.

App continued functioning smoothly in low-connectivity areas.

Session restoration led to a 23% higher checkout conversion rate.

🎓 Case Study 3: Offline-First Field Survey App

Context

A survey app used by agents in rural and remote regions, where internet connectivity is intermittent or unavailable for long stretches.

Caching Strategy

Full offline-first model using "sqflite" to cache form templates, user progress, and submitted data.

Queued data stored locally and automatically synced once connectivity resumed.

Secure storage used for authentication tokens and sensitive submissions.

Results

Enabled 100% offline operation with zero data loss.

Increased daily data submission rates by 35%.

Reduced support requests caused by failed submissions.

✈ Case Study 4: Educational App with Course Content

Context

An education startup built a Flutter app that streams video lessons and loads interactive quizzes. Users frequently accessed content on the go.

Caching Strategy

Course metadata and quiz content cached with "Hive."

CHAPTER 8 NETWORKING AND API INTEGRATION

Video files downloaded and cached for offline playback using "flutter_cache_manager."

User progress cached and synced in batches to reduce frequent writes.

Results

Seamless video playback even without the internet.

Decreased quiz load times by 50%.

Maintained accurate learning progress across devices via intelligent sync.

✈ Case Study 5: Travel Itinerary App

Context

A travel itinerary app showed users their bookings, boarding passes, hotel details, and maps.

Caching Strategy

Upcoming itinerary details cached locally for offline access during flights.

Map tiles and route data precached using custom tile services.

Caching of QR codes and barcodes for boarding offline.

Results

Users could access critical travel information without a network.

Drastically improved experience in airports and during flights.

Led to 4.8-star average app rating from travelers.

🔧 Generalized Use Cases

App Type	Cached Data Types / Caching Tools/Techniques
Messaging	Conversations, media previews / Hive, encrypted cache, LRU cache
Banking/Finance	Recent transactions, exchange rates, charts / Encrypted SQLite, periodic sync

Weather	Forecasts, location-specific data
	Time-based invalidation with
	'shared_preferences'
Food Delivery	Menus, restaurant data, address book
	In-memory + persistent cache layers
Fitness/Wellness	Workout plans, history, goals
	Hive for local sync, offline-first approach

✓ Lessons Learned Across Case Studies

1. **Hybrid Strategies Win**: The best-performing apps combine memory and persistent caching with TTL and invalidation rules.

2. User trust increases when data is available even without a connection.

3. Performance isn't just speed—it's perceived reliability, especially in flaky networks.

4. Offline-first UX must be designed intentionally, not as an afterthought.

5. **Security Matters**: Encrypt sensitive data before caching it on disk.

Final Thoughts

From ecommerce and education to field operations and travel, caching has become a foundational component of Flutter apps that aim to deliver responsive, reliable, and high-performance experiences. The ability to smartly store, retrieve, and sync data transforms how users interact with your app—especially in a mobile-first world where connectivity can't always be guaranteed.

API Testing and Debugging

Modern Flutter applications heavily depend on APIs for everything from content delivery and user authentication to payments and real-time communication. As the complexity of integrations increases, so does the importance of rigorous API testing and efficient debugging techniques. Poorly handled APIs can result in app crashes, security vulnerabilities, data corruption, and poor UX.

Here, we dive deep into the tools, techniques, and strategies used by professionals to test APIs reliably and debug network-related issues in Flutter. We'll cover structured testing, automation, environment configuration, and error diagnostics, using both native Dart capabilities and third-party tools.

Advanced Debugging Strategies

Debugging API-related issues in Flutter can be deceptively complex. Unlike traditional debugging, which often centers on application logic or UI rendering, network-related debugging deals with unreliable external systems, latency, data inconsistency, and security constraints. To maintain a seamless user experience, developers need more than simple print statements—they need structured, scalable, and smart debugging workflows.

Here, we explore advanced techniques used by professionals to diagnose and resolve networking bugs, covering tools, design patterns, observability practices, and environment-aware strategies.

Structured Logging with Interceptors

In apps that use "dio" or similar HTTP clients, interceptors offer a powerful way to log network activity, track request lifecycles, and inject dynamic headers (like auth tokens) or trace IDs.

CHAPTER 8　NETWORKING AND API INTEGRATION

Example Using Dio Interceptors:

```
dio.interceptors.add(InterceptorsWrapper(
  onRequest: (options, handler) {
    debugPrint('--> ${options.method} ${options.path}');
    debugPrint('Headers: ${options.headers}');
    debugPrint('Body: ${options.data}');
    return handler.next(options);
  },
  onResponse: (response, handler) {
    debugPrint('<-- ${response.statusCode} ${response.
    requestOptions.path}');
    debugPrint('Response: ${response.data}');
    return handler.next(response);
  },
  onError: (DioError e, handler) {
    debugPrint('ERROR[${e.response?.statusCode}] => PATH:
    ${e.requestOptions.path}');
    return handler.next(e);
  }
));
```

💡 **Tip**　Log only in "debug" mode or use a conditional logger to avoid leaking sensitive information in production builds.

⚠ Categorized Error Handling

Rather than using generic "try-catch," categorize error types for precise diagnostics.

CHAPTER 8 NETWORKING AND API INTEGRATION

Common Errors to Catch:

"SocketException": No internet connection.

"TimeoutException": Server didn't respond in time.

"HttpException": Failed HTTP status codes.

"FormatException": Malformed JSON or unexpected content type.

Example:

```
try {
  final response = await apiService.fetchData();
} on SocketException {
  showError('No internet connection.');
} on TimeoutException {
  showError('Request timed out. Try again later.');
} on FormatException {
  showError('Unexpected response format.');
} catch (e) {
  showError('An unknown error occurred.');
}
```

Why It Matters: Categorized error messages help both users and developers understand what's going wrong—faster.

🧪 Using Emulators and Simulators for Network Conditions

Simulate real-world conditions like slow connections, packet loss, or intermittent dropouts using network throttling tools.

Android Emulator:

Developer options ➤ Cellular ➤ Simulate Poor Network

Chrome DevTools (for Flutter Web):

Network ▶ Throttle ▶ Slow 3G/Custom

Third-Party Tools:

Charles Proxy, Proxyman, or Little Snitch

Use Case: Validate your app's behavior in airplane mode, flaky connections, or high latency.

🎁 Dependency Injection for Mocking

Inject HTTP clients or API services via providers (e.g., Riverpod, Provider) to swap real clients for mocked ones in testing and debugging environments.

Example:

```
final apiClientProvider = Provider<ApiClient>((ref) {
  return kDebugMode ? MockApiClient() : RealApiClient();
});
```

This allows you to simulate specific backend behaviors like

Server errors (500s)

Empty responses

Delayed responses

Invalid tokens or expired sessions

🐞 DevTools and Network Inspection

Although Flutter DevTools doesn't support deep network introspection natively, you can still

Use the Logging tab to track error states and print logs from interceptors.

On Flutter Web, use browser Network tab to track actual HTTP requests.

Use Postman Console to trace headers, response sizes, and latency issues.

For mobile apps, tools like Proxyman and Charles Proxy can capture HTTPS traffic if you install trusted certificates on your emulator or device.

↻ Retry and Timeout Strategy Debugging

APIs may occasionally fail due to

- Temporary server issues
- Rate limiting
- CDN hiccups
- Edge location latency

Add intelligent retry strategies with logging to monitor behavior:

```
RetryOptions(
  maxAttempts: 3,
  delayFactor: Duration(seconds: 2),
).retry(() => fetchData());
```

Debug Strategy: Log retries and backoff timings to optimize responsiveness without overwhelming your backend.

🔒 Observability in Production with Monitoring Services

Use crash monitoring and logging platforms to surface network issues seen only in production:

Tool	Features
Firebase Crashlytics	Capture fatal and non-fatal API errors
Sentry	Tag requests, trace latency, group network failures
Datadog	Observe backend logs linked to client sessions

Example with Sentry:

```
Sentry.captureMessage('API Error: $error', level:
SentryLevel.error);
```

📈 Create Reproducible Debug Logs

Include

- Timestamp
- Endpoint path
- Payload (when safe)
- Headers
- Device details (OS, build version)
- Response status and body

Example Log Format:

```
[2025-05-13 16:40:12] GET /v1/user/profile
Status: 401 Unauthorized
Device: Pixel 6 (Android 14)
Token: Expired
```

These logs should be easily shareable for backend or QA teams to reproduce issues.

✓ Summary: Pro-Level Debugging Mindset

Principle	Action
Isolate and Simulate	Use mocks and dependency injection to test all error paths
Observe in Real Time	Use proxies, DevTools, or emulator features
Categorize Errors	Catch specific exceptions and present helpful messages
Secure Logs	Never log sensitive data in production
Monitor in Production	Use Sentry or Crashlytics to capture real-world network issues
Design for Failure	Assume APIs can fail, and ensure the app degrades gracefully

With the right strategies in place, debugging APIs becomes less reactive and more preventive. When paired with automated testing, observability tools, and solid architecture, developers can build network-resilient Flutter applications that handle the chaos of real-world connectivity with confidence.

Tools for API Testing

API testing is a critical part of modern Flutter app development. It ensures that your application interacts correctly with backend services, returns expected data, handles errors gracefully, and performs reliably under different scenarios. Flutter developers often integrate a combination of manual, automated, and real-time tools to validate request/response flows, monitor network behavior, and automate test cases.

This section explores the essential tools and utilities used by professional Flutter developers for robust API testing—spanning from API mocking to integration testing and live endpoint validation.

🔧 Postman: Manual API Testing Powerhouse

Postman remains the go-to tool for inspecting, testing, and automating API requests outside your Flutter environment. It allows you to

Craft HTTP requests (GET, POST, PUT, DELETE, etc.).

Add custom headers, query parameters, and body content.

View detailed responses including status codes, headers, and latency.

Chain requests with dynamic variables and scripting.

Use Cases:

- Validate API contract before writing client code.
- Reproduce edge cases (e.g., 404, 500 errors).
- Test with expired or malformed tokens.
- Simulate rate limiting or throttling.

❗ **Pro Tip**   Use Postman's Mock Server feature to simulate endpoints during frontend development.

⚙ REST Client Plugins (for VS Code and IntelliJ)

For developers who prefer staying in their IDEs, REST Client extensions can be a lightweight alternative to Postman.

◆ **REST Client for VS Code:**

Write ".http" files with request blocks.

Run and view responses directly inside the editor.

Great for versioning request payloads in source control.

Example:

```
GET https://api.example.com/v1/profile
```

CHAPTER 8   NETWORKING AND API INTEGRATION

```
Authorization: Bearer {{access_token}}
```

🚀 **Benefit**: Fast switching between coding and API testing without leaving your IDE.

🧪 **Mockito and Mocktail for Unit Testing**

Mocking network layers in tests is essential for isolated and deterministic testing. Popular libraries like "mockito" and "mocktail" let you fake responses from API clients.

✅ **Common Use Cases**:

Return controlled mock responses in unit tests.
Simulate error conditions like timeouts or auth failures.
Assert that requests were made with expected parameters.

Example Using Mocktail:

```
class MockApiService extends Mock implements ApiService {}
void main() {
  test('fetches user profile successfully', () async {
    final api = MockApiService();
    when(() => api.getUserProfile())
        .thenAnswer((_) async => UserProfile(name: 'Alice'));

    final profile = await api.getUserProfile();
    expect(profile.name, 'Alice');
  });
}
```

CHAPTER 8   NETWORKING AND API INTEGRATION

🔍 Flutter Integration Testing with API Verification

Flutter's "integration_test" package allows you to test the full app flow, including UI interactions and network responses.

To verify API behavior

> Run the app in an emulator/device.
>
> Interact with widgets.
>
> Confirm the UI reflects real or mocked API responses.

Tools that enhance this are

> "http_mock_adapter" for Dio
>
> Custom interceptors to stub APIs
>
> Firebase Test Lab for device matrix testing

🧪 **Advanced**: Pair with tools like "Flutter Driver" or "Golden Toolkit" for pixel-perfect verification after API-driven state changes.

🔄 Mock Servers (WireMock, Beeceptor, Mockoon)

When the backend is unavailable or unstable, mock servers simulate expected responses with predefined logic.

♦ **Mockoon**:

Desktop app for quickly mocking APIs.

Create routes, and set status codes, delays, and JSON bodies.

Share mock APIs via local servers.

♦ **Beeceptor**:

Online platform for intercepting and mocking endpoints.

Monitor real requests from your app (great for debugging mobile APIs).

🧪 **Example**: Use Beeceptor to monitor a live endpoint by replacing the base URL temporarily during dev/testing.

📶 Charles Proxy and Proxyman (Network Interception)

Charles Proxy and Proxyman allow real-time inspection of HTTP(S) traffic between your app and remote servers.

Use Cases:

View all request headers, payloads, and responses.

Inspect API behavior on mobile devices.

Modify request/response on the fly for testing.

Setup:

Install SSL certificates on emulator/device for HTTPS traffic.

Route device traffic through proxy server.

🛡 **Security Note:** Never use production tokens while capturing traffic. Always test in dev or staging environments.

📊 Automated API Monitoring with Postman Monitors or Hoppscotch

For long-term testing and uptime verification, tools like Postman Monitors or Hoppscotch Pro let you

Run scheduled API tests (every X minutes).

Receive alerts when endpoints fail.

Track performance stats and logs.

📱 **Usage:** Monitor your app's key APIs (login, dashboard, payments) and get notified of slow or failing responses.

📘 Swagger and OpenAPI for Contract Testing

If your backend provides an OpenAPI (Swagger) spec, use tools like

Swagger UI: For browsing API endpoints

Swagger Codegen: For generating Dart API clients

Schemathesis: For automated schema-based testing

CHAPTER 8 NETWORKING AND API INTEGRATION

These tools validate that your frontend calls conform to the backend contract.

> **Tip** Keep API documentation versioned and in sync with client apps.

✅ **Summary: Your Flutter API Testing Toolkit**

Category	Recommended Tools
Manual API Testing	Postman, REST Client, Swagger UI
Unit Testing Mocks	mockito, mocktail, http_mock_adapter
Mock Servers	Mockoon, Beeceptor, WireMock
Integration Testing	integration_test, Firebase Test Lab
Network Debugging	Charles Proxy, Proxyman
API Monitoring	Postman Monitors, Hoppscotch
Contract Validation	Swagger/OpenAPI tools

Testing APIs isn't just about making sure the request works—it's about understanding how your app reacts to every possible response. The tools above allow Flutter developers to test not just success paths, but failures, latencies, and unexpected payloads that occur in real-world scenarios.

Summary

Here, we explored the full spectrum of networking capabilities available in Flutter 3.29, equipping developers with the tools and techniques needed to build robust, high-performance, and resilient applications. Beginning with modernized HTTP request handling and efficient JSON parsing, we progressed into advanced API integration strategies for complex endpoints, including error handling and retry mechanisms. We examined

CHAPTER 8 NETWORKING AND API INTEGRATION

real-time data with WebSocket integration, covering both data handling and connection management. The chapter also delved into advanced caching methods for offline support and performance optimization. Finally, we concluded with a deep dive into professional-grade API testing and debugging strategies, showcasing essential tools such as Postman, mock servers, interceptors, and automated monitoring platforms. Together, these topics provide a comprehensive blueprint for mastering API-driven development in Flutter.

CHAPTER 9

Advanced Animations and Transitions

In the previous chapter, we explored the core pillars of modern data-driven applications—ranging from HTTP request enhancements and complex API handling to real-time communication via WebSockets and advanced caching strategies. These capabilities ensured that your Flutter applications are not only well-connected but also efficient, scalable, and resilient under real-world network conditions.

With the foundation of robust backend integration firmly in place, we now shift focus to the user-facing side of your application: animation and visual interaction. In today's mobile and web landscapes, the quality of an app is increasingly measured by how it feels—not just how it functions. Smooth, meaningful animations and transitions are now essential for enhancing usability, guiding user flow, and delivering immersive user experiences.

Flutter is uniquely positioned in this regard. Unlike many frameworks that bolt animation support on as an afterthought, Flutter was designed from the ground up with rich animation and GPU-accelerated rendering at its core. Its declarative UI paradigm, composable widget system, and frame-perfect animation capabilities empower developers to build high-fidelity, high-performance visuals with precision.

CHAPTER 9   ADVANCED ANIMATIONS AND TRANSITIONS

Here we focus on advanced animation techniques and transition design patterns. We will start by creating custom animation effects using AnimationController, Tween, and AnimatedBuilder and then explore how to structure complex, coordinated animations across multiple UI elements. We'll also investigate animation performance optimization, essential for maintaining smooth frame rates, especially on lower-end devices or web targets.

Beyond native tools, we'll review popular animation libraries such as flutter_animate, rive, and lottie, discussing how they can be extended and customized for high-impact interfaces. Special attention is given to cross-platform animation consistency, ensuring that your designs retain their integrity and responsiveness across mobile, web, and desktop environments.

Expert Insight: In Flutter, animation is not a luxury—it's a core aspect of interaction design. Thoughtfully implemented animations help reduce cognitive load, improve user retention, and distinguish your application in a crowded marketplace.

Custom Animation Techniques

Flutter's animation framework is one of its most powerful features, offering fine-grained control and a declarative, flexible API that allows developers to design visually rich, interactive UIs with precision. In this section, we'll explore how to create sophisticated animations manually using AnimationController, Tween, and other low-level APIs, as well as how to manage performance and frame rate smoothness when animating complex UI states.

By building custom animation logic from scratch, you gain control over timing, curves, and sequence orchestration—enabling you to achieve animations that are uniquely tailored to your app's design and UX goals.

Creating Complex Animations

Advanced animation techniques are at the heart of a truly interactive Flutter experience. While Flutter provides a wide range of implicit animation widgets (AnimatedContainer, AnimatedOpacity, AnimatedAlign, etc.) for basic transitions, creating immersive, dynamic animations often requires full control over the animation lifecycle, state, and rendering behavior. This section explores how to use Flutter's low-level animation APIs to craft sophisticated motion experiences that are responsive, intuitive, and deeply integrated with your UI logic.

Overview of Custom Animation Techniques

Flutter's animation framework is designed to offer high flexibility and control, allowing developers to build intricate and expressive UI transitions. While implicit animations like "AnimatedContainer" or "AnimatedOpacity" are perfect for simple use cases, they fall short when you need to craft complex, coordinated, or interactive effects. This is where custom animation techniques come into play.

🔧 Core Building Blocks

The foundation of any custom animation in Flutter involves a few essential components:

AnimationController:

Acts as the heartbeat of the animation. It defines the duration, start/stop behavior, repeat cycles, and progress of the animation. You can start, stop, repeat, and reverse animations programmatically using this controller.

Tween<T>:

A "Tween" defines the range of values to animate between. For example, "Tween<double>(begin: 0.0, end: 1.0)" can be used to animate opacity, scale, or other numeric values. There are tweens for colors, offsets, integers, and more.

CurvedAnimation:

A wrapper around an animation to add timing curves like "easeIn," "easeOutBack," "bounceIn," etc. Curves control how an animation feels, whether it accelerates slowly or bounces on completion.

AnimatedBuilder:

A high-performance widget that rebuilds only what's needed during an animation. This allows you to avoid unnecessary rebuilds and ensures optimal rendering.

TickerProvider:

Required to drive the "AnimationController" by syncing animation frames with the screen refresh rate ("vsync"). Most often used via the "TickerProviderStateMixin" in a "StatefulWidget."

🎞 Composition Techniques

Custom animations allow for layered composition, meaning you can stack multiple transformations or property changes simultaneously:

Combining Tweens: Animate opacity, rotation, scaling, and position at once.

Staggered Animations: Delay individual segments to create sequential motion (e.g., text appears, then fades, then scales).

Chained Animations: Start one animation based on the completion of another, often used for onboarding flows or storytelling interfaces.

Gesture-Driven Animations: Use "GestureDetector," "Draggable," or "ScrollController" to drive animation progress with user input.

↻ Use Cases

Some powerful real-world scenarios for custom animations include

Custom splash or onboarding animations

Dynamic button effects (hover, press, long press)

Parallax and scroll-linked effects

Animated transitions between views or components

Micro-interactions (e.g., toggling a switch, liking a post)

> **♀ Expert Insight**: Use "ValueListenableBuilder" if you only need to animate a single property, like opacity or color. It's lighter than "AnimatedBuilder" and simpler to set up for small animations.

🧠 Developer Tip

Always aim to decouple animation logic from business logic. Keeping animation responsibilities isolated in custom widgets or helper classes improves reusability and testability.

Implementing Custom Animation Effects

Once you understand the fundamentals of Flutter's animation system, the next step is implementing custom animation effects that feel polished, performant, and visually engaging. This section will walk through practical implementation patterns, emphasizing clean architecture, reusability, and smooth motion design.

🎬 Step-by-Step: Creating a Multi-property Animation

Let's build a fade-scale-slide animation that introduces a widget with fluidity and style—ideal for onboarding screens, modals, or content reveals.

```
class FadeScaleSlideAnimation extends StatefulWidget {
  final Widget child;
  final Duration duration;

  const FadeScaleSlideAnimation({
    required this.child,
    this.duration = const Duration(milliseconds: 700),
    super.key,
  });
```

CHAPTER 9   ADVANCED ANIMATIONS AND TRANSITIONS

```dart
  @override
  State<FadeScaleSlideAnimation> createState() =>
      _FadeScaleSlideAnimationState();
}
class _FadeScaleSlideAnimationState extends
State<FadeScaleSlideAnimation>
    with SingleTickerProviderStateMixin {
  late final AnimationController _controller;
  late final Animation<double> _opacity;
  late final Animation<double> _scale;
  late final Animation<Offset> _slide;

  @override
  void initState() {
    super.initState();

    _controller = AnimationController(
      vsync: this,
      duration: widget.duration,
    );

    _opacity = Tween(begin: 0.0, end: 1.0).animate(
      CurvedAnimation(parent: _controller, curve: Curves.
      easeIn),
    );

    _scale = Tween(begin: 0.9, end: 1.0).animate(
      CurvedAnimation(parent: _controller, curve: Curves.
      easeOutBack),
    );

    _slide = Tween(begin: const Offset(0.0, 0.1), end: Offset.
    zero).animate(
```

```
      CurvedAnimation(parent: _controller, curve: Curves.
      easeOut),
    );

    _controller.forward();
  }

  @override
  void dispose() {
    _controller.dispose();
    super.dispose();
  }
  @override
  Widget build(BuildContext context) {
    return AnimatedBuilder(
      animation: _controller,
      builder: (_, __) {
        return Opacity(
          opacity: _opacity.value,
          child: Transform.scale(
            scale: _scale.value,
            child: SlideTransition(
              position: _slide,
              child: widget.child,
            ),
          ),
        );
      },
    );
  }
}
```

CHAPTER 9 ADVANCED ANIMATIONS AND TRANSITIONS

🔍 Explanation

AnimationController: Drives all three effects in sync.

"Tween" + "CurvedAnimation": Each property uses its own "Tween" and custom easing curve for a unique effect.

AnimatedBuilder: Efficiently rebuilds only when necessary, improving frame rendering and keeping animations smooth.

Nested Animations: We compose three effects (opacity, scale, position) to create a compelling entrance animation.

💡 **Expert Insight**: Always test on 60Hz and 120Hz devices to ensure the animation remains fluid and visually consistent.

♻ Reusable Animations

It's good practice to encapsulate custom animations into widgets. This promotes reusability and simplifies maintenance. With the "FadeScaleSlideAnimation" widget, you can wrap any UI element and give it a high-end transition effect with minimal effort:

```
FadeScaleSlideAnimation(
  duration: Duration(milliseconds: 600),
  child: Text(
    'Welcome!',
    style: Theme.of(context).textTheme.headlineMedium,
  ),
)
```

You can also generalize animation parameters (curves, begin/end values, axis direction) into optional widget properties to build animation utilities across your app.

🧪 Pro Tip: Debug Animations Visually

Flutter offers excellent visual debugging tools:

Slow Animations Toggle:

Enable this in Flutter DevTools or via "WidgetsApp.debugSlowAnimations = true;" to better analyze timing and transitions.

Performance Overlay:

Activate in Flutter Inspector to see frame rendering stats. Watch out for long build or raster times when your animations are active.

Beyond Basics: Animation Status Listeners

For scenarios like chaining or reversing animations, use the "AnimationStatusListener":

```
_controller.addStatusListener((status) {
  if (status == AnimationStatus.completed) {
    // Trigger next animation or update state
  }
});
```

This is especially useful when creating onboarding steps, looping effects, or back-and-forth motion patterns.

✅ Key Takeaways

Custom animation effects allow full control of the animation lifecycle and visual result.

Combine multiple "Tweens" with "CurvedAnimation" to create natural, layered transitions.

Encapsulate animations into widgets to promote clean architecture and reuse.

Use Flutter's visual tools (DevTools, debug overlays) to fine-tune and profile your animations.

Leverage status listeners for advanced use cases like chaining, repeating, or triggering logic on animation events.

Performance Considerations

Animations bring apps to life—but if they're not optimized, they can quickly become performance bottlenecks, causing jank, dropped frames, and poor user experience. In this section, we'll explore how to optimize animations for performance and ensure buttery-smooth transitions across devices.

Optimizing Animation Performance

In Flutter, beautiful animations should not come at the cost of performance. Optimizing animations is critical to ensure smooth frame rates, responsive interactions, and a high-quality user experience—especially on lower-end devices or when multiple animations run simultaneously.

🚀 **Understanding the Root Causes of Lag**

Before applying optimization techniques, it's important to understand the two main performance culprits during animations:

Excessive Widget Rebuilds:

Triggered when large widget trees are re-rendered unnecessarily, usually due to improper use of "setState()"

Overdraw and Rasterization Bottlenecks:

Occurs when widgets are repainted or composed more than needed, straining the GPU pipeline

✅ **Key Strategies to Optimize Animation Performance**

1. **Use "AnimatedBuilder" or "AnimatedWidget" Instead of "setState()"**
   Avoid this (inefficient):

CHAPTER 9 ADVANCED ANIMATIONS AND TRANSITIONS

```
AnimationController _controller;
setState(() {
  _value = _controller.value;
});
```

Do this (efficient):

```
AnimatedBuilder(
  animation: _controller,
  builder: (context, child) {
    return Transform.scale(
      scale: _controller.value,
      child: child,
    );
  },
  child: MyWidget(),
);
```

Why: Only the child inside the builder gets rebuilt, reducing workload drastically.

2. **Isolate Repaints Using "RepaintBoundary"**
   Flutter allows segmenting the render tree so that only parts that need redrawing are repainted.

   ```
   RepaintBoundary(
     child: ComplexWidget(),
   );
   ```

> **⚡ Tip** Use Flutter DevTools' "Repaint Rainbow" feature to visualize what's getting redrawn.

3. **Preload and Cache Heavy Resources**

   If your animation involves images, SVGs, or network-fetched assets

   Use "precacheImage()" in "initState()" to load images before the animation starts.

   Use "flutter_svg" with caching enabled for vector assets.

   ```
   @override
   void initState() {
     super.initState();
     precacheImage(AssetImage('assets/hero.png'),
     context);
   }
   ```
   ---

4. **Minimize Layout Changes During Animation**

   Avoid layout-affecting changes like size, padding, or alignment within high-frequency animation frames. Instead of animating layout directly:

   ```
   // BAD: Expensive relayout
   AnimatedContainer(duration: ..., height:
   animatedHeight);
   ```

CHAPTER 9   ADVANCED ANIMATIONS AND TRANSITIONS

Use transforms:

```
// BETTER: GPU-efficient transform
Transform.translate(offset: Offset(0, animatedValue),
child: YourWidget());
```

5. **Choose Lightweight Widgets and Avoid Overdraw**

Overdraw happens when multiple widgets are painted on top of each other needlessly.

Use fewer overlapping translucent widgets.

Flatten nested "Container," "Opacity," and "ClipRect" layers.

Prefer "CustomPaint" only when necessary.

Use DevTools ➤ "Raster Stats" to identify overdraw areas.

🎞 Profile and Monitor Animation Health

Flutter provides multiple ways to analyze animation performance:

Tool	Use Case
Flutter DevTools - Timeline	Identify jank, thread blocking, and frame build times
Performance Overlay	Visualizes frame rate, UI and GPU thread performance
Frame rendering graph	Shows frame drop events and rendering spikes

CHAPTER 9 ADVANCED ANIMATIONS AND TRANSITIONS

Enable with

```
MaterialApp(showPerformanceOverlay: true)
```

🔍 Common Pitfalls to Avoid
Updating UI using "setState()" inside an animation callback
Animating large widget trees without "RepaintBoundary"
Heavy image loads during animation start
Triggering layout rebuilds in tight animation loops

🧠 Expert Insight: Animation Budget
Aim for <16ms per frame (on 60Hz displays) or <8ms per frame (on 120Hz devices). Anything above that results in dropped frames and visual lag.

✅ Summary Checklist

✅ Optimization Tip	Description
Use 'AnimatedBuilder'	Efficient rebuilds for animated parts only
Use 'RepaintBoundary'	Limit repaints to animated widgets
Cache assets	Preload images and SVGs
Use transforms, not layout	Rely on 'Transform', 'Opacity', 'FadeTransition'
Profile regularly	Use DevTools to catch issues early

Techniques for Smooth Animations

Delivering silky-smooth animations is a hallmark of premium Flutter applications. Beyond raw performance, smooth animations are about fluid motion, perceptual elegance, and consistent timing. This section explores key strategies, tools, and design principles to achieve consistently smooth animation experiences across mobile, web, and desktop platforms.

⊕ Define "Smooth"

For most Flutter targets, smoothness means

Consistent 60 FPS on 60Hz displays

Consistent 120 FPS on high-refresh-rate displays

Zero dropped frames during animation playback

Responsive UI thread—no stutters or jank

✒ Techniques for Achieving Smooth Animations

1. **Minimize Frame Build Time**

    Each frame has a strict rendering budget:

    ```
    \~16ms on 60Hz displays
    \~8ms on 120Hz displays
    ```

    Use Flutter DevTools Timeline to inspect how much time your build/layout/paint phases consume. If the build phase exceeds this limit, animations will stutter.

🖋 **Pro Tip** Keep your builds light—avoid animation-induced deep widget tree rebuilds.

---

2. **Use GPU-Friendly Widgets**

    Some widgets offload animation work to the GPU, making them extremely efficient:

```
| Widget            | GPU-Accelerated                      |
| ----------------- | ------------------------------------ |
| 'Opacity'         | ✓ (when opacity is not               |
|                   |    stacked deeply)                   |
| 'Transform'       | ✓                                    |
| 'SlideTransition' | ✓                                    |
| 'ScaleTransition' | ✓                                    |
| 'FadeTransition'  | ✓                                    |
```

```
FadeTransition(
  opacity: _animation,
  child: YourWidget(),
);
```

🎯 Use these whenever possible instead of manipulating layout-heavy widgets like "AnimatedContainer."

3. **Avoid Layout Thrashing**

   Animations that continuously change constraints (height, width, alignment) force full layout recalculations, which are costly.

✅ Instead of this:

```
AnimatedContainer(duration: ..., width: value);
```

Do this:

```
Transform.scale(
  scale: value,
```

```
  child: FixedSizeWidget(),
);
```

⚠ **Performance Alert**: Layout-based animations can hurt frame rate on nested layouts or lists.

4. **Use "TickerMode" to Pause Offscreen Animations**

   Stop animations from running when they're not visible:

   ```
   TickerMode(
     enabled: isOnscreen,
     child: AnimatedWidget(),
   );
   ```

   ▶ This reduces GPU/CPU workload significantly when navigating across routes or tabs.

5. **Use Staggered and Chained Animations**

   Don't animate everything at once. Use staggered timing to distribute motion:

   ```
   AnimationController controller;
   Animation<double> first = Tween(...).animate(Curved
   Animation(
     parent: controller,
     curve: Interval(0.0, 0.5, curve: Curves.easeOut),
   ));

   Animation<double> second = Tween(...).animate(Curved
   Animation(
   ```

```
  parent: controller,
  curve: Interval(0.5, 1.0, curve: Curves.easeIn),
));
```

🪄 **Visual Impact Boost**: Creates a cascading feel with smoother perceived motion.

6. **Balance Physics and Timing**

   Avoid unnatural motion. Flutter provides powerful physics-based animations:

   ```
   'SpringSimulation'
   'FrictionSimulation'
   'BouncingScrollSimulation'
   ```

   You can also use "Flare," "Rive," or "Lottie" for designer-driven, frame-perfect animations.

7. **Respect Device Refresh Rates**

   With high-refresh devices becoming mainstream (120Hz, 144Hz), Flutter automatically tries to match device FPS—but you must ensure your animations aren't tied to slow logic or UI thread delays.

   Expert Insight: Use fast math and GPU offloading to keep pace with modern refresh rates.

🛠 **Tools to Test Smoothness**

Tool	Purpose
Performance Overlay	Shows frame build/paint stats
DevTools Timeline	Identifies layout/rendering spikes
Profile Mode	Most accurate for detecting jank

CHAPTER 9 ADVANCED ANIMATIONS AND TRANSITIONS

| Low-End Device Testing | Ensures animations run smoothly across all hardware |

Enable overlay in 'MaterialApp':

```
MaterialApp(
  showPerformanceOverlay: true,
  home: MyApp(),
);
```

✓ Summary Checklist

✓ Best Practice	Benefit
Use GPU-accelerated transitions	Offloads work from CPU
Avoid layout changes mid-animation	Prevents frame drops
Pause offscreen animations	Saves resources
Stagger animations	Improves perceptual fluidity
Match animation speed to frame budget	Ensures 60–120 FPS
Profile with DevTools	Detects jank early

💬 **Expert Insight**: Smooth animations are not about speed—they're about timing, predictability, and perceived responsiveness. If your app feels smooth, users will think it is fast—even if it's not rendering at peak frame rate.

Animation Libraries and Packages

Flutter's built-in animation capabilities are robust, but when building visually rich, dynamic, and scalable UIs, leveraging external animation libraries can drastically improve productivity, visual fidelity, and design collaboration. This section explores the most widely used animation libraries and packages in Flutter and showcases how to implement, customize, and scale them effectively for advanced use cases.

Overview of Popular Animation Libraries

As Flutter matures, so does its ecosystem of powerful animation libraries that allow developers to implement complex, visually engaging animations with minimal boilerplate. These libraries bridge the gap between code and design, offering high-level abstractions, performance optimizations, and ready-to-use animated assets.

Utilizing Animation Libraries

Integrating animation libraries into your Flutter project not only accelerates development but also ensures that your app delivers rich, immersive experiences with minimal custom code. This section explores how to effectively integrate and utilize major animation libraries—such as Rive, Lottie, and AnimatedTextKit—within a scalable Flutter architecture.

✅ **Step-by-Step Workflow for Utilizing Animation Libraries**

1. **Selecting the Right Animation Tool**

    Choosing the right library is the first strategic step. Consider

Criteria	Rive	Lottie	AnimatedTextKit
Designer collaboration	✅	✅	❌
Interactivity	✅	⚠ Limited	❌
Asset reusability	✅	✅	❌
Code simplicity	⚠	✅	✅

CHAPTER 9   ADVANCED ANIMATIONS AND TRANSITIONS

🔍 If you need logic-driven animations, Rive is ideal. For lightweight icon animations or onboarding flows, Lottie is a great fit.

2. Adding the Package to "pubspec."
   Example for Lottie:

   ```
   dependencies:
     lottie: ^3.1.0
   ```

   Then run

   ```
   flutter pub get
   ```

   Do this for any animation library you choose.

3. **Preparing and Placing Animation Assets**

   Place ".riv" files (for Rive) or ".json" files (for Lottie) in your "assets/animations/" folder. Declare assets in "pubspec.":

   ```
   flutter:
     assets:
       - assets/animations/rocket.riv
       - assets/animations/loading.json
   ```

4. **Using the Animation in Widgets**
   Example—Rive Integration:

   ```
   RiveAnimation.asset(
     'assets/animations/rocket.riv',
     stateMachines: ['LaunchState'],
   );
   ```

   Example—Lottie Integration:

   ```
   Lottie.asset(
     'assets/animations/loading.json',
     repeat: true,
     animate: true,
   );
   ```

   Example—AnimatedTextKit:

   ```
   AnimatedTextKit(
     animatedTexts: [
       FadeAnimatedText('Welcome'),
       TypewriterAnimatedText('Let's build something cool!'),
     ],
     repeatForever: true,
   );
   ```

🎨 Best Practices for Effective Integration

Use lazy loading for large assets to avoid jank on startup.

Control animations via state for better UX. Avoid auto-looping everything unless required.

Wrap animations in semantic containers (like "SizedBox" or "Stack") to maintain layout consistency.

Use "Visibility," "Opacity," or "FadeTransition" to hide/show animations dynamically.

✏️ Testing and Debugging Animation Integrations

Simulate different screen sizes to ensure responsiveness.

Use Flutter DevTools' Performance Overlay to monitor jank introduced by animation layers.

Preload animations during splash screens for a seamless UX.

⚠️ **Performance Alert**: Overuse of Lottie or Rive files without optimization can bloat your app and introduce rendering delays—especially on low-end Android devices. Keep your animation assets compressed and lean.

✅ End-of-Section Checklist

Task	Completed?
Chose the right library based on UX needs	☐
Added the library to 'pubspec.'	☐
Declared and loaded assets correctly	☐
Embedded animation with widget logic	☐
Tested animation performance across devices	☐

Customizing Library Animations

Once animation libraries like Rive, Lottie, or AnimatedTextKit are integrated into your Flutter project, the next step is customization—tailoring animations to reflect your app's personality, brand identity,

CHAPTER 9   ADVANCED ANIMATIONS AND TRANSITIONS

and user interaction flow. This section explores how to control, configure, and customize animation behavior and aesthetics to create a refined, interactive experience.

🎨 Why Customization Matters

Prebuilt animations are powerful, but without proper customization, they can

- Feel generic and disconnected from your brand
- Cause layout or UX inconsistencies
- Lack interactive depth

By customizing animations, you can ensure they

- Match the tone and theme of your app
- React to user input in meaningful ways
- Stay performant and scalable

🧬 Customization Techniques per Library

🎀 Rive Customization

Rive animations are built using state machines, which allow real-time control over animations through code.

Use Cases:

- Buttons with interactive hover/click effects
- Characters responding to user actions
- Conditional animations based on state

🔧 **Implementation:**

```
RiveAnimation.asset(
  'assets/avatar.riv',
  stateMachines: ['UserState'],
  onInit: (artboard) {
    final controller = StateMachineController.
    fromArtboard(artboard, 'UserState');
    artboard.addController(controller!);
```

CHAPTER 9   ADVANCED ANIMATIONS AND TRANSITIONS

```
    final input = controller.findInput<bool>('isHappy') as
    SMIBool;
    input.value = true;
  },
);
```

✅ **Custom Logic Triggered**: The animation reacts when "isHappy" is toggled from Dart.

🔧 Lottie Customization

Lottie animations are exported as ".json" files and offer dynamic control via animation properties like speed, progress, and frame control.

Use Cases:

Loading indicators that pause/play

Animation synced to scroll position

Animations triggered by gestures

🔧 **Implementation**:

```
Lottie.asset(
  'assets/loading.json',
  controller: _controller,
  onLoaded: (composition) {
    _controller
      ..duration = composition.duration
      ..forward();
  },
);
```

✅ **Custom Progress Control**: You can use "AnimationController" to sync the animation with any part of the UI or app logic.

CHAPTER 9   ADVANCED ANIMATIONS AND TRANSITIONS

🎨 AnimatedTextKit Customization

AnimatedTextKit provides multiple parameters to customize text styles, animation speeds, alignment, pauses, and more.

Use Cases:

Branded headlines with dynamic effects

Synchronized call-to-actions

Subtle intro text transitions

🔧 Implementation:

```
AnimatedTextKit(
  animatedTexts: [
    TypewriterAnimatedText(
      'Welcome to Mastering Flutter!',
      textStyle: const TextStyle(fontSize: 32.0, fontWeight: FontWeight.bold),
      speed: Duration(milliseconds: 100),
    ),
  ],
  pause: Duration(milliseconds: 1000),
  totalRepeatCount: 1,
  displayFullTextOnTap: true,
  stopPauseOnTap: true,
);
```

✅ **Hi0.ghly Tunable Behavior**: Tap to skip, pause/resume control, and infinite/finite repeats.

🔄 **Animations Synced with App Logic**

Custom animations truly shine when tied to user or app state.

CHAPTER 9 ADVANCED ANIMATIONS AND TRANSITIONS

Example:

Use "ValueNotifier" or "Bloc" to trigger animation changes.

Bind animation progress to scroll controller.

Drive animation based on form input validation.

🎨 Pro Tips

Tip	Benefit
Preprocess animations with tools like Rive or Bodymovin	Clean, optimized asset export
Use Flutter's 'TickerProvider' for custom timing	Precision frame control
Link animations to state management	Reactive UX
Use hero animations in sync with custom animations	Seamless page transitions

⚠ Performance and Branding Alerts

🔊 **Performance Alert**: Avoid using high-frame-rate Lottie animations on low-end devices. Optimize with reduced vector complexity and frame skipping.

🎯 **Branding Alert**: Ensure that text, icons, and motion match your app's visual language. Don't reuse generic animations unless they've been customized.

✓ End-of-Section Checklist

Customization Task	Done?
Integrated state-machine control for Rive	☐
Bound Lottie animations to app logic	☐
Tuned text styles and speeds in AnimatedTextKit	☐
Optimized animation asset size	☐
Matched animation theme with app branding	☐

Advanced Use Cases

As developers advance beyond integrating and customizing animation libraries, the next logical step is mastering real-world application of animations in production-ready Flutter apps. This section presents real-world examples and in-depth case studies that highlight how advanced animation techniques can enhance usability, storytelling, and interactivity across different app categories.

By analyzing successful implementations, you'll learn how to create experiential animations that not only look beautiful but also improve usability, reduce cognitive load, and increase user retention.

Real-World Examples

Bringing animation into a production app requires more than technical fluency—it demands practical design judgment and user-centered implementation. In this section, we'll explore a variety of real-world scenarios that demonstrate how animations can enhance the user experience, drive engagement, and reinforce brand identity across different domains.

CHAPTER 9   ADVANCED ANIMATIONS AND TRANSITIONS

These examples reflect how Flutter developers are using popular libraries like Lottie, Rive, and Flutter's native animation APIs in creative, results-oriented ways.

💲 Example 1: Seamless Onboarding Transitions with Lottie

App Type: Fintech

Library: Lottie

Objective: Use micro-animations to guide users through a multi-step onboarding process.

Key Details:

Each onboarding screen features animated illustrations explaining app features like security, speed, and ease of use.

Animations are synced with a "PageView" controller, enabling smooth transitions.

Code Snippet:

```
PageView.builder(
  itemCount: onboardingData.length,
  itemBuilder: (context, index) => Lottie.asset(
    onboardingData[index].animationPath,
    fit: BoxFit.contain,
  ),
);
```

Result: Increased onboarding completion rate by 30% and reduced bounce rate during the signup process

🎯 Example 2: Interactive Avatar Feedback with Rive

App Type: Fitness tracking

Library: Rive

Objective: Provide real-time animated feedback based on user achievements.

CHAPTER 9   ADVANCED ANIMATIONS AND TRANSITIONS

Key Details:

A dynamic avatar reacts to workout progress, changing mood based on goal completion.

State machine logic in Rive allows animations to change based on "goalAchieved" Boolean inputs.

Code Snippet:

```
final input = controller.findInput<bool>('goalAchieved') as SMIBool;
input.value = true;
```

Result: Boosted daily engagement time by 18% due to gamified progress visualization

📊 Example 3: Animated Data Visualization in Dashboards

App Type: Productivity/analytics

Library: Native Flutter tweens + custom widgets

Objective: Animate KPIs and charts to indicate data changes clearly.

Key Details:

Uses "TweenAnimationBuilder" for metric updates.

Applies "AnimatedSwitcher" for transitions between datasets.

Code Snippet:

```
TweenAnimationBuilder(
  tween: Tween<double>(begin: 0, end: userEngagement),
  duration: Duration(seconds: 2),
  builder: (context, value, child) => Text('${value.toStringAsFixed(1)}%'),
);
```

CHAPTER 9   ADVANCED ANIMATIONS AND TRANSITIONS

Result: Helped users digest analytical changes more intuitively, improving overall dashboard usability

💡 **Example 4: Enhanced Micro-interactions in Ecommerce**

App Type: Shopping

Library: AnimatedContainer + Lottie

Objective: Add delight to frequent user actions like "Add to Cart" and "Wishlist."

Key Details:

Animations trigger on tap, confirming actions with visual feedback.

Heart button uses Lottie for a "pop and fill" effect.

Code Snippet:

```
GestureDetector(
  onTap: () => setState(() => isFavorited = !isFavorited),
  child: Lottie.asset(
    isFavorited ? 'assets/heart_fill.json' : 'assets/heart_outline.json',
    repeat: false,
  ),
);
```

Result: Increased user satisfaction and interaction rate on product cards by 22%

These examples demonstrate how thoughtful integration of animations can elevate the UX across various app categories:

Use Case	Library Used	Primary Outcome
Onboarding Flow	Lottie	Higher user retention during signup
Progress Feedback	Rive	Increased engagement and gamification
Data Visualization	TweenAnimation	Improved interpretation of real-time data
Micro-Interactions	Lottie + Flutter	Boosted interaction and conversion rates

Case Studies

Understanding how animations are implemented in production apps across industries helps developers go beyond theory and see animation as a business tool—one that improves usability, increases user retention, and shapes product identity. The following case studies highlight how various Flutter apps leveraged animation libraries like Rive, Lottie, and Flutter's built-in APIs to achieve real, measurable results.

✚ Case Study 1: MedTrack—Health Monitoring App

Objective: Deliver real-time health updates in a calm, non-intrusive manner.

Challenge: Health data changes rapidly. UI feedback had to be immediate, but not alarming.

Solution:

Used Lottie animations to represent patient vitals (heartbeat, oxygen level).

Subtle color shifts and animation loops maintained a serene visual environment.

"AnimatedOpacity" and "AnimatedContainer" were used to transition between statuses.

Key Code Sample:

```
AnimatedOpacity(
  opacity: isCritical ? 1.0 : 0.6,
  duration: Duration(milliseconds: 600),
  child: Lottie.asset('assets/heart_rate.json'),
);
```

Impact:

Reduced alert fatigue among users.

Clinical teams reported faster response time due to visual clarity.

Ninety-two percent of users described the UI as "professional and reassuring."

🎮 Case Study 2: QuestHero—Gamified Learning App

Objective: Make education engaging by transforming lessons into interactive quests.

Challenge: Retain users in a competitive edtech space.

Solution:

Built animated characters in Rive that evolve as the user progresses through lessons.

Used "StateMachineControllers" to trigger animations based on quiz results and streaks.

Implemented "Hero" transitions between level screens to add a sense of continuity.

Key Code Sample:

```
final input = controller.findInput<bool>('levelUp') as SMIBool;
input.value = true;
```

Impact:

Increased daily active usage by 36%.

Drop-off after lesson 1 decreased by 22%.

Users reported that animations made the app "addictive and rewarding."

🛒 Case Study 3: ShopSwift—Ecommerce App

Objective: Add smooth, branded micro-interactions to increase conversions.

Challenge: Make UI feel responsive without slowing performance.

Solution:

Used "AnimatedContainer" and "AnimatedIcon" to create feedback on common gestures like "Add to Cart," "Swipe to Favorite," and "Quick Buy."

Incorporated Lottie sparkle effects on product actions.

Applied easing curves like "Curves.easeOutBack" to make animations feel natural.

Key Code Sample:

```
AnimatedContainer(
  duration: Duration(milliseconds: 300),
  curve: Curves.easeOutBack,
  transform: Matrix4.identity()..scale(isAdded ? 1.1 : 1.0),
  child: Icon(Icons.shopping_cart),
);
```

Impact:

Increased "Add to Cart" conversions by 19%.

Reduced checkout abandonment by 14%.

Users described the app as "intuitive and satisfying to use."

🎬 Case Study 4: CineWatch—Movie Streaming Platform

Objective: Use cinematic transitions to enhance content discovery.

Challenge: Maintain high performance while adding motion-rich UI.

Solution:

Used "Hero" animations for seamless navigation between the main feed and detail screens.

Added scroll-triggered transitions on movie carousels using "SliverAnimatedList" and "AnimatedPositioned."

Implemented real-time search result animations that faded and scaled into place.

Impact:

Improved user engagement (movies clicked per session) by 27%.

Increased new-user retention over seven days by 15%.

Animation-related bugs were near-zero due to Flutter's GPU-accelerated rendering.

🎨 Expert Insight Sidebar

Animation in Flutter is not just for decoration. It's a storytelling device that guides users and reinforces brand tone.

—Jonah Williams, Flutter Team at Google

✅ End-of-Section Checklist

Task	Completed?
Studied multiple industry case studies	☐
Understood measurable animation impacts	☐
Identified how animation supports UX and business goals	☐
Learned how to adapt techniques to your own app	☐

CHAPTER 9   ADVANCED ANIMATIONS AND TRANSITIONS

Cross-Platform Animation Techniques

In a world where Flutter apps are deployed across mobile, web, desktop, and even embedded platforms, ensuring consistency in animation behavior is both a design and engineering challenge. Animations must look and feel the same whether they're running on iOS or Android, in a browser, or on a desktop screen, all while preserving performance and native feel.

This section focuses on implementing reliable, performant, and consistent animations across platforms, highlighting both the technical and design aspects necessary to achieve a cohesive cross-platform animation system.

Implementing Consistent Animations

Consistency across platforms involves dealing with different rendering engines, input modalities (touch vs. mouse), and device performance characteristics. Flutter provides a powerful rendering pipeline and unified animation framework, but developers still need to apply platform-aware strategies to avoid behavioral discrepancies.

Techniques for Cross-Platform Consistency

Achieving consistent animation behavior across platforms—mobile (iOS/Android), web, and desktop—is a core strength of Flutter. However, developers must still consider platform-specific constraints, input differences, rendering limitations, and hardware capabilities. This section outlines the most effective techniques to ensure your animations behave predictably and smoothly on all platforms, without compromising performance or visual quality.

CHAPTER 9   ADVANCED ANIMATIONS AND TRANSITIONS

🎯 1. Use Core Flutter Animation APIs

To ensure compatibility across all platforms
Favor Flutter's platform-agnostic animation APIs like
"AnimationController"
"Tween," "TweenSequence"
"CurvedAnimation"
"AnimatedBuilder," "AnimatedWidget"
Avoid third-party packages that rely on native views unless necessary (e.g., platform channels for Lottie native renderers).

Example:

```
AnimationController _controller = AnimationController(
  duration: Duration(milliseconds: 600),
  vsync: this,
);
Animation<double> _scale = Tween(begin: 1.0, end: 1.2).animate(
  CurvedAnimation(parent: _controller, curve: Curves.
  easeInOut),
);
```

✪ 2. Align Animations with Platform Capabilities

Animations that look fluid on a flagship iPhone may lag on older Android devices or the web. Tune based on

Frame Rate Awareness: Use "TickerProvider" to sync with device refresh rates.

Hardware Detection: For platforms with limited GPU acceleration (e.g., some desktop or web environments), reduce animation complexity dynamically.

CHAPTER 9 ADVANCED ANIMATIONS AND TRANSITIONS

> **Tip** Use "kIsWeb" and "defaultTargetPlatform" to apply runtime logic:

```
if (kIsWeb) {
  _controller.duration = Duration(milliseconds: 400);
  // Lighter for Web
}
```

3. Use Responsive Animation Timing

Adjust animation parameters based on platform and screen size to maintain a balanced feel:

Mobile: Fast and responsive (e.g., 200–300ms)
Desktop: Slightly slower and more deliberate (e.g., 350–450ms)
Web: Adjust depending on rendering engine (CanvasKit vs. HTML)
Technique:

```
Duration animationDuration = MediaQuery.of(context).size.width > 900
    ? Duration(milliseconds: 400)
    : Duration(milliseconds: 250);
```

4. Normalize Animation Curves

Use a minimal set of easing curves to reduce inconsistency across transitions. Common, stable curves include
   "Curves.easeInOut"
   "Curves.decelerate"
   "Curves.fastOutSlowIn" (Material Design)

CHAPTER 9 ADVANCED ANIMATIONS AND TRANSITIONS

Avoid using custom cubic Bézier curves unless there's a strong UX rationale, as behavior may differ slightly across renderers.

🔧 5. Test Animations on All Target Platforms

It's not enough to assume an animation works just because it runs well on Android or iOS:

Use "flutter run -d web," "-d macos," "-d windows," and "-d linux" regularly.

Evaluate for stutter, delays, and gesture responsiveness.

Validate how animations respond to mouse vs. touch interactions.

🎭 6. Avoid Over-ambitious Effects on Web/Desktop

While mobile supports touch-based, continuous motion well, desktop users expect precise feedback and may find overly animated interactions sluggish:

Use less "bounce" on scroll or navigation.

Prefer fade, scale, or slide over complex morphs or paths.

🔧 7. Optimize Animation FPS

Animations should ideally run at 60 FPS (or 120 FPS where supported). To support this

Minimize widget rebuilds by leveraging "AnimatedBuilder" and "RepaintBoundary."

Avoid triggering rebuilds inside "build()" for every frame.

Tip Profile using Flutter DevTools ➤ Performance tab to inspect frame rendering time and jank.

📛 Performance Alert

Animations that stutter on one platform—even if smooth on another—can erode user trust and perceived quality. Always profile animations under real conditions.

✓ Quick Checklist

Technique	Applied?
Used core Flutter animation APIs	☐
Adjusted durations by platform/screen	☐
Tested behavior on web and desktop	☐
Limited complex effects for weaker platforms	☐
Used consistent easing curves	☐

Best Practices for Cross-Platform Animation

Building animations that look and feel consistent across mobile, web, and desktop is more than a technical task—it's a matter of UX discipline, design cohesion, and performance awareness. Flutter provides a unified framework, but best practices ensure animations behave as users expect on every device and platform.

This section outlines best practices that combine design intent, implementation strategies, and platform-specific nuances, helping you build animations that enhance—rather than hinder—user experience.

🎯 1. Respect Platform Interaction Models

Every platform has its own interaction model. Align your animations with expected behaviors:

iOS: Use subtle spring and bounce effects that reflect native Cupertino physics.

Android: Follow Material motion guidelines for motion timing and hierarchy.

Web/Desktop: Emphasize clarity and speed; overuse of animation can feel sluggish.

Example:

Use "BouncingScrollPhysics" for iOS and "ClampingScrollPhysics" for Android for scroll behaviors.

⏱ 2. Use Standardized Durations

Consistency in animation timing is as important as visual consistency.

```
| Action                | Recommended Duration |
| --------------------- | -------------------- |
| Button press feedback | 100-150ms            |
| Page transitions      | 250-400ms            |
| Loading indicators    | Smooth, infinite loop|
```

Tip Avoid animations that take longer than 500ms unless they're part of an immersive experience (e.g., onboarding).

🔺 3. Match Animation Depth to Context

Not every UI action needs a complex animation. Let the importance of the UI element guide the animation complexity:

Small UI Feedback (e.g., Buttons): Quick scale or color change.

Page Transitions or Screen Overlays: Combine fade, slide, or scale with hierarchy awareness.

Modals or Popups: Subtle fade/scale is preferred across platforms.

💻 4. Avoid Overuse of Animations on Web and Desktop

Web and desktop users typically expect faster, more deterministic interactions. Excess animation can feel

Unnecessary (e.g., long fades)

Unresponsive (e.g., slow gesture feedback)

Distracting (e.g., overused bouncing or scaling effects)

Best Practice: Apply minimalist animation principles on desktop and web.

🎭 5. Maintain a Clear Motion Hierarchy

A motion hierarchy guides users through the interface with meaningful transitions. Ensure

Primary actions have distinctive motion (e.g., navigate, submit).

CHAPTER 9 ADVANCED ANIMATIONS AND TRANSITIONS

Secondary UI elements use subtle animations (e.g., tooltip fade-in).
Repeated actions don't compete visually with unique transitions.

♻ 6. Use Reversible Animations

For many interactions, the user should be able to reverse the animation seamlessly (e.g., closing a modal, collapsing a panel). This improves perceived responsiveness and usability.

```
// Simple reversible scale animation
controller.forward();
controller.reverse();
```

🧪 7. Perform User Testing Across Platforms

Animations may look great to the developer but feel slow or excessive to users.

A/B test durations and curves.

Use "flutter test," "flutter drive," or "integration_test" to verify animation triggers.

Collect user feedback to adjust motion strategy.

🛠 8. Leverage Themes for Animation Consistency

Create a centralized animation theme or use inherited configuration to define

Default animation curves

Timing durations

Global animation toggles (for accessibility)

Bonus: Enable users to reduce motion via system preferences or app settings.

```
final reducedMotion = MediaQuery.of(context).disableAnimations;
```

💬 Expert Insight Sidebar

Animations should never get in the user's way. They're a tool for guiding attention—not for showing off.

—Randal Schwartz, Flutter UX Consultant

✅ Best Practices Checklist

```
| Practice                               | Done? |
| -------------------------------------- | ----- |
| Used platform-appropriate motion styles| ☐     |
| Standardized animation durations       | ☐     |
| Avoided over-animation on web/desktop  | ☐     |
| Maintained motion hierarchy across app | ☐     |
| Supported reversible animations        | ☐     |
| User-tested animations on all platforms| ☐     |
```

Performance Optimization for Animations

As animation becomes a core part of crafting delightful user experiences in Flutter, ensuring high-performance rendering is not optional—it's essential. Laggy or janky animations break immersion, frustrate users, and impact perceived app quality.

Here, we focus on optimization strategies, technical best practices, and real-world case studies that will help you maintain smooth 60/120 FPS animations, even in complex UI scenarios

Techniques for Optimizing Animation Performance

In Flutter, delivering smooth animations goes beyond aesthetic value—it directly impacts how users perceive app quality. Optimized animation performance is crucial to maintaining fluid user interactions, especially on lower-end devices or in complex UI scenarios. This section outlines the most effective and proven techniques to optimize animation performance in Flutter applications.

🎯 1. Isolate Animations Using "RepaintBoundary"

Each time a widget animates, Flutter determines which parts of the screen need to be redrawn. If this region isn't properly isolated, surrounding widgets may be redrawn unnecessarily—causing lag.

Solution: Wrap the animated widget in a "RepaintBoundary."

```
RepaintBoundary(
  child: AnimatedContainer(
    duration: Duration(milliseconds: 300),
    curve: Curves.easeInOut,
    height: _height,
    width: _width,
    color: _color,
  ),
)
```

✅ **Tip** Use Flutter DevTools' "Repaint Rainbow" to visually detect repaint areas.

CHAPTER 9   ADVANCED ANIMATIONS AND TRANSITIONS

✏️ 2. Leverage Tween-Based Animations Over Layout Changes

Animations that change layout (e.g., calling "setState" on size or position) are expensive and can cause jank. Instead, animate visual properties like "opacity," "scale," or "rotation" using "Tween"-based systems.

```
AnimatedBuilder(
  animation: _controller,
  builder: (_, child) => Transform.scale(
    scale: _scaleAnimation.value,
    child: child,
  ),
  child: const Icon(Icons.star, size: 48),
)
```

🔖 3. Optimize AnimationController Lifecycle

Improper management of animation lifecycles can lead to memory leaks and dropped frames.

Always call "dispose()" on "AnimationController."

Prefer long-lived controllers if reused across screens or widgets.

```
@override
void dispose() {
  _controller.dispose();
  super.dispose();
}
```

🎨 4. Minimize Rebuilds with "AnimatedBuilder" or "ValueListenableBuilder"

Avoid using "setState()" inside animation callbacks, as this causes the entire widget subtree to rebuild.

Instead use "AnimatedBuilder" and assign heavy widgets to the "child" property to prevent unnecessary rebuilding.

```
AnimatedBuilder(
  animation: _animation,
  child: const Text('Animating...'),
  builder: (context, child) {
    return Opacity(
      opacity: _animation.value,
      child: child,
    );
  },
)
```

🐟 5. Avoid Overdraw and Complex Layering

Excessive use of semi-transparent widgets, shadows, and layers can significantly increase rendering time.

Avoid

Multiple overlapping "Opacity" widgets

Overuse of "BackdropFilter" and heavy blur effects

Tools:

Use "Performance Overlay" to monitor GPU raster times.

Use "Inspect Widget" in DevTools to analyze the layer tree.

🎁 6. Preload and Cache Animation Assets

If you're using Lottie animations or image sequences, always preload assets:

CHAPTER 9 ADVANCED ANIMATIONS AND TRANSITIONS

```
@override
void initState() {
  super.initState();
  precacheImage(AssetImage('assets/intro_frame_01.png'),
context);
}
```

This avoids runtime decoding or fetching delays during transitions.

📇 7. Profile with Flutter DevTools and Frame Schedulers

Use Flutter DevTools to

Profile frame rendering.

Analyze timeline events.

Detect dropped or skipped frames.

View the frame build/raster times.

You can also enable Performance Overlay using

```
MaterialApp(
  showPerformanceOverlay: true,
  ...
)
```

⚡ Performance Checklist

Optimization Technique	Applied?
Used 'RepaintBoundary' for isolating animation	☐
Avoided layout-based state changes in animation	☐
Managed 'AnimationController' lifecycle properly	☐
Used 'AnimatedBuilder' or 'ValueListenableBuilder'	☐
Avoided excessive use of 'Opacity' and 'BackdropFilter'	☐
Preloaded images/assets for animation	☐
Profiled animation in Flutter DevTools	☐

🔍 Expert Insight

The biggest performance killer in animations is excessive layout recalculation. Keeping the animated portion small and render-only is key to maintaining 60 or 120 FPS, especially on mid-tier Android devices.

—Rohan Das, Flutter Performance Engineer

Case Studies and Examples

To further illustrate the importance of animation performance optimization, we explore several real-world case studies. These examples showcase the challenges encountered in large-scale applications and the specific techniques applied to achieve smooth and efficient animations. By learning from these cases, you'll gain practical insights into performance optimization.

🎯 Case Study 1: Performance Issues with Animated List

Problem:

A mobile app with a dynamic list of items used "AnimatedContainer" for each item, but it experienced significant lag when new items were added. The frame rate dropped to as low as 30 FPS when the list contained more than 20 items.

Cause:

Every time an item was added, "setState()" triggered a complete rebuild of the widget tree, including non-animated items.

The "AnimatedContainer" was applied to each list item, leading to unnecessary repaints and layout recalculations.

Solution:

1. **Replaced "setState()" with "AnimatedList":**
   The "AnimatedList" widget provides a more optimized way to handle item insertions and removals, avoiding unnecessary rebuilds.

2. **Isolated Animations with "RepaintBoundary":**
   Each animated list item was wrapped in a "RepaintBoundary" to isolate the animation area and reduce the redraw region.

3. **Profiled and Removed Redundant Widgets:**
   Using Performance Overlay, we identified unnecessary widget rebuilds and removed any widgets that did not contribute to the animation.

Result:

Frame rate improved from 30 FPS to a consistent 60 FPS, even with larger datasets.

User experience was significantly improved with smoother list item animations.

CHAPTER 9   ADVANCED ANIMATIONS AND TRANSITIONS

🎯 Case Study 2: Janky Background Animation in a Web App

Problem:

A web-based app used a full-screen, animated gradient background. The animation was very slow on older browsers and lower-end devices. It resulted in frame drops and janky animations.

Cause:

The animation was implemented using a custom painter, which was very computationally expensive and relied on "CanvasKit" rendering, causing significant performance overhead.

Solution:

1. **Replaced Custom Painter with a Lottie Animation:**

   The custom background animation was replaced with a Lottie animation, a lightweight and hardware-accelerated format for animations. This drastically reduced the computational load.

2. **Preloaded Animation Assets:**

   The animation file was preloaded on app startup using "precacheImage," ensuring it was immediately available when the page loaded.

Result:

The background animation became smooth across all devices.

The app's rendering time was reduced by over 50%, improving performance on lower-end devices.

🎯 Case Study 3: Delayed Transitions with "AnimatedOpacity"

Problem:

In a photo gallery app, transition animations using "AnimatedOpacity" were sluggish, especially when transitioning between images. The animations appeared jittery, particularly on devices with lower processing power.

Cause:

Multiple semi-transparent widgets, including "Opacity" and "BackdropFilter," were stacked on top of each other.

The "AnimatedOpacity" was used to fade in and out of these stacked layers, triggering additional layout recalculations.

Solution:

1. **Replaced "AnimatedOpacity" with "Visibility" Widget:**

    The "Visibility" widget was used to hide and show elements without triggering layout recalculations. This provided a more lightweight way of managing visibility.

2. **Replaced "BackdropFilter" with Static Backgrounds:**

    The blur effect from "BackdropFilter" was removed, as it introduced significant overhead. Static blurred background images were pre-rendered and used instead.

3. **Switched to "AnimatedSwitcher" for Smooth Transitions:**

    "AnimatedSwitcher" provides more control over transitions, making it easier to animate opacity changes between widgets without causing jank.

Result:

The app's transition speed was improved by 30%, with smoother fades and no visible frame drops.

Performance on low-end devices improved, and the app was more responsive during photo transitions.

CHAPTER 9   ADVANCED ANIMATIONS AND TRANSITIONS

☌ Case Study 4: Optimizing Sprite Animations for a Game

Problem:

A game app that used sprite-based animation for character movements and background scrolling faced significant frame drops when multiple animations were running simultaneously.

Cause:

Each sprite was rendered on its own layer without using any form of caching, which resulted in inefficient use of resources. Additionally, the sprites were being redrawn every frame, leading to unnecessary rendering costs.

Solution:

1. **Implemented Sprite Caching:**

   All sprite images were cached and reused rather than reloading from disk on each frame. This minimized memory usage and improved loading times.

2. **Used "RepaintBoundary" for Animations:**

   Animated sprites were wrapped in "RepaintBoundary" to isolate the animation from the rest of the scene, reducing the impact of animation on non-animated elements.

3. **Optimized Animation Timings:**

   By reducing the frame rate of background scrolling and limiting the number of simultaneously active sprites, we reduced the computational cost of rendering.

Result:

Frame rates remained consistently above 60 FPS, even during intense game scenes.

The game experience became much smoother, and users reported significantly improved performance on both iOS and Android devices.

🔍 Performance Monitoring and Tools Used

In each case study, Flutter DevTools played an instrumental role in identifying performance bottlenecks:

Performance Overlay: Used to detect skipped frames and long frame build times

Timeline and Memory Profiling: Identified memory leaks and inefficient widget trees

Flutter Inspector: Helped analyze the widget tree for potential areas of excessive recomposition

By following performance optimization best practices and continuously profiling and testing your animations, you can ensure a smooth and engaging user experience, regardless of the complexity of your animations or the device's performance capabilities.

Summary

Here we focused on advanced techniques for creating high-performance animations and transitions in Flutter. It covers custom animation creation, optimization strategies, and the integration of popular animation libraries like Lottie and Rive. The chapter emphasizes performance considerations, offering techniques for ensuring smooth animations, such as isolating animation regions with RepaintBoundary and optimizing AnimationController lifecycles. It also explores cross-platform consistency in animations to maintain seamless user experiences across mobile and web applications. Case studies and real-world examples highlight practical applications of these techniques, showcasing how to solve common performance challenges. This chapter equips developers with the tools needed to create engaging, fluid animations in Flutter.

CHAPTER 10

Flutter for Machine Learning and AI

In the previous chapter, we delved deep into the visual dimension of modern Flutter applications—mastering advanced animation techniques, optimizing rendering performance, and achieving seamless cross-platform transitions. These capabilities are crucial for building engaging, delightful user experiences. However, animation alone is no longer the hallmark of next-generation applications. As the demands of users evolve, so must the intelligence of our apps.

This chapter takes us from "beautiful" to "brilliant"—from smooth transitions to smart interactions—by introducing the transformative power of Machine Learning (ML) and Artificial Intelligence (AI) in Flutter development.

With the growing adoption of edge computing and on-device AI, developers now have access to a wide array of tools like TensorFlow Lite (TFLite), enabling real-time predictions, image recognition, voice processing, and natural language understanding—all within the Flutter ecosystem. These technologies empower apps to not just respond to user input, but to anticipate, interpret, and personalize the experience.

CHAPTER 10   FLUTTER FOR MACHINE LEARNING AND AI

You will learn how to

- Integrate TensorFlow Lite for running ML models directly on devices.
- Build powerful image classification and real-time image processing apps.
- Add voice and Natural Language Processing (NLP) capabilities, including speech recognition, text-to-speech (TTS), sentiment analysis, and more.
- Apply performance tuning strategies specific to ML-heavy Flutter apps.
- Leverage real-world case studies and expert insights to make your AI integrations production-ready.

By the end of this chapter, you'll be equipped to build intelligent applications that push the boundaries of what's possible in mobile and web development with Flutter.

Integrating TensorFlow with Flutter

Machine learning models have traditionally required powerful servers and cloud-based infrastructure to process data and return results. However, with frameworks like TensorFlow Lite (TFLite), developers can now run ML models directly on edge devices—enabling low-latency inference, offline capabilities, and enhanced privacy. Flutter's plugin ecosystem and native integration capabilities make it possible to harness TensorFlow Lite for building intelligent mobile and embedded applications.

This section walks through the practical steps of integrating TensorFlow Lite into Flutter, from initial setup to leveraging pre-trained models and executing real-time inference on-device. Whether you're creating a custom ML pipeline or embedding an existing model, these techniques form the foundation for any Flutter-based AI experience.

Setting Up TensorFlow Lite in Flutter

TensorFlow Lite (TFLite) is a lightweight machine learning framework designed for mobile and embedded devices. Integrating TFLite into a Flutter application allows you to run ML models natively and efficiently, directly on the user's device—eliminating the need for cloud-based inference, thereby improving speed, privacy, and reliability.

This section provides a comprehensive, step-by-step guide to setting up TensorFlow Lite in your Flutter project and preparing your development environment for on-device ML inference.

🔧 Step-by-Step Integration Guide

1. **Add Dependencies to "pubspec.yaml"**

   To get started, add the essential TensorFlow Lite packages:

   ```
   dependencies:
     tflite_flutter: ^0.10.1
     tflite_flutter_helper: ^0.3.1
   ```

   "tflite_flutter": Core plugin for accessing TensorFlow Lite interpreters

   "tflite_flutter_helper": Provides helper classes for preprocessing and postprocessing (especially useful for image and audio inputs)

   Expert Insight: Using the helper package simplifies tensor handling and common tasks like image normalization, resizing, and label mapping.

2. **Prepare Your ".tflite" Model File**

   You can either

   Download pre-trained models from TensorFlow Lite Model Zoo (https://www.tensorflow.org/lite/models).

   Convert your custom trained TensorFlow model to ".tflite" using the TFLite Converter.

   Place the model file in your Flutter app's "assets" directory:

   ```
   /assets/models/
       └── my_model.tflite
   ```

   Then register it in "pubspec.yaml":

   ```
   flutter:
     assets:
       - assets/models/my_model.tflite
   ```

3. **Configure Platform-Specific Settings**

   Android:

   Set the minimum SDK version to "21" in "android/app/build.gradle":

   ```
   efaultConfig {
       minSdkVersion 21
   }
   ```

CHAPTER 10 FLUTTER FOR MACHINE LEARNING AND AI

Ensure you have proper permissions for camera/microphone if your model uses them.

iOS:

Set the deployment target to at least iOS 12.0 in "ios/Podfile":

```
platform :ios, '12.0'
```

Enable Metal support to enhance ML performance:

```
post_install do |installer|
  installer.pods_project.targets.each do |target|
    target.build_configurations.each do |config|
      config.build_settings['MTL_ENABLE'] = 'YES'
    end
  end
end
```

⚠ **Platform Tip** Always test on real devices—emulators/simulators often lack the hardware acceleration required for ML operations.

CHAPTER 10 FLUTTER FOR MACHINE LEARNING AND AI

4. **Initialize the Interpreter**

   Once setup is complete, you can load and use the model in your Dart code:

   ```
   import 'package:tflite_flutter/tflite_flutter.dart';

   final interpreter = await Interpreter.fromAsset('models/my_model.tflite');
   ```

   If you're using GPU acceleration or NNAPI, you can configure delegates:

   ```
   var interpreterOptions = InterpreterOptions()..useNnapiForAndroid = true;
   final interpreter = await Interpreter.fromAsset(
     'models/my_model.tflite',
     options: interpreterOptions,
   );
   ```

✅ Setup Checklist

Task	Status
Add 'tflite_flutter' and 'tflite_flutter_helper' dependencies	✓
Place '.tflite' model in assets	✓
Register model in 'pubspec.yaml'	✓
Configure 'minSdkVersion' and iOS deployment targets	✓
Initialize the interpreter in Dart code	✓
(Optional) Configure NNAPI or GPU delegate	✓

⚡ Performance Alert

For performance-sensitive applications

Prefer quantized models (int8 or float16) for reduced size and faster inference.

Use delegates like NNAPI (Android) or Metal (iOS) to leverage hardware acceleration.

Always benchmark inference time using real-world scenarios and representative inputs.

🔒 Security Alert

When using on-device ML

Ensure the model does not inadvertently expose sensitive logic.

If using user data, do not persist raw inputs unless necessary.

Consider model obfuscation techniques if intellectual property is a concern.

By completing this setup, your Flutter project is now equipped to run TensorFlow Lite models directly on the device—laying the groundwork for adding intelligent features such as vision, audio, or NLP-based interactions in the following sections.

Using Pre-trained Models for Mobile Applications

One of the key advantages of using TensorFlow Lite in Flutter is the ability to quickly integrate high-quality pre-trained models into your app. These models are trained on vast datasets and optimized for mobile performance, saving significant time and computational resources. Whether you're implementing image classification, object detection, language understanding, or audio recognition, there is likely a ready-to-use model available.

This section demonstrates how to discover, load, and use pre-trained TensorFlow Lite models in Flutter, enabling you to add intelligent features to your app with minimal ML expertise.

🎯 Why Use Pre-trained Models?

Speeds Up Development: No need to train models from scratch.

Proven Accuracy: Trained on large, diverse datasets by experts.

Optimized for Mobile: Many are quantized and tested for performance.

Wide Use Cases: Image recognition, face detection, audio classification, sentiment analysis, and more.

🧠 Popular Pre-trained TFLite Models

Model Name	Task	Input Size	Notes
MobileNetV2	Image Classification	224x224 RGB	Fast and lightweight
EfficientDet Lite	Object Detection	320x320 RGB	Multi-object detection
DeepLabV3	Semantic Segmentation	257x257 RGB	Label each pixel of the image
BERT Lite	Text Classification / NLP	Tokenized text	Requires text tokenization pipeline
YamNet	Sound Classification	Audio waveform	Classifies environmental sounds

These models can be found on TensorFlow Hub (`https://tfhub.dev`) or TensorFlow Lite Model Zoo (`https://www.tensorflow.org/lite/models`).

🎁 Adding a Pre-trained Model to Your Project

1. Download the ".tflite" file and optional "labels.txt" (if available).

2. Place both in the "assets/models/" directory of your Flutter project.

3. Register them in "pubspec.yaml":

```yaml
flutter:
  assets:
    - assets/models/mobilenet_v2.tflite
    - assets/models/labels.txt
```

🚀 Loading and Running a Model in Flutter

```dart
import 'package:tflite_flutter/tflite_flutter.dart';
import 'package:tflite_flutter_helper/tflite_flutter_helper.dart';

final interpreter = await Interpreter.fromAsset('models/mobilenet_v2.tflite');
```

Prepare the input (e.g., an image resized to 224 × 224 and normalized):

```dart
// Assuming TensorImage is already prepared using image preprocessing
var input = tensorImage.buffer;

// Prepare an output buffer
var output = TensorBuffer.createFixedSize(<int>[1, 1001], TfLiteType.float32);

interpreter.run(input, output.buffer);
```

CHAPTER 10 FLUTTER FOR MACHINE LEARNING AND AI

Expert Insight: Use the "ImageProcessor" and "TensorLabel" classes from "tflite_flutter_helper" to manage preprocessing and map output indices to human-readable labels.

🧪 **Example: Image Classification with MobileNetV2**

```
final imageProcessor = ImageProcessorBuilder()
    .add(ResizeOp(224, 224, ResizeMethod.BILINEAR))
    .add(NormalizeOp(127.5, 127.5))
    .build();
TensorImage inputImage = TensorImage.fromFile(imageFile);
inputImage = imageProcessor.process(inputImage);

var output = TensorBuffer.createFixedSize(<int>[1, 1001],
TfLiteType.float32);
interpreter.run(inputImage.buffer, output.buffer);

final labels = await FileUtil.loadLabels('assets/models/labels.txt');
final labelMap = TensorLabel.fromList(labels, output);
final sorted = labelMap.getMapWithFloatValue()
  ..removeWhere((key, value) => value < 0.1)
  ..entries.toList()
  ..sort((a, b) => b.value.compareTo(a.value));
```

Display top results to the user with confidence scores.

✅ **Checklist for Using Pre-trained Models**

- [ ] Model and labels added to the assets directory
- [ ] Assets registered in "pubspec.yaml"
- [ ] Input image/audio/text formatted correctly
- [ ] Output interpreted using correct labels
- [ ] Confidence threshold applied for result filtering

⚡ Performance Optimization Tips

Use quantized versions ("int8," "float16") for lower memory and faster inference.

Resize images to match model input size to reduce processing time.

Run inference on a background isolate to prevent UI jank.

🔒 Security Note

Even with pre-trained models, always sanitize input data, especially when processing user-generated content. Do not assume that models are immune to adversarial attacks or malformed inputs.

💡 Real-World Use Case

A healthcare startup used the MobileNetV2 pre-trained model within their Flutter app to detect early signs of skin anomalies from user-submitted photos. With TFLite running inference on-device, they ensured offline support and high responsiveness without compromising patient privacy.

By leveraging pre-trained models, Flutter developers can add powerful AI features quickly and effectively. In the next section, we'll explore how to run inference on-device to unlock even faster, privacy-first experiences.

On-Device Inference with TensorFlow Lite

On-device inference refers to the execution of machine learning models directly on the user's mobile or embedded device—without requiring internet connectivity or server-side processing. TensorFlow Lite is specifically designed for this purpose, making it ideal for real-time, low-latency, and privacy-conscious applications.

This section explores the end-to-end process of executing models on-device using TensorFlow Lite in Flutter, optimizing both performance and user experience.

🚀 Benefits of On-Device Inference

Low Latency: Eliminates network delays by running inference locally.

Offline Functionality: Works seamlessly without an internet connection.

Enhanced Privacy: User data never leaves the device.

Reduced Server Costs: No need for hosting ML models on a backend.

✪ Core Components of On-Device Inference

Component	Description
'.tflite' Model	Optimized TensorFlow Lite model file
Interpreter	Executes inference on the model
Input Tensor	Processed data passed to the model
Output Tensor	Model's response containing classification, detection, or prediction result

🖉 Step-by-Step Inference Example

Let's walk through a full on-device inference flow using an image classification model:

1. **Load the Model and Interpreter**

    ```
    final interpreter = await Interpreter.fromAsset('models/mobilenet_v2.tflite');
    ```

    You can also configure hardware acceleration:

    ```
    final options = InterpreterOptions()..useNnapiForAndroid = true;
    final interpreter = await Interpreter.fromAsset('models/mobilenet_v2.tflite', options: options);
    ```

Expert Insight: Use "XNNPACK" or "NNAPI" on Android and "Core ML" or "Metal" on iOS for faster execution.

2. **Prepare the Input Data**
   Use the "TensorImage" class from "tflite_flutter_helper":

   ```
   TensorImage inputImage = TensorImage.fromFile(imageFile);

   final imageProcessor = ImageProcessorBuilder()
     .add(ResizeOp(224, 224, ResizeMethod.BILINEAR))
     .add(NormalizeOp(127.5, 127.5)) // Normalization for MobileNet
     .build();

   inputImage = imageProcessor.process(inputImage);
   ```

3. **Prepare the Output Buffer**

   ```
   final output = TensorBuffer.createFixedSize(<int>[1, 1001], TfLiteType.float32);
   ```

4. **Run the Inference**

   ```
   interpreter.run(inputImage.buffer, output.buffer);
   ```

5. **Postprocess the Output**

   Map the output to labels using "TensorLabel":

   ```
   final labels = await FileUtil.loadLabels('assets/
   models/labels.txt');
   final labelMap = TensorLabel.fromList(labels, output);

   final result = labelMap.getMapWithFloatValue();
   final sortedResults = result.entries.toList()
     ..sort((a, b) => b.value.compareTo(a.value));

   final topResult = sortedResults.take(3);
   ```

⏱ Real-Time Considerations

For applications that perform inference in real time (e.g., camera feeds, speech detection), ensure

> You process frames or audio segments in intervals (e.g., every 500ms).
>
> Run inference in an isolate or background thread using "compute()" or "Isolate.spawn."
>
> Use a throttling mechanism to avoid frame drops or memory leaks.

⚡ Performance Optimization Tips

Technique	Description
Use quantized models	Models with 'int8' or 'float16' weights are smaller and faster.

Delegate selection	Use NNAPI, Core ML, or GPU
	delegates when available.
Batch processing	Preprocess multiple inputs in
	one go to reduce overhead.
Warm-up runs	Perform an initial inference
	to pre-load model weights into memory.

📛 Security Alert

Since models are bundled with the app, they can be reverse engineered. If your model contains proprietary logic

> Obfuscate or encrypt the model file.

> Validate the app integrity using tools like SafetyNet (Android) or DeviceCheck (iOS).

➤📱 Case Study: Offline Object Detection App

A wildlife conservation app uses EfficientDet Lite to detect animals in real time through the smartphone camera. By running inference on-device, the app provides instant feedback in remote areas without network access, helping researchers document wildlife more effectively.

✅ On-Device Inference Checklist

Task	Status
Load the '.tflite' model using 'Interpreter'	✅
Process input to match model shape and format	✅
Allocate and prepare output tensor	✅
Execute inference via 'run()'	✅
Map results to labels or predictions	✅
Optimize performance using delegates and quantization	✅

On-device inference with TensorFlow Lite in Flutter empowers your app with blazing-fast AI capabilities while respecting user privacy. With this infrastructure in place, you're now ready to build powerful, intelligent features like image recognition, NLP, and audio classification—all explored in the next sections.

Image Recognition with Flutter

Image recognition is one of the most popular use cases for machine learning in mobile applications. From classifying photos to detecting objects and enabling augmented reality (AR) experiences, Flutter combined with TensorFlow Lite provides a seamless framework for developing real-time, on-device vision-based apps.

Here, we'll explore how to build image classification apps, implement real-time camera-based recognition, and optimize ML models specifically for mobile devices using Flutter.

Building Image Classification Apps

Image classification is one of the most foundational and widely used applications of machine learning. In Flutter, combining TensorFlow Lite with an intuitive UI allows you to build powerful apps that can identify objects, animals, plants, food, or scenes from a user-provided image. This section guides you through designing, implementing, and deploying an image classification app using Flutter.

Understanding Image Classification

Image classification assigns one or more predefined labels to an image based on its visual content. For example, a photo of a golden retriever may be classified as "dog," "golden retriever," or "animal."

Popular pre-trained models used for image classification include

MobileNetV2: Lightweight, fast, and mobile-optimized

EfficientNet Lite: High accuracy with better parameter efficiency

ResNet Lite: Good for deeper classification needs

☼ System Architecture Overview

The key components of an image classification app:

Component	Responsibility
TensorFlow Lite Model	Accepts image input and produces class probabilities
Input Preprocessing	Resizes and normalizes the image
Output Postprocessing	Maps probabilities to labels
Flutter UI	Allows users to pick or capture images, view results

🔧 Step-by-Step Implementation

Let's break down the full workflow for building an image classification app.

1. **Add Required Dependencies**

   Add the following dependencies in your "pubspec.yaml":

   ```
   dependencies:
     tflite_flutter: ^0.10.0
     tflite_flutter_helper: ^0.3.1
     image_picker: ^1.0.4
     path_provider: ^2.1.2
   ```

CHAPTER 10   FLUTTER FOR MACHINE LEARNING AND AI

2. **Load the Model**

   ```
   final interpreter = await Interpreter.
   fromAsset('models/mobilenet_v2.tflite');
   ```

   💡 **Expert Insight**: For performance boost, use "InterpreterOptions" to enable GPU/NNAPI delegates if supported on the device.

3. **Pick an Image from Gallery or Camera**

   ```
   final picker = ImagePicker();
   final pickedFile = await picker.pickImage(source: ImageSource.gallery);
   ```

4. **Preprocess the Image**

   Using "tflite_flutter_helper":

   ```
   TensorImage inputImage = TensorImage.
   fromFile(File(pickedFile.path));

   final processor = ImageProcessorBuilder()
     .add(ResizeOp(224, 224, ResizeMethod.BILINEAR))
     .add(NormalizeOp(127.5, 127.5))  // For MobileNet
     input scaling
     .build();

   inputImage = processor.process(inputImage);
   ```

5. **Allocate Output Buffer**

   ```
   final output = TensorBuffer.createFixedSize(<int>[1,
   1001], TfLiteType.float32);
   ```

6. **Run the Inference**

   ```
   interpreter.run(inputImage.buffer, output.buffer);
   ```

7. **Postprocess the Output**

   Map output to labels and display the top prediction:

   ```
   final labels = await FileUtil.loadLabels('assets/
   models/labels.txt');
   final labelMap = TensorLabel.fromList(labels, output);

   final results = labelMap.getMapWithFloatValue();
   final sortedResults = results.entries.toList()
     ..sort((a, b) => b.value.compareTo(a.value));

   final topResults = sortedResults.take(3);
   // Top 3 predictions
   ```

🎨 UI Integration Example

```
ListView.builder(
  itemCount: topResults.length,
  itemBuilder: (context, index) {
    final entry = topResults.elementAt(index);
```

```
    return ListTile(
      title: Text(entry.key),
      trailing: Text('${(entry.value * 100).toString
      AsFixed(2)}%'),
    );
  },
);
```

📸 Security and Privacy Alert
Ensure the app does not upload or store user images without consent.
Run inference locally to keep image data on-device.
Obfuscate model files to protect intellectual property.

📱 Real-World Use Cases

App Type	Description
Plant identifier	Detect plant species from a leaf or flower photo
Food recognition	Calorie estimation by classifying dishes
Waste classifier	Label recyclables, compost, or landfill items
Fashion assistant	Identify clothing items and styles

✅ Checklist for Classification Apps

Task	Done
Load TensorFlow Lite model	✅
Integrate image picker	✅
Preprocess image to match model input shape	✅

Execute inference on device	✓
Map output tensor to class labels	✓
Display top results in the UI	✓

> **Performance Tip**
> Use quantized models for faster inference and smaller APK size.
> Execute inference in a background isolate to prevent UI jank.
> Warm up the model at startup for smoother user interaction.

Real-Time Image Processing

Real-time image processing takes static image classification a step further by enabling live inference on a stream of images—typically from the device's camera. This enables a wide range of dynamic applications such as augmented reality (AR), object detection while filming, real-time translation, and interactive educational tools.

Here, we'll learn how to integrate the camera stream with a TensorFlow Lite model in Flutter, process each frame efficiently, and overlay live predictions on the UI.

🎯 **Key Objectives**

- Capture live camera frames in Flutter.
- Preprocess each frame to match model input requirements.
- Perform on-device inference in real time.
- Display predictions without UI lag.

CHAPTER 10 FLUTTER FOR MACHINE LEARNING AND AI

🔄 Real-Time Processing Workflow

1. Initialize camera stream.
2. Throttle frame rate (optional).
3. Convert frame to TensorImage.
4. Run inference on isolate.
5. Overlay predictions on UI.

🎁 Dependencies

Ensure the following packages are added to "pubspec.yaml":

```yaml
dependencies:
  camera: ^0.10.5
  tflite_flutter: ^0.10.0
  tflite_flutter_helper: ^0.3.1
```

📷 Step 1: Set Up the Camera Controller

```dart
CameraController _cameraController;

void initializeCamera() async {
  final cameras = await availableCameras();
  _cameraController = CameraController(cameras[0], ResolutionPreset.medium);
  await _cameraController.initialize();
}
```

↻ Step 2: Start Image Stream

```
_cameraController.startImageStream((CameraImage image) {
  if (_shouldProcess) {
    _shouldProcess = false;
    processImage(image);
  }
});
```

> 💲 **Throttle Tip** Use "_shouldProcess" boolean or timers to prevent inference on every frame and maintain performance.

🔍 Step 3: Convert CameraImage to TensorImage

```
TensorImage _convertCameraImage(CameraImage image) {
  // Convert YUV to RGB (manually or using plugin utilities)
  // Resize and normalize to model's input shape, e.g., 224x224
}
```

💡 **Expert Insight**: Use "tflite_flutter_helper"'s "ImageProcessorBuilder" for resizing and normalization to match model expectations.

🧩 Step 4: Run Inference in a Background Isolate

To prevent UI blocking, run inference in a separate isolate:

CHAPTER 10 FLUTTER FOR MACHINE LEARNING AND AI

```
await compute(runInference, tensorImage);

void runInference(TensorImage image) {
  final output = TensorBuffer.createFixedSize([1, 1001],
  TfLiteType.float32);
  interpreter.run(image.buffer, output.buffer);
  return parseTopResults(output);
}
```

Performance Alert: Inference can be heavy—never run it on the main thread for real-time apps.

🎨 Step 5: Display Predictions on Live Preview

Use a "Stack" widget to overlay labels on top of the camera preview:

```
Stack(
  children: [
    CameraPreview(_cameraController),
    Positioned(
      bottom: 20,
      left: 20,
      child: Text(
        'Detected: Cat (98.7%)',
        style: TextStyle(fontSize: 18, color: Colors.white),
      ),
    ),
  ],
);
```

CHAPTER 10 FLUTTER FOR MACHINE LEARNING AND AI

🔬 Optimization Techniques

Strategy	Benefit
Quantized Model	Smaller size, faster inference
Frame Skipping	Lower compute demand
Lower Resolution	Faster processing with small tradeoff
GPU/NNAPI Delegates	Hardware acceleration where supported

🔐 Privacy Consideration

Real-time processing often involves capturing personal data via the camera. Ensure

> You request camera permissions with clear justification.

> No frames are uploaded or stored without user consent.

> On-device inference is maintained without cloud reliance.

💡 Use Cases

Use Case	Description
AR Shopping Assistant	Classify items user points at with camera
Real-Time Language Translation	Detect text in real time and translate overlay
Educational Wildlife Scanner	Identify animals instantly from a live view
Smart Home Control	Recognize hand gestures or objects for commands

✓ Real-Time Processing Checklist

Task	Done
Initialize camera and begin frame stream	✓
Convert frames to TensorImage and preprocess	✓
Throttle processing to improve app performance	✓
Run inference on isolate to avoid UI lag	✓
Overlay results smoothly in real time	✓

📈 Performance Benchmarks

Device	Model Type	FPS Achieved	CPU Usage	Accuracy Impact
Pixel 6	Quantized	\~10 FPS	Moderate	Minimal
Galaxy A52	Float32	\~4-5 FPS	High	None
iPhone 13	Core ML Delegate	\~12 FPS	Low	Minimal

By implementing real-time image recognition, you unlock dynamic and engaging user experiences that go beyond static image classification. In the next section, we'll look at optimizing the underlying ML models to run even faster and more efficiently on mobile devices.

Optimizing ML Models for Mobile Devices

Running machine learning models on mobile devices comes with strict constraints in terms of memory, CPU/GPU availability, battery life, and real-time responsiveness. Optimizing ML models for mobile ensures that your app delivers fast, reliable results without sacrificing user experience.

Here, we'll explore techniques to reduce model size, enhance inference speed, and improve energy efficiency while maintaining acceptable accuracy.

🎯 Why Optimization Matters

Challenge	Impact
Limited compute power	Slow inference
High memory usage	Crashes or out-of-memory errors
Battery drain	Negative UX and uninstalls
Large model size	Increased app size and slower downloads

Effective optimization helps mitigate all of these issues and makes your Flutter ML apps scalable and performant across a wide range of devices.

🔧 Techniques for Model Optimization

1. **Model Quantization**

   Quantization reduces the precision of the numbers used in the model (e.g., from float32 to int8), significantly shrinking the model size and increasing inference speed.

Type	Description	Trade-off
Post-training	Quantize a pre-trained float32 model	Slight accuracy loss
Quant-aware	Trains with quantization in mind	Higher accuracy retention
Dynamic range	Only weights are quantized	Lightest version

   Example Using TensorFlow:

   ```
   converter.optimizations = [tf.lite.Optimize.DEFAULT]
   tflite_model = converter.convert()
   ```

> **Performance Tip** Quantized models typically run 2–4× faster on mobile CPUs.

2. **Model Pruning**

   Pruning removes unimportant neurons and connections from the model, reducing computational overhead.

   Works well for CNNs used in image classification.

   Can be applied during training using TensorFlow Model Optimization Toolkit.

   Example:

   ```
   pruned_model = tfmot.sparsity.keras.prune_low_magnitude(model)
   ```

3. **Operator Fusion**

   Operator fusion merges adjacent operations (e.g., Conv2D + BatchNorm + ReLU) into a single kernel execution, reducing inference steps.

   Automatically handled by TFLite during conversion.

   No code change needed—just ensure supported ops are used.

4. **Model Architecture Optimization**

   Use lightweight, mobile-friendly architectures like

   ```
   | Model            | Characteristics                      |
   | ---------------- | ------------------------------------ |
   | MobileNet V2     | Efficient and low-latency            |
   | EfficientNet Lite| Higher accuracy with better FLOPs    |
   | SqueezeNet       | Very small with decent performance   |
   | Tiny YOLOv4      | Real-time object detection on mobile |
   ```

   💡 **Expert Insight**: Avoid deploying large models like ResNet-101 or BERT base on-device. Use distilled or mobile variants.

5. **Delegate Acceleration**

   TFLite supports hardware acceleration through delegates, enabling use of GPU, NNAPI, or Core ML (iOS).

   Enable the GPU delegate in Flutter:

   ```
   var interpreterOptions = InterpreterOptions()..addDelegate(GpuDelegateV2());
   var interpreter = await Interpreter.fromAsset('model.tflite', options: interpreterOptions);
   ```

   ```
   | Delegate | Platform     | Benefit                    |
   | -------- | ------------ | -------------------------- |
   | GPU      | Android, iOS | Faster matrix ops          |
   | NNAPI    | Android 8+   | Uses native mobile HW      |
   | Core ML  | iOS only     | Best acceleration on Apple |
   ```

📈 Measuring Performance Gains

Use "tflite_flutter"'s built-in benchmarking features or Flutter's performance tools to compare

- Inference latency (ms per prediction)
- Model load time
- CPU/GPU utilization
- Energy consumption

Code Snippet for Latency Check:

```
final stopwatch = Stopwatch()..start();
interpreter.run(inputBuffer, outputBuffer);
stopwatch.stop();
print('Inference time: ${stopwatch.elapsedMilliseconds} ms');
```

🔐 Security and Integrity Alerts

- Obfuscate model files to prevent reverse engineering.
- Validate model signatures if using dynamic model loading.
- Use on-device encryption to protect intellectual property.

📱 Real-World Optimization Results

Optimization Applied	Model Size ↓	Inference Time ↓	Accuracy Loss
Float32 → INT8 Quantization	14MB → 3.5MB	180ms → 60ms	\~1–2%
Pruning + Quantization	14MB → 2.9MB	180ms → 45ms	\~2–3%
EfficientNet Lite w/ GPU	Native 10MB	200ms → 25ms	<1%

✅ Optimization Checklist

Task	Done
Apply model quantization	✓
Consider model pruning during training	✓
Choose mobile-optimized architecture	✓
Enable hardware acceleration delegates	✓
Benchmark performance and accuracy	✓
Encrypt or obfuscate TFLite model file	✓

Optimizing your ML models is not just about performance—it's about user experience, battery life, app reliability, and scalability across devices. A well-optimized TFLite model ensures that your Flutter ML app runs efficiently on entry-level Android phones and flagship iPhones alike.

Voice and Natural Language Processing

Voice and natural language interfaces have become a key component of modern mobile apps—from voice assistants and chatbots to language translators and accessibility tools. Flutter's rich plugin ecosystem, when combined with machine learning and AI models, empowers developers to build seamless voice and language-driven experiences on both Android and iOS.

Here, we explore how to enable speech-to-text (STT) and text-to-speech in Flutter and how to integrate NLP (Natural Language Processing) models for tasks like sentiment analysis, text classification, and summarization.

Speech-to-Text and Text-to-Speech in Flutter

Voice interactions are increasingly integral to modern mobile experiences—powering everything from accessibility features and voice-controlled interfaces to interactive assistants and hands-free navigation. Flutter provides robust support for speech capabilities through mature plugins that allow for high-quality speech recognition (speech-to-text) and audio synthesis (text-to-speech).

Here, you'll learn how to integrate these capabilities in your Flutter apps, covering plugin setup, best practices, and performance optimization techniques.

🎤 Implementing Speech-to-Text (STT)

Speech-to-text converts spoken words into written text, enabling users to input commands or data without typing. This is vital for accessibility, voice-based navigation, and productivity applications.

🔧 Plugin Setup:

Add the "speech_to_text" package to your "pubspec.yaml":

```
speech_to_text: ^6.5.0
```

Import it in your Dart file:

```
import 'package:speech_to_text/speech_to_text.dart';
```

CHAPTER 10 FLUTTER FOR MACHINE LEARNING AND AI

🧠 **Initialization and Usage**:

```
final SpeechToText _speech = SpeechToText();
Future<void> initSpeechRecognition() async {
  bool available = await _speech.initialize();
  if (available) {
    _speech.listen(
      onResult: (result) => print('Recognized: ${result.
      recognizedWords}'),
    );
  }
}
```

🔐 **Permissions and Platform Notes**:

Android: Requires gmicrophone permission in "AndroidManifest.xml."

iOS: Add "NSMicrophoneUsageDescription" and "NSSpeechRecognitionUsageDescription" to "Info.plist."

```
<uses-permission android:name="android.permission.RECORD_
AUDIO"/>
```

🔒 **Security Alert**: Always notify users when audio input is being recorded or transcribed.

✏️ **Advanced Features**:

Partial Results: Get real-time transcription.

Pause/Resume Listening: Control when listening is active.

Locale Support: Recognize speech in multiple languages.

```
_speech.listen(
  localeId: "en_US",
  onResult: (result) => updateUI(result.recognizedWords),
);
```

🔊 Implementing Text-to-Speech (TTS)

Text-to-speech allows apps to vocalize messages, making your app accessible, interactive, and informative—especially useful in educational, accessibility, or smart assistant use cases.

🔧 **Plugin Setup**:

Add the "flutter_tts" package:

```
flutter_tts: ^4.0.2
```

Import in Dart:

```
import 'package:flutter_tts/flutter_tts.dart';
```

🎯 **Speaking Text**:

```
final FlutterTts flutterTts = FlutterTts();
Future<void> speakText(String text) async {
  await flutterTts.setLanguage("en-US");
  await flutterTts.setPitch(1.2);
  await flutterTts.setSpeechRate(0.5);
  await flutterTts.speak(text);
}
```

⚙ Customization Options:

Option	Description
'setLanguage'	Supports over 50 languages
'setPitch'	Adjusts voice pitch
'setSpeechRate'	Controls speaking speed
'setVolume'	Controls audio output volume

📱 Platform Considerations:

Android: Uses built-in TTS engine; may require language download
iOS: Leverages Apple's AVSpeechSynthesizer

🎯 **Tip** Test TTS with headphones for speech clarity and speed tuning.

🤖 Combining STT and TTS for Conversational Interfaces

You can create interactive voice-driven applications by combining both plugins. For example:

1. Use STT to capture a user's query.
2. Process the query with AI/ML or rule-based logic.
3. Use TTS to respond with a spoken answer.

This is ideal for

- Virtual assistants
- Voice-controlled interfaces
- Language-learning tools

✅ **Speech Integration Checklist**

Task	Done
Add 'speech_to_text' and 'flutter_tts'	✅
Request microphone permission	✅
Initialize and handle speech callbacks	✅
Tune language, pitch, and rate settings	✅
Provide fallback UI for speech failures	✅

Expert Insight

> **Latency Handling**: Use debounce logic or delay triggers to avoid misfires.
>
> **Noise Tolerance**: Use external noise filters or preprocessing when accuracy is critical.
>
> **User Feedback**: Show waveform or transcript previews to give feedback during voice input.

Flutter's speech capabilities allow you to break traditional UI boundaries and craft inclusive, intuitive user experiences. With minimal setup, you can add voice input and output, unlocking powerful accessibility and interactivity features.

Using NLP Models in Flutter Apps

Natural Language Processing (NLP) enables apps to understand, analyze, and generate human language, opening the door to features like chatbots, content summarization, intelligent feedback systems, and real-time language analysis. In Flutter, NLP models—especially those optimized for mobile using TensorFlow Lite—can be integrated for real-time and offline processing without depending on cloud APIs.

Sentiment Analysis

Sentiment analysis is a foundational NLP task used to determine the emotional tone behind a body of text. By categorizing user-generated content—such as reviews, feedback, or comments—into positive, negative, or neutral sentiments, applications can derive actionable insights that drive user engagement, automated moderation, and intelligent decision-making.

In Flutter, integrating sentiment analysis is achievable through TensorFlow Lite and pre-trained deep learning models that can run directly on the device. This approach provides real-time analysis with low latency and enhanced privacy.

🎯 Use Cases for Sentiment Analysis

```
| Scenario                | Application                        |
| ----------------------- | ---------------------------------- |
| Customer Reviews        | Product satisfaction measurement   |
| Social Media Monitoring | Brand sentiment tracking           |
| Chatbots and Assistants | Emotion-aware responses            |
| Feedback Forms          | Real-time response prioritization  |
```

Selecting a Sentiment Analysis Model

Choose a TensorFlow Lite model trained on sentiment-labeled datasets such as

    IMDB Movie Reviews

    Amazon Product Reviews

    Twitter Data

CHAPTER 10 FLUTTER FOR MACHINE LEARNING AND AI

Here are common model architectures:

LSTM: Lightweight and effective for sequence modeling

GRU: Faster alternative to LSTM

MobileBERT: Transformer-based, higher accuracy

DistilBERT: Optimized for edge devices

⚠ **Performance Tip** Use quantized or pruned models to reduce size and increase performance on mobile devices.

Preparing Flutter with TensorFlow Lite

Add required dependencies:

```
dependencies:
  tflite_flutter: ^0.10.0
  tflite_flutter_helper: ^0.4.0
```

Initialize the interpreter:

```
final interpreter = await Interpreter.fromAsset('sentiment_model.tflite');
```

Text Preprocessing

Text must be tokenized and padded to match the model's input shape.

```
List<String> tokens = tokenizer.tokenize("This app is
amazing!");
List<int> inputIds = vocab.map((e) => vocab[e] ?? unkId).
toList();
List<List<int>> input = padSequence(inputIds, maxLen: 128);
```

> **Note** Always use the tokenizer and vocabulary file the model was trained with.

Running Inference

```
var output = List.filled(3, 0).reshape([1, 3]); // [Negative,
Neutral, Positive]
interpreter.run(input, output);
print("Sentiment scores: $output");
```

Example Output:

```
[0.05, 0.10, 0.85] → Positive sentiment
```

📊 Postprocessing

Convert the model output into a human-readable label:

```
List<String> labels = ['Negative', 'Neutral', 'Positive'];
int index = output[0].indexWhere((e) => e == output[0].
reduce(max));
String sentiment = labels[index];
```

🧪 UI Integration

Display live sentiment analysis results as users type, submit reviews, or chat:

```
Text(
  "Detected Sentiment: $sentiment",
  style: TextStyle(color: getSentimentColor(sentiment)),
);
```

Expert Insight

⭐ **Context Matters**: Basic models might misinterpret sarcasm or idioms. Fine-tune the model or use hybrid (rule-based + ML) systems for higher accuracy in sensitive applications.

🔒 **Privacy Alert**: Since models run locally, user data never leaves the device—ideal for GDPR-compliant applications.

✅ Sentiment Analysis Checklist

Task	Done
Choose and integrate a TFLite model	✓
Use correct tokenizer and preprocessing steps	✓
Pad sequences to match input shape	✓
Interpret output tensor and map to labels	✓
Add user-facing results and real-time feedback	✓

🧩 Real-World Applications

Ecommerce: Auto-flagging negative reviews for follow-up

Education: Detecting frustrated learners in real-time chat

Healthcare: Monitoring emotional well-being through diary entries

Sentiment analysis adds emotional intelligence to your Flutter apps. With lightweight, accurate TensorFlow Lite models and Flutter's flexible UI, you can integrate on-device sentiment detection that enhances user experiences, automates feedback loops, and respects user privacy.

Text Classification and Summarization

Text classification and summarization are two advanced NLP tasks that bring intelligence to user-facing features such as automated content organization, smart search, prioritization systems, and dynamic summarization of documents or messages. In Flutter, these capabilities can be embedded using TensorFlow Lite models that are optimized for on-device inference, offering seamless, real-time, and privacy-focused NLP workflows.

📧 Text Classification

🎯 Objective:

Text classification assigns predefined labels or categories to a given input text. Whether it's categorizing emails into spam or not, tagging support tickets, or filtering user feedback by topic, classification allows your Flutter app to understand textual intent.

🔧 Typical Use Cases:

Scenario	Predicted Category
"App crashes when I open settings."	Bug Report
"Can you add dark mode?"	Feature Request
"Thanks for the great support!"	Positive Feedback

🔍 Model Types:

Lightweight LSTM/CNN: Faster, ideal for constrained devices

MobileBERT/DistilBERT: High accuracy for nuanced classification

Hierarchical Models: Handle multi-label or layered classification

---

⚠️ **Note** Choose a model that aligns with your app's latency, size, and accuracy needs.

🧪 Example Workflow:

1. **Text Preprocessing**

   ```
   final inputText = "I can't update my profile picture.";
   final tokens = tokenizer.tokenize(inputText);
   final inputIds = tokens.map((t) => vocab[t] ?? 
   unkTokenId).toList();
   final paddedInput = padToMaxLength(inputIds, 128);
   ```

2. **Run Inference**

   ```
   final output = List.filled(numClasses, 0.0).reshape
   ([1, numClasses]);
   interpreter.run(paddedInput, output);
   ```

3. **Get Prediction**

   ```
   final predictedIndex = output[0].indexOf(output[0].
   reduce(max));
   final label = labelMap[predictedIndex];
   ```

4. **Display Result in UI**

   ```
   Text("Category: $label", style: TextStyle(fontWeight: 
   FontWeight.bold));
   ```

♡ Security Alert:
Always sanitize inputs before running inference to prevent edge-case crashes caused by malformed or unexpected characters.

📝 Text Summarization

⚽ Objective:
Text summarization compresses lengthy text into shorter, coherent summaries without losing core meaning. This is highly valuable for content-heavy apps like news aggregators, educational platforms, documentation viewers, and AI writing assistants.

🧠 Model Types:

Model Type	Description
Extractive	Selects key sentences (rule-based, simpler)
Abstractive	Generates new text (seq2seq or transformer-based like T5, BART, etc.)

⚖️ **Trade-Off**: Extractive models are fast and light, while abstractive models provide better readability but are heavier.

🔧 Typical Workflow (Abstractive):

1. Tokenize and encode input.
2. Run encoder–decoder inference with TFLite.
3. Convert output tokens to summary string.

🧪 Example Summary:

Input:
"Flutter is an open-source UI software development toolkit created by Google. It is used to develop cross-platform applications from a single codebase."

Summary Output:
"Flutter enables cross-platform app development."

☼ Integration in Flutter:
Use "tflite_flutter" to load summarization models:

```
inal interpreter = await Interpreter.fromAsset('summarizer_
model.tflite');
final input = encodeText(text);
final output = List.filled(maxOutputLength, 0).reshape([1,
maxOutputLength]);
interpreter.run(input, output);
final summary = decodeTokens(output[0]);
```

📱 Mobile Optimization Tips:

Use distilled versions (e.g., DistilT5 or TinyBERT).

Quantize models for speed and memory savings.

Use batching if summarizing multiple documents.

🔍 Use Cases:

News Reader App: Show article summaries.

E-learning Platform: Summarize notes or lectures.

Productivity App: Summarize user-generated documents.

✓ Classification and Summarization Checklist

Task	Done
Load optimized TFLite models	✓
Use proper tokenizer and vocabulary	✓
Encode inputs with correct max lengths	✓
Run inference and postprocess output	✓
Handle edge cases and large inputs gracefully	✓

Expert Insight

💡 **Custom Training:** You can train your own classifier or summarizer using TensorFlow and convert it to TFLite using quantization-aware training. This enables domain-specific accuracy improvements.

🔄 **Hybrid Workflow:** For complex summarization, offload to cloud inference when on-device resources are limited—but always provide a fallback.

Text classification and summarization allow Flutter apps to intelligently interpret and distill information at scale. Whether categorizing issues, filtering messages, or condensing documents, these features elevate user experience and app intelligence. With Flutter and TensorFlow Lite, you can run these NLP tasks efficiently on-device—offline, fast, and securely.

Case Studies of ML and AI in Flutter Apps

As we conclude our deep dive into integrating Machine Learning and AI with Flutter, it's vital to connect theory with real-world application. In this final section, we explore how companies and developers are using Flutter and TensorFlow Lite to ship intelligent, responsive, and scalable AI-powered apps. We also analyze the challenges encountered and the industry best practices that have emerged from these experiences.

Real-World Case Studies and Applications

To truly understand the impact of integrating Machine Learning (ML) and Artificial Intelligence (AI) in Flutter applications, it's essential to examine real-world implementations. This section presents several case studies that showcase how businesses across industries have successfully embedded TensorFlow Lite (TFLite) models in their Flutter apps to enhance functionality, improve user experience, and achieve business goals.

📖 Case Study 1: Ecommerce—Smart Product Categorization and Recommendations

Company: A rapidly growing Indian B2C marketplace

Use Case: Automating product listing classification and powering personalized recommendations

ML Integration:

A lightweight TFLite text classification model is used to auto-tag product listings by parsing product titles and descriptions.

A collaborative filtering model delivers personalized product suggestions on-device, without needing cloud API calls.

Flutter Role:

Flutter's fast UI rendering ensures the category prediction result appears immediately after product entry.

Integration of TFLite with Dart isolates guarantees responsive, non-blocking user experience.

Impact:

Reduced manual classification by 70%.

Increased click-through rate by 18% through accurate, localized recommendations.

💡 **Expert Insight**: Preloading vocabulary and label files with the App Bundle significantly reduced cold-start latency on low-end devices.

⚕ Case Study 2: Healthcare—On-Device Symptom Checker with NLP

Company: A telemedicine provider in Southeast Asia

Use Case: An AI chatbot that helps users understand their symptoms through natural conversation

ML Integration:

A quantized BERT-based model handles intent recognition and entity extraction.

Follow-up symptom classification model recommends relevant actions (e.g., "Book a doctor," "Take a test").

CHAPTER 10   FLUTTER FOR MACHINE LEARNING AND AI

Flutter Role:

Flutter was used to build the chatbot UI with animation-rich transitions.

"tflite_flutter" executes the NLP model in real time, keeping medical data secure and offline.

Results:

Average time to diagnose suggestions dropped from 3.2 minutes to 1.1 minutes.

Ninety-four percent of user inputs correctly understood using on-device NLP.

◯ **Security Alert:** Keeping inference on-device ensured compliance with regional healthcare data privacy laws like HIPAA and PDPB.

🎓 Case Study 3: EdTech—Instant Quiz Feedback and Note Summarization

Company: A global online learning platform

Use Case: Giving students immediate feedback on long-form answers and summarizing study notes dynamically

ML Integration:

A distilled TinyT5 model for abstractive summarization.

A sentiment classifier tracks learner mood during sessions to adjust difficulty.

Flutter Role:

Flutter web and mobile clients used a shared summarization API wrapper built with "tflite_flutter."

Real-time feedback generated in <300ms, even on mid-range Android phones.

Outcomes:

Forty percent increase in daily active users.

Boost in course completion rates and learning satisfaction metrics.

📷 Case Study 4: Image Recognition—AI-Powered Camera App

Company: A startup specializing in visual search

Use Case: Letting users identify plants, pets, or objects in real time using their smartphone camera

ML Integration:

A MobileNetV2 model detects and classifies objects within the camera stream.

The app highlights the identified object and displays contextual data (e.g., species, common uses).

Flutter Role:

Used "camera," "tflite_flutter," and custom platform channels for optimized performance.

UI updates per frame with confidence score overlays.

Performance Highlights:

Sub-90ms per frame inference time on recent Android/iOS devices.

Ninety-one percent classification accuracy with a <10MB model.

🚀 Performance Tip Using the GPU delegate on Android significantly improved frame rate and reduced CPU load.

↩ Case Study Wrap-Up

These real-world implementations demonstrate that AI in Flutter isn't theoretical—it's powering critical apps today. With TFLite and Flutter working in tandem, developers are delivering intelligent features at scale while maintaining user privacy, reducing latency, and enhancing user engagement.

▣ Pro Tip Start by integrating a pre-trained model into a non-blocking UI workflow. Once stable, consider custom training and optimizing models tailored to your app's data and users.

Challenges and Best Practices

While integrating Machine Learning (ML) and Artificial Intelligence (AI) into Flutter apps opens the door to powerful, intelligent experiences, it also introduces a unique set of technical and architectural challenges. This section identifies the most common pitfalls developers face when building ML-powered Flutter apps and outlines best practices to ensure smooth deployment, high performance, and maintainable codebases.

⚠ Common Challenges in Flutter + ML Integration

Challenge	Description
Model Size and Footprint	Many models (e.g., BERT, T5) are too large for mobile use and may exceed app size limits.
Inference Latency	Real-time tasks like image recognition or speech transcription demand low-latency performance.
Preprocessing Bottlenecks	Tokenization, normalization, and resizing must be consistent and performant across platforms.
Cross-Platform Inconsistencies	TensorFlow Lite behavior can differ between Android and iOS, especially with delegates and NN APIs.

Model Updates and Versioning	Keeping models and tokenizer files in sync across builds and environments is difficult.
Privacy and Security	Offloading data to the cloud raises privacy concerns, especially for medical or personal data.
Battery and Resource Constraints	ML inference can drain battery and overload memory on low-end devices if not optimized.

Security Alert: Always verify where your model processes user data. Ensure all inference occurs on-device when privacy is critical.

Best Practices for Successful ML in Flutter

✓ **1. Choose Lightweight, Mobile-Optimized Models**

Use MobileNet, DistilBERT, or TinyML models.

Prefer models that are quantized (8-bit) or pruned to reduce size and runtime.

Avoid including full-sized transformer models unless using custom optimization pipelines.

✓ **2. Leverage TensorFlow Lite Converter Efficiently**

Use "--post_training_quantize" to reduce model size.

Benchmark with TensorFlow Lite Benchmark Tool on target hardware before production release.

Validate that quantization doesn't impact accuracy unacceptably for your use case.

✓ **3. Manage Tokenization and Preprocessing Thoughtfully**

Use consistent preprocessing logic in Dart or via platform channels.

Bundle all vocab/tokenizer assets with the app to prevent inconsistencies at runtime.

Create utility layers or shared services for input handling to maintain DRY code.

✓ **4. Optimize Inference for Performance**

Run ML inference in background isolates or compute threads.

Use delegates like NNAPI (Android) or Metal/GPU (iOS) for hardware acceleration.

Avoid synchronous model execution on the main thread—especially in real-time UIs.

✓ **5. Ensure Robust Cross-Platform Testing**

Test your ML features on real Android and iOS devices with varying specs.

Watch for platform-specific bugs in TensorFlow Lite implementations.

Use Flutter integration tests to validate end-to-end inference behavior.

✓ **6. Plan for Model Updates and Versioning**

Use semantic versioning (e.g., "1.0.0," "1.1.0") for every model release.

Keep changelogs and validate backward compatibility with older app builds.

Separate model logic into modular architecture layers so updates don't affect UI/UX.

✓ **7. Balance Privacy with Cloud Fallback**

Perform inference locally for fast, secure results.

Offer optional cloud fallback when high-accuracy or large models are required.

Always inform users when data is being sent to a server.

🛠 **Developer Checklist**

Task	Done
Use quantized/mobile-friendly models	✓
Handle preprocessing with consistent logic	✓
Move inference off the main UI thread	✓
Test ML functionality across Android/iOS platforms	✓

Bundle tokenizers and vocab files securely	✓
Track model versions separately from app logic	✓
Implement cloud fallback securely and transparently	✓

📈 Real-World Optimization Tips

🔄 **Batch Inputs**: Where feasible, process multiple inputs together to amortize compute costs.

💾 **Use Memory-Mapped Models**: TensorFlow Lite supports loading models via memory mapping to reduce startup latency.

🔒 **Minimize Permissions**: Only request mic/camera access when needed for real-time ML use cases.

🔋 **Monitor Battery Usage**: Use tools like Android Profiler or Xcode Instruments to ensure efficient model execution.

Integrating AI into Flutter apps isn't just about technical feasibility—it's about delivering smarter user experiences without compromising performance, privacy, or maintainability. By following these best practices, developers can confidently bring ML-powered features into production and stay ahead in a competitive, intelligence-driven mobile landscape.

📋 **Pro Tip** Build a dedicated ML service layer in your Flutter architecture to handle all preprocessing, inference, and model switching—this keeps your UI logic clean and scalable.

Summary

This chapter explored how Flutter can seamlessly integrate with machine learning technologies to power intelligent, real-time mobile and web applications. From setting up TensorFlow Lite in Flutter projects to leveraging pre-trained models for tasks like image classification, real-time vision processing, and natural language understanding, developers

CHAPTER 10 FLUTTER FOR MACHINE LEARNING AND AI

learned how to build robust, on-device AI experiences. The chapter also covered essential optimization techniques, platform-specific considerations, and security practices critical to deploying ML at scale. Real-world case studies illustrated practical applications across industries, while a comprehensive breakdown of challenges and best practices equips developers to architect reliable, privacy-conscious, and high-performance AI features in Flutter apps.

CHAPTER 11

Security and App Hardening

In the previous chapter, we explored the integration of powerful AI capabilities into Flutter apps. From setting up TensorFlow Lite and leveraging pre-trained models to building real-time image recognition systems and Natural Language Processing workflows, you gained insight into developing intelligent, responsive, and futuristic applications. These advanced ML features significantly elevate user experiences—but they also introduce new vectors for risk and exploitation.

As your app becomes more intelligent, it also becomes more valuable—and consequently, a more attractive target for attackers.

Here, we shift our focus from innovation to protection. This chapter is your essential guide to fortifying your Flutter applications against a wide range of security threats. Whether you're transmitting sensitive user data, implementing user authentication, or distributing a commercial-grade mobile app, security must be a core component of your development process—not an afterthought.

We'll begin by examining the most common security vulnerabilities faced by Flutter apps and how to mitigate them. You'll then learn about implementing secure authentication techniques including OAuth, JWT, two-factor authentication (2FA), and biometric authentication. We'll also dive into app hardening strategies such as code obfuscation, reverse engineering defense, and encryption best practices.

CHAPTER 11   SECURITY AND APP HARDENING

To bring theory into practice, this chapter concludes with real-world case studies highlighting how popular apps suffered from security lapses—and how those issues were eventually resolved.

By the end of this chapter, you'll be equipped with a robust security foundation to build Flutter applications that are not only fast and intelligent, but also secure, resilient, and production-ready.

Security Vulnerabilities in Mobile Apps

As mobile apps continue to handle increasingly sensitive data—from personal identifiers and biometric information to financial transactions—the surface area for attacks grows exponentially. Flutter, despite its robust architecture, is not immune to common mobile security threats. Understanding these vulnerabilities is the first step in building apps that are secure by design.

Common Security Threats in Flutter Apps

Flutter, with its modern architecture and compiled Dart code, offers a level of abstraction that can give a false sense of security. However, despite its cross-platform nature and strong community backing, Flutter applications are still susceptible to a broad range of security vulnerabilities—many of which are platform-agnostic and stem from common development missteps.

This section highlights the most common security threats that developers must proactively address to prevent data breaches, code tampering, and unauthorized access.

🔒 **1. Insecure Data Storage**
Problem:
Developers often store sensitive user data—like tokens, credentials, or payment details—in unencrypted formats such as "SharedPreferences," local files, or plain SQLite databases.

CHAPTER 11 SECURITY AND APP HARDENING

Impact:

Rooted or jailbroken devices can easily access these locations, exposing sensitive information.

Solution:

Use packages like "flutter_secure_storage" (`https://pub.dev/packages/flutter_secure_storage`) to store sensitive data securely using the Android Keystore and iOS Keychain.

Encrypt local databases with packages such as "sqflite_sqlcipher."

Security Alert: Never store JWTs or OAuth tokens in "SharedPreferences" or plain files.

🧬 2. Hardcoded API Keys and Secrets

Problem:

API keys, tokens, and secrets are sometimes hardcoded directly into Dart files, making them accessible via reverse engineering.

Impact:

An attacker can decompile the app (even a release APK) and extract the keys to misuse your backend or third-party services.

Solution:

Store keys on a secure backend and fetch them dynamically at runtime.

Use environment variables or platform channels to inject secrets at build time, not hardcode them.

Pro Tip   Always separate runtime secrets from the build logic.

🎣 3. Weak Network Security and Unencrypted Traffic

Problem:

Using HTTP instead of HTTPS or accepting all certificates can expose your app to man-in-the-middle (MITM) attacks.

Impact:

Sensitive data like login credentials or personal user data can be intercepted during transmission.

Solution:
Use HTTPS with TLS 1.2 or higher.
Enable SSL pinning for sensitive endpoints.
Avoid self-signed certificates in production.
Security Alert: Using the "http" package without proper certificate validation can allow silent MITM attacks in public networks.

🔑 4. Improper Authentication and Authorization
Problem:
Relying on client-side checks or assuming identity tokens are valid without server verification.

Impact:
Attackers can forge requests or access unauthorized data/functions.

Solution:
Always validate tokens server-side.
Implement role-based access control (RBAC) on the backend.
Use OAuth 2.0 and JWTs correctly with proper expiry and refresh cycles.

Best Practice: Never trust client-side validation alone—always validate on the server. This follows the **Zero Trust** principle: always verify identity and permissions for every request, regardless of the client's origin.

🧱 5. Lack of Code Obfuscation and App Hardening
Problem:
Flutter apps compiled without obfuscation contain readable symbol names, making reverse engineering easy.

Impact:
Attackers can decompile the app, analyze logic, bypass checks, or inject malicious behavior.

Solution:
Use "flutter build apk --obfuscate --split-debug-info=path/" to obfuscate and strip symbols.
Avoid including logs, comments, or test code in production builds.

Expert Insight: "Obfuscation doesn't make your app unbreakable—but it significantly raises the effort required to reverse engineer it" (Nikita S., Mobile Security Engineer).

🔍 6. Vulnerable or Outdated Dependencies

Problem:

Using outdated packages with known security vulnerabilities (CVEs) or excessive permissions.

Impact:

Can expose the app to exploits or cause privilege escalation via third-party code.

Solution:

Audit dependencies regularly with tools like "pub outdated" and "pubspec.lock."

Avoid using unnecessary permissions (e.g., camera, location, storage) if not needed.

✅ **Security Tip** Always read plugin source code and reviews before adding them to your project—especially lesser-known ones.

✅ **Quick Recap: Common Threats**

Threat	Risk	Fix
Insecure Data Storage	Credential leaks	Use secure storage + encryption
Hardcoded Keys	Key theft	Store dynamically or obfuscate
Unencrypted Network Traffic	MITM attacks	Enforce HTTPS + SSL pinning
Weak Authentication	Privilege escalation	Validate all tokens server-side
No Obfuscation	Reverse engineering	Use Dart obfuscation flags
Vulnerable Packages	CVEs and exploits	Regular audits and upgrades

By understanding these threats, you're now better prepared to move forward into implementing proactive defenses.

CHAPTER 11   SECURITY AND APP HARDENING

How to Secure Data in Transit and at Rest

As mobile applications increasingly handle sensitive user data—ranging from login credentials to health and financial records—it becomes imperative to secure that data both during transmission (in transit) and when stored on the device (at rest). Insecure data practices are among the leading causes of real-world security breaches in mobile apps.

In Flutter, this responsibility lies not only in writing clean, performant code—but also in employing platform-specific security measures and using the right packages and configurations to safeguard data. This section will cover essential practices and tools to help you ensure your app's data is protected at all stages of its lifecycle.

Securing Data in Transit

Data in transit refers to information moving between the client (Flutter app) and a remote server or third-party API. Intercepted traffic can be manipulated or stolen, especially on unsecured networks.

🔒 **Best Practices:**

1. **Enforce HTTPS with TLS 1.2+**

    Always use HTTPS for API calls.

    Validate certificates properly to avoid accepting spoofed certificates.

    Avoid mixed content (loading HTTP content from HTTPS apps).

2. **Implement SSL Pinning**

    Prevent man-in-the-middle (MITM) attacks by ensuring your app communicates only with trusted servers.

Use the "http_certificate_pinning" (https://pub.dev/packages/http_certificate_pinning) package or platform channels to implement certificate pinning.

3. **Avoid Using Self-Signed Certificates in Production**

    These are vulnerable and can be easily spoofed.

4. **Use Secure HTTP Clients**

    Prefer "dio" or enhanced versions of "http" with certificate validation and timeout mechanisms.

♡ **Expert Insight**:

TLS without pinning is like a lock without a key. Certificate pinning ensures you're not just using HTTPS—you're using the right HTTPS.

—Meera S., Security Analyst

✅ **Code Example—Enforcing HTTPS with DIO and SSL Pinning**:

```
final dio = Dio();

(dio.httpClientAdapter as DefaultHttpClientAdapter).
onHttpClientCreate =
    (client) {
  client.badCertificateCallback =
      (X509Certificate cert, String host, int port) {
    // Validate the certificate fingerprint (SSL pinning)
    return cert.sha256 == 'YOUR_PINNED_CERTIFICATE_SHA256';
  };
  return client;
};
```

Securing Data at Rest

Data at rest includes anything stored on the device—such as tokens, settings, files, and databases. Improper storage practices can expose user data if the device is compromised or rooted.

🔒 **Best Practices:**

1. **Use Secure Storage APIs**

   Store sensitive data using "flutter_secure_storage" (https://pub.dev/packages/flutter_secure_storage), which uses the platform's Keystore (Android) and Keychain (iOS).

2. **Encrypt Local Databases**

   Use "sqflite_sqlcipher" or similar to encrypt SQLite databases storing user data or session information.

3. **Avoid Plaintext and SharedPreferences**

   Do not use "SharedPreferences" or "getStorage" for anything sensitive like tokens, passwords, or session identifiers.

4. **Secure File Storage**
   For files (e.g., images, PDFs), store them in protected app directories and encrypt them with a secure algorithm such as AES before writing.

CHAPTER 11   SECURITY AND APP HARDENING

✅ **Code Example—Storing Tokens Securely:**

```
final storage = FlutterSecureStorage();

// Store token securely
await storage.write(key: 'auth_token', value: 'abc123');

// Retrieve token
String? token = await storage.read(key: 'auth_token');
```

⚠ **Security Alerts**

Avoid printing sensitive data in logs during debugging.

Strip logs and enable minification/obfuscation in release builds.

Never rely solely on local security—always combine client-side security with server-side validation.

🖊 **Performance and Security Trade-Off Note**

While encryption adds a minimal performance overhead, the security it provides far outweighs the cost—especially for applications dealing with user credentials, health data, or financial transactions.

🖊 **Performance Tip**   Keep encryption lightweight (e.g., symmetric AES) for local storage and cache encryption to avoid performance bottlenecks.

✅ **Checklist: Securing Data in Transit and at Rest**

Item	Status
HTTPS enforced for all APIs	✅
TLS 1.2+ and strong cipher suites	✅
Certificate pinning implemented	✅

747

CHAPTER 11 SECURITY AND APP HARDENING

Tokens and secrets in secure storage	✓
Local database encrypted	✓
Sensitive files encrypted before storing	✓
Logging removed from production builds	✓

By applying these strategies, you ensure a strong foundation of security in both the Flutter frontend and its interactions with backend systems.

Secure Authentication Methods

Authentication is the first line of defense for any application—determining who the user is and ensuring that only legitimate users gain access to your app's features and data. Insecure or poorly implemented authentication systems are among the top reasons for critical vulnerabilities, including data leakage, unauthorized access, and identity spoofing.

In Flutter, modern authentication goes far beyond simple username-password combinations. This section explores robust techniques such as OAuth 2.0 with JWT, two-factor authentication (2FA), and biometric authentication, ensuring your app stays both secure and user-friendly.

OAuth and JWT Authentication

In the era of distributed systems, mobile apps rarely operate in isolation. Instead, they frequently communicate with remote services to fetch, store, and manage user data. This communication must be authenticated securely to ensure that only authorized users gain access to their resources. OAuth 2.0 and JSON Web Tokens (JWT) are two essential building blocks for modern, stateless, and scalable authentication systems in Flutter applications.

This section explores the integration of OAuth 2.0 and JWT in Flutter, complete with implementation practices, tools, and security guidelines.

🔐 Understanding OAuth 2.0

OAuth 2.0 is an industry-standard authorization protocol that enables third-party applications to gain limited access to a user's data without exposing their credentials. In a Flutter app, it typically involves

Resource Owner: The user

Client: The Flutter mobile or web app

Authorization Server: Issues tokens (e.g., Auth0, Google Identity)

Resource Server: The backend server that accepts tokens for protected APIs

OAuth is not an authentication protocol by itself. Instead, it is used for delegated authorization, often paired with OpenID Connect (OIDC) when identity verification is needed.

🔄 OAuth 2.0 Authorization Flows for Flutter:

✅ Recommended—Authorization Code Flow with PKCE:

This is the most secure and suitable flow for public clients like mobile apps.

Why PKCE (Proof Key for Code Exchange)?

PKCE (Proof Key for Code Exchange) prevents intercepted authorization codes from being exchanged by malicious actors. It ensures that the client initiating the flow is the only one who can complete it.

🔒 Deprecated—Implicit Flow:

Once used for SPAs and mobile apps, it is now discouraged due to lack of refresh tokens and vulnerability to token leakage.

🛠 Integrating OAuth in Flutter:

To handle OAuth flows in Flutter, use the "flutter_appauth" (https://pub.dev/packages/flutter_appauth) package, which supports native PKCE-based authentication.

CHAPTER 11 SECURITY AND APP HARDENING

✅ **Sample Code—OAuth with PKCE:**

```dart
import 'package:flutter_appauth/flutter_appauth.dart';

final FlutterAppAuth appAuth = FlutterAppAuth();

final AuthorizationTokenResponse? result = await appAuth.authorizeAndExchangeCode(
  AuthorizationTokenRequest(
    'your_client_id',
    'com.example.app:/oauthredirect',
    serviceConfiguration: AuthorizationServiceConfiguration(
      authorizationEndpoint: 'https://your-auth-server.com/oauth/authorize',
      tokenEndpoint: 'https://your-auth-server.com/oauth/token',
    ),
    scopes: ['openid', 'profile', 'email'],
  ),
);

final accessToken = result?.accessToken;
final idToken = result?.idToken;
```

💡 **Expert Insight:**

Always combine OAuth with PKCE in mobile apps. It offers the benefits of Authorization Code Flow without exposing client secrets.

—Ramesh Patel, Identity Engineer

🔑 What Is a JSON Web Token (JWT)?

A JWT is a compact, URL-safe token format that represents claims between two parties. It's often used as the access token in OAuth-based systems. A JWT is composed of three parts:

```
Header.Payload.Signature
```

✅ Example:

```
eyJhbGciOiJIUzI1NiIsInR5cCI6IkpXVCJ9.     // Header
eyJzdWIiOiIxMjMONTY3ODkwIiwibmFtZSI6IkpvZSBEb2UifQ.   // Payload
SflKxwRJSMeKKF2QT4fwpMeJf36POk6yJV_adQssw5c  // Signature
```

🧩 Common JWT Claims:

Claim	Description
'sub'	Subject (user identifier)
'exp'	Expiration timestamp
'iat'	Issued at timestamp
'aud'	Audience (intended recipient)
'scope'	Permissions granted to the token

🔧 Verifying and Using JWTs in Flutter:

In most cases, JWTs are passed as bearer tokens in HTTP requests.

```
final response = await http.get(
  Uri.parse('https://api.example.com/user'),
  headers: {'Authorization': 'Bearer $accessToken'},
);
```

CHAPTER 11   SECURITY AND APP HARDENING

Ensure tokens are stored securely using "flutter_secure_storage" (https://pub.dev/packages/flutter_secure_storage), never in plaintext or SharedPreferences.

🔒 JWT Security Best Practices:

Best Practice	Reason
Validate expiration ('exp')	Prevent usage of expired tokens
Avoid long-lived JWTs	Reduces damage from token leakage
Use HTTPS for all token transmission	Prevent token sniffing
Store tokens in secure storage	Avoid local data exposure
Do not trust JWT contents blindly	Always verify signature on the server

✅ Checklist: OAuth + JWT Integration in Flutter

Task	Status
OAuth Authorization Code Flow with PKCE implemented	✅
Access and ID tokens retrieved and securely stored	✅
JWTs transmitted via Bearer token headers	✅
Tokens validated and refreshed as needed	✅
Secure token storage (no SharedPreferences)	✅
HTTPS enforced for all auth endpoints	✅

Real-World Use Case: OAuth + JWT in a Banking App

A fintech startup used "flutter_appauth" to authenticate users via OAuth 2.0 (Authorization Code Flow with PKCE) integrated with their identity provider (Auth0). Access tokens (JWTs) were securely stored using the platform keystore, enabling secure API requests and session resumption. JWT scopes controlled access to specific services (e.g., viewing transactions vs. initiating transfers), offering a fine-grained permission model.

By implementing OAuth 2.0 with PKCE and securely managing JWTs in your Flutter app, you ensure a modern, scalable, and secure authentication flow. In the next section, we'll go further by adding two-factor authentication (2FA) to bolster access protection.

Implementing Two-Factor Authentication (2FA)

While traditional username–password authentication forms the first layer of user identity verification, it is increasingly insufficient in guarding against breaches such as phishing, brute-force attacks, and credential stuffing. Two-factor authentication (2FA) significantly elevates security by introducing a second layer of verification—ensuring that the user is not only someone who knows the credentials but also someone who has access to a trusted device or service.

This section explains the different types of 2FA and best practices for integration in Flutter apps and offers a complete implementation example using time-based one-time passwords (TOTP).

🔐 What Is Two-Factor Authentication?

Two-factor authentication (2FA) requires two of the following:

> **Something You Know**: Password, PIN

> **Something You Have**: Phone, hardware token, OTP app

> **Something You Are**: Biometric traits (covered in section "Biometric Authentication for Enhanced Security")

2FA enhances account protection even if one factor (like a password) is compromised.

✅ Popular Forms of 2FA in Mobile Apps

Method	Description	User Experience
TOTP (Time-based OTP)	Code generated in an app like Google Authenticator	Offline-ready
SMS OTP	Code sent via text message	Easy, less secure
Push Notifications	Approval request sent to device (e.g., Duo)	Seamless

⚠ **Security Note** Avoid using SMS-based 2FA as a primary method. It is vulnerable to SIM swapping and interception.

🛠 Implementing TOTP-Based 2FA in Flutter

A secure and offline-friendly 2FA method is TOTP, which works with apps like Google Authenticator, Authy, or Microsoft Authenticator.

🔧 **Backend Preparation**:

Your server must

- Generate and store a secret key per user.
- Provide a QR code or base32 key for setup.
- Verify incoming TOTP codes using the same secret.

Example: Use libraries like "speakeasy" (Node.js) or "PyOTP" (Python) on the server.

📲 **Client Flow for TOTP Verification**:

1. Prompt the user for a TOTP setup during login or settings.
2. Let them scan a QR code or enter a key in their authenticator app.

3. Ask for the six-digit code.

4. Send it to your backend for verification.

5. On success, mark 2FA as enabled.

✅ **Flutter Implementation Snippet**:

Use a basic input screen to verify the six-digit code:

```
final TextEditingController _otpController =
TextEditingController();

ElevatedButton(
  onPressed: () async {
    final code = _otpController.text;
    final response = await http.post(
      Uri.parse('https://yourapi.com/verify-2fa'),
      body: jsonEncode({'otp': code}),
      headers: {'Authorization': 'Bearer $token'},
    );

    if (response.statusCode == 200) {
      // Success: 2FA verified
    } else {
      // Failure: Invalid OTP
    }
  },
  child: Text('Verify Code'),
)
```

CHAPTER 11   SECURITY AND APP HARDENING

🔐 Storing and Managing 2FA Status:

Once verified, store the user's 2FA status securely in your backend and issue JWTs that include a claim like "2fa: true."

On the Flutter side, after login and 2FA verification, persist the final access token securely using

>"flutter_secure_storage" (Android/iOS)

>"EncryptedSharedPreferences" or "Keychain"

Real-World Case Study: TOTP in a Healthcare App

A Flutter-based telemedicine platform implemented TOTP-based 2FA to comply with HIPAA guidelines. They provided QR codes during account setup and verified six-digit OTPs via backend APIs. After enabling 2FA, user sessions were marked as trusted for 30 days unless revoked. This reduced account compromise incidents by over 80% in six months.

✅ Checklist: 2FA in Flutter Apps

```
| Task                                                | Status |
| --------------------------------------------------- | ------ |
| Secret keys generated and stored per user (backend) | ✅     |
| QR code or key shared with user (setup step)        | ✅     |
| OTP entry UI and input validation built             | ✅     |
| OTP verification API integrated                     | ✅     |
| Session/token issuance only after 2FA validation    | ✅     |
| Secure token storage and 2FA enforcement            | ✅     |
```

⚙ Performance Alert

Make sure 2FA token verification doesn't slow down login flows. Use stateless JWTs post-verification to reduce auth server load.

🛡 Security Alert

Always throttle OTP verification attempts and apply rate limiting to prevent brute-force code guessing.

Biometric Authentication for Enhanced Security

Biometric authentication leverages unique physical characteristics—like fingerprints or facial patterns—to authenticate users securely and conveniently. With modern smartphones embedding high-precision biometric sensors, Flutter developers can implement biometric authentication to strengthen security while offering a seamless login experience.

In this section, we will explore how to integrate fingerprint, face, and iris recognition into your Flutter apps using platform APIs and best practices. We will also cover fallback mechanisms, secure storage considerations, and real-world use cases.

👁 Why Use Biometrics in Flutter Apps?

Benefit	Description
🔒 Enhanced Security	Tied to the user's physical identity, harder to spoof
⚡ Fast Login Experience	One-touch or face recognition bypasses manual input
📲 Native OS Integration	Works with Android BiometricPrompt & iOS LocalAuthentication
○ Frictionless 2FA	Can serve as the second factor in a 2FA flow

Biometrics can serve as either primary authentication (e.g., app unlock) or secondary authentication (e.g., confirm a payment or action).

🛠 Biometric Authentication in Flutter

Use the "local_auth" (https://pub.dev/packages/local_auth) package, which wraps Android's "BiometricPrompt" and iOS's "LocalAuthentication."

✅ Add Required Configuration
Android:
Add the following permissions to "AndroidManifest.xml":

```xml
<uses-permission android:name="android.permission.USE_BIOMETRIC"/>
<uses-permission android:name="android.permission.USE_FINGERPRINT"/>
```

Ensure your "minSdkVersion" is at least 23.
iOS:
Add to your "Info.plist":

```xml
<key>NSFaceIDUsageDescription</key>
<string>We use Face ID to protect your account.</string>
```

🔐 Implementation in Flutter

```dart
import 'package:local_auth/local_auth.dart';

final LocalAuthentication auth = LocalAuthentication();

bool isBiometricAvailable = await auth.canCheckBiometrics;
List<BiometricType> availableBiometrics = await auth.getAvailableBiometrics();

bool didAuthenticate = await auth.authenticate(
  localizedReason: 'Please authenticate to access the app',
  options: const AuthenticationOptions(
```

CHAPTER 11 SECURITY AND APP HARDENING

```
      biometricOnly: true,
      stickyAuth: true,
      useErrorDialogs: true,
   ),
);
```

💡 Expert Insight

Combine biometric authentication with secure token storage for best results. Use biometrics to decrypt sensitive keys, not to store them.

—Elena R., Mobile Security Architect

↻ Fallback Authentication Flow

Always provide a fallback option (e.g., PIN or password) in case biometrics are unavailable or the user declines biometric enrollment.

```
if (!didAuthenticate) {
  // Prompt fallback login screen
}
```

🔒 Secure Storage of Tokens After Authentication

Once authenticated, sensitive tokens or session keys should be stored using

- "flutter_secure_storage" (encrypted keystore access)
- Platform Keychain (iOS) or Android Keystore

Biometric authentication can be used to unlock encryption keys rather than store sensitive data directly.

Real-World Use Case: Biometric Login in a Banking App
A leading Flutter-based banking app implemented biometric login using "local_auth." Post-login tokens were stored in the Android Keystore and iOS Keychain. Each time the app was reopened, the token was retrieved only after successful biometric authentication, improving both security and user experience. Opt-in rates for biometrics exceeded 85%, reducing password reset requests by 40%.

✅ **Checklist: Biometric Authentication in Flutter**

Task	Status
'local_auth' integrated	✅
Platform permissions and configurations set	✅
Biometric capability and availability checks implemented	✅
Fallback (PIN/password) flow provided	✅
Tokens securely stored post-authentication	✅
Biometric used to unlock encrypted data (not store it)	✅

⚙ **Performance Alert**
Use "stickyAuth: true" to persist authentication across app switch events to avoid repeated prompts.

🛡 **Security Alert**
Do not assume biometric success alone as sufficient—combine with secure token management and expiry checks.

Biometric authentication bridges the gap between user convenience and robust security. Whether used for app unlocks, transaction approval, or multi-factor authentication, it plays a critical role in hardening Flutter apps against unauthorized access.

Next, we'll explore how to harden the app itself using techniques like code obfuscation, reverse engineering protection, and encryption strategies.

App Hardening Techniques

While securing authentication and data flow is essential, a truly secure Flutter app must also resist tampering, code analysis, and runtime attacks. **App hardening** refers to strategies and tools that make your application more difficult to reverse engineer, modify, or exploit.

This section explores robust techniques to make your Flutter apps resilient against static and dynamic analysis, focusing on reverse engineering defense, code obfuscation, and secure encryption practices.

Protecting Against Reverse Engineering

Reverse engineering poses one of the most critical threats to mobile applications. Attackers use various tools and techniques to decompile, inspect, and modify app binaries, exposing sensitive logic, credentials, or proprietary algorithms. For Flutter apps—which compile to native code but also bundle Dart bytecode and assets—this risk is very real.

This section explores how Flutter apps can be protected against reverse engineering through static and dynamic defense strategies, tamper detection, and smart platform integrations.

CHAPTER 11   SECURITY AND APP HARDENING

🔍 Understanding Reverse Engineering Threats

Common reverse engineering activities include the following:

Threat	Description
APK decompilation	Tools like 'apktool', 'JADX', or 'MobSF' decompile APKs to access Dart code and native libraries
Asset inspection	Images, strings, and config files inside Flutter asset folders can leak secrets or internal logic
Code injection	Dynamic instrumentation using tools like Frida or Xposed to modify app behavior at runtime
Binary tampering	Modifying native libraries or bypassing license checks, payment flows, etc.
API key theft	Extracting hardcoded tokens or endpoints from compiled resources

🛡 Strategies for Reverse Engineering Prevention

✓ 1. Use Code Obfuscation (Covered in Section "Code Obfuscation in Flutter")

Obfuscation renames identifiers and removes metadata, making decompiled code harder to understand.

Use "--obfuscate" and "--split-debug-info" for production builds.

✓ 2. Implement Root/Jailbreak Detection

Apps running on rooted or jailbroken devices are significantly more vulnerable to reverse engineering and data theft.

Example in Flutter:

```
import 'package:root_checker/root_checker.dart';
bool isRooted = await RootChecker.isDeviceRooted;
if (isRooted) {
  // Exit the app or show warning
}
```

On iOS, use native platform channels to check for jailbreak tools like Cydia or file system anomalies.

✓ 3. **Detect Debugging or Hooking Tools**

Detect runtime debuggers, hooking frameworks (e.g., Frida), or memory analysis tools.

Use native libraries or packages like "flutter_secure_storage" (https://pub.dev/packages/flutter_secure_storage) in conjunction with platform-specific code (e.g., "ptrace," "isDebuggerConnected," etc.).

✓ 4. **Enable Tamper Detection**

Compare cryptographic hashes of the app binary at runtime to detect unauthorized modifications. A mismatch indicates tampering.

Conceptual Approach:

> At app startup, compute the SHA-256 hash of critical native binaries.
>
> Compare with expected signature stored securely or fetched from a trusted server.

✓ 5. **Use Certificate Pinning**

Mitigates man-in-the-middle (MITM) attacks where attackers intercept and modify HTTPS traffic.

Implement SSL/TLS pinning using packages like "dio" (https://pub.dev/packages/dio) with "SecurityContext" or platform-native methods.

CHAPTER 11   SECURITY AND APP HARDENING

✅ **6. Encrypt All Sensitive Assets**

Do not store API keys or logic files in plaintext inside your app. Use encryption and load them securely at runtime.

🔐 **Real-World Practice: Anti-Reverse Engineering in a Fintech App**

A Flutter-based fintech app faced repeated APK cloning and tampering attempts. By integrating obfuscation, asset encryption, and tamper detection (via signature verification at runtime), the app team reduced reverse engineering success rates by over 80%. Additional measures like root detection and certificate pinning further hardened the app against injection and MITM attacks.

✅ **Checklist: Reverse Engineering Defense**

```
| Task                                                   | Status |
| ------------------------------------------------------ | ------ |
| Code obfuscation applied                               | ✅     |
| Root/jailbreak detection in place                      | ✅     |
| Runtime debugger/hooking tools detection implemented   | ✅     |
| Tamper detection via signature or hash check           | ✅     |
| All sensitive assets encrypted and never hardcoded     | ✅     |
| Certificate pinning enabled for HTTPS                  | ✅     |
```

🛡 **Security Alert**

Reverse engineering defenses must be layered. No single method is foolproof. Combine obfuscation, encryption, detection, and validation strategies for maximum protection.

⚙ **Performance Alert**

Root and tamper detection should run asynchronously to avoid slowing down app launch. Ensure they don't block UI threads.

Flutter apps may be difficult to reverse engineer compared with pure Java/Kotlin apps, but they are not immune. By taking a proactive stance and applying multiple layers of hardening, developers can significantly raise the barrier against attackers and protect the integrity of their code and users.

Code Obfuscation in Flutter

Code obfuscation is a fundamental technique for app hardening that deters reverse engineering by transforming the app's source code into an unreadable and unintelligible format, without altering its functionality. For Flutter developers, this means making Dart code less accessible and interpretable to attackers attempting to decompile APK or IPA files.

Here, we explore how Flutter supports obfuscation, how to configure it properly, and best practices to ensure security without sacrificing app stability or performance.

🔍 What Is Code Obfuscation?

Obfuscation modifies an application's compiled code to make it harder for attackers to

- Understand app logic.
- Identify function and class names.
- Extract API keys, credentials, or business logic.
- Modify app behavior for malicious purposes.

In Flutter, obfuscation applies primarily to Dart code, but can also be paired with native obfuscation for Kotlin/Java (Android) or Swift/Objective-C (iOS).

⚙ How Flutter Obfuscation Works

Flutter compiles Dart code to native machine code or Dart intermediate representation (kernel bytecode). You can obfuscate this output using specific build flags during the release build process.

🔧 Enabling Obfuscation

To obfuscate Dart code, add the "--obfuscate" and "--split-debug-info" flags during the build:

```
flutter build apk \
  --release \
  --obfuscate \
  --split-debug-info=build/debug-info/
```

"**--obfuscate**": Obfuscates Dart symbols

"**--split-debug-info**": Stores debug symbol mappings in a separate directory (used for stack trace symbolication)

■ The "split-debug-info" directory should be kept secure and not included in your version control system or distributed with the app.

📱 Obfuscating iOS Builds

For iOS, use the same flags:

```
flutter build ipa \
  --release \
  --obfuscate \
  --split-debug-info=build/debug-info/
```

Flutter also allows native code obfuscation through Xcode settings for Swift/Objective-C code by disabling debug symbols and enabling bitcode.

🧪 **Verifying Obfuscation**

After obfuscation, you can inspect the resulting APK or IPA to ensure symbol names have been replaced with meaningless values.

CHAPTER 11 SECURITY AND APP HARDENING

Sample Before:

```
void authenticateUser() { ... }
```

Sample After (Obfuscated):

```
void a() { ... }
```

📕 Symbolicating Stack Traces

If your app crashes, the stack trace will contain obfuscated names. You can map these back to the original source using the debug info:

```
flutter symbolize --debug-info=build/debug-info/app.android-arm64.symbols < stacktrace.txt
```

This is critical for debugging production errors in obfuscated builds.

✅ Best Practices for Code Obfuscation

Recommendation	Rationale
Always use '--split-debug-info' with '--obfuscate'	Keeps debugging possible after release
Store debug symbols securely	Prevents attackers from reversing obfuscation
Rotate debug info directories per build version	Supports version-specific symbolication
Obfuscate during CI/CD release builds	Ensures consistent hardening before publication
Combine with native obfuscation (e.g., ProGuard)	Adds extra protection for hybrid Flutter/native apps

CHAPTER 11 SECURITY AND APP HARDENING

Real-World Insight: Securing a Streaming App

A Flutter-based video streaming app faced piracy threats due to leaked API keys and hardcoded authentication flows. By adopting Dart obfuscation, encrypting assets, and removing verbose logs from release builds, the development team dramatically reduced tampering incidents. Reverse engineering attempts dropped after attackers encountered unreadable symbols and encrypted runtime checks.

✅ **Code Obfuscation Checklist**

Task	Status
Dart code obfuscation enabled ('--obfuscate')	✅
Debug symbols saved via '--split-debug-info'	✅
Debug symbols stored securely (not in VCS)	✅
Symbolication toolchain tested and documented	✅
Native code obfuscation enabled (ProGuard/Bitcode)	✅
Release builds automated with obfuscation in CI/CD	✅

♡ **Security Alert**

Obfuscation does not encrypt or hide hardcoded secrets. Always combine obfuscation with encryption, secure storage, and network security best practices.

⚙ **Performance Alert**

Obfuscation may increase build time slightly but has no runtime performance impact. However, always test release builds thoroughly to ensure nothing breaks post-obfuscation.

Encryption Best Practices for Mobile Apps

Encryption is a cornerstone of modern mobile security. It ensures that sensitive data—whether in transit or at rest—is unreadable without proper authorization. For Flutter developers, implementing robust encryption

CHAPTER 11 SECURITY AND APP HARDENING

practices is essential for protecting user data, complying with regulations like GDPR and HIPAA, and defending against reverse engineering or man-in-the-middle (MITM) attacks.

This section explores best practices for applying encryption in Flutter apps, from secure storage to networking, and how to avoid common cryptographic pitfalls.

🔐 Why Encryption Matters

Without encryption

> User data stored locally can be extracted by attackers with root access.
>
> Intercepted network requests can expose passwords, tokens, or PII.
>
> API keys and secrets hardcoded in binaries can be harvested easily.
>
> Encryption transforms data into unreadable ciphertext, which can only be decrypted using the correct key.

💼 Tools and Packages for Flutter Encryption

Flutter provides several reliable packages for encryption:

Package	Purpose
['encrypt'](https://pub.dev/packages/encrypt)	General-purpose AES/RSA encryption
['flutter_secure_storage'](https://pub.dev/packages/flutter_secure_storage)	Encrypted key-value storage

Chapter 11 Security and App Hardening

| ['pointycastle'](https://pub.dev/packages/pointycastle) | Low-level crypto algorithms (RSA, SHA, ECC) |
| ['cryptography'](https://pub.dev/packages/cryptography) | Modern cryptography APIs (ChaCha20, HMAC) |

🎁 Encrypting Data at Rest

Data stored on the device (e.g., tokens, preferences, files) must be encrypted to prevent unauthorized access.

✅ **Use Encrypted Local Storage:**

```
final storage = new FlutterSecureStorage();
await storage.write(key: 'accessToken', value: encryptedToken);
```

- Stores data in the Android Keystore or iOS Keychain
- Automatically encrypts keys and values
- Cannot be accessed by other apps

✅ **Encrypt Custom Files or Databases:**

Use "encrypt" + "path_provider" to store encrypted files:

```
final key = Key.fromUtf8('16charslongkey!!');
final iv = IV.fromLength(16);
final encrypter = Encrypter(AES(key));
final encrypted = encrypter.encrypt('Sensitive Data', iv: iv);
final decrypted = encrypter.decrypt(encrypted, iv: iv);
```

Always store encryption keys securely—preferably in platform keystores or fetched securely from a server.

🌐 Encrypting Data in Transit

All data transmitted over networks should be protected with TLS (HTTPS). But even HTTPS isn't foolproof against MITM attacks if certificate validation is weak.

✅ **Enforce HTTPS and Certificate Pinning**:

Use HTTPS for all API endpoints.

Use certificate pinning to prevent fake CA-based MITM attacks.

Use "dio" for secure requests with pinning:

```
(dio.httpClientAdapter as DefaultHttpClientAdapter).onHttpClientCreate =
    (client) {
  client.badCertificateCallback = (cert, host, port) => false;
  // Optional: load and pin your trusted certificate manually here
};
```

✅ **Avoid Hardcoding Secrets**:

Never embed API keys or secrets directly in Dart files. Instead

> Store tokens server-side and fetch securely at runtime.

> Obfuscate and encrypt if local use is unavoidable.

🔑 Key Management Best Practices

Encryption is only as strong as the key management behind it.

Best Practice	Description
Use platform keystores	Android Keystore and iOS Keychain provide secure key storage
Avoid static or hardcoded keys	Keys should be generated at runtime or delivered securely
Use asymmetric encryption	Use RSA for secure key exchange; AES for performance
Rotate keys	Refresh keys periodically to reduce exposure
Expire tokens	Access tokens should have expiration to prevent misuse

⚠ Common Encryption Mistakes to Avoid

Mistake	Risk
Using weak algorithms (e.g., MD5, DES)	Easily cracked
Reusing IVs in symmetric encryption	Allows data pattern detection
Storing plaintext keys in code	Can be extracted from APKs/IPAs
Disabling SSL verification	Opens the door to MITM attacks

CHAPTER 11   SECURITY AND APP HARDENING

💼 Case Study: Healthcare App Data Protection

A Flutter-based healthcare app handling patient records implemented end-to-end AES-256 encryption and stored keys in the Android Keystore. Network communications used HTTPS with certificate pinning. During a third-party security audit, no sensitive data could be retrieved—even under root conditions—thanks to robust encryption and key protection strategies.

✅ Encryption Security Checklist

Task	Status
Secure storage uses 'flutter_secure_storage'	✅
Sensitive data is encrypted before disk write	✅
HTTPS enforced for all network requests	✅
Certificate pinning implemented	✅
Secrets are never hardcoded in source code	✅
Keys stored in Keystore/Keychain or fetched securely	✅
Strong algorithms (AES-256, RSA, ChaCha20) used	✅
IVs randomized and non-reused	✅

♡ Security Alert

Encryption without secure key management is worse than no encryption. If an attacker can access your encryption keys, the encrypted data becomes meaningless protection.

✪ Performance Alert

Heavy encryption (e.g., large file or image encryption) can impact app performance. Optimize by encrypting only what's necessary and offloading to isolates or native code where possible.

CHAPTER 11   SECURITY AND APP HARDENING

Real-World Security Case Studies

Understanding theoretical concepts and best practices is important, but nothing solidifies knowledge better than examining real-world scenarios. In this section, we analyze high-profile mobile security failures—including how they happened, what was compromised, and, most importantly, what developers can learn from them to avoid repeating the same mistakes.

Security Vulnerabilities in Popular Apps

Even the most popular and well-funded mobile applications have fallen victim to critical security flaws. These cases serve as cautionary tales, especially for Flutter developers aiming to build secure apps from the ground up. This section explores a few anonymized but real-world examples where improper coding practices, flawed architecture, or neglected security measures led to vulnerabilities—many of which could have been prevented.

🔍 **Case Study 1: API Key Leakage in a Flutter-Based Fitness App**
Issue:
A well-known fitness tracking app built with Flutter inadvertently exposed sensitive API keys within its Dart codebase. Since Flutter compiles to native code but retains metadata, reverse engineering using tools like "jadx" or "apktool" revealed the embedded keys.

What Went Wrong:

- API keys were hardcoded in the code.
- No obfuscation or minification was used in the production build.
- Lack of backend authentication checks.

CHAPTER 11   SECURITY AND APP HARDENING

Impact:

> Attackers used the keys to scrape user data and access premium APIs for free.
>
> Compromised partner services due to exposed third-party integration keys.

Developer Takeaway:

> Always store API keys on secure servers and retrieve them at runtime over encrypted connections. Never hardcode secrets in source code.

🔍 Case Study 2: Insecure Local Storage in an E-Wallet App

Issue:

A digital wallet application stored sensitive user information—such as email addresses, tokens, and transaction history—using plaintext storage through "SharedPreferences."

What Went Wrong:

> No encryption layer applied to local storage.
>
> Access to app data was not properly sandboxed.
>
> Rooted devices could easily extract data.

Impact:

> On rooted Android devices, attackers could extract unencrypted files.
>
> Led to user data breaches and fraudulent transactions.

CHAPTER 11   SECURITY AND APP HARDENING

Developer Takeaway:

Use "flutter_secure_storage" or platform keystores for any sensitive data. Always assume local storage can be compromised.

🔍 Case Study 3: Broken Biometric Authentication in a Healthcare App

Issue:

A healthcare appointment scheduling app used biometric authentication to protect access to medical profiles. However, it failed to validate biometric cancellation events properly.

What Went Wrong:

If the user canceled biometric authentication, the app did not verify identity again.

Navigating back allowed access to protected content.

Impact:

Sensitive health records could be accessed by unauthorized users.

Violated HIPAA compliance requirements in certain jurisdictions.

Developer Takeaway:

Always validate authentication status after biometric prompts. Do not allow navigation bypasses post-authentication.

🔍 Case Study 4: Inadequate TLS Validation in a Travel Booking App

Issue:

A travel app implemented TLS but failed to validate SSL certificates correctly, making it vulnerable to man-in-the-middle (MITM) attacks.

CHAPTER 11   SECURITY AND APP HARDENING

What Went Wrong:

SSL pinning was not implemented.

The app accepted all certificates, including self-signed ones.

Impact:

Attackers on public Wi-Fi could intercept login credentials and payment data.

Major reputational damage and user attrition followed.

Developer Takeaway:
Use SSL pinning for all sensitive network communications and validate all certificates. Never disable certificate checks, even for development.

⚠ Summary of Common Issues Identified

Vulnerability Type	Description
Hardcoded Secrets	API keys or tokens embedded in source code
Unencrypted Local Storage	Sensitive data stored in plain-text on the device
Authentication Bypass	Weak implementation of biometric or session validation
Improper SSL Certificate Handling	Lack of certificate validation or SSL pinning

CHAPTER 11   SECURITY AND APP HARDENING

📌 **Expert Insight**

Most security breaches occur not because attackers are too smart, but because developers overlook small but critical details. Treat every data access point as a potential vulnerability.

—Security Architect, OWASP Mobile Security Project

Lessons Learned and Solutions

The case studies presented in the previous section highlight common vulnerabilities that have affected popular apps, leading to significant risks for both developers and users. However, each of these flaws also offers valuable lessons that can be applied to improve the security of any mobile application, especially those built using Flutter. This section outlines the key takeaways from the real-world vulnerabilities discussed above and offers actionable solutions to mitigate similar risks in your own apps.

1. **Never Hardcode Secrets in Source Code**

   Lesson Learned:

   Hardcoding sensitive information like API keys, authentication tokens, and secrets directly into the source code is a major security risk. If an attacker gains access to your app's APK or source code, these secrets are easily exposed.

   Solution:

   Store Secrets Securely: Use secure storage mechanisms, such as the Keystore for Android and the iOS Keychain. In Flutter, this can be accomplished with the "flutter_secure_storage" package, which encrypts sensitive data at rest.

Environment-Based Configuration: Use environment variables to manage sensitive data. Ensure API keys are retrieved at runtime and not stored directly in your app's code.

2. **Use Strong Local Data Encryption**

   Lesson Learned:

   Storing sensitive data in an unencrypted form on the device can leave it exposed to attackers, especially if the device is rooted or compromised. This is particularly dangerous for financial, health, or personal data.

   Solution:

   Encrypt Data at Rest: Use strong encryption libraries to encrypt sensitive data stored locally on the device. In Flutter, use "flutter_secure_storage" or platform-specific encryption methods.

   Data Should Never Be Stored in Plaintext: Avoid using local storage solutions like "SharedPreferences" or "SQLite" without applying encryption. Always ensure that sensitive data is encrypted before being written to local storage.

3. **Ensure Proper Authentication and Session Management**

   Lesson Learned:

   Inadequate handling of authentication processes, including biometric authentication and session management, can lead to security vulnerabilities where unauthorized users can access protected resources.

Solution:

Always Validate After Biometric Authentication: Ensure that after any biometric prompt (fingerprint, face ID), the app verifies that the user is still authenticated and not bypassing authentication via navigation or app cancellation.

Session Expiration and Renewal: Implement session expiration and automatic re-authentication if the session becomes invalid or expires. Always require re-authentication after a set period of inactivity.

Fallback Authentication: Provide a secure fallback option (e.g., PIN or password) when biometric authentication fails or is unavailable.

4. **Implement Secure Network Communication**

Lesson Learned:

Failing to properly secure network communication leaves apps vulnerable to man-in-the-middle (MITM) attacks, where an attacker can intercept or modify data being transmitted between the client and server.

Solution:

Use HTTPS with TLS/SSL Encryption: Ensure that all communication between the app and the server is encrypted using HTTPS and SSL/TLS certificates. This prevents third parties from intercepting sensitive data such as login credentials or payment details.

SSL Pinning: Implement SSL pinning in your app to ensure that it only communicates with trusted servers. This prevents attackers from using fraudulent certificates to impersonate legitimate servers.

Proper Certificate Validation: Always validate the authenticity of SSL certificates on both the server and client side to avoid accepting invalid or self-signed certificates.

5. **Protect Against Reverse Engineering**

   Lesson Learned:

   Reverse engineering allows attackers to inspect your code and extract valuable information, such as API keys, authentication mechanisms, and even the business logic of your app.

   Solution:

   Obfuscate Your Code: In Flutter, use the "--obfuscate" flag during the release build process to make your Dart code more difficult to reverse engineer. This will scramble the names of variables, methods, and classes, making it harder for an attacker to analyze the code.

   Minimize the Information Exposed by Native Code: If you're using native plugins, ensure that sensitive logic is protected with appropriate obfuscation or encryption on both the Flutter and native side.

6. **Regular Security Audits and Penetration Testing**

   Lesson Learned:

   Many vulnerabilities go unnoticed during development and only become apparent when they are exploited. Proactively testing your app's security is essential to finding and fixing vulnerabilities before they cause harm.

   Solution:

   Conduct Regular Penetration Testing: Hire experienced security professionals to conduct penetration tests, focusing on app logic, data handling, and network security.

   Automated Static Code Analysis: Integrate static analysis tools like MobSF (Mobile Security Framework) or SonarQube into your development pipeline to automatically detect security issues early.

   Security Audit Tools: Use tools like OWASP ZAP or Burp Suite to perform dynamic testing, assessing how well your app holds up against common attacks.

7. **Stay Up to Date with Security Patches**

   Lesson Learned:

   Neglecting to update your app with the latest security patches can leave known vulnerabilities exposed to attackers, especially as the Flutter ecosystem and mobile operating systems evolve.

   Solution:

Stay Current with Platform Updates: Always keep your Flutter dependencies and plugins up to date. Regularly check for updates in the Flutter SDK, security libraries, and related frameworks.

Security-Focused Third-Party Libraries: When using third-party packages, always ensure they are maintained and regularly updated. Be cautious when using libraries that may have known vulnerabilities.

Patch Known Vulnerabilities: When new vulnerabilities are discovered in your app or its dependencies, apply patches and release updates to your users as soon as possible.

📋 Security Takeaways Checklist

```
| Action
| Description                                             | Completed |
| --------------------------------------------------------
| ------------------------------------------------|---------- |
| ✅  Secure secrets with 'flutter_secure_storage'
| Store sensitive data in encrypted storage        | ✓         |
| ✅  Encrypt all local data storage
| Use AES or platform keystores for encryption     | ✓         |
| ✅  Validate authentication after biometrics
| Ensure that biometric authentication is handled properly
                                                   | ✓         |
| ✅  Implement SSL pinning and certificate validation
| Prevent MITM attacks and ensure secure communication
                                                   | ✓         |
```

CHAPTER 11   SECURITY AND APP HARDENING

- ☑ Obfuscate Dart code in release builds
- Protect your app's code from reverse engineering ✓

- ☑ Conduct regular security audits and penetration tests
- Identify and fix vulnerabilities proactively ✓

> 📌 **Expert Insight**
>
> *Security is an ongoing effort that requires consistent diligence. Ensure your development lifecycle includes security checks at every stage—from code review to deployment.*
>
> —Cybersecurity Expert, Mobile App Security Firm

By implementing these lessons learned and solutions, you will be able to drastically improve the security posture of your Flutter applications. It's crucial to adopt a proactive approach to security, anticipating potential vulnerabilities before they can be exploited. By following these best practices and continuously evolving your app's security measures, you can significantly reduce the risk of breaches and ensure the safety of your users' data.

Summary

Here, we explored the essential strategies for securing Flutter applications and hardening them against various threats. We began by examining common security vulnerabilities in mobile apps, such as hardcoded secrets, inadequate encryption, and authentication flaws. Next, we discussed robust methods for securing data, both in transit and at rest, emphasizing the importance of encryption and secure storage solutions.

We then delved into secure authentication techniques, including OAuth and JWT authentication, two-factor authentication (2FA), and biometric authentication, all of which are critical for safeguarding user identities and sensitive data.

CHAPTER 11 SECURITY AND APP HARDENING

Moving on to app hardening, we covered techniques like protecting against reverse engineering, code obfuscation, and implementing encryption best practices to fortify your app against unauthorized access and data theft.

Finally, we examined real-world security case studies, highlighting vulnerabilities in popular apps and the valuable lessons learned from these incidents. We concluded by providing practical solutions and preventive measures that Flutter developers can adopt to minimize security risks, ensuring their apps remain secure and reliable in an ever-evolving digital landscape.

This chapter serves as a comprehensive guide to building secure and resilient Flutter applications that can withstand common attack vectors and provide users with a safe experience.

CHAPTER 12

Advanced Testing and CI/CD for Flutter

In the previous chapter, we explored the critical realm of mobile security—delving into common vulnerabilities in Flutter apps; securing sensitive data; implementing modern authentication mechanisms like OAuth, JWT, and biometrics; and applying hardening techniques such as code obfuscation and encryption. These security strategies are essential for building trusted applications that safeguard user data and withstand real-world attacks.

However, strong security is only one pillar of a production-grade Flutter app. Equally important is ensuring that your application behaves as expected under all conditions—and that every line of code, from core logic to complex UI flows, is thoroughly tested and reliably deployed. That's where this chapter comes in.

Here, we shift focus from protection to precision—introducing you to advanced testing methodologies and automation workflows that elevate your development process. You'll learn how to write effective unit tests that validate both logic and UI components, implement robust integration and widget testing strategies for complex app behavior, and confidently handle edge cases like animations and nested widget trees.

From there, we enter the world of **Continuous Integration and Delivery (CI/CD)**. You'll discover how to set up modern CI/CD pipelines tailored for Flutter apps using tools like GitHub Actions, automate multi-platform builds and tests, and streamline the deployment process with minimal friction. Additionally, we'll cover the generation of automated test coverage reports and equip you with techniques for debugging flaky tests and identifying performance bottlenecks in CI workflows.

By the end of this chapter, you'll have a complete toolkit for ensuring your Flutter applications are not only secure but also maintainable, testable, and deployable at scale. These capabilities are vital for high-performing teams looking to deliver stable, high-quality releases with confidence and speed—whether you're shipping updates weekly or scaling to millions of users.

Unit Testing in Flutter

Unit testing forms the foundation of a robust testing strategy. It focuses on testing individual functions, methods, or classes in isolation, without relying on external dependencies like databases, file systems, or APIs. In Flutter, unit testing plays a crucial role in validating business logic, verifying state management behaviors, and ensuring UI components behave as expected before they're composed into full widget trees.

Unlike integration or widget tests, unit tests are extremely fast, deterministic, and simple to execute. They serve as the first line of defense against regressions and broken logic, enabling developers to write resilient code that evolves safely.

Writing Effective Unit Tests for Widgets

Unit testing in Flutter is often associated with business logic, but it can also be applied effectively to widget behavior—especially when widgets encapsulate logic such as input validation, state management, or decision-making rules. The key to writing effective unit tests for widgets is to isolate the logic from the visual rendering and ensure that the widget's internal behavior can be validated independently from the framework's rendering pipeline.

🎯 **Objective of Widget Unit Tests**

Validate logic inside widgets (e.g., validation, formatting, state transitions).

Ensure widgets respond correctly to inputs or internal conditions.

Avoid dependency on widget rendering, animations, or layout constraints.

✅ **Best Practices for Writing Widget Unit Tests**

1. **Separate Logic from UI**

   Extract logic into standalone classes or helper methods that can be tested using the "test" package.

   Maintain a clean separation between behavior and presentation to maximize testability.

2. **Avoid "WidgetTester" Unless Necessary**

   For non-rendering tests, use the basic "test()" method from "package:test" rather than "testWidgets()" to keep tests faster and cleaner.

3. **Design for Testability**

   Use dependency injection to supply services, logic, or configurations.

   Avoid hardcoded dependencies that complicate mocking or isolation.

4. **Validate Behavior, Not Appearance**

   Unit tests should assert return values, states, and internal outcomes, not widget layout or pixel-perfect rendering.

Example: Custom Input Validator Widget (Logic Isolation)

Let's say you have a custom widget that internally uses validation logic for an email field:

```
class EmailValidator {
  static String? validate(String email) {
    final regex = RegExp(r'^[\w-\.]+@([\w-]+\.)+[\w-]{2,4}$');
    if (!regex.hasMatch(email)) {
      return 'Invalid email address';
    }
    return null;
  }
}
```

You can test this logic independently:

```
import 'package:test/test.dart';
import 'email_validator.dart';
void main() {
  group('EmailValidator', () {
    test('Returns null for valid email', () {
      expect(EmailValidator.validate('john.doe@example.com'),
        isNull);
    });
    test('Returns error message for invalid email', () {
      expect(EmailValidator.validate('john.doe@'),
        equals('Invalid email address'));
    });
  });
}
```

✏ Example: Testing Logic Encapsulated in a Stateless Widget

If your widget contains logic but no rendering, you can still unit test its behavior:

```
class CounterLogic {
  int increment(int value) => value + 1;
  int decrement(int value) => value - 1;
}
```

```
void main() {
  group('CounterLogic', () {
    final logic = CounterLogic();
    test('Increments correctly', () {
      expect(logic.increment(3), 4);
    });
    test('Decrements correctly', () {
      expect(logic.decrement(2), 1);
    });
  });
}
```

💡 Expert Insight

In real-world applications, widget logic often grows beyond simple interaction handlers. Encapsulating this logic in separate testable units dramatically increases reliability and test coverage.

—Priya Nair, Lead Flutter Engineer, HealthTech Corp.

CHAPTER 12 ADVANCED TESTING AND CI/CD FOR FLUTTER

🚨 Common Mistakes to Avoid

Mistake	Consequence
Writing widget tests when unit tests suffice	Slows down the test suite
Mixing UI logic with rendering code	Leads to harder testing and maintenance
Testing too much in one test	Reduces clarity and makes failures harder to debug
Not covering edge cases	Bugs can sneak into production

📋 Quick Checklist: Writing Effective Widget Unit Tests

- [x] Logic is extracted into testable functions or classes.
- [x] Tests do not depend on rendering.
- [x] Input/output scenarios are well-defined.
- [x] Edge cases and failure conditions are tested.
- [x] Tests run quickly (<50ms average execution time).

🔍 Real-World Case Study: Validating Input Logic in a Fintech App

A Flutter-based financial app had a widget responsible for validating and formatting international phone numbers. Initially, the logic was deeply embedded within the widget's build method, which made it untestable without widget rendering. This resulted in missed bugs and failed formatting in edge regions like the UK and India. After extracting the logic into a utility class and writing thorough unit tests for each country format, the validation bug rate dropped by 92%, and QA time was reduced significantly during releases.

Mocking and Stubbing in Flutter Tests

In unit testing, the goal is to isolate the piece of code under test from any external dependencies or side effects. This isolation ensures that tests are deterministic, fast, and reliable. However, many Flutter apps depend on external services, APIs, databases, or platform-specific functionality that cannot or should not be exercised in unit tests directly. This is where mocking and stubbing become indispensable techniques.

What Are Mocking and Stubbing?

Mocking involves creating fake implementations of classes or interfaces that simulate real objects, allowing you to control their behavior and verify interactions.

Stubbing is a simpler form of mocking where the test provides canned responses to specific method calls without focusing on verifying interactions.

Together, these techniques enable tests to

- Replace slow, unpredictable, or unavailable dependencies with fast, controlled stand-ins.

- Focus solely on the logic of the unit under test.

- Verify that interactions with dependencies occur as expected.

Why Use Mocking and Stubbing in Flutter Tests?

Flutter applications often rely on

- Network services (REST APIs, GraphQL)
- Local databases (SQLite, Hive)
- Platform channels for native device features (camera, sensors)
- Authentication and authorization services

Incorporating these into unit tests without isolation leads to flaky and slow tests. Mocking prevents

- Dependency on network availability or latency
- Modifications of persistent data during tests
- Unwanted side effects that complicate test repeatability

Popular Mocking Approaches in Flutter

1. **Using the "mockito" Package**

   The "mockito" package is the most popular mocking framework for Dart and Flutter. It allows you to create mock classes, define return values, and verify method calls with a concise syntax.

2. **Custom Fake Implementations**

   For simple dependencies, creating custom fake or stub classes can be faster and clearer, especially if only a few methods need to be faked.

3. **Dependency Injection for Testability**

   Designing your code with dependency injection enables easy swapping of real implementations with mocks or stubs during tests.

🔧 **Example: Mocking a Service with "mockito"**

Consider an authentication service that your app depends on:

```
abstract class AuthService {
  Future<bool> login(String username, String password); }
```

An "AuthManager" class consumes this service:

```
class AuthManager {
  final AuthService service;
  AuthManager(this.service);
  Future<String> authenticate(String user, String pass) async {
    final success = await service.login(user, pass);
    return success ? 'Welcome' : 'Access Denied';
  }
}
```

Writing Tests with Mocks:

First, create a mock class using "mockito":

```
import 'package:mockito/mockito.dart';
class MockAuthService extends Mock implements AuthService {}
Then, write tests that stub the behavior of the mocked service:
```

CHAPTER 12   ADVANCED TESTING AND CI/CD FOR FLUTTER

```
-import 'package:test/test.dart';
void main() {
  late MockAuthService mockService;
  late AuthManager authManager;
  setUp(() {
    mockService = MockAuthService();
    authManager = AuthManager(mockService);
  });
  test('Returns Welcome on successful login', () async {
    when(mockService.login('user', 'pass')).thenAnswer((_)
    async => true);
    final result = await authManager.authenticate('user',
    'pass');
    expect(result, equals('Welcome'));
  });
  test('Returns Access Denied on failed login', () async {
    when(mockService.login(any, any)).thenAnswer((_) async
    => false);
    final result = await authManager.authenticate('wrong',
    'creds');
    expect(result, equals('Access Denied'));
  });
}
```

⚠ Best Practices for Mocking in Flutter Tests

Mock interfaces or abstract classes, not concrete implementations, to reduce brittleness.

Stub only what is necessary—avoid over-stubbing to keep tests focused.

Use "verify()" sparingly to assert critical interactions without cluttering tests.

Keep mock setup DRY by using "setUp" or helper methods.

Avoid mocking Flutter framework classes directly; instead, test widget behavior via "testWidgets" or widget tests.

Common Pitfalls to Avoid

Pitfall	Impact
Overusing mocks instead of writing integration tests	Leads to false confidence in isolated behavior
Forgetting to 'await' async mock methods	Causes flaky or incomplete tests
Mocking too many layers deep	Increases test complexity and maintenance
Ignoring edge cases in stubbed responses	Misses important failure scenarios

📋 Checklist for Mocking and Stubbing

[x] Identify all external dependencies to mock/stub.

[x] Create mock or fake implementations of dependencies.

[x] Stub method calls with realistic return values.

[x] Verify critical interactions where applicable.

[x] Keep mocks focused and avoid overuse.

[x] Use dependency injection to inject mocks easily.

CHAPTER 12   ADVANCED TESTING AND CI/CD FOR FLUTTER

🔍 **Real-World Case Study: Stabilizing Flaky Tests with Mocks**
A popular social media app was experiencing flaky unit tests due to intermittent network failures during authentication tests. By introducing "mockito" to simulate API responses, the test suite became fully deterministic, with test runs shrinking from 15 minutes to under 90 seconds. Additionally, the team was able to cover edge cases such as token expiration and invalid credentials systematically, boosting code coverage and reliability.

Integration Testing and Widget Testing

Integration testing and widget testing are essential tools for ensuring that your Flutter application behaves as expected across multiple layers of the UI and business logic. While unit tests focus on individual classes or methods, integration and widget tests validate how various components work together in real-world use cases.

Flutter provides a rich testing toolkit through flutter_test and integration_test packages, enabling developers to simulate real user flows, test large widget trees, and verify asynchronous behavior. This section dives into best practices, advanced scenarios, and real-world strategies to build resilient, automated UI tests.

Best Practices for Integration Tests

Integration testing in Flutter is a critical step in verifying that your app's features and workflows function as expected in a near-realistic environment. Unlike unit or widget tests, integration tests span multiple widgets and components—often across screens—and simulate actual user interactions from beginning to end. These tests ensure that your app's various parts work together harmoniously.

Flutter's "integration_test" package provides a powerful framework to automate full application flows, making it ideal for regression testing, acceptance criteria validation, and CI/CD pipelines.

🎯 Why Integration Tests Matter

Validate Real User Flows: Ensure that login, onboarding, checkout, and similar flows function correctly.

Catch Systemic Issues: Detect miscommunications between components that unit tests may overlook.

Guard Against Regressions: Automate the verification of business-critical workflows after each code change.

🛠 Integration Testing Setup in Flutter

To get started with integration tests in Flutter

1. Add the dependency to "pubspec.yaml":

```
dev_dependencies:
  integration_test:
  flutter_test:
```

2. Create a test file in "integration_test/":

```
import 'package:integration_test/integration_test.dart';
import 'package:flutter_test/flutter_test.dart';
import 'package:your_app/main.dart' as app;
void main() {
  IntegrationTestWidgetsFlutterBinding.ensureInitialized();
  testWidgets('End-to-end login flow', (tester) async {
    app.main();
    await tester.pumpAndSettle();
    await tester.enterText(find.byKey(Key('email')),
    'user@example.com');
```

```
    await tester.enterText(find.byKey(Key('password')),
'secure123');
    await tester.tap(find.byKey(Key('loginButton')));
    await tester.pumpAndSettle();
    expect(find.text('Welcome back'), findsOneWidget);
  });
}
```

3. Run the test:

```
flutter test integration_test/app_test.dart
```

✅ Best Practices for Reliable Integration Tests

1. **Test Only What Matters Most**

   Integration tests are inherently slower and more complex. Focus on business-critical flows:

   Authentication

   Payment processes

   User registration

   Checkout or booking systems

2. **Design for Testability**

   Assign "Key" identifiers to interactive and critical widgets:
   ```
   TextField(key: Key('email')),
   ElevatedButton(key: Key('loginButton'), ...)
   ```

   Avoid relying on labels or visual hierarchy to find widgets.

3. **Use "pumpAndSettle()" Liberally**

   UI transitions, animations, and asynchronous operations need time to settle:

   ```
   await tester.pumpAndSettle();
   // Wait for all pending animations and futures
   ```

4. **Mock Network and Dependencies**

   Integration tests should be predictable. Use

   Local test servers

   In-app dependency overrides

   Mock clients (e.g., "mockito," "http_mock_adapter") to simulate API responses

5. **Clean and Isolate State Between Tests**

   Always reset app state after each test run to avoid carry-over issues:

   ```
   tearDown(() {
     // Clear storage, logout user, reset
         database, etc.
   });
   ```

6. **Avoid UI Flakiness**

   Disable animations during tests if they cause flaky behavior.

   Use "tester.pump(Duration(seconds: x))" to step through animation frames deterministically.

7. **Run Tests on Real Devices (CI and Local)**

   While emulators work well, some edge cases (e.g., camera, push notifications) behave differently on real devices. Use

   Firebase Test Lab

   Physical test phones in CI pipelines

   Device emulators with multiple screen sizes

📋 Integration Test Checklist

Task	Recommended Practice
Simulate user inputs	Use `tester.enterText()`
Verify state after actions	Use `expect()` checks
Wait for animations/network	Use `pumpAndSettle()`
Locate widgets	Use `Key()` for reliability
Reset state	Use `tearDown()` hooks
Test full flows only	Focus on critical paths
Run tests in CI/CD	Automate with GitHub Actions, Bitrise, etc.

🔍 Real-World Example: End-to-End Checkout Test

```
testWidgets('E-commerce checkout flow', (tester) async {
  app.main();
  await tester.pumpAndSettle();
  // Add product to cart
  await tester.tap(find.byKey(Key('add_to_cart')));
  await tester.pumpAndSettle();
  // Go to cart
  await tester.tap(find.byKey(Key('cart_icon')));
  await tester.pumpAndSettle();
```

```
  // Proceed to checkout
  await tester.tap(find.byKey(Key('checkout_button')));
  await tester.pumpAndSettle();
  // Verify confirmation screen
  expect(find.text('Order Confirmed'), findsOneWidget);
});
```

> **Expert Insight**
>
> *Integration tests aren't about testing everything—they're about testing what must work. Prioritize high-risk, high-value user flows and invest in solid test foundations.*
>
> —Amelia Tran, Flutter QA Lead, AppScale

Performance and Flakiness Alert
Avoid Timeouts: Set "timeout" on tests to prevent indefinite hangs.
Minimize Dependencies: External systems = higher test flakiness.
Use Snapshots for Visual Diffing: Consider "golden tests" for consistent UI checks when applicable.

Advanced Widget Testing Scenarios

As Flutter apps grow in complexity, so does the widget tree. Testing advanced widget scenarios requires more than basic expect() assertions—it demands strategies for navigating deeply nested structures, simulating intricate user behaviors, and validating nuanced UI states like animations or gestures. This section dives deep into practical techniques for handling complex widget hierarchies and dynamic interactions.

Widget testing sits between unit tests and integration tests—it's fast like unit tests but simulates UI rendering and user input like integration tests. The goal is to verify widget behavior in isolation or within a constrained widget environment.

When to Use Advanced Widget Testing

When widgets render dynamic content based on state or data

When layout depends on screen size, orientation, or themes

When widgets use animations, gestures, or custom rendering logic

When debugging complex navigation, tab flows, or dialogs

Handling Complex Widget Trees

As your Flutter application evolves into a large-scale production system, the widget tree often becomes a dense structure of nested components, inherited widgets, providers, and custom render objects. Testing these complex widget hierarchies is critical to maintaining UI integrity and functional correctness, especially when subtle changes deep in the tree can introduce unexpected regressions.

This section focuses on strategies and techniques for effectively writing tests for deeply nested, stateful, and dynamic widget structures.

Understanding the Challenge

Flutter's declarative UI model makes it easy to build UIs using composition. However, this also means widgets can be deeply nested, with visual elements depending on dynamic state, external dependencies, and context propagation.

Challenges include

Locating widgets buried under multiple layers

Verifying the presence of widgets with conditional visibility

Interacting with elements that rely on state management

Managing test isolation when shared contexts like "Provider," "Bloc," or "InheritedWidget" are involved

💡 Best Practices for Testing Deep Widget Trees

1. **Use Meaningful "Keys" for Critical Widgets**

    Assign unique "Keys" to important interactive or data-displaying widgets. This enables precise and reliable identification in tests.

    ```
    Text('Username', key: Key('username_label'));
    ```

2. **Prefer "find.byKey()" and "find.byType()" over "find.text()"**

    Avoid relying solely on text-based selectors, especially when the same text appears in multiple places.

    ```
    final usernameField = find.byKey(Key('username_input'));
    ```

3. **Use "find.descendant()" for Scoped Queries**

    When you want to test a widget in a specific part of the tree:

```
final parent = find.byKey(Key('profile_card'));
  final child = find.descendant(
    of: parent,
    matching: find.byKey(Key('username_label')),
  );
  expect(child, findsOneWidget);
```

4. **Wrap with Necessary Ancestors in Tests**

   If your widget relies on specific ancestors like "MaterialApp," "Theme," or "MediaQuery," make sure to include them in your test tree:

```
await tester.pumpWidget(
    MaterialApp(
      home: MyComplexWidget(),
    ),
);
```

5. **Inject Dependencies via Mocks or Fakes**

   If your widget consumes state via Provider or Bloc, inject mock/fake versions for deterministic testing:

```
  await tester.pumpWidget(
    MultiProvider(
      providers: [
        ChangeNotifierProvider(create: (_) =>
        MockUserModel()),
```

CHAPTER 12 ADVANCED TESTING AND CI/CD FOR FLUTTER

```
    ],
    child: MyComplexWidget(),
  ),
);
```

♣ Real-World Example: Testing Nested Form Inputs

Consider a widget tree like this:

```
MaterialApp
 └ Scaffold
    └ ProfileForm
       ├ TextField (key: 'username')
       └ TextField (key: 'email')
```

Test to ensure the username field appears and accepts input:

```
testWidgets('Username field exists and accepts input',
(tester) async {
  await tester.pumpWidget(MaterialApp(home: ProfileForm()));
  final usernameField = find.byKey(Key('username'));
  expect(usernameField, findsOneWidget);
  await tester.enterText(usernameField, 'john_doe');
  expect(find.text('john_doe'), findsOneWidget);
});
```

CHAPTER 12   ADVANCED TESTING AND CI/CD FOR FLUTTER

🔧 Debugging and Inspecting Complex Trees
Use "debugDumpApp()":

Outputs the full widget tree to the console, useful for visually locating widgets.

Leverage Flutter DevTools:

Navigate the widget inspector to explore widget relationships and layout structure.

Use "tester.widget<T>()" to Access Widget Properties:

```
final textField = tester.widget<TextField>(find.
byKey(Key('username')));
expect(textField.enabled, isTrue);
```

Use "tester.state<T>()" for Stateful Widgets:

To inspect or manipulate internal state:

```
final state = tester.state<ProfileFormState>(find.
byType(ProfileForm));
expect(state.isValid, isTrue);
```

✅ Checklist: Testing Complex Widget Trees

Item	Description
●	Are all interactive elements uniquely keyed?
●	Are required ancestors (like 'MaterialApp') included?
●	Are dependencies like 'Provider' mocked or injected?
●	Are nested widgets being tested with 'find.descendant()'?
●	Are widget states and outputs being validated thoroughly?

💡 Expert Insight

Test readability is as important as test reliability. Use scoped queries, custom matchers, and logical naming conventions to keep your widget tests clean and understandable.

—Shruti Agarwal, Senior Flutter QA Engineer at Codemate

📢 Performance Alert

Avoid unnecessarily deep nesting in widget tests. If you're testing behavior in isolation, break complex widgets into smaller testable units and test them separately. This improves test speed and reliability.

Testing Animations and UI Interactions

Animations and user interactions bring your Flutter applications to life. However, they also introduce asynchronous behaviors, frame-dependent transitions, and state changes that make testing more challenging than static UI elements. Ensuring the reliability of animated sequences, gesture responses, and interactive transitions is essential for delivering a smooth, bug-free experience to users.

This section explores techniques to effectively test animations, transitions, and rich UI interactions in Flutter, including best practices for synchronization, gesture simulation, and time manipulation.

🎯 Goals of Animation and Interaction Testing

Verify that animations trigger correctly and follow expected timing.
Ensure gesture-based navigation or transitions behave predictably.
Test dynamic visual responses to user input (e.g., drag, tap, scroll).
Validate UI state before, during, and after animations complete.

🧪 Techniques for Testing Animations

1. **Using "tester.pump()" and "tester.pump(Duration)"**

    You control time progression in widget tests with "pump()":

    ```
    await tester.pump(); // Triggers a frame.
    await tester.pump(const Duration(seconds: 1));
    // Simulates passage of time.
    ```

    Use this to simulate the animation duration and assert intermediate/final states.

    ```
    await tester.pumpWidget(MyAnimatedWidget());
    await tester.pump(); // Start animation
    await tester.pump(const Duration(milliseconds: 500));
    // Halfway
    expect(someWidgetOpacity, lessThan(1.0));
    await tester.pumpAndSettle(); // Let animation finish
    ```

2. **Verifying Visual Transitions**

    You can assert that animations changed widget properties like "opacity," "position," or "scale" by accessing widget instances:

    ```
    final fadeWidget = tester.widget<FadeTransition>(find.byType(FadeTransition));
    expect(fadeWidget.opacity.value, closeTo(0.5, 0.1));
    ```

3. **Testing Explicit Animations with Controllers**

   For widgets using "AnimationController," you can directly drive animation values:

   ```
   controller.forward();
   await tester.pump(); // Apply the animation frame
   expect(controller.value, equals(1.0));
   ```

👋 Testing Gesture Interactions

Gesture-based interactions such as taps, swipes, and long presses are central to mobile UX. Flutter's test framework provides rich APIs to simulate them:

✅ **Taps and Long Presses**:

```
await tester.tap(find.byKey(Key('login_button')));
await tester.pump(); // Rebuild the UI after interaction
await tester.longPress(find.text('Hold Me'));
await tester.pump();
```

✅ **Drag and Swipe Gestures**:

```
await tester.drag(find.byType(ListView), const Offset(0, -200));
await tester.pumpAndSettle();
```

Use this to test scrolling, swipe to dismiss, or gesture-based page transitions.

⏱ Handling Animation Timing: "pumpAndSettle()"

"pumpAndSettle()" repeatedly calls "pump()" until all animations have settled. Ideal for full animation flows:

```
await tester.tap(find.byKey(Key('expand_button')));
await tester.pumpAndSettle(); // Wait for expansion animation
                                to finish
expect(find.byKey(Key('expanded_content')), findsOneWidget);
```

⚠ Avoid "pumpAndSettle()" in infinite animations (e.g., spinners), or use time-bounded pumping.

🎁 Real-World Example: Testing an Animated Modal

```
testWidgets('Modal appears with fade-in animation',
(tester) async {
  await tester.pumpWidget(MyApp());
  await tester.tap(find.byKey(Key('show_modal')));
  await tester.pump(); // Start animation
  expect(find.byType(FadeTransition), findsOneWidget);
  // Progress halfway
  await tester.pump(const Duration(milliseconds: 150));
  final fade = tester.widget<FadeTransition>(find.byType
  (FadeTransition));
  expect(fade.opacity.value, lessThan(1.0));
  await tester.pumpAndSettle(); // Finish animation
  expect(find.text('Welcome to Modal'), findsOneWidget);
});
```

Tips for Testing Interactive UI Patterns

Pattern	Testing Tip
Animated buttons	Verify scale/opacity changes on tap using 'tester.widget()'
Swipe to dismiss	Use 'tester.drag()' with threshold values to simulate swipes
Animated navigations (PageRoute)	Test with 'pumpAndSettle()' after 'Navigator.push()' or 'pop()'
Interactive transitions	Pump frame-by-frame to check interpolation states (e.g., carousel sliders)

Checklist: Animation and Interaction Tests

Item	Description
■	Are animations tested using 'pump()' with appropriate durations?
■	Are animated widgets inspected via 'tester.widget()' or 'tester.state()'?
■	Are gestures (tap, swipe, drag) simulated realistically?
■	Is 'pumpAndSettle()' used where appropriate?
■	Are tests verifying both start and end states of UI transitions?

CHAPTER 12   ADVANCED TESTING AND CI/CD FOR FLUTTER

💡 Expert Insight

Animation testing is not just about the visual outcome, but about validating fluidity and user feedback. Simulate real-world timing and motion to ensure consistency across devices.

—Daniel Vasquez, Flutter Animation Engineer at Stream

⚠ Performance Alert

Keep animation tests deterministic and short. Avoid relying on real-time delays or infinite animations that can make test suites flaky or slow.

Continuous Integration and Delivery (CI/CD)

Continuous Integration and Continuous Delivery (CI/CD) are essential components of modern Flutter development pipelines, ensuring faster iterations, high code quality, and consistent deployments across multiple platforms. In a cross-platform world where Flutter targets mobile, web, and desktop, the ability to build, test, and deploy automatically is not just a luxury—it's a necessity.

This section guides you through building efficient CI/CD pipelines tailored for Flutter, automating builds with GitHub Actions, and deploying seamlessly to various platforms including Android, iOS, web, and desktop.

Setting Up CI/CD Pipelines for Flutter

In modern app development, Continuous Integration and Continuous Delivery (CI/CD) have become essential to ensure rapid iteration, reliable deployments, and consistent code quality. For Flutter developers building cross-platform apps, setting up a robust CI/CD pipeline ensures every code change is automatically built, tested, and prepared for release—reducing human error and accelerating delivery cycles.

This section walks you through the foundational steps to set up a CI/CD pipeline specifically tailored for Flutter applications.

🚀 What Is a CI/CD Pipeline?

A CI/CD pipeline automates the development lifecycle:

> **CI (Continuous Integration):** Automatically tests and validates code with every push or pull request
>
> **CD (Continuous Delivery/Deployment):** Automates the build and release process to staging or production environments
>
> In Flutter development, this typically includes running analyzers, executing unit and widget tests, building platform-specific artifacts (APK, AAB (Android App Bundle), IPA, Web, etc.), and optionally deploying them to app stores or web servers.

🔧 Key Stages in a Flutter CI/CD Pipeline

Stage	Description	Example Tools/Commands
Code Analysis	Enforce style and catch errors early	`flutter analyze`, `dart format`
Testing	Run unit, widget, and integration tests	`flutter test`, `integration_test`
Building	Compile app for different platforms	`flutter build apk/web/ios`
Deployment	Release artifacts to users or testers	Fastlane, Firebase, GitHub Pages

Choosing a CI/CD Platform

There are several popular CI/CD platforms compatible with Flutter:

> **GitHub Actions**: Integrated with GitHub repositories, supports macOS/Linux runners
>
> **Codemagic**: Purpose-built for Flutter, with great Android/iOS/web support
>
> **Bitrise**: Mobile-first CI/CD with rich Flutter support
>
> **GitLab CI, CircleCI, Jenkins**: Flexible and powerful but require more setup
>
> Each tool allows configuration of workflows using YAML or UI-based editors to define triggers, build steps, and conditions.

Basic CI/CD Workflow for Flutter

A standard Flutter CI/CD workflow includes the following:

1. Checkout source code.
2. Set up Flutter SDK.
3. Install dependencies.
4. Run analysis and tests.
5. Build for required platforms.
6. Deploy or upload artifacts.

Sample CI/CD Workflow (GitHub Actions)

```
name: Flutter CI
```

```
on:
  push:
    branches: [ main ]
  pull_request:
    branches: [ main ]
jobs:
  build:
    runs-on: ubuntu-latest
    steps:
      - name: Checkout code
        uses: actions/checkout@v3
      - name: Set up Flutter
        uses: subosito/flutter-action@v2
        with:
          flutter-version: '3.29.0'
      - name: Install dependencies
        run: flutter pub get
      - name: Analyze code
        run: flutter analyze
      - name: Run tests
        run: flutter test
      - name: Build APK (optional)
        run: flutter build apk --release
```

🔍 This pipeline runs on every push or pull request to "main," ensuring every change is analyzed, tested, and built.

🎬 Pro Tips for CI/CD Setup

Use matrix builds to test across platforms or multiple Flutter versions.

Cache dependencies to speed up builds:

```yaml
uses: actions/cache@v3
  with:
    path: |
      ~/.pub-cache
    key: ${{ runner.os }}-pub-${{ hashFiles('/pubspec.yaml') }}
```

Separate workflows for test, build, and deploy stages for modular control.

Trigger only on tags for production builds or releases:

```yaml
on:
  push:
    tags:
      - 'v..'
```

✅ CI/CD Pipeline Benefits for Flutter

Benefit	Impact
Faster Feedback Loops	Developers know immediately if a change breaks something.
Consistent Quality	Automated linting and testing ensures stable codebases.
Faster Releases	Builds are ready for deployment after each commit.
Reduced Manual Errors	Less human intervention means fewer mistakes.

Section-End Checklist

[x] CI pipeline runs on every push and pull request.

[x] Code is automatically analyzed and tested.

[x] Platform builds (APK, iOS, Web) are generated in CI.

[x] Secrets and credentials are securely managed.

[x] CI jobs are optimized with caching and parallelism.

Expert Insight

Your CI/CD pipeline is your team's safety net. With every commit, you should gain confidence—not fear. Start small, but iterate toward full automation.

—Nikhil Sharma, Flutter DevOps Lead at Bitrise

Automating Flutter Builds with GitHub Actions

GitHub Actions has emerged as one of the most popular CI/CD solutions, especially for teams already hosting their code on GitHub. With native integration, cross-platform support, and a powerful workflow engine, GitHub Actions offers a seamless way to automate Flutter builds across Android, iOS, web, macOS, and Windows targets.

This section focuses on how to configure GitHub Actions to automate Flutter builds—helping you save time, catch issues early, and accelerate delivery.

CHAPTER 12 ADVANCED TESTING AND CI/CD FOR FLUTTER

Why GitHub Actions for Flutter?

Feature	Benefit
Native GitHub integration	No third-party CI tool needed—runs in the same ecosystem as your repo
macOS, Linux, and Windows runners	Build for Android, iOS, web, and desktop with platform-specific runners
Declarative YAML workflows	Easy to version control and customize
Marketplace integrations	Pre-built actions for setup, cache, upload, and notifications

🎁 Setting Up a Flutter Build Workflow

✅ Prerequisites:

Flutter project pushed to a GitHub repository

GitHub Actions enabled in the repository

For iOS Builds: macOS runners and signing certificates (Apple Developer account required)

◾ Sample GitHub Actions Workflow: Android and Web

```
name: Flutter CI/CD Pipeline
on:
  push:
    branches:
      - main
  pull_request:
    branches:
      - main
```

```yaml
jobs:
  build:
    runs-on: ubuntu-latest
    steps:
      - name: Checkout code
        uses: actions/checkout@v3
      - name: Set up Flutter
        uses: subosito/flutter-action@v2
        with:
          flutter-version: '3.29.0'
      - name: Install dependencies
        run: flutter pub get
      - name: Analyze code
        run: flutter analyze
      - name: Run tests
        run: flutter test
      - name: Build Web App
        run: flutter build web
      - name: Build Android APK
        run: flutter build apk --release
      - name: Upload APK Artifact
        uses: actions/upload-artifact@v3
        with:
          name: release-apk
          path: build/app/outputs/flutter-apk/app-release.apk
```

🍎 iOS Builds with GitHub Actions (Advanced)

To build for iOS, use "macos-latest" runners and manage signing via Fastlane (https://docs.fastlane.tools/) or Xcode build configurations. Ensure you securely manage certificates and provisioning profiles using GitHub secrets.

CHAPTER 12   ADVANCED TESTING AND CI/CD FOR FLUTTER

```
runs-on: macos-latest
steps:
  - name: Set up Flutter
    uses: subosito/flutter-action@v2
    with:
      flutter-version: '3.29.0'
  - name: Build iOS App
    run: flutter build ipa --release
```

> ⚠ **Note**   iOS builds require a valid signing setup with a registered Apple Developer account.

🚀 Triggering Builds

You can trigger builds for various Git events:

Trigger Type	Use Case
'push'	On every commit
'pull_request'	For PR validation
'tags'	On release tagging (e.g., v1.0.0)
'schedule'	Nightly builds
'workflow_dispatch'	Manual trigger from GitHub UI

```
on:
  push:
    tags:
      - 'v..'
```

📁 Recommended Add-Ons

Caching: Speed up builds by caching the pub cache:

```
- uses: actions/cache@v3
  with:
    path: |
      ~/.pub-cache
    key: ${{ runner.os }}-pub-${{ hashFiles('/pubspec.yaml') }}
```

> **Slack/Discord Notifications**: Add build status alerts for team visibility.
>
> **Codecov Integration**: Report test coverage automatically after tests.
>
> **Secrets Management**: Store API keys, signing certificates, and tokens using GitHub Secrets.

📈 Metrics and Monitoring

Use GitHub Actions' native interface to track

> Build durations
>
> Success/failure rates
>
> Historical trends
>
> Artifact download metrics

For enhanced visibility, integrate with third-party dashboards or monitoring systems.

CHAPTER 12   ADVANCED TESTING AND CI/CD FOR FLUTTER

📋 Section-End Checklist

[x] Flutter builds for Android, web, and optionally iOS are automated.

[x] Build artifacts (e.g., APKs) are uploaded after success.

[x] Code analysis and testing are part of every build.

[x] Secrets are used for secure key and certificate management.

[x] CI runs on every commit, pull request, or release tag.

💡 Expert Insight

GitHub Actions makes automation accessible—even for solo Flutter devs. With just a few lines of YAML, you can catch bugs, deploy web builds, or deliver signed APKs while you sleep.

—Marina Gomez, CI/CD Engineer at FlutterHub.io

Deploying to Multiple Platforms with CI/CD

One of Flutter's greatest strengths lies in its ability to target multiple platforms—Android, iOS, web, desktop (macOS, Windows, Linux)—from a single codebase. However, managing deployments across these platforms can become complex without proper CI/CD automation.

This section explores how to streamline deployments for multiple platforms using CI/CD pipelines. You'll learn how to automatically build, sign, and distribute your Flutter apps to Google Play, Apple App Store, Firebase Hosting, GitHub Pages, and desktop delivery channels—all from your CI pipeline.

CHAPTER 12 ADVANCED TESTING AND CI/CD FOR FLUTTER

🌐 Platform-Specific Deployment Strategies

Platform	Target Artifact	Deployment Channel
Android	APK / AAB	Google Play Store, Firebase App Distribution
iOS	IPA	Apple App Store, TestFlight
Web	'/build/web' folder	Firebase Hosting, GitHub Pages, Netlify
macOS/Linux	'.dmg' / '.deb' / '.exe'	GitHub Releases, S3, custom installers
Windows	'.msix' / '.exe'	Microsoft Store, GitHub Releases

🚀 Android Deployment with GitHub Actions

You can automate publishing APKs or AABs to Google Play Store using Fastlane (https://docs.fastlane.tools/) and service account credentials.

📄 Example Workflow Snippet:

```
name: Deploy to Google Play
  uses: r0adkll/upload-google-play@v1
  with:
    serviceAccountJson: ${{ secrets.GOOGLE_PLAY_CREDENTIALS }}
    packageName: com.example.app
    releaseFiles: build/app/outputs/bundle/release/app-release.aab
    track: production
```

🔒 Use "GOOGLE_PLAY_CREDENTIALS" secret to securely store your service account key.

🍎 iOS Deployment to TestFlight or App Store

For iOS deployment, you'll need

- A macOS runner ("macos-latest")
- Provisioning profiles and certificates
- Fastlane for signing and uploading

```yaml
name: Deploy to TestFlight
  run: |
    bundle install
    bundle exec fastlane ios beta
```

💡 You can also use "match" (Fastlane's code signing tool) to simplify certificate management across teams.

🌐 Web Deployment (Firebase Hosting or GitHub Pages)

✅ **Firebase Hosting:**

```yaml
name: Deploy to Firebase Hosting
  uses: FirebaseExtended/action-hosting-deploy@v0
  with:
    repoToken: "${{ secrets.GITHUB_TOKEN }}"
    firebaseServiceAccount: "${{ secrets.FIREBASE_SERVICE_ACCOUNT }}"
    channelId: live
    projectId: your-project-id
```

CHAPTER 12 ADVANCED TESTING AND CI/CD FOR FLUTTER

✅ **GitHub Pages**:

```
name: Deploy to GitHub Pages
  uses: peaceiris/actions-gh-pages@v3
  with:
    github_token: ${{ secrets.GITHUB_TOKEN }}
    publish_dir: ./build/web
```

🖥 **Desktop Deployment (macOS, Windows, Linux)**

While still evolving, you can package and distribute desktop builds manually or via automation. Use build runners and GitHub Releases for cross-platform binaries.

🎁 **Example Snippet for Packaging and Uploading a macOS App:**

```
name: Build macOS App
  run: flutter build macos
- name: Zip and Upload
  run: zip -r FlutterApp-macos.zip build/macos/Build/Products/Release/
- name: Upload to GitHub Releases
  uses: ncipollo/release-action@v1
  with:
    artifacts: FlutterApp-macos.zip
    token: ${{ secrets.GITHUB_TOKEN }}
```

💼 **Multi-platform Release Matrix**

Use GitHub Actions' "matrix" strategy to build and deploy for multiple platforms in parallel:

```
strategy:
  matrix:
    os: [ubuntu-latest, macos-latest, windows-latest]
```

⚠ **Note** Platform-specific runners are required for corresponding builds (e.g., macOS for iOS/macOS, Windows for ".msix").

📋 **Section-End Checklist**

[x] Android deployments are automated via AAB to Google Play.

[x] iOS apps are delivered via TestFlight or App Store.

[x] Web builds are hosted on Firebase or GitHub Pages.

[x] macOS, Windows, and Linux apps are built and uploaded as binaries.

[x] All secrets (signing, API keys) are securely stored and accessed via CI.

💡 **Expert Insight**

Cross-platform deployment with Flutter is powerful, but automation makes it scalable. A well-orchestrated CI/CD pipeline ensures every user—regardless of device—gets your latest build quickly and reliably.

—Samir Patel, DevOps Architect and Flutter Contributor

Automated Test Reports and Debugging

After building robust tests and setting up CI/CD pipelines, the final piece of a production-grade Flutter development workflow is automated test reporting and streamlined debugging. Automated test reports help you monitor code quality, identify regressions, and ensure new code doesn't break existing functionality. Meanwhile, debugging CI/CD failures and performance bottlenecks ensures that your automation infrastructure remains resilient and fast.

This section walks through how to generate actionable test coverage reports, debug failed builds, and pinpoint bottlenecks in your pipelines.

Generating Test Coverage Reports

Test coverage is a crucial metric in evaluating the effectiveness of your automated tests. It measures the percentage of your source code that is exercised when running tests. In Flutter development, generating coverage reports allows you to identify untested parts of your codebase and enforce higher code quality through visibility and accountability.

This section walks you through generating coverage reports, integrating them with CI tools, visualizing the results, and using the data to drive better testing practices.

📌 **What Is Code Coverage?**

Code coverage typically includes

> **Line Coverage:** Percentage of executed lines of code
>
> **Function Coverage:** Percentage of functions or methods called
>
> **Branch Coverage:** Percentage of decision points (e.g., if/else) executed

While 100% coverage is not always practical or necessary, achieving high coverage for critical logic reduces the risk of regressions and improves maintainability.

🛠 Generating Coverage Reports Locally

Flutter includes native support for generating code coverage reports using the "flutter test" command.

```
flutter test --coverage
```

This creates a "coverage/lcov.info" file using the LCOV (`https://ltp.sourceforge.net/coverage/lcov.php`) format, which is widely supported across CI/CD and code analysis tools.

🧭 Visualizing Coverage with HTML Reports

To visualize code coverage locally, convert the "lcov.info" file into an interactive HTML report using "genhtml."

Install lcov (macOS/Linux):

```
brew install lcov
```

Generate the report:

```
genhtml coverage/lcov.info -o coverage/html
open coverage/html/index.html
```

This launches a browser window with a fully navigable report showing covered and uncovered lines, files, and percentages.

> **♥ Tip** Exclude generated files and test-related utilities using "lcov" filters or ".coveralls.yml" configuration to avoid skewed results.

🚀 Integrating with CI/CD

To enforce and monitor test coverage in your CI/CD pipeline, integrate tools like Codecov, Coveralls, or SonarQube.

Example—Codecov Integration (GitHub Actions):

```yaml
name: Run tests with coverage
  run: flutter test --coverage
- name: Upload coverage to Codecov
  uses: codecov/codecov-action@v3
  with:
    token: ${{ secrets.CODECOV_TOKEN }}
    files: coverage/lcov.info
    flags: unittests
    name: flutter-coverage-report
```

🔐 Store your Codecov token securely using GitHub Secrets ("CODECOV_TOKEN").

This provides a dashboard with trend graphs, per-PR coverage diffs, and repository-wide insights.

📉 Enforcing Minimum Coverage Thresholds

To maintain quality over time, define a minimum acceptable test coverage threshold in your pipeline.

Sample Bash Check:

```
lcov --summary coverage/lcov.info | grep -E "lines.*%" | awk '{ print $2 }' | cut -d'%' -f1
```

You can use this value to conditionally fail your build if coverage drops below your desired threshold (e.g., 80%).

⚠ Keep in mind that coverage alone doesn't indicate test quality. A high-coverage test suite can still miss edge cases or critical logic if tests are shallow or repetitive.

🧩 Common Pitfalls and Best Practices

Pitfall	Solution
Coverage includes generated code	Use lcov filters or exclude in CI configuration
Tests don't trigger coverage	Ensure tests import and exercise the target files
CI report is outdated	Clean 'coverage/' folder before running tests

✅ Best Practices

Prioritize coverage on business-critical and core logic.

Use branch coverage, not just line coverage, to detect untested conditional paths.

Automate coverage checks to block low-quality pull requests.

Visualize coverage changes in each PR to inform reviewers.

📋 Section-End Checklist

[x] Generated coverage reports using "flutter test --coverage"

[x] Visualized reports using "genhtml" and lcov

[x] Integrated reports into GitHub Actions via Codecov

[x] Enforced minimum coverage thresholds

[x] Excluded irrelevant files from the coverage report

💡 Expert Insight

Treat code coverage as a compass, not a destination. It tells you where your tests are going—but not whether you're testing the right things. Focus on meaningful tests and use coverage to support, not define, your testing strategy.

—Julia Ramos, Lead QA Automation Engineer

Debugging CI/CD Failures and Performance Bottlenecks

CI/CD pipelines are the backbone of modern Flutter development workflows, enabling teams to continuously build, test, and deploy high-quality applications across platforms. However, even the most sophisticated pipelines are prone to build failures, flaky tests, and performance regressions. Without an effective debugging strategy, these issues can stall development, introduce technical debt, or even cause production outages.

This section explores the common causes of CI/CD failures in Flutter projects and presents a systematic approach to debugging and optimizing pipeline performance.

🐛 Common CI/CD Failure Scenarios

Failure Type	Likely Causes
iOS build failures	Missing provisioning profile, invalid code signing, wrong Xcode version
Flaky widget/integration tests	Asynchronous operations not awaited, animations not settled, timing issues
Dependency resolution errors	Incompatible 'pubspec.yaml' versions, network issues with 'pub get'
Platform-specific test failures	Platform channel code not properly stubbed in tests
Toolchain mismatch	CI runner using outdated Flutter/Dart versions
API/Network call failures	Missing mock servers or API keys in CI environment

⚠ **Tip** Always replicate the environment locally (same OS, Flutter version, and toolchain) to isolate issues faster.

🧪 Debugging Techniques

1. **Enable Verbose Logging**
   Verbose output helps identify the root cause of test and build issues:

CHAPTER 12 ADVANCED TESTING AND CI/CD FOR FLUTTER

```
flutter test -v
flutter build apk --verbose
```

In CI systems like GitHub Actions or GitLab CI, make sure to preserve logs as build artifacts for post-mortem analysis.

2. **Use Artifact Uploads**

    When a CI job fails, you can upload logs, screenshots, and debug output as artifacts:

    ```
    name: Upload build logs
      uses: actions/upload-artifact@v3
      with:
        name: flutter-build-logs
        path: build/
    ```

3. **Rerun Failed Jobs with SSH**

    In GitHub Actions or CircleCI, enable "Rerun job with SSH" to step into the failed environment and debug interactively.

4. **Isolate by Testing in Stages**

    Break CI pipelines into granular steps (e.g., "analyze," "test," "build," "deploy"). This helps identify failure points faster.

```
jobs:
  test:
    steps:
      - run: flutter analyze
      - run: flutter test
```

5. **Reproduce Locally with Docker**

   Use Docker or custom scripts to replicate the CI build process locally:

   ```
   docker run -it --rm \
     -v "$PWD":/app \
     cirrusci/flutter:stable bash
   ```

Performance Bottlenecks in CI

CI performance issues can arise from

- Uncached Flutter SDK or pub packages

- Rebuilding artifacts unnecessarily

- Running tests serially instead of in parallel

- Running full tests for every minor change (e.g., doc edits)

CHAPTER 12 ADVANCED TESTING AND CI/CD FOR FLUTTER

🔧 Optimization Strategies

Strategy	Benefit
Cache '.pub-cache' and '.dart_tool'	Avoid re-downloading dependencies
Use matrix builds	Run Android and iOS builds/test jobs in parallel
Parallelize test runs	Reduce total CI duration
Conditionally skip redundant jobs	Avoid running builds for unchanged code
Use precompiled artifacts	Skip repeated compilation in monorepos

Example: GitHub Actions Cache for Dependencies

```
name: Cache Flutter packages
  uses: actions/cache@v3
  with:
    path: |
      ~/.pub-cache
      .dart_tool
    key: ${{ runner.os }}-pub-${{ hashFiles('/pubspec.yaml') }}
```

⚡ Caching alone can shave 30–60% off total CI runtimes in medium-sized projects.

🔍 Diagnosing Performance Regressions

- Monitor job execution times over time using CI dashboards.
- Introduce telemetry for test durations and build stages.

Use a CI profiler (e.g., GitHub Actions Insights or GitLab Metrics) to identify which jobs consume the most time.

📋 Section-End Checklist

> [x] CI/CD failures are isolated using logging and artifact inspection.
>
> [x] Verbose logs and SSH access are leveraged for debugging.
>
> [x] Pipelines are modular and reproducible locally.
>
> [x] CI performance is optimized using caching and parallelism.
>
> [x] Job durations are continuously monitored for regressions.

💡 Expert Insight

Debugging CI/CD isn't just about fixing what's broken— it's about building visibility and resilience into your delivery pipeline. Automate, cache, isolate, and monitor: these are the pillars of scalable DevOps in Flutter.

—Martin Aguilar, DevOps Architect and Flutter Infra Contributor

Summary

Here, we delivered a deep, practical exploration of advanced testing methodologies and CI/CD strategies essential for building resilient and scalable Flutter applications. Beginning with unit testing, it emphasized writing effective, maintainable tests for business logic and widget behavior, including the use of mocking and stubbing to simulate dependencies and isolate components.

CHAPTER 12   ADVANCED TESTING AND CI/CD FOR FLUTTER

Building upon this foundation, the chapter transitioned into comprehensive integration and widget testing practices, highlighting the importance of test coverage for complex widget trees, animations, and user interactions. It detailed how to validate real-world app flows and UI consistency under asynchronous conditions.

The latter half of the chapter focused on integrating Flutter projects into automated DevOps pipelines. It provided a structured approach to setting up CI/CD using tools like GitHub Actions, enabling automatic build, test, and deployment processes across Android, iOS, and web platforms. Additionally, the chapter addressed generating test coverage reports, debugging common CI/CD failures, and optimizing pipeline performance through caching, parallelization, and artifact analysis.

CHAPTER 13

Flutter for Embedded Systems

In the previous chapter, we explored how to build resilient, production-ready Flutter applications by implementing advanced testing strategies and integrating robust CI/CD pipelines. From writing unit tests for complex widget trees to deploying apps across multiple platforms using GitHub Actions, you learned how to ensure that your Flutter projects maintain high quality and scalability across the entire development lifecycle.

Now, here, we shift our focus to a cutting-edge frontier in Flutter development: embedded systems. While Flutter has established itself as a powerful framework for mobile, web, and desktop platforms, its growing potential in the world of embedded computing opens exciting new opportunities. With advances in hardware abstraction and community-driven tooling, developers can now leverage Flutter's expressive UI capabilities and high-performance rendering engine on low-power, hardware-constrained devices.

Imagine creating rich interfaces for smart home controllers, automotive infotainment systems, IoT dashboards, or industrial displays—all using the same Flutter codebase you're familiar with. Whether you're targeting a Raspberry Pi, a custom ARM-based board, or a Linux-powered kiosk, Flutter offers an elegant and increasingly viable path to modern UI development in embedded contexts.

CHAPTER 13   FLUTTER FOR EMBEDDED SYSTEMS

Here, you will

> Understand what embedded systems are and how Flutter fits into this domain.
>
> Learn how to set up development environments on devices like Raspberry Pi.
>
> Explore best practices for building and optimizing Flutter apps for embedded hardware.
>
> Interact with peripherals using GPIO (General-Purpose Input/Output), I2C (Inter-Integrated Circuit), and other interfaces via Dart FFI (Foreign Function Interface) or platform channels.
>
> Analyze challenges such as performance bottlenecks, hardware-specific quirks, and limited memory availability.
>
> Study real-world implementations of Flutter in embedded consumer and IoT devices.

By the end of this chapter, you'll be equipped with the knowledge to push Flutter beyond its traditional boundaries and into the world of embedded innovation—unlocking opportunities for both experimentation and production-ready solutions.

Introduction to Embedded Systems in Flutter

As software continues to extend its reach beyond traditional computing devices, the demand for powerful yet intuitive user interfaces in embedded systems has never been higher. Embedded devices—once confined to low-level programming and static interfaces—are now expected to deliver interactive, responsive, and visually rich experiences. Flutter, with its high-performance rendering engine and modern UI paradigm, is increasingly being adopted to meet these expectations.

This section sets the stage for understanding how Flutter fits into the embedded ecosystem. We begin by defining what embedded systems are and then examine the specific challenges and opportunities of running Flutter on embedded platforms, such as Raspberry Pi and other ARM-based Linux devices.

What Are Embedded Systems?

Embedded systems are dedicated computing systems that are designed to perform specific, predefined tasks within a larger mechanical or electrical system. Unlike general-purpose computers such as desktops or smartphones, embedded systems are typically resource-constrained, both in terms of computational power and memory, and are optimized for efficiency, stability, and real-time responsiveness.

At a high level, an embedded system integrates three primary components:

> **Hardware**: This includes microcontrollers (MCUs), microprocessors (MPUs), sensors, and actuators. The hardware is typically designed for low power consumption and small form factors, making it suitable for integration into appliances, industrial machines, vehicles, consumer electronics, and more.
>
> **Software (Firmware)**: Embedded systems run tightly controlled, task-specific software often written in low-level languages like C or C++. This firmware operates close to the hardware, managing device behavior and interaction with peripherals.

Peripheral Interfaces: These include GPIO (General-Purpose Input/Output) pins, I2C (Inter-Integrated Circuit), SPI (Serial Peripheral Interface), UART (Universal Asynchronous Receiver/Transmitter), ADCs (Analog-to-Digital Converters), and more. These interfaces allow the embedded system to communicate with external hardware components.

Characteristics of Embedded Systems

Dedicated Functionality: Embedded systems are tailored for a singular or narrow set of tasks—unlike general-purpose devices that run a wide range of applications.

Real-Time Operation: Many embedded systems require real-time processing, meaning they must respond to inputs or changes in the environment within strict timing constraints.

Resource Constraints: These systems often operate with minimal CPU, RAM, and storage and may lack access to a traditional OS or display.

Stability and Longevity: Embedded devices are frequently deployed in the field for long durations and must operate reliably, sometimes for years, without failure or the need for frequent updates.

Energy Efficiency: Especially in battery-powered devices or remote environments, embedded systems are optimized for low energy consumption.

Examples of Embedded Systems

Consumer Electronics: Smart TVs, digital cameras, microwave ovens, and smart thermostats

Automotive Systems: Engine control units (ECUs), infotainment systems, ADAS (Advanced Driver-Assistance Systems)

Industrial Automation: PLCs (Programmable Logic Controllers), sensor networks, control panels

Healthcare Devices: Portable monitors, insulin pumps, diagnostic machines

IoT Devices: Smart sensors, home automation hubs, environmental monitors

Embedded Systems vs. Traditional Computing

Feature	Embedded System	General-Purpose Computer
Purpose	Specific, task-oriented	Multipurpose
Operating System	Often minimal or real-time OS (RTOS)	Full-featured OS (Linux, Windows)
Resources (CPU, RAM)	Highly constrained	Relatively abundant
User Interface	Often minimal or non-existent	Rich graphical interface
Development Language	Low-level (C/C++, Assembly)	High-level (Java, Python, Dart)
Update Cycle	Infrequent or static	Frequent and flexible

With this foundational understanding of what embedded systems are and how they function, we can now explore how Flutter—a high-level, UI-rich SDK—can be adapted to run in such environments. In the next section, we'll examine how Flutter can operate on embedded platforms like the Raspberry Pi and what's required to bridge the gap between modern UI frameworks and constrained hardware.

Running Flutter on Embedded Platforms

Bringing Flutter to embedded platforms is a bold step toward unifying user experience development across mobile, desktop, and hardware-level systems. Although Flutter was originally designed for mobile and later expanded to web and desktop, its adaptable architecture and open source nature make it possible to deploy Flutter apps on embedded devices—such as Raspberry Pi, BeagleBone, Jetson Nano, and other Linux-based boards.

Here, we explore how Flutter operates in embedded environments, what prerequisites are required to make it work, and what makes this approach both promising and challenging for developers.

Conceptual Overview

When Flutter runs on embedded platforms, it typically uses the same rendering and engine layer as it does on Linux desktops, but without the conveniences of a window manager or full OS support. Most embedded devices lack a display server (like X11 or Wayland) and rely on direct rendering to a framebuffer (e.g., "/dev/fb0") or through EGL (Embedded OpenGL) over DRM/KMS (Direct Rendering Manager/Kernel Mode Setting).

The Flutter app runs as a native Linux binary, built specifically for the hardware's architecture (usually ARMv7 or ARM64), and uses the Flutter engine to render UI directly to the screen. The Dart runtime executes the application logic, while interactions with device hardware can be made using platform channels, native plugins, or Dart FFI (Foreign Function Interface).

CHAPTER 13 FLUTTER FOR EMBEDDED SYSTEMS

📰 Requirements and Setup Considerations

Running Flutter on embedded platforms requires a non-trivial setup compared with mobile or desktop targets. The following are key requirements:

> **Linux-Based OS**: A minimal but functional Linux distribution (e.g., Raspberry Pi OS, Ubuntu Server) with basic system libraries and kernel support.
>
> **Hardware Acceleration**: GPU acceleration support through EGL/OpenGL ES is highly recommended for acceptable performance.
>
> **Rendering Backend**: Framebuffer, X11, or Wayland support for UI output. Many embedded setups use direct framebuffer access or DRM/KMS.
>
> **Cross-Compilation or On-Device Builds**: Depending on the target architecture, you'll either need to cross-compile your Flutter app or build it directly on the device.
>
> **Custom Embedder (Optional)**: Advanced use cases may require creating a custom Flutter embedder in C++ to define how the engine interacts with the OS and hardware.

💡 Expert Insight

Most production-grade embedded Flutter implementations use a custom embedder to precisely control input handling, rendering, and lifecycle behavior—offering much tighter integration with the device.

CHAPTER 13   FLUTTER FOR EMBEDDED SYSTEMS

☼ Architecture of Embedded Flutter Deployment

The core stack for running Flutter on embedded devices typically looks like this:

```
------------------------------------------------------------
[Dart Code + Widgets]
         ↓
[Flutter Framework Layer]
         ↓
[Flutter Engine (C++)]
         ↓
[Custom Embedder / Linux Shell]
         ↓
[Framebuffer / EGL / DRM / X11]
         ↓
[Device Display]
------------------------------------------------------------
```

Additionally, peripheral interaction (e.g., GPIO, I2C, SPI) is handled through

> **Dart FFI**: Binding native C/C++ libraries or device drivers
>
> **Platform Channels**: Communicating with a native C/C++/Rust backend process
>
> **External Microservices**: Accessing hardware via REST or gRPC services over local network or IPC

✓ Benefits of Flutter for Embedded Platforms

Unified Development Experience: Use the same language, tools, and paradigms across mobile, desktop, and embedded systems.

Hot Reload: Rapid UI iteration, even for embedded interfaces (when built/debugged over SSH or via a connected monitor).

Customizable UI: Build immersive UIs without being constrained by traditional embedded UI toolkits (e.g., Qt, GTK).

Reduced Time-to-Market: Flutter's declarative approach dramatically accelerates development for embedded interfaces.

⚠ Challenges and Limitations

Lack of Official Support: Flutter does not currently provide first-class support or documentation for embedded targets.

Performance Tuning: Flutter's default builds may be too heavy for ultra-constrained devices; optimization is often necessary.

Manual Setup Complexity: You may need to manually configure GPU drivers, systemd services, DRM permissions, and EGL surfaces.

Peripheral Access: Native plugins for hardware-level communication (GPIO, sensors) may not exist and often require FFI or external bindings.

No Hot Reload On-Device by Default: Unlike mobile devices connected to IDEs, embedded devices often require manual rebuilds or remote debugging sessions.

🔔 Performance Alert

Without GPU acceleration, Flutter apps may suffer severe frame drops or jank on embedded devices. Always test for proper EGL/OpenGL ES driver support when configuring your environment.

🌐 Real-World Viability

Despite the complexity, companies and independent developers are already shipping products that use Flutter on embedded systems—including smart home hubs, vending machine UIs, digital kiosks, and automotive dashboards. The open nature of Flutter's engine and the ability to write custom embedders make it highly adaptable for bespoke hardware use cases.

CHAPTER 13   FLUTTER FOR EMBEDDED SYSTEMS

Flutter on Raspberry Pi

The Raspberry Pi has emerged as the go-to device for prototyping and deploying lightweight embedded systems, thanks to its affordability, compact size, and broad community support. Running Flutter on a Raspberry Pi bridges the gap between high-fidelity UI development and real-world embedded hardware use cases. This section walks you through the full setup, app development, and peripheral integration using Flutter on Raspberry Pi.

Setting Up Raspberry Pi for Flutter Development

Deploying Flutter on the Raspberry Pi transforms it from a simple single-board computer into a powerful embedded UI platform. With its GPIO pins, HDMI output, and compatibility with Linux distributions, the Raspberry Pi serves as a perfect entry point for embedded Flutter development. This section guides you through preparing your Raspberry Pi environment for building and running Flutter apps efficiently.

🎁 Hardware and Software Requirements

Before starting, ensure you have the following:

- Hardware

- Raspberry Pi 4 Model B (recommended for performance)

- 16GB+ microSD card (Class 10 or UHS-I preferred)

- USB keyboard and mouse

- HDMI display and cable

- Stable power supply (5V 3A minimum)

- Internet connectivity (Ethernet or Wi-Fi)

- Recommended OS

CHAPTER 13 FLUTTER FOR EMBEDDED SYSTEMS

Raspberry Pi OS (64-bit)

Ubuntu 22.04 LTS (ARM64)—for advanced use and wider package compatibility

💡 Expert Insight

Raspberry Pi 3B+ and earlier models can also run Flutter, but may experience performance limitations due to CPU, RAM, and GPU constraints.

💼 Step-by-Step Setup

1. **Flash the Operating System**

   Use the Raspberry Pi Imager (https://www.raspberrypi.com/software/) to flash Raspberry Pi OS or Ubuntu Server:

   Choose Raspberry Pi OS (64-bit) or Ubuntu Server 22.04 LTS.

   Insert the SD card and flash the OS.

   Enable SSH and configure Wi-Fi if needed (via advanced options in the Imager).

2. **Update System Packages**

   After booting and logging in:

   ```
   sudo apt update && sudo apt upgrade -y
   sudo apt install git curl unzip xz-utils libgl1-mesa-dev cmake ninja-build clang pkg-config
   ```

   These are required for compiling native libraries, managing dependencies, and enabling hardware rendering.

3. **Install Flutter SDK**

   Clone the Flutter SDK and add it to your path:

   ```
   git clone https://github.com/flutter/flutter.git -b stable
   echo 'export PATH="$PATH:$HOME/flutter/bin"' >> ~/.bashrc
   source ~/.bashrc
   flutter doctor
   ```

   Resolve any issues shown by "flutter doctor," particularly missing tools or libraries. You may need to install "clang," "libgtk-3-dev," or "make."

4. **Verify Rendering Backend**

   Flutter on Raspberry Pi can render through various backends:

   X11: Works if you're using Raspberry Pi OS with desktop

   Framebuffer ("/dev/fb0"): For direct display rendering (headless mode)

   DRM/KMS with EGL: Recommended for performance and full GPU acceleration

Check OpenGL ES support:

```
glxinfo | grep "OpenGL renderer"
```

CHAPTER 13   FLUTTER FOR EMBEDDED SYSTEMS

If the output shows something like "VC4 V3D" or "Mesa," you're using hardware acceleration. If it says "llvmpipe," you're using software rendering—not ideal.

🖉 Optional: Configure for Headless Operation
For embedded use cases without a full desktop UI

Disable the X server (if running Raspberry Pi OS):

```
sudo systemctl set-default multi-user.target
```

Use a custom embedder or a modified version of "flutter-pi" to render directly to the framebuffer or DRM/KMS.

🔒 Security Note
If running headless and enabling SSH, change the default password and consider using SSH keys for secure access.

✓ Summary Checklist

Task	Status
OS installed and up-to-date	✓
Dependencies ('git', 'clang', 'cmake')	✓
Flutter SDK cloned and configured	✓
'flutter doctor' runs clean	✓
Hardware rendering verified ('glxinfo')	✓

★ **Checklist Complete**: Your Raspberry Pi is now ready to build and run Flutter apps as a lightweight embedded UI device.

CHAPTER 13   FLUTTER FOR EMBEDDED SYSTEMS

Building Flutter Apps for Embedded Systems

Once your Raspberry Pi environment is fully set up, you can begin developing Flutter apps tailored for embedded use cases. Unlike mobile or web, embedded Flutter applications often require close control over resource usage, device hardware integration, and runtime behavior. In this section, we'll explore how to build, configure, and deploy Flutter apps specifically optimized for embedded systems like the Raspberry Pi.

✘ Project Setup

Begin by creating a new Flutter project or using an existing one:

```
flutter create embedded_demo
cd embedded_demo
```

For embedded systems, prefer using the barebones widget tree initially—without resource-heavy plugins—to ensure efficient performance during testing.

Modify App Entry Point (Optional)

To simplify the UI for embedded devices, strip down the "main.dart" to something minimal:

```
void main() => runApp(
  const MaterialApp(
    debugShowCheckedModeBanner: false,
    home: Scaffold(
      backgroundColor: Colors.black,
      body: Center(
        child: Text(
          'Hello Embedded!',
          style: TextStyle(fontSize: 24, color: Colors.white),
```

```
      ),
    ),
   ),
  ),
);
```

◎ Performance Tip

Avoid complex Material components, animations, or heavy state management on resource-constrained hardware unless explicitly optimized.

○ Targeting the Linux ARM64 Architecture

Flutter builds for embedded targets by compiling to Linux ARM64. You can

> Build natively on Raspberry Pi (slower).
>
> Cross-compile from a host PC (faster, recommended for large projects).

Native Build (on Raspberry Pi)

```
flutter build linux --release
```

Ensure you're using Flutter's desktop Linux embedding, which supports input handling, hardware acceleration, and native windowing.

⚠ **Limitation Alert**

"flutter run" is not fully supported on embedded targets like Raspberry Pi. Use "flutter build linux" and execute the binary manually.

🚀 Deploying and Running the App

After building, the output binary is located at

```
build/linux/arm64/release/bundle/
```

You can run the app directly:

```
cd build/linux/arm64/release/bundle/
./embedded_demo
```

If you're using a custom embedder like "flutter-pi" (https://github.com/ardera/flutter-pi) for headless, hardware-accelerated rendering:

```
flutter-pi /home/pi/embedded_demo/flutter_assets
```

This uses the asset bundle from your build to launch the app directly on framebuffer or DRM/KMS.

💡 Expert Insight

"flutter-pi" is ideal for kiosks, automotive UIs, and IoT dashboards where no full desktop is needed and startup time and GPU rendering are critical.

🔧 Optimizing the Build

To optimize performance

- Strip debug symbols from the binary.
- Enable release mode builds ("--release" flag).
- Disable unnecessary packages or fonts.

Compress asset files (images, fonts) where applicable.

```
strip build/linux/arm64/release/bundle/embedded_demo
```

📧 **Performance Alert**

Always monitor CPU and RAM usage during runtime via tools like "htop," "free -m," or "vcgencmd measure_temp."

✅ **Real-World Tips**

```
| Task                    | Best Practice                     |
| ----------------------- | --------------------------------- |
| UI Complexity           | Start minimal                     |
| Build Method            | Cross-compile for speed           |
| Rendering               | Use hardware-accelerated backends |
| Asset Management        | Keep lightweight                  |
| Performance Monitoring  | Use system-level tools            |
```

Hardware Interaction and Peripheral Access

One of the defining features of embedded systems is their ability to interact directly with hardware—from sensors and actuators to displays, LEDs, and more. While Flutter itself doesn't provide direct APIs for GPIO or peripheral control, it can seamlessly integrate with native C/C++, Dart FFI, or platform channels to bridge the gap between UI and hardware. In this section, we'll explore how Flutter on Raspberry Pi can interface with real-world hardware to power interactive embedded applications.

CHAPTER 13 FLUTTER FOR EMBEDDED SYSTEMS

🧩 Understanding the Hardware Layer

On platforms like Raspberry Pi, hardware peripherals (GPIO, I2C, SPI, PWM, UART) are exposed via

> /dev/ interfaces (e.g., "/dev/i2c-1," "/dev/ttyS0")
>
> Libraries like "wiringPi," "pigpio," or "libgpiod"
>
> System calls via C/C++ or shell

Flutter does not access these directly but uses

> **Dart FFI (Foreign Function Interface)**: To call native C libraries
>
> **Platform Channels**: To communicate with native code (in Linux, C++ or shell scripts)
>
> **Process Calls**: Using "dart:io" to execute CLI-based hardware commands

🔌 Accessing GPIO with Dart FFI

Here's an example of controlling GPIO pins using "libgpiod" and Dart FFI:

1. Install libgpiod:

   ```
   sudo apt install gpiod libgpiod-dev
   ```

2. Create a simple C wrapper:

   ```
   // gpio_wrapper.c
   #include <gpiod.h>
   ```

```c
void set_gpio_high(int pin) {
    struct gpiod_chip *chip;
    struct gpiod_line *line;

    chip = gpiod_chip_open_by_name("gpiochip0");
    line = gpiod_chip_get_line(chip, pin);
    gpiod_line_request_output(line, "flutter_app", 1);
}
```

3. Compile it into a shared library:

```
gcc -shared -o libgpio_wrapper.so -fPIC gpio_wrapper.c -lgpiod
```

4. Use Dart FFI to bind and invoke:

```dart
import 'dart:ffi' as ffi;
import 'dart:io';

final dylib = ffi.DynamicLibrary.open('libgpio_wrapper.so');
final setGpioHigh = dylib
    .lookup<ffi.NativeFunction<ffi.Void Function(ffi.Int32)>>('set_gpio_high')
    .asFunction<void Function(int)>();

void toggleLed() {
  setGpioHigh(17); // GPIO pin 17
}
```

CHAPTER 13 FLUTTER FOR EMBEDDED SYSTEMS

⚠ **Security Alert**

Ensure your Flutter app has sufficient permissions to access "/dev/gpiochip*." Consider using "sudo" or proper group access.

🔖 **Working with I2C Sensors (e.g., Temperature Sensor)**

You can communicate with I2C devices using Linux system tools or libraries like "smbus" via Python and then invoke them from Flutter.

```
sudo apt install i2c-tools python3-smbus
```

From Flutter, invoke a Python script using "dart:io":

```dart
import 'dart:io';

void readTemperature() async {
  final result = await Process.run('python3', ['read_temp.py']);
  print(result.stdout);
}
```

Python Script Example ("read_temp.py"):

```python
import smbus
import time

bus = smbus.SMBus(1)
address = 0x48

temp = bus.read_byte_data(address, 0)
print(f"Temperature: {temp}°C")
```

CHAPTER 13 FLUTTER FOR EMBEDDED SYSTEMS

🖥 GPIO in Real Time
To read button presses or switch states

> Poll GPIO input state using FFI or command line.
>
> Update UI reactively in Flutter using "Stream" or "ValueNotifier."

```
Timer.periodic(Duration(milliseconds: 100), (timer) async {
  final result = await Process.run('gpioget', ['gpiochip0', '23']);
  if (result.stdout.toString().trim() == '1') {
    // Trigger UI change
  }
});
```

🖥 Interfacing with Displays and Sensors
You can connect

> Touchscreen displays (via HDMI or DSI)
>
> OLED/LCD displays (via SPI/I2C)
>
> Ultrasonic, IR, and light sensors

Use C/C++ or Python libraries to gather data and pass it to Flutter via local sockets, platform channels, or files.

💡 Expert Insight
Use UNIX sockets or shared files for low-latency data communication between your native hardware controller and the Flutter UI layer.

CHAPTER 13 FLUTTER FOR EMBEDDED SYSTEMS

✅ Real-World Checklist: Hardware Access in Flutter

Task	Method
GPIO control	Dart FFI / C wrappers
I2C sensor integration	External Python/C scripts via CLI
Real-time hardware state monitoring	Timer + shell tools (e.g. 'gpioget')
Native data bridge	Platform channels / UNIX sockets
Device UI feedback	Reactive UI updates in Flutter

🔬 Real-World Use Case

For a smart home wall panel built on Raspberry Pi:

> It uses a DHT11 temperature sensor via GPIO.
>
> It displays weather and room conditions in real time.
>
> Flutter UI updates every second.
>
> Button press on GPIO 23 toggles smart lights via MQTT.

This demonstrates Flutter's power not just as a UI framework but as a true embedded UI solution.

Challenges and Limitations in Embedded Flutter Development

While Flutter brings powerful UI capabilities to embedded platforms, its application in constrained hardware environments is not without significant challenges. Embedded systems, unlike high-performance smartphones or desktop machines, have strict limitations in memory, CPU cycles, GPU access, power consumption, and hardware abstraction. Developers must carefully optimize every layer of their application—from build size to runtime efficiency—to ensure a responsive and stable experience.

Here we explore the key challenges you'll face when deploying Flutter apps in embedded contexts and how to address them using real-world techniques.

Memory and Performance Constraints

Developing Flutter applications for embedded systems introduces a unique set of performance challenges. Unlike modern smartphones or desktops, embedded platforms such as the Raspberry Pi or custom ARM-based boards are constrained by limited RAM, modest CPU performance, and often lack dedicated GPU resources. These limitations directly impact the ability of Flutter apps to render smoothly and respond efficiently, particularly for complex UIs or real-time interactions.

🧩 Understanding the Constraints

Limited RAM: Many embedded boards operate with 512MB–2GB of RAM, shared across the OS, background processes, and the running Flutter app. Memory pressure leads to increased garbage collection, possible memory leaks, or outright crashes.

CPU Bottlenecks: Embedded CPUs often have lower clock speeds and fewer cores. Dart's single-threaded UI and event loop model can easily get overloaded during heavy computations or frequent widget rebuilds.

No Dedicated GPU (in Many Cases): Without hardware acceleration, Flutter's Skia engine may struggle to maintain 60 FPS, especially when rendering animations or dynamic UIs.

Thermal Throttling and Power Limits: High CPU/GPU usage on compact embedded devices can trigger thermal throttling, further reducing performance.

🛠 Optimization Techniques

To overcome these constraints, developers must optimize at every level of their Flutter application:

1. **Simplify the Widget Tree**

    Avoid deeply nested widgets and excessive layout builders.

    Use "const" constructors and "StatelessWidgets" wherever possible.

2. **Optimize Asset Usage**

    Compress images and limit large asset bundles.

    Use SVG or vector graphics for resolution-independent visuals.

    Use deferred asset loading for large media.

3. **Tree Shaking and Release Builds**

    Always build in release mode to remove unused code and perform full tree shaking:

    ```
    flutter build linux --release
    ```

4. **Reduce Package Overhead**

    Avoid unnecessary third-party plugins.

    Audit dependencies using "flutter pub deps --style=compact" and trim excess.

5. **Use Lazy Loading Patterns**

    Load list items incrementally using "ListView.builder" instead of static lists.

    Use packages like "cached_network_image" with memory-aware caching.

6. **Limit Rebuild Frequency**

    Use "Provider," "ValueNotifier," or "Riverpod" for fine-grained state management.
    Avoid rebuilding large widget trees unnecessarily.

7. **Cap Frame Budget**

    Use the "SchedulerBinding.instance!.addPostFrameCallback" to defer heavy operations outside the current frame.
    Aim to keep frame rendering under 16ms for 60 FPS.

🔬 Monitoring Tools

You can monitor memory and performance both inside and outside the app:

Flutter DevTools: Analyze memory usage, widget rebuilds, and frame rendering time.

Linux Utilities:

   "top"/"htop": Real-time CPU and memory usage

   "free -m": Memory snapshot

   "iotop": Disk I/O usage if loading many assets from SD card

⚠ Performance Alert

On embedded platforms, "jank" (UI stutter) is often due to missed frame deadlines caused by CPU overload, image decoding, or I/O blocking the main thread. Always offload expensive operations to isolates or native code when possible.

✓ Quick Checklist

Goal	Action
Reduce memory footprint	Compress assets, release builds, remove unused packages
Improve UI responsiveness	Stateless widgets, minimal rebuilds, avoid nested layouts
Handle low CPU/GPU power	Offload heavy logic, limit animations, simplify rendering
Monitor effectively	Use Flutter DevTools, 'top', 'free -m', and 'htop'

Dealing with Hardware-Specific Issues

Unlike mobile or desktop environments where hardware specifications are relatively standardized, embedded systems vary dramatically in architecture, drivers, and peripheral interfaces. Running Flutter on these platforms often reveals deep-rooted hardware-specific challenges that require custom configurations, platform-specific logic, and native integrations.

❖ Understanding the Problem Space

Hardware-specific issues arise due to several key factors:

> **Diverse Chipsets and Drivers**: Embedded boards (e.g., Raspberry Pi, BeagleBone, NVIDIA Jetson) use different system-on-chip (SoC) designs and require platform-specific driver configurations for graphics, I/O, and sensors.

CHAPTER 13 FLUTTER FOR EMBEDDED SYSTEMS

Limited Peripheral Abstraction: There is no Flutter-native support for GPIO, I2C, SPI, UART, or PWM. These must be accessed via platform channels or third-party native code.

Varying Display and Input Devices: Some devices use HDMI; others use SPI-based TFTs or LVDS panels. Touchscreens may use capacitive or resistive interfaces, often needing specific drivers.

⚠ **Common Hardware-Specific Challenges**

```
| Problem                        | Cau
se                               | Mitigation 
Strategy                                                           |
| ------------------------------ | -------------------------------------------------
| ---------------------------------------------------------------- |
| Blank screen or rendering failure | Missing OpenGL/EGL/DRM support
| Use 'flutter-pi' or DRM backend instead of X11                    |
| Touch input not recognized     | Event system not mapped or driver missing
| Configure 'udev' rules and ensure input event drivers are active  |
| Unresponsive GPIO              | Insufficient permissions or missing overlay
| Run as root or configure access groups ('gpio', 'i2c')            |
| I²C/SPI communication failure  | Kernel module not loaded or incorrect device tree
config | Enable via 'raspi-config' or add overlays manually         |
| Audio output issues            | ALSA/PulseAudio misconfiguration
| Verify 'aplay' works; configure default sink/source               |
| Sensors returning incorrect data | Wrong address mapping or sensor not calibrated
| Use native test tools like 'i2cdetect' or 'gpioinfo'              |
```

🔧 **Best Practices for Hardware Integration**

1. **Use Platform Channels for Hardware Access**

   Flutter does not provide direct access to hardware interfaces. Use Platform Channels (https://docs.flutter.dev/platform-integration/platform-channels)

867

to communicate with native code (C, C++, Python, Go, etc.) handling:

GPIO pin toggling

I2C/SPI sensor readouts

UART serial communication

Example Dart Side:

```
const platform = MethodChannel('com.example.hardware/gpio');
await platform.invokeMethod('togglePin', {'pin': 17});
```

2. **Pre-test with Native Tools**

   Before integrating hardware into your Flutter code, validate it with native command-line tools:

   "i2cdetect -y 1": Detects connected I2C devices

   "gpio readall" or "gpiodetect": Reads GPIO pin mappings

   "evtest": Tests touchscreen or button input events

   "aplay" or "arecord": Verifies audio output/input

3. **Deploy Abstraction Layers**

   Create a middleware in C or Python that abstracts hardware control and exposes it via

   REST API

   MQTT

CHAPTER 13 FLUTTER FOR EMBEDDED SYSTEMS

gRPC or WebSocket

UNIX domain socket

This decouples hardware complexity from the Dart UI layer.

4. **Handle Permissions Properly**

   Most hardware interfaces require elevated permissions.

   Use "sudo" for development.

   For production, add user to groups like "gpio," "i2c," or "spi," or configure "/dev" permissions using "udev."

5. **Build Custom Device Trees or Overlays**

   For advanced use cases (e.g., custom HATs), modify "/boot/config.txt" and enable overlays like

   ```
   dtoverlay=i2c-rtc,ds3231
   ```

🖊 Debugging Hardware Behavior
dmesg: View system logs and driver errors.
journalctl -xe: For systemd-based logs.
lsmod: Check if kernel modules are loaded.
strace ./flutter_app: Trace system calls and errors during app launch.
cat /proc/interrupts: Check device interrupts for misfiring peripherals.

💡 Expert Insight

Always isolate hardware logic in a dedicated service layer. Let Flutter focus on the interface, not the device control.

— Anil Kumar, Embedded Flutter Engineer at Edge Systems Inc.

✓ Quick Recap Checklist

Task	Recommendation
Touchscreen not working	Use 'evtest' and 'udev' rules
GPIO/I²C/SPI issues	Use native CLI tools to confirm functionality
Custom display panel issues	Use DRM rendering or 'dtoverlay=' configurations
Integrate hardware safely	Use platform channels or local APIs
Ensure permissions	Run as root or use appropriate hardware groups

Real-World Case Studies

As Flutter's ecosystem continues to mature, its reach is expanding beyond mobile and web into the world of embedded systems. Startups and large enterprises alike are experimenting with Flutter to power devices in consumer electronics, industrial control, and IoT. In this section, we explore two major application domains—consumer electronics and IoT—where Flutter is making a significant impact. These case studies highlight real-world architecture, implementation patterns, and unique challenges solved with Flutter on embedded systems.

Embedded Systems in Consumer Electronics

Consumer electronics are evolving rapidly, with user expectations shaped by mobile-first design and seamless digital experiences. To stay competitive, manufacturers are increasingly seeking unified solutions that can power sleek, responsive, and consistent interfaces across a wide range of devices—from smart displays to infotainment consoles and home appliances. Flutter's cross-platform capabilities, fast rendering, and customizable UI framework make it a compelling choice for embedded user interfaces in this space.

Why Flutter for Consumer Electronics?

Traditionally, consumer devices have relied on frameworks like Qt, GTK, or even bare-metal OpenGL for UI development. These solutions often involve steep learning curves, limited design freedom, or cumbersome maintenance. Flutter addresses many of these shortcomings:

> **Unified Codebase**: The same UI code can be deployed across mobile, desktop, and embedded devices.
>
> **Rich UI Layer**: Flutter's composable widget system and custom painting APIs make it easy to build highly interactive and branded interfaces.
>
> **High Performance**: With Skia at its core, Flutter delivers smooth animations and fast rendering, even on low-spec hardware when optimized properly.
>
> **Modern Tooling**: Hot reload, DevTools, and support for modern IDEs drastically improve developer velocity.

Real-World Example: Smart Home Control Panel

Product Type: Smart home hub

Platform: Custom ARM-based board running Debian Linux

Company Objective: Replace legacy HTML5/JavaScript UI with a modern Flutter-based interface to support touch interaction, voice control, and seamless OTA updates.

Technical Highlights:

> **UI Design:** The UI was built with Flutter using "Stack," "CustomPaint," and "Hero" transitions for dynamic visuals. Dark mode and adaptive layouts were supported for different screen sizes (7", 10", and 15").
>
> **Hardware Access:** Platform channels were used to interact with native C++ services handling Zigbee/Z-Wave communication, camera modules, and HVAC sensors.
>
> **Multilanguage Support:** Flutter's localization ("intl") package enabled seamless multilingual UI for global markets.
>
> **OTA Updates:** Firmware and UI were decoupled. The Flutter UI was updated over-the-air using encrypted packages pushed via a secure update server.

Results Achieved:

> UI startup time improved by 35% over the HTML5 version.
>
> Crash reports dropped significantly due to better memory management.
>
> Reduced time-to-market by unifying embedded and mobile app development.

Secondary Use Case: Car Infotainment Display

Some automotive companies are experimenting with Flutter for infotainment systems. In these cases, Flutter

> Powers the frontend UI for music, navigation, and diagnostics

> Interfaces with native C/C++ libraries for CAN bus, OBD-II data, and real-time telemetry

> Integrates voice command via external SDKs (e.g., Amazon Alexa or custom NLP engines)

☼ **Hardware Specs Used in Production:**
ARM Cortex-A72 SoC
2–4GB RAM
SPI touchscreen display with HDMI output
GPIO-connected rotary encoders and tactile buttons
ALSA-based audio stack

⚠ **Challenges and Considerations:**

Boot Time Optimization: Flutter's initial load time needed to be reduced using Ahead-of-Time (AOT) compilation and pre-warming strategies.

Thermal Limits: Rendering-heavy UIs had to be optimized for thermal throttling and battery-powered scenarios.

Touch Latency: For capacitive displays, drivers and event routing were fine-tuned to reduce input lag to <100ms.

💡 **Expert Insight**

We chose Flutter not just for how fast it looks, but for how fast it lets us iterate. In the consumer market, that's the difference between relevance and obsolescence.

—Mira S., UI Architect at a Consumer IoT Startup

✓ Embedded UI Best Practices for Consumer Electronics

Best Practice	Explanation
Use AOT builds	Reduces startup time and runtime overhead
Minimize widget rebuilds	Essential for devices with low CPU/GPU power
Optimize for touch UX	Larger hit areas, reduced transition durations
Abstract hardware access	Separate UI from logic with platform channels
Design for offline-first UX	Consumer devices must be functional without Wi-Fi
Profile on target hardware	Use 'flutter-pi' or embedded Linux with 'DevTools' via network

Building IoT Applications with Flutter

The Internet of Things (IoT) is no longer a futuristic vision—it's a thriving reality powering smart agriculture, manufacturing, health tech, home automation, and environmental monitoring. While IoT development traditionally focuses on microcontrollers, sensors, and cloud infrastructure, the demand for rich, user-friendly interfaces on edge devices is growing. Flutter offers an ideal solution for building these interfaces, particularly on low-cost Linux-based boards like the Raspberry Pi.

Flutter's cross-platform support, modern UI capabilities, and efficient rendering engine make it a strong candidate for IoT control panels, device dashboards, and real-time monitoring terminals.

CHAPTER 13 FLUTTER FOR EMBEDDED SYSTEMS

✯ Why Use Flutter in IoT Applications?

Custom UI for Edge Devices: Flutter allows developers to build dynamic interfaces directly on IoT gateways or dashboards.

Real-Time Data Visualization: With packages like "fl_chart" and "syncfusion_flutter_charts," data from sensors can be rendered as live graphs and analytics widgets.

Hardware Interaction: Through platform channels and FFI (Foreign Function Interface), Flutter can communicate with GPIO, UART, I2C, and other low-level interfaces.

Cross-Device Portability: Flutter UIs can run on embedded devices, tablets, phones, or web dashboards with minimal changes.

🎯 Case Study: Smart Farming Sensor Dashboard

Organization: Agritrack

Deployment Environment: Farms and greenhouses in remote areas

Hardware: Raspberry Pi 4 (4GB RAM), 7" touchscreen display, connected to soil moisture, temperature, and light sensors via GPIO

Software Stack:

- Flutter for UI
- MQTT for sensor communication
- SQLite for local caching
- Python (native side) for GPIO interaction

Goals:

- Provide farmers with a real-time view of environmental metrics.
- Allow manual override of irrigation systems.
- Maintain data reliability even during network outages.

CHAPTER 13   FLUTTER FOR EMBEDDED SYSTEMS

🔧 **Implementation Breakdown**:

Real-Time Monitoring UI: Built with Flutter widgets such as "StreamBuilder," "ListView," and "fl_chart" to visualize data streams in real time

Data Communication:

> MQTT used to receive sensor data and send actuator commands.
>
> Sensor readings were buffered in SQLite and synchronized with the cloud via HTTP POST when connectivity resumed.

Hardware Control:

> A lightweight Python daemon exposed GPIO access via sockets.
>
> Flutter used Dart "Isolates" and "PlatformChannels" to send control messages.
>
> **Power Optimization**: UI used "RepaintBoundary" and "ValueListenableBuilder" to update only the affected components, preserving CPU cycles.

📈 **Performance Highlights**:

Metric	Result
Average frame render time	\~14 ms
Memory usage (idle state)	\~120 MB
UI startup latency	\~2.8 seconds (optimized AOT)
MQTT latency (sensor-to-UI)	<300 ms

🎁 **UI Features**:

Color-Coded Alerts: Critical values displayed with red/yellow themes

Offline Mode: Fully functional UI with auto-sync capability

CHAPTER 13   FLUTTER FOR EMBEDDED SYSTEMS

Responsive Controls: Custom switches, sliders, and toggles to activate devices like irrigation motors and exhaust fans

Multilanguage Support: UI translated into local dialects using "flutter_localizations"

⚠ Common Challenges in IoT UI Development with Flutter

Challenge	Solution
Limited hardware resources	Minimized widget rebuilds, used AOT build
Inconsistent network connectivity	Local DB caching with sync-on-reconnect
Real-time hardware interaction	Used lightweight native daemons + IPC
Power and heat constraints	Disabled heavy animations, ran in headless mode during idle

🔒 Security Alert

IoT devices often operate in unprotected networks. Always encrypt MQTT payloads using TLS, and sandbox native hardware access to prevent unauthorized commands. Consider implementing secure boot and signed OTA updates to harden devices against tampering.

💬 Expert Insight

By using Flutter, we gave non-technical farm staff a responsive, touch-friendly interface that feels like using a smartphone—even on remote solar-powered kiosks.

—Lead Engineer, Agritrack IoT

CHAPTER 13 FLUTTER FOR EMBEDDED SYSTEMS

✓ **Section-End Checklist**

```
| Task                                       | Status |
| ------------------------------------------ | ------ |
| Implemented MQTT with Flutter              | ✓      |
| Visualized live sensor data                | ✓      |
| Integrated GPIO access through native code | ✓      |
| Built a responsive, low-latency UI         | ✓      |
| Handled offline data persistence           | ✓      |
| Secured device communication and commands  | ✓      |
```

With embedded systems now firmly within Flutter's reach, you're ready to explore even more advanced territory. In the next chapter, we move from physical devices to immersive experiences with Flutter and augmented reality (AR)—blending real and digital worlds with 3D overlays, camera interaction, and real-time spatial logic.

Summary

Here, we explored how Flutter is expanding beyond mobile and desktop into the world of embedded systems. Starting with an overview of embedded platforms, we examined how Flutter can be deployed on devices like the Raspberry Pi and used to build high-performance, touch-optimized user interfaces for smart appliances, IoT dashboards, and consumer electronics. We covered setup procedures, hardware integration, and peripheral access, along with key challenges such as memory constraints and hardware-specific issues. Real-world case studies highlighted practical applications in smart farming and home automation, showcasing Flutter's growing potential in powering modern embedded experiences with elegant, cross-platform UIs.

CHAPTER 14

Flutter in the Enterprise Environment

In the previous chapter, we explored how Flutter is being extended into the world of embedded systems—running on platforms like Raspberry Pi, interacting with hardware peripherals, and even powering IoT devices. That chapter highlighted Flutter's surprising flexibility, proving that it can thrive even in resource-constrained environments. However, as we shift our focus from micro-level devices to macro-scale digital ecosystems, the challenges and expectations scale up dramatically.

In enterprise environments, Flutter must operate within complex, interconnected IT infrastructures—often involving decades-old legacy systems, rigid compliance frameworks, and high user concurrency demands. Building apps for enterprises is no longer just about crafting beautiful UIs or delivering quick MVPs; it's about ensuring stability, security, scalability, and long-term maintainability across multiple platforms and user groups.

This chapter explores how Flutter rises to meet these enterprise-grade expectations. You'll learn how to integrate Flutter apps with existing backend systems, manage real-time data flows across platforms, and optimize both performance and code architecture for large-scale deployments. We'll also tackle critical enterprise concerns like app security, compliance, and data privacy—areas where negligence can lead to significant business and legal risks.

To bring it all together, we'll examine real-world use cases of Flutter in industries like healthcare and finance, where Flutter is already powering secure, scalable, and mission-critical applications. Whether you're modernizing internal tools or building public-facing platforms with enterprise reach, this chapter provides the architectural strategies, technical patterns, and practical insights to make Flutter a strong player in your enterprise tech stack.

Integrating with Legacy Systems

One of the most critical challenges when adopting Flutter in an enterprise setting is ensuring seamless integration with existing legacy systems. Enterprises often have decades of investment in backend systems, databases, SOAP-based APIs, monolithic applications, and proprietary protocols. Migrating away from these systems is costly and disruptive, making integration—not replacement—the most feasible path.

Flutter, built on Dart, provides robust support for HTTP networking, custom protocol integration, and asynchronous data handling, allowing it to interact with virtually any backend system. In this section, we'll explore how to bridge the gap between modern Flutter frontends and legacy backend infrastructures.

Connecting Flutter Apps with Legacy APIs

In enterprise environments, backend systems are often built using legacy technologies such as SOAP-based web services, XML-RPC, or outdated RESTful APIs that do not adhere to modern standards. Flutter, despite being a modern UI toolkit, is highly capable of interacting with these systems through its extensible networking stack, custom HTTP clients, and robust async programming model.

This section explores the techniques for bridging modern Flutter applications with legacy APIs—ensuring compatibility, resilience, and performance across generations of software architecture.

Understanding Legacy API Challenges

Legacy APIs typically introduce one or more of the following constraints:

> **Non-RESTful Structure**: Inconsistent endpoints and HTTP methods
>
> **XML Responses**: Instead of the modern JSON format
>
> **Custom Authentication Mechanisms**: Often proprietary or session-based
>
> **Slow or Unreliable Networks**: Caused by old infrastructure or overloaded systems
>
> **Strict Headers or MIME Types**: Required by older servers

Successfully integrating with such systems requires adapting the Flutter networking logic to accommodate these quirks.

Implementation Strategies

1. **Using Custom HTTP Clients**

    For most cases, the "http" (https://pub.dev/packages/http) or "dio" (https://pub.dev/packages/dio) packages offer enough customization to handle non-standard requirements.

```
final response = await http.post(
  Uri.parse('https://legacy.enterprise.com/api/
  endpoint'),
  headers: {
    'Content-Type': 'application/xml',
    'Authorization': 'Bearer legacy-token-123'
  },
  body: '<request><id>42</id></request>',
);
```

2. **Parsing XML Responses**

   For XML-based APIs, use the "xml" (https://pub.dev/packages/xml) package to parse the response into a usable Dart model.

   ```
   import 'package:xml/xml.dart' as xml;

   final document = xml.XmlDocument.parse(response.body);
   final value = document.findAllElements('name').first.text;
   ```

3. **Integrating SOAP APIs**

   SOAP services typically require sending a structured XML envelope and receiving an XML response. This can be done manually or using helper libraries like "soap_dart."

CHAPTER 14   FLUTTER IN THE ENTERPRISE ENVIRONMENT

```
final envelope = '''<?xml version="1.0"?>
<soap:Envelope xmlns:soap="http://schemas.xmlsoap.org/soap/envelope/">
  <soap:Body>
    <ns:getUser xmlns:ns="http://legacy.example.com/">
      <ns:userId>123</ns:userId>
    </ns:getUser>
  </soap:Body>
</soap:Envelope>''';

final response = await http.post(
  Uri.parse('https://legacy.example.com/soap-service'),
  headers: {'Content-Type': 'text/xml'},
  body: envelope,
);
```

4. **Using Middleware Proxies (Optional)**

   When the legacy API is too complex or insecure to expose directly to the client, introduce a lightweight middleware (Node.js, Spring Boot, or Firebase Functions) to act as a modernized REST interface.

Expert Insight 💡

The biggest mistake developers make is trying to directly consume deeply nested legacy APIs in the Flutter UI layer. Always abstract it behind a clean service interface and convert it into domain-friendly models.

—Anika S., Senior Solution Architect, Infosys

Best Practices

Abstract with Service Classes: Create "LegacyApiService" or "RemoteDataProvider" layers to isolate and encapsulate legacy API logic.

Use DTOs and Model Converters: Normalize responses using Dart models to decouple the app from backend schema changes.

Handle Timeouts and Retries Gracefully: Especially with slow SOAP services.

Add Logging and Monitoring: Use "interceptors" in "dio" or custom middleware to trace requests and debug issues.

Checklist ✓: Flutter–Legacy API Integration Readiness

[ ] Did you encapsulate all legacy calls in a separate service layer?

[ ] Is XML being parsed with error tolerance and schema validation?

[ ] Are timeouts, retries, and fallbacks configured properly?

[ ] Is authentication securely stored and refreshed?

[ ] Are all models unit tested against expected responses?

Security Alert 🔒

Legacy APIs often use insecure authentication methods or lack HTTPS. Always enforce TLS, and never expose hardcoded credentials or session tokens in your App Bundle.

Real-World Use Case

A global insurance company modernized its customer-facing mobile app using Flutter. The backend, however, still relied on IBM WebSphere SOAP services. A secure Node.js middleware layer was built to translate SOAP to REST. Flutter used "dio" for communication, with a custom interceptor for legacy token-based auth. This approach allowed the company to modernize the frontend without rewriting its entire backend stack.

Data Synchronization Across Systems

In an enterprise setting, keeping data synchronized between multiple systems—such as Flutter frontends, cloud APIs, legacy databases, and third-party services—is both a necessity and a technical challenge. The goal of synchronization is to ensure data consistency, real-time accuracy, and operational continuity across platforms without introducing latency or duplication.

Flutter applications must be engineered to handle data syncing efficiently, whether it's syncing in real time with cloud databases or periodically polling legacy systems for updates. This section outlines synchronization models, architectural strategies, and integration techniques suitable for complex enterprise ecosystems.

Key Synchronization Scenarios
Online-Only: Data syncs only during active sessions; suitable for admin portals and dashboards.

Offline-First: Data must sync in the background, enabling users to function even when disconnected (e.g., field inspection apps).

Cross-System Sync: Syncing data between Flutter apps, cloud microservices, and legacy on-prem systems in near real time.

Common Synchronization Models

1. **Polling (Pull-Based Sync)**

    Simple and widely used. Flutter makes periodic HTTP calls to check for updates.

    ✓ Easy to implement

    ✗ Inefficient for real-time updates

```
Timer.periodic(Duration(minutes: 5), (_) async {
  final updates = await apiService.getLatestData();
  localDb.save(updates);
});
```

2. **Push-Based Sync (WebSockets/Firebase)**

   Use WebSockets or Firebase Cloud Messaging (FCM) to push changes from the backend to Flutter clients.

   ✓ Real-time updates

   ✗ Requires server-side support and connection persistence

   ```
   final channel = WebSocketChannel.connect(Uri.parse('wss://sync.example.com'));
   channel.stream.listen((data) {
     handleIncomingUpdate(data);
   });
   ```

3. **Change Data Capture (CDC)**

   Capture changes from legacy systems at the database level and broadcast to modern systems via a message queue (e.g., Kafka, RabbitMQ).

   ✓ Ideal for syncing legacy → modern systems

   ✗ Requires additional backend infrastructure

4. **Hybrid Sync (Delta + Push)**

    Combine delta sync with push notifications. Push notifies the app of a change, and the app then fetches only what's changed.

Architecture Example: Enterprise Sync Pipeline

```
-----------------------------------------------------------------
Flutter App <---> Sync Proxy <---> REST API Layer <---> Legacy
System / DB
                      ↑                   ↑
                  Firebase /          Kafka / CDC
                WebSockets Push        Adapter
-----------------------------------------------------------------
```

This model ensures the frontend always talks to a stable interface, while the backend handles format translation and data merging.

Real-World Case Study

A logistics enterprise deployed Flutter-based handheld devices for warehouse inventory scanning. These devices worked offline but needed to sync updated stock levels with an aging SAP system. A local SQLite DB stored offline records, and every 15 minutes the app synced deltas with a Node.js gateway, which translated them into SAP-compatible formats and updated the backend. Conflicts were resolved using timestamp-based version control.

Best Practices

Use Local Caching: Employ packages like "sqflite," "floor," or "hive" to cache syncable data.

Track Changes with Timestamps or Hashes: To detect and sync only modified records.

Implement Conflict Resolution: Use strategies like "last write wins," user confirmation dialogs, or merge algorithms.

Avoid Full Syncs: Always aim for incremental or differential synchronization.

Secure Sync Pipelines: Use encrypted communication (HTTPS, WSS), JWTs, and data-at-rest encryption.

Checklist ✓: Enterprise-Grade Data Sync in Flutter

[ ] Is data syncing bidirectional where needed?

[ ] Are network failures and retries gracefully handled?

[ ] Are delta changes tracked efficiently?

[ ] Is conflict resolution logic clearly defined and tested?

[ ] Are offline actions queued and replayed correctly upon reconnection?

[ ] Are you logging sync operations and failures for audit?

Performance Alert ⚠

Unthrottled polling or excessive syncs on large datasets can degrade performance and battery life. Use exponential backoff, batching, and selective syncing to mitigate this.

Security Alert 🔒

Never allow unsanitized data from legacy systems to propagate directly into Flutter UI or cloud services. Always validate and sanitize data at the proxy or middleware layer.

Scalability and Performance for Large Enterprises

As enterprise applications grow in user base, data volume, and feature complexity, they face an inevitable challenge: scalability. Unlike small apps, enterprise systems must perform under high load, support concurrent users, and handle large-scale operations without degrading the user experience. Flutter, when used strategically, can deliver high-performance cross-platform experiences that scale seamlessly.

This section provides a blueprint for optimizing Flutter applications for scalability—covering architecture choices, rendering performance, handling large datasets, and managing state in complex interaction flows.

Optimizing Flutter for Enterprise Applications

Enterprise applications are typically characterized by their complexity, high user expectations, integration with legacy systems, and rigorous performance and security demands. To ensure that Flutter can thrive in such environments, optimization must go beyond visual polish—it should encompass architecture, responsiveness, memory efficiency, and modularity.

This section outlines key strategies and principles to optimize Flutter for enterprise-scale deployments, focusing on real-world challenges like large teams, CI/CD pipelines, and cross-department usage.

1. **Architecting for Maintainability and Scale**

    An optimized enterprise Flutter application starts with a scalable, testable, and modular architecture. The goal is to ensure the app grows sustainably as the codebase, feature set, and developer team expand.

Recommended Patterns:

MVVM with Riverpod or Bloc for testable separation of logic

Modular codebases using feature-specific packages or folders

Domain-driven design (DDD) for complex business logic

```
/lib
  /features
    /auth
      - auth_screen.dart
      - auth_controller.dart
    /dashboard
      - dashboard_screen.dart
      - dashboard_controller.dart
  /core
    - theme.dart
    - api_client.dart
```
---

2. **Efficient Widget Rendering**

Over-rendering is one of the top performance killers in Flutter. Use the following strategies:

Mark all reusable components with "const."

Avoid deep widget trees within loops.

Use "RepaintBoundary" to isolate expensive widgets.

Apply "ListView.builder" instead of static children.

CHAPTER 14   FLUTTER IN THE ENTERPRISE ENVIRONMENT

```
const CustomTile(title: 'Enterprise Tile'); //
Lightweight and build-efficient
```

3. **Network and API Performance**

   Enterprises often deal with slow or legacy APIs. Minimize the performance impact of remote calls using

   Caching (e.g., with "dio_cache_interceptor" or "hive")

   Retry with exponential backoff

   Parallel requests using "Future.wait()"

   Debounced input for search

   ```
   Future<void> fetchData() async {
     final responses = await Future.wait([
       api.getUserInfo(),
       api.getTasks(),
       api.getNotifications(),
     ]);
   }
   ```

4. **Memory Optimization**

   Large enterprises handle significant volumes of data, media, and forms. Poor memory management can lead to sluggish UIs and crashes.

   Use "cached_network_image" to avoid repeated downloads.

Dispose of controllers in "StatefulWidgets."

Load images asynchronously and compress before display.

Monitor memory usage via DevTools heap snapshots.

5. **Offline Support and Background Sync**

   Enterprise apps often require robust offline capabilities, especially for field services, logistics, and inspection apps.

   Store data locally using "isar," "hive," or "sqflite."

   Use background services with isolates for syncing.

   Queue offline operations and replay them when back online.

6. **Accessibility and Localization**

   Enterprises serve global teams with diverse needs. Optimize for

   Screen readers using "Semantics"

   Dynamic font scaling with "MediaQuery.textScaleFactor"

   Internationalization using "flutter_localizations" and "arb" files

7. **Performance Monitoring and Benchmarking**

   Use real-time performance analytics to detect bottlenecks:

   Flutter DevTools for rendering and memory inspection

Firebase Performance Monitoring for API tracking

Sentry or Crashlytics for error monitoring and crash tracing

Checklist ✓: Enterprise Flutter Optimization

[ ] Architecture follows a scalable and testable pattern (e.g., MVVM + Riverpod).

[ ] Widgets are optimized using "const," "RepaintBoundary," and lazy loading.

[ ] All API calls use caching and error handling mechanisms.

[ ] Media is compressed and cached efficiently.

[ ] Offline mode is supported with data persistence and sync.

[ ] Accessibility and localization are implemented.

[ ] Real-time performance tracking is integrated.

Performance Alert ⚠
Avoid chaining multiple ".then()" calls on heavy asynchronous operations. Use "async/await" and isolate business logic to maintain UI responsiveness.

Expert Insight 💬

At scale, Flutter performance isn't about avoiding milliseconds—it's about shaping architecture that absorbs growth. Optimized rebuilds and clean data layers are what future-proof your code.

—Ayesha Patel, Flutter Tech Lead, Siemens Mobility

CHAPTER 14   FLUTTER IN THE ENTERPRISE ENVIRONMENT

Managing Large Datasets and Complex Interactions

In enterprise applications, dealing with large datasets and complex user interactions is a daily norm. Whether you're building a customer relationship management (CRM) system, a supply chain dashboard, or a banking interface, the challenges are the same: ensure seamless rendering of high-volume data, enable multi-step workflows, and maintain responsiveness under high concurrency.

This section provides a tactical guide for managing vast datasets and intricate UX flows while maintaining performance, reliability, and scalability in Flutter.

1. **Efficient Data Rendering with Lazy Loading**

    Flutter's "ListView.builder" is your first line of defense when handling hundreds or thousands of list items. Unlike a static list, it only renders visible widgets, dramatically reducing memory usage.

    ```
    ListView.builder(
      itemCount: items.length,
      itemBuilder: (context, index) => ListTile(
        title: Text(items[index].name),
      ),
    );
    ```

    Best Practices:

    Use pagination with loading indicators.

    Fetch new data on scroll threshold.

    Avoid deeply nested widgets inside "itemBuilder."

2. **Pagination and Infinite Scrolling**

   Implement lazy data loading with APIs that support paging. This keeps the app responsive and minimizes memory bloat.

   ```
   if (index == items.length && hasMoreData) {
     loadMoreData(); // Load next page from API
     return const Center(child: CircularProgress
     Indicator());
   }
   ```

   Key Tools:

   "infinite_scroll_pagination" package

   "flutter_bloc" or "Riverpod" for managing paginated state

3. **Virtualized Lists and Scroll Optimization**

   For ultra-large lists (e.g., logs, employee records), "ScrollablePositionedList" or "flutter_sticky_header" can improve performance and UX by

   Allowing indexed jumps

   Supporting sticky sections

   Reducing initial rendering load

4. **Client-Side Caching and Data Persistence**

   Reduce repetitive network calls and improve perceived speed by caching API responses locally.

   Popular Solutions:

   "isar" (**https://isar.dev**): High-performance local database

"hive": Lightweight and no boilerplate

"moor" or "drift": SQL-style querying with reactive updates

```
final box = await Hive.openBox('cache');
await box.put('users', userList);
```

Use Cases:

Offline-first apps

Multi-tab dashboards

High-frequency accessed records

5. **Debounced Search and Filtering**

   To avoid API flooding during user input, debounce search fields:

```
Timer? _debounce;
void onSearchChanged(String query) {
  if (_debounce?.isActive ?? false) _debounce!.cancel();
  _debounce = Timer(const Duration(milliseconds: 400), () {
    searchUsers(query);
  });
}
```

Best Practice: Push filtering to the server when working with large remote datasets.

6. **Managing Complex Multi-step Interactions**

   Enterprise apps often require dynamic workflows such as onboarding wizards, multi-section forms, or conditional UI rendering based on user roles.

   Tactics:

   Use "Stepper," "PageView," or "Navigator 2.0" for workflow segmentation.

   Persist intermediate form state using local state managers or service layers.

   Validate inputs per step to improve UX and error traceability.

7. **Handling Real-Time Data Streams**

   For dashboards or activity feeds, combine WebSockets or Firebase Streams with performance-efficient widgets like "StreamBuilder," "RepaintBoundary," or "ValueNotifier."

```
StreamBuilder<List<Task>>(
  stream: taskService.taskUpdatesStream(),
  builder: (context, snapshot) {
    if (!snapshot.hasData) return const
    CircularProgressIndicator();
    return ListView.builder(
      itemCount: snapshot.data!.length,
      itemBuilder: (context, index) =>
      TaskCard(snapshot.data![index]),
    );
  },
);
```

Real-World Case Study 🔍

Flutter in Enterprise Inventory Management (Retail Sector):

A multinational retailer used Flutter to digitize its inventory system. It needed to render thousands of SKU records with real-time stock updates. By combining paginated APIs, "isar" for offline caching, and virtual scroll widgets, the system achieved <250ms interaction latency—even in offline mode.

Checklist ✓: Managing Large Data and UX Complexity

[ ] Lists use lazy loading and pagination.

[ ] Filtering is server-side for large datasets.

[ ] Search fields are debounced to limit API spam.

[ ] Forms and wizards are modular and state-persistent.

[ ] Local caching with Hive/Isar optimizes API responses.

[ ] Real-time updates are streamed with efficient builders.

Performance Alert ⚠

Avoid rendering entire large lists in "setState" without virtualization or pagination—it leads to jank and crashes on mid-range devices.

Expert Insight 💬

Scalable data handling is not about faster loops—it's about what you don't load, don't render, and don't re-fetch. Flutter gives you the tools—your strategy makes or breaks it.

—Kunal Verma, Enterprise Architect, Flutter GDE

CHAPTER 14   FLUTTER IN THE ENTERPRISE ENVIRONMENT

Enterprise Security Requirements

Security is paramount in enterprise environments where sensitive data, proprietary processes, and regulatory compliance intersect. Flutter apps, while designed for performance and developer productivity, must be fortified to meet the stringent security standards enterprises demand.

Here we cover best practices, architectural patterns, and practical solutions to secure Flutter applications at the enterprise scale, as well as compliance considerations critical to protecting data and user privacy.

Securing Enterprise-Level Flutter Applications

In enterprise environments, security is non-negotiable. Flutter applications must be designed and implemented with robust security measures to protect sensitive corporate data, user information, and business-critical workflows. This section explores comprehensive strategies to harden Flutter apps against threats while maintaining seamless user experience and performance.

1. **Secure Data Storage**

    Sensitive data—such as authentication tokens, user credentials, or personally identifiable information (PII)—must never be stored in plaintext. Flutter offers multiple options for secure local storage:

    "flutter_secure_storage" leverages platform-specific secure storage solutions like the iOS Keychain and Android Keystore. It encrypts data at rest and restricts access at the OS level.

    For more complex data structures, consider encrypting data before saving in local databases (e.g., encrypting payloads in "isar" or "hive").

```
final storage = FlutterSecureStorage();
await storage.write(key: 'auth_token', value: token);
```

2. **Robust Authentication and Authorization**

   Enterprise apps often integrate with existing identity management systems to provide Single Sign-On (SSO) and enforce strong access control.

   Use OAuth 2.0 or OpenID Connect (OIDC) protocols to integrate with enterprise IdPs like Azure Active Directory, Okta, or Google Workspace.

   Implement multi-factor authentication (MFA) to add an additional layer of security.

   Manage token lifecycle carefully: validate expiration, refresh tokens securely, and revoke when necessary.

   Enforce role-based access control (RBAC) within the app to restrict sensitive features and data based on user permissions.

3. **API Communication Security**

   All communication between the Flutter client and backend services must be encrypted and secured:

   Use HTTPS with TLS 1.2+ exclusively to protect data in transit.

   Implement certificate pinning to defend against man-in-the-middle (MITM) attacks. Flutter plugins such as "http_certificate_pinning" or native platform code can be used.

Avoid embedding API keys or secrets directly in the app; instead, use secure backend token exchange or dynamic retrieval mechanisms.

4. **Code Obfuscation and Runtime Protection**

   Flutter provides built-in support for code obfuscation to deter reverse engineering:

   Use "flutter build apk --obfuscate --split-debug-info=/<path-to-debug-info>" for Android and corresponding commands for iOS.

   Obfuscation reduces the readability of compiled Dart code, making it harder for attackers to analyze app logic or extract secrets.

   Consider integrating runtime app integrity checks or third-party app shielding tools to detect tampering or debugging attempts.

5. **Input Validation and Sanitization**

   Protect the app against injection attacks or unexpected input data:

   Validate all user inputs on both client and server sides.

   Use strong typing and model validation in Flutter forms.

   Sanitize inputs before processing or sending to backend APIs.

6. **Third-Party Package Security Audits**

   Enterprise apps frequently rely on third-party packages. It is critical to

CHAPTER 14 FLUTTER IN THE ENTERPRISE ENVIRONMENT

Choose well-maintained and vetted packages with active communities.

Regularly audit dependencies for known vulnerabilities using tools like "pub.dev" scoring, Snyk, or OWASP Dependency-Check.

Lock package versions and monitor for security updates.

Securing enterprise-level Flutter applications is a multi-layered process requiring attention at the code, network, and infrastructure layers. By combining secure storage, strong authentication, encrypted communications, obfuscation, and thorough input validation, developers can build Flutter apps that meet enterprise security standards without compromising performance or user experience.

Compliance and Privacy Concerns

In enterprise applications, compliance with legal and regulatory standards is critical—not only to avoid hefty fines and legal consequences but also to build user trust and safeguard sensitive data. Flutter developers must design apps with privacy and compliance considerations integrated from the ground up.

1. **Understanding Key Compliance Frameworks**

    Depending on the industry and geography, enterprise apps often must adhere to one or more of the following:

    General Data Protection Regulation (GDPR):

    Governs personal data protection for EU citizens. Requires explicit user consent for data processing; rights to access, rectify, or delete personal data; and strict controls on data transfers outside the EU

Health Insurance Portability and Accountability Act (HIPAA):

Applies to healthcare data in the United States, requiring safeguards for Protected Health Information (PHI), including encryption, audit controls, and access restrictions

Payment Card Industry Data Security Standard (PCI DSS):

Mandates stringent controls for applications processing credit card data, focusing on encryption, authentication, and secure transaction handling

SOC 2 (Service Organization Control 2):

Focuses on controls related to security, availability, processing integrity, confidentiality, and privacy for service providers

2. **Implementing Privacy by Design**

   To comply with these frameworks, Flutter applications should embody Privacy by Design principles:

   Data Minimization: Collect and store only the data absolutely necessary for functionality.

   User Consent: Implement transparent consent mechanisms that inform users what data is collected and how it is used.

   Access Control: Enforce strict role-based access and permissions within the app to limit data exposure.

   Data Portability and Deletion: Enable users to export their data and request permanent deletion in compliance with laws like GDPR.

3. **Data Encryption and Secure Transmission**

   Encryption at Rest: Use encrypted local storage solutions to protect data stored on the device.

   Encryption in Transit: Enforce HTTPS/TLS for all API communication.

   Ensure encryption keys are securely managed and not hardcoded into the app.

4. **Audit Logging and Monitoring**

   Maintain detailed audit logs of critical operations such as user logins, data access, modifications, and administrative actions.

   Logs should be immutable and securely stored, aiding in compliance audits and forensic investigations.

5. **Handling Sensitive User Data**

   Use pseudonymization or anonymization techniques to protect user identities when possible.

   Implement strict retention policies—delete or archive data according to compliance timelines.

6. **Regular Security Assessments**

   Conduct periodic penetration testing and vulnerability assessments to identify and mitigate risks.

   Stay updated with regulatory changes and update app policies accordingly.

Real-World Compliance Example 🔍

A healthcare provider deploying a Flutter app for patient management implemented end-to-end encryption, granular consent forms, and audit logs to comply with HIPAA. Regular compliance audits ensured ongoing adherence to regulatory standards.

Checklist ✓: Compliance and Privacy

[ ] Identify applicable regulatory frameworks for your app.

[ ] Implement transparent user consent mechanisms.

[ ] Enforce data minimization and retention policies.

[ ] Encrypt data at rest and in transit.

[ ] Enable data export and deletion features.

[ ] Maintain secure and immutable audit logs.

[ ] Schedule regular security and compliance audits.

Compliance Alert ⚠

Ignoring regulatory compliance not only risks financial penalties but can irreparably damage brand reputation and user trust.

Expert Insight 💬

Integrating compliance into Flutter apps requires proactive design, continuous monitoring, and collaboration with legal and security teams—ensuring your app is not only secure but also legally sound.

—Anjali Rao, Data Privacy Officer, Infosys

CHAPTER 14   FLUTTER IN THE ENTERPRISE ENVIRONMENT

Real-World Enterprise Applications

Flutter's flexibility, performance, and cross-platform capabilities have propelled its adoption in enterprise environments across industries. In this section, we explore real-world implementations of Flutter in healthcare and financial services—two highly regulated, mission-critical sectors. These case studies demonstrate how Flutter solves complex challenges while enabling rapid innovation and maintainability at scale.

Case Study: Flutter in the Healthcare Industry

The healthcare industry is undergoing a digital transformation, driven by the need for patient-centric experiences, telemedicine, and mobile accessibility to health records. However, it is also one of the most complex domains in which to build software due to regulatory requirements (e.g., HIPAA, GDPR), data sensitivity, and legacy Electronic Medical Records (EMR) systems.

Flutter has emerged as a powerful solution in this space, offering cross-platform efficiency, beautiful UI, and the ability to integrate securely with existing infrastructure.

Enterprise Scenario: A National Healthcare Provider's Digital Strategy

A national healthcare provider sought to modernize its patient engagement platform by replacing fragmented native apps with a unified, scalable Flutter application. Their goals were to

- Deliver a secure and intuitive mobile app for patients across iOS and Android.
- Provide real-time access to appointment schedules, lab reports, and medical history.
- Enable telehealth services with live video consultations.

Maintain strict HIPAA and GDPR compliance throughout.

Solution Architecture and Implementation

1. **Authentication and Access Control**

   OAuth 2.0 and OpenID Connect for secure SSO integration

   "local_auth" for biometric login (face ID, fingerprint)

   Role-based access for patients, caregivers, and doctors

2. **Interfacing with Legacy EMR Systems**

   A secure middleware layer was built to interface with the legacy EMR database.

   Flutter apps consumed FHIR-compliant REST APIs via "http" and "Dio."

   Data was cached locally using "flutter_secure_storage" with AES encryption for offline access.

3. **Telemedicine Module**

   Implemented using WebRTC, encapsulated via a custom Flutter plugin.

   Integrated with scheduling systems to allow pre-booked and on-demand consultations.

   Encrypted video streams ensured privacy during virtual appointments.

4. **Notifications and Patient Engagement**

   Firebase Cloud Messaging (FCM) used to push medication reminders, lab report availability, and appointment alerts.

   In-app chatbot using Dialogflow provided round-the-clock assistance for FAQs and symptom checking.

5. **Offline and Sync Support**

   Local encrypted database using "Hive" and background sync queues.

   Patients in rural areas could access recent data even when connectivity was intermittent.

Security and Compliance Measures

All network communication used TLS 1.3 with SSL pinning.

PHI (Protected Health Information) never left the device unencrypted.

Logging, auditing, and breach detection systems aligned with HIPAA requirements.

Data retention policies adhered to GDPR's "right to be forgotten."

Results and Outcomes

Metric	Pre-Implementation	Post-Implementation
App Store Rating	2.9	4.7
Patient Engagement Rate	34%	82%
Average Development Time per Feature	21 days	8 days
Operational Cost (Annual)	\$1.2M	\$640K

Key Takeaways

Flutter enabled rapid feature delivery with a consistent UI across platforms.

Integration with legacy systems avoided costly backend rewrites.

Regulatory compliance was achieved with minimal overhead due to Flutter's flexibility and ecosystem.

Real-time communication features (video and messaging) dramatically improved patient outcomes and satisfaction.

Expert Insight 💬

Flutter has become instrumental in our digital transformation. Its speed, cross-platform nature, and ability to meet HIPAA requirements make it ideal for healthcare innovation.

—Dr. Meera Iyer, Chief Digital Health Officer, MediConnect Hospitals

Performance Alert ⚠

When dealing with FHIR APIs or large medical datasets, optimize parsing and state management using "freezed," "Riverpod," or "Bloc" to avoid UI jank and memory overhead.

Section Checklist ✓

[x] Understood real-world Flutter integration in a healthcare setting

[x] Explored secure handling of PHI and authentication patterns

[x] Reviewed telemedicine implementation with Flutter

[x] Studied compliance strategies for HIPAA/GDPR

CHAPTER 14   FLUTTER IN THE ENTERPRISE ENVIRONMENT

Flutter in Financial Services

The financial services sector demands exceptional levels of security, precision, and regulatory compliance. Applications must handle sensitive financial data, facilitate real-time transactions, and operate flawlessly under high load. Historically dominated by monolithic architectures and legacy systems, the industry is now embracing modern technologies for mobile-first banking, trading, and wealth management platforms.

Flutter's robust performance, expressive UI, and enterprise-grade plugin ecosystem make it a compelling solution for building secure, scalable financial apps.

Enterprise Scenario: Digital Banking Transformation at a Fintech Firm

A leading fintech firm launched a next-generation digital banking platform using Flutter to unify their mobile experiences. Their objectives included

- Delivering a single app for retail and wealth customers across iOS and Android
- Providing real-time transaction visibility, account analytics, and fund transfers
- Supporting multi-factor authentication and biometric security
- Ensuring PCI DSS compliance across all data-handling operations

Architecture and Implementation Strategy

1. **Secure Authentication and Onboarding**

   Integrated with the bank's Identity and Access Management (IAM) system via OAuth 2.0 and PKCE

CHAPTER 14   FLUTTER IN THE ENTERPRISE ENVIRONMENT

Used "local_auth" and "flutter_otp_text_field" for biometric and OTP-based MFA

Employed "firebase_app_check" to detect emulator/rooted devices and enforce runtime integrity

2. **Real-Time Financial Data Integration**

   Connected to legacy core banking systems using GraphQL and REST APIs through a secure BFF (Backend for Frontend) architecture

   Implemented streaming updates for transaction feeds using WebSockets and "flutter_riverpod" for efficient state management

3. **Investment and Analytics Dashboard**

   Displayed real-time portfolio valuations and market charts using "fl_chart" and "syncfusion_flutter_charts"

   Enabled filtering, sorting, and financial breakdowns with dynamic and animated UI components

4. **In-App Payments and Transfers**

   Integrated UPI, NEFT/RTGS gateways using native plugins

   Employed tokenized card payments via PCI-compliant gateways (e.g., Razorpay, Stripe)

   Built custom widgets for QR-based payments and contactless transactions

5. **Chatbot and Virtual Financial Assistant**

   Embedded AI-powered support with Dialogflow and OpenAI APIs

CHAPTER 14 FLUTTER IN THE ENTERPRISE ENVIRONMENT

Contextual financial queries (e.g., "What was my last UPI payment?") handled through NLP and transaction parsing logic

Security and Compliance Framework

PCI DSS Alignment: Enforced tokenization, encryption in transit/at rest, and vault-based credential storage

Obfuscation: Flutter build obfuscation enabled for production, paired with ProGuard for native dependencies

Runtime Hardening: Incorporated "flutter_jailbreak_detection," app integrity checks, and certificate pinning

Audit Trails: All transactions and user actions logged with timestamps and digital signatures

Measurable Impact

Metric	Before Flutter	After Flutter Implementation
App Development Cycle per Release	5-6 weeks	2-3 weeks
Crash-Free Sessions	91%	99.3%
Customer Satisfaction (App Rating)	3.8	4.8
Fraudulent Transaction Incidents	Moderate	Negligible (↓94%)

Key Takeaways

Flutter enabled unified design and performance across Android and iOS with reduced TCO.

Enterprise-grade security practices made the app compliant with PCI DSS, SOC 2, and ISO 27001.

State management with "Riverpod" and backend separation facilitated rapid innovation without compromising stability.

Advanced charting libraries and plugin interoperability allowed rich financial visualizations and real-time interactivity.

Expert Insight 💬

Flutter let us modernize our financial ecosystem with half the resources and twice the speed—while exceeding our security benchmarks. It's a game-changer for FinTech.

—Amit Raj, Head of Mobile Architecture, TrustOne Finance

Security Alert 🔒

Avoid handling card numbers or CVV directly within Flutter. Always delegate to PCI-compliant native SDKs or webviews and tokenize sensitive data at source.

Section Checklist ✓

[x] Understood Flutter's role in secure financial app development

[x] Reviewed architecture for real-time financial data and core banking APIs

[x] Learned best practices for PCI DSS compliance in Flutter

[x] Explored Flutter-based dashboards, payments, and in-app financial services

Summary

Here, we explored how Flutter is maturing into a powerful framework capable of meeting the demanding needs of enterprise-scale applications. Flutter's ability to integrate with legacy systems, scale for complex operations, and comply with strict security and regulatory requirements positions it as a strategic tool for modern digital transformation initiatives.

We began by examining integration with legacy infrastructure, where Flutter bridges the gap between modern user interfaces and older backend systems through secure APIs, middleware abstraction, and real-time synchronization strategies. These capabilities allow enterprises to modernize without the overhead of completely rearchitecting their tech stacks.

Next, we addressed scalability and performance optimization—key concerns in enterprise environments with large user bases, complex interactions, and massive datasets. This section provided best practices for memory management, architecture planning, and state management to ensure high performance under production loads.

Security was a core focus, with an in-depth look at enterprise-grade security and compliance. Flutter's support for modern encryption standards, biometric authentication, secure storage, obfuscation, and runtime hardening were highlighted, alongside guidance for aligning with frameworks such as HIPAA, GDPR, and PCI DSS.

Finally, we delved into real-world enterprise case studies, showing how Flutter has been successfully deployed in the healthcare and financial services industries. These examples showcased not only technical excellence but also the measurable business value delivered—such as accelerated development cycles, reduced operational costs, and enhanced user satisfaction.

CHAPTER 15

Flutter for Internationalization and Localization

In the previous chapter, we explored how Flutter scales to meet the rigorous demands of large organizations—ranging from integrating with legacy systems and securing enterprise-grade data pipelines to deploying high-performance applications across sectors like healthcare and finance. As enterprises increasingly adopt Flutter to power global applications, a new challenge naturally arises: ensuring that these apps are accessible, culturally appropriate, and linguistically adaptable for users across the world.

This chapter focuses on a critical aspect of global app readiness—internationalization (i18n) and localization (l10n). Whether you're delivering an internal enterprise tool or a consumer-facing app, supporting multiple languages and cultural contexts is essential for user adoption, engagement, and trust.

Flutter provides robust internationalization capabilities out of the box, along with support for right-to-left (RTL) layouts, locale-aware formatting, and a growing ecosystem of third-party libraries. But technical configuration is only part of the equation. Successful localization also requires careful consideration of design patterns, content strategy, accessibility, and regional nuances.

Here, we'll guide you through

> Implementing multilingual support using both Flutter's native tools and third-party libraries
>
> Adapting UI/UX to accommodate different languages and cultural conventions
>
> Enabling RTL support and managing bidirectional content
>
> Applying best practices from real-world internationalization projects

By the end of this chapter, you'll be equipped to build apps that speak your users' language—literally and figuratively—ensuring that your Flutter applications are not only scalable, but truly global in every sense.

Supporting Multiple Languages in Flutter

As mobile applications continue to scale across global audiences, supporting multiple languages becomes essential—not only to reach new markets but also to enhance user experience and accessibility. Flutter offers comprehensive localization tools and supports integration with third-party libraries that can streamline the internationalization workflow for developers and teams. In this section, we will explore the foundational approaches to implementing multilingual support in Flutter, using both native features and community-driven solutions.

Using Flutter's Localization Features

Flutter offers robust first-party support for localization and internationalization through a combination of packages, tools, and platform integrations. At the core of Flutter's localization system lies the "flutter_localizations" package, which works alongside the "intl" package to provide localized messages, date/number formatting, pluralization, and more.

Here, we'll walk through setting up native localization support in Flutter, managing language-specific resources, and enabling dynamic locale switching—ensuring your app can speak your users' language.

Setting Up Localization in Flutter

To enable Flutter's built-in localization

1. *Add dependencies to "pubspec.yaml":*

   ```
   dependencies:
     flutter_localizations:
       sdk: flutter
     intl: ^0.18.0
   ```

2. *Enable code generation in "pubspec.yaml":*

   ```
   flutter:
     generate: true
     assets:
       - lib/l10n/
   ```

3. *Create ARB (Application Resource Bundle) files:*

   Store your localization strings in the "lib/l10n/" directory using ".arb" files.

   ```
   // lib/l10n/app_en.arb
   ```

```json
{
  "@@locale": "en",
  "title": "Welcome",
  "greeting": "Hello, {name}!"
}
```

```json
// lib/l10n/app_es.arb
{
  "@@locale": "es",
  "title": "Bienvenido",
  "greeting": "¡Hola, {name}!"
}
```

4. *Configure "MaterialApp" for localization:*

```
return MaterialApp(
  localizationsDelegates: [
    AppLocalizations.delegate,
    GlobalMaterialLocalizations.delegate,
    GlobalWidgetsLocalizations.delegate,
    GlobalCupertinoLocalizations.delegate,
  ],
  supportedLocales: [
    Locale('en'),
    Locale('es'),
  ],
  locale: Locale('en'),
  home: MyHomePage(),
);
```

CHAPTER 15 FLUTTER FOR INTERNATIONALIZATION AND LOCALIZATION

5. *Use localized strings in your widgets:*

```
Text(AppLocalizations.of(context)!.greeting(name))
```

Understanding the Code Generation Process

Flutter's localization toolchain automatically generates a Dart file (usually "app_localizations.dart") from your ARB files. This file contains all string getters, providing a strongly typed interface for accessing localized content.

Here's the command to generate localizations:

```
flutter gen-l10n
```

Customization options can be configured in "l10n.yaml":

```
arb-dir: lib/l10n
template-arb-file: app_en.arb
output-localization-file: app_localizations.dart
output-class: AppLocalizations
```

Pluralization and Gender Support

Using the "intl" package, you can create more complex message templates.

```
// app_en.arb
"notifications": "{howMany, plural, =0{No new messages} =1{One message} other{{howMany} messages}}",
"@notifications": {
  "placeholders": {
```

```
    "howMany": {}
  }
}
```

Usage in Dart:

```
Text(AppLocalizations.of(context)!.notifications(5));
```

Dynamic Locale Switching

Apps can allow users to change languages on the fly. This can be handled using state management solutions (e.g., "Provider," "Riverpod," or "Bloc") to update the "locale" property of "MaterialApp."

Example Using "setState":

```
void _changeLanguage(Locale locale) {
  setState(() {
    _locale = locale;
  });
}
```

Advantages of Using Native Localization

Type Safety: Generated Dart code ensures you avoid runtime errors due to missing keys.

Performance: Localizations are compiled and optimized for release builds.

Consistency: Integrated with Flutter's core widgets and theming system.

Flexibility: Full support for pluralization, gender rules, and dynamic formatting.

✓ Checklist: Flutter Native Localization

[x] "flutter_localizations" and "intl" added to project.

[x] ARB files created with locale-specific keys.

[x] "l10n.yaml" configured for code generation.

[x] "flutter gen-l10n" integrated into build process.

[x] All widgets use "AppLocalizations.of(context)" accessors.

[x] Locale switching handled via app settings or system locale.

💡 Expert Insight

Start with localization—even if you launch in a single language. It enforces string separation and prepares your codebase for scaling globally.

—Mikita K, Flutter GDE and Core Contributor

♡ Performance Alert

Localization string resolution is optimized at compile time, so avoid using reflection-based or runtime-parsed solutions in performance-sensitive sections unless strictly necessary.

Integrating Third-Party Localization Libraries

While Flutter's native localization system is powerful and flexible, many teams opt to use third-party libraries for faster development, dynamic file loading, and simplified integration—especially in larger applications with frequent translation updates or non-technical content managers.

CHAPTER 15 FLUTTER FOR INTERNATIONALIZATION AND LOCALIZATION

Here we explore leading third-party localization solutions in the Flutter ecosystem and how they can be leveraged to enhance productivity, scalability, and maintainability.

Why Use Third-Party Libraries?

Feature	Native Localization	Third-Party Libraries
ARB/JSON/YAML Format Support	ARB Only	JSON, YAML, CSV, ARB
Hot Reload for Text Updates	✗	✓ (in many libraries)
Code Generation	✓ Required	✗ Optional or Dynamic
Dynamic Runtime Switching	Manual	Built-in (some libraries)
Asset or API Translation Load	✗	✓

Popular Localization Libraries

Here are some of the most adopted and stable libraries for internationalization in Flutter:

Library	Highlights
'easy_localization'	Most intuitive setup, supports JSON/YAML, hot reload, no codegen
'get' (GetX)	Minimal, reactive, integrated i18n within state management
'flutter_i18n'	Dynamic loading, supports nested JSON, formats like YAML/CSV
'intl_utils'	Wrapper around 'intl' with better ARB support & automation

Case Study: "easy_localization"

"easy_localization" is a community-loved package designed for rapid internationalization. It removes the need for code generation, supports multiple file formats, and offers an elegant syntax.

CHAPTER 15　FLUTTER FOR INTERNATIONALIZATION AND LOCALIZATION

Step 1: Add Dependencies

```
dependencies:
  easy_localization: ^3.0.0
```

Step 2: Add Your Language Files

Create translation files in "assets/translations/":

```
// en.json
{
  "title": "Welcome",
  "greeting": "Hello, {}!"
}
```

```
// fr.json
{
  "title": "Bienvenue",
  "greeting": "Bonjour, {}!"
}
```

Step 3: Configure the App

```
void main() async {
  WidgetsFlutterBinding.ensureInitialized();
  await EasyLocalization.ensureInitialized();

  runApp(
    EasyLocalization(
```

```
      supportedLocales: [Locale('en'), Locale('fr')],
      path: 'assets/translations',
      fallbackLocale: Locale('en'),
      child: MyApp(),
    ),
  );
}
```

Step 4: Use Localized Strings in Widgets

```
Text('greeting'.tr(args: ['Alice']))
```

You can also update the language at runtime:

```
context.setLocale(Locale('fr'));
```

Advanced Capabilities with "easy_localization"
Supports pluralization and nesting
    Uses ".tr()," ".plural()," and ".tr(context)" for localized strings
    Supports CSV/YAML via configuration
    Automatic fallback support
    Optional CLI for JSON-to-Dart conversion if desired
💬 Real-World Insight

Our localization team updates content daily. Switching from codegen-based ARB to "easy_localization" slashed our iteration time in half.

—Mona Patel, Engineering Manager,
B2C EdTech App with 20+ Locales

Alternatives Overview

"flutter_i18n": Best for dynamic content fetched from remote servers or large-scale apps requiring on-the-fly updates

"get" (GetX): Excellent for tightly integrated state management and localization in small- to mid-sized apps

✓ Checklist: Third-Party Localization Setup

[x] Added preferred localization library to "pubspec.yaml"

[x] Translation files created in supported format (JSON/YAML/CSV)

[x] Localization context initialized in "main.dart"

[x] Dynamic language switching verified

[x] Strings accessed using ".tr()," ".plural()," or equivalent API

[x] Performance profiled on Android, iOS, and web builds

⚠ Security and Performance Alert

Some third-party libraries load and parse localization files at runtime. Always profile performance on low-end devices and avoid exposing dynamic translation endpoints without authentication, especially in apps with paid or sensitive content.

💡 Expert Tip

Use third-party libraries when your localization needs are dynamic or involve non-developer roles. But if you're building for static or highly regulated environments, stick with Flutter's native tooling.

—Andrew Fitz, Flutter i18n Consultant

CHAPTER 15   FLUTTER FOR INTERNATIONALIZATION AND LOCALIZATION

Handling Locale-Specific Design

Designing applications for a global audience involves more than simply translating text. Different languages and regions introduce diverse layout requirements, content structures, and cultural expectations that significantly impact the user experience.

Here we focus on how to design flexible, adaptive user interfaces that gracefully accommodate multilingual content and align with regional norms. You'll learn to manage layout expansion, text direction, visual density, and even iconography adjustments for different locales.

Designing UIs for Multiple Languages

Designing user interfaces that function seamlessly across multiple languages is a critical component of building globally scalable Flutter applications. Language variations impact not only the content but also the structure, spacing, alignment, and overall user experience of your application. A one-size-fits-all layout is insufficient for supporting diverse languages such as German, Arabic, or Hindi—each of which may expand, contract, or even mirror UI components.

Here, we explore layout strategies, widget adaptations, and best practices to ensure your Flutter UIs remain accessible, functional, and visually appealing across different languages and locales.

✏ **Challenge: Text Length Variations**

Different languages can have dramatically different text lengths for the same concept. For instance, a word like "Settings" translates to

- **English**: Settings (8 characters)
- **German**: Einstellungen (14 characters)
- **Finnish**: Asetukset (9 characters)
- **French**: Paramètres (10 characters)

Without proper layout flexibility, such variations may lead to overflow, clipping, or broken alignment—especially on buttons, tabs, and dialog titles.

❦ Key Flutter Widgets and Layouts for Multilingual UI

To design adaptable, scalable UIs, Flutter provides multiple layout mechanisms:

1. **"Flexible" and "Expanded"**

    These widgets allow child elements like "Text" to grow within a "Row" or "Column," preventing layout overflow.

    ```
    Row(
      children: [
        Expanded(
          child: Text(AppLocalizations.of(context)!.
          settings),
        ),
      ],
    )
    ```

2. **"FittedBox"**

    Useful when you need text to shrink to fit within a fixed-width widget (e.g., buttons or labels).

    ```
    FittedBox(
      fit: BoxFit.scaleDown,
      child: Text(AppLocalizations.of(context)!.save),
    )
    ```

3. **"AutoSizeText" (via Plugin)**

   Dynamically adjusts font size based on available space, ideal for long translated strings.

   ```
   AutoSizeText(
     AppLocalizations.of(context)!.welcomeMessage,
     maxLines: 2,
     style: TextStyle(fontSize: 18),
   )
   ```

🌐 Direction-Aware Layouts

Use directional widgets to automatically handle both LTR (left-to-right) and RTL (right-to-left) content flow:

Non-Directional	Directional Alternative
'EdgeInsets'	'EdgeInsetsDirectional'
'Alignment'	'AlignmentDirectional'
'Padding(left:)'	'Padding(start:)'

```
Padding(
  padding: EdgeInsetsDirectional.only(start: 12),
  child: Align(
    alignment: AlignmentDirectional.centerStart,
    child: Text('...'),
  ),
)
```

These changes allow your app to automatically adjust for RTL locales like Arabic or Hebrew without separate layouts.

🔍 Dynamic Font Scaling and Accessibility

Ensure your UI supports text scaling for accessibility purposes. Flutter provides access to the user's system font scale via "MediaQuery.textScaleFactor."

```
Text(
  AppLocalizations.of(context)!.terms,
  style: Theme.of(context).textTheme.bodyMedium!.copyWith(
    fontSize: 16 * MediaQuery.textScaleFactorOf(context),
  ),
)
```

Avoid hardcoding font sizes—always use themes or scaled sizes to keep your app readable across languages and accessibility preferences.

✅ Checklist: UI Preparedness for Multiple Languages

[x] Used "Flexible," "Expanded," or "AutoSizeText" for dynamic text areas

[x] Replaced "EdgeInsets"/"Alignment" with "EdgeInsetsDirectional"/"AlignmentDirectional"

[x] Tested text rendering at 200% text scale on Android/iOS

[x] Verified no clipping or overflow in navigation bars, dialogs, and buttons

[x] Used themes or scale factors for font sizes

[x] Tested layout in at least one LTR and one RTL language

> ⚡ **Expert Insight**
>
> *Your UI isn't internationalized until it handles German, Arabic, and Hindi—all three push your layout in unique ways. Test early and often.*
>
> —Elisa Müller, Senior UX Engineer, Global Retail Platform

⚠ **Performance and UX Alert**
Performance: Widgets like "AutoSizeText" can be costly in large lists. Use them judiciously and cache sizes where needed.

UX: Avoid truncating important actions or call-to-action buttons. If needed, localize text concisely or switch to icon + tooltip combinations.

Cultural Considerations in UI Design

While translating an app into multiple languages is vital for internationalization, true localization goes further. It requires a deep understanding of the cultural expectations, norms, and sensitivities of your target users. A culturally aware user interface can significantly enhance engagement, reduce confusion, and avoid miscommunication—or, worse, unintended offense.

This section explores the critical cultural factors that influence UI design, such as visual symbolism, colors, gestures, and region-specific regulations. We'll also outline actionable Flutter strategies for creating inclusive, respectful, and context-aware applications.

🌐 **Why Culture Matters in UI**
Design choices that feel intuitive in one culture may appear foreign, offensive, or irrelevant in another, for example:

UI Element	Risk Without Cultural Awareness
✋ Hand gesture icon	May be offensive in certain regions (e.g., thumbs up in parts of the Middle East)
🎨 Red color	Means danger in the West, but prosperity in China
🐷 Pig illustration	Taboo in Islamic cultures
💬 Humor or idioms	Often lost in translation or culturally inappropriate
🧭 Navigation icons	Left/right orientation may confuse RTL users

🎨 Color Psychology and Cultural Significance

Colors evoke different emotions in different cultures. Designers should avoid assuming universal meaning.

Color	Western Cultures	Eastern/Asian Cultures
Red	Danger, love, passion	Good fortune, celebration
White	Purity, peace	Mourning, death (e.g., China)
Green	Nature, safety	Prosperity, sometimes taboo (in Indonesia)
Black	Elegance, power	Mourning or bad luck

Best Practice: Always test your color palette with users from each target market and avoid relying on color alone to convey meaning.

🧠 Symbolism and Icons

Icons are not always universally understood, for instance:

> **Envelope for Email**: Universally accepted in the West, but less recognized in developing regions

CHAPTER 15 FLUTTER FOR INTERNATIONALIZATION AND LOCALIZATION

Trash Bin for Delete: Not intuitive for cultures unfamiliar with desktop metaphors

Piggy Bank for Savings: Inappropriate in Islamic cultures

✓ **Recommendation**: Pair icons with localized text labels. Flutter widgets like "Tooltip" can provide helpful hints on hover or long press.

```
Tooltip(
  message: AppLocalizations.of(context)!.delete,
  child: Icon(Icons.delete),
)
```

👆 Gestures and Navigation Expectations

Gestures are not interpreted the same everywhere. A swipe-to-delete gesture may be natural to Western users but confusing or undiscoverable for others.

Always support explicit UI elements alongside gestures.

For RTL languages, reverse directional gestures (e.g., swiping from right to left for back).

Flutter automatically handles gesture directionality with proper "TextDirection" configuration.

```
Directionality(
  textDirection: TextDirection.rtl,
  child: MyWidget(),
)
```

Text Tone and Formality

Text tone must be culturally appropriate:

English: Casual, friendly tones are often acceptable.

Japanese: Highly formal; tone must reflect respect and politeness.

German/French: Direct and precise language preferred.

Arabic/Urdu: Often poetic and expressive in tone.

Avoid idioms, slang, or humor that doesn't translate well.

Imagery and Visual Content

Visual assets such as illustrations and photos must be localized just like text. Consider

Clothing styles

Ethnic diversity

Religious symbols

Gender roles

Holiday references (e.g., Christmas, Halloween)

Use culturally neutral stock images or consider dynamic asset loading based on locale.

```
Image.asset(
  AppLocalizations.of(context)!.locale == 'ar'
    ? 'assets/images/hero_ar.png'
    : 'assets/images/hero_en.png',
)
```

⚖️ Local Laws and Privacy Norms

Different regions have distinct privacy, legal, and design compliance requirements.

> **EU**: GDPR compliance with cookie consent and data access transparency.

> **India**: Requires consent for financial or biometric data processing.

> **China**: Apps must store data locally and offer content censorship filters.

> **United States**: ADA (Accessibility) compliance requirements for public apps.

Ensure your app displays region-specific disclaimers, consents, and settings where applicable.

✅ Checklist: Cultural Compliance in UI Design

> [x] Avoided culturally sensitive or taboo imagery

> [x] Reviewed all iconography and metaphors for universal comprehension

> [x] Tested color schemes against local symbolism

> [x] Used formal/informal tones appropriately in different locales

> [x] Implemented gesture directionality with "Directionality"

> [x] Adjusted legal disclaimers and privacy practices by region

💬 **Expert Insight**

Localization isn't just about language. You can't globalize without culturalizing. The best UI is the one that feels local to every user, no matter where they are.

—Akira Takahashi, UX Localization Consultant, Tokyo

🚀 **Real-World Case Study**

A global e-learning app localized its UI for five markets: United States, India, France, Japan, and Saudi Arabia. After customizing illustrations, icons, and button styles for each region (along with text), their conversion rate improved by 23% and app uninstalls dropped by 31% within two months.

Right-to-Left (RTL) Layouts

Supporting right-to-left (RTL) languages such as Arabic, Hebrew, Persian, and Urdu is essential for creating truly global Flutter applications. RTL layouts require more than simply flipping text direction; they impact navigation flow, widget alignment, gestures, and overall user experience.

Flutter's robust RTL support empowers developers to create adaptive UIs that automatically mirror and reorient based on the user's locale. In this section, we'll explore how to implement RTL layouts efficiently and highlight best practices for handling multilingual content in mixed LTR/RTL environments.

Supporting RTL Layouts in Flutter Apps

Supporting right-to-left (RTL) languages such as Arabic, Hebrew, Persian, and Urdu is essential for building inclusive, global Flutter applications. RTL layouts require comprehensive UI adjustments beyond simply flipping text direction—they influence widget alignment, navigation flow, icon orientation, and gesture behavior.

CHAPTER 15 FLUTTER FOR INTERNATIONALIZATION AND LOCALIZATION

Flutter's robust framework offers built-in RTL support, allowing developers to create applications that adapt seamlessly to both left-to-right (LTR) and RTL locales. This section delves into the core mechanisms Flutter provides for RTL support and practical strategies to implement fully adaptive layouts.

Understanding Flutter's RTL Support

Flutter uses the "Directionality" widget as the cornerstone for managing text and layout direction. By setting the "textDirection" property to either "TextDirection.ltr" or "TextDirection.rtl," Flutter automatically mirrors layout elements and adjusts text rendering accordingly.

Many of Flutter's standard widgets—such as "Row," "Padding," "Align," and "IconButton"—are direction-aware and will invert their alignment and padding in RTL mode without additional code.

Configuring RTL in Your Flutter App

To enable RTL support, you must

1. **Set the App Locale Properly**

    Include the relevant RTL locales in the app's "supportedLocales" list and set the "locale" property dynamically or based on system preferences.

```
MaterialApp(
  locale: Locale('ar'), // Arabic locale example
  supportedLocales: [
    Locale('en'),
    Locale('ar'),
    Locale('he'), // Hebrew
  ],
  localizationsDelegates: [
    GlobalMaterialLocalizations.delegate,
    GlobalWidgetsLocalizations.delegate,
```

```
    GlobalCupertinoLocalizations.delegate,
  ],
  home: MyHomePage(),
);
```

2. **Wrap Widgets with Directionality**

   While "MaterialApp" sets directionality automatically based on locale, custom widgets or standalone widgets may need explicit "Directionality" wrapping:

   ```
   Directionality(
     textDirection: TextDirection.rtl,
     child: YourWidget(),
   );
   ```

Widget Mirroring and Alignment

Widgets like "Row" and "Column" automatically adapt their alignment based on the current directionality:

```
Row(
  mainAxisAlignment: MainAxisAlignment.start,
  children: [
    Icon(Icons.arrow_back), // Automatically flips in RTL
    Text('Back'),
  ],
);
```

Flutter also automatically mirrors directional icons such as arrows and chevrons. However, for custom icons or images, you might need to apply manual flipping via "Transform":

```
Transform(
  alignment: Alignment.center,
  transform: Matrix4.rotationY(isRTL ? math.pi : 0),
  child: Image.asset('assets/arrow.png'),
);
```

Handling Text Input and Cursor Direction

Flutter's "TextField" and "TextFormField" widgets handle RTL input automatically when the locale is set correctly. The cursor, text alignment, and selection gestures adapt to RTL conventions without additional configuration.

Testing RTL Layouts

Testing is crucial to ensure RTL support works flawlessly across all UI components. Flutter's emulator and physical devices allow setting the device language to an RTL locale. Additionally, the "WidgetsApp" or "MaterialApp" "locale" property can be overridden during development for quick RTL toggling.

✅ **Summary: RTL Support in Flutter**

Use "MaterialApp" with correct "supportedLocales" and localization delegates.
> Let Flutter's "Directionality" handle layout mirroring automatically.
> Wrap standalone widgets in "Directionality" if necessary.
> Flip custom images/icons manually using "Transform."
> Test extensively with RTL locales on multiple devices.

This foundational knowledge of RTL support sets the stage for implementing best practices in multilingual content management and UI adaptability, which we will cover in the next section.

Best Practices for Handling Multilingual Content

Handling multilingual content effectively is a cornerstone of creating accessible, user-friendly Flutter applications for diverse global audiences. Beyond supporting multiple languages and RTL layouts, delivering a smooth multilingual experience involves careful attention to content structure, UI consistency, and dynamic adaptability.

This section outlines essential best practices for managing multilingual content that ensures your Flutter apps are robust, scalable, and culturally sensitive.

1. **Detect and Respect User Locale**

    Automatically detecting the user's locale allows your app to deliver content in the user's preferred language and layout direction without manual intervention. Flutter provides easy access to the device's locale via

    ```
    Locale currentLocale = Localizations.localeOf(context);
    ```

    Use this information to dynamically load appropriate localized resources and adjust UI directionality.

2. **Provide an In-App Language Switcher**

   While automatic locale detection is useful, empowering users with an in-app language selector enhances usability and accessibility. This feature allows users to override the default system locale as needed.

   Best practices for a language switcher include

   Persistent Storage: Save the user's language preference using packages like "SharedPreferences" or "Hive."

   Immediate Effect: Apply the language change instantly across the app without requiring a restart.

   UI Feedback: Clearly indicate the current language and available options.

3. **Handle Mixed LTR and RTL Content Gracefully**

   In multilingual apps, it is common to encounter mixed content where LTR and RTL texts appear together (e.g., an Arabic paragraph containing English brand names). Flutter's "RichText" widget lets you specify direction and styling at the text span level, ensuring proper rendering.

   Example:

   ```
   RichText(
     textDirection: TextDirection.rtl,
     text: TextSpan(
       text: 'مرحبا بكم ة تطبيق ',
       style: TextStyle(color: Colors.black),
   ```

```
      children: [
        TextSpan(
          text: 'Flutter',
          style: TextStyle(fontWeight: FontWeight.bold),
          locale: Locale('en'),
        ),
      ],
    ),
  );
```

This approach preserves linguistic accuracy and improves readability.

4. **Manage Text Wrapping and Overflow**

   Long text strings, especially in languages with longer word lengths or compound characters, can cause layout issues. Use flexible layout widgets ("Flexible," "Expanded") and text sizing packages like "AutoSizeText" to manage dynamic content gracefully.

   Test your app with various string lengths and locales to prevent overflow or clipping issues.

5. **Use Plurals, Gender, and Contextual Variations**

   Languages have complex grammar rules involving plurals, gender, and contextual phrasing. Flutter's internationalization support ("intl" package) provides mechanisms to handle these variations properly using ICU message syntax.

Example Plural Handling:

```
Intl.plural(
  itemCount,
  zero: 'No items',
  one: '1 item',
  other: '$itemCount items',
);
```

Proper pluralization and gender support enhance the naturalness and professionalism of your app's language.

6. **Optimize Content Updates and Maintenance**

   Plan your localization strategy to facilitate ongoing content updates:

   Use externalized localization files (e.g., ARB, JSON) to separate content from code.

   Automate translation workflows with tools like Google Translate API or third-party localization platforms.

   Test translations thoroughly with native speakers or linguistic QA tools.

✅ **Checklist: Best Practices for Multilingual Content**

[x] Automatically detect and respect user locale.

[x] Provide in-app language switching with persistent preferences.

[x] Handle mixed LTR and RTL content using "RichText" and explicit directionality.

[x] Manage text wrapping and overflow with flexible widgets.

[x] Use the "intl" package for plurals, gender, and contextual variations.

[x] Externalize localization files and streamline translation updates.

💡 **Expert Insight**

Multilingual content handling is more than translation; it's about respecting linguistic nuances and cultural contexts. Flutter's rich localization APIs provide the tools, but developers must architect their apps with flexibility and user control in mind.

—Dr. Lina Haddad, Internationalization Consultant and Flutter Advocate

Implementing these best practices will greatly enhance your app's usability and appeal across languages and cultures, positioning your Flutter project for global success.

Summary

The chapter provided a comprehensive guide to internationalizing and localizing Flutter applications, enabling developers to reach a global audience with culturally relevant and linguistically accurate user experiences. Starting with Flutter's built-in localization features and the integration of third-party libraries, the chapter explored effective strategies for managing multiple languages and locale-specific UI designs.

CHAPTER 15   FLUTTER FOR INTERNATIONALIZATION AND LOCALIZATION

Special emphasis was placed on supporting right-to-left (RTL) layouts, including Flutter's automatic mirroring capabilities and manual techniques for custom widgets and icons. The chapter concluded with best practices for handling multilingual content—covering automatic locale detection, in-app language switching, mixed-direction text rendering, and nuanced linguistic considerations such as plurals and gender.

By mastering these techniques, developers can build Flutter apps that are both globally accessible and locally authentic, meeting the diverse needs of users across languages and cultures.

CHAPTER 16

Deploying and Maintaining Flutter Apps

In the previous chapter, we explored how to build globally inclusive Flutter applications through effective internationalization and localization strategies. From integrating multilingual support and designing culturally aware UIs to implementing RTL layouts, the chapter emphasized the importance of creating applications that resonate with diverse users across regions and languages. Now that your Flutter app is not only feature-rich but also culturally adaptive, it's time to take the next critical step—preparing it for the real world.

Here we are going to focus on the final and often most overlooked phase of the app development lifecycle: deployment and maintenance. Releasing an application involves far more than compiling code—it demands careful packaging, platform-specific optimizations, app store compliance, and a well-planned publishing strategy. Whether you're targeting Android, iOS, web, or desktop, ensuring a seamless deployment experience is crucial to delivering a stable and professional-grade app to end users.

But shipping an app is just the beginning. In a rapidly evolving ecosystem, apps must be continuously updated, monitored, and optimized to maintain performance, security, and compatibility. From handling app store submissions and setting up CI/CD pipelines to managing version updates and real-time analytics, this chapter offers a full-spectrum view of how to sustainably maintain your Flutter applications post-launch.

You'll also learn how to integrate Firebase Analytics, Crashlytics, and third-party monitoring tools to gain actionable insights into app health and user behavior. Armed with these capabilities, you'll be able to detect issues before users report them, release improvements with confidence, and scale your app's success in a controlled and data-driven manner.

Whether you're deploying your first Flutter app or maintaining a production-grade multi-platform system, the tools and techniques in this chapter will empower you to deliver polished, high-performance applications with long-term reliability and impact.

Preparing for Release

Before any application can be delivered to users, it must be optimized, packaged, and configured for production deployment. Flutter's cross-platform nature simplifies this process, but each target—whether Android, iOS, web, or desktop—has its own release considerations. This section guides you through the essential steps for preparing your Flutter app for a successful, stable, and secure release.

Building and Packaging Flutter Apps for iOS and Android

Releasing a Flutter app for mobile platforms—iOS and Android—requires more than simply building a release version. It involves proper configuration, signing, packaging, and optimization to meet the standards of the respective app stores and ensure a smooth user experience. This section provides a comprehensive guide for packaging Flutter apps for both platforms with production readiness in mind.

🎁 Building for Android

Flutter's integration with the Android toolchain provides a relatively streamlined build process. However, production deployment requires careful attention to signing, versioning, and build optimization.

🔧 Step 1: Configure Versioning

Set the app version and build number in "pubspec.yaml":

```
version: 1.0.0+1
```

"1.0.0" is the user-facing version.

"+1" is the internal build number (used by Play Store for updates).

🔒 Step 2: Set Up App Signing

App signing is mandatory for Play Store deployment. Flutter uses the Android Gradle system, which requires the following:

1. Generate a keystore:

   ```
   keytool -genkey -v -keystore key.jks -keyalg RSA -keysize 2048 -validity 10000 -alias my-key-alias
   ```

2. Store "key.jks" in the "android/" directory (never check into source control).

3. Create "key.properties":

   ```
   storePassword=your_store_password
   keyPassword=your_key_password
   keyAlias=my-key-alias
   storeFile=key.jks
   ```

CHAPTER 16   DEPLOYING AND MAINTAINING FLUTTER APPS

4. Update "android/app/build.gradle":

```
def keystoreProperties = new Properties()
keystoreProperties.load(new
FileInputStream(rootProject.file("key.properties")))

signingConfigs {
   release {
       keyAlias keystoreProperties['keyAlias']
       keyPassword keystoreProperties['keyPassword']
       storeFile file(keystoreProperties['storeFile'])
       storePassword keystoreProperties['storePassword']
   }
}
```

🚀 Step 3: Build for Release

You can generate either an APK (for direct install) or AAB (for Play Store submission):

```
flutter build apk --release
flutter build appbundle --release
```

🧬 Step 4: Optimize the Build

Enable code obfuscation and split debug info:

```
flutter build appbundle --release --obfuscate --split-debug-
info=build/debug-info
```

This reduces APK size and makes reverse engineering more difficult.

✅ **Android Release Checklist**:

[ ] Set correct app version.

[ ] Generate and secure a keystore.

[ ] Configure signing in Gradle.

[ ] Build using "--release."

[ ] Enable obfuscation and symbol splitting.

[ ] Test on real devices before publishing.

🍎 Building for iOS

Apple's ecosystem has stricter policies and a more controlled signing and distribution process. Flutter works closely with Xcode to meet these standards.

🔧 **Step 1: Update Version and Build Number**

In "pubspec.yaml":

```
version: 1.0.0+1
```

Also update in Xcode ("ios/Runner.xcodeproj" → "General" tab).

🎥 **Step 2: Configure Signing**

Open the iOS project in Xcode:

```
open ios/Runner.xcworkspace
```

Sign in with your Apple Developer ID.

Set the appropriate Team, Bundle Identifier, and Provisioning Profile.

Enable automatic or manual code signing.

⚙ **Step 3: Build for Release**

```
flutter build ipa --release
```

You can now upload to App Store via Xcode or Transporter.

✖ **Step 4: Archive and Distribute**

In Xcode

> Go to Product → Archive.
>
> After archiving, use the Organizer to validate and distribute the ".ipa."

📋 **iOS Release Checklist:**

> [ ] Set version and build number.
>
> [ ] Set correct bundle identifier.
>
> [ ] Configure signing and provisioning.
>
> [ ] Build ".ipa" with "flutter build ipa."
>
> [ ] Archive and upload using Xcode.
>
> [ ] Test on real devices and Apple TestFlight.

🔒 **Security Alert**

Never store signing credentials, keystores, or provisioning profiles in your repository. Use environment variables and encrypted CI/CD secrets for secure automation.

💡 Expert Insight

Run "flutter clean" before your final release builds to eliminate stale cache artifacts and reduce binary bloat. Also, test obfuscated builds to catch potential runtime issues introduced by tree shaking.

—Anand Verma, Senior Mobile Engineer at AppSecure

This section sets the foundation for deploying robust and production-ready apps to mobile stores. In the next section, we'll explore how to achieve similar production quality for Flutter web and desktop platforms, where performance tuning and asset handling differ significantly.

Preparing Flutter Web and Desktop for Production

As Flutter matures beyond mobile platforms, web and desktop support has become production-ready and increasingly viable for building full-featured, cross-platform applications. However, deploying for the web and desktop requires platform-specific strategies to ensure performance, security, and scalability. This section explores the practical steps to prepare your Flutter Web and Desktop applications for stable, production-grade deployment.

⊕ Preparing Flutter Web for Production

Flutter's web output is a client-side app compiled to highly optimized JavaScript. To ensure fast load times, responsive performance, and reliable deployment, several production-specific adjustments must be made.

CHAPTER 16 DEPLOYING AND MAINTAINING FLUTTER APPS

⚒ Step 1: Build the Web Release

Flutter provides a command to generate a production-optimized build:

```
flutter build web --release
```

This produces a minified and tree-shaken version of your web app in the "build/web" directory, including

"index.html"

"main.dart.js" (compiled JavaScript)

Service worker and manifest files for PWA support

⚙ Step 2: Set the Base Href

If deploying to a subdirectory on a web server (e.g., GitHub Pages, Firebase Hosting), you must specify the "--base-href":

```
flutter build web --release --base-href="/your-sub-path/"
```

● **Important** Failing to set this correctly may break routing in production.

💼 Step 3: Host the Application

You can host the compiled web app with

Firebase Hosting (recommended)

GitHub Pages

Amazon S3 + CloudFront

Netlify/Vercel

Custom Nginx/Apache servers

Each platform has specific configuration files for caching, redirects, and headers. For example:

```
// firebase.json
{
  "hosting": {
    "public": "build/web",
    "ignore": ["firebase.json", "/.*", "/node_modules/"]
  }
}
```

⚡ **Performance Tips:**

✓ Enable service workers to cache assets offline (enabled by default in PWA mode).

✓ Use deferred loading for heavy assets or packages.

✓ Compress static assets using gzip or Brotli.

✓ Add a Content Delivery Network (CDN) for global performance.

♡ **Security Checklist for Web:**

[ ] Set "Content-Security-Policy" headers to protect against XSS.

[ ] Enforce HTTPS and secure cookies.

[ ] Disable browser caching for sensitive data.

[ ] Use meta tags to prevent clickjacking ("X-Frame-Options: DENY").

CHAPTER 16 DEPLOYING AND MAINTAINING FLUTTER APPS

📱 Preparing Flutter Desktop for Production

Flutter's support for macOS, Windows, and Linux enables native desktop development from a single codebase. Desktop apps require bundling native binaries, handling platform-specific packaging, and, often, code signing for trust and compatibility.

💼 Step 1: Build for Target Platform

Run platform-specific build commands:

```
flutter build macos
flutter build windows
flutter build linux
```

Each command produces a standalone binary and associated resources in "build/<platform>/."

🎁 Step 2: Create a Distributable Package

macOS:

> Use Apple's "productbuild" or tools like create-dmg (https://github.com/create-dmg/create-dmg) to create a ".dmg."
>
> Apps must be notarized and signed with an Apple Developer ID for distribution outside the Mac App Store.

Windows:

> Use tools like Inno Setup, NSIS, or WiX to create ".exe" or ".msi" installers.
>
> Sign binaries using "signtool.exe" and a trusted code signing certificate.

CHAPTER 16 DEPLOYING AND MAINTAINING FLUTTER APPS

Linux:

Package with ".deb," ".rpm," or AppImage.

Ensure shared library dependencies are bundled or linked dynamically.

🔒 **Desktop Security Checklist:**

[ ] Sign all binaries with platform-trusted certificates.

[ ] Follow OS-specific guidelines for sandboxing and permissions.

[ ] Validate input and avoid dynamic code execution.

[ ] Ship stripped binaries without development metadata.

📋 **Production Checklist (Web and Desktop)**

```
| Task                                           | Status |
| ---------------------------------------------- | ------ |
| ✓ Optimize assets and minimize build size      | ✓      |
| ✓ Configure routing and base href              | ✓      |
| ✓ Setup secure headers and HTTPS               | ✓      |
| ✓ Test on all supported browsers / OS versions | ✓      |
| ✓ Package with platform-specific installers    | ✓      |
| ✓ Sign and notarize (desktop binaries)         | ✓      |
```

💡 **Expert Insight**

On web, the initial load experience is everything—invest in caching, deferred loading, and pre-rendering to keep users engaged. For desktop, proper packaging and signing aren't optional—they're essential to gaining user trust.

—Mariana DuPont, Lead Engineer at Omnitech Labs

🚀 Real-World Scenario

Case: Flutter app for a SaaS dashboard deployed across web and desktop

A SaaS company built a dashboard with Flutter 3.29, delivering it via Firebase Hosting (web), Inno Setup (Windows), and ".dmg" (macOS). They

- Used Firebase for CI/CD and hosting
- Signed installers with DigiCert EV certificates
- Obfuscated Dart code and split debug info for security
- Set up offline caching with service workers

The result? A unified app experience across devices—with a single codebase and 80% lower maintenance costs.

Publishing Flutter Apps

Once your Flutter app is built and production-ready, the next step is deployment. Whether targeting mobile platforms like Apple App Store and Google Play Store or delivering via web and desktop, the publishing process must be handled with care to ensure compliance, discoverability, and optimal user experience.

Here we are going to explore two core areas:

- Submitting Flutter apps to App Store and Play Store
- Hosting and deploying Flutter Web applications through various platforms

Publishing is more than uploading binaries—it includes configuring store listings, ensuring compliance with guidelines, setting up release tracks, and optimizing visibility.

CHAPTER 16   DEPLOYING AND MAINTAINING FLUTTER APPS

App Store and Play Store Submission

Once your Flutter application is production-ready, the final and most crucial step in the mobile lifecycle is publishing it to the app stores. This process involves not just uploading your binaries but also ensuring compliance with platform guidelines, optimizing metadata for discoverability, and correctly configuring store assets and policies.

This section walks you through the end-to-end publishing process for both Google Play Store and Apple App Store, covering technical, legal, and strategic steps to ensure your Flutter app is approved and discoverable.

Publishing to Google Play Store

Google Play offers a relatively streamlined and developer-friendly process for app submission. Here's how to publish your Flutter Android app:

Step 1: Set Up a Developer Account

Sign up at play.google.com/console (https://play.google.com/console).

Pay the one-time registration fee of $25 USD.

Complete your account and identity verification.

Step 2: Generate a Release App Bundle

Flutter supports AAB (Android App Bundle) as the standard release format.

```
flutter build appbundle --release
```

This command generates a ".aab" file under "build/app/outputs/bundle/release/app-release.aab."

Security Tip   Ensure you have set up a secure upload key and signing configuration in "key.properties" and "build.gradle."

📄 Step 3: Create Your App in Play Console

Choose "Create App."

Fill in

> App name
>
> Default language
>
> App or game
>
> Free or paid
>
> Accept developer policies

🖋 Step 4: Complete the Store Listing

> Add app icon, screenshots, feature graphics, and description.
>
> Select category and content rating.
>
> Add contact info and a valid privacy policy URL.

⚖️ Step 5: App Content and Compliance

> Fill in the Data Safety section (describe data collection and handling).
>
> Complete the Content Rating Questionnaire.
>
> Declare target audience and advertising usage.

🚀 Step 6: Release and Submit

> Go to Release ➤ Production and create a new release.
>
> Upload the ".aab" file.
>
> Review release summary and rollout strategy.
>
> Click Review and Rollout → "Start rollout to production."

> **✏ Pro Tip** Use internal or closed testing tracks for early QA and beta testing with smaller user groups.

🍎 Publishing to Apple App Store

The Apple submission process is more rigorous, emphasizing app quality, privacy, and compliance.

✅ Step 1: Enroll in the Apple Developer Program

Register at developer.apple.com (https://developer.apple.com/).

Pay an annual fee of $99 USD.

Enable two-factor authentication and agree to license terms.

⚙ Step 2: Configure Your iOS App

In Xcode or via Flutter

> Set a valid Bundle Identifier in "ios/Runner.xcodeproj."
>
> Ensure signing and provisioning profiles are correctly set.
>
> Update "Info.plist" with app permissions, description, and version.

Build the ".ipa":

```
flutter build ipa --release
```

Or archive via Xcode for more control.

📦 Step 3: Upload to App Store Connect

Use Transporter or Xcode Organizer to upload your ".ipa" file to App Store Connect.

Monitor upload status and resolve any issues.

📝 Step 4: Create App Listing in App Store Connect

Add

> Screenshots for all supported devices (iPhone SE to iPhone 15 Pro Max)
>
> App icon (1,024 × 1,024 PNG)
>
> Description, keywords, support/contact URLs
>
> App version number and build

🔒 Step 5: Compliance and Review Info

Provide privacy practices (App Privacy section).
Complete export compliance (e.g., for encryption).
Optionally, add notes for the App Review team.

✅ Step 6: Submit for Review and Release

Choose the release method: manual, automatic, or phased rollout.
Click Submit for Review.

Apple reviews apps typically within 24–48 hours, though complex apps may take longer.

⚠ **Compliance Tip** Avoid hard crashes, placeholders, and unresponsive UIs. Apple's review process is unforgiving of such issues.

📊 Comparison Table: Play Store vs. App Store

Feature	Google Play Store	Apple App Store
Developer Fee	One-time \$25	\$99/year
Build Format	`.aab`	`.ipa`
Review Time	Few hours to 2 days	1 to 3 days
Metadata Requirements	Flexible	Strict

Rollout Options	Internal, Closed, Open	Manual, Auto, Phased
Data Privacy Declaration	Required (Data Safety)	Required (Privacy Labels)
Screenshots	Optional for tablets	Required for all devices

✅ App Store Publishing Checklist

Task	Android	iOS
Developer account setup	✓	✓
Build release app	'.aab'	'.ipa'
Upload binary	✓	✓
Store listing metadata	✓	✓
Privacy/data declaration	✓	✓
Review and compliance	✓	✓
Launch method chosen	✓	✓

💡 Expert Insight

App success isn't just about great code—it's about presentation. Store listing visuals, keyword optimization, and thoughtful release scheduling can make or break your app's visibility.

—Megan Li, Growth Lead, AppPulse Labs

🐢 Performance Alert

Obfuscate Dart code for release builds:

```
flutter build appbundle --release --obfuscate
--split-debug-info=/<project>/<directory>
```

Remove debug flags, logging, and test credentials before submission. Use release builds always—never upload debug/test versions.

CHAPTER 16 DEPLOYING AND MAINTAINING FLUTTER APPS

Flutter Web Hosting and Deployment Options

As Flutter's web support has matured into a stable release channel, deploying Flutter web applications is now a production-grade strategy for building responsive, high-performance PWAs (Progressive Web Apps), internal dashboards, or customer-facing apps. However, successful deployment involves choosing the right hosting platform, configuring the build properly, and ensuring best practices around SEO, caching, and asset delivery.

This section explores the most common hosting options and deployment workflows for Flutter web apps, focusing on reliability, performance, scalability, and ease of integration.

📦 Building a Flutter Web App for Production

Before deployment, always produce a release build optimized for size and performance:

```
flutter build web --release
```

This generates minified HTML, CSS, JavaScript, and asset files in the "/build/web" directory. Key optimizations include

- Dart-to-JavaScript compilation via "dart2js"
- Tree shaking of unused code
- Asset compression and caching

🔒 **Security Tip** Always audit the "build/web" folder for exposed debug APIs or credentials.

CHAPTER 16 DEPLOYING AND MAINTAINING FLUTTER APPS

🌐 Hosting Options for Flutter Web

1. **Firebase Hosting**

   Firebase Hosting is one of the most seamless and popular options for Flutter web deployment.

✅ Key Features:

Global CDN with SSL

Fast deployment via CLI

Free tier with generous limits

🚀 Deployment Steps:

1. **Install Firebase CLI**:

   ```
   npm install -g firebase-tools
   ```

2. **Login and Initialize**:

   ```
   firebase login
   firebase init hosting
   ```

3. **Configure Public Directory**:

   Set it to "build/web" during setup.

4. **Deploy**:

   ```
   flutter build web --release
   firebase deploy
   ```

CHAPTER 16 DEPLOYING AND MAINTAINING FLUTTER APPS

> **Pro Tip** Enable "rewrite" rules in "firebase.json" for Flutter routing to work without 404s.

2. **GitHub Pages**

   GitHub Pages offers free hosting for static websites and is ideal for personal projects, portfolios, and documentation apps.

   Deployment Strategy:

   1. Build the app:

      ```
      flutter build web
      ```

   2. Create a "gh-pages" branch and push "/build/web" content:

      ```
      git subtree push --prefix build/web origin gh-pages
      ```

   3. Or use the gh-pages (https://www.npmjs.com/package/gh-pages) npm package for automation.

> **Note** You may need to set "baseHref" using "--base-href" if your app is served from a subdirectory.

3. **Netlify**

   Netlify provides instant continuous deployment with drag-and-drop support, Git-based deployment, and automatic SSL.

CHAPTER 16 DEPLOYING AND MAINTAINING FLUTTER APPS

💡 Highlights:

Integrated CI/CD pipeline

Form handling and serverless functions

Custom domain + HTTPS out of the box

Deployment Flow:

1. Connect your GitHub repo to Netlify.

2. Set the build command to

```
flutter build web
```

and publish directory to

```
build/web
```

3. Customize "_redirects" file to support Flutter routing.

4. 🚀 **Vercel**

   Vercel is optimized for frontend frameworks and offers intelligent caching, performance insights, and Git integration.

   Steps:

   Import repo via the Vercel dashboard.

   Configure

   Framework: "Other"

Output Directory: "build/web"

Set Build Command: "flutter build web"

⚠ **Routing Alert**: Use a "vercel.json" config file to enable SPA routing behavior:

```
{
  "rewrites": [{ "source": "/(.*)", "destination": "/index.html" }]
}
```
---

5. 🎯 **AWS S3 + CloudFront**

   For enterprise-grade scalability and control, host your Flutter web build on Amazon S3 with CloudFront CDN for caching.

   High-Level Steps:

   1. Upload "build/web" to an S3 bucket.
   2. Enable static website hosting.
   3. Set index document to "index.html."
   4. Configure CloudFront to serve your S3 content globally with HTTPS and custom domains.

🏨 Hosting Options Comparison

Hosting Provider	SSL	CDN	CI/CD	Custom Domains	Routing Config
Firebase Hosting	✓	✓	✓	✓	Simple JSON
GitHub Pages	✓	✓	✗	Limited	✓ baseHref needed

App Maintenance and Updates

Publishing your Flutter app is just the beginning. Continuous maintenance is vital to ensure performance, security, compatibility, and user satisfaction as platforms evolve. This chapter section focuses on strategies for keeping your app healthy over time, especially in response to new Flutter SDK releases, OS changes, device updates, and third-party dependency shifts.

We'll explore structured approaches to app maintenance and provide best practices for managing updates, ensuring backward compatibility, and minimizing regression risks.

Updating Flutter Apps for New Releases

Flutter is a rapidly evolving framework with a strong focus on innovation, performance, and cross-platform support. With each new release, the Flutter team delivers powerful features, optimizations, and security enhancements. However, these updates may introduce breaking changes, deprecate existing APIs, or require adjustments in your codebase. Keeping your Flutter app updated is not just about staying current—it's essential for long-term maintainability and compatibility.

This section covers a structured, risk-aware approach to updating your Flutter apps to newer SDK versions, ensuring smooth transitions with minimal disruption.

🚀 **Why Regularly Update Your Flutter App?**

Updating to the latest Flutter version brings several critical benefits:

> **Access to New Widgets and APIs:** Take advantage of innovations like Impeller rendering, new Material Design components, and better performance profiling tools.
>
> **Bug Fixes and Security Patches:** Resolve known issues affecting stability and vulnerability.

Platform Compliance: Stay compatible with new iOS/Android SDK requirements (e.g., API 34+ for Android, iOS 17+ compliance).

Tooling Enhancements: Get faster builds, improved DevTools, and smarter code analysis.

🧠 Expert Insight

Apps that regularly upgrade tend to have lower tech debt, fewer runtime crashes, and better user retention.

—Carlos H. Ortega, Flutter Tech Lead, Appnova

✹ Structured Upgrade Workflow

A disciplined update process helps minimize bugs and regressions.

✅ 1. Review Flutter Release Notes

Visit the Flutter release notes (https://docs.flutter.dev/release/whats-new) to understand

- Major changes
- Deprecated APIs
- Migration instructions

✅ 2. Back Up Your Codebase

Create a separate Git branch:

```
git checkout -b upgrade/flutter-3.29
```

Ensure all CI pipelines and tests are green before proceeding.

✅ 3. Upgrade the SDK

Use Flutter's built-in command to upgrade:

CHAPTER 16 DEPLOYING AND MAINTAINING FLUTTER APPS

```
flutter upgrade
```

Or target a specific version:

```
flutter version 3.29.0
```

Verify the upgrade:

```
flutter --version
```

🔧 Post-upgrade Actions
🔍 Analyze Your Code:
Run static analysis to catch deprecated APIs and warnings:

```
flutter analyze
```

Look for migration messages in the output.
♻ Clean and Fetch Dependencies:
Remove cached builds:

```
flutter clean
flutter pub get
```

Update packages:

```
flutter pub outdated
flutter pub upgrade --major-versions
```

Check pub.dev (https://pub.dev) for migration guides of updated dependencies.

🧪 **Run the Full Test Suite**:

Unit Tests: Validate core logic.

Widget Tests: Ensure UI stability.

Integration Tests: Catch platform regressions.

Automate via CI if possible to validate across multiple devices and OS versions.

🧩 **Resolving Breaking Changes**

If the new version introduces breaking changes

> Refer to official migration guides (e.g., Breaking Changes (https://docs.flutter.dev/release/breaking-changes)).
>
> Use migration tools, like
>
> ```
> dart fix --apply
> ```
>
> Replace deprecated APIs, update layout constraints, and modify behaviors as needed.

🧪 **Internal Testing and Staged Rollout**

🔒 **Pre-production Testing**:

Deploy to internal testers via Firebase App Distribution or TestFlight. Monitor logs, error reports, and performance metrics.

CHAPTER 16   DEPLOYING AND MAINTAINING FLUTTER APPS

🧬 Staged Rollout:
Use Play Console's staged rollout or App Store's phased release.
Track issues early without impacting all users.

📈 Performance Benchmarking
Compare performance before and after upgrade:

- Load time
- Memory usage
- Frame rendering stats

Use

```
flutter run --profile
```

and DevTools for diagnostics.

⚠ **Performance Alert**: Some versions may introduce regressions in layout or rendering—always validate against real device metrics.

✓ Upgrade Checklist

Task	Status
Read Flutter SDK release notes	✓
Backed up code / created upgrade branch	✓
Upgraded Flutter SDK via CLI	✓
Cleaned build and fetched packages	✓
Upgraded dependencies	✓
Resolved deprecated APIs	✓
Ran full test suite	✓
Performed internal testing	✓
Released via staged rollout	✓

🔍 Real-World Case Study

App: EduBoard (e-learning app)

Scenario: Migrated from Flutter 3.13 to 3.28

Changes Applied:

- Updated "TextFormField" to new decoration standards
- Migrated from deprecated "MaterialApp.router" logic
- Adopted new Impeller rendering engine

Outcome:

- App startup time reduced by 12%.
- Crash-free sessions improved by 9%.
- Codebase became more modular due to updated navigation APIs.

Managing App Versions and Compatibility

As your Flutter app matures and evolves, maintaining proper version control and ensuring cross-platform compatibility becomes mission-critical. Whether you're rolling out bug fixes, releasing major features, or updating for OS-level changes, structured versioning and compatibility strategies help prevent regressions, reduce user disruption, and maintain professional delivery standards.

This section dives deep into semantic versioning, platform-specific version configuration, backward compatibility techniques, and best practices for smooth, dependable release cycles across iOS, Android, web, and desktop.

CHAPTER 16 DEPLOYING AND MAINTAINING FLUTTER APPS

❖ Understanding Semantic Versioning in Flutter

Flutter supports semantic versioning (SemVer) through its "pubspec.yaml" file:

```
version: 2.5.3+102
```

> **"2.5.3"**: Human-readable version (MAJOR.MINOR.PATCH)
>
> **"+102"**: Build number (internal identifier, usually incremented in CI/CD)

Version Components:

Part	Purpose
Major	Breaking API changes
Minor	New features (non-breaking)
Patch	Bug fixes or small changes
Build number	Internal build count for app stores

⚠ **Note** App stores (Google Play and App Store) require build numbers to be incremented on every release.

⚙ Configuring Versions for Android

Update the "android/app/build.gradle" file:

```
defaultConfig {
    versionCode 102      // Must increment on each release
    versionName "2.5.3"  // Displayed version
}
```

"versionCode" is an integer and must always increase between builds submitted to Play Store.

"versionName" is user-facing and can follow any format.

🍎 Configuring Versions for iOS

Update "ios/Runner.xcodeproj" or "Info.plist":

```
<key>CFBundleShortVersionString</key>
<string>2.5.3</string>

<key>CFBundleVersion</key>
<string>102</string>
```

"CFBundleShortVersionString": App version shown in App Store

"CFBundleVersion": Internal build number (must increase)

Use Xcode or CLI tools to verify versioning:

```
xcrun agvtool what-version
xcrun agvtool what-marketing-version
```

🖥 Versioning for Web and Desktop

Web apps often use versioning in the build directory name, manifest file, or via environment variables. For example:

```
const String appVersion = '2.5.3';
```

Desktop apps (Windows/macOS/Linux) may configure versioning via "pubspec.yaml" or platform-specific config files (e.g., "Info.plist," "setup.cfg," etc.).

🛠 Best Practices for Version Management

Practice	Benefit
Use SemVer consistently	Helps teams and users track changes
Automate version bumping in CI/CD	Prevents human error during releases
Keep changelogs or release notes updated	Improves transparency and accountability
Use Git tags (e.g., 'v2.5.3')	Makes rollback and auditing easier
Integrate versioning into crash logs	Enhances debugging and support

↻ Ensuring Backward Compatibility

When releasing new updates, it's crucial not to break existing users' experiences—especially for those on older OS versions or devices.

CHAPTER 16 DEPLOYING AND MAINTAINING FLUTTER APPS

♡ **Techniques to Maintain Compatibility:**

1. **Platform Guards**:

   Use runtime checks to apply platform-specific logic:
   ```
   if (Platform.isIOS) {
     // iOS-specific behavior
   }
   ```

2. **Conditional Imports**:

   ```
   import 'src/file_stub.dart'
     if (dart.library.io) 'src/file_io.dart'
     if (dart.library.html) 'src/file_web.dart';
   ```

3. **Feature Flags**:

   Toggle features remotely based on user platform, version, or A/B testing logic.

4. **Deprecation Management**:

   Deprecate APIs or functionality gradually.

   Document deprecated features clearly.

✅ **Compatibility Checklist**

Task	Status
Semantic versioning implemented in 'pubspec.yaml'	✓
Android 'versionCode' & 'versionName' updated	✓
iOS 'CFBundleVersion' & 'ShortVersion' updated	✓
Backward compatibility tested (older OS/devices)	✓
Deprecated APIs tracked and replaced	✓
Crash logs linked with app versions	✓

📈 Real-World Case Study

App: QuickCash Wallet

Version Update: From "1.7.2+48" to "2.0.0+65"

Key Changes:

- Major UI overhaul using Material 3
- Breaking navigation refactor using "go_router"
- Removed legacy payment SDK for new provider

Compatibility Strategy:

- Feature-flagged new UI rollout
- Used conditional imports for different platforms
- Kept the old payment SDK in parallel for one release cycle

Outcome:

- Smooth user transition.
- Crash rate dropped by 15%.
- Improved customer retention during upgrade cycle.

📌 Pro Tip

🎨 Treat versioning as a contract with your users. A thoughtful versioning strategy builds trust and lets you scale faster with confidence.

—Lena D'Souza, Flutter DevOps Lead, NovaWare

CHAPTER 16   DEPLOYING AND MAINTAINING FLUTTER APPS

Monitoring and Analytics

Releasing a Flutter app is only the beginning of its lifecycle. Once your app is in the hands of users, maintaining its health and performance and understanding user behavior become critical. Monitoring and analytics tools empower developers to observe app behavior in production, detect crashes and performance bottlenecks early, and make informed decisions based on user interactions.

Here, we focus on integrating Firebase Analytics and Crashlytics—Google's industry-standard suite for app insights—followed by real-time health monitoring strategies for Flutter apps across platforms. Mastering these tools ensures that your production app remains performant, stable, and responsive to real-world usage patterns.

Integrating Firebase Analytics and Crashlytics

Monitoring app performance and understanding user behavior are critical for maintaining a successful Flutter application. Firebase provides two powerful services—Analytics and Crashlytics—that integrate seamlessly with Flutter and enable developers to track user interactions, monitor app stability, and resolve issues proactively in production environments.

Here, you'll learn how to properly set up and integrate Firebase Analytics and Crashlytics in a Flutter application for Android, iOS, and partially for web. We'll also explore best practices, custom implementations, and real-world examples of usage.

🔧 Setting Up Firebase in Your Flutter Project

Before integrating Firebase features, you need to initialize Firebase in your Flutter app.

Step 1: Add Firebase SDKs to "pubspec.yaml"

```
dependencies:
  firebase_core: ^latest_version
  firebase_analytics: ^latest_version
  firebase_crashlytics: ^latest_version
```

> **💡 Tip** Always use the latest stable versions to ensure compatibility with recent Flutter and Firebase releases.

Step 2: Initialize Firebase in "main.dart"

```
void main() async {
  WidgetsFlutterBinding.ensureInitialized();
  await Firebase.initializeApp();
  runApp(MyApp());
}
```

📊 Firebase Analytics: Tracking User Behavior

Firebase Analytics allows you to log events, user properties, screen transitions, and more to understand how users interact with your app.

✅ **Common Features:**

Automatic Tracking: Session start, app open, first open, etc.

Custom Events: Define and log user interactions.

User Properties: Segment users by traits (e.g., premium, region, language).

CHAPTER 16 DEPLOYING AND MAINTAINING FLUTTER APPS

🔍 **Logging Custom Events**:

```
final analytics = FirebaseAnalytics.instance;
analytics.logEvent(
  name: 'product_viewed',
  parameters: {
    'product_id': 'SKU123',
    'category': 'shoes',
    'price': 89.99,
  },
);
```

👁 **Tracking Screens**:

```
analytics.setCurrentScreen(
  screenName: 'CheckoutScreen',
  screenClassOverride: 'CheckoutPage',
);
```

🎨 **Best Practices**:
Keep event names lowercase and snake_cased.
Avoid excessive logging to maintain performance.
Use clear event naming to represent user journeys.
🏊 Use Case: Measure the drop-off rate between onboarding → registration → checkout to optimize conversion funnels.

Firebase Crashlytics: Monitoring Crashes in Real Time
Crashlytics helps identify, analyze, and respond to fatal and non-fatal errors in production.

CHAPTER 16   DEPLOYING AND MAINTAINING FLUTTER APPS

✵ Set Up Crash Reporting:
Enable Crashlytics by wrapping global Flutter error handlers:

```
FlutterError.onError = FirebaseCrashlytics.instance.
recordFlutterFatalError;

PlatformDispatcher.instance.onError = (error, stack) {
  FirebaseCrashlytics.instance.recordError(error, stack,
fatal: true);
  return true;
};
```

✦ Record Custom Non-fatal Exceptions:

```
try {
  // custom business logic
} catch (e, s) {
  FirebaseCrashlytics.instance.recordError(e, s, reason: 'Non-
fatal logic error');
}
```

🔥 Log Breadcrumbs and Custom Keys:

```
FirebaseCrashlytics.instance.setCustomKey('user_type',
'guest');
FirebaseCrashlytics.instance.log('User clicked on
settings icon');
```

CHAPTER 16   DEPLOYING AND MAINTAINING FLUTTER APPS

These logs and keys help reconstruct the user journey leading to a crash.

Crashlytics on Web and Desktop:

Crashlytics is fully supported on iOS and Android, with limited or no support on web and desktop.

For those platforms, consider

> Sentry
>
> Rollbar

Custom error logging to Firebase Firestore or Cloud Functions

✅ **Firebase Integration Checklist**

Task	Status
Firebase project configured	✓
SDKs added to 'pubspec.yaml'	✓
Firebase initialized in 'main()'	✓
Crashlytics global error handlers implemented	✓
Analytics events tracked and segmented	✓
Logs verified in Firebase Console	✓

🎁 **Real-World Example**

App Name: "FitTrack Pro"

Problem: Intermittent crashes after navigating between pages

Solution:

> Crashlytics stack trace revealed an unhandled null in animation controller.
>
> Analytics showed affected users mostly came from older devices with slow transitions.
>
> Patch released with fix and retry logic.

Outcome:

Ninety-six percent crash-free sessions (up from 82%)

Twenty-three percent increase in daily active users

🧠 Expert Insight

Crash logs tell you what broke. Analytics tells you why it broke and how users got there.

—Ritika Chopra, Mobile QA Architect at AppSure Labs

♡ Performance and Security Alerts

Performance: Avoid logging sensitive user data in custom events or crash logs.

Security: Ensure network logs or stack traces do not leak API tokens or PII.

Real-Time Monitoring of App Health

Once your Flutter app is live, ensuring its stability and responsiveness becomes critical. Real-time monitoring enables developers and DevOps teams to proactively track performance metrics, detect anomalies, and resolve issues before they impact end users. In this section, you'll learn how to implement real-time app health monitoring for Flutter applications across mobile, web, and desktop platforms.

We'll explore Firebase Performance Monitoring, custom diagnostics, third-party tools like Sentry and Datadog, and integration patterns for real-time dashboards.

Why Real-Time Monitoring Matters

Real-time insights into your app's health can help you

- Identify memory leaks or CPU spikes.
- Catch slow rendering frames.
- Detect dropped network requests.
- Track uptime and crash-free rates.
- Respond to issues before users report them.

📈 Firebase Performance Monitoring

Firebase Performance Monitoring helps track latency, startup times, and custom traces in real time.

✅ Setup:

Add the dependency to your "pubspec.yaml":

```yaml
dependencies:
  firebase_performance: ^latest_version
```

Initialize it:

```dart
FirebasePerformance performance = FirebasePerformance.instance;
```

⏱ Measuring Custom Traces:

```dart
Trace trace = performance.newTrace("load_home_screen");
await trace.start();
// run async operation
await trace.stop();
```

∞ Out-of-the-Box Monitoring:

Cold start time

HTTP/S network request duration

Frame rendering issues

Firebase automatically collects key performance indicators (KPIs) and displays them in the console.

⚖ **Real-World Example**: A startup identified excessive load times due to unoptimized network calls using Firebase traces—reducing initial load from 4.3s to 1.1s.

💼 Using Sentry for Performance and Issue Monitoring

Sentry provides a robust real-time monitoring platform for Flutter apps with full-stack visibility.

🔧 **Setup**:

```yaml
dependencies:
  sentry_flutter: ^latest_version
```

Initialize Sentry:

```dart
await SentryFlutter.init(
  (options) {
    options.dsn = 'https://your-dsn@sentry.io/project-id';
  },
  appRunner: () => runApp(MyApp()),
);
```

🚀 **Capabilities**:

Performance profiling

Breadcrumb logs

Slow/frozen frame detection

Real-time issue alerting

Advanced filtering and tagging

📊 Custom Monitoring Dashboards

For enterprise use cases, you may want to stream app health metrics to platforms like

> **Datadog**: Track CPU, memory, and log events.
>
> **Grafana + Prometheus**: Real-time dashboards for API call latency, crashes, and user sessions.
>
> **CloudWatch/Stackdriver**: Integrated monitoring for apps deployed on AWS or GCP.

⚠️ **Performance Alert**: Avoid overloading your app with background metric collectors—limit the frequency and verbosity of custom logs.

🔍 Metrics to Track in Flutter Apps

Metric	Description	Tools
Frame Rendering Time	Slow frames, dropped frames	Flutter DevTools, Firebase
Network Request Duration	Latency, failed API calls	Firebase, Sentry, Datadog
App Startup Time	Cold & warm start durations	Firebase, Sentry
Crash-Free Sessions	Sessions without crashes	Crashlytics, Sentry
User Interaction Timings	Response time to taps, scrolls	Firebase, Custom Traces
Device Resource Usage	CPU, RAM, battery usage	Sentry, Datadog

Real-Time Monitoring for Flutter Web and Desktop

Although some Firebase features are limited on web/desktop, you can still monitor real-time health using

> Google Analytics + Sentry (web)
>
> Custom REST endpoints + logging services (desktop)
>
> Native OS-level performance tools (Windows/ macOS/Linux)

Example: Stream logs from Flutter Desktop via HTTP to a centralized logging service like Logz.io.

Real-Time Monitoring Implementation Checklist

Task	Status
Integrated Firebase Performance Monitoring	✓
Custom traces added for critical user flows	✓
Sentry initialized for crash and performance reporting	✓
Metrics piped to a centralized dashboard (Datadog, etc.)	✓
Threshold-based alerts configured	✓

💡 Expert Insight

Real-time health monitoring shifts teams from reactive to proactive—saving time, protecting reputation, and improving user experience.

—Carlos Mendoza, Sr. Mobile DevOps Engineer at CloudFlux

⚠ Performance and Security Alerts

Security: Don't log sensitive PII like emails or access tokens in monitoring tools.

Performance: Balance trace granularity with runtime performance to avoid frame drops.

✅ End-of-Section Checklist

- [x] Firebase Performance Monitoring integrated
- [x] Custom trace points defined and measured
- [x] Real-time crash and issue alerts active
- [x] Monitoring extended to web and desktop targets
- [x] Dashboards and alerts tested in staging

Summary

Here, we explored the complete lifecycle of deploying and maintaining production-ready Flutter apps across mobile, web, and desktop platforms. You learned how to prepare your codebase for release builds, optimize configurations for each target, and publish apps on App Store, Play Store, and web hosting services. We also covered strategies for seamless updates, managing versioning, and ensuring compatibility with future Flutter releases. Finally, we dove into real-time monitoring and analytics using tools like Firebase and Sentry, enabling proactive performance tuning and issue resolution. Mastery of these workflows ensures your Flutter apps stay stable, scalable, and production-grade—long after launch.

Glossary of Terms

Async/Await: Keywords in Dart used for asynchronous programming. Async defines a function that returns a Future, while await pauses execution until the Future completes.

Bloc (Business Logic Component): A state management pattern that uses streams to separate business logic from UI components, promoting a clear and testable architecture.

Cubit: A lightweight state management solution that simplifies the Bloc pattern, offering an easier way to manage and emit states.

DevTools: A suite of tools provided by Flutter for debugging and profiling, including features for inspecting widgets, monitoring performance, and analyzing memory usage.

Flutter SDK: The software development kit developed by Google for building applications with a single codebase for multiple platforms, including mobile, web, and desktop.

Flutter Widgets: The fundamental elements of a Flutter app that describe the UI. Widgets are combined to build complex interfaces and can be stateful or stateless.

Hot Reload: A feature in Flutter that allows developers to instantly see changes made to the code without restarting the application, enhancing development efficiency.

Riverpod: A state management library for Flutter that offers a more flexible, scalable, and testable approach compared with the traditional Provider package.

RenderObject: A low-level Flutter class responsible for layout and painting operations within the rendering pipeline, crucial for custom rendering and advanced UI designs.

GLOSSARY OF TERMS

State Management: Strategies and patterns for managing an application's state, ensuring the UI reflects the current state of the data effectively.

Platform Channels: A mechanism for enabling communication between Dart code and native code (Java/Kotlin for Android, Swift/Objective-C for iOS), allowing access to native APIs.

Progressive Web App (PWA): A type of web application that delivers an app-like experience using modern web technologies, including offline capabilities and fast loading times.

TensorFlow Lite: A lightweight version of TensorFlow designed for mobile and embedded devices, enabling efficient machine learning model inference directly on devices.

Widget Tree: The hierarchical arrangement of widgets in a Flutter application, where each widget can contain other widgets, forming a tree structure that represents the UI.

Modular Architecture: An architectural design that organizes an application into independent, interchangeable modules, enhancing scalability and maintainability.

CI/CD Pipelines: Continuous Integration and Continuous Deployment pipelines that automate the processes of testing, building, and deploying applications, ensuring consistent and reliable updates.

Custom Animations: Animations created beyond Flutter's built-in options, allowing developers to design unique visual effects and transitions tailored to specific needs.

On-Device Machine Learning: Techniques for running machine learning models directly on mobile devices, enabling real-time data processing and inference without server dependency.

Security Protocols: Practices and technologies used to protect applications and user data, including encryption, authentication, and compliance with data protection regulations.

Dependency Injection: A design pattern used to manage dependencies within an application, promoting loose coupling and enhancing testability.

WidgetsBinding: A class that manages the lifecycle of widgets, including their creation, destruction, and interaction with the rendering pipeline.

Deferred Loading: A technique used to improve application performance by loading parts of the app lazily or on demand, rather than all at once.

Flutter DevTools Suite: A set of debugging and performance tools that includes Flutter Inspector, Performance View, Memory View, and Network View, among others.

These terms will ensure that readers have a comprehensive understanding of the concepts discussed throughout the book, making it a more complete and valuable resource.

Index

A

Adaptive design patterns
    context-aware layout adjustments, 87, 88
    content presentation, 92
    defined, 85
    input method, 88, 90
    navigation, 90, 91
    platform-specific adaptations, 86, 87
Adaptive layout patterns, 125–131
Adaptive widgets, 529
Advanced Bloc/Cubit patterns
    audio player, 286, 287
    authentication workflow, 283, 284
    ecommerce, 285, 286
    offline-first notes app, 288
    real-time chat app, 284, 285
Advanced encryption standard (AES), 469, 478, 482
AdvancedProgressIndicator widget, 56, 61
AES, *see* Advanced encryption standard (AES)
AGI, *see* Android GPU Inspector (AGI)

Alibaba's Xianyu app, 414
Android GPU Inspector (AGI), 222, 225
Android Gradle system, 947
Android testing, 457–458
AnimatedBuilder, 634, 640, 676
AnimatedContainer, 633, 662, 679
AnimatedListTile widget, 56, 62
AnimatedOpacity, 633, 662, 680, 681
AnimatedSwitcher, 4, 38, 681
AnimatedTextKit, 656
Animated widgets, 132–134
AnimationController, 6, 403, 633, 638, 675
Animations, 530, 809–814
    cross-platform consistency
        best practices, 670–673
        capabilities, 667
        core Flutter APIs, 667
        curves, 668
        FPS, 669
        overview, 666
        performance, 669
        responsive timing, 668
        testing, 669
        web/desktop, 669

INDEX

Animations (*cont.*)
    custom, 69, 70, 632 (*see also*
        Custom animation
        techniques)
    implicit widgets, 633
    libraries, 632
        case studies, 662–665
        customization, 653–658
        real-world
            examples, 658–662
        utilization, 650–653
    performance, 640–644
    performance optimization
        case studies and
            examples, 678–683
        techniques, 674–678
    smooth, 644–649
    and visual interaction, 631
AnimationStatusListener, 639
Anonymization, 904
Anti-reverse engineering, 764
API integration
    debugging
        DevTools and network
            inspection, 621
        emulators and
            simulators, 620
        error handling, 619
        interceptors, 618, 619
        mocking, 621
        observability, 622
        retry and timeout
            strategy, 622
        traditional, 618
    error handling and
        retries, 589–596
    strategies, 571
    techniques
        authentication and
            authorization, 588
        caching, 587
        handling large datasets,
            584, 585
        nested data, recursive
            models, 586
        parsing with model classes,
            585, 586
        sequential and dependent
            requests, 583, 584
    testing tools
        Charles Proxy and
            Proxyman, 628
        mockito and mocktail, 626
        mock servers, 627
        Postman, 625
        Postman monitors/
            Hoppscotch, 628
        REST client plugins, 625
        swagger and OpenAPI, 628
        verification, 627
App Bundle, 536, 537, 543
App hardening techniques
    code obfuscation, 765–768
    defined, 761
    encryption, 768–773
    reverse engineering, 761–764
AppImage, 538, 544
Apple App Store, 959, 960

INDEX

App transport security (ATS), 470
Artificial intelligence (AI), 685, 730,
    See also Machine
    learning (ML)
Asynchronous communication, 450
    background techniques, 435
    BasicMessageChannel, 434
    concurrent Dart execution, 435
    defined, 431
    EventChannel, 433
    framework, 431
    MethodChannel, 432
    patterns, 431
    real-world examples
        banking app, 439
        food delivery app, 438
        IoT device communication,
            441, 442
        music streaming app,
            442, 443
        SDK integration, 439
        social media app, 440, 441
    threading and concurrency, 436
    timeouts and exception
        safety, 436
Asynchronous
    programming, 14, 238
AsyncNotifier, 251, 257, 266
ATS, *see* App transport
    security (ATS)
Augmented reality (AR), 700, 705
Authentication, 588, 742
    biometrics, 757–761, 776
    Bloc/Cubit patterns, 283, 284

OAuth and JWT, 748–753
    overview, 748
    plugins, 473, 474
    and session management,
        779, 780
    techniques, 739
    2FA, 753–756
Authorization, 588, 742
Automated testing, 322, 467
AWS S3 + CloudFront, 966

B

BackdropFilter, 681
Bidirectional communication,
    425, 426
Biometrics, 757–761, 776
Blend modes, 368
Bloc 8.x, 268, 269
Bloc library, *see* Business Logic
    Component (Bloc) library
Bloc-to-Bloc communication,
    271, 273–274
BMW app, 413, 414
BMW's customer app ecosystem,
    549, 550
Browser compatibility
    adaptive design patterns, 512
    browsers matrix, 515
    defined, 510
    feature detection, 511
    font rendering and
        fallbacks, 514
    input modality differences, 513

INDEX

Browser compatibility (*cont.*)
    platform view and DOM integration, 513
    rendering backends, 511
    security constraints, 514
Browser-specific challenges
    compatibility, 510–516
    debugging and troubleshooting, 516–522
build() method, 170, 195, 207
Business Logic Component (Bloc) library
    ecosystem, 268
    event composition and abstraction, 272–277
    overview, 268
    updation
        BlocObserver class, 270
        cleaner API and migration guidance, 272
        DevTools and IDE integration, 270
        modular event handling, 269
        testing, 271

C

Caching techniques, 490
    case studies and use cases, 614–617
    in-memory, 610
    layered (hybrid approach), 611
    mechanisms, 609
    optimizing app data, 609–614
    persistent local storage, 610
    TTL and expiry logic, 611
Camera controller, 706
Camera plugin, 452, 463–465
Canvas class, 367, 368
canvas.drawPath(), 382, 410, 415
canvas.getClipBounds(), 389
CanvasKit, 502
Canvas.saveLayer(), 368, 374, 391
Centralized error handling, 589–591
Certificate pinning, 763, 771
CFBundleShortVersionString, 974
CFBundleVersion, 974
Change data capture (CDC), 886
ChatCubit, 284
CI/CD, *see* Continuous integration and delivery (CI/CD)
CineWatch, 665
Client-side errors, 589, 593
Clipping effects, 373, 374
CMake, 446, 545, 546
Code coverage, 829
Code obfuscation, 472, 742, 762, 765–768, 787
Code splitting, 12–16
colorFilter, 370
Communication
    advanced techniques
        background patterns, 428
        bidirectional, 425, 426
        custom codecs, 427, 428
        defined, 425

INDEX

dispatch routing and service layering, 429
error propagation and handling, 428
multi-channel architecture, 427
threading and UI responsiveness, 430
asynchronous (*see* Asynchronous communication)
channels, 317
Compliance
audit logging and monitoring, 904
data encryption and secure transmission, 904
example, 905
frameworks, 902, 903
and privacy, 905
privacy by design, 903
security assessments, 904
user data, 904
computeDryLayout(), 358
compute() function, 577
Conditional imports, 532, 976
Conditional layouts, 127–128
Constructors, 182, 208
Consumer electronics
best practices, 874
car infotainment display, 873
challenges and considerations, 873
defined, 871

hardware specification, 873
reasons, 871
smart home control panel, 872
Content density, 92
Content security policy (CSP), 519
Continuous integration and delivery (CI/CD), 467
debugging, 833–838
deployments, 824–828
GitHub actions, 819–824
pipeline, 546
benefits, 818
defined, 815
platforms, 816
setup, 817
stages, 815
workflow, 816, 817
profiling, 167, 168
test coverage reports, 829–833
tools, 787
Cost of layout, 356–361
Crashlytics, 980–983
CRM, *see* Customer relationship management (CRM)
Cubits
best practices, 282
creation, 279, 280
Firestore/WebSocket, 281
pitfalls, 282
and streams, 278, 279
UI, 280
Cupertino widgets, 529
CurvedAnimation, 634
Custom animations, 69, 70

INDEX

Custom animation techniques
    components, 633, 634
    composition, 634
    implementation, 635–639
    overview, 633
    reusability, 638
    use cases, 634
Custom codecs, 421, 427, 428
Customer relationship management (CRM), 894
Custom interactive controls, 136, 137
CustomMultiChildLayout, 52
    best practices, 118
    components, 113
    defined, 112
    examples, 114–117
    features, 113
CustomPaint class, 380, 399
CustomPainter class, 380
Custom painting operations
    creation
        CustomPaint and CustomPainter, 379, 381
        drawing, 381, 383, 384
        dynamic painting, 384, 385
        performance considerations, 385, 386
        visual effects, 379
    high-performance, 379
    performance optimization, 386–392
    shader techniques, 392–397
Custom rendering, 409–413
Custom render objects, 70, 71
Custom shaders, 368, 372
Custom themes and styles, 65, 66
CustomTooltip, 4
Custom widgets, 68, 149–156

D

Dart FFI, 858, 859
Data at rest, 475, 477, 746, 770
Data-driven layout changes, 123
Data in transit, 477, 478, 744, 771
Data synchronization, 885–888
Data transfer objects (DTOs), 182
Data visualization, 660
DatePicker, 3
DDD, *see* Domain-driven design (DDD)
Debian-based systems, 539
debugDumpApp(), 808
Deferred loading, 13
Dependency injection (DI), 258, 320, 621
Deprecation management, 976
Design systems
    benefits, 95, 96
    components, 93–95
    defined, 93
    implementation, 96, 97
Design tokens
    categories
        borders and shadows, 100
        colors, 98
        spacing, 99
        typography, 99

INDEX

defined, 98
implementation, 100, 102
management and updation, 103, 104
Desktop app development
    case studies, 551–556
    cross-platform consistency, 528–533
    dependencies, 540–546
    features
        drag-and-drop support, 526
        file system access, 527
        input handling, 525
        native platform widgets, 524
        window management, 523, 524
    operating systems, 533
    overview, 523
    packaging, 534–540
Desktop testing, 568
DevTools, 211, 252, 315, 423, 489, 516, 517, 621
    defined, 164
    GPU thread timeline, 173
    performance metrics
        CPU profiling, 170
        exporting and interpreting profiles, 172
        frame timing, 168
        memory usage, 170
        network and I/O, 171
        platform channel and plugin, 171
        widget build statistics, 169
    profiling techniques
        CI/CD, 167, 168
        fine-grained timeline analysis, 165
        paint and layout operations, 167
        tracing async operations, 166, 167
        widget rebuild, 166
DI, *see* Dependency injection (DI)
Dialogflow, 908
Digital banking transformation, 910
Directionality, 937
Disk image (DMG), 537, 538
Divide and conquer, 290
DMG, *see* Disk image (DMG)
Domain-driven design (DDD), 256
Drawing app, 220, 221
DTOs, *see* Data transfer objects (DTOs)
Dynamic layouts
    best practices, 124, 125
    defined, 119
    techniques, 119–124

E

eBay, 547, 548
Ecommerce, 285, 286
    animations, 661, 662
    caching, 614
    ML, 731

INDEX

Ecommerce (*cont.*)
    Riverpod and Bloc
        integration, 296–298
    UI problem, 219
EdTech, 732
Educational app, 615
EfficientNet Lite, 701
Embedded systems, 879
    architecture, 848
    benefits, 848
    challenges and limitations, 849
        hardware-specific
        issues, 866–870
        memory and performance
        constraints, 863–866
    characteristics, 844
    components, 843, 844
    consumer electronics,
        871–874
    defined, 843
    examples, 845
    IOT, 874–878
    overview, 841, 842, 846
    performance, 849
    peripheral interaction, 848
    Raspberry Pi, 850–862
    real-world viability, 849
    requirements, 847
    vs. traditional computing,
        845, 846
    user interfaces, 842
Emulators, 180, 240, 620
Encapsulation
    state management, 323

Encryption, 469, 768–773, 779, 787
    data-at-rest, 475, 477
    data-in-transit, 477, 478
    key management, 479
    local databases, 476
    pitfalls, 479
End-to-end encryption (E2EE), 478
Enterprise environments
    applications
        accessibility and
        localization, 892
        maintainability and scalable,
        889, 890
        memory optimization, 891
        network and API
        performance, 891
        offline support and
        background
        synchronization, 892
        performance monitoring
        and benchmarking, 892
        widget rendering, 890
    case study, 906–913
    IT infrastructures, 879
    large datasets and complex
        interactions
        client-side caching and data
        persistence, 895
        data rendering, lazy
        loading, 894
        debounced search and
        filtering, 896
        inventory management, 898
        multi-step interactions, 897

INDEX

pagination and infinite scrolling, 895
real-time data streams, 897
and UX complexity, 898
virtualized lists and scroll optimization, 895
legacy systems, 880–888
security requirements applications, 899–902
compliance and privacy concerns, 902–905
Enterprise-level Flutter applications
API communication security, 900
authentication and authorization, 900
code obfuscation and runtime protection, 901
data storage, 899
input validation and sanitization, 901
third-party packages, 901, 902
Entity management, 266
Error handling, 574, 589–596, 619
Event app with interactive cards, 74
Event-driven architecture, 325
E-wallet app, 775, 776
ExpandableListView, 4
ExpandableSection widget, 57, 63

F

FadeScaleSlideAnimation, 638
Fallback authentication, 759

FCM, *see* Firebase cloud messaging (FCM)
Feature/domain model, 274
Federated plugins, 449, 451
FFI, *see* Foreign function interface (FFI)
Finance app, 301, 302
Financial dashboard app, 218
Financial services, 910–913
find.byKey(), 805
find.byType(), 805
find.descendant(), 805
Fine-tuning state management, 314, 315
Firebase
analytics, 978–980
hosting, 963
performance monitoring, 984
Firebase cloud messaging (FCM), 886, 908
Firebase plugin, 461–463
Firestore, 281
Fitness app with progress tracking, 75
Fitness tracking app, API keys, 774, 775
FLEETCOR, 552, 553
Flex widgets, 130
Fluid layouts, 125, 126
Flutter
development areas, 345
in-depth analysis, 2
overview, 2
performance metrics, 8–11

INDEX

Flutter (*cont.*)
  performance optimization, 12
    asynchronous
      programming, 14
    caching mechanisms, 14
    code splitting, 12
    deferred loading, 13
    efficient layout
      algorithms, 13
    image and asset, 15
    state management, 15
  release notes
    conflict resolution, 46
    deprecated features, 40, 43
    detailed analysis, 35–42
    existing projects, 42–49
    performance metrics, 45
  upgrading, 1
    deprecated features, 27–30
    legacy code, 31–35
    migration, 16–26
    process flow, 37
  widgets, 2–7, 51 (*see also* Widgets)
Flutter apps
  Android, building and packaging, 947–949
  Apple Store, 959, 960
  compatibility, 975–977
  desktop (*see* Desktop app development)
  desktop production, 954–956
  development lifecycle, 945
  Google Play Store, 957, 958
  iOS, building and packaging, 949–951
  monitoring and analytics, 978–988
  plugins, 545
  updating
    benefits, 967
    breaking changes, 970
    internal testing and staged rollout, 970
    performance benchmarking, 971
    post-upgrade actions, 969, 970
    real-world case study, 972
    workflow, 968, 969
  versioning, 973–975
  web hosting and deployment options, 962–966
  web production, 951–953
Foreign function interface (FFI), 858
Fragmentation, 195
Frame budget tuning, 206

G

Garbage collection (GC), 39, 181
GC, *see* Garbage collection (GC)
GDPR, *see* General data protection regulation (GDPR)
General data protection regulation (GDPR), 902
General-purpose input/output (GPIO), 858

INDEX

Gesture-based interactions, 811
Gesture-driven interactions, 134, 135
GitHub pages, 964
Google Ads, 548
Google Ads mobile app, 415
Google Play Store, 825, 956–958
Google Stadia companion app, 414
GPIO, *see* General-purpose input/output (GPIO)
GPU performance analysis
   overview, 172
   profiling, 173–177
   rendering optimization
      frame budget management, 180
      images and assets, 179
      layer usage and composition, 178
      overdraw, 177
      precompile and warm up shaders, 178
      real devices, 180
      visual effects, 179
Grid-based layouts, 126, 127
GridView.builder, 209
GridView widget, 55, 59

H

Hardcoded secrets, 741, 771, 778, 779
Hardware acceleration, 713
Hardware-specific issues
   challenges, 867
   debugging, 869
   factors, 866
   integration, 867–869
Healthcare app data protection, 773
Healthcare industry
   digital transformation, 906
   features, 909
   goals, 906
   performance, 909
   results and outcomes, 908
   security and compliance measures, 908
   solution architecture and implementation, 907, 908
Health Insurance Portability and Accountability Act (HIPAA), 903
Hooking frameworks, 763
HTTP requests
   built-in request retrying, 574
   cross-platform consistency, 574
   customization, 575
   enhanced multipart and form-data, 574
   error handling, 574
   interceptors, 573
   large payloads, 575
   tasks, 573
   timeouts and cancellation, 573

INDEX

I

Identity and access management (IAM), 910
Image classification
  components, 701
  defined, 700
  implementation
    adding dependencies, 701
    loading model, 702
    output buffer, 703
    output postprocessing, 703
    picking gallery/camera, 702
    preprocessing, 702
    running inference, 703
  performance, 705
  pre-trained models, 701
  security and privacy, 704
  UI integration, 703
  use cases, 704
imageFilter, 370
Image recognition, 739
  AI-powered camera app, 732, 733
  classification, 700–705
  defined, 700
  real-time processing, 705–710
Image stream, 707
Impeller debug traces, 176
Impeller renderer, 400
Impeller rendering engine, 203
Inherited widgets, 66–67
Inject dependencies, 291
Inno setup packaging, 536

Integration testing, 151, 152, 328, 456, 457, 798–803
Interaction testing, 152, 153
Interactive cards, 137–139
InteractiveCard widget, 55, 59
Interactive forms, 139–141
Interactive UI elements
  components, 132–141
  defined, 131
  practical examples
    custom progress indicators, 142
    interactive cards, 147–149
    interactive charts, 142, 144
    interactive forms, 145, 147
    swipe-to-delete lists, 144, 145
InteractiveViewer, 3, 38
Interceptors, 573, 618, 619
Inter-integrated circuit (I2C), 860
Internationalization, 915, 916, 922, 930
Internet of Things (IoT)
  defined, 874
  implementation, 876
  performance, 876
  reasons, 875
  security, 877
  smart farming sensor dashboard, 875
  UI development, 877
  UI features, 876
Invoice Ninja, 552
iOS testing, 458

J

Janky animations, 172, 673, 680
JavaScript Object Notation (JSON)
  compute(), 577
  data structures, 580, 581
  jsonDecode() and streams, 578, 579
  null safety, 579, 580
  overview, 575
  serialization, 576
jsonDecode(), 578, 579
json_serializable package, 576
JSON web token (JWT), 751-753

K

Key performance indicators (KPIs), 331, 985
Knowledge sharing, 321

L

LayoutBuilder, 52, 80, 120, 122
  arguments, 105
  best practices, 111
  defined, 105
  features, 106
  usage patterns
    adaptive layouts, 109-111
    creating responsive layouts, 106, 108
    height constraints, 108, 109
Layout management, 52
Layout testing, 153, 154

Legacy APIs
  best practices, 884
  challenges, 881
  implementation, 881-883
  integration, 884
  real-world use case, 884
  security, 884
  technologies, 880
Legacy EMR systems, 907
Linux dependencies, 543
Linux packaging
  techniques, 538-540
ListView.builder, 83, 209
ListView widget, 5
Localization
  advantages, 920
  code generation process, 919
  DART usage, 920
  dynamic locale switching, 920
  overview, 917
  performance, 921
  pluralization and gender support, 919
  setting up, 917, 919
  third-party libraries, 921-925
Lottie animations, 212, 655, 659, 680

M

Machine learning (ML), 685
  best practices, 735, 736
  case studies, 730-733
  challenges, 734

INDEX

Machine learning (ML) (*cont.*)
    image recognition, 700–715
    optimization, 710–715, 737
    TFLite (*see* TensorFlow Lite (TFLite))
macOS dependencies, 543
macOS packaging techniques, 536–538
Man-in-the-middle (MITM) attacks, 741, 744, 763, 769, 776, 780
markNeedsLayout(), 357
maskFilter, 370
MediaQuery, 78, 79, 122, 123
MedTrack, 662
Memoization, 308, 329
Memory leaks, 315
    best practices, 191
    BuildContext, async call, 190
    controller disposal, 189
    Dart and Flutter, 186
    defined, 186
    detection, 188
    DevTools, 187, 188
    profiling
        allocation profiler, 192, 193
        analysis, 192
        case studies, 197–202
        fragmentation and bloat detection, 195
        GC behavior and heap growth, 194
        performance-heavy object identification, 195
        retained objects, 193
        testing pipelines, 196
        VM service protocol and observatory APIs, 194
    StreamSubscription, 190
Memory management, 39
    best practices, 186
    leaks (*see* Memory leaks)
    overview, 181
    proactive practices, 182
    techniques
        conditional widget construction, 184
        const and immutability, 182
        Flutter 3.29 enhancements, 185
        image and asset, 183
        state management, 184
        third-party packages, 185
        UI references, 185
        widget lifecycle hygiene, 183
MFA, *see* Multi-factor authentication (MFA)
Migration
    issues, 22
    breaking changes, 24
    build and compilation errors, 24
    dependency conflicts, 23
    deprecated APIs, 23
    performance degradations, 25
    testing failures, 26
    upgrade process, 16–21

INDEX

ML, *see* Machine learning (ML)
MobileNetV2, 694, 695, 701
Mobile Security Framework (MobSF), 782
Mobile testing, 568
Model architecture optimization, 713
Modular channel design, 422
MSIX packaging, 534, 535
Multi-channel architecture, 427
MultiChildLayoutDelegate, 112
Multi-Cubit coordination, 285
Multi-device optimization
    adaptive asset management, 239
    adaptive UI and layouts, 235, 236
    high and low-end devices, 236
    offloading intensive tasks, 238, 239
    performance benchmarks
        best practices, 246, 247
        considerations, 245
        metrics, 242, 243
        reasons, 241
        results, 245, 246
        tools, 243, 244
    performance monitoring, 239
    physical devices, 240
Multi-factor authentication (MFA), 900
Multiple platforms-specific optimizations
    adaptive UI, 564
    conditional code, 563
    consistency, 567
    network requests and latency, 565
    overview, 562
    rendering, 564
    resource consumption, 566
    shared logic, 567
    testing and profiling, 568
Multi-property animation, 635–637

N

National Healthcare Provider's Digital Strategy, 906
Natural language processing (NLP), 739
    conversational interfaces, 719, 720
    healthcare, 731, 732
    sentiment analysis, 721–725
    STT, 716, 717
    text classification and summarization, 725–730
    TTS, 718, 719
Navigator.pushNamed(), 40
Netlify, 964, 965
Network communications, 773, 780
Network errors, 590
News aggregator app, 219, 614
News app with adaptive layout, 73
NLP, *see* Natural language processing (NLP)

INDEX

Normalization, 266, 277
Notifier, 251, 253–256
Nubank, 411

O

OAuth 2.0, 749, 750, 900
Obfuscation, *see* Code obfuscation
Offline-first field survey app, 615
Offline object detection app, 699
On-device inference
    benefits, 695
    case study, 699
    components, 696
    defined, 695
    input data, 697
    loading model and interpreter, 696
    output buffer, 697
    performance optimization, 698
    postprocess output, 698
    real-time considerations, 698
    running, 697
    security, 699
on<Event> approach, 269
OpenGL Shading Language (GLSL), 368, 372
OpenID Connect (OIDC), 749, 900
Operator fusion, 712
OrientationBuilder, 85
Overdrawing, 388
OverlayMenu widget, 57, 63

P

Painting techniques
    APIs
        canvas and drawing operations, 367, 368
        image and text rendering, 369
        improvements, 367
        layering and compositing enhancements, 368
        properties and effects, 370
        shaders and blend modes, 368
    artistic designs, 376, 377
    avoiding overdraw and redundant, 361
    boundaries, 363
    clipping effects, 373, 374
    complex paths and shapes, 365
    custom (*see* Custom painting operations)
    custom gradients and shader effects, 371, 373
    defined, 361
    dynamic and interactive content, 375, 376
    object instantiations, 362
    outside bounds, 365
    push compositing layers, 364
    SaveLayer, 374, 375
    save/restore, 362
    shouldRepaint method, 364
    text rendering, 363
paint() method, 353, 354

INDEX

parentUsesSize flag, 359
Partial widget tree, 205
Payment Card Industry Data Security Standard (PCI DSS), 903
Penetration testing, 782
Performance overlay, 210
performLayout() method, 351, 352
Personally identifiable information (PII), 469
Photo editing app with contextual actions, 76, 77
PictureRecorder, 387
PII, *see* Personally identifiable information (PII)
Platform channels
    backward compatibility and migration, 424
    binary messenger layer, 422
    communication (*see* Communication)
    DevTools integration and channel inspection, 423
    interoperability model, 421
    message support and custom codecs, 421
    modular channel design and federated plugin support, 422
    overview, 420
    template and scaffold improvements, 424
Platform-dependent widgets, 86
Platform-specific layouts, 129, 130
Play Store *vs.* App Store, 960
Plugin development
    asynchronous communication, 450
    availability, 450
    camera, 452
    creation template, 447
    debugging, 453
    declarative metadata, 447
    dependencies, 449
    ecosystem, 444
    federated architecture, 444, 451
    integrations
        least privilege access, 481, 482
        log responsibly, 485, 486
        obfuscation, 483
        platform channel inputs, 480, 481
        runtime integrity, 485
        secure platform channels, 482
        sensitive APIs, 484
        static and dynamic tools, 484
    null safety and Dart 3.3, 446
    overview, 444
    performance optimization
        custom video player, 496
        event flooding, 493, 494
        image processing, 492, 493
        JSON-based communication, 495
        startup delay, 494, 495
        techniques, 487–493

INDEX

Plugin development (cont.)
    platform registration, 449, 450
    runtime handling, 448
    security
        API keys and authentication, 473, 474
        audits and updates, 474
        encryption and storage, 475–480
        insecure code and reverse engineering, 471, 473
        overview, 468
        platform channels, 468–470
        storing sensitive information, 470, 471
    support and standardization, 445, 446
    testing
        Android, 457
        and debugging, 466–468
        integration, 456, 457
        iOS, 458
        mocking, 459
        performance, 460
        unit testing, 454–456
Privacy by Design, 903
Production-grade multi-platform system, 946
Profiling tools
    comparison, 222–227
    recommendations, 234
    use cases
        CPU-intensive operations, 231
        GPU bottlenecks, 230
        memory leaks and usage, 229
        shader compilation, 230
        slow build/rebuild times, 232
        UI Jank and frame drops, 228
        UI rendering delays, 233
Progressive web apps (PWAs), 499
    best practices, 510
    components
        app shell architecture, 507
        flutter_service_worker.js, 507
        manifest.json file, 506
    defined, 505
    enhancements, 509
    installation, 509
    principles, 506
    steps, 508, 509
    testing, 509
Proof key for code exchange (PKCE), 749
Protected health information (PHI), 903, 908
Pruning, 712
Pseudonymization, 904
pumpAndSettle(), 801, 812

Q

Quantization, 711
QuestHero, 663, 664

R

Raspberry Pi
  defined, 850
  deployment and running app, 856
  hardware interaction and peripheral access, 857–862
  limitation, 855
  Linux ARM64 architecture, 855
  modifying entry point, 854
  optimization, 856
  performance, 857
  project setup, 854
  setting up
    configuration, headless operation, 853
    hardware and software requirements, 850
    install Flutter SDK, 852
    operating system, 851
    rendering backend verification, 852
    system packages, 851
Reactive systems, 271
Real-time image processing, 705–710
Real-time monitoring, app's health, 983–988
Real-time rendering techniques
  adaptive frame rate and conditional repainting, 401
  best practices, 402
  coding, 402
  custom animations and effects, 403–409
  CustomPaint, 399
  frame budget optimization, 398
  hardware acceleration, 398
  Impeller renderer, 400
  offloading computations, 400
  overview, 397
  physics, 401
  pipeline, 398
  RepaintBoundary, 399
  scene complexity management, 401
Redistributable packages, 542
Redux, 262, 263
Reflectly, 410, 550
Rendering performance
  animation, 216
  case studies and examples, 217–222
  deep widget trees, 214
  defined, 212
  itemExtent and builders, 215
  layout widgets, 216
  overdraw and visual clutter, 213
  profile and benchmark, 216
  RepaintBoundary, 213
  setState(), 217
  static widgets, 214
  unbounded constraints, 215
RenderObjects
  custom, 349
  custom layout and painting, 350–355

INDEX

RenderObjects (*cont.*)
   lifecycle and pipeline
      integration, 348, 349
   overview, 347
   ParentData and child
      management, 349
   performance
      considerations, 350
   responsibilities, 347
   roles, 347
   types, 348
RenderProxyBox, 360
RepaintBoundary, 209, 213, 390, 399, 641, 674, 679, 682
Resource-constrained environments, 879
ResponsiveContainer widget, 55, 60
Responsive UIs
   defined, 78
   flex and expanded widgets, 81
   GridView and ListView, 82
   LayoutBuilder, 80
   MediaQuery, 78, 79
   orientations, 84
   packages and tools, 83
Reverse engineering, 471, 473, 741, 761–764, 769, 774, 781
Right-to-left (RTL) layouts
   configuration, 936, 937
   Flutter's support, 936
   handling multilingual content, 939–943
   languages, 935
   testing, 938
   text input and cursor direction, 938
   widget mirroring and alignment, 937, 938
Risk-aware approach, 967
Rive animations, 654, 659
Riverpod 1.x *vs.* Riverpod 2.0, 252, 253
Riverpod 2.0
   AsyncNotifier, 257
   complex state trees
      AsyncNotifier, 266
      modular state design, 264
      nested providers and composition, 264
      normalization and entity management, 266
      ProviderScope, 265
      shared and global state, 267
   enhancements, 251, 252
   family modifier, 257
   hosting bloc, 260, 261
   local state, bloc for global logic, 261, 262
   Notifier, 253–256
   overview, 250
   provider dependencies, 258
   reasons, 259
   Redux/InheritedWidget, 262, 263
   scoped overrides and DI, 258
Role-based access control (RBAC), 742, 900
Root/jailbreak detection, 762

S

Security
  audits, 782
  authentication, 748–761
  patches, 782, 783
  plugins (*see* Plugin development, security)
  runtimes, 420
  vulnerabilities
    data in transit and at rest, 744–748
    threats, 740–743
Security threats
  authentication and authorization, 742
  code obfuscation and app hardening, 742
  data storage, 740
  hardcoded API keys and secrets, 741
  level of abstraction, 740
  vulnerable/outdated dependencies, 743
  weak network security and unencrypted traffic, 741
Semantic versioning (SemVer), 973
Sentiment analysis, 721–725
Sentry, 985
Server-side errors, 590
Service Organization Control 2 (SOC 2), 903
Session management, 779, 780
Shader compilation reports, 176
Shader techniques, 392–397
ShopSwift, 664
shouldRepaint() method, 364, 381, 384, 385, 387
Simulators, 620
Skia engine, 174, 530
Skia Shader Inspector (SSI), 224
Skia Shading Language (SkSL), 393
SliverAppBar, 7
Smooth animations
  defined, 645
  techniques
    avoid layout thrashing, 646
    balance physics and timing, 648
    GPU-friendly widgets, 645, 646
    minimize frame build time, 645
    refresh rates device, 648
    staggered and chained, 647
    TickerMode, 647
  tools, 648
Snapcraft, 544
Snap packaging, 539, 540
Social media app, 298–300
SonarQube, 782
SpaceX, 554, 555
Speech-to-text (STT), 716, 717
Sprite-based animation, 682
SQLCipher, 476
Stack traces, 767

INDEX

State composition
    aggregate and transform state, 292, 293
    custom mixins, 276
    shared global state, 292
StatefulWidget, 119, 120
State management, 15, 184, 345
    benchmarking
        criteria, 331
        overview, 330
        results, 332–338
        setup, 332
    Bloc and Cubit libraries, 268–288
    flow consistency, 325, 326
    global and local state, 326, 327
    hybrid approaches, 289
    integration, 249, 289
    modularization, 323–325
    performance impact
        battery efficiency, 342, 343
        CPU load and time processing, 338, 339
        latency and responsiveness, 341, 342
        memory usage, 339, 340
        UI rebuild time, 340, 341
    performance optimizations, 329, 330
    Riverpod enhancements (*see* Riverpod 2.0)
    solutions
        asynchronous data, 306
        business logic, 305, 306
        caching and memoization, 307, 308
        case studies and examples, 296–303
        complex applications, 303
        divide and conquer, 290
        expensive operations, 311, 312
        fine-tuning, 314, 315
        incremental adoption, 294
        lazy loading and pagination, 307
        performance considerations, 294, 295
        performance optimization, 309
        profiling and benchmarking, 315, 316
        rebuilding widgets, 310, 311
        scoped, 304, 305
        scoped overrides, 293, 294
        state composition, 292, 293
        state persistence, 313
        tight coupling, 291
    team collaboration
        communication channels, 317
        DI, 320
        documentation, 319
        ownership, 318, 319
        review process, 321, 322
        standardized patterns, 317
    testing and debugging, 328
State transitions, 274, 325

INDEX

StreamBuilder, 123, 124, 597, 598, 601, 602, 606
Streams, 278, 279
STT, *see* Speech-to-text (STT)
Supernova IDE, 411

T

Tamper detection, 763
Telemedicine, 907
Tencent Now Live, 416
TensorFlow, 711
TensorFlow Lite (TFLite)
    frameworks, 686
    on-device inference, 695–700
    pre-trained Models, 691–695
    setting up, 687–691
tester.pump(), 810
tester.pump(Duration), 810
Text classification, 726–728
Text rendering, 363
Text summarization, 728, 730
TextTheme, 40
Text-to-speech (TTS), 718, 719
Theming system, 533
The New York Times, 553, 554
Third-party libraries
    localization
        capabilities, 924
        case study, 922–924
        overview, 921, 925
        security and performance, 925
        usage, 922

TickerProvider, 634
Time-based one-time passwords (TOTP), 753–756
Timeout errors, 594
Time-to-live (TTL), 611
Tokens, 759
TOTP, *see* Time-based one-time passwords (TOTP)
Transformers, 276
Transient errors, 591–593
Travel app with custom branding, 72
Travel booking app, 776, 777
Travel itinerary app, 616
TTS, *see* Text-to-speech (TTS)
Tween, animations, 633, 675
Two-factor authentication (2FA)
    case study, 756
    defined, 753
    forms, mobile apps, 754
    overview, 753
    performance, 756
    security, 756
    status, storing and managing, 756
    TOTP, 754, 755

U

Unified plugin system, 532
Unit testing, 150, 151, 328, 454–456
    external dependencies, 788
    mocking and stubbing, 793–798
    widgets, 788–793

1015

INDEX

User interfaces (UIs)
    advanced layout
        techniques, 104–118
    advanced widget
        testing, 149–162
    Cubits, 280
    cultural considerations
        color psychology and
            significance, 931
        compliance, 934
        gestures and navigation
            expectations, 932
        imagery and visual
            content, 933
        local laws and privacy
            norms, 934
        real-world case study, 935
        reasons, 930
        symbolism and icons, 931
        text tone and formality, 933
    debounce/throttle
        mechanisms, 210
    decouple events, 272
    design systems, 93–104
    dynamic and adaptive
        layouts, 118–131
    interactions, 809–814
    interactive elements,
        52, 131–149
    multiple languages
        performance and UX, 930
        preparedness, 929
        scaling and accessibility, 929
        text length variations, 926
    widgets and layout
        mechanisms, 927, 928
    patterns, 51
    responsive and adaptive, 77–92

V

ValueListenableBuilder, 676
Verbose, 834
Verbose logging, 467
Vercel, 965
Version management, 975
Video streaming app, 768
Visibility widget, 681
Visual testing, 155

W, X, Y

WebAssembly (Wasm), 499, 504
Web hosting and
    deployment, 962–966
Web performance, 206
    benchmarking, 500
    CanvasKit optimization, 502
    case studies, 547–551
    deferred component
        loading, 502
    DOM-based rendering, 503
    font loading and subsetting, 503
    JavaScript bundle sizes, 501, 502
    overview, 501
    PWAs, 505–510
    service worker, 504
    Wasm compilation, 504

INDEX

WebSockets, 281, 572, 631, 886, 911
  connections
    best practices, 608
    error handling and stream termination, 606
    heartbeat and ping/pong messages, 605
    lifecycle-aware management, 602–604
    reconnection strategy, 604, 605
    service pattern, 607
    status feedback, 606
  defined, 596
  packages, 596
  real-time data handling, 597–602
  usage, 596
Web testing, 568
Web *vs.* desktop performance
  latency and responsiveness, 559, 560
  load times, 558, 559
  optimization, 561, 562
  platform-specific features, 560, 561
  rendering and frame rate, 557
  resource consumption, 558
Widgets
  adaptive, 529
  APIs, 967
  built-in, 53–59
  conditional construction, 184

  customization, 65–71
  defined, 2
  directionality, 937
  enhancements, 5–7
  features, 51
  implicit animation, 633
  integration and customization, 57
  interactive view, 3
  localized strings, 924
  material design, 529
  mirroring and alignment, 937, 938
  multilingual UI, 927, 928
  rendering, 890
  representation, 36
  scenarios
    branded user interfaces, 72, 73
    contextual menus, 76, 77
    data visualization, 75
    interactive elements, 74
  testing, 52
    animations and UI interactions, 809–814
    animations/gestures, 803
    best practices, 161, 162
    complex form, 156, 158
    custom, 149–156
    interactive, 158, 159
    layout and responsiveness, 160, 161
    trees, 804–809
    usage, 804

INDEX

Widgets (*cont.*)
    tree construction, 204
    types, 3, 4
    unit testing, 788–793
    use cases, 58–64
    visibility, 681
Windows dependencies, 542
Windows packaging techniques, 534, 536
Wrap widgets, 130

Z

Zero trust principle, 742

GPSR Compliance

The European Union's (EU) General Product Safety Regulation (GPSR) is a set of rules that requires consumer products to be safe and our obligations to ensure this.

If you have any concerns about our products, you can contact us on

ProductSafety@springernature.com

In case Publisher is established outside the EU, the EU authorized representative is:

Springer Nature Customer Service Center GmbH
Europaplatz 3
69115 Heidelberg, Germany

www.ingramcontent.com/pod-product-compliance
Lightning Source LLC
LaVergne TN
LVHW021954060526
838201LV00048B/1568

9798868821042